D0631074

Walt Whitman & the World

Walt

Edited by GAY WILSON ALLEN & ED FOLSOM

UNIVERSITY OF IOWA PRESS ᛟ *Iowa City*

COMMUNITY COLLEGE OF
ALLEGHENY COUNTY

PS
3238
.W356
1995

Whitman
& the World

University of Iowa Press, Iowa City 52242

Copyright © 1995 by the University of Iowa Press

All rights reserved

Printed in the United States of America

Design by Richard Hendel

No part of this book may be reproduced or used
in any form or by any means, electronic or
mechanical, including photocopying and
recording, without permission in writing from
the publisher.

Printed on acid-free paper

Library of Congress Cataloging-in-Publication Data

Walt Whitman and the world / edited by

Gay Wilson Allen and Ed Folsom.

   p.   cm.

   Includes bibliographical references (p.).

ISBN 0-87745-497-3 (cloth),

ISBN 0-87745-498-1 (paper)

   1. Whitman, Walt, 1819–1892 — Criticism
and interpretation — History.   2. Whitman,
Walt, 1819–1892 — Appreciation — Foreign
countries.   3. American literature —
Appreciation—Foreign countries.
4. National characteristics in literature.
I. Allen, Gay Wilson, 1903–1995.
II. Folsom, Ed, 1947–
PS3238.W356   1995
811′.3 — dc20   95-479
                                                      CIP

01 00 99 98 97 96 95 C 5 4 3 2 1

01 00 99 98 97 96 95 P 5 4 3 2 1

GAY WILSON ALLEN, 1903–1995

Gay Wilson Allen died while this book was in press.
The contributors to *Walt Whitman and the World* join me
in dedicating this, his last book, to him. For half a century,
he towered above the field of Whitman studies and was a
friend and mentor to hundreds of scholars worldwide.
His generosity of spirit was legendary. He will be missed.

He had been anxious to see this book appear; it was his
labor of love during his final years. Well, Gay, now that
you've set out on your cosmic journey, the ultimate open
road, here it is. This book is not only *by* you, it's *for* you.
Allons!

Ed Folsom
August 7, 1995

Contents

Acknowledgments

This project was made possible by a grant from the National Endowment for the Humanities (NEH) and by the generosity of C. Esco Obermann. The NEH grant and Mr. Obermann's support allowed the editors to bring together most of the contributors to this volume in 1992 at the University of Iowa Center for Advanced Studies, where a two-day seminar on Whitman in translation was held. The details of this book were hammered out at that meeting. The editors are grateful to the NEH for continuing support during the completion of the book and to the University of Iowa Center for Advanced Studies and its director, Jay Semel, for extraordinary help and hospitality throughout the years of the Whitman Centennial Project.

Dan Lewis played a major role in the complex job of gathering and editing the materials for this volume. Victoria Brehm offered valuable editorial and organizational help in the project's early stages. Abigail Metcalf helped in the later stages.

Roger Asselineau wishes to express his debt to a number of Italian colleagues who supplied him with books, articles, and information: Marina Camboni, Mario Corona, Andrea Mariani, and Francesca Orestano in particular, as well as Alessandra Pinto Surdi, whose updated bibliography of Whitman's reception in Italy was especially precious. He is also grateful to José Augusto Seabra, Portuguese ambassador with UNESCO in Paris, and Susan Brown for their help with Portugal. Ezra Greenspan thanks Riki Greenspan for help with gathering and translating material and Yehoiadah Amir for turning his attention to the work of Gershom Scholem. Guiyou Huang is grateful to Kenneth M. Price for encouragement and help in writing the essay on Whitman and China.

The editors also wish to recognize the many scholars, poets, translators, and Whitman enthusiasts who have worked tirelessly over the years to carry Whitman's work into various cultures through a variety of media and languages. One outstanding example is Robert Strassburg, one of the most prolific composers of musical interpretations of Whitman's poems. Strassburg, professor emeritus of music at California State University, Los Angeles, has set many Whitman texts to music. His *Leaves of Grass* symphony had its premiere performance in Japan, and a recording of the symphony continues to be played frequently on Japanese national radio. He is now at work on an opera about Whitman in New Orleans. He edits a quarterly newsletter dedicated to worldwide Whitman activities, and his tireless efforts to foster an international understanding of Whitman serve as a model of committed scholarship.

ED FOLSOM & GAY WILSON ALLEN

Introduction: "Salut au Monde!"

If it hadn't been for Emerson's electrifying letter greeting Whitman at "the beginning of a great career," the first edition of *Leaves of Grass*, published in 1855, would have been a total failure; few copies were sold, and Emerson and Whitman seemed about the only people who recognized much promise in it. Undaunted, Whitman published an expanded second edition in 1856, in which he included a visionary poem (then called "Poem of Salutation," later to become "Salut au Monde!") containing this prophetic exclamation:

> My spirit has pass'd in compassion and determination around the whole earth,
> I have look'd for equals and lovers and found them ready for me in all lands,
> I think some divine rapport has equalized me with them. (LG, 148)

He boasted that this new edition would sell several thousand copies, but it turned out to be an even greater failure than the first. What we now see as prophecy appeared in 1856 as nothing more than boastful fantasy, for it would be many years before Whitman would become known in other lands. Throughout his life, though, he would maintain this international dream; in 1881, while expressing hope that a projected Russian translation of *Leaves* would soon become a reality, he noted:

As my dearest dream is for an internationality of poems and poets, binding the lands of the earth closer than all treaties and diplomacy — As the purpose beneath the rest in my book is such hearty comradeship, for individuals to begin with, and for all the nations of the earth as a result — how happy I should be to get the hearing and emotional contact of the great Russian peoples.[1]

Eventually Whitman would find "equals and lovers" quite literally around the world, a true "internationality" of "hearty comradeship." Today, complete translations of *Leaves of Grass* have been published in France, Germany, Spain, Italy, Japan, and China, and selections of Whitman's poetry have appeared in every major language except Arabic. Scores of biographical and critical books on Whitman have been published on every continent.

This book sets out to trace some of the ways Whitman has been absorbed into cultures from around the world for more than a century. From nation to nation, Whitman's poetry and prose have generated a wide variety of aesthetic, political, and religious responses. Since no American writer has been more influential in more nations than Whitman, the materials in this book demonstrate some important ways that American culture, as articulated in Whitman's work, has helped redefine older and more established national traditions and how it has helped emerging nations define themselves. These materials also show how various national cultures have reconstructed Whitman in order to make him fit their native patterns. This book presents and examines, then, some radically realigned versions of Whitman, as his writing — translated into other languages and absorbed into other traditions — undertakes a different kind of cultural work than it performs in the United States.

To accomplish this overview of responses, we organized an international group of writers and scholars, each with expertise in both Whitman and the culture about which they write. This group of distinguished scholars corresponded with each other and eventually met in Iowa City in 1992 to discuss the project in detail; their collaboration has resulted in one of the first sustained explorations of a major American writer's influence on world literature. Our goal has been to bring together the most illuminating responses to Whitman from every culture in which we could identify significant work on Whitman. The book is organized in sections, each one offering a careful analysis of the ways that Whitman has been absorbed into a particular culture and then offering selections from writings about Whitman by poets and critics from that culture.

The size and detail of each section of this book reflect the range and depth of the particular national response to Whitman. For cultures that have long and manifold responses to *Leaves of Grass*, like Great Britain, we have chosen to present brief excerpts from a large number of respondents, indicating the wealth of materials available. Where particular essays have had a dramatic impact on Whitman's reputation in a given culture, as José Martí's did in Spanish-speaking countries or as Ferdinand Freiligrath's and Johannes Schlaf's did in Germany, we have devoted more space to those individual responses. In countries where the response to Whitman has so far been fragmentary but still noteworthy, we offer only a historical and critical overview, with few or no selections. Selected bibliographies at the back of the volume list major translations and key critical writings.

This book began as an updating of Gay Wilson Allen's *Walt Whitman Abroad* (1955), but it quickly turned into a project that involved reconceptualizing and vastly revising the earlier work. While we reprint some pieces that appeared in *Walt Whitman Abroad*, much of the material is new, and the overviews have been completely rewritten to reflect the overwhelming changes of the past forty years — changes both in the cultures represented and in their views of Whitman. *Walt Whitman Abroad* contained no section on Great Britain, since at that time Harold Blodgett's *Walt Whitman in England* (1934) still seemed to cover the ground adequately. Blodgett's study now needs to be supplemented, however, and we are pleased to present M. Wynn Thomas's up-to-date overview of Whitman in the British Isles. *Walt Whitman Abroad* also did not include any of the poems that poets from around the world have addressed to Whitman over the past century. In 1981, in *Walt Whitman: The Measure of His Song*, Jim Perlman, Ed Folsom, and Dan Campion collected many of the poems that demonstrated how poets from Whitman's time to the present have continued to engage in a dialogue with Whitman, literally "talking back" to him just as he talked forward to "Poets to Come." This ongoing poetic dialogue with Whitman was not limited to American poets, and in this book we present a selection of poems, many appearing for the first time in English translation, that demonstrates just how remarkably international the "talking back" to Whitman has been.

We had hoped to present a study of Whitman in African nations, but that important topic remains to be done. Certainly Whitman has generated African responses, from white South Africans like Jan Christiaan Smuts, a former prime minister who wrote one of the earliest critical studies of Whitman, and novelist Alan Paton, to important black writers like Ngugi wa T'hiongo, who has used Whitman's poetry as epigraphs for his novels, and Syl Cheney-Coker, a Sierra Leone poet who has written Whitman-inspired poems, including his own "Children of Adam." But the responses have yet to be gathered, studied, and sorted according to the multitude of national and tribal traditions in Africa. This important project awaits a generation of critics to come.

From the 1860s to the present, Whitman's poetry has been remarkably influential in an international context. Before he was widely viewed as a significant writer in the United States, Whitman was already taken seriously by readers in many countries as an author who carefully and imaginatively defined the problematics of democracy. Until well into the twentieth century, in fact, he was more highly regarded and more widely read in several European countries than he was in the United States. His international impact has continued to grow throughout this century, and he has helped generations of writers — in Europe, Latin America, the Indian subcontinent, and emerging African nations — to formulate and challenge democratic assumptions and attitudes. As Gay Wilson Allen noted in his preface to *Walt Whitman Abroad*, "Time after time the critics in other lands have seen in Whitman's crudities—or fancied crudities—the awkwardness of a young nation, an immature giant which has not yet learned its own strength." Allen suggested that "these foreign critics of Whitman may help Americans to understand themselves [and] to understand the misconceptions about themselves that they must overcome."[2]

Now, forty years later, the United States perhaps seems less of an "immature giant," but the culture clearly remains just as much in need of help in defining itself. Critics and poets from other cultures still turn to Whitman for the materials out of which they define the United States. Huck Gutman has observed, in the introduction to a recent collection of essays investigating international perspectives on American literature, that the great value of such a global view "is the manner in which the study and reception of American literature reveals national identity. When one culture abuts another, the way in which one encounters or assimilates the other is defining in special ways."

Gutman's collection (in which Whitman is notably absent) sets out to provide "a sense of just how thoroughly—or partially—American culture has penetrated other cultures, and with what sort of impact."[3] *Walt Whitman and the World* provides a case study of how one of the best-known representatives of American culture has carried his democratic message into an array of other cultures and how those cultures have responded to that message.

Questions concerning the nature of a democratic political system, a democratic art, a democratic sexuality, and a democratic religion are central concerns of Whitman's, and they have been key components of countless international responses to Whitman. His impact was felt in the Soviet Union, where he was read as a kind of socialist prophet (it will be interesting to see just where and how he continues to be read in the myriad countries emerging from the collapse of the USSR), and it is beginning to be felt in China, where a full translation of *Leaves of Grass* is now available (after having been delayed by Chinese authorities for fear of the impact it might have had during the Tiananmen Square student democratic uprisings a few years ago). It is no accident that Whitman's influence has been most dramatically apparent in countries that are in the midst of democratic revolutions and deep social change. Whitman's poetry has in the last few years been translated into Slovenian and Serbo-Croatian and was published in Yugoslavia just before that country disintegrated into ethnic states, and the first major edition of his prose work to appear in East Germany was published less than five years before the Berlin Wall came down.

From early on, Whitman has been read in other cultures as a poet of revolution, and his influence has been notably cross-cultural, as writers from one nationality export or import him with ease into another. One of the earliest critics to become interested in Whitman was the German poet Ferdinand Freiligrath, who published an essay on Whitman in 1868; he first encountered Whitman's works while he was living in England as an exile because of his rebellion against political tyranny in Germany. Several radicals in Britain had recently discovered

Whitman (he was embraced there mostly by liberals, militant democrats, and proto-socialists), and it was their discussion of him in periodicals that attracted Freiligrath's attention. In 1871 Algernon Swinburne addressed a poem to Whitman, celebrating him as a prophet of liberty, a "strong-winged soul with prophetic lips hot with the blood-beats of song" (Swinburne would eventually include this poem in his *Songs Before Sunrise*, a book dedicated to Giuseppe Mazzini, leader of a revolution in Italy), and in 1878 Edward Dowden hailed the American poet as the "poet of democracy." Some Chinese poets came to know Whitman first while living in exile in France, and the German Erich Arendt engaged Whitman's work while exiled in Latin America. Wherever he was first encountered, and in whatever language, his writings usually seemed to speak democratic revolution.

Actually, Whitman wrote very few poems about political revolution, though his 1855 edition did contain two: a satirical poem later entitled "A Boston Ballad" and another that lamented and celebrated the failed revolts in various European countries in 1848–49 (later entitled "Europe, the 72nd and 73d Years of These States"). His "Europe" poem offered both consolation and prophecy: "Not a grave of the murder'd for freedom but grows seed for freedom, in its turn to bear seed, / Which the winds carry afar and re-sow, and the rains and the snows nourish" (LG, 268). Such sentiments appealed to some of the young Russian poets and journalists during the abortive Russian revolt in 1905 and again, more widely, during the Bolshevik revolution of 1917. Earlier, a Russian journalist named V. Popov had called Whitman "the spirit of revolt," the champion of all those oppressed by tyranny: this was the Whitman who appealed to the Bolsheviks, who distributed translations of his poems in military camps.

But Whitman was not read only for his revolutionary political impulses. Others turned to him for what he could teach them about poetry or about themselves: Franz Kafka, for example, found him "among the greatest formal innovators in the modern lyric," and in Portugal Fernando Pessoa celebrated Whitman's "wild and gentle brotherhood with everything," finding in the American poet wonderfully incongruous personalities that opened up new possibilities for subjectivity. Whitman's ability to reconcile contradictions, to resist the valorization of soul over body, has led many Indian writers to hear ancient Hindu voices at the heart of Whitman's poetry.

Whatever his sources, the remarkable thing about Whitman's appeal to his readers is that everyone seems to find in his poetry what she or he wants and needs. So the Russians, unhappy under their czar, perceived in Whitman's poems "the spirit of revolt and pride," while later Soviet Communists admired the way he "defines the solidarity of interests of working people . . . and foretells the advent of brotherhood of all nations." In France he was admired early in the twentieth century by the Symbolists and a few years later by the pan-social Unanimists, while still others, like André Gide, found fellowship in Whitman the homosexual. During the first Whitman cult in Germany, he was admired for his cosmic world outlook and was compared to Beethoven and Bismarck; during World War I,

German soldiers were attracted by *Drum-Taps* and carried translations of his poems in the trenches; after the war, the German labor press discovered Whitman and used him for their propaganda; in 1922 Thomas Mann, in his famous "Von Deutscher Republik" speech, praised Whitman and Novalis as archetypes of American democracy and German humanity. Once we begin to trace the fertile and shifting responses, the examples proliferate; this book provides an abundance of materials out of which illuminating new international influence studies can be constructed.

In a surprisingly large number of nations, then, important writers have responded in significant ways to Whitman — ways that help define the intersections between American culture and other cultures, ways that help define the varied possibilities for the construction of democracies, and ways that help define an emerging international culture. Jorge Luis Borges said that Whitman "wrote his rhapsodies in the role of an imaginary self, formed partly of himself, partly of each of his readers." This is why so many readers find not only Whitman but also themselves in his poems, and it is why so many nations find in his work aspects of and challenges to their own cultures. No other poet in English since Shakespeare has appealed to so many people in so many places in so many ways.

In the United States, during this century, an awareness of Whitman's international influence has slowly evolved. Even in Whitman's own lifetime, the poet's disciples were actively involved in gathering and responding to essays on the poet published in European countries, and Whitman's follower Horace Traubel used his wide association of socialist contacts to form an International Walt Whitman Fellowship. As Whitman scholarship developed in the twentieth century, however, most American critics lost touch with the developing foreign reputation of Whitman and instead turned their attention to Whitman's American connections and to his native roots. During the era of New Criticism, with its insistence on viewing poetic texts as self-enclosed art objects, Whitman's poetry came to seem both loosely symbolic and embarrassingly nationalistic.

Meanwhile, Whitman's reputation in other countries was developing along quite different lines, lines that were invisible to most American scholars until Gay Wilson Allen's *Walt Whitman Handbook* was published in 1946. Allen devoted a chapter to Walt Whitman and world literature, and he developed his analysis in *Walt Whitman Abroad*, which offered the first gathering of international responses. In 1955 that book came as something of a shock to scholars who had learned to view Whitman in more insular ways. Books gradually began to appear that viewed Whitman in particular cultural contexts: Harold Blodgett had already written on Whitman in England, as had Fernando Alegría on Whitman in Hispanoamerica; soon, V. K. Chari would write on Whitman and Indian traditions; later, Betsy Erkkila on Whitman among the French; and most recently, Walter Grünzweig on Whitman in German-speaking cultures. Essays appeared tracing Whitman's influence on countries as diverse as Russia, Brazil, Israel,

China, and Finland. It became clear that a multinational and quite diverse response to Whitman had been forming for more than a century, but, while individual pockets were known, there had been no attempt to assess the full range of responses.

The ways that a writer of one nationality begins to influence writers of another nationality—and then becomes more generally absorbed into the culture—are obviously complex. When language barriers exist, the patterns of influence become even more difficult to trace, especially in the case of poetry, where the radical and innovative use of language embeds the text even more firmly in the originating culture. Usually some significant translation of the author's work into the host country's language is the first step in developing international influence, and that is generally followed by critical responses to the work in translation. This book takes the next step, translating this international critical response to Whitman back into English and investigating the nature of the response, so that the international reaction can in turn begin to have an impact on Americans' comprehension of Whitman's importance. *Walt Whitman and the World* completes the circle, allowing the insights that have been gained by reading Whitman in other cultural contexts to impinge on the rather provincial understanding of Whitman held by many American readers and writers, who tend still to view him only in an American context and who tend to be oblivious to the variety of ways that Whitman has been construed for the purposes and needs of other cultures.

One of the most persistent concerns about the field of American Studies and American Literature in the past half century has been its provincialism, its insistence that American literature can only be understood in national terms, in relation to the opening of the American West, in relation to the Civil War, in relation to the search for a distinctly American literature. Such approaches to American literature were necessary to offset the earlier perception of the nation's writing as simply a subset of British literature, a colonial literature best read in the context of and judged in relation to the tradition of English literature in the old country. But the work of defining the national origins and goals of American literature is largely complete, and more recent concerns in the field now call for a wider understanding of the multicultural forces that have combined to form what we call "American" literature: Spanish influences, Japanese and Chinese contributions, Amerindian influences, African influences. It is vital to see the melding of various ethnic traditions that form American literature, and such a melding was exactly what Whitman celebrated about his country's emerging literary and political traditions. He saw a time when democratic literature would transcend national boundaries, and he did his best to encourage an international reaction to his work, to generate a debate on the nature of democratic literature that would eventually produce poets from around the world who would carry on and refine the project he began.

But even Whitman would have been startled by the variety of reactions to his work and by the multitude of ways that his call for a democratic literature has been heard. The tracking of this international response, then, is one way that American literature can be conceptualized outside of national boundaries and outside of "English" influences and reactions. This book internationalizes our perception of American literature by demonstrating how various cultures appropriate an American writer who ceases to sound quite so narrowly "American" as soon as he is read into another culture's traditions.

Those readers interested primarily in American literature will find this study yielding fascinating insights into and responses to American cultural concerns and will discover how differently American literary traditions appear to those who are more distant from the localized historical, political, and economic factors that surrounded nineteenth-century writers. We have set out to challenge narrow nationalistic views of American authors by placing America's most important poet clearly and fully in a remarkably wide international context and by assessing the ways that other cultures have adapted an important American writer for their own political, artistic, and religious needs.

Those readers interested in reception theory and those interested in the problematics of translation will find here a detailed case study of the multicultural reception of a major figure. If, as is often claimed, poetry is what is lost in translation, this book demonstrates just what new poetry emerges *in* the act of translation itself, so that often it is not Whitman who influences another culture so much as Whitman-as-rendered-by a particularly influential translator (as was the case with Ferdinand Freiligrath and Johannes Schlaf in German-speaking cultures).

No poet has generated more responses from other writers than Whitman has. Authors from around the world have written poems and essays and books that directly respond to questions that Whitman raised; they literally talk back to him, across time, across cultures, across languages. Whitman always addressed his work to "poets to come," and those later writers have taken up his challenge by arguing with him, adapting his innovations, realigning his sympathies, and developing his insights. This gathering of a wide array of international responses forms a tapestry that reveals for the first time the overall patterns of the century-long response to Whitman, a pattern that has much to do with the way democratic ideals, democratic attitudes, and democratic institutions are perceived around the world. It should be emphasized that, while the nature of democracy and of democratic art is at the heart of Whitman's influence, the patterns of his reception in other cultures are complex and far from jingoistic. There is little evidence of any such phenomenon as Whitman/America conquering the world in the name of democracy. Instead, there are complex weaves of influence, resistance, realignment, and application — a kind of resistant "talking back" to Whitman by other cultures, a dialogue that challenges as much as it affirms.

Whitman thus enters each culture as a singular figure; his views of democracy and of democratic art are distinctly reconfigured by every culture he enters. The act of translation itself alters his poetry and makes it conform in ways it otherwise would not to the traditions and tones of the receiving nation. His free verse forms—connected as intimately as they are to American speech rhythms, oratorical styles, and colloquial diction—are difficult to reproduce in other languages; in some cases, simply to be able to reproduce his work as something that would be perceived *as* poetry by readers in the host culture, translators have reformed his free verse style into patterned and rhymed verse. Moreover, each translated version of his work is produced with specific motivations and is read in specific contexts, so certain elements of Whitman's work are emphasized, others silenced. Whitman thus enters Indian culture as a western version of a Hindu prophet, and his work is perceived as endorsing a democracy of the spirit, while his poems are read as a kind of yoga discipline. This version of Whitman is very different from the political revolutionary, often seen as a prophet of socialism, that defined the Whitman who entered the cultures of many European nations in the late nineteenth century. And, in turn, that radical version of Whitman contrasts the politically conservative apologist for American imperialism that was the Whitman often perceived (and resisted) in Latin American cultures. But even such rough generalizations do a disservice to the complex dynamics that generate each national version of Whitman, where he is finally far from a simplistic construct but rather emerges as a figure who incorporates many and often conflicting strands of any given culture's concerns and obsessions. This text contains many possibilities for understanding Whitman, gathered from many different times and places. Out of these possibilities, the reader is invited to construct not only a new understanding of Walt Whitman but also a new understanding of how national literatures might function in a dawning era of internationalism.

As this book was being prepared for press, international events continued to remind us how fluid and unstable many national identities are. With the breakup of the Soviet Union and the dismantling of Yugoslavia and Czechoslovakia, studies of Whitman's international influence echo the increasing fragmentation. What formerly seemed like relatively simple absorptions of Whitman into a single nationality now reveal themselves to be much more complex and multiple patterns of influence. We have tried to trace some of these emerging new patterns, especially in the former country of Yugoslavia, where Whitman's entry had several distinct sources in Slovenian, Croatian, and Serbian traditions. With the swift changes in national boundaries and the resurgence of long-repressed ethnic affinities, it becomes clear that any book like this one can only be a snapshot of the current state of an ongoing process. Whitman continues to be an active agent in cultures that are themselves undergoing unpredictable changes. Joking about the bewildering array of photographs of himself that he kept encountering, Whitman once said, "I meet new Walt Whitmans every day. There are 'a dozen of me afloat."[4] He would no doubt feel the same way were he able to see the versions of Walt Whitman that continue to emerge in cultures around the world: year after year in country after country, there are new Whitmans afloat.

NOTES

1. Justin Kaplan, ed., *Complete Poetry and Selected Prose* (New York: Library of America, 1982), 1049.

2. Gay Wilson Allen, ed., *Walt Whitman Abroad* (Syracuse: Syracuse University Press, 1955), viii.

3. Huck Gutman, *As Others Read Us: International Perspectives on American Literature* (Amherst: University of Massachusetts Press, 1991), 16, 11.

4. Horace Traubel, *With Walt Whitman in Camden* (Boston: Small Maynard, 1906), 1: 108.

ABBREVIATIONS

LG: Walt Whitman, *Leaves of Grass*, Comprehensive Reader's Edition, ed. Harold Blodgett and Sculley Bradley. New York: New York University Press, 1965.

M. WYNN THOMAS

Whitman in the British Isles

"Those blessed gales from the British Isles probably (certainly)
saved me. . . . That emotional, audacious, open-handed, friendly-mouthed, just-
opportune English action, I say, plucked me like a brand from the burning, and
gave me life again. . . . I do not forget it, and I shall never forget it." [1] Whitman's ef-
fusively favorable view of his standing in Britain has not been fully endorsed by
scholars, who point to the distinctly stormy reception accorded *Leaves of Grass* by
an outraged cultural establishment, from the hostile early *Critic* review onward
(see selection 2). But as the excited response of the elderly Charles Ollier, onetime
friend of Shelley, shows (see selection 1), the book — and its author — did appeal
immensely to those writers and intellectuals who belonged to the radical subcul-
ture of Victorian Britain.[2] To such progressives, his blatant Americanness was important, since it confirmed his status as prophet of the social and political future,
but they also saw him as the heir to a distinguished British and European tradition
of libertarianism, represented in literature by figures such as Burns, Blake, and
Shelley.[3] So by 1894 Henry Salt (see selection 21) could construct around Whitman
an anthology deliberately meant as a challengingly radical alternative to that
influential Victorian fashioner of an Arnoldian "great tradition," *The Golden
Treasury*. Although Palgrave's famous anthology purported to be purely literary
and strictly apolitical, Salt set out to expose its covert cultural conservativism
by following the example of critics like Edward Dowden, who had discovered,

through reading Whitman, how instinct with political assumptions was the form, as well as the content, of works of literature (see selection 9). Dowden was one of the first critics to use Tocqueville's *Democracy in America* as a commentary on *Leaves of Grass*.

In 1885 another radical, the militant democrat and protosocialist Ernest Rhys, set out to save Whitman not only from his enemies but also from his cultivated middle-class friends, in order to make his revolutionary gospel of thoroughgoing egalitarianism known to the masses newly made literate by the education acts of the 1870s. Rhys's letter (selection 13) reminds us that Whitman's initial appeal had been to a small, maverick, middle-class elite of academics, bohemian artists, and men of letters who discovered in his classlessness and sexual frankness, his robust "healthiness" and bold optimism, a relief from the inhibitions and prohibitions of their own sickly culture (see J. A. Symonds's comments in selection 20).[4] The activities of this coterie of devotees, which bore several of the hallmarks of a religious cult, are too well known to need further documentation, but it may be worth emphasizing that many of the critical "monologues" printed here are in fact only one side of a complex dialogue. Swinburne, for instance, was already attempting in 1872 (see selection 7) to distance himself from the more uncritically adulatory of Whitman's supporters, an increasingly violent process of self-extrication that culminated in his notorious attack on "Whitmania" in 1887.[5] Even the urbane and measured style of conspicuously accomplished writers like George Saintsbury and Edmund Gosse (see selections 8 and 22) can be regarded as a standing rebuke to the gushing rhapsodies of the faithful.[6] But John Addington Symonds makes a challenging point when he claims that established, conventional critical discourse is incapable of dealing adequately with the revolutionary character of this poetry (see selection 20). His call for a new and answerable style of critical discussion is relevant both to Anne Gilchrist's powerfully informal, torrentially impetuous manner of writing (selection 6) and to the later vatic stance of John Cowper Powys (selection 30) or the fluid explorations of D. H. Lawrence (see selection 27 and *Studies in Classic American Literature*). Bearing Symonds's remark in mind, it is worth noting that the best early British (selection 1) and American (Emerson's 1855 response to Whitman) reactions to *Leaves of Grass* came in the unstudied and unbuttoned form of a private letter.

It wasn't only members of the intelligentsia who were intensely attracted to Whitman's writings. From 1885 onward a devoted group of skilled workers and lower-middle-class professionals in industrial Bolton met regularly on Monday evenings to study his work. Many of them saw in him a great prophet of the new socialist "religion," and they succeeded in spreading his "gospel" of universal brotherhood to the Labour Church and to the Independent Labour Party, whose revered leader, Keir Hardie, came to regard Whitman as a fellow spirit. Edward Carpenter formed a close association with the circle; two of its members went on pilgrimages to Camden for an audience with Whitman himself; and in turn his beloved, distinguished disciple R. M. Bucke paid the group a visit in 1891. As a last token, at once touching and funny, of Whitman's special affection for the ordinary "fellows" of the "Bolton College," the poet allowed them to stuff the body of his dead pet canary — the caged bird that had comforted him during his last, gloomy years — and carry it back to England with them. In their turn, his Bolton followers remained staunchly true to his memory (see selection 25). "Whitman Day" remained a labor holiday in that part of Lancashire right down to the 1950s.[7]

Whitman's early followers may have congregated in small groups and formed exclusive coteries, but they were nevertheless also usually part of what became a broad movement for social, political, and cultural reform in Victorian Britain. By the turn of the century this movement included radical Liberals, utopian socialists, supporters of Lib-Lab politics, and members of the Independent Labour Party, and activists in these disparate groups were usually exposed to Whitman's influence through the distorting medium of Edward Carpenter's prose and poetry (particularly *Towards Democracy*, which has been aptly described as "Whitman and water"). The reaction to *Leaves of Grass* during the nineteenth and early twentieth centuries can, in fact, be usefully charted against the background of the initially doubtful and then irresistible rise of broad-based Victorian progressivism and radicalism, culminating, however, in the emergence of a new politics of class conflict.[8] When *Leaves of Grass* first appeared in 1855, the American republican "experiment" was viewed with hostile skepticism by conservatives and with considerable misgivings even by liberals (see selection 4). But by the time of the publication in 1860 of Rossetti's influential sanitized selection of Whitman's poetry (see selection 5), Britain had already embarked on a program of social and political reconstruction that was broadly parallel to the American example. Special enthusiasm for Whitman was therefore grounded in a general optimism about "democracy," although an occasional renegade supporter, such as Roden Noel, could still express reservations about the indiscriminately "levelling" spirit of the poetry (selection 14). The prevailing climate of opinion partly accounts for the great increase of interest in American literature during the last third of the century, with Emerson and Hawthorne in particular being regarded as major writers. American authors accounted for 10 percent of all titles bought in Britain during the 1880s. The first complete and uncensored British edition of *Leaves of Grass* appeared in 1881, and twenty editions of Whitman's poetry had been published by 1900.[9]

But if there was no longer condescending talk about the naive provincialism and comical brashness of the States, little attempt was made to examine in detail the complex historical background from which *Leaves of Grass* had actually emerged. (J. A. MacCulloch's comments [selection 23] are an exception.) Instead, Whitman was welcomed as the embodiment of all that was progressive — in his enlightened attitude toward science, religion, sex (see selection 16), and women (see selection 6). As the century drew to its close, however, the confidence of some liberal humanists began to wane, and even previously ardent supporters like Dowden and Robert Louis Stevenson began to revise their views of Whitman's philosophy. Even Henry Bryan Binns's 1905 *Life of Walt Whitman*, which registered the poet's loose affiliation with socialism, reflected the decline in Whitman's reputation as a social prophet; Binns set out to write an "objective" biography, not a polemical one. Forster's wistful little article (selection 26), addressed to "working men" during a time of bitter labor disputes, is clearly the product of this twilight period of liberalism and can be regarded as a relic of the 1890s, when Whitman's poetry had appealed to a whole generation of young Cambridge intellectuals, including Lowes Dickinson, Roger Fry, G. M. Trevelyan, and G. E. Moore.[10] The decline in Whitman's status as a social prophet may well have helped Basil de Selincourt to concentrate almost exclusively on Whitman's standing as a poet (selection 28). His brilliant, innovative study of the unconventional and much-derided artistry of *Leaves of Grass* appeared just as the First World War was finally pulverizing the world of liberalism. A year later Pound's *Cathay* was published, helping to usher in an aggressive literary modernism whose British followers and opponents alike were mostly to treat Whitman as a mere irrelevance.

Those late-nineteenth-century texts that testify to Whitman's power as a great liberator, and even as a savior, are particularly fascinating cultural documents precisely because they now seem so historically remote; once more, the most striking of them comes in the form of a series of letters sent by Anne Gilchrist to Rossetti (see selection 6). Her startlingly unguarded response may in many respects repel rather than inspire modern feminists, but taken in its totality it provides a quite fearsome insight into the plight of Victorian women. In particular, Gilchrist defends Whitman's treatment of sexuality with a fiercely passionate intelligence completely unmatched elsewhere in all the Victorian verbiage about his "obscenity." By comparison, Pauline Roose's discussion of Whitman as a "childpoet" may at first seem coyly sentimental and cutely maternal (selection 18). But it has its own subversive aspects, since it adroitly avoids passing conventional moral judgment on the sexual morality of the poetry by radically changing the terms of the discussion and incidentally points the way forward to later psychoanalytic readings of Whitman's "infantilism" and polymorphous-perverse tendencies.

Two other daring explorers of the sexual content of the poetry returned with findings very different from those of Gilchrist and Roose. Havelock Ellis and Symonds both strongly suspected that Whitman's secret erotic preference was for the homophile relationships celebrated so ambiguously in the *Calamus* sequence (see selections 16 and 20). Like his friend Edward Carpenter, Ellis exulted in this discovery, but Symonds's anguished uncertainty about both Whitman's real sexual orientation and Symonds's own attitude toward homosexuality permeates his writing.[11] Yet although these Britons were among the first to crack Whitman's sexual code, he seems never to have assumed the kind of importance in gay men's circles in Britain that he has in the culture of American gays.[12]

Both for its quantity and for its quality, then, the best of British reactions to *Leaves of Grass* deserved Whitman's gratitude. "Those blessed gales from the British Islands" he called the support he had received, before lapsing into a description of it as "a just-opportune English action." He was right the first time, since it was not only England but each of the countries of the British Isles that played its part in establishing Whitman's reputation. Wales did least, because its culture, strongly nonconformist, continued to exist mainly in the Welsh language, but it nevertheless contributed through the Anglo-Welshman Ernest Rhys and later through the adopted Welshman John Cowper Powys.[13] P. Mansell Jones's comparison of Whitman to the great Belgian poet Verhaeren (selection 29) was an interesting cultural by-product of Lloyd George's recruitment appeal to his countrymen to remember that other small beleaguered European country, gallant little Belgium. Yet during the First World War, T. E. Nicholas (Niclas y Glais) used a crude form of free verse modeled on Whitman's example to produce a savage attack in Welsh on the carnage which capitalism was sponsoring. As for Scotland, the interest it showed in Whitman was quite remarkable and can perhaps best be attributed both to the pronounced liberal and libertarian strain in the culture since the period of the Scottish enlightenment and to a degree of sympathetic fellow-feeling by the Scots for another non-English but English-speaking nation. No fewer than three books on Whitman were published in Scotland during his lifetime, including John Robertson's incisively intelligent polemical pamphlet (selection 11).[14] Leading Scottish writers from Robert Louis Stevenson to the redoubtable Hugh MacDiarmid have acknowledged the significant debt they've owed to Whitman's example, and since the Second World War David Daiches has been an accomplished and prolific interpreter of his poetry (selection 35).[15]

It was in Ireland, though, that Whitman had the greatest impact of all, as W. B. Yeats's letter best illustrates (selection 19). Dowden was, of course, an Anglo-Irishman and the center of a Whitman circle well known to the poet himself. Whitman's deepest influence on Irish literature was, however, transmitted by different means, through figures who played a key part at different stages in the Irish Renaissance.[16] These included Standish O'Grady, AE (George Russell), Sean O'Casey, and Frank O'Connor.[17] Even Joyce, in *Finnegans Wake*, registered Whitman's presence as a force in modern Irish culture,[18] and the letters written by Yeats in his youth show how he looked to Whitman to provide a model and an inspiration for the development of an independent, indigenous Irish literature in English.[19] Padraic Colum anticipated Lawrence in his sensitive discussion of Whitman's work as, both in form and content, a poetry of "Becoming" (see selection 31).[20] Nor was Whitman's influence confined to the writers. The freedom fighter James Connolly took Whitman's "Defiant Deed" as the text of his address to his followers during the Easter Rising in 1916, and his friend, the famous labor leader James Larkin, claimed his love of humanity derived from the writings of Thoreau, Emerson, and "the greatest man of all next to Whitman — Mark Twain."[21] The warmth of Irish attachment to Whitman continues to be evident in the panache of the recent studies by Denis Donoghue (selection 38), while the comments of the contemporary Ulster poet Tom Paulin (selection 43) represent a fascinating attempt, reminiscent of Henry Salt's a century ago, to link Whitman to a native British republican tradition.

What, though, of Whitman's creative influence on the *writers* of the British Isles? While poets as diverse as Hopkins (selection 10), Wilde, Isaac Rosenberg, and Dylan Thomas have been fascinated by his work,[22] it seems that W. H. Auden (see selection 36) and Charles Tomlinson are pretty close to the mark when they single out Lawrence as the sole example of a major writer whose imagination was certainly informed, and had perhaps been transformed, by Whitman's poetry.[23] Lawrence's resultant attitude toward the American was so prickly and so chronically ambivalent that between 1913 and 1923 he made at least three separate and significantly different attempts to write him out of his system. The last two essays are already very well known, while the first must await publication by Cambridge University Press, but Lawrence's marvelously suggestive letter to Henry Savage deserves more attention, since everything he says later is there in embryo (selection 27).[24] Tomlinson's recent demonstration of the extent of Whitman's influence on Ivor Gurney is revealing (selection 42), but in spite of his sensitive tribute to Whitman in "Crossing Brooklyn Ferry" and other poems (selection 40),[25] Tomlinson offers in his own work a perfect example of the preference most important modern British poets have shown, whenever they have turned to American literature, for Pound and his fellow-modernists over Whitman. At the same time, those writing determinedly in the British grain have — with the occasional memorable exception such as Geoffrey Grigson (selection 39) — regarded Whitman as the epitome of all that is foreign (and wrong) in American writing. The case with modern British composers has been intriguingly different, as the novelist Anthony Burgess points out (selection 37).

In retrospect, Lawrence's essay in *Studies in Classic American Literature* (1923) can be seen to have been the culmination of almost seventy years of intense and frequently controversial discussion by British writers and critics of *Leaves of Grass* and its author. For almost half a century thereafter, however, Whitman was virtually ignored. Hugh l'Anson Faussett's comments (selection 32) illuminate the situation during the thirties and remind us that Whitman's philosophy of a kind of corporate or cooperative individualism was unconvincing and unsympathetic to those who believed in the need for collectivist solutions to modern social problems. Published to mark the fiftieth anniversary of Whitman's death in 1942, Faussett's book was reviewed in the *Times Literary Supplement*, where the reviewer understandably warmed to those aspects of Whitman that had left Faussett cold — his advocacy of a personal freedom that was the antithesis of totalitarianism in both its Fascist and its Communist forms.[26] A renewed interest in democracy not only as a political system but also as a human ideal is evident in the elderly J. Middleton Murry's postwar, and Cold War, study (selection 34).

In 1955 the *Times Literary Supplement* welcomed Gay Wilson Allen's *The Solitary Singer*: "a good biography of Whitman is particularly needed in this country, for most of us are only lightly acquainted with the social and political background of the America of his day."[27] Since then the growth of American Studies in British universities has done much to improve the situation, and most of the discussion of Whitman over the past thirty years has taken place within that specialized professional context. The evident strengths of such a delimiting approach have, however, their corresponding weaknesses, which is why the cross-cultural comparisons effortlessly made by an elegantly perceptive nonacademic like V. S. Pritchett and a gifted general practitioner like John Bayley are such vitally important correctives (selections 33 and 41). After all, Whitman's appeal in Britain had, from the very first, extended well beyond the academy and has frequently been deliciously unpredictable.[28]

NOTES

1. Floyd Stovall, ed., *Prose Works 1892* (New York: New York University Press, 1964), 2: 699–700. Whitman is referring specifically to the kindness of Rossetti and his friends who supported him through subscriptions in 1875 and 1876.

2. For further information about Charles Ollier, see M. Wynn Thomas, "'A New World of Thought': Whitman's Early Reception in England," *Walt Whitman Review* 27 (June 1981): 74–78. This article also argues the case for identifying Edmund Ollier as the probable author of *The Leader* review (selection 3).

3. See, for instance, Swinburne's discussion of Whitman in *William Blake: A Critical Essay* (London: John Camden Hotten, 1868).

4. Note, for instance, the comment of J. A. MacCulloch in *Westminster Review* (July–December 1899): 550: "He is in marked contrast to Clough and Arnold, poets of despair, of those moods of the soul which are suited to so many in our time." The standard study of Whitman's early admirers is still Harold Blodgett, *Walt Whitman in England* (Cornell: Cornell University Press, 1934; reprint, New York: Russell and Russell, 1973). His succinct summary of the nineteenth-century British reaction is worth recording: "As the British reader turned the pages [of *Leaves of Grass*], he was confronted, according to his temperament, by Whitman the magnetic lover and glorifier of life, Whitman the archetype of the American democrat, Whitman the great prophet of the world's hope, Whitman the innovating artist, or Whitman the vulgar and ignorant charlatan" (216). See also the section on Britain in Gay Wilson Allen, *The New Walt Whitman Handbook* (New York: New York University Press, 1975), and the section on *Leaves of Grass* in Benjamin Lease, *Anglo-American Encounters* (Cambridge: Cambridge University Press, 1981), 229–254.

5. On the vexed question of Swinburne's "defection," see Blodgett, *Walt Whitman*, chapter 7; Georges Lafourcade, "Swinburne and Walt Whitman," *Modern Language Review* 22 (1927): 84–86; W. B. Cairns, "Swinburne's View of Whitman," *American Literature* 3 (May 1931): 125–135; Clyde K. Hyder, "Swinburne's 'Changes of Aspect' and Short Notes," *PMLA* 58 (March 1943): 241; William J. Gaede, "Swinburne and the Whitmaniacs," *Victorian Newsletter* 33 (1968): 16–21.

6. For Gosse, see Robert L. Peters, "Edmund Gosse's Two Whitmans," *Walt Whitman Review* 11 (1965): 19–21.

7. The fullest account of the Bolton group is to be found in Paul Salvesen, *Loving Comrades: Lancashire's Links to Walt Whitman* (a pamphlet published by the author in conjunction with the Bolton Branch of the Workers' Educational Association, 1984); the poem by Hawkins included here is reprinted from page 6 of Salvesen's book. See also Blodgett, *Walt Whitman*, chapter 12.

8. For this interpretation and related material, I am deeply indebted to R. H. Jellema's

unpublished doctoral dissertation, "Victorian Critics and the Orientation of American Literature, with Special Reference to the Reception of Walt Whitman and Henry James" (University of Edinburgh, 1962–1963).

9. See Clarence Gohdes, *American Literature in Nineteenth Century England* (Carbondale: Southern Illinois University Press, 1944). He also makes the point that after the Franco-Prussian War, Britain increasingly looked on America as an ally against the rising European superpower of Germany.

10. For an analysis of Binns's biography, see Jerome Loving, "The Binns Biography," in Ed Folsom, ed., *Walt Whitman: The Centennial Essays* (Iowa City: University of Iowa Press, 1994), 10–18. I am grateful to my friend, Tony Brown, UCNW, Bangor, for drawing Forster's article to my attention. Whitman's influence on the Cambridge liberals, and thereby eventually on the Bloomsbury group, is discussed by Howard Howarth, "Whitman and the English Writers," in Lister F. Zimmerman and Winston Weathers, eds., *Papers on Walt Whitman* (Tulsa, Oklahoma: University of Tulsa, 1970), 6–25.

11. For Carpenter, see A. D. Brown, ed., *Edward Carpenter and Late Victorian Radicalism* (London: Frank Cass, 1990).

12. For the history of gay culture in Britain and its representation in literature, see Eve Kosofsky Sedgwick, *Between Men: English Literature and Male Homosocial Desire* (New York: Columbia University Press, 1985).

13. For Rhys, see M. Wynn Thomas, "Walt Whitman's Welsh Connection: Ernest Rhys," *Anglo-Welsh Review* 82 (1986): 77–85; J. Kimberley Roberts, *Ernest Rhys* (Cardiff: University of Wales Press, 1983). Welsh-language writers influenced by Whitman are discussed in M. Wynn Thomas, "From Walt to Waldo: Whitman's Welsh Admirers," *Walt Whitman Quarterly Review* 10 (Fall 1992): 61–73.

14. The Scottish context is well discussed by Jellema, "Victorian Critics." Allen, however, believes that "Scotland was slow in accepting Whitman" (*Handbook*, 275). The importance of Burns to Whitman is discussed in Robert Crawford, *Devolving English Literature* (Oxford: Clarendon Press, 1992), 208–213.

15. Hugh MacDiarmid, *Lucky Poet* (London: Jonathan Cape, 1972), 188–189.

16. See Terence Diggory, *Yeats and American Poetry* (Princeton: Princeton University Press, 1983); Herbert Howarth, "Whitman among the Irish," *London Magazine* (1960): 48–55; James E. Quinn, "Yeats and Whitman, 1887–1925," *Walt Whitman Review* 20 (1974): 106–109.

17. See Standish O'Grady, "Walt Whitman, the Poet of Joy," *Gentleman's Magazine* 15 (n.s.) (London, 1875): 704–716. Patrick Kavanagh's refreshingly irreverent reaction to AE's solemn enthusiasm for Whitman is worth recalling: "I was a peasant and a peasant is a narrow surveyor of generous hearts. He read me Whitman, of whom he was very fond, and also Emerson. I didn't like Whitman and said so. I always thought him a writer who tried to bully his way to prophecy" (*The Green Fool* [London: Martin, Brian & O'Keefe, 1971], 301).

18. *Finnegans Wake* (New York: Viking Press, 1959), 263, 551. See also Don Summerhayes, "Joyce's *Ulysses* and Whitman's 'Self,'" *Wisconsin Studies in Contemporary Literature* 4 (1963): 216–224.

19. Yeats's comments on Whitman in his letters should be read in conjunction with the

very different opinion he expressed in *A Vision*, Book One, phase six (London: Macmillan, 1978), 113–114.

20. See D. H. Lawrence's introduction to the American edition of *New Poems*, in Anthony Beal, ed., *D. H. Lawrence: Selected Literary Criticism* (London: Heinemann, 1964), 84–89.

21. Robert Flack, "A Note on Whitman in Ireland," *Walt Whitman Review* 21 (1975): 160–162.

22. Oscar Wilde, "The Gospel According to Walt Whitman," *Pall Mall Gazette* 49 (London, January 25, 1889), 3. Rosenberg expresses a touching admiration for *Drum-Taps* in his wartime letters (see G. Bottomley and D. Harding, eds., *The Collected Works of Isaac Rosenberg* [London: Chatto and Windus, 1937], 348, 358). More about Hopkins's interest can be found in Jerry A. Herndon, "Hopkins and Whitman," *Walt Whitman Review* 24 (1978): 161–162. Whitman's portrait had a place of honor on the wall of the Laugharne boathouse where Dylan Thomas worked. His mentions of Whitman occur in numbers 117 and 145 of Paul Ferris, ed., *The Collected Letters* (London: Dent, 1985). For Whitman's influence on Thomas, see Stanley Friedman, "Whitman and Laugharne," *Anglo-Welsh Review* 18 (1969): 81; Paul J. Ferlazzo, "Dylan Thomas and Walt Whitman: Birth, Death and Time," *Walt Whitman Review* 23 (1977): 136–141; James E. Miller, Jr., Karl Shapiro, and Bernice Slote, *Start with the Sun* (Lincoln: University of Nebraska Press, 1960). Other interesting material on Whitman's connection with British writers includes John M. Ditsky, "Whitman-Tennyson Correspondence: A Summary and Commentary," *Walt Whitman Review* 18 (1972): 75–82; George Ray Eliott, "Browning's Whitmanism," *Sewanee Review* 37 (April 1929): 164–171; W. E. Fredeman, "Whitman and William Morris," *Victorian Poetry* 15 (Autumn/Winter 1977); George Soule, "Rupert Brooke and Whitman," *Little Review* (April 1914): 15–16.

23. For the complicated history of Lawrence's treatment of Whitman, see George Y. Trail's comprehensive essay, "Lawrence's Whitman," *D. H. Lawrence Review* 14, no. 2 (Summer 1981): 172–190; Richard Swigg, *Lawrence, Hardy and American Literature* (London: Oxford University Press, 1977); R. W. French, "Whitman and the Poetics of Lawrence," in Jeffrey Meyers, ed., *D. H. Lawrence and Tradition* (Amherst: University of Amherst Press, 1985), 91–114; Rosemarie Arbour, "'Lilacs' and 'Sorrow': Whitman's Effect on the Early Poems of D. H. Lawrence," *Walt Whitman Review* 24 (1978): 17–21.

24. I am very grateful to my friend and colleague John Worthen, one of the senior editors of the Cambridge University Press edition of Lawrence's works, for his attempt, though unsuccessful, to obtain permission for me to include Lawrence's unpublished essay in this collection. A summary (already out of date) of the various essays on Whitman written by Lawrence can be found in Warren Roberts, *A Bibliography of D. H. Lawrence* (Cambridge: Cambridge University Press, 2d ed., 1982). Even more succinct than Lawrence's remarks in the letter is his poem "Retort to Whitman": "And whoever walks a mile full of false sympathy / walks to the funeral of the whole human race" (V. de Sola Pinto and W. Roberts, eds., *The Complete Poems of D. H. Lawrence* [London: Heinemann, 1967], 2: 633).

25. See also "A Garland for Thomas Eakins," *Selected Poems, 1951–1974* (Oxford: Oxford University Press, 1978), 76, and "Hero Sandwiches," *Notes from New York* (Oxford: Ox-

ford University Press, 1984), 23. Tomlinson first discovered Pound when he went up to Cambridge in 1945, and what Pound "had to teach survived the only other reading of an American that I accomplished in bulk at Cambridge. This was Whitman. He, along with Nietzsche, formed the style of the earliest unfortunate poems that I wrote on going down in 1948" (*Some Americans: A Personal Record* [Berkeley: University of California Press, 1981], 3).

26. "Whitman: Poet of Democracy," *Times Literary Supplement,* Saturday, March 14, 1942, 126; also the lead article, "Masses or Men," 127.

27. *TLS,* Friday, June 10, 1955, 316.

28. Douglas Grant's remark should always be borne in mind: "The history of Whitman's reception in England [*sic*] . . . is almost as important to an understanding of English taste and sensibility as it is to the appraisal of the poet, and may help to show why we should be unwise to neglect American literature, or to allow it to be always treated as if it existed on its own" ("Walt Whitman and His English Admirers," University of Leeds inaugural lecture, University of Leeds Press, 1962; reprinted in *Purpose and Place* [London: Macmillan, 1965]).

1. CHARLES OLLIER

Letter to Leigh Hunt, February 19, 1856

[Whitman] says he is "one of the roughs," a "kosmos" etc; and in another part of his poem, he tells us his age & that he is six feet high.

"Well!" say you, "What care I? Who the deuce is Walt. Whitman?"

Let me be the first to tell you.

Walt. is an American — a sensualist — a "rough" — a "rowdy" — a "kosmos" (this is odd) — a poet — a humanist — an egotist — a transcendentalist, and a philosopher. Except the first book ever written (and who can tell what that was?) Walt. has given to the world the most original book ever composed. Other writers are derivations from their predecessors. Chaucer had his precursors; so had Spenser; so had Shakespeare; so Milton, and the rest. But Walt. is himself *alone:* himself in his mode of utterance, in his all-embracing philosophy, in his imagery, his description, his word-craft, and in every thing else. O the delight of getting into a new intellectual region!

Walt's book, just arrived from New York, is a quarto with very full pages, published without any publisher's name or any author's; but he faces the title with what our ancestors used to call the writer's true effigies, as much as to say "Here is the man who wrote this work. How do you like me? What do you think of me?" And there he stands in his shirt sleeves and bare neck and rough beard. He lets out his name in the course of the poem.

Walter Whitman is very fleshly as well as intellectual; and is too "particular" in the former respect. I wish it were not so. But one must be careful how one judges so large a mind. Perhaps he finds on that "side of things" as much to love and to wonder at as any other; and not only in that, but in "things evil," the soul of goodness in which he "observingly distils out." He says he is "the poet of the body, and the poet of the soul: the poet of goodness, and the poet of wickedness." And wonderfully does he work out his purpose, which appears to be the universal reconcilement of things. He is obscure — he is occasionally *slangy* and vulgar with his Yankeeisms and plain-speaking; and his mysticism is too frequent. But his pages open a new world of thought. He is profound and far-seeing: profound because he digs to the roots of things; & far-seeing because he looks at space. He is not a driveller, like Wordsworth who is a flat variation of Cowper. He lies at the feet of no man; but stands like a great statue on a mountain-top seen from afar or like that lonely warder on the summit of one of the towers in Claude's Enchanted Castle, whom the artist has posted there forever, grasping his spear, and forever gazing over the wide, weltering waste of water. Walt. is sure to be laughed at and derided. But he evidently does not write for tavern-wits, though he may be one of them — a rake, a rough, a rowdy. In his universal love (for it is nothing short of that) of his fellow-men, he can find the friendliest words for drunkards, prostitutes & fools. He scans with a learned eye the mysteries of our nature, & cannot detect anything to hate. I can already understand half his book, and hope some day to comprehend the remainder. Very very few things in the English language are so fine — so strong — so juicy — so marrowy — so eloquent as some of Walt's passages. He will not tolerate pattern-writing (like that of Longfellow) or transmitted phrases; but is ever fresh and surprising. His poem is not in rhyme nor in blank verse; but in what one of his Yankee reviewers calls "excited prose." He divides his paragraphs like stanzas: he has long & short lines: and sometimes lines so long as to run three or four times across the page. I cannot yet find out his music though I believe him to be musical for he talks with rapture of music, classical & otherwise. Plenty of ridicule awaits him, and he is the very man to bear it, for he is himself a droll; and he is a weeper too, making his reader weep with him whenever he pleases. His main endeavour, nevertheless, is to elevate his reader with the grandeur of his philosophy and his conceptions and to make the world happier than it is. Walt. is a great poet — almost a prophet. His poem is about nothing, because it is about everything.

Manuscript in British Museum.

2. ANONYMOUS REVIEW

We had ceased, we imagined, to be surprised at anything that America could produce. We had become stoically indifferent to her Woolly Horses, her Mermaids, her Sea Serpents, her Barnums, and her Fanny Ferns; but the last monstrous importation from Brooklyn, New York, has scattered our indifference to the winds. Here is a thin quarto volume without an author's name on the title-page; but to atone for which we have a portrait engraved on steel of the notorious individual who is the poet presumptive. This portrait expresses all the features of the hard democrat, and none of the flexile delicacy of the civilized poet. The damaged hat, the rough beard, the naked throat, the shirt exposed to the waist, are each and all presented to show that the man to whom those articles belong scorns the delicate arts of civilisation. The man is the true impersonation of the book—rough, uncouth, vulgar. It was by the merest accident that we discovered the name of this erratic and newest wonder: at page 29 we find that he is—

Walt Whitman, an American, one of the roughs, a Kosmos,
Disorderly, fleshly and sensual.

The words, "an American" are a surplusage, "one of the roughs" too painfully apparent; but what is intended to be conveyed by a "Kosmos" we cannot tell, unless it means a man who thinks that the fine essence of poetry consists in writing a book which an American reviewer is compelled to declare is "not to be read aloud to a mixed audience." We should have passed over this book, *Leaves of Grass*, with indignant contempt, had not some few Transatlantic critics attempted to "fix" this Walt Whitman as the poet who shall give a new and independent literature to America—who shall form a race of poets as Banquo's issue formed a line of kings. Is it possible that the most prudish nation in the world will adopt a poet whose indecencies stink in the nostrils? We hope not; and yet there is a probability, and we will show why, that this Walt Whitman will not meet with the stern rebuke which he so richly deserves. America has felt, oftener perhaps than we have declared, that she has no national poet—that each one of her children of song has relied too much on European inspiration, and clung too fervently to the old conventionalities. It is therefore not unlikely that she may believe in the dawn of a thoroughly original literature, now there has arisen a man who scorns the hellenic deities, who has no belief in, perhaps because he has no knowledge of, Homer and Shakespeare; who relies on his own rugged nature, and trusts to his own rugged language, being himself what he shows in his poems.

Once transfix him as the genesis of a new era, and the manner of the man may be forgiven or forgotten. But what claims has this Walt Whitman to be thus considered, or to be considered a poet at all? We grant freely enough that he has a strong relish for nature and freedom, just as an animal has; nay, further, that his crude mind is capable of appreciating some of nature's beauties; but it by no means follows that, because nature is excellent, therefore art is contemptible. Walt Whitman is as unacquainted with art, as a hog is with mathematics. His poems—we must call them so for convenience—twelve in number, are innocent of rhythm, and resemble nothing so much as the war-cry of the Red Indians. Indeed, Walt Whitman has had near and ample opportunities of studying the vociferation of a few amiable savages. Or rather perhaps, this Walt Whitman reminds us of

Caliban flinging down his logs, and setting himself to write a poem. In fact Caliban, and not Walt Whitman, might have written this:

I too am not a bit tamed—I too am untranslatable.
I sound my barbaric yawp over the roofs of the world.

Is this man with the "barbaric yawp" to push Longfellow into the shade, and he meanwhile to stand and "make mouths" at the sun? The chance of this might be formidable were it not ridiculous. That object or that act which most develops the ridiculous element carries in its bosom the seeds of decay, and is wholly powerless to trample out of God's universe one spark of the beautiful. We do not, then, fear this Walt Whitman, who gives us slang in the place of melody, and rowdyism in the place of regularity. The depth of his indecencies will be the grave of his fame, or ought to be if all proper feeling is not extinct. The very nature of this man's compositions excludes us from proving by extracts the truth of our remarks; but we, who are not prudish, emphatically declare that the man who wrote page 79 of the *Leaves of Grass* deserves nothing so richly as the public executioner's whip. Walt Whitman libels the highest type of humanity, and calls his free speech the true utterance of a *man*: we, who may have been misdirected by civilisation, call it the expression of *a beast* . . .

Critic 15 (April 1, 1856): 170–171.

3. EDMUND OLLIER (?)

"Transatlantic Latter-Day Poetry"

"Latter-day poetry" in America is of a very different character from the same manifestation in the old country. Here, it is occupied for the most part with dreams of the middle ages, of the old knightly and religious times: in America, it is employed chiefly with the present, except when it travels out into the undiscovered future. Here, our latter-day poets are apt to whine over the times, as if Heaven were perpetually betraying the earth with a show of progress that is in fact retrogression, like the backward advance of crabs: there, the minstrels of the stars and stripes blow a loud note of exultation before the grand new epoch, and think the Greeks and Romans, the early Oriental races, and the altar men of the middle centuries, of small account before the outward tramping of these present generations. Of this latter sect is a certain phenomenon who has recently started up in Brooklyn, New York—one Walt Whitman, author of "Leaves of Grass," who has been received by a section of his countrymen as a sort of prophet, and by Englishmen as a kind of fool. For ourselves, we are not disposed to accept him as the one, having less faith in latter-day prophets than in latter-day poets; but assuredly we cannot regard him as the other. Walt is one of the most amazing, one of the most startling, one of the most perplexing, creations of the modern American mind; but he is no fool, though abundantly eccentric, nor is his book mere food for laughter, though undoubtedly containing much that may most easily and fairly be turned into ridicule.

The singularity of the author's mind — his utter disregard of ordinary forms and modes — appears in the very title-page and frontispiece of his work. Not only is there no author's name (which in itself would not be singular), but there is no publisher's name — that of the English bookseller being a London addition. Fronting the title is the portrait of a bearded gentleman in his shirt-sleeves and a Spanish hat, with an all-pervading atmosphere of Yankee-doodle about him; but again there is no patronymic, and we can only infer that this roystering blade is the author of the book. Then follows a long prose treatise by way of Preface (and here once more the anonymous system is carried out, the treatise having no heading whatever); and after that we have the poem, in the course of which, a short autobiographical discourse reveals to us the name of the author. . . .

The poem is written in wild, irregular, unrhymed, almost unmetrical "lengths," like the measured prose of Mr. Martin Farquhar Tupper's *Proverbial Philosophy*, or of some of the Oriental writings. The external form, therefore, is startling, and by no means seductive, to English ears, accustomed to the sumptuous music of ordinary metres; and the central principle of the poem is equally staggering. It seems to resolve itself into an all-attracting egotism — an eternal presence of the individual soul of Walt Whitman in all things, yet in such wise that this one soul shall be presented as a type of all human souls whatsoever. He goes forth into the world, this rough, devil-may-care Yankee; passionately identifies himself with all forms of being, sentient or inanimate; sympathizes deeply with humanity; riots with a kind of Bacchanal fury in the force and fervour of his own sensations; will not have the most vicious or abandoned shut out from final comfort and reconciliation; is delighted with Broadway, New York, and equally in love with the desolate backwoods, and the long stretch of the uninhabited prairie, where the wild beasts wallow in the reeds, and the wilder birds start upwards from their nests among the grass; perceives a divine mystery wherever his feet conduct or his thoughts transport him; and beholds all beings tending towards the central and sovereign Me. Such, as we conceive, is the key to this strange, grotesque, and bewildering book; yet we are far from saying that the key will unlock all the quirks and oddities of the volume. Much remains of which we confess we can make nothing; much that seems to us purely fantastical and preposterous; much that appears to our muddy vision gratuitously prosaic, needlessly plain-speaking, disgusting without purpose, and singular without result. There are so many evidences of a noble soul in Whitman's pages that we regret these aberrations, which only have the effect of discrediting what is genuine by the show of something false; and especially do we deplore the unnecessary openness with which Walt reveals to us matters which ought rather to remain in a sacred silence. It is good not to be ashamed of Nature; it is good to have an all-inclusive charity; but it is also good, sometimes, to leave the veil across the Temple.

The Leader (June 7, 1856): 547.

4. MATTHEW ARNOLD

Letter to W. D. O'Connor, September 16, 1866

As to the general question of Mr. Walt Whitman's poetical achievement, you will think that it savours of our decrepit old Europe when I add that while you think it is his highest merit that he is so unlike anyone else, to me this seems to be his demerit; no one can afford in literature to trade merely on his own bottom and to take no account of what the other ages and nations have acquired: a great original literature America will never get in this way, and her intellect must inevitably consent to come, in a considerable measure, into the European movement. That she may do this and yet be an independent intellectual power, not merely as you say an intellectual colony of Europe, I cannot doubt; and it is on her doing this, and not on her displaying an eccentric and violent originality that wise Americans should in my opinion set their desires.

Bliss Perry, *Walt Whitman: His Life and Work* (Boston: Houghton Mifflin, 1906), 177–179.

5. WILLIAM MICHAEL ROSSETTI

Introduction, *Poems by Walt Whitman*

[*Leaves of Grass*], then, taken as a whole, is the poem both of Personality and Democracy; and, it may be added, of American nationalism. It is *par excellence* the modern poem. It is distinguished also by this peculiarity — that in it the most literal view of things is continually merging into the most rhapsodic or passionately abstract. Picturesqueness it has, but mostly of a somewhat patriarchal kind, not deriving from the "word-painting" of the *littérateur*; a certain echo of the old Hebrew poetry may even be caught in it, extra-modern though it is. Another most prominent and pervading quality of the book is the exuberant physique of the author. The conceptions are throughout those of a man in robust health, and might alter much under different conditions.

Further, there is a strong tone of paradox in Whitman's writings. He is both a realist and an optimist in extreme measure: he contemplates evil as in some sense not existing, or if existing, then as being of as much importance as anything else. Not that he is a materialist; on the contrary, he is a most strenuous assertor of the soul, and, with the soul, of the body as its infallible associate and vehicle in the present frame of things. Neither does he drift into fatalism or indifferentism; the energy of his temperament, and ever-fresh sympathy with national and other developments, being an effectual bar to this. The paradoxical element of the poems is such that one may sometimes find them in conflict with what has preceded, and would not be much surprised if they said at any moment the reverse of whatever they do say. This is mainly due to the multiplicity of the aspects of things, and to the immense width of relation in which Whitman stands to all sorts and all aspects of them.

But the greatest of this poet's distinctions is his absolute and entire originality. He may be termed formless by those who, not without much reason to show for themselves, are wedded to the established forms and ratified sentiments of poetic art; but it seems reasonable to enlarge the canon till it includes so great and startling a genius, rather than to draw it close and exclude him. His work is practically certain to stand as archetypal for many future poetic efforts — so great is his power as an originator, so fervid his initiative. It forms incomparably the *largest* performance of our period in poetry. Victor Hugo's *Légende des Siècles* alone might be named with it for largeness, and even that with much less of a new starting-point in conception and treatment. Whitman breaks with all precedent. To what he himself perceives and knows he has a personal relation of the intensest kind: to anything in the way of prescription, no relation at all. But he is saved from isolation by the depth of his Americanism; with the movement of his predominant nation he is moved. His comprehension, energy and tenderness, are all extreme, and all inspired by actualities. And, as for poetic genius, those who, without being ready to concede that faculty to Whitman, confess his iconoclastic boldness and his Titanic power of temperament, working in the sphere of poetry, do in effect confess his genius as well. . . .

Besides originality and daring, which have already been insisted upon, width and intensity are leading characteristics of his writings — width both of subject-matter and of comprehension, intensity of self-absorption into what the poet contemplates and expresses. He scans and presents an enormous panorama, unrolled before him as from a mountain-top; and yet whatever most large or most minute or casual thing his eye glances upon, that he enters into with a depth of affection which identifies him with it for the time, be the object what it may. There is a singular interchange also of actuality and of ideal substratum and suggestion. While he sees men, with even abnormal exactness and sympathy, as men, he sees them also "as trees walking," and admits us to perceive that the whole show is in a measure spectral and unsubstantial, and the mask of a larger and profounder reality beneath it, of which it is giving perpetual intimations and auguries. He is the poet indeed of literality, full of indirections as well as directness, and of readings between the lines. If he is the "cutest of Yankees," he is also as truly an enthusiast as any the most typical poet. All his faculties and performance glow into a white heat of brotherliness; and there is a *poignancy* both of tenderness and of beauty about his finer works which discriminates them quite as much as their modernness, audacity, or any other exceptional point. . . .

There is a singular and impressive intuition or revelation of Swedenborg's; that the whole of heaven is in the form of one man, and the separate societies of heaven in the forms of the several parts of man. In a large sense, the general drift of Whitman's writings, even down to the passages which read as most bluntly physical, bear a striking correspondence or analogy to this dogma. He takes man, and every organism and faculty of man, as the unit — the datum — from which all that we know, discern, and speculate, of abstract and supersensual, as well as of concrete and sensual, has to be computed. He knows of nothing nobler than that unit man; but, knowing that, he can use it for any multiple, and for any dynamical extension or recast.

Let us next obtain some idea of what this most remarkable poet — the founder of *American* poetry rightly to be so called, and the most sonorous poetic voice of the tangibilities of actual and prospective democracy — is in his proper life and person. . . .

A few words must be added as to the indecencies scattered through Whitman's writings. Indecencies or improprieties — or, still better, deforming crudities — they may rightly be termed; to call them immoralities would be going too far. Whitman finds himself, and other men and women, to be a compound of soul and body; he finds that body plays an extremely prominent and determining part in whatever he and other mundane dwellers have cognizance of; he perceives this to be the necessary condition of things, and therefore, as he fully and openly accepts it, the right condition; and he knows of no reason why what is universally seen and known, necessary and right, should not also be allowed and proclaimed in speech. That such a view of the matter is entitled to a great deal of weight, and at any rate to candid consideration and construction, appears to me not to admit of a doubt; neither is it dubious that the contrary view, the only view which a mealy-mouthed British nineteenth century admits as endurable, amounts to the condemnation of nearly every great or eminent literary work of past time, whatever the century it belongs to, the country it comes from, the department of writing it illustrates, or the degree or sort of merit it possesses.

(London: John Camden Hotten, 1868), 5–7, 9–11, 20–21.

6. ANNE GILCHRIST

An Englishwoman's Estimate of Walt Whitman

I had not dreamed that words could cease to be words, and become electric streams like these. I do assure you that, strong as I am, I feel sometimes as if I had not bodily strength to read many of these poems. In the series headed "Calamus," for instance, in some of the "Songs of Parting," the "Voice out of the Sea," the poem beginning "Tears, tears," etc., there is such a weight of emotion, such a tension of the heart, that mine refuses to beat under it — stands quite still — and I am obliged to lay the book down for a while. Or again, the piece called "Walt Whitman," and one or two others of that type, I am as one hurried through stormy seas, over high mountains, dazed with sunlight, stunned with a crowd and tumult of faces and voices, till I am breathless, bewildered, half-dead. Then come parts and whole poems in which there is such calm wisdom and strength of thought, such a cheerful breadth of sunshine, that the soul bathes in them renewed and strengthened. Living impulses flow out of these that make me exult in life, yet look longingly towards "the superb vistas of Death." Those who admire this poem, and do not care for that, and talk of formlessness, absence of metre, and so forth, are quite as far from any genuine recognition of Walt Whitman as his bitter detractors. Not, of course, that all the pieces are equal in power and beauty, but that all are vital; they grew — they were not made. We criticise a palace or a cathedral; but what is the good of criticising a forest? . . .

Nor do I sympathize with those who grumble at the unexpected words that turn up now and then. A quarrel with words is always, more or less, a quarrel with meanings; and here we are to be as genial and as wide as nature, and quarrel with nothing. If the thing a word stands for exists by divine appointment (and what does not so exist?) the word need never be ashamed of itself; the shorter and more direct, the better. It is a gain to make friends with it, and see it in good company. Here, at all events, "poetic diction" would not serve — not pretty, soft, colourless words, laid by in lavender for the special uses of poetry, that have had none of the wear and tear of daily life; but such as have stood most, as tell of human heartbeats; as fit closest to the sense, and have taken deep hues of association from the varied experiences of life — those are the words wanted here. We only ask to seize and be seized swiftly, overmasteringly, by the great meanings. We see with the eyes of the soul, listen with the ears of the soul; the poor old words that have served so many generations for purposes, good, bad, and indifferent, and become warped and blurred in the process, grow young again, regenerate, translucent. It is not mere delight they give us — *that* the "sweet singers," with their subtly wrought gifts, their mellifluous speech, can give too in their degree; it is such life and health as enable us to pluck delights for ourselves out of every hour of the day, and taste the sunshine that ripened the corn in the crust we eat — I often seem to myself to do that. . . .

You argued rightly that my confidence would not be betrayed by any of the poems in this book. None of them troubled me even for a moment; because I saw at a glance that it was not, as men had supposed, the heights brought down to the depths, but the depths lifted up level with the sunlit heights, that they might become clear and sunlit too. Always, for a woman, a veil woven out of her own soul — never touched upon even, with a rough hand, by this poet. But, for a man, a daring, fearless pride in himself, not a mock-modesty woven out of delusions —

a very proper imitation of a woman's. Do they not see that this fearful pride, this complete acceptance of themselves, is needful for her pride, her justification? What! is it all so ignoble, so base, that it will not bear the honest light of speech from lips so gifted with "the divine power to use words?" Then what hateful, bitter humiliation for her, to have to give herself up to the reality! Do you think there is ever a bride who does not taste more or less this bitterness in her cup? But who put it there? It must surely be man's fault, not God's, that she has to say to herself, "Soul, look another way—you have no part in this. Motherhood is beautiful, fatherhood is beautiful; but the dawn of fatherhood and motherhood is not beautiful." Do they really think that God is ashamed of what He has made and appointed? And, if not, surely it is somewhat superfluous that they should undertake to be so for Him.

The full-spread pride of man is calming and excellent to the soul.

Of a woman above all. It is true that instinct of silence I spoke of is a beautiful, imperishable part of nature too. But it is not beautiful when it means an ignominious shame brooding darkly. Shame is like a very flexible veil, that follows faithfully the shape of what it covers—beautiful when it hides a beautiful thing, ugly when it hides an ugly one. It has not covered what was beautiful here; it has covered a mean distrust of a man's self and of his Creator. It was needed that this silence, this evil spell, should for once be broken, and the daylight let in, that the dark cloud lying under might be scattered to the winds. It was needed that one who could here indicate for us "the path between reality and the soul" should speak. That is what these beautiful, despised poems, the "Children of Adam," do, read by the light that glows out of the rest of the volume: light of a clear, strong faith in God, of an unfathomably deep and tender love for humanity—light shed out of a soul that is "possessed of itself."

Herbert H. Gilchrist, ed., *Anne Gilchrist: Her Life and Writings* (London: T. F. Unwin, 1887), 287–307.

7. ALGERNON CHARLES SWINBURNE

Under the Microscope

There are in him two distinct men of most inharmonious kinds; a poet and a formalist. . . . It is from no love of foolish paradox that I have chosen the word "formalist" to express my sense of the radical fault in the noble genius of Whitman. For truly no scholar and servant of the past, reared on academic tradition under the wing of old-world culture, was ever more closely bound in with his own theories, more rigidly regulated by his own formularies, than this poet of new life and limitless democracy. Not Pope, not Boileau, was more fatally a formalist than Whitman; only Whitman is a poet of a greater nature than they. It is simply that these undigested formulas which choke by fits the free passage of his genius are to us less familiar than theirs; less real or less evident they are not. . . . What he says is well said when he speaks as of himself and because he cannot choose but speak; whether he speak of a small bird's loss or a great man's death, of a nation rising for battle or a child going forth in the morning. What he says is not well said when he speaks not as though he must but as though he ought; as though it behooved one who would be the poet of American democracy to do this thing or to be that thing if the duties of that office were to be properly fulfilled, the tenets of that religion worthily delivered. Never before was high poetry so puddled and adulterated with mere doctrine in its crudest form. Never was there less assimilation of the lower dogmatic with the higher prophetic elements. . . . [It] is one thing to sing the song of all trades, and quite another thing to tumble down together the names of all possible crafts and implements in one unsorted heap; to sing the song of all countries is not simply to fling out on the page at random in one howling mass the titles of all divisions of the earth, and so leave them. At this rate, to sing the song of the language it should suffice to bellow out backwards and forwards the twenty-six letters of the alphabet. And this folly is deliberately done by a great writer, and ingeniously defended by able writers, alike in good faith, and alike in blind bondage to mere dogmatic theory, to the mere formation of foregone opinion. They cannot see that formalism need not by any means be identical with tradition; they cannot see that because theories of the present are not inherited they do not on that account become more proper than were theories of the past to suffice of themselves for poetic or prophetic speech.

E. Gosse and T. J. Wise, eds., *The Complete Works of Algernon Charles Swinburne*, vol. 16 (London: Heinemann, 1926), 411–420.

8. GEORGE SAINTSBURY

"Leaves of Grass"

It is not difficult to point out the central thesis of Walt Whitman's poetical gospel. It is briefly this: the necessity of the establishment of a universal republic, or rather brotherhood of men. And to this is closely joined another, or rather a series of others, indicating the type of man of which this universal republic is to consist, or perhaps which it is to produce. The poet's language in treating the former of these two positions is not entirely uniform; sometimes he speaks as of a federation of nations, sometimes as if mankind at large were to gravitate towards the United States, and to find in them the desired Utopia. But the constitution of the United States, at least that constitution as it ought to be, is always and uniformly represented as a sufficient and the only sufficient political means of attaining this Utopia, nay, as having to some extent already presented Utopia as a fact. Moreover, passing to the second point, the ideal man is imaged as the ideal Yankee, understanding that word of course as it is understood in America, not in Europe. He is to be a rather magnificent animal, almost entirely uncultured (this is not an unfair representation, although there are to be found certain vague panegyrics on art, and especially on music), possessing a perfect *physique*, well nourished and clothed, affectionate towards his kind, and above all things resolved to admit no superior. As is the ideal man, so is the ideal woman to be. Now it may be admitted frankly and at once, that this is neither the creed nor the man likely to prove attractive to many persons east of the Atlantic. If it be said that the creed is a vague creed, and the man a detestable man, there will be very little answer attempted. Many wonderful things will doubtless happen "when," as the poet says, "through these States walk a hundred millions of superb persons"; but it must be allowed that there is small prospect of any such procession. One is inclined for very many sound reasons, and after discarding all prejudices, to opine that whatever salvation may await the world may possibly come from quarters other than from America. Fortunately, however, admiration for a creed is easily separable from admiration for the utterance and expression of that creed, and Walt Whitman as a poet is not difficult to disengage from Walt Whitman as an evangelist and politician. The keyword of all his ideas and of all his writings is universality. His Utopia is one which shall be open to everybody; his ideal of man and woman one which shall be attainable by everybody; his favourite scenes, ideas, subjects, those which everybody, at least to some extent, can enjoy and appreciate. He cares not that by this limitation he may exclude thoughts and feelings, at any rate phases of thought and feeling, infinitely choicer and higher than any which he admits. To express this striving after universality he has recourse to methods both unusual and (to most readers) unwelcome. The extraordinary jumbles and strings of names, places, employments, which deface his pages, and which have encouraged the profane to liken them to auctioneers' catalogues or indexes of encyclopaedias, have no other object than to express this universal sympathy, reaching to the highest and penetrating to the lowest forms of life. The exclusion of culture, philosophy, manners, is owing also to this desire to admit nothing but what is open to every human being of ordinary faculty and opportunities. Moreover, it is to this that we may fairly trace the predominance in Whitman's writings of the sexual passion, a prominence which has given rise, and probably will yet give rise, to much unphilosophical hubbub. This passion, as the poet has no doubt observed, is almost the only one which is peculiar to man as man, the presence of which denotes virility if not humanity, the absence of which is a sign of abnormal temperament. Hence he elevates it to almost the principal place, and treats of it in a manner somewhat shocking to those who are accustomed to speak of such subjects (we owe the word to Southey) *enfarinhadamente.* As a matter of fact, however, the treatment, though outspoken, is eminently "clean," to use the poet's own word; there is not a vestige of prurient thought, not a syllable of prurient language. Yet it would be a great mistake to suppose that sexual passion occupies the chief place in Whitman's estimation. There is according to him something above it, something which in any ecstasies he fails not to realize, something which seems more intimately connected in his mind with the welfare of mankind, and the promotion of his ideal republic. This is what he calls "robust American love." He is never tired of repeating "I am the poet of comrades" — Socrates himself seems renascent in this apostle of friendship.

The Academy (October 10, 1874): 398–400.

9. EDWARD DOWDEN

"The Poetry of Democracy"

The principle of political and social equality once clearly conceived and taken to heart as true, works outward through one's body of thought and feeling in various directions. As in the polity of the nation every citizen is entitled by virtue of the fact of his humanity to make himself heard, to manifest his will, and in his place to be respected, so in the polity of the individual man, made up of the faculties of soul and body, every natural instinct, every passion, every appetite, every organ, every power, may claim its share in the government of the man. If a human being is to be honoured as such, then every part of a human being is to be honoured. In asserting one's rights as a man, one asserts the rights of everything which goes to make up manhood. . . .

Having acknowledged that Whitman at times forgets that the "instinct of silence," as it has been well said, "is a beautiful, imperishable part of nature," and that in his manner of asserting his portion of truth there is a crudity which perhaps needlessly offends, everything has been acknowledged, and it ought not to be forgotten that no one asserts more strenuously than does Whitman the beauty, not indeed of asceticism, but of holiness or healthiness, and the shameful ugliness of unclean thought, desire and deed. If he does not assert holiness as a duty, it is because he asserts it so strongly as a joy and a desire, and because he loves to see all duties transfigured into the glowing forms of joys and of desires. The healthy repose and continence, and the healthy eagerness and gratification of appetite, are equally sources of satisfaction to him. If in some of his lyrical passages there seems entire self-abandonment to passion, it is because he believes there are, to borrow his own phrase, "native moments," in which the desires receive permission from the supreme authority, conscience, to satisfy themselves completely. . . .

In the way of crude mysticism Whitman takes pleasure in asserting the equality of all natural objects, and forces, and processes, each being as mysterious and wonderful, each as admirable and beautiful as every other; and as the multitude of men and women, so, on occasions, does the multitude of animals, and trees, and flowers press into his poems with the same absence of selection, the same assertion of equal rights, the same unsearchableness, and sanctity, and beauty, apparent or concealed in all. By another working of the same democratic influence (each man finding in the world what he cares to find) Whitman discovers everywhere in nature the same qualities, or types of the same qualities, which he admires most in men. For his imagination the powers of the earth do not incarnate themselves in the forms of god and demi-god, faun and satyr, oread, dryad, and nymph of river and sea — meet associates, allies or antagonists of the heroes of an age, when the chiefs and shepherds of the people were themselves almost demi-gods. But the great Mother — the Earth — is one in character with her children of the democracy, who, at last, as the poet holds, have learnt to live and work in her great style. She is tolerant, includes diversity, refuses nothing, shuts no one out; she is powerful, full of vitality, generous, proud, perfect in natural rectitude, does not discuss her duty to God, never apologizes, does not argue, is incomprehensible, silent, coarse, productive, charitable, rich in the organs and instincts of sex, and at the same time continent and chaste. The grass Whitman loves as much as did Chaucer himself; but his love has a certain spiritual significance which Chaucer's had not. It is not the "soft, sweet, smale grass," embroidered with flowers, a fitting carpet for the feet of glad knights and sportive ladies, for which he cares. In the grass he beholds the democracy of the fields, earthborn, with close and copious companionship of blades, each blade like every other, and equal to every other, spreading in all directions with lusty life, blown upon by the open air, "coarse, sunlit, fresh, nutritious."

Studies in Literature (London: Kegan Paul, Trench, Trubner & Co., 1878), 500–501, 504–505, 515–516.

10. GERARD MANLEY HOPKINS

Letter to Robert Bridges, October 18, 1882

I have read of Whitman's (1) "Pete" ["Come up from the Fields, Father"] in the library at Bedford Square (and perhaps something else; if so I forget), which you point out; (2) two pieces in the *Athenaeum* or *Academy*: this is all I remember. I cannot have read more than a half dozen pieces at most.

This, though very little, is quite enough to give a strong impression of his marked and original manner and way of thought and in particular of his rhythm.

It might be even enough, I shall not deny, to originate or, much more, influence another's style: they say the French trace their whole modern school of landscape to a single piece of Constable's exhibited at the Salon early this century.

The question then is only about the fact. But first I may as well say what I should not otherwise have said, that I always knew in my heart Walt Whitman's mind to be more like my own than any other man's living. As he is a very great scoundrel this is not a pleasant confession. And this also makes me the more desirous to read him and the more determined that I will not.

Nevertheless I believe that you are quite mistaken about this piece and that on second thoughts you will find the fancied resemblance diminish and the imitation disappear.

And first for the rhythm. Of course I saw that there was to the eye something in my long lines like this, that the one would remind people of the other. And both are in irregular rhythms. There the likeness ends. The pieces of his I read were mostly in an irregular rhythmic prose: that is what they are thought to be meant for and what they seemed to me to be. Here is a fragment of a line I remember: "or a handkerchief designedly dropped." This is in a dactylic rhythm — or let us say anapaestic; for it is a great convenience in English to assume that the stress is always at the end of the foot; the consequence of which assumption is that in ordinary verse there are only two English feet possible, the iamb and the anapaest, and even in my regular sprung rhythm only one additional, the fourth paeon: for convenience' sake assuming this, then the above fragment is anapaestic

> 1 2   3   1 2   3 1 2 3   1   2   3
> "or a hańd kerchief. . . . desígn edly drópped"

— and there is a break down, a designed break of rhythm, after "handkerchief," done no doubt that the line may not become downright verse, as it would be if he had said "or a handkerchief purposedly dropped." Now you can of course say that he meant pure verse and that the foot is a paeon

> 1 2   3   1   2   3 4 1 2   3
> "or a hańd kerchief desígn edly drópped";

or that he means, without fuss, what I should achieve by looping the syllable *de* and calling that foot an outriding foot — for the result might be attained either way. Here then I must make the answer which will apply here and to all like cases and to the examples which may be found up and down the poets of the use of sprung rhythm — *if they could have done it they would*; sprung rhythm, once you hear it, is so eminently natural a thing and so effective a thing that if they had known of it they would have used it. Many people, as we say, have been "burning," but they all missed it; they took it up and mislaid it again. So far as I know — I am inquiring and presently I shall be able to speak more decidedly — it existed in full force in Anglo-Saxon verse and in great beauty; in a degraded and doggerel shape in *Piers Ploughman* (I am reading that famous poem and am coming to the conclusion that it is not worth reading); Greene was the last who employed it at all consciously and he never continuously; then it disappeared — for one cadence in it here and there is not sprung rhythm and one swallow does not make a spring. (I put aside Milton's case, for it is altogether singular.) In a matter like this a thing does not exist, is not *done* unless it is wittingly and willingly done; to recognize the form you are employing and to mean it is everything. To apply this: there is (I suppose, but you will know) no sign that Whitman means to use paeons or outriding feet where these breaks in rhythm occur; it seems to me a mere extravagance to think he means people to understand of themselves what they are slow to understand even when marked or pointed out. If he does not mean it then he does not do it; or in short what he means to write — and writes — is rhythmic prose and that only. And after all, you probably grant this.

Good. Now prose rhythm in English is always one of two things (allowing my convention about scanning upwards or from slack to stress and not from stress to slack) — either iambic or anapaestic. You may make a third measure (let us call it) by intermixing them. One of these three simple measures then, all iambic or all anapaestic or mingled iambic and anapaestic, is what he in every case means to write. He dreams of no other and he *means* a rugged or, as he calls it in that very piece "Spirit that formed this scene" (which is very instructive and should be read on this very subject) a "savage" art and rhythm.

Extremes meet, and (I must for truth's sake say what sounds pride) this savagery of his art, this rhythm in its last ruggedness and decomposition into common prose, comes near the last elaboration of mine. For that piece of mine is very highly wrought. The long lines are not rhythm run to seed: everything is weighed and timed in them. Wait till they have taken hold of your ear and you will find it so. No, but what it *is* like is the rhythm of Greek tragic choruses or of Pindar; which is pure sprung rhythm. And that has the same changes of cadence from point to point as this piece. If you want to try it, read one till you have settled the true places of the stress, mark these, then read it aloud, and you will see. Without this these choruses are prose bewitched; with it they are sprung rhythm, like that piece of mine.

Besides, why did you not say *Binsey Poplars* was like Whitman? The present piece is in the same kind and vein, but developed, an advance. The lines and the stanzas (of which there are two in each poem and having much the same relation to one another) are both longer, but the two pieces are greatly alike: just look. If so how is this a being untrue to myself? I am sure it is no such thing.

The above remarks are not meant to run down Whitman. His "savage" style has advantages, and he has chosen it; he says so. But you cannot eat your cake and keep it: he eats his offhand, I keep mine. It makes a very great difference. Neither do I deny all resemblance. In particular I noticed in *Spirit that Formed this Scene* a preference for the alexandrine. I have the same preference: I came to it by degrees, I did not take it from him.

About diction the matter does not allow me so clearly to point out my independence as about rhythm. I cannot think that the present piece owes anything to him. I hope not, here especially, for it is not even spoken in my own person but in that of St. Winefred's maidens. It ought to sound like the thoughts of a good but lively girl and not at all like—not at all like Walt Whitman. But perhaps your mind may have changed by this.

C. C. Abbott, ed., *The Letters of Gerard Manley Hopkins to Robert Bridges* (Oxford: Oxford University Press, 1935), 154–158.

11. JOHN ROBERTSON

Walt Whitman: Poet and Democrat

The essential thing is that the singer of democracy shall be full charged with his theme; and that an idea which feeds on optimism and confidence shall be carried with a confidence that no adversity will dash. And how Whitman's confidence rays out from his first page! Other poets have sung democracy in moments of expansion, or when goaded by the sight of war and depression: he alone ecstatically points a prosperous demos to new heights of ideal life. . . .

But Whitman is too enormously in earnest, too intensely faithful to laugh. Carlyle, let it be noted, is the one really earnest moralist who has indulged much in humour, and Carlyle's humour grew out of his profound unfaith in humanity. Whitman's faith is as strong as Carlyle's scepticism; and though he may meet one of Carlyle's favourite moral tests by a capacity to laugh broadly at the broadly and simply laughable, he is never heartily humorous in his writing. The humorous propensities of his countrymen get little recognition from him; when he is in a minatory mood—he frequently is in his later prose—he sees in the American habit of jesting on all things one of the unhealthy aspects of things democratic. . . . It may be doubted, however, whether Whitman's lack of humour is not a weakness in him as a propagandist, relatively to the average intellect of his time. Which of us can remain resolutely grave over the intimation that, among other things, the "picturesque looseness of carriage" of the American common people, and "the president's taking off his hat to them, not they to him," are "unrhymed poetry"? The thing is said in all good faith, and a momentary sympathy is possible, though it is not clear why the president should take off his hat to his fellow-citizens save to win their votes; but the smile will break through.

Mr. Meredith makes a character observe that cynicism is intellectual dandyism. Perhaps the dictum is truer than its acute author really believed. Take it that cynicism is humour overdone, and we arrive at a conception of humour as the soul's clothing for its nakedness, acutely experienced after modern indulgence in the fruit of the tree of knowledge of good and evil. It may be that the adoption of this is demonstrably an irrational act; but to demonstrate that a joke is an absurdity is but to make the joker a present of another. Logical progress, however, is possible on the understanding that he is a weak creature, and that a stronger may get on in vigorous nakedness. Such a son of Adam is Whitman. He positively does not need humour to protect him from his atmosphere, and he has no self-critical qualms about his appearance; being, indeed, by his enemies' account, far too naked to be ashamed.

(Edinburgh: William Brown, 1884), 13, 14–16; originally published in the Round Table Series 4.

12.

Sonnet-epigraph to John Robertson's
Walt Whitman: Poet and Democrat

Strong poet of the sleepless gods that dwell
    As far above the stars as we beneath,
    Thy melody, disdaining the soft sheath
Of dainty modern music, snaps the spell,
And heedless of old forms and fettered plan,
    Clothes itself carelessly in rough free words,
    And strikes with giant's hand the inner chords
That vibrate in the strong and healthful man!

What if our brothers in an age to be,
    Emerging from the Titan war of Thought,
      Seize hollow Custom, and with one keen blow
Strike off her seven heads, and having smote,
      Pass on, and with their larger veins aglow
With new found vigour, mould themselves to thee!

A.A.

Last stanza of the second poem which serves as epigraph to Robertson's *Walt Whitman: Poet and Democrat*:

Better forgiveness serene as the sun than the bolt of the storm-god:
Better the large faith of love than the Coriolanian cry:
Better the eye still bright with the dream of a glorious distance
Than the sad grey world of the sage scanning his race from on high;
Better the pride of the comrade, great in his vision of greatness,
Than the pride of the sage or the scorner, letting his kind pass by.

(Anon.)

(Edinburgh: William Brown, 1884); originally published in the Round Table Series 4.

Letter to Walt Whitman, July 7, 1885

At first it seemed rather out of place to have your work in a series of this kind called, rather stupidly, The Canterbury Poets, and got up in a cheap and prettified fashion, with red lines etc. But afterwards it struck me that there might be gain in the end through it. . . . The very including of *Leaves of Grass* in a series like this gives them a chance of reaching people who would otherwise never see them. What I — and many young men like me, ardent believers in your poetic initiative — chiefly feel about this is, however, that an edition at a price which will put it in the hands of the poorest member of the great social democracy is a thing of imperative requirement. You know what a fervid stir and impulse forward of Humanity there is today in certain quarters! and I am sure you will be tremendously glad to help us here, in the very camp of the enemy, the stronghold of caste and aristocracy and all selfishness between rich and poor!

Some people want to class you as the property of a certain literary clique — a *rara avis,* to be carefully kept out of sight of the uneducated mob as not able to understand and appreciate the peculiar qualities of your work. This does harm in many ways, and it would be a very good thing to make a fair trial of the despised mob. . . . What we want then is an edition for the poor, and this proposed one at only a shilling would be within reach of every man willing and caring to read.

Horace Traubel, *With Walt Whitman in Camden*, vol. 1 (New York: D. Appleton, 1908; reprint, New York: Rowman Littlefield, 1961), 451–453.

"A Study of Walt Whitman"

But is equality a truth in the manner in which he asserts it? I believe not; and if not, it must be so far mischievous to assert it. That common manhood is a greater, more cardinal fact than any distinctions among men which raise one above another I most firmly believe. Still these distinctions do exist, and so palpable a fact cannot be ignored without very serious injury. If great men could not have been without average men, and owe most to the grand aggregate soul of the ideal unit, humanity — which is a pregnant truth — yet, on the other hand, this grand aggregate soul could never have been what it is, could never have been enriched with the treasures it now enjoys, without those most personal of all personalities — prophets, heroes, men of genius. . . . If these men need to be reminded, as they do, of the rock whence they are hewn, there is yet a danger of average men mistaking such a message as that of modern democracy through so powerful a spokesman as Whitman, and insisting upon paring down the ideal superiority of their great ones too much to the level of their own inorganic uniformity, rather than acknowledging and venerating what is verily superior in these; taking them for leaders in regions where they are appointed by Nature to lead, and generally aiming to raise themselves as far as possible to the standard of a higher excellence thus set before them.

In order to satisfy this law of *inequality* among men, I do not believe that the mere proclamation of friendly love as between comrades (any more than of sexual love and equal union between man and woman) is at all sufficient. Veneration, reverence, also must be proclaimed, as likewise necessary; and the great point we ought to aim at, in helping to solve the momentous question of the social future, seems in that respect to be this—that mankind be taught, and gradually accustomed, to place their reverence where reverence is indeed due, and not upon mere idols of popular superstition. . . . But what Whitman does see so clearly is that, even when men have themselves elected a ruler, or been concerned in the choice of a form of government, there is a sort of glamour of the imagination which immediately invests any actual depositary of power; and bows them in a kind of unreasonable stupor before it. He therefore reminds them—Government exists for you, not you for government. Obey it intelligently; modify it when reason requires.

Essays on Poetry and Poets (London: Kegan, Paul, Trench, 1886), 330, 331, 332.

15. ANONYMOUS REVIEW

"American Poets"

Such pieces as the burial hymn to Lincoln "When Lilacs Last etc.," or "Out of the Cradle Endlessly Rocking," stamp Whitman as a lyric genius of the highest order. In creative force and imaginative vigour Whitman stands, in our opinion, first among American poets. But he has not justified his claim to initiate a new departure in the form or the substance of poetry. His finest passages are written when, in the sweep of his lyric passion, he forgets his system and his purpose. His poems come before the world in a shape which is as attractive to some as it is repulsive to others. In either case the audacity of the strange attire rivets attention. Yet the form is not new. At their best his lines have the sweep of the Hebrew prophets; they roll in upon the ear, rythmic as the waves beating on the shore. But just as often they resemble the baldest prose of Tupper. Whitman denounces rhyme as the medium of inferior writers and trivial subjects. His slatternly prose irresistibly suggests the conclusion, that his revolt against the tinkling serenader's style was confirmed, if it was not stimulated, by mechanical incapacity or at least by a want of artistic patience. In the first heat of his revolutionary enthusiasm, he claimed to throw art to the winds, and to demonstrate its futility when applied to the higher forms of poetry. In his maturer judgement he poses as the Wagner of poetry. It is possible, and even probable, that poetry, like music, may undergo great rythmical changes; but whatever change takes place will be in the direction, not of the neglect, but of the development of Art. It is no defence of Whitman's theory, that he wished to render poetry inartistic; it is a complete and adequate defence, that he attempts to reproduce in verse the cosmical symphony, the strong musical pulse that beats throughout the world, the great undersong of the universal surge of Nature. Had this conception been in his mind from the first, had he been an innovator and not a mere iconoclast, he might have worked out his system less crudely. His vocabulary is strong and rich. He bows to no aristocracy of words. He hopes to see the Versailles of verse invaded by the language of the "Halles." He uses whatever expression most forcibly conveys his meaning, without regard to conventionalities. Thus his language is piercingly direct, and he repeatedly strikes out original epithets or phrases which create a picture in themselves.

In the protest which Whitman makes against conventionalities of form and language, he did good service, but he only echoes the voice of Emerson.

Quarterly Review 163 (July–October 1886): 390–391.

16. HAVELOCK ELLIS

The New Spirit

Beneath the vast growth of Christianity, for ever exalting the unseen by the easy method of pouring contempt on the seen, and still ever producing some strange and exquisite flower of *ascesis*—a slow force was working underground. A tendency was making itself felt to find in the theoretically despised physical— in those everyday stones which the builders of the Church had rejected—the very foundation of the mysteries of life; if not the basis for a new vision of the unseen, yet for a more assured vision of the seen. . . .

Whitman appeared at a time when this stream of influence, grown mighty, had boldly emerged. At the time that "Leaves of Grass" sought the light Tourgenieff was embodying in the typical figure of Bassaroff the modern militant spirit of science, positive and audacious—a spirit marked also, as Hinton has pointed out, by a new form of asceticism, which lay in the denial of emotion. Whitman, one of the very greatest emotional forces of modern times, who had grown up apart from the rigid and technical methods of science, face to face with a new world and a new civilization, which he had eagerly absorbed so far as it lay open to him, had the good inspiration to fling himself into the scientific current, and so to justify the demands of his emotional nature; to represent himself as the inhabitant of a vast and coordinated cosmos, tenoned and mortised in granite. . . . That Whitman possessed no trained scientific instinct is unquestionably true, but it is impossible to estimate his significance without understanding what he owes to science. Something, indeed, he had gained from the philosophy of Hegel — with its conception of the universe as a single process of evolution, in which vice and disease are but transient perturbations — with which he had a second-hand acquaintance, that has left distinct, but not always well assimilated marks on his work; but, above all, he was indebted to those scientific conceptions which, like Emerson, he had absorbed or divined. It is these that lie behind "Children of Adam."

This mood of sane and cheerful sensuality, rejoicing with a joy as massive and calm-eyed as Boccaccio's, a moral-fibred joy that Boccaccio never knew, in all the manifestations of the flesh and blood of the world — saying, not: "Let us eat and drink, for tomorrow we die," but, with Clifford: "Let us take hands and help, for this day we are alive together" — is certainly Whitman's most significant and impressive mood. Nothing so much reveals its depth and sincerity as his never-changing attitude towards death.

(London: Bell and Sons, 1890), 112–114.

17. R. W. RAPER

"The Innings"

1

    To take your stand at the wicket in a posture of haughty defiance:
    To confront a superior bowler as he confronts you:
    To feel the glow of ambition, your own and that of your side:
    To be aware of shapes hovering, bending, watching around — white-
        flannelled shapes — all eager, unable to catch you.

2

    The unusually fine weather,
    The splendid silent sun flooding all, bathing all in joyous evaporation.
    Far off a gray-brown thrush warbling in hedge or in marsh;
    Down there in the blossoming bushes, my brother, what is it that you are
        saying?

3

    To play more steadily than a pendulum; neither hurrying nor delaying, but
        marking the right moment to strike.

4

> To slog:

5

> The utter oblivion of all but the individual energy:
> The rapid co-operation of hand and eye projected into the ball;
> The ball triumphantly flying through air, you too flying.
> The perfect feel of a fourer!
> The hurrying to and fro between the wickets: the marvellous quickness of all
>   fields:
> The cut, leg hit, forward drive, all admirable in their way;
> The pull transcending all pulls, over the boundary ropes, sweeping, orotund,
>   astral:
> The superciliousness of standing still in your ground, content, and masterful,
>   conscious of an unquestioned six;
> The continuous pavilion-thunder bellowing after each true lightning stroke;
> (And yet a mournful note, the low dental murmur of one who blesses not,
>   I fancied I heard through the roar
> In a lull of the deafening plaudits;
> Could it have been the bowler? or one of the fields?)

6

> Sing on, gray-brown bird, sing on! now I understand you!
> Pour forth your rapturous chants from flowering hedge in the marsh,
>   I follow, I keep time, though rather out of breath. . . .

Echoes from the Oxford Magazine (London: Henry Frowde, 1890); reprinted in Henry S. Saunders, ed., *Parodies on Walt Whitman* (New York: American Library Series, 1923), 76–77.

18. PAULINE W. ROOSE

"A Child-Poet: Walt Whitman"

This attitude of admiration and ever-fresh surprise, as of a stranger in the world, is accompanied by most of the characteristics of early childhood. Without a grain of egotism, he has a child's intense interest in himself and absorbing sense of his own importance. Thus, to a series of his poems he ushers himself in in words recalling the formula one so often sees inscribed on the title-page of some child's diary, and which, with its innocent unsuspiciousness of fate, brings a pang to the heart:

"Afternoon this delicious ninth month in my forty-first year."

Independently of all witchcraft and fairy lore, he can create for himself the very miracles and transformations of which the little ones are always dreaming. The old woodland kings, in his belief, hold great thoughts, which they drop down upon him as he passes beneath them. There was a small boy who once prayed that God would make the trees walk. This very conceit was almost realised by the vivid fancy of Walt Whitman, who, in a "sort of dream-trance," as he calls it, beheld his favourite trees "step out and promenade up, down, and around very curiously, — with a whisper from one, leaning down as he passed me: 'We do all this on the present occasion, exceptionally, just for you.'" That they could do it if they chose seems indeed to be his deliberate opinion.

Children are notably devoid of humour, and in Whitman that quality is conspicuous by its absence. Who, however, better than children — or than Whitman — can appeal to the humour of others? There is something touching in the unconsciousness with which he lays himself open to the sneers of whoever may be willing to avail himself of the opportunity. His sense of fun, of which he has his full share, never interferes with the most preposterous statements on his own part, even while he allows no oddity of life nor any ludicrous effect of nature to escape him. Of what has been called the *cockneyism* of the nineteenth century not a trace is to be found in him, nor of the modern smartness and indifference. He cannot content himself with superficial views any more than childhood can be put off with the flippant answers which grown-up persons of a certain calibre amuse themselves by returning to its earnest questionings. . . .

His coarseness is as the coarseness of the earth, which, with "disdainful innocence," takes all for clean. Or rather, to maintain our point of view, he is a "vulgar child" indeed, but after the fashion of the youngster to whose harmless improprieties Sterne, in justification of his own deliberate offences, drew its mother's attention — not after that of the sentimentalist himself. The "chaste indecency of childhood" is not so hard to forgive.

The Gentleman's Magazine 272 (January–June 1892): 467, 474, 480.

19. W. B. YEATS

Letters to the Editor of *United Ireland*

[December 17, 1892] Is there, then, no hope for the de-Anglicising of our people? Can we not build up a national tradition, a national literature, which shall be none the less Irish in spirit from being English in language? Can we not keep the continuity of the nation's life, not by trying to do what Dr. Hyde has practically pronounced impossible, but by translating or retelling in English, which shall have an indefinable Irish quality of rhythm and style, all that is best of the ancient literature? Can we not write and persuade others to write histories and romances of the great Gaelic men of the past, from the son of Nessa to Owen Roe, until there has been made a golden bridge between the old and the new?

America, with no past to speak of, a mere *parvenu* among the nations, is creating a national literature which in its most characteristic products differs almost as much from English literature as does the literature of France. Walt Whitman, Thoreau, Bret Harte, and Cable, to name no more, are very American, and yet America was once an English colony. It should be more easy for us, who have in us that wild Celtic blood, the most un-English of all things under heaven, to make such a literature. If we fail it shall not be because we lack the materials, but because we lack the power to use them.

[December 1, 1894] I know perfectly well what Emerson wrote about the "wit and wisdom" of the *The Leaves of Grass*, but cannot see how his praise alters the fact that while Mr. W. M. Rossetti was bringing out an English selection from Whitman's poems, and Mr. Ruskin and George Eliot celebrating their power and beauty, the American public was hounding their author from a Government post because of their supposed immorality, or that when in his old age all Europe had learned to honour his name the leading magazines of his country were still not ashamed to refuse his contributions. Whitman appealed, like every other great and earnest mind, not to the ignorant many, either English or American, but to that audience, "fit though few," which is greater than any nation, for it is made up of chosen persons from all, and through the mouths of George Eliot, Ruskin, and Emerson it did him honour and crowned him among the immortals.

John Kelly, ed., *The Collected Letters of W. B. Yeats* (Oxford: Clarendon Press, 1986), 338–339, 416.

20. JOHN ADDINGTON SYMONDS

Walt Whitman, a Study

To bear the yoke of universal law is the plain destiny of human beings. If we could learn to bear the yoke with gladness, to thrill with vibrant fibres to the pulses of the infinite machine we constitute — (for were it possible that the least of us should be eliminated, annihilated, the whole machine would stop and crumble into chaos) — if, I say, we could feel pride and joy in our participation of the cosmic life, then we might stand where Whitman stood with "feet tenoned and mortised in granite." I do not think it is a religion only for the rich, the powerful, the wise, the healthy. For my own part, I may confess that it shone upon me when my life was broken, when I was weak, sickly, poor, and of no account; and that I have ever lived thenceforward in the light and warmth of it. In bounden duty toward Whitman, I make this personal statement; for had it not been for the contact of his fervent spirit with my own, the pyre ready to be lighted, the combustible materials of modern thought awaiting the touch of the fire-bringer, might never have leapt up into the flame of life-long faith and consolation. During my darkest hours, it comforted me in the illimitable symphony of cosmic life. When I sinned, repined, sorrowed, suffered, it touched me with a gentle hand of sympathy and understanding, sustained me with the strong arm of assurance that in the end I could not go amiss (for I was a part, an integrating part of the great whole); and when strength revived in me, it stirred a healthy pride and courage to effectuate myself, to bear the brunt of spiritual foes, the slings and arrows of outrageous fortune. For this reason, in duty to my master Whitman, and in the hope that my experience may encourage others to seek the same source of inspiration, I have exceeded the bounds of an analytical essay by pouring forth my personal confession. . . .

I am not sure whether a loose, disjointed method, the mere jotting down of notes, would not be the best way of illustrating so intangible an author. And then I think of many metaphors to express a meaning irreducible to propositions.

He is Behemoth, wallowing in primitive jungles, bathing at fountain-heads of mighty rivers, crushing the bamboos and the crane-brakes under him, bellowing and exulting in the torrid air. He is a gigantic elk or buffalo, trampling the grasses of the wilderness, tracking his mate with irresistible energy. He is an immense tree, a kind of Yggdrasil, stretching its roots deep down into the bowels of the world, and unfolding its magic boughs through all the spaces of the heavens. His poems are even as the rings in a majestic oak or pine. He is the circumambient air, in which float shadowy shapes, rise mirage-towers, and palm-groves; we try to clasp their visionary forms; they vanish into ether. He is the globe itself; all seas, lands, forests, climates, storms, snows, sunshines, rains of universal earth. He is all nations, cities, languages, religions, arts, creeds, thoughts, emotions. He is the beginning and the grit of these things, not their endings, lees and dregs.

The section of Whitman's works which deals with adhesiveness, or the love of comrades, is full as important, and in some ways more difficult to deal with, than his "Children of Adam." . . . Here the element of spirituality in passion, of romantic feeling, and of deep enduring sentiment, which was almost conspicuous by its absence from the section on sexual love, emerges into vivid prominence, and lends peculiar warmth of poetry to the artistic treatment. . . .

It is clear then that, in his treatment of comradeship, or the impassioned love of man for man, Whitman has struck a keynote, to the emotional intensity of which the modern world is unaccustomed. It therefore becomes of much importance to discover the poet-prophet's *Stimmung*—his radical instinct with regard to the moral quality of the feeling he encourages. Studying his works by their own light, and by the light of their author's character, interpreting each part by reference to the whole and in the spirit of the whole, an impartial critic will, I think, be drawn to the conclusion that what he calls the "adhesiveness" of comrades is meant to have no interblending with the "amativeness" of sexual love. . . . It is obvious that those unenviable mortals who are the inheritors of sexual anomalies, will recognise their own emotion in Whitman's "superb friendship, exalté, previously unknown," which "waits, and has been always waiting, latent in all men," the "something fierce in me, eligible to burst forth," "ethereal comradeship," "the last comradeship," "the last athletic reality." Had I not the strongest proof in Whitman's private correspondence with myself that he repudiated any such deductions from his "Calamus," I admit that I should have regarded them as justified; and I am not certain whether his own feelings upon this delicate topic may not have altered since the time when "Calamus" was first composed. . . .

[We may inquire] whether anything like a new chivalry is to be expected from the doctrines of "Calamus," which shall in the future utilise for noble purposes some of those unhappy instincts which at present run to waste in vice and shame. It may be asked what these passions have in common with the topic of Whitman's prophecy? They have this in common with it. Whitman recognises among the sacred emotions and social virtues, destined to regenerate political life and to cement nations, an intense, jealous, throbbing, sensitive, expectant love of man for man: a love which yearns in absence, droops under the sense of neglect, revives at the return of the beloved: a love that finds honest delight in hand-touch, meeting lips, hours of privacy, close personal contact. He proclaims this love to be not only a daily fact in the present, but also a saving and ennobling aspiration. While he expressly repudiates, disowns, and brands as "damnable" all "morbid inferences" which may be drawn by malevolence or vicious cunning from his doctrine, he is prepared to extend the gospel of comradeship to the whole human race. He expects democracy, the new social and political medium, the new religious ideal of mankind, to develop and extend "that fervid comradeship," and by its means to counterbalance and to spiritualise what is vulgar and materialistic in the modern world.

(London: John C. Nimmo, 1893), 34–35, 155–156, 74–76, 81–82.

21. HENRY SALT

Songs of Freedom

A new impulse was given to democratic songs by the political and social excitement that commenced with the Reform Bill of 1832, and culminated in the outbreak of 1848 — a movement which was represented in England by the Anti-Corn Law and Chartist agitations, and in Ireland by a revival of national spirit which led to an abortive rebellion, while in America it was the abolition of negro-slavery that formed the ideal of the emancipators. . . .

Where, then, is the great singer of modern democracy? Who can voice its myriad demands for freedom and justice as Shelley voiced the high and sanguine aspirations of the early years of the century? In England no such poet has yet made his appearance; but in Walt Whitman we find another epoch-making writer, a worthy successor to Shelley—unlike him, it is true, in a thousand ways, yet manifesting in a sterner and rougher form the same unquenchable spirit of freedom, the same unalterable spirit of love. We know, of course, all the critical objections that are urged against Whitman's "barbaric yawp" and alleged lack of style; but then we remember that Shelley's poetry—a "drivelling prose run mad" as the Quarterly described it—was scarcely less distasteful to the artistic susceptibilities of seventy years back! And if, as seems probable, there be needed not only a fresh impulse of thought, to create a new wave of poetry, but also a new vehicle of poetic expression (a need which would certainly arise, if anywhere, in the case of that poetry which has revolutionary import), we can realise the supreme significance of Walt Whitman as a singer of democracy. He has given us a new ideal of universal comradeship; and he has given us a new method of embodying that ideal. His name inevitably stands at the head of the present era of revolutionary song.

(London: Walter Scott, 1894), xx–xxi, xxii.

22. EDMUND GOSSE

"Walt Whitman"

To me, at least, after all the oceans of talk, after all the extravagant eulogy, all the mad vituperation, he remains perfectly cryptic and opaque. I find no reason given by these authorities why he should have made his appearance, or what his appearance signifies. I am told that he is abysmal, putrid, glorious, universal and contemptible. I like these excellent adjectives, but I cannot see how to apply them to Whitman. Yet, like a boy at a shooting-gallery, I cannot go home till I, too, have had my six shots at this running-deer.

On the main divisions of literature it seems that a critic should have not merely a firm opinion, but sound argument to back that opinion. It is a pilgarlicky mind that is satisfied with saying, "I like you, Dr. Fell, the reason why I cannot tell." Analysis is the art of telling the reason why. But still more feeble and slovenly is the criticism that has to say, "I liked Dr. Fell yesterday and I don't like him today, but I can give no reason." The shrine of Walt Whitman, however, is strewn around with remarks of this kind. Poor Mr. Swinburne has been cruelly laughed at for calling him a "strong-winged soul, with prophetic lips hot with the blood-beats of song," and yet a drunken apple-woman reeling in a gutter. But he is not alone in this inconsistency. Almost every competent writer who has attempted to give an estimate of Whitman has tumbled about in the same extraordinary way. Something mephitic breathes from this strange personality, something that maddens the judgment until the wisest lose their self-control.

Therefore, I propound a theory. It is this, that there is no real Walt Whitman, that is to say, that he cannot be taken as any other figure in literature is taken, as an entity of positive value and defined characteristics. . . . Whitman is mere *bathybius*; he is literature in the condition of protoplasm — an intellectual organism so simple that it takes the instant impression of whatever mood approaches it. Hence the critic who touches Whitman is immediately confronted with his own image stamped upon that viscid and tenacious surface. He finds, not what Whitman has to give, but what he himself has brought. And when, in quite another mood, he comes again to Whitman, he finds that other self of his own stamped upon the provoking protoplasm. . . . Almost every sensitive and natural person has gone through a period of fierce Whitmanomania; but it is a disease which rarely afflicts the same patient more than once. It is, in fact, a sort of highly-irritated kind of egotism come to a head, and people are almost always better after it. . . .

Every reader who comes to Whitman starts upon an expedition to the virgin forest. He must take his conveniences with him. He will make of the excursion what his own spirit dictates. There are solitudes, fresh air, rough landscape, and a well of water, but if he wishes to enjoy the latter he must bring his own cup with him. When people are still young and like roughing it, they appreciate a picnic into Whitman-land, but it is not meant for those who choose to see their intellectual comforts round them.

Critical Kit-Kats (New York: Dodd, Mead, 1896), 96–111.

23. J. A. MACCULLOCH

"Walt Whitman: The Poet of Brotherhood"

But before coming to that stumbling-block to the *bourgeois* and to the verse-reading public alike, Whitman's style, a further word may be spoken of the tendencies in American thought when he began to write. The wave of revolution, of illumination, of romanticism which had swept over Europe, passed in succession to America. Puritanism, an uncompromising and bigoted orthodoxy, utilitarianism, Philistinism, had petrified the nation into a rock on which idealism could find scanty foothold. When the new movement arrived it disintegrated these unyielding elements, and was welcomed by a group of men and women who saw in it the dawn of a new age of poetry, of social reform, of religious fervour. A Transcendental Club was formed, and found choice spirits in George Ripley, Charles Dana, Margaret Fuller, Theodore Parker, Hawthorne and Emerson. With loud voice they proclaimed to the world, *Ecce, nunc acceptabile tempus*. But the movement became discredited by the wild enthusiasm of many bizarre, crack-brained, and absurd persons; and, though it never lost its possession of a noble ideal, it had to adapt itself to the circumstances of the modern world. Yet it formed a current which has continued to warm and to colour American thought since then. It has resulted in a certain freshness and crispness in literature, such as may readily be seen in the writings of Emerson, of Thoreau, of Lowell, of Longfellow. Nor did Whitman escape it. He is the finest product of the Transcendental movement, the prophet who will sound it forth to future ages. We see in his work the stirring of a new life in America, which we in the Old World cannot eventually escape.

Westminster Review (July–December 1899): 550.

24. G. K. CHESTERTON

"Conventions and the Hero"

Walt Whitman is, I suppose, beyond question the ablest man America has yet produced. He also happens to be, incidentally, one of the greatest men of the nineteenth century. Ibsen is all very well, Zola is all very well and Maeterlinck is all very well; but we have begun already to get to the end of them. And we have not yet begun to get to the beginning of Whitman. The egoism of which men accuse him is that sense of human divinity which no one has felt since Christ. The baldness of which men accuse him is simply that splendidly casual utterance which no sage has used since Christ. But all the same, this gradual and glowing conservatism which grows upon us as we live leads us to feel that in just those points in which he violated the chief conventions of poetry, in just those points he was wrong. He was mistaken in abandoning metre in poetry; not because in forsaking it he was forsaking anything ornamental or anything civilized, as he himself thought. In forsaking metre he was forsaking something quite wild and barbarous, something as instinctive as anger and as necessary as meat. He forgot that all real things move in a rhythm, that the heart beats in harmony, that the seas rise and ebb in harmony. He forgot that any child who shouts falls into some sort of repetition and assonance, that the wildest dancing is at the bottom monotonous. The whole of Nature moves in a recurrent music; it is only with a considerable effort of civilization that we can contrive to be other than musical. The whole world talks poetry; it is only we who, with elaborate ingenuity, manage to talk prose.

The same that is true of Whitman's violation of metre is true, though in a minor degree, of his violation of what is commonly called modesty. Decorum itself is of little social value; sometimes it is a sign of social decay. Decorum is the morality of immoral societies. The people who care most about modesty are often those who care least about chastity; no better examples could be given than Oriental Courts or the west-end drawing-rooms. But all the same Whitman was wrong. He was wrong because he had at the back of his mind the notion that modesty or decency was in itself an artificial thing. This is quite a mistake. The roots of modesty, like the roots of mercy or of any other traditional virtue, are to be found in all fierce and primitive things.

D. Collins, ed., *Lunacy and Letters* (New York: Sheed and Ward, 1958), 62–65.

25. W. T. HAWKINS

Poem Read at Celebration of Whitman's Birthday, May 31, 1906

Once more we meet — as pilgrims at a shrine,
    To reassert our Comradeship sincere:
Around the Master's head a wreath t'entwine
    Then lay it lovingly upon his bier.

To dear, dead Walt, who, being dead, yet speaks,
    In us and through us with the same old tone;
Breathing his message, as the ripple breaks
    Upon the shingle, kissing sand and stone.

That message, which the world has scarcely heard,
    Or, having heard it, has not understood;
His life-thought centred in one sacred word,
    The password of true Comrades — "Brotherhood!"

We leave behind the traffic of the mart,
    We steal away from busy, bustling street;
As Comrades, Brothers, standing heart to heart,
    Breathing the fragrance of his presence sweet.

His birthday! The one day of all the year
    Kept in remembrance by his Comrades true;
We chant no mournful dirge, we shed no tear,
    But joy that we our spirits thus renew.

"Joy, shipmate, joy!" There sounds his cheery hail!
    No longer troubles vex, or cares annoy;
Do riches flee us? Do we fear to fail?
    List to the good, glad, cry — "Joy, shipmates, joy!"

Have men betrayed us? He will not betray!
    Have Comrades left us in the hour of need?
They were no Comrades: let them pass away;
    The slaves of passion, prejudice or greed.

Hark to the glad old cry that greets us still!
    Sounding above the ocean's mighty roar;
What other message can our bosoms thrill
    Like that grand greeting from Paumanok's shore?

Comrades, join hands! So shall we symbolise
    The love that binds us with its golden chain.
True Comrades; linked in love! Though all else dies,
    Let this sweet bond of Comradeship remain.

Amid the turmoil of the striving days
    One night each year at least we'll call a halt,
And in his memory our glasses raise.
    And drink the same old toast — "Here's to you, Walt."

Annandale Observer, June 15, 1906; reprinted in Paul Salveson, *Loving Comrades* (Bolton, 1984).

26. E. M. FORSTER

"The Beauty of Life"

Whitman knew what life was. He was not praising its beauty from an armchair. He had been through all that makes it hideous to most men — poverty, the battlefield, the hospitals — and yet could believe that life, whether as a whole or in detail, was perfect, that beauty is manifest wherever life is manifested. He could glorify the absurd and the repulsive; he could catalogue the parts of a machine from sheer joy that a machine has so many parts; he could sing not only of farming and fishing, but also of "leather-dressing, coach-making, boiler-making, rope-twisting, distilling, sign-painting, lime-burning, cotton-picking, electro-plating, electro-typing, stereo-typing"; one of the lines in one of his poems runs thus! He went the "whole hog" in fact, and he ought to be writing this article.

But most of us have to be content with a less vigorous attitude. We may follow the whole-hogger at moments, and no doubt it is our fault and not his when we don't follow him; but we cannot follow him always. . . . One might define the average educated man as optimist by instinct, pessimist by conviction. . . .

Here then is what one may call the irreducible minimum, the inalienable dowry of humanity: Beauty in scraps. It may seem a little thing after the comprehensive ecstasies of Whitman, but it is certain; it is for all men in all times, and we couldn't avoid it even if we wanted to. . . .

One final tip; read Walt Whitman. He is the true optimist — not the professional optimist who shuts his eyes and shirks, and whose palliatives do more harm than good, but one who has seen and suffered much and yet rejoices. He is not a philosopher or a theologian; he cannot answer the ultimate question and tell us what life is. But he is absolutely certain that it is grand, that it is happiness, and that "wherever life and force are manifested, beauty is manifested."

George H. Thomson, ed., *Albergo Empedocle and Other Writings* (New York: Liveright, 1971), 170, 171, 175.

27. D. H. LAWRENCE

Letter to Henry Savage, December 22, 1913

What a rum chap you are. Now you're discovering Whitman and humanity. But don't you see, he says all men are my brothers, and straightway goes into the wilderness to love them. Don't let yourself in for a terrific chagrin. But I'm glad you've discovered Humanity: it is fearfully nice to feel it round one. If you read my poetry — especially the earlier rough stuff which was published in the *English Review*, and isn't in the book of poems, you would see how much it has meant to me. Only, the bitterness of it is, that while one is brother to all men, and wrote *Macbeth* with Shakespeare and the Bible with James the First's doctors, one still remains Henry Savage or D. H. Lawrence, with one's own little life to live, and one's own handful of thoughts to write. And it is so hard to combine the two, and not to lose oneself in the generalisation, and not to lose the big joy of the whole in being narrowly oneself. Which is a preach. But perhaps you, like Whitman or Christ, can take the Church to bride, and give yourself, bodily and spiritually, to the abstract. The fault about Whitman is, strictly, that he is too self-conscious to be what he says he is: he's not Walt Whitman, I, the joyous American, he is Walt Whitman, the Cosmos, trying to fit a cosmos inside his own skin: a man rongé with unsatisfiedness not at all pouring his seed into American brides to make Stalwart American Sons, but pouring his seed into the space, into the idea of humanity. Poor man, it is pathetic when he makes even an idea of his own flesh and blood. He was a martyr like Christ, in a slightly different sort. — I don't mind people being martyrs in themselves, but to make an idea of the flesh and blood is wrong. The flesh and blood must go its own road. There is something wrong with Whitman, when he addresses American women as his Stalwart brides in whom he is to pour the seed for Stalwart Sons. One doesn't think like that. Imagine yourself addressing English women like that, in the mass. One *doesn't* feel like that — except in the moments of wide, gnawing desire when everything has gone wrong — Whitman is like a human document, or a wonderful treatise in human self-revelation. It is neither art nor religion nor truth: Just a self-revelation of a man who could not live, and so had to write himself. But writing should come from a strong root of life: like a battle song after a battle. — And Whitman did this, more or less. But his battle was not a real battle: he never gave his individual self into the fight: he was too much aware of it. He never fought with another person — he was like a wrestler who only wrestles with his own shadow — he never came to grips. He chucked his body into the fight and stood apart saying "Look how I am living." He is really false as hell. — But he is fine too. Only, I am sure, the generalisations are *no good* to the individual: the individual comes first, then the generalisation is a kind of game, not a reality: just a surplus, an excess, not a whole.

About spiritual pride, I think you are right. I can't understand you when you think so much of books and genius. They are great too — but they are the cake and wine of life — there is the bread and butter first, the ordinary human contact, the exchange with individuals of a bit of our individual selves, like beggars might exchange bits of crust on the road side. But Whitman did not take a person: he took that generalised thing, a Woman, an Athlete, a Youth. And this is wrong, wrong, wrong. He should take Gretchen, or one Henry Wilton. It *is* no use blanking the person out to have a sort of representative.

George J. Zytaruk and James T. Bolton, eds., *The Letters of D. H. Lawrence*, vol. 2 (Cambridge: Cambridge University Press, 1981), 129–130.

28. BASIL DE SELINCOURT

"The Problem of the Form"

[In] the example that follows, the tone of conversation has passed into that of soliloquy; the mood is too intimate, too remote, to admit of the idea of any but an impersonal utterance; we picture the soul of the poet addressing as it were some shadow of itself:

Tears! tears! tears!
In the night, in solitude, tears,
On the white shore dripping, dripping, suck'd in by the sand,

Tears, not a star shining, all dark and desolate,
Moist tears from the eyes of a muffled head;
O what is that ghost? that form in the dark, with tears?
What shapeless lump is that, bent, crouch'd there on the sand?
Streaming tears, sobbing tears, throes, choked with wild cries;
O storm, embodied, rising, careering with swift steps along the beach!
O wild and dismal night storm, with wind — O belching and desperate!
O shade so sedate and decorous by day, with calm countenance and regulated
  pace,
But away at night as you fly, none looking — O then the unloosen'd ocean,
Of tears! tears! tears!

The form here is of such exquisite sensitiveness that it is with an effort we remember the offences its author could commit. The lines "O who is that ghost" and "What shapeless lump is that" serve just to maintain the air of realistic familiarity that Whitman loves. He takes advantage of the ballast they provide to soar up into heights of suggestion and impressionism where he is equally at home. The storm, the human creature out in it, exchange forces, appearance, personality almost, from line to line. The tears are the rain, but who is it that is weeping? The night, the tempest, the seashore are part of the solitude and the despair they cover, part of the outpouring of passion and sorrow which they liberate, echo and absorb. And how does language take the impress of hints so vague and so conflicting and of an integration so profound? All through the piece alliteration, though never obtruding itself, and indeed never appearing till it is sought out, adds significance to the choice of the words by coaxing the reader to dwell upon them and so helping him to pass naturally over gaps whether of grammar or idea which might otherwise check him; he may observe next how every line, sensitive to the cadence of the first, divides itself sympathetically into a succession of lesser impulses, of which there are usually, but not always, three; and finally, as the sign of a still more vital sensitiveness, he will note the repetition of the keynote of the piece, the word "tears." The word is not only repeated, but variously placed in successive lines, so that by maintenance of the emphasis upon it its structural significance may be fully brought out. Then, at what is structurally the centre of the piece, there is a cessation; four lines of release and tumult follow which are silent of it; and so we are prepared for the beauty and inevitability of the final cadence in which it returns.

In *Tears! Tears! Tears!* we have a piece of poetic architecture which is at once completely original and completely satisfying. . . . The sincerer our devotion to poetry, the more readily we recognise that even in works called great, the form is apt to be a convenient mantle which, though it serves indeed to reveal the living gestures of the poet, serves also to give an average effect of dignity to transitional moments, when he is recovering from one gesture and preparing for the next. Form, as Whitman made use of it, avoids this pitfall. Not pre-existing as a mould to be filled, it cannot attract the feeling that is to fill it. It waits upon the feeling, and the feeling when it comes is the more likely to be genuine and sincere.

Walt Whitman: A Critical Study (London: Martin and Secker, 1914; reprint, New York: Russell and Russell, 1965), 79–81, 82.

29. P. MANSELL JONES
"Whitman and Verhaeren"

In considering together Whitman and Verhaeren, it is at once evident that they are, so to speak, poetic anomalies: they are alike in being unlike most other poets. And their importance lies in the fact that they are great not by the standards and virtues of the past, but because they have rebelled greatly and conquered. Yet that which distinguishes them from the vast majority of poets unites them more closely to one another. Both have chosen as themes, not any of the so-called "poetic subjects," but the world as it is today, the world of commerce and industry, of democracy and science. But apart from this modern, universal aspect of their work, each finds in the development of his country a source of inspiration which offers many points of similarity.

As young as America, Belgium is still adolescent and feels the joy of newly-acquired strength. As in America, the mixture of peoples and fertility of the soil have engendered a superb and powerful race. Walt Whitman was the cry of America, at last conscious of her power. Verhaeren proclaims the triumph of the Belgian — the European race. Each is the first adequate singer of his country. For this audacious task, both poets were by nature equally well equipped. Each embodies his country's two main sources of character: French and Flemish in the case of the Belgian poet, English and Dutch in that of the American. Moreover, their composite characters were moulded by similar environments: both combine, in a striking manner, a whole-hearted worship of nature with a love of "populous pavements." They have given the people — their needs and aspirations — a primary place in their works. Verhaeren truly loves the life of the humble. Though he belongs by birth to the middle-classes, his sympathy for the lowest in the social scale enables him to transform the commonplace details of their life into poems of extraordinary beauty and tenderness. He is one of them, says Zweig, and they feel their nearness to him. . . .

Surveying his work towards the end of his life, the author of *Leaves of Grass* said: "The word I myself put primarily for the description of them as they stand at last is the word Suggestiveness." And a last glance at Whitman's work, so rough and unpolished, yet so rich in the stuff and substance of poetry, seems to drive home the conclusion that Whitman is the fountain-head whence, all unconsciously, Verhaeren proceeds. Yet there is no intention to suggest that the former is of less significance than the latter. For if the "comradeship" of *Calamus* finds its reflection in the "admiration" of *La multiple Splendeur*, and if, as a song of the modern, *Leaves of Grass* is excelled by *Les Villes tentaculaires*, if, finally, Verhaeren is a greater artist than Whitman, it must not be forgotten that many themes — like those of democracy and death — have been treated more fully by the American than by the Belgian poet.

Aberystwyth Studies (Aberystwyth: University College) 2 (1914): 73–74, 104–105.

30. JOHN COWPER POWYS

Walt Whitman, in Visions and Revisions

I want to approach this great Soothsayer from the angle least of all profaned by popular verdicts. I mean from the angle of his poetry. We all know what a splendid heroic Anarchist he was. We all know with what rude zest he gave himself up to that "Cosmic Emotion," to which in these days the world does respectful, if distant, reverence. We know his mania for the words "en masse," for the words "ensemble," "democracy" and "libertad." We all know his defiant celebrations of Sex, of amorousness, of maternity; of that Love of Comrades which "passeth the love of women." We know the world-shaking effort he made — and to have made it at all, quite apart from its success, marks him a unique genius! — to write poetry about every mortal thing that exists, and to bring the whole breathing palpable world into his Gargantuan Catalogues. It is absurd to grumble at these Inventories of the Round Earth. They may not all move to Dorian flutes, but they form a background — like the lists of the Kings in the Bible and the lists of the Ships in Homer — against which, as against the great blank spaces of Life itself, "the writing upon the wall" may make itself visible.

What seems much less universally realized is the extraordinary genius for sheer "poetry" which this Prophet of Optimism possessed. . . .

The "free" poetry of Walt Whitman obeys inflexible, occult laws, the laws commanded unto it by his own creative instinct. We need, as Nietzsche says, to learn the art of "commands" of this kind. Transvaluers of old values do not spend all their time sipping absinthe. Is it a secret, then, the magical unity of rhythm, which Walt Whitman has conveyed to the words he uses? Those long, plangent, wailing lines, broken by little gurgling gasps and sobs; those sudden thrilling apostrophes and recognitions; those far-drawn flute-notes; those resounding sea-trumpets; all such effects have their place in the great orchestral symphony he conducts.

Take that little poem — quite spoiled before the end by a horrible bit of democratic vulgarity — which begins:

Come, I will build a Continent indissoluble;
I will make the most splendid race the sun ever shone upon—

Is it possible to miss the hidden spheric law which governs such a challenge? Take the poem which begins:

In the growths, by the margins of pond-waters—

Do you not divine, delicate reader, the peculiar subtlety of that reference to the rank, rain-drenched *anonymous weeds*, which every day we pass in our walks inland? A botanical name would have driven the magic of it quite away.

Walt Whitman, more than anyone, is able to convey to us that sense of the unclassified pell-mell, of weeds and stones and rubble and wreckage, of vast, desolate spaces, and spaces full of debris and litter, which is most of all characteristic of your melancholy American landscape, but which those who love England know where to find, even among our trim gardens. No one like Walt Whitman can convey to us the magical *ugliness* of certain aspects of Nature—the bleak, stunted, God-forsaken things; the murky pools where the grey leaves fall; the dead reeds where the wind whistles no sweet fairy tunes; the unspeakable margins of murderous floods; the tangled sea-drift, scurfed with scum; the black sea-windrow of broken shells and dead fishes' scales; the roots of willow trees in moonlit places crying out for demon-lovers; the long, moaning grass that grows outside the walls of prisons; the leprous mosses that cover paupers' graves; the mountainous wastes and blighted marsh-lands which only unknown wild-birds ever touch with their flying wings, and of which madmen dream—these are the things, the ugly, terrible things, that this great optimist turns into poetry. "Yo honk!" cries the wild goose, as it crosses the midnight sky. Others may miss that mad-tossed shadow, that heart-breaking defiance—but from amid the drift of leaves by the roadside, this bearded Fakir of Outcasts has caught its meaning; has heard, and given it its answer.

(London: Macdonald & Co., 1915; reprint, London: Vintage Books, 1974), 209, 212–213.

31. PADRAIC COLUM

"The Poetry of Walt Whitman"

Somewhere in the beginning of our histories of Philosophy is the name of the thinker who first announced that the World was a Becoming. That intuition was left to the philosophers until Walt Whitman arrived. And with Whitman the Becoming seems not only to be realized, but to be participated in. All is urge in his poetry. His rhythms flow and break like waves. His stanzas have not the measure that belongs to the poets of a world that is established — poets like Dante and Spenser, for instance — but the balances that are set in nature — one living member balancing another living member, as in a branching tree.

His verse not merely departs from traditional forms. It creates a new and special norm. It is special in as much as it exists only for Whitman's purpose, but it is a norm — that is to say, any departures from it can be perceived. . . . Hardly any poet has revised his original texts more than Whitman has. And it can be perceived that all his revision has the effect of making his lines conform to his verse-norm. "Flood-tide of the river, flow on! I watch you face to face," is the opening he once had for Crossing Brooklyn Ferry. If one substitutes this line for the line that opens the poem now, one can see that the norm is disturbed:

> Flood-tide below me! I watch you face to face;
> Clouds of the west! sun there half an hour high! I see you also face to face.
> Crowds of men and women attired in the usual costumes! how curious you
>   are to me! . . .

Whitman is a master of language as well as a master of his special verse-form. His is one of the greatest vocabularies of any poet who has written in English. What an array of words is in his volume! squatter's words; hobo's words; drummer's words; foreign phrases; words out of scientific and philosophic texts, with all the words of literary and journalistic English. And he uses all these words with such precision and vigor that he stamps them anew. . . . Every line in his verse is so vividly felt and so powerfully realized that it stands as solid as a bar of iron. . . .

Then there is in Whitman the clear and tender-toned poet. The themes of the poet are affection, reconciliation, death. When he sings of death he has a strangely beautiful accent. It is as if all the things that had kept him company — those tremendous shows and processions that his will and his vision bound him to — were folded away from him. He is Ruth to the Universe's Naomi. "Whither thou goest I will go," he says, and his trust makes beautiful his most haunting poems — Passage to India, the lovely Death Carol beginning "Come, Lovely and Soothing Death," Whispers of Heavenly Death; Darest Thou Now, O Soul; Out of the Cradle Endlessly Rocking, and The Last Invocation with its hushed lyricism. Did Whitman feel an unwonted power upon him when he sang of death? It would seem as if he did. It is something outside himself that prompts the lines of the Death Carol, a bird singing. And in Out of the Cradle Endlessly Rocking the bird that sings of separation is named demon. Whitman surely was aware when he gave that strange name to the bird that the demon in tradition is the spiritual power beyond our own soul that prompts to extraordinary manifestations.

New Republic (June 14, 1919): 213–214.

32. HUGH L'ANSON FAUSSETT

Walt Whitman: Poet of Democracy

It was . . . increasingly difficult to avoid seeing the scramble for wealth as the dominating motive of the time, not merely in the feverish gold-rush to California in 1849–50, but in the city government itself. Yet it was neither in his nature nor his experience to question the individualism of which a ruthless pursuit of self-interest was an extreme expression. He was born into a tenaciously individual class, nourished on the self-reliant gospels of Franklin and Jefferson, and suspicious of any encroachments by a central government upon independent rights. The phase of material development during which he lived as well as his own pronounced egoism prevented him from being in any radical sense a socialist.

Even today in America the conception of a society reorganised so that the co-operative impulse supersedes the competitive grows very slowly. And Whitman was too naively of his time to be a hundred years in front of it. His sympathies were all for brotherhood, but for a brotherhood of individuals who had surrendered none of their private rights. The acquisitive individual was an unfortunate by-product of such freedom, but less dangerous to the health of a society than an intrusive Government.

It was and is an understandable view. But it was based on a serious underestimate of the vicious strength of the acquisitive impulse, through which democracy in America has been persistently defeated by plutocracy, and on a very limited conception of Government. Whitman resisted any extension of Governmental authority because he viewed it always as something imposed upon individuals. He never seems to have conceived of it as a possibly organic expression of their social consciousness and as such liberating them from a conflict of selfish impulses. At bottom his political views were limited by his own gospel of egoism. Seeing, as he did, so imperfectly what a real self-hood entailed, he was equally blind to the sacrifice of selfish independence necessary to the individual who would lose and find himself in an integrated society. And so, in theory at least, he was always to remain a merely humanitarian democrat despite all the inhumanities which a *laissez-faire* system was increasingly to display.

(London: Cape, 1942), 93–94.

33. V. S. PRITCHETT

"Two Writers and Modern War"

The American Civil War was the first modern war. . . . [In the work of writers before this] there is no suggestion that war is a human tragedy. This suggestion is not made until the civilian fights. He cannot shrug his shoulders and say, "C'est la guerre." He is stunned by his own fears, stupefied by his own atrocities, amazed at his happiness, incredulous at the point of death. When all people are at war, no code, no manner, can contain the experience. The nearest writers to Whitman are Tolstoy and Erckmann-Chatrian — it is interesting to note that they were all writing about war at the same time — but Tolstoy's ironical pacifism and Erckmann-Chatrian's mildness and peaceableness are a branch of the main stream of popular feeling. They are not, like Whitman, the stream itself. The *Histoire d'un Conscrit de 1813* was written in 1864. It has been called *l'Iliade de la peur* and it portrays the pathos of the conscript's situation. The tragedy of the conscript is a passive one: that a quiet, peaceable man like himself should be killed. But in Whitman — as in Wilfred Owen — the tragedy is not passive; it lies not only in what is done to a man but in what he himself does and in what happens to him inside. . . . [Tolstoy and Erckmann-Chatrian] are propagandists with an uncommonly delicate ear. They write to warn opinion in the fond domestic parlour behind the little shop.

Compared with them, Whitman does not know his mind. He is all over the place. He is the public. It is typical of *Specimen Days* that its first picture of the war is of the news spreading in the streets at night. The emotion of the street catches him. He is not intoxicated with patriotism but he does not deny the message of the pennants and the flags in the street. He is the man in the parlour who goes out into the street and loses his head. He feels the herd instinct. Two great wars have made us guarded, and when we read *Specimen Days* and especially the poems called *Drum-Taps*, we resist that old-fashioned war. The sun has faded the defiant and theatrical photograph, and paled the headlines to a weak-tea brown. The uniforms are shabby. We suspect Whitman's idea that out of this a nation is born; it sounds like the cracked bugle and slack drum of propaganda. And yesterday's propaganda puts no one in a flurry. Yet, in all this, the loquacious Whitman is right. It is the bewildering thing in all his work, that this dressed-up egotist with all the air of a ham actor, is always half-right when he is most dubious. He is the newspaper man who reflects the ambiguous quality of public feeling. His virtue is that he begins on the pavement and that, like the streets, he has no shame and no style. Excitement and incantation take the place of it. . . .

After this the reality begins. And the reality, as the first modern war drags on, is the casualty list. In the classical narratives men are merely shot. Sometimes they are blown up. The aftermath was not minutely described. "Bloodshed," "carnage," generalise it. Whitman too, uses those words but with all his voice. . . . That discovery marks the beginning of the modern attitude to war. We write as followers, not leaders. And though Whitman likes the heroic act, the message in the leader's eye, enjoys seeing the President ride past with his escort of cavalry and feels the public emotion of the "great convulsive drums," he writes more surely when he goes back to the rank and file, when he recovers his sense of anonymity. (Odd that this huge and often so flaccid egotist should be able to puff himself large enough until he is identified with all the people and lost in them; it is his paradox.) It is his paradox, too, that doggerel and the real thing traipse along together like the blind leading the blind, unable to see, unable to stop. . . .

Drum-Taps describes the general scene, what the unknown and anonymous man did and saw and how filthily he died. Patriotism has not decayed; but the human being has emerged. He emerged first of all, it is interesting to observe, in a civil war, a war of ideas; and in the country which, to so many people, had seemed the Promised Land, where no formal tradition of war existed. Whitman himself observed, in his confused groping way, that a new way of warfare was necessary to America. A new way of writing about war certainly emerged; perhaps that is what he was trying to say.

The Living Novel (London: Chatto and Windus, 1946), 166–172.

34. J. MIDDLETON MURRY

"Walt Whitman: Prophet of Democracy"

The universal of which "these States" were the particular in Whitman's poetry is Democracy; and all over the world democrats, in Whitman's peculiar and profound sense of the word—that is, those who believe that a self-governing society of free and responsible individuals offers the only way of progress towards the Good—have had no difficulty in regarding Whitman's America as the city of their own soul. It is for them a symbol of the ideal, of the same order as Blake's Albion and Jerusalem; and Whitman in rhapsodizing over the rivers and prairies of America, is behaving as Shakespeare's poet, "who gives to airy nothing a local habitation and a name"—except that the ideal Democracy is much more than "an airy nothing." It is at least a compelling vision of the society towards which humanity must stumble on, if it is not to cease to be human. . . .

[Writing] as late as 1904 Henry Bryan Binns, his English biographer, speaking of Whitman's dismissal in 1865 from his clerkship in the Indian Bureau in Washington, as the result of the reading of *Leaves of Grass* by his Methodist chief, says: "Average American opinion was then undisguisedly hostile, as, of course, it still remains." If that was really the situation in America in 1904, it was distinctly different from that in England, where by that time his book had been accepted as a classic by the Liberal intellectuals, and as a sort of bible by the native British Socialist movement, which, though it had a fair sprinkling of intellectuals, had a solid working-class core. Perhaps the explanation of this discrepancy is that quite early in the nineteenth century the British working class had become more or less completely urbanized, and Whitman's poetry had, for the part of it which was sufficiently alert to become Socialist, a powerful nostalgic attraction as a poetry of the open country and the open air. And it is very probable that the curious, but very marked association of the early Socialist movement in England with camping and hiking, on foot or cycle in the countryside is almost entirely due to the influence of Whitman. . . .

[The] matrix is more important than the gems; the total Whitman far more dynamic, far more charged with potential for humanity, than his rounded utterances. The Whitman who gropes his way from the basis of his deep and new-discovered personality, his identified soul, into the vast variety of his incomplete affirmations; who offers himself with all his hesitations, his contradictions, and his deep unformulable faith, to his comrades of the future is a truly prophetic man. He is, in part, the attractive image of the citizen of the new completely human society of which the crude integument is what we call Democracy; he is, in a yet more important part, the tongue-tied soul in his travail of the idea of which he is the instinctive vehicle. And this part of him, which is quite inseparable from the other, is perhaps even more durable than the image of the rounded man which he communicates. For it is inherent in this conception of Democracy, as the constant, endless breaking of the fallows of humankind for the sowing of the seed of personality, that it should never reach finality.

Milton Hindus, ed., *Leaves of Grass One Hundred Years After* (Stanford: Stanford University Press, 1955), 125, 136, 143.

35. DAVID DAICHES
"Walt Whitman's Philosophy"

How could Whitman take a normative attitude to the civilization of his day if at the same time he accepted everything in existence merely because it was in existence? I think the answer to this question lies in Whitman's view of the nature of a real person. Inanimate Nature and animals were all to be accepted; they were what they were, part of the process of things. But men — who were alone capable of betraying their identities by leading second-hand lives in which their real selves were not involved — could be judged in accordance with the degree to which they fulfilled the true laws of their own personalities. It is significant that after Swinburne turned against Whitman, to write a stinging attack on the man and his poetry, Whitman remarked of the furious English poet: "Ain't he the damndest simulacrum?" Swinburne, in talking this frenzied nonsense, was acting as a simulacrum, a pale image of his real self, not in his true capacity as a person. And this is the way in which Whitman tended to speak of those he disliked and, indeed, of all evil in the universe. He did not hold simply that "whatever is, is right," but rather that whatever exists in its true, undistorted nature is good. The "parcel of helpless dandies" that he attacked were denounced as "all second-hand, or third, fourth, or fifth hand," and that was the real burden of his complaint.

Now I think that this helps to explain, too, Whitman's increasing insistence on his originality as he grew older. In repudiating an obvious debt to Emerson and — as Esther Shephard has pointed out — concealing a significant debt to two novels of George Sand, Whitman cannot be acquitted of disingenuousness; but we can see why it was important to him to keep stressing his originality. The real poet was essentially original, true to his own vision, transcribing nothing at second-hand. If Whitman had thought more carefully about the problem of originality, he would have seen that it is not necessarily incompatible with borrowing: nobody now denies the originality of Shakespeare's genius because he took his plots from other writers. But he was so obsessed with the importance of renouncing the second-hand, of exploiting only his own true self, that he felt it necessary to repudiate with increasing urgency any suspicion of borrowing.

Literary Essays (Edinburgh: Oliver and Boyd, 1956), 79–80.

36. W. H. AUDEN

"D. H. Lawrence"

The difference between formal and free verse may be likened to the difference between carving and modelling; the formal poet, that is to say, thinks of the poem he is writing as something already latent in the language which he has to reveal, while the free verse poet thinks of language as a plastic passive medium upon which he imposes his artistic conception. One might also say that, in their attitude towards art, the formal verse writer is a catholic, the free verse writer a protestant. And Lawrence was, in every respect, very protestant indeed. As he himself acknowledged, it was through Whitman that he found himself as a poet, found the right idiom of poetic speech for his demon.

On no other English poet, so far as I know, has Whitman had a beneficial influence; he could on Lawrence because, despite certain superficial resemblances, their sensibilities were utterly different. Whitman quite consciously set out to be the Epic Bard of America and created a poetic *persona*, not an actual human being, even when he appears to be talking about the most intimate experiences. When he sounds ridiculous, it is usually because the image of an individual obtrudes itself comically upon what is meant to be a statement about a collective experience. *I am large. I contain multitudes* is absurd if one thinks of Whitman himself or any individual; of a corporate person like General Motors it makes perfectly good sense. The more we learn about Whitman the man, the less like his *persona* he looks. On the other hand it is doubtful if a writer ever existed who had less of an artistic *persona* than Lawrence; from his letters and the reminiscences of his friends, it would seem that he wrote for publication in exactly the same way as he spoke in private. (I must confess that I find Lawrence's love poems embarrassing because of their lack of reticence; they make me feel a Peeping Tom.) Then, Whitman looks at life extensively rather than intensively. No detail is dwelt upon for long; it is snapshotted and added as one more item to the vast American catalogue. But Lawrence in his best poems is always concerned intensively with a single subject, a bat, a tortoise, a fig tree, which he broods on until he has exhausted its possibilities.

The Dyer's Hand (London: Faber and Faber, 1963), 287–288.

37. ANTHONY BURGESS

"The Answerer"

British musicians have been better Whitman publicists than British men of letters. Whitman, a bad poet to quote (as Uncle Ponderevo admits in *Tono-Bungay*), was learned by heart by thousands of provincial choral singers — those who tackled Delius's *Sea-Drift*, Vaughan Williams's *A Sea Symphony*, Holst's *Dirge for Two Veterans*, eventually Bliss's *Morning Heroes*. Because Whitman, like the Bible, seemed to stand on the margin of art, composers saw that they could add some art to him. More than that, he was democratic, even sweaty, and the right librettist for a musical renaissance that turned against Mendelssohnian salons and went to the sempiternal soil. Whitman's free verse (not *vers libre*, a very salony thing) was a corrective to the four-square folkiness that bedevilled so many rural rhapsodies and even *The Planets*, but his rhythms were lyrical or declamatory, not — like Eliot and Pound (who eventually made a peace with Whitman, having "detested him long enough") — muffled, arhetorical, conversational.

Whitman's verse-technique is still of interest to the prosodist. His basic rhythm is an epic one — the Virgilian dactyl-spondee — and his line often hexametric. . . . He sometimes sounds like Clough's *Amours de Voyage*, though it would be hard to imagine a greater disparity of tone and attitude than that which subsists between these two Victorians. Nevertheless, both Clough and Whitman saw that the loose hexameter could admit the contemporary and sometimes the colloquial. . . . When Whitman becomes "free," it is as though he justifies truncation or extension of the basic hexameter by some unspoken theory of a line-statement or line-image. Flouting classical procedure in refusing to allow any spill-over from line to line, he invokes a tradition older than Virgil — that of Hebrew poetry. British composers, their noses well-trained, sniffed the Bible in Whitman.

Urgent Copy (New York: W. W. Norton, 1968), 48–49.

38. DENIS DONOGHUE

"Walt Whitman"

[We] have to ask what Whitman's freedom gave him, besides ease. In one sense he was, indeed, free; he put down burdens which other men sustained. But it may be argued that in another sense he was bound, because he was ignorant of what he disowned. There is no evidence that he conn'd old times sufficiently to know them as sturdy and different from his own: certainly, he did not propose a relation to the past based upon that knowledge. So it is necessary to say that he freed himself from human history without taking the precaution, in the first instance, of thoroughly understanding it. Whatever worth we ascribe to his freedom, it must allow for that limitation, that its facility was not profoundly earned. That is why his message, so far as it may be described as such, is dispensable. He was, by his own assertion, a prophet and a sage, but his prophecy was somewhat meretricious, his wisdom untested. What matters, after all, is the poetry.

To get the beauty of Whitman's poetry hot, one must read it in long, rolling stretches. No poet is less revealed in the single phrase, the image, or even the line. The unit of the verse is indeed the phrase, a loose-limbed structure of several words easily held together and moving along because the cadence goes with the speaker's breath. This is what William Carlos Williams learned from Whitman, the natural cadence, the flow of breath as a structure good enough for most purposes and better for humanity than the counting of syllables. For both poets the ideal is what Whitman called "a redeeming language," a language to bridge the gap between subject and object, thereby certifying both and praising bridges. Again in both poets the function of language is to verify an intricate network of affinities and relationships, contacts, between person and person, person and place, person and thing. In Whitman, the number of completely realized poems is small: many poems contain wonderful passages, but are flawed, often by a breach of taste, a provincialism. Where the poem fails, it fails because Whitman thought too well of his excess to curb it; the words converge upon the poem, and he will not turn them aside. Some of his greatest writing is in "Song of Myself," but on the other hand that poem, too, is often provincial, awkward. The best of Whitman, certainly one of his greatest achievements, is a shorter poem, "Crossing Brooklyn Ferry." William Carlos Williams once praised a poem by Marianne Moore as an anthology of transit, presumably because the words secured a noiseless progression from one moment to another: they did not sit down to admire themselves. Whitman's favourite subject is movement, process, becoming: no wonder he loved bridges and ferries, which kept things moving while defining relationships, one thing with another.

Marcus Cunliffe, ed., *American Literature to 1900* (London: Sphere Books, 1975), 275–276.

39. GEOFFREY GRIGSON

The Private Art: A Poetry Notebook

A poem should be words locked into a form and so made indestructible or hard to destroy, whether the words are fitted into already determined forms, or whether they find their own form as they go along, to each poem its own form. So there isn't really a contradiction between the tight compressed regularity of a poem by an Icelandic or Norwegian scald of the Middle Ages and a poem by Whitman or St.-John Perse, or between a poem by Hopkins and a poem by Whitman.

Hopkins was upset to have to recognize his kinship with Whitman. . . .

From North America I once had a ninny poet in the house. He could not be persuaded that poets occur in a population by rare genetic accident, little related to numbers, although their nurture and their maturation will much depend on culture and economics.

He wasn't going to accept from me that in the great population of his conti-nent there might have been — there may have been — no very remarkable poet since John Crowe Ransom, and Whitman.

The most — at any rate the best — in fewest words. Which condemns, if that were necessary, Olson and the upright or vertical paper poets of America. But not Whitman. And then what is always required, from each if possible, isn't too little of the most in the fewest words, but plenty of it, plenty of risks undertaken. . . .

How Whitman's rhetoric deflates to a wrinkled toy balloon when he unhooks too long from the objectivity of his great America — stars, lilac, rivers, wharfs, fer-ries, the cavalry in the ford, the net around the fish, and all of his "eternal uses of the earth," his "primal sanities" of Nature. How he conveys when his exclamation is particular!

Whitman thrilled to a high voltage of new America, a beginning, a continent flowering (into what subsequent flowers, if only he had known). Hopkins, his contemporary in small England, thrilled, while it was still possible, to a high volt-age of the divine, opening its apparent flowers to him. It is hard to see how there can again be grandly equivalent coincidences of the poet and the situation. But doesn't Whitman say that the best poems are still to be written, and that in his opinion "no definition that has ever been made sufficiently encloses the name Po-etry; nor can any rule or convention ever so absolutely obtain but some great ex-ception may arise and disregard it and overturn it"?

Anyhow the company chairman and the Foreign Minister and the editor and the union boss and the detective inspector and the engineer mayn't believe it, but no poetry, in whatever future convention, would mean no humanity.

(London and New York: Allison and Busby, 1982), 78, 187, 216, 219.

40. CHARLES TOMLINSON

"Crossing Brooklyn Ferry"

To cross a ferry that is no longer there,
The eye must pilot you to the further shore:
It travels the distance instantaneously
And time also: the stakes that you can see
Raggedly jettying into nothingness
Are the ghosts of Whitman's ferry: their images
Crowding the enfilade of steel and stone
Have the whole East River to reflect upon
And the tall solidities it liquifies.

Notes from New York and Other Poems (Oxford: Oxford University Press, 1984), 16.

41. JOHN BAYLEY

"Songs of a Furtive Self: Whitman"

The fact is that Whitman was not really doing anything American at all in *Song of Myself,* whatever the appearances; he was creating a new language and style for self-expression — the physical sense of self — as Keats had done thirty years or so before. Keats's sensuality of language can often be slightly shamefaced, but it is not furtive; furtiveness implies a carefully worked out undercover programme, such as the genius of Whitman could organize.

The effects of Keats's language, though, are remarkably similar to Whitman's — "The Eve of St. Agnes" and *Sleep and Poetry* are in terms of their verbal world the nearest kind of poetry to *Song of Myself.* Even Keats's neologisms have an exact parallel in Whitman's exuberances and demotic oddities. . . . Whitman's gallicisms are an essential part of his style, its total and original "campness," and like Keats's intuitions in language of the nature and feel of the body Whitman's sense of it seems also to need that posture of touching and unwitting absurdity and vulnerability which belongs to human nakedness. This his fervency of language, like Keats's provides. . . . Like Keats's Whitman's language has what might be termed erectile tendencies ("Those movements, those improvements of our bodies," as Byron blandly remarks) and its exuberance and oddities seem wholly natural for this reason. There is nothing pretentious or metaphysical about the neologisms of either poet; they seem to expand into a world not of ingenuity but of vivid physical simplicity, a verbal equivalent of what Whitman calls "the curious sympathy one feels when feeling with the hand the naked meat of the body," and its "thin red jellies."

Discovering the body in poetry was not quite the same thing as discovering America. More fortunate than Keats in this as in other ways, Whitman did not feel that he had to pass himself for the higher life in order to discover America. Furtiveness came naturally to him, but it had the simple health of inner shamelessness: he was not in thrall to romantic ideas of the European tradition, the spirit and its lofty destiny, as Keats was. The age and the expectations that ordained for Keats the romantic hero's role, in opposition to his own poetic genius, left Whitman wholly free to loaf about on fish-shaped Paumanok, clam-digging and declaiming Shakespeare to the waves.

Selected Essays (Cambridge: Cambridge University Press, 1984), 2–3.

42. CHARLES TOMLINSON
"Ivor Gurney's 'Best Poems'"

[The first London performance] of the Sea Symphony brought together two of [Ivor] Gurney's heroes—Vaughan Williams and Walt Whitman. Vaughan Williams's spacious and dramatic settings of Whitman's poems deal with texts that were to be increasingly important for Gurney. Except for Lawrence, it is hard to think of any other English poet who has known what to do with Whitman. Gurney—dangerously, one might have thought—identified himself with Whitman and earned his right to do so not only in his excellent "New England poems" but in masterpieces like "Felling a Tree." He wrote this last, having emerged from the war, in 1922 when his days of freedom were already numbered.

During his asylum years, evidently round about 1925, Gurney compiled a forgotten selection entitled "Best poems," the manuscript of which has only recently come to light in a Gloucestershire sale room. . . . It contains "Felling a Tree" and many other Whitmanian pieces. One of these, "Of the Sea," has never appeared in selections of Gurney and is a remarkable celebration of that poet who helped give him a standard beyond the constrictions of English Georgianism:

Cornwall surges round Zennor like the true delight
Of earth all savage with a force enemy to man—
Bude streams a long roller of curled gathering foam.
But nothing more than Masefield I have come truly
To know, Great Ocean with huge strength untamed or stilly,
Or Marryat's sea affairs so local and snug of the foc'sle.
Mightiness of the wide Atlantic hiding its strength,

Or tempested Long Island or Massachusetts land
Bretagne, and Baltic, the Californian long sand length;
The dark October lowering of South Dorset
"Dynasts" has shown to me, these are not to forget —
Seen of my deep mind reading the northeast blind
Dawn through. But of all things most of the sea to me —
There is Longney Reach to Priding beating victoriously
In a great June exultation of half-tide Severn.
And Trafalgar ships moving like painted things
Over a painted sea — and Walt Whitman true sight, haunted sea.
"The perfume, the faint creaking of the cordage — melancholy
Rhythm —" And this is ocean's poem to compel
Poetry in the heart of a boy late night working;
Men giving life of the huge unseen mid Atlantic swell.

One of the surprising things about Gurney's attachment to Whitman was that it did not lead to mere superfluity. The piled-up, almost laborious effects of "Felling a Tree" serve the theme of the poem itself. "Of the Sea," though shorter, achieves a comparable massive simplicity of utterance in a style which characterizes another poem in Kavanagh's collection, "Portraits," which Donald Davie has justly referred to as "perhaps the finest reflection on American history by an Englishman." These Whitmanesque yet unmistakably Gurney poems take him beyond Gloucestershire and the Severn meadows and also beyond the trenches.

Times Literary Supplement, January 3, 1986.

43. TOM PAULIN

Minotaur: Poetry and the Nation State

With hindsight we can see that the mansion-house of liberty passage in *Areopagitica* reads like an anticipation of Whitman's "Song of Myself":

Many sweating, ploughing, thrashing, and then the chaff for payment
    receiving,
A few idly owning, and they the wheat continually claiming.

This is the city and I am one of the citizens,
Whatever interests the rest interests me, politics, wars, markets, newspapers,
    schools,
The mayor and councils, banks, tariffs, steamships, factories, stocks, stores,
    real estate and personal estate.

The Whitman who hears "all sounds running together, combined, fused or following" is true to the social relatedness of different individual activities which Milton sings in the prose. Especially at the close — "others as fast reading, trying all things" — Milton sounds uncannily like Whitman democratically trying to pack every last rapid action in.

Both poets share an ecstatic primitivism ("Smile O voluptuous cool-breath'd earth!") that can also be a figure for the procreant urge of the market: "millions of spinning worms, / That in their green shops weave the smooth-haired silk." However, Milton's commitment to the busy hum of mercantile republics is not entirely wholehearted, for he assigns this vision of productive "natural" labour to Comus, the tempter. . . . Milton's egotism, like Whitman's, has a generous, wonderfully innocent optimism that springs from their absolute confidence in the liberating possibilities of the free individual conscience.

By comparing Milton and Whitman, we start to see the republican poetics that structure the prose. Whitman asserts, "Not words of routine this song of mine," and Milton is constantly striving to break down inert routines in order to free the imagination from "linen decency," "a gross confirming stupidity, a stark and dead congealment." To adapt Hazlitt's terms, the "momentum" and "elasticity" of this republican visionary force which confidently insists that of all governments a Commonwealth aims "most to make the people flourishing, virtuous, noble and high-spirited." It seems appropriate that scholars working in the United States should invite readers congealed in the royalist kitsch of present-day Britain to remember and admire this great servant of human liberty.

(London: Faber, 1991), 29–31.

FERNANDO ALEGRÍA

Whitman in Spain and Latin America

Jorge Luis Borges, an admirer but not a worshipper of Whitman, has said with typical irony:

> Almost everything written about Whitman is ruined by two persistent errors. One is the summary identifying of Whitman, the conscientious man of letters, with Whitman the semi-divine hero of *Leaves of Grass.* . . . The other, the senseless adoption of the style and vocabulary of his poems, that is to say, the adoption of the very same amazing phenomenon which one wishes to explain. (Borges, 70)

But the majority of persons who have written about Whitman in Spain and Latin America have simply identified the hero of "Song of Myself" with the man who created him. To them, Whitman achieved one of the great ambitions of his life: convincing the reader that his book and his person bear one single identity — that in saying "Camerado, this is no book, who touches this touches a man" he was not attempting a metaphor but demanding to be taken literally.

HISPANIS WHITMANISTAS: WHITMAN'S GOSPEL ACCORDING TO MARTÍ

José Martí, the Cuban poet who introduced Whitman to Hispanic literature in 1877, laid the foundations for this glorification (see selection 1). So brilliantly inspired was Martí's exegesis that no one dared contradict him; thus, Whitman was considered an apostle without blemish, the representative poet of the democratic genius of America. This image of a bard as the poet-prophet speaking for a chosen nation was not unfamiliar to the Latin American readers of Rubén Darío, Leopoldo Lugones, and José S. Chocano. Martí opens his essay on Whitman by quoting a newspaper report about Whitman's 1887 Lincoln lecture: "Last night he seemed a god, sitting in his red velvet chair, his hair completely white, his beard upon his breast, his brows like a thicket, his hand upon a cane." Martí then built upon this divine image to create a "muscular and angelic" bard: "All literate New York attended that luminous speech in religious silence, for its sudden grace notes, vibrant tones, hymnlike fugues and Olympian familiarity seemed at times the whispering of stars." The Nobel laureate Spanish poet Juan Ramón Jiménez, referring to Martí's essay, suggested that

> Darío owed much to him, Unamuno a great deal. Spain and Spanish America owed to him the poetic discovery of the United States. Through his travels in exile Martí incorporated the United States into Hispanic America and Spain better than any other Spanish-language writer. . . . Whitman came to us, and to all Spaniards, through Martí. (Jiménez, 33)

Following Martí's lead, later Hispanic authors tended to take at face value Whitman's own statements about his family and the Long Island surroundings of his youth. They idealized his ancestors and his legendary youthful years of "absorption" when the poet stored knowledge as the result of direct experience. They enumerated the positions he held; they emphasized the triumph of his bohemian inclinations over bureaucratic routines. His wanderings along Broadway, his passion for opera, his meanderings along the wharves, his bus rides and evenings spent in taverns with his worker-friends were all described as examples of Whitman's democratic and progressive spirit. His trip to New Orleans provided romance (as well as six phantom children). Whitman's activities as a nurse during the Civil War were described as an apostolate. His literary career was exalted as the struggle of an isolated poet against the power of a strong and prejudiced political establishment. Whitman was typically described as having suffered economic and physical hardships during his old age, all of which he overcame through extraordinary stoicism, aided by a small group of loyal friends.

Despite this idealization, these biographical sketches have a peculiar significance which is difficult to explain. In them, the ghost of Whitman finds a language that creates a unity between his personality and his poetic hero. Never was Whitman more bohemian than in Spanish; never was he more prophetic than when shuffling centuries and sidereal spheres in the modernistic discourse of Darío. Who can make Whitman more apocalyptic than Lugones? And how can Whitman sound more proletarian than in Pablo Neruda's "Let the Woodcutter Awaken"? Every detail of Whitman's life, however insignificant and hackneyed, gains new life in the lyrical drive of Martí, in the metaphors of Amando Vasseur, in the avant-garde imagery of Luis Franco. "This man loves the world with the fire of Sappho," exclaims Martí. "He sees the world as a gigantic bed." Whitman's sea roars aggressively in the paraphrases of León Felipe, while in Armando Donoso's descriptions it pounds with philosophic resonance. *Leaves of Grass* is a patriotic book for Torres-Ríoseco, a social document for Gilberto Freyre, a demiurgic text for Miguel de Unamuno.

However, to consider all commentary on Whitman that derives from Martí as simply lyrical fireworks would be a mistake. Martí characterizes Whitman's poetry as representative of a society based on freedom to work and on the liberty to develop spiritually. Whitman's poetry is one "of inclusiveness and faith, soothing and solemn." Its greatness derives from its desire to serve man's constant struggle for liberty: "Whitman sings what the working masses aspire to sing and brings into an atmosphere of collective endeavor the exercise of an art which could not prosper in any other way."

This idea of the necessary freedom of man leads the poet to organize an optimistic philosophical system. Consider the conception of death in the poem honoring Lincoln, "When Lilacs Last in the Dooryard Bloom'd." Nature, Martí says, accompanies the dead man across the States. The stars had announced the death of the hero, the clouds had darkened, the thrush sang its sad song in the swamps: "When the poem is finished it seems all Earth has been clothed in black and the dead man has covered it from sea to sea." On the threshold of death the secret visions of the poet become illuminated; then Whitmanian lovers can reintegrate themselves into eternity.

This harmonious relationship between the concepts of life and death is a basic link in Whitman's dialectic chain. His understanding of the universe is based on the Hegelian principle of the harmony of opposites, and, for Martí, the poet is the unifying cosmos: "His duty is to create and his creation shares in the divine, so that when Whitman intones the 'Song of Myself' he is expressing the identity of the Universe." Whitman's sensuality so compellingly draws Martí's attention that most modernist and postmodernist critics and poets following in his footsteps could not avoid being influenced. Martí describes the sensual enjoyment that Whitman experiences in the contemplation and experience of his own body and proceeds to formulate a theory of autoeroticism quite similar to ideas expressed by European and North American readers:

> Why be surprised then if the poet chooses to sing the body as much as the soul exalting the beauty of the spirit and the disturbing presence of matter? . . . He depicts truth as a frantic lover who invades his body and, eager to possess him, rids him of his clothes. . . . Such language has seemed lascivious to some who are incapable of understanding its grandeur. . . . He gives himself to the atmosphere like a tremulous bridegroom.

It must be emphasized that for Martí — and later on, for Neruda and Borges — Whitman's sensuality is an essential derivative of his pantheistic ideas. Love is one of the bonds that unites humans with God and with nature.

Montoliú, Donoso, and Others

Many Hispanic critics and poets developed Martí's ideas, among them Gómez Carrillo, Pérez Jorba, Jaime Brossa, Angel Guerra, Cebría Montoliú, Armando Donoso, Luis Franco, and José Gabriel. Of these—all writing during the first half of the twentieth century—Montoliú, Donoso, and Gabriel are the most interesting.

Montoliú's book *Walt Whitman, L'home i sa tasca* (1913), in Catalan (later translated in Argentina into Spanish as *Walt Whitman, el hombre y su obra* [1943]), may be considered the first systematic study of Whitman published in the Hispanic world (see selection 3). The Catalan critic states that his purpose is to vindicate the memory of a poet who was denied recognition in his country even after being accepted in Europe as one of the greatest poets of the nineteenth century. Montoliú's main sources of information were *Specimen Days*, "A Backward Glance O'er Travel'd Roads," and Richard Maurice Bucke's *Walt Whitman*; from these he could draw only an idealized image. However, he offers historical comments that have influenced Hispanic readers. He describes the failure of the first edition of *Leaves of Grass*, and he offers a fine analysis of Emerson's letter to Whitman. Montoliú explains why the transcendentalists accepted Whitman and proclaimed his genius, even though Emerson used harsh words to criticize the "excessive crudity" of some sexual passages in *Leaves of Grass*. Analyzing the Civil War, Montoliú describes Lincoln's influence upon Whitman. He emphasizes the strong support Whitman received from British writers such as William Michael Rossetti, and he notes how Whitman's popularity grew in England. Montoliú remains faithful to Whitman's autobiographical writings and to the idealization of his life which the poet himself promoted. He does not tamper with historical facts; rather, the facts that reached him are deeply glorified. He deals with Whitman's metaphysics, politics, aesthetics, and, more warily, his prosody. In an appendix, he candidly discusses Whitman's sexual attitudes. Montoliú also published the first Hispanic translations of poems from *Leaves of Grass* (1909), but in Catalan, not Spanish.

However, in the same year as Montoliú's book, there also appeared a brilliant essay on Whitman's catalogs by the great Spanish scholar Miguel de Unamuno, the rector of the University of Salamanca: "El canto adánico," later published in his *El espejo de la muerte* (1930; see selection 4). It was a clever and lyric justification of Whitman's use of enumerations. Unamuno discovered *Leaves of Grass* in 1906 during a visit to America, and he adopted Whitman's disregard of traditional poetic diction and musicality, as his poem "Credo poético" shows. He even imitated Whitman's rhythmic liberties in "El Cristo de Velasquez" (1920) and remained faithful to Whitman during the rest of his life, admiring his indifference to contradictions and his bold assertion of himself in his poems.

Not long after the appearance of Montoliú's book and Unamuno's essay, the Chilean critic Armando Donoso published two articles on Whitman that attempted to discover the roots of his philosophy outside of traditional American patriotism. Donoso was an unusual social thinker himself. As a literary critic he fostered avant-garde tendencies; as an editorialist for the venerable Chilean daily *El Mercurio* he defended extremely conservative causes. A man of culture and sensibility, he had been educated in Germany and lived in Spain, where he published an anthology of the most advanced Chilean poetry and an excellent scholarly book on Goethe. What is particularly appealing in Donoso's writing on Whitman is that, drawing away from the usual idealization of "Song of Myself," he searches for the philosophical and religious roots underlying the poet's ideas. "Walt Whitman, born into an admirable family (his father was a working man and his mother a fine Dutch woman, a Quaker), inherited that spiritual strength which comes only from a life full of hardships leading towards the highest apostolates" (Donoso, 199). From the Quakers he inherited his love of nature, a love which is not expressed in the form of a "sickly mysticism" but as an exaltation of his strong personality, leading him to identify with the universe and to define himself as a cosmos. Whitman's spirituality involved an idea of limitless progress, which Donoso links to Emerson's idea of the "representative man" and to Nietzsche's *Übermensch*. Donoso believes that this "superman" is contained in the very person of the poet and gains expression through Whitman's literary work.

Donoso's greatest achievement may be his analysis of "Drum-Taps," a section of *Leaves of Grass* which generally has had little attraction for Hispanic readers. The presence of Whitman on the battlefront is not just a simple humanitarian act, Donoso believes. Rather, Whitman is giving expression to "the warlike happiness which exalts him to an apocalyptic hate and holy fire which overflows the poems of 'Drum-Taps.'" On the other hand, in Lincoln's death Whitman "finds the poetic motive that allows him to find a universal significance to the feelings that the Civil War had aroused in him" (Donoso, 203, 205).

During the years of the First World War, Hispanic Whitmanism went through a period of lethargy, even though Whitman's name was mentioned repeatedly in literary manifestos and articles dealing with the theory and the poetry of the avant-garde. In 1922 the Chilean critic and poet A. Torres-Ríoseco broke this silence by publishing a volume of criticism, biography, and translations which initiated a renewed impulse in the Whitmanist movement. Torres-Ríoseco's book is a mixture of idealization and bombastic contradictory statements:

Studied as man, Walt Whitman proves to be proud and egotistical. The Horace Traubels and the O'Connors with their bowing and scraping made him believe that he was the greatest man of all times. . . . At times, reading his biography, it seems easy to believe that Walt was an astute man. . . . Walt Whitman was very fond of pontificating and discussing topics about which he didn't have the slightest notion. . . . Nevertheless, his lyric work is a categorical denial of any superficial misunderstanding of his personality. (Torres-Ríoseco, 54–55)

Perhaps Torres-Ríoseco initiated a trend. The Peruvian critic Luis A. Sánchez was no less bold in his surprising comparison between Whitman and Oscar Wilde in his volume *Panorama de la literatura actual* (1935):

Wilde, in spite of everything, was less immoral than Queensberry and Whitman. Wilde was sociable, artistic, gentlemanly, beyond morality, comfortable, lovable, humorous, individualistic, optimistic. Whitman was unsociable but approachable, active, rude, laborious, shy, affirmative, prophetic, tumultuous, optimistic, without morals. . . . The sons of those who yesterday outlawed *Leaves of Grass* are today founding Whitmanian societies. . . . (Sánchez, 61–62)

Soon after Sánchez wrote these words the Cuban José A. Ramos attempted to contradict him. Ramos complained that some ill-informed critics were using the case of Whitman and Poe to blame the United States for having misunderstood and persecuted their greatest literary figures. Whitman was not a man who coveted material advantages, said Ramos; his struggle against the bourgeois environment of his era was due to his own temperament, which impelled him to despise conventional institutions. The admiration that intellectuals such as Thoreau, Emerson, and Burroughs felt for Whitman proves that Whitman was never completely rejected by the literary circles of his time. As for the attitude of the reading public, Ramos notes that "from 1881 until his death in 1892, Walt Whitman lived on the income from the sale of his books" (Ramos, 76).

José Gabriel, a Spaniard who was a nationalized Argentinean, reacted against the most obvious exaggerations of the Latin American Whitmanists when he published *Walt Whitman, la voz democrática de América* (*Walt Whitman, the Democratic Voice of America*) (1944). He set some family matters straight. Whitman, according to Gabriel, did nothing but share family obligations in supporting his brother Eddie, a congenital idiot, and his brother Jesse, who died in a mental institution. Then he refers to Whitman's "spiritual awkwardness, running parallel to his physical ungainliness." Of the youthful work, Gabriel's opinion is that Whitman was "young and naive; he also indulged in moralistic preaching that made his work mediocre. . . . His novel *Franklin Evans* is nothing more than a hygienic argument in favor of the temperance cause." His predilection for the opera exhibits "a certain bourgeois optimism," the imprint of which is not difficult to find in his literary work. Whitman has a "superb image. But already Europeanized: Jehovah, Abraham, Moses, Jupiter. . . . The portrait of his old age already shows the *mise-en-scène* prepared by the poet himself." The image of Whitman, that of the "rough" who appears facing the title page of the first edition of *Leaves of Grass*, an image that was then almost unknown among Hispanic Americans (for whom he was always the old bearded poet), is "the image of a cowboy of the western plains" (Gabriel, 23, 30, 40–41). In dealing with the Civil War, Gabriel draws an interesting parallel with the Spanish Civil War (1936–1938), and thus Whitman's actions and the poems of *Drum-Taps* become filled with a clearly revolutionary élan.

The great merit of Gabriel's essay lies in its restraint and, particularly, in the poetic passages that accompany each chapter, some of them direct translations from *Leaves of Grass* meant to illustrate the facts narrated by the biographer.

Whitman and Santayana

Idealizing interpreters of Whitman's life and poetry might be held responsible for driving George Santayana to write his dubious attack against what he called "The Poetry of Barbarism" (1921). Santayana's piece provoked a spirited reaction among Latin American Whitmanists — particularly José Gabriel and Luis Franco — in sharp contrast to the favorable North American reaction, where Santayana's whimsical opinions on *Leaves of Grass* were generally admired. Santayana may have been influenced by the journalistic criticism that bombarded the first edition of *Leaves of Grass* and by opinions of British writers like Swinburne, whose work Santayana read and admired during his years at Harvard (Santayana 1944, 201). Santayana may also have been inspired by the Guatemalan Enrique Gómez Carrillo, who wrote that

> shades of meaning are unknown to Whitman; psychological mysteries do not reach him; intellectual complications are foreign to him. . . . For him life levels all things with its unconscious force. He finds nothing despicable: neither vice, nor ugliness, nor crime. His universal sympathy recognizes no limits going from the Flesh to the Idea, from Good to Evil. (Carrillo, 22)[1]

Santayana, a poet himself, was an admirer of classical tradition, indifferent to the vociferous clamor associated with Whitman's pronouncements, particularly among the early disciples of Futurismo and Marinetti. Trained as a philosopher, Santayana, like Unamuno, searched for poetic abstractions and symbols. He was shocked by Whitman's "lack of distinction, absence of beauty, confusion of ideas and incapacity to please permanently. . . . The order of his words, the procession of his images, reproduce the method of a rich, spontaneous, absolutely lazy fancy." In most poets this natural order is modified by regulating motives: "the thought," "the metrical art," "the echo of other poems in the memory" (Santayana 1921, 177–178). For Whitman, these conventional regulators do not exist:

> We find the swarms of men and objects rendered as they might strike the retina in a sort of waking dream. It is the most sincere possible confession of the lowest — I mean the most primitive — type of perception. All ancient poets are sophisticated in comparison and give proof of longer intellectual and moral training. Walt Whitman has gone back to the innocent style of Adam, when the animals filed before him one by one and he called each of them by its name. (177–178)[2]

Santayana reduces Whitman to the size of an engaging "primitive" who had the faculty of understanding only "the elementary aspects of things" (Santayana 1921, 181). Whitman was not interested in their inner structure; his attitude was that of a person without knowledge of the uses of practical or theoretical interpretation:

> He basked in the sunshine of perception and wallowed in the stream of his own sensibility, as later at Camden in the shallows of his favorite brook. Even dur-

ing the Civil War, when he heard the drum-taps so clearly, he could only gaze at the picturesque and terrible aspects of the struggle, and linger among the wounded day after day with a canine devotion; he could not be aroused either to clear thought or to positive action.

The world has no inside for Whitman, according to Santayana: "This abundance of detail without organization, this wealth of perception without intelligence, and of imagination without taste, makes the singularity of Whitman's genius." Thus we must discover his qualities in his very defects: Whitman is interesting, even in moments when he is simply "grotesque or perverse." He has seen life not in contrast with an ideal but rather as an expression of more indeterminate and elemental forces than life itself, and therefore "the vulgar, in this cosmic setting, has appeared to him sublime" (180–181).

Santayana concludes by analyzing Whitman's seldom-discussed political attitude. If Whitman is the poet of democracy, it is because "there is clearly some analogy between a mass of images without structure and the notion of an absolute democracy. . . . Surrounded by ugly things and common people, he felt himself happy, ecstatic, overflowing with a kind of patriarchal love." Whitman's only hero is his own self. As for Whitman's perfect man of the future, he "is to work with his hands, chanting the poems of some future Walt, some ideally democratic bard." With a premonition of Borges's modern irony, Santayana implies that the women of Whitman's utopia will be as much like the men as possible, and the men will be "vigorous, comfortable, sentimental, and irresponsible" (Santayana 1921, 181–183).

In a significant way, Santayana's Whitman is a poet not of the future but of the past: Whitman became "the prophet of a lost cause. That cause was lost, not merely when wealth and intelligence began to take shape in the American Commonwealth, but . . . at the foundation of the world, when those laws of evolution were established which Whitman, like Rousseau, failed to understand" (Santayana 1921, 183). So Whitman does not represent "the tendencies of his country," nor does he attract the masses, but only the dilettanti whom he always despised. Santayana concludes that only "foreigners, who look for some grotesque expression of the genius of so young and prodigious a people," can consider him the spokesman for the United States. Feeling, perhaps, that he was being unfair in his general judgment on Whitman, Santayana added a rather condescending final note, suggesting that Whitman's appeal was to something more primitive and general than an ideal: "When the intellect is in abeyance, when we would 'turn and live with the animals, they are so placid and self-contained,' when we are weary of conscience and of ambition, and would yield ourselves for a while to the dream of sense, Walt Whitman is a welcome companion" (186–187). Whitman's images, full of vigor and radiance, direct and beautiful, are particularly attractive because they come "from a hideous and sordid environment" (187). They offer a sort of escape from conventional life and allow his readers to sink back comfortably into "a lower level sense and instinct" (187). Santayana's words seem to indicate that Whitman's mysticism is no more than an excuse to act unintelligently, an effort to convince us that we are divine by remaining "imperfectly human" (187).

Latin American admirers of Whitman found it difficult to sympathize with Santayana's snobbishness. What they detected in the Harvard philosopher's critique was his attempt to defend a pseudoaristocratic aestheticism against a powerful antibourgeois social attack. "America" for Whitman symbolized the transformation of an aggressively individualistic, materialistic system into a society of "comrades" in which spiritual values were as essential as material ones and where the concept of individuality was accepted as a factor of universal unity. Santayana, on the other hand, brought the full weight of his scholarly background in defense of a hierarchical, pragmatic establishment. He attempted to portray Whitman as the champion of a lost cause, a poet of the disappearing era of the pioneers, already surpassed by the pragmatism and intelligence of the American Commonwealth. Unfortunately, he seems to be referring to the political machinery organized at the turn of the century, so his measure of progress is heavily dependent on geopolitical dominance.

It is instructive to compare the attitude of Eduardo Mallea, a distinguished Latin American novelist and essayist, with Santayana's scornful view of Whitman's ideology. Searching for the image of an individual who would embody the noblest qualities of the Argentine people, Mallea recalls ideas expressed by Whitman in his poem "Me Imperturbe": "Is that imperturbability an attitude, a pose? No, it is a form of being which can exist unmanifested, which can remain implicit in man, unknown but natural . . ." (Mallea, 340). One of Mallea's characters in *La Bahía de silencio* (*The Bay of Silence*) (1945) says, "The more I think of it I feel that there could be no other ideal possible for men than that of wishing to grow from the earth toward the sky like trees, unperturbable, sure of the sense of their growth. Without theoretical arguments about this or anything else. Do you recall the poem by Whitman, Walt Whitman?" (340). José Gabriel, too, felt that Santayana did not understand Whitman: "From his country he received the same old rebukes, whose echoes, less noisy but perhaps more passionate, are still present in the classical pettiness of Santayana, that Hispanic-Roman relic in America (personal talent included)" (Gabriel, 177).

According to the Argentine Luis Franco, Santayana scorned Whitman's poetry because he found in it a lack of restraint and good taste, because he considered it irrational (although powerfully imaginative), chaotic, too simple and primitive. Santayana believed that poetry could not limit itself to expressing a purely poetic impulse; it had, in addition, to be enriched by an objective content. Most poets, according to Santayana, capture only segments of the world, without accomplishing an intelligent coordination of their institutions. Franco, however, set out to prove that behind Whitman's sharp perception of concrete reality was a profound understanding of the unity of the universe: "Whitman is not a modernist poet, but a fundamentally modern spirit. . . . The greatness of Whitman's poetic art lies in the fact that the substance makes one forget the form, that, as in organic life, form and substance are undistinguishable. . . . The enlightened consciousness and the great boldness with which Whitman brought the necessities of modern man into poetry are so evident that it is difficult to imagine how Santayana could call him a primitive poet" (Franco, 232, 227). Franco, Gabriel, and other Hispanic Whitmanists are unanimous in condemning Santayana's prudishness. Santayana, they feel, was offended by Whitman's haste, his improvisations, and his confidence in intuitive powers.

WHITMAN'S INFLUENCE ON SPANISH AMERICAN POETRY

The role Whitman has in the development of contemporary Hispanic poetry can best be studied in relation to two movements: modernism and the avant-garde. One might say that Spanish American modernist poets did not really grasp the essence of Whitman's message. Whitman's voice often is present in their work, but seldom his spirit. To them, Whitman was mainly a legend. They knew only fragments of his work and those mostly through translations. They admired him for having dared to break away from England's traditions, and they thought of him as a Victor Hugo of the new world.

Inspired by Martí, Rubén Darío wrote his famous sonnet to Whitman and then paid homage to him in an article published by the Chilean newspaper *La Epoca*. Later on, he left testimony of his admiration for Whitman in his *Autobiografía* (1918) and in the prologue to *Prosas profanas* (1917). Following his example, other important figures in the modernist movement approached *Leaves of Grass* with a mixture of curiosity and apprehension: in Mexico, J. J. Tablada and Amado Nervo; in Peru, José S. Chocano (who melodramatically claimed, "Walt Whitman has the North, I have the South") and Alfredo González Prada, who translated into Spanish "A Woman Waits for Me." In Argentina, Leopoldo Lugones praised the social struggles of his people in a free verse style echoing Whitman's. In Puerto Rico, Luis Llorena Torrens brought about radical literary changes by expressing his zest for life in poetic forms reminiscent of Whitman.[3]

Whitman's philosophical, religious, and political ideas were not really discovered until later, after the Mexican poet E. González Martínez gave the coup de grace to modernism in his memorable sonnet "Tuércele el cuello al cisne" ("Wring the Swan's Neck") found in his *Los senderos ocultos* (1915). These postmodernists went beyond Whitman's verbalism to discover in his poetry much more than the romantic nationalism that had impressed Darío and Chocano. Armando Vasseur published the first anthology of *Leaves of Grass* in Spanish translation and started a Whitmanist movement in Uruguay. He was joined by young poets of high merit such as Sabat Ercasty and Parra del Riego. Then, numerous disciples appeared in Argentina: Luis Franco, González Tuñón, and Ezequiel Martínez Estrada (who wrote in his 1929 poem "Walt Whitman": "I will follow your trail with the zeal of the hound, / among the rhythmic stars or the earth-molded human, / wherever you are now repeating, Walt Whitman, / the autochthonous canticles of your iron land"). Antonio Arraíz began a Whitmanist trend in Venezuela with the publication of *Aspero* (1924). Chile also awakened to the Whitman call when the Nobel laureate Gabriela Mistral paraphrased sections of *Leaves of Grass* in her masterful "Motivos del barro," found in her *Desolación* (1945).

During the years of the First World War, Spanish American poets turned away from social themes and immersed themselves in the experimentation promoted by schools such as creationism and surrealism. Lautreamont and Rimbaud—and Apollinaire, Reverdy, and Breton, their most famous contemporaries—became the supreme masters. Once the obsession to experiment died down, however, Spanish American avant-garde poets began their return to realism and found their way back to Whitman. After World War I, the poets belonging to the so-called Generation of 1895 absorbed *Leaves of Grass* with enthusiasm. During the Spanish Civil War, some of these poets praised the heroism of the antifascist fighters in a tone clearly akin to Whitman's. Pablo Neruda and César Vallejo in Latin America and León Felipe, García Lorca, and Jorge Guillén in Spain are the leading examples of such a trend. Felipe captured the tone of querulous identification when he said, "And so what if I call myself Walt Whitman? I have justified this poet of Democracy, I have extended him and I have contradicted him" (Felipe, 18; see selection 5). Lorca was as fervent an admirer of Whitman as Felipe and turned him into a cosmic and mythical figure in "Oda a Walt Whitman," which he wrote while in New York in 1929–1930, but unlike Felipe, he never lost his own identity, never melted into Whitman, and remained faithful to traditional means of expression and to Spanish subjects. As a homosexual, Lorca also was one of the first poets to directly address Whitman's homosexuality. Jorge Guillén had no such reason for admiring Whitman. In his *Cántico*, the first edition of which appeared in Madrid in 1928, he sang with elegance and transparent clarity—in a form closer to Valéry than to Whitman—his sense of wonder before all forms of life, the mystery of the physical world, the happiness of merely existing; in short, he expressed a pantheistic vision of the world, which he shared with Whitman (see selection 8). Like Whitman, during the greater part of his career he kept enriching the same collection of poems, his *Cántico*, his hymn to Universal Life, which went through four constantly revised editions. A slightly younger poet, Rafael Alberti, also fell under Whitman's spell, but he was attracted by the social rather than by the cosmic themes of *Leaves of Grass*, and thus he wrote in "Siervos": "I send you a greeting / and I call you comrades." The poets who raised their voices during the Spanish Civil War and the Franco regime were similarly often inspired by Whitman, notably Antonio Machado and later Gabriel Celaya (the pseudonym of Rafael Múgica, an engineer), who occasionally resorted to Whitman's technique of enumerations.

I will turn now to a more detailed and specific account of Whitman's influence on the poetry of Hispanic America during the twentieth century, considering the works of Darío, Lugones, Vasseur, Sabat, Neruda, Mistral, Rokha, and Huidobro. This is by no means an exhaustive list, however, for many other poets from Spanish American countries were followers of Whitman: in Venezuela, Jacinto Fombona Pachano, author of "Un alerta para Abraham Lincoln" (*Las torres desprevenidas*, Caracas, 1940); in Guatemala, Melvin René Barahona ("Listen, Walt Whitman") and Pedro Mir (*Contracanto a Walt Whitman, Canto a nosotros mismos*, 1952); in Nicaragua, Alfredo Cardona Peña (*Los jardines amantas*, Mexico, 1952), Ernesto Cardenal, and José Coronel Urtecho.

Rubén Darío

Rubén Darío probably did not know Whitman's work before the publication of *Azul*. His first contact with Whitman's poetry came indirectly, through three articles that fell into his hands when *Azul* was already partially published in newspapers and magazines in Chile and Central America. The first edition of *Azul* (1888) does not include his poem to Whitman. This sonnet and other "Medallions" were added by Darío in the second edition of his book in 1890 (see selection 2). It is not known when Darío wrote his sonnet to Whitman. In his book *Revelaciones íntimas de Rubén Darío* (1925), Máximo Soto Hall says that some of Darío's sonnets in *Azul*—"Catulle Mendès," "Whitman," and "J. J. Palma"—were written in 1890 while Darío was in Guatemala. Although this is plausible (the second edition of *Azul* did appear in that country), it could also be that Darío wrote them in 1889 during his sojourn in El Salvador. Moreover, in his book *A. de Gilbert*—hastily written in Sonsonate, El Salvador, as a lyric testimony of grief at the death of Pedro Balmaceda Toro, the son of Chilean president J. M. Balmaceda—Darío makes a surprising reference to Whitman. "My friend," says Darío, referring to Balmaceda,

> was proud of knowing the Araucanian language and he enjoyed narrating many quaint anecdotes about the sons of "Untamed Arauco." He used to tell that if they had something to ask of the head of the republic, they would go to Santiago dressed in their strange costumes and never took off their hats to anything or anyone, just as the Yankee prophet Walt Whitman says he does. (Darío 1927, 361–362)

In 1889, also in El Salvador, Darío wrote the prologue for Narciso Tondreau's book *Asonantes*, and again he mentioned Whitman's name, this time in regard to metrical experiments which he judged of particular interest: "Some poets have attempted to introduce the Greek and Latin hexameters into Spanish. At the present time in Italy, Giosuè Carducci is trying to popularize the Spanish ballad and the Yankee prophet Walt Whitman repeats the Hebrew versicle in English" (Darío 1934, 290).

Darío's admiration for Whitman had its limitations, however; he was careful to point out his own aristocratic preferences in contrast to Whitman's populism: "If there is poetry in our America, it will be found in ancient things: in Palenke and Utatlán, in the legendary Indian, and in the sensual, refined Inca, in the great Montezuma of the golden chair. The rest is yours, democrat Walt Whitman" (Darío 1945, 606–607). In *El viaje a Nicaragua e historia de mis libros* (1919) Darío reiterates this idea: "But abominating democracy, fatal to poets—regardless of what Whitman may think—I look toward the past, toward the ancient mythologies and their splendid stories" (Darío 1919, 188).

Darío was, of course, an admirer and a follower of French Parnassianism and symbolism. His knowledge of *Leaves of Grass* was at best superficial and probably indirect. When he addressed himself to the imperialistic attitude of the United States toward Latin America, he borrowed from Whitman a certain grandiloquence he thought adequate and proper. This explains his poems to Theodore Roosevelt.[4] Later, in his "Ode to Mitre," Darío would be more specific in his mention of Whitman and would quote him directly (if not correctly): "Oh captain! Oh my captain! called Whitman." He even gave proof of his attachment to Whitman: "One morning, after spending the night without sleep, Alejandro Sawa brought Charles Morice, the critic of the symbolists, to my hotel. . . . He found a few books on my table, among them a Walt Whitman with which he was not acquainted" (Darío 1977, 3–6).

Admiring Whitman as he did, why did Darío not include him among his *Los Raros* (1896)? He did include Edgar Allan Poe. He admired both, but Poe, an incarnation of French decadence and a bohemian hero, lost in the midst of a prosaic, mechanistic civilization, was his brother, so he exalted his poetry as a model of sensitivity and refinement for Spanish American young poets (Englekirk, 181–182). In Whitman, Darío admired the iconoclast, the reformer, the dynamic pioneer, the defender of the sacred right to remain an individual isolated in the world of his own artistic creation. "I do not have a literature 'of mine' to show the way to others, as a great critic has expressed," said Darío; "my literature is deeply rooted in me; he who servilely follows my footsteps will lose his personal wealth and, either page or slave, will never be able to hide his brand or his livery" (Darío 1977, 179).

Leopoldo Lugones

One of the earliest examples of Whitman's influence in Spanish American poetry is *Las montañas del oro*, the first book by the Argentine poet Leopoldo Lugones, published in 1897. In time, Lugones would change radically; his revolutionary inspiration gave way to a lofty rhetoric in which the sensual tones of French decadentism mixed freely with epic descriptions of the Argentine land. Reading the story of his life, it is not difficult to explain why the young Lugones was more convincing than Darío in expressing his admiration for Whitman. In the midst of a bitter struggle against critics who could not condone his poetic experiments and his revolutionary pronouncements, disillusioned by the apathy of the public, Lugones found a new source of energy in the writings of the great rebels of his time: Nietzsche, Bakunin, Tolstoy, Zola. He sacrificed his economic welfare and went on waging an implacable war against conservative reaction. Commenting on Lugones's line, "And I decided to put myself on the side of the stars," Pedro Miguel Obligado has said:

> It is a profession of faith, and in order to be loyal to it during all his life, the author became a poet-hero. He did not like the poetry of those who imitated him, nor did he desire followers whose ideas might limit his freedom. He longed to be spiritually alone, like Leonardo whom he venerated so much, "in order to be himself," although it might cost him the loss of his best friends, this disposition to correct himself, to change if he thought it was his duty to change, was one of the norms which he imposed on his conscience. (Obligado, 16)

At the onset of his literary career Lugones searched for a definition of his personality and for the purpose of his art in the realm of history and in the critical evaluation of the aesthetic systems of the past. *Las montañas del oro* is a poem written with a cosmic vision of the world and in the biblical tone that readers identify with Whitman's. The language appears to be poetic prose, but since Lugones's sentences are rhythmical and separated by hyphens, they can be considered free verse. As in "Song of Myself," the Whitmanian "I" also acquires in Lugones's discourse a biblical resonance because of the prophetic quality of the sentences it introduces. Also, like Whitman, Lugones uses enumerations in a cumulative, catalog-like form.

In the introduction to his book, Lugones names the writers who best represent his ideal conception of the poet: Homer, Dante, Hugo, and Whitman. "The poet is the star of his own exile — he has his head next to God — but his flesh is the fruit of the cosmic mud of life." He then says:

> Whitman sings a song serenely noble.
> Whitman is the glorious artisan of the oak,
> He adores life that springs forth from the harvest,
> The great love that smooths the flanks of a female.
> And all that is power, creation, universe,
> Weighs upon the huge vertebrae of his verse. (Lugones, 55–56)

Although Lugones's pantheistic doctrine is usually expressed in rather naive terms, the reader senses the existence of a certain bond between him and Whitman:

> It is an eternal miracle of faith. That which is fecund
> Or luminous, or beautiful — love, star, rose —
> Certifies the ruling of a mysterious law
> Which combines the scheme of destinies, and draws
> Together the efforts of everything that is born
> Upon an eternal light which performs and thinks
> As the clump of muscles of an immense right. (Lugones, 57)

Lugones singles out the "democratic dynamism" of the United States as an ideal for Latin Americans to follow. His vocabulary then becomes reminiscent of Whitman's in phrases like "he found the fraternal dogmas on new altars" and "God has said words to the leaves of grass: People of the New World, you are the great reserve of the Future" (57–59).

In the first section of his book, Lugones includes an "Ode to Nakedness" in which he displays a strong sensualism obviously rooted in "Song of Myself":

> . . . and wailing with love under the rustic virility of my beard,
> upon the violets that anoint it, squeezing its blue blood
> on its noble hair, my love grows pale like a big, naked lily in the night.

Other lines in this and other poems bring to memory the lyric sensuality of "Calamus" (Lugones, 62).

In the second section of the book, however, Lugones returns to descriptive prose. The third part, called "Hymn to the Towers," is without doubt the most influenced by Whitman. Lugones attempts an epic evocation of human history in which the towers are symbols of humanity's great conquests. In the tenth section Lugones mentions Emerson and, in the eleventh, Whitman and Poe. The language is biblical, and the rhythmical repetition and the abundance of images create effects of intense poetic brilliance. Lugones seems to be adapting into Spanish Whitman's recitative form (Lugones, 93, 96–97).

Growing old, Lugones withdrew from social and political struggles and joined the comfortable circle of literary salons. One section of his book *Los crepúsculos del jardin* (*Twilights*) (1926), however, still recalls the Whitmanism of his youth, the series of sonnets entitled "The Twelve Pleasures." Once again one finds in them an intense sensuality, an erotic imagination, and a tender melancholy. In *Las horas doradas* (*The Golden Hours*) (1922), there are two poems—"Triumphant Clearness" and "Last Roses"—in which Lugones attempts to express a Whitmanian metaphysical vision of nature. In these poems, he tries to capture moments of perfect balance between humans and nature, a mystic unity that demands a poetic expression of deep simplicity. The pantheism is again lyrical and nostalgic.

Poets such as Whitman and Gabriela Mistral have successfully expressed this idea of metaphysical continuity—Whitman willing himself to the grass, Mistral to the dust of the road, to be reborn in nature. Lugones, like other poets of modernist romanticism, conceives such a process as a mere literary metaphor without philosophical content. Lugones's Whitmanism is reduced, then, to a heartfelt admiration in his initial book *Las montañas del oro* and to isolated echoes throughout his poetic work. But it is fair to say that Lugones owes to Whitman his enumerative style used at times in the form of rhythmic prose, at times in rhymed poetry, as well as his type of optimistic, healthful sensualism endowed with deep pantheistic resonances.

Armando Vasseur

To the Uruguayan Armando Vasseur we owe the first anthological translation of *Leaves of Grass* into Spanish, *Hojas de hierba* (1912). The first section of his book *Cantos augurales* (1904), entitled "Epic of the Abyss," is inscribed: "To the memory of Walt Whitman, rhapsodist of democracy." The third part, dedicated to Alma Fuerte, begins with a few resounding lines from Whitman quoted in Italian! These lines are taken from "To Him That Was Crucified" and, because they appear in Italian, indicate that Vasseur was not yet familiar with *Leaves of Grass* in the original. "Ode to a Couple of Introvert Women," the fourth section of the book, also carries an epigraph from Whitman in Italian, this time taken from "Song of the Redwood Tree": "You womanhood divine, mistress and source of all, whence life and love and aught that comes from life and love."

Vasseur's *Cantos del nuevo mundo* (*Songs of the New World*) (1907) begins with a symbol that was dear to Whitman — the tree symbolizing the creative impulse of life. Vasseur tries to trace the literary history of trees, including the trees of the Bible, of classical mythology, and of the Greco-Roman Golden Age. Then, in a cosmic flight through the centuries, he describes the American landscape, naming its typical trees in a three-page enumeration, after which *wood* is made transcendental and is viewed as the motivator of contemporary civilization. Because of its cumulative form, its glorification of matter and labor, and its Americanist ideal, this enumeration seems rooted in *Leaves of Grass* and apparently inspired by "A Song for Occupations":

> Let come forth from your entrails, opened by the axes of mountaineer Lincolns, the cross pieces of the bridges, stretched across rivers and mountain depths . . . the millions of railroad links uniting the three Americas, and the internal framework of the electric trains, speeding in the great lightning of their time-tables, transporting the cargoes of harvests, the abundant catch from the fisheries, the firstlings of the flocks, the mine treasures, the works of art, the scientific discoveries, the languages, the ideas, the wealth and loves of the voyagers. (Vasseur, 12)

Vasseur continues his enumeration, accumulating material objects and striving to create a vision of modern industry and cultural life in great cities. In one of the most notable poems of the book, "La Atlántida," Vasseur expresses his social utopianism, upholding as a basic idea the proposition of a perfect democracy.

El vino de la sombra (1917) is one of Vasseur's greatest achievements. In it there is a composition which shows a clear Whitman influence, "El afilador" ("The Grinder"). Vasseur included "Sparkles from the Wheel" in his 1912 translation of *Leaves of Grass*. Of the three elements that Whitman uses in his poem — the street scene and the grinder surrounded by children, the figure of the grinder himself, and the golden sparks symbolizing the magic of the day and the miracle of the worker creating life around him — only the first is lacking in Vasseur's poem. Although Whitman prefers to let facts express his dynamic conception of the world,

Vasseur is more interested in the emotional content of the man and in his wandering life, aspects Whitman ignores.

Carlos Sabat Ercasty

In 1917 Carlos Sabat Ercasty published *Pantheos* and established himself as the pioneer of Spanish American avant-garde poetry and the precursor of the great social poets who began writing around 1920. He was not an imitator of Whitman but — like Vasseur, and later Neruda and León Felipe — he was a continuator and apostle of his message. Sabat confronted the great enigma of the universe with a metaphysical creed rooted in Hindu philosophy. Federico de Onís describes his poetry as "characterized by its strength and abundance, by the courage with which he confronts the great human themes: man, time, sea, life. In free form, which has something of the biblical verse and of Walt Whitman's poetry, he sings his exuberant, vital, cosmic optimism at the top of his voice" (Onís, 783). In poems such as "Urania," Sabat struggles to express his "cosmic consciousness." "In the world, the sidereal trace of my life still persists, when all possible lives circulated in the cosmic desire for God" (Sabat 1917, 41–42). From a cosmic vision he moves to the consideration of his own body, and his words echo "Song of Myself," where Whitman writes,

> I am an acme of things accomplish'd, and I am an encloser of things to be.
> My feet strike an apex of the apices of the stairs,
> On every step bunches of ages, and larger bunches between the steps,
> All below duly travel'd, and still I mount and mount. (LG, 80–81)

Sabat writes:

> When I inquire from my flesh and my bones and my blood,
> I have the certainty
> that during innumerable cycles,
> I wandered in remote zones of space . . .
> I know that in those stars
> is already reliving my distant sons' flesh,
> and that of friends of other cycles . . .
> My eyes contemplated other stars
> and other men and other flora and fauna
> and other mountains and harmonies . . .
> My soul is a celestial traveller! (44–46)

In one of his *Poems of Man*, Sabat addresses the question of identity; paraphrasing Whitman, he states that his body is the product of centuries of preparation and that his life reflects the cosmic plan of creation encompassing the energy and dynamism of the worlds. Compare, for example, Sabat's poem that begins "It is night time" with Whitman's "Night on the Prairies." In Sabat's poem "The Tree," there is a reiteration of a pantheistic, dynamic idea related to a "cosmic plan" symbolized by the structure of a tree (Sabat 1917, 45, 56–57). A similar idea served Whitman as a basis for the "organic" plan of *Leaves of Grass*, also elaborated in "Song of the Redwood Tree." In the climax of his poem, Whitman's tree speaks directly to humans, describing the qualities of the race that will build a better world. In Sabat's poem, the tree also assumes this prophetic role. For both poets the tree, imperturbable to the passage of time, is the witness to the gestation of life and the symbol of immortality in this world.

Once Sabat learned Whitman's ideology, he explained it in his own words, without specific references. In "The Beginning," "Further," and "The Hero and the Road," Sabat offers a synthesis, admirable for its lyrical beauty and clarity, of the philosophical ideas that are the foundation of *Pantheos*, and Whitman is very much present: "America! The poets of the future will be the verb of the race which will give concrete form to your immortal being and will orient your eternally renewed action" (Sabat 1917, 119).

Just as Whitman's descriptions of nature are usually activated by touches of unequivocal sensuality, the erotic enters Sabat's pantheistic poetry through images in which sea, air, sun, and the human body anxiously seek to be fused in an embrace which symbolizes the unity of all created. In *Libro del mar* (*Book of the Sea*) (1922), Sabat makes the ocean a symbol of creation; he uses images similar to Section 22 of "Song of Myself" — "You sea! I resign myself to you also" (LG, 49) — or poems such as "Elemental Drifts," "On the Beach at Night Alone," and "With Husky-Haughty Lips, O Sea":

Sensual sea, voluptuous, awesome.
Bed of the sun. Desperate sex of the earth.
Womb of life.
The vertical noon penetrates your entrails
And you roar with love like a mother,
and break your large waves
on the stones of all the shores of the world. (Sabat 1922, 18–19)

In this series of poems, Sabat adapts his poetic discourse to the subtle movements of the sea, from a description in which the ocean becomes a "cosmic uterus" and the "womb of life" to a subjective interpretation in which the sea takes on shapes that awaken erotic responses (18–19). Sabat ends with the sea becoming a symbol of the cosmic plan of the universe.[5] There is a unity of thought and poetic intuition between Whitman and Sabat, both striving to achieve a philosophical synthesis through the idea of the sea.

Despite these similarities, there is an important difference between Whitman's and Sabat's poems. For Whitman, the sea is a cosmic symbol and a poetic motif, which allows him to evoke intimate past experiences; for Sabat, the ocean is invariably a symbol stripped of sentimental connotations, a metaphysical riddle leading to a feeling of ecstasy which might reveal the mystery of life. Using the sea as a poetic element, Whitman wrote one of his most impassioned and intimate lyric poems, "Out of the Cradle Endlessly Rocking," but the sea itself, in its unfathomable mystery, never awakened in him the metaphysical and philosophical depth of Sabat's *Libro del mar*. Sabat Ercasty was a kindred spirit of Whitman rather than a disciple. Like Whitman, he was possessed by a feverish anxiety to discover God in nature and to unite himself with God in an ardent, amorous embrace. He believed, like Whitman, that America had found in his poetry the true expression of a unique utopia.

Pablo Neruda

Of all Spanish American poets, the Chilean Pablo Neruda is most often compared to Whitman, sometimes negatively. A *London Times* reviewer once criticized Neruda by comparing him to Whitman: "Señor Neruda's hoarse and strident tones are not hard to imitate. But it is difficult to imagine what purpose such concentrated shrillness and indignation serve, or to whom exactly such a book can be recommended; certainly were the rail splitter — Lincoln — to awake, he would make very little of this new Whitman." At first glance Whitman and Neruda seem to express a similar message in a surprisingly related form, but there is a great deal of optical and aural illusion in those similarities. They share certain rhetorical forms of speech, but between the two poets there is more than fifty years of intense experimental literature, most of it thoroughly absorbed by Neruda. Moreover, by the time he published *Canto general* (1950), Neruda had already become a militant member of the Communist Party.

Neruda seldom expressed his indebtedness to Whitman, yet he left indications of his admiration. Speaking of Mayakovsky, he wrote that "the strength, the tenderness and fire of Mayakovsky make him the greatest example of contemporary poetry. Whitman would have adored him. Whitman would have heard his voices coming over the steppes, answering for the first time and through the years his great civic orations" (Neruda 1976, 396). In *Canto general*, Neruda names Whitman among the greatest literary figures of the United States and considers him with Lincoln as the representative of North American democracy. Nowhere, however, has he detailed his admiration for Whitman or elaborated on the relationship between his own poetry and Whitman's. The closest he came was in a 1966 interview conducted by Robert Bly, when he spoke in broad generalities:

> Whitman was a great teacher. Because what is Whitman? He was not only intensely conscious, but he was open-eyed! He had tremendous eyes to see everything — he taught us to see things. . . . He had eyes opened to the world and he taught us about poetry and many other things. (Neruda 1967, 87)

The first literary and ideological links between Neruda and Whitman become noticeable in the more mature work of *Residencia en la tierra* (*Residence on Earth*) (1935) and *Canto general*. Perhaps the most obvious similarity between the two poets is a sensualism which Whitman's critics have described as autoeroticism. It reveals itself in Neruda's poem "Ritual de mis piernas" ("Ritual of My Legs") and in "Juntos nosotros" ("We Together"), both in *Residencia en la tierra*. Neruda seems to have been inspired particularly by Section 9 of "I Sing the Body Electric." But even though both poets describe the human body in autoerotic terms, the degree of sensualism is more intense in Neruda. After following Whitman's bare enumeration, Neruda rises to express a materialistic exaltation of his body, totally deprived of metaphysical implications. By emphasizing the realism of his description with a mixture of concrete detail and sexual metaphors, he succeeds in presenting his body as an independent creature, with a life of its own, vegetating in a purely sexual atmosphere where the solitary observation and examination of its organs seems the prelude to decay. In the last lines of his poem, Neruda assigns an unusual significance to his feet, which are, for him, the frontier between the world and himself, that which decisively separates his life from the "invincible and unfriendly" earth. The second volume of *Residencia* contains two poems charged with organic eroticism and detailed physiological descriptions, "Materia nupcial" and "Agua sexual." Although Neruda's language may seem more metaphorical than Whitman's, the mention of human organs is equally direct in both poets. Neruda's phrase "un espeso río de semen" (Neruda 1967, 231) recalls Whitman's image of semen in his poem "From Pent-up Aching Rivers": "From pent-up aching rivers, / From that of myself without which I were nothing" (LG, 91).

Neruda's autoeroticism disappeared in *Canto general*. Neruda liberated himself from morbidness, and references to sex take the form of remote and isolated memories from younger years. He accomplishes this change by applying his metaphors to the American environment to discover the intrinsic unity between humans and the world that surrounds them. Whitman endows nature with sexual power because he makes nature human in the process of identifying himself with it. Neruda, on the other hand, sees nature an opposite sex which, as the object of his love, he must conquer and possess. Neruda's struggle to re-create the American landscape is both epic and lyric, epic because he is living the experience of the Spanish American man defending himself against physical forces much superior to his own, and lyric because in this struggle he cannot fail to appreciate the tragic beauty of his enemy and glorify it romantically. Even though Whitman and Neruda personalize nature in their poems by means of sexual metaphors, they differ in their aims. Whitman is inspired by a pantheistic ideal, Neruda by dynamic materialism.

One more theme links Whitman and Neruda: comradeship. Whitman transformed an earthy passion into a sentiment of universal significance, furthering love as a form of total unity and as the social basis for a true democracy. Neruda glorified friendship and comradeship.[6] But Neruda espoused a social creed of proletarian and revolutionary friendship in which the word "comrade" assumes an edge absent in Whitman's work. This is the subject of Neruda's "Oda a Walt Whitman," written in the 1950s (see selection 6).

Nothing illustrates more graphically Neruda's love and admiration for Whitman than an anecdote told by Mexican writer Wilberto Cantón in *Posiciones* (1950).

When Neruda and a group of friends were trying to start a new magazine in 1943, he was chosen to gather the necessary funds and to keep them in a safe place. At one meeting, someone suggested that Neruda should give a report and display the funds already gathered, one thousand pesos. Neruda obliged. He mentioned that the money was kept among the pages of a handsome edition of *Leaves of Grass*. His friends smiled. Neruda brought the book and searched. He kept searching. Nothing. No matter how hard he tried, he could not find the one thousand pesos. "He ran to his desk, emptied the drawers, he rolled up the rug." Canton picked up the book and, lo and behold, he found a notation: "See Bernal Díaz del Castillo, vol. II, p. 309." They all went to see the book, and on page 309 they found another direction: "See Santa Teresa, p. 120." And from Santa Teresa "they were referred to Milozc, to César Vallejo, Elizabeth Barrett Browning, Aeschylus, Dante, Rilke, Plato, Tagore, Ercilla, Goethe, Dostoievski. . . . At last, on page 213 of Andersen's *Tales*," they found the treasure (quoted in Alegría, 334). This practical joke has given us the opportunity to know what books Neruda kept with him during his years of exile, but what we must never forget is that Neruda originally placed the one thousand pesos in *Leaves of Grass*.

Gabriela Mistral

Whitman has left his imprint on the work of Chilean Nobel laureate Gabriela Mistral. A brief examination of her first book, *Desolación* (1922), will convince the reader that her mysticism, steeped in Hindu tradition, is closely allied to Whitman's ideas. She believes in giving herself to be born again in a plural life of the spirit. There are as many popular roots in Mistral as there are in Whitman and Neruda; she shows equal devotion to working people, and she expresses the same ambition to make her work and her life a living gospel which must be carried directly to the masses.

Mistral speaks for Latin American women in their struggle for social liberation in the same tone Whitman used when speaking for a new democracy in the United States. Like Whitman, she looks to mystic experiences for the secret of creation. *Desolación* includes a prose poem in which the pantheist doctrine shines as purely and intensely as in the work of Whitman or Tagore. Whitman's "I bequeath myself to the dirt to grow from the grass I love, / If you want me again look for me under your boot-soles" (LG, 89) perhaps inspired Mistral's poem "A los niños" ("To Children"), the fourth in "Motivos del barro" ("Themes in Clay"): "I'd rather be the dust with which you play in the country roads. Oppress me: I have been yours; undo me, for I made you; step on me, because I did not give you all the truth and all the beauty. Or, simply sing and run over me, so that I may kiss your beloved feet . . ." (Mistral, 150).

But it is not only mysticism that joins Mistral to Whitman. She also follows him in the glorification of motherhood. Few poets have expressed more eloquently than Whitman the creative function of woman, and few have defended with so much frankness and boldness the right of women to share with men the rights and responsibilities of social life. Mistral has said that "holiness in life begins with motherhood, which is, therefore, sacred. Let them feel the deep tenderness with which a woman who cares for children not her own considers the mothers of all the children in the world" (Mistral, 141). The Spanish critic Enrique Diez-Canedo recalled Whitman's name to prove that Mistral's work embodies, better than any other contemporary poet's work, the soul of a woman: "For *Desolación* is so much a woman's work that it is hardly a book. 'Comrade,' says Whitman, 'this is no book; whoever touches it, touches a man'" (Diez-Canedo, 300).

Pablo de Rokha and Vicente Huidobro

Whitman's influence has been more direct on the work of Pablo de Rokha, another contemporary Chilean poet. Beginning with his early works, de Rokha has cultivated a proletarian and enumerative language to attack capitalistic society and to promote a socialistic revolution. His poetic vision is cosmic in a social and political sense, and a number of his themes derive directly from Whitman. "I am as old as the world," he states in *Morfología del espanto* (*Morphology of Fear*) (1942), "as tall and wide as the world" (quoted in Alegría, 339). He speaks of himself as the embodiment of humanity; he reviews human history, identifying himself with the universe in the process of its centuries-old preparation. His image of cosmic creation is a surrealistic dramatization, and his mention of Whitman comes as a shock: "I am going to create the world, again, in seven days . . . on the fifth I shall create a cow, Walt Whitman's widow . . ." (de Rokha, 2). De Rokha's embrace, far from being a sentimental love of comrades, is a symbol of political solidarity within the proletarian revolution. De Rokha is, like Neruda, essentially materialistic, and pessimism runs as an undercurrent in his poetry.

Whitman's popularity in Spanish America declined during the years of the First World War. It was then that the "isms" of the avant-garde burst forth. Whitman's name was temporarily forgotten and replaced by new artistic leaders: Apollinaire, Tzara, Reverdy, Breton, Aragon. The futurists made an attempt to reaffirm Whitman's ideas but ended up singing the virtues of fascism. Another Chilean poet, Vicente Huidobro, took over the Creationist movement, restating Emerson's ideas as expressed in "The Poet." Huidobro had already mentioned Emerson in his book *Adán* (1916), and in his famous poem "Altazor" (1931) he compared himself to Whitman: "Ah, ah, I am Altazor, the great poet. . . . / I'm the one who has seen all, who knows all the secrets, without being Walt Whitman, for I've never had a white beard like the pretty nurses and the frozen rivulets" (Huidobro 1981, 58). Huidobro's "Ars Poetica" is a more accurate reflection of his relationship to Whitman:

Let the poem be like a key that opens a thousand doors.
A leaf falls; something goes by flying;
all that my eyes see is being created,
and the listener's soul will be trembling.
Invent new worlds and be careful with your word;
adjectives that don't give life, kill. . . .

Why do poets sing to a rose?
Make it bloom in your poem.
Things under the sun live only for us.
The poet is a small God. (Huidobro 1945, 42)

The earliest Spanish translation of Whitman's poetry (eighty-three poems) was the work of Armando Vasseur, the Uruguayan poet discussed earlier. Other translations of *Leaves of Grass* may be more literal or even more poetic than Vasseur's, and two versions (Francisco Alexander's and Jorge Luis Borges's)[7] are certainly more complete, but Vasseur's translation is the breviary in which Hispanic poets learned their Whitman. Vasseur was thirty-five years old and a diplomatic representative of Uruguay in Spain when the first edition of his *Walt Whitman, Poemas* was published in Valencia in 1912.[8] That he intended his translation to be a literary manifesto is borne out by the fact that he did not translate all of *Leaves of Grass* but only enough to stir the world of Spanish letters. Vasseur omitted approximately 750 lines of "Song of Myself," even though he knew Whitman's work was conceived in such a manner that any attempt to abridge it could be fatal. He was prone to making additions and deletions, he substituted a full metaphor for Whitman's "phrenological" terms, and at times he selected only a section of a poem whose real value was precisely in its contextual relation to the whole. Vasseur edited according to his personal taste. He was particularly attracted by Whitman's bits of formal and lyrical beauty; if something more philosophical came his way, he was inclined to omit it or shorten it considerably.

In addition to indulging in a game of making new poems out of excerpts from *Leaves of Grass*, Vasseur was not always accurate in his rendition of Whitman's vocabulary; he was usually defeated by the formidable mechanism of Whitman's present participles and gerunds. In Whitman's language, the present participle expresses, besides movement, an everlasting present which provides a transcendental quality to images which, described in different terms, would appear insignificant. The Spanish preterit that Vasseur used as a substitute truncates the action. Vasseur often added to Whitman's text in order to clarify it, but he used the occasion to display his own lyrical power. Like Bazalgette in France, he also toned down Whitman's sexual poems.

Perhaps the influence of the Whitman legend determined Vasseur's revisions, even in a text which the poet himself changed a hundred times in order that it might conform with that legend he so ardently wished to maintain. There have been other translations as well. A. Torres-Ríoseco's attempt resulted in a thoroughly harmonious text, authentically Whitmanist and unquestionably Spanish. León Felipe's 1941 translation, limited to "Song of Myself," suffered from a rhetorical emphasis superimposed on a poetry that is lyrically subdued, in spite of its powerful social message; however, this translation has enjoyed immense popular-

Fernando Alegría [93]

ity in Spain and Spanish America because of Felipe's undeniable lyrical genius and his resounding Castilian eloquence. Concha Zardoya's 1946 translation, *Obras Escogidas*, includes 112 compositions from *Leaves of Grass* (plus extracts from *Specimen Days*), translated with dynamism and a genuine Whitmanist tone. Though she avoided some of Vasseur's errors, she contributed some of her own, but on the whole she rendered the meaning satisfactorily and, above all, she translated all the important poems. So Spanish readers could at long last have a fairly complete idea of Whitman's Weltanschauung. Her handsomely bound translation was well received by the general public, was considered a successful critical revision of Vasseur's translation, and was reprinted several times.

Leaves of Grass was thus gradually acclimatized in Spain, and there was such a demand for it that translations multiplied. In 1971 a Catalan publisher brought out a complete translation by Francisco Alexander, which had originally appeared in Ecuador in 1953, and another Catalan publisher reprinted in 1972 a partial translation by Jorge Luis Borges, who on the whole followed Alexander's translation toward whom he recognized his debt in his preface. He was a great admirer of Whitman and, in his old age, could still recite some of his poems, which he knew by heart.

Then in 1981 there appeared, this time in Madrid, two slim volumes of translations by the same author, Enrique Lopez Castellon, a professor at the free University of Madrid. The first volume contained *Canto a mí mismo* ("Song of Myself") and the second one *El Calamo, Hijos de Adan* ("Calamus," "Children of Adam"). The translations are close to the text and correct, the introductions well informed and sensible without any romantic or fanciful embellishments.

"Song of Myself" attracted still another translator in 1984, Mauro Armiño, who, he claimed, tried to improve on his predecessors and probably did. His very clear introduction to *Canto de mí mismo* is based on James E. Miller's *A Critical Guide to "Leaves of Grass"* and Miller's *Whitman's "Song of Myself": Origin, Growth, Meaning*. In the same year, two very elegant minivolumes in a series entitled Mini-Vision came out, containing the translation of a selection from *Leaves of Grass* by Alberto Manzano. All the longer poems were included, but there was no introduction. Finally, there appeared in 1978 the first volume of what was intended to be a complete bilingual edition of *Leaves of Grass*. The translator's ambition was very modest. Pablo Mañé Garzón simply wanted his translation to be as literal as possible, leaving to the reader the responsibility of filling it out with the English text on the opposite page. Borges, in his own introduction, said that the translator had to choose between (i.e., free and arbitrary) interpretation, a resigned and modest rigor, or a compromise between the two. He personally chose the compromise, and Mañé Garzón very humbly the rigor, yielding a pedagogically useful translation.

The proliferation of translations denotes the growing appetite of the Spanish-speaking peoples for *Leaves of Grass*. Whitman appeared to them as a liberator both aesthetically and politically, though at first many critics thought that his genius was alien to Latin minds and that his work would never be popular in Spain, even if he was the great American poet and the poet of the future.

NOTES

1. Their ideas are quite similar, and Carrillo's article, although it appeared in 1895, was written years before, perhaps in 1890 or 1891 judging by the introduction: "This article was written when Walt Whitman was still living, in answer to the sonnet . . . of Rubén Darío's." See Carrillo's *Primeros estudios cosmopolitas* (Madrid, 1920).

2. The last sentence of this quotation contains the leading motive inspiring Unamuno in his interpretation of Whitman in "Adamic Song" (selection 4).

3. For all sources, see Luis Llorena Torrens, *Revista Iberoamericana* (October 1947), 6–11.

4. See Rubén Darío, *Cantos de vida y esperanza* (Madrid, 1905) and *El canto errante* (Madrid: M. Perez Villavicencio, 1907).

5. See Sabat, *El vuelo de la noche* (Montevideo: Talleres Grafico de la Escuela: Industrial no. 1, 1925). Pablo Neruda later accomplished a philosophical synthesis of the sea symbolism in his masterpiece "The Great Ocean," in *Canto general* (1950; reprint, Caracas: Biblioteca Ayacucho, 1976).

6. See "T.L." in Pablo Neruda, *Anillos, prosas de Pablo Neruda y de Tomás Lago* (Santiago, Chile: Nascimento, 1926). See also "Tomás Lago," "Rubén Azócar," "Juvenico Valle," and "Diego Muñoz," a collection of poems to his worker friends, ditchdiggers, shoemakers, sailors, fishermen, and miners; in "La tierra se llama Juan" ("Earth Is Called Juan"); in his poem-letters to "Miguel Otero Silva," "Rafael Alberti," and "González Carballo"; in his elegies to García Lorca, Rojas Jiménez, Silvestre Revueltas, and Miguel Hernández, all in *Canto general*.

7. See Francisco Alexander, *Hojas de Hierba* (Quito: Casa de la Cultura Ecuatoriana, 1953); and Jorge Luis Borges, *Hojas de Hierba* (Buenos Aires: Juárez, 1969).

8. See the study of Vasseur's translation in Fernando Alegría, *Walt Whitman en Hispanoamérica* (Mexico: Ediciones Studium, 1954).

WORKS CITED

Alegría, Fernando. *Walt Whitman en Hispanoamérica*. Mexico: Ediciones Studium, 1954.

Borges, Jorge Luis. *Discusión*. Buenos Aires: M. Gleizer, 1932.

Carrillo, E. Gómez. *Whitman y otras crónicas*. Washington, D.C.: Unión Panamericana, 1950.

Darío, Rubén. *El viaje a Nicaragua e historia de mis libros*. Madrid: Editorial "Mundo latino," 1919.

———. *Obras de juventud*. Santiago, Concepción, Chile: Nascimento, 1927.

———. *Obras desconocidas de R. D.* Santiago: Prensas de la Univ. de Chile, 1934.

———. *Obras poéticas completas.* Madrid: Aguilar, 1945.

———. *Poesía.* Vol. 9. Caracas: Biblioteca Ayacucho, 1977.

de Rokha, Pablo. *Morfología del espanto.* Santiago de Chile: Editorial "Multitud," 1942.

Diez-Canedo, Enrique. *Letras de América.* Mexico: El Colegio de Mexico, 1944.

Donoso, Armando. "Walt Whitman." *Cuba Contemporánea* 7 (February 1915): 198–208.

Englekirk, John Eugene. *Edgar Allan Poe in Hispanic Literature.* New York: Institutío de las Espanas en los Estados Unidos, 1934.

Felipe, León. *Walt Whitman: Canto a mí mismo.* Buenos Aires: Losada, 1941. (With prologue in verse, 9–21.)

Franco, Luis. *Walt Whitman.* Buenos Aires: Ed. Américalee, 1945.

Gabriel, José. *Walt Whitman, la voz democrática de América.* Montevideo: Ed. Ceibo, 1944.

Huidobro, Vicente. *Antología.* Santiago de Chile: Zig-Zag, 1945.

———. *Altazor.* Madrid: Ediciones Editions, Cátedra, 1981.

Jiménez, Juan Ramón. *Españoles de tres mundos.* Buenos Aires: Losada, 1942.

Lugones, Leopoldo. *Las montañas del oro.* Buenos Aires: Imp. J. A. Kern, 1897.

Mallea, Eduardo. *La Bahía de silencio.* 2d ed. Buenos Aires: Editorial Sudamericana, 1945.

Martí, José. *Norteamericanos.* In *Obras completas.* La Habana: Editorial de Ciencas Sociales, 1975.

Mistral, Gabriela. *Desolación.* Buenos Aires, 1945.

Neruda, Pablo. *Canto general.* 1950. Reprint, Caracas: Biblioteca Ayacucho, 1976.

———. *Obras completas.* 3d ed., Vol. 1. Buenos Aires: Losada, 1967.

Obligado, Pedro Miguel. In Leopoldo Lugones, *Obras poéticas completas.* Madrid: Aguilar, 1952.

Onís, Federico de. *Anthología de la poesíe española e hispanoamericana.* Madrid: Imp. de la Lib., 1934.

Ramos, José A. *Panorama de la literatura norteamericana.* Mexico: Botas, 1935.

Sabat Ercasty, Carlos. *Pantheos.* Montevideo: O. M. Bertani, 1917.

———. *Libro del mar.* Montevideo: Tallers graficos de la Escuela Industrial no. 1, 1922.

Sánchez, Luis A. *Panorama de la literatura actual.* 2d ed. Santiago de Chile: Ercilla, 1935.

Santayana, George. "The Poetry of Barbarism." In *Interpretations of Poetry and Religion.* New York: Charles Scribner's Sons, 1921, 166–216.

———. *Persons and Places.* New York: Charles Scribner's Sons, 1944.

Torres-Ríoseco, A. *Walt Whitman.* San José de Costa Rica: Ed. J. García Monge, 1922.

Vasseur, Armando. *Cantos del nuevo mundo.* Montevideo: A. Diaz, 1907.

1. JOSÉ MARTÍ

"The Poet Walt Whitman"

"Last night he seemed a god, sitting in his red velvet chair, his hair completely white, his beard upon his breast, his brows like a thicket, his hand upon a cane." This is what a newspaper says today of the poet Walt Whitman, a man of seventy whom the deeper critics—always in the minority—assign to an extraordinary place in the literature of his country and times. Only the holy books of antiquity, with their prophetic language and sturdy poetry, afford a doctrine comparable to that which is given out in grand, sacerdotal apothegms, like bursts of light, by this elderly poet, whose amazing book has been banned.

And why not, since it is a natural book? Universities and Latin quotations have brought men to such a state as to recognize each other no longer. Instead of throwing themselves into mutual embrace, attracted by essential, eternal qualities, they draw apart, exchanging compliments like village gossips; and all because of chance differences. Like a pudding in a mold, a man takes on the shape of an energetic teacher or a book with which mere fortune or fashion has placed him in contact. Philosophical, religious, or literary schools set a uniform on a man's back, like livery on a footman's; men let themselves be branded like horses or bulls, and show the mark to the world. Therefore when they find themselves in the presence of a man who is naked, virginal, loving, sincere, and strong—a man who goes forward, who contends, who pulls on his oar—a man who, not letting himself be blinded by misfortune, reads a promise of final happiness in the balance and harmony of the world; when they find themselves in the presence of Walt Whitman the father-man, muscular and angelic, they flee as from their own consciences and refuse to recognize this specimen of fragrant, superior humanity as the true type of their species, which appears faded, standardized, and puppetlike.

The newspaper says that yesterday, when another venerable man, Gladstone, had finished giving his rivals in Parliament a list of instructions concerning the rightfulness of granting Ireland a government of its own, he was like a mighty mastiff, standing erect and unchallenged in the midst of the crowd, which lay at his feet like a pack of bull terriers. So seems Whitman, with his "natural persons," with his "Nature without check with original energy," with his "myriads of youths, beautiful, gigantic," with his belief that "the smallest sprout shows there is really no death," with the impressive naming of peoples and races in his "Salut au Monde!," with his resolve that "knowing the perfect fitness and equanimity of things, while they discuss I am silent, and go bathe and admire myself"; so seems Whitman, "he who does not say these things for a dollar"; he who says, "I am satisfied—I see, dance, laugh, sing"; he who has no professorship or pulpit or school. So seems he when compared to the spiritless poets and philosophers—philosophers of a detail or of a single aspect—sweetness-and-light poets, patterned poets, bookish poets, philosophical or literary figurines.

You must study him, for while he is not a poet of the most refined taste, he is the most daring, inclusive, and uninhibited of his times. In his frame cottage, standing on the verge of poverty, he displays in a window a portrait of Victor Hugo, bordered in black. Emerson, whose words purify and uplift, used to put his arm on Whitman's shoulder and call him his friend. Tennyson, the kind of man who sees to the roots of things, sends affectionate messages to "the grand old man," from his oaken armchair in England. Robert Buchanan, the Englishman of

the fiery words, cries out to the North Americans, "What can you know of literature if you let the old age of your colossal Walt Whitman run out without the honors it deserves?"

"The truth is that reading him, although it causes amazement at first, leaves a
delightful feeling of convalescence in the soul, which has been tormented by universal pettiness. He creates his own grammar and logic. He reads in the eye of a
bull and in the sap of a leaf." "The man who cleanses your house of dirt — that
man is my brother!" His apparent irregularity, disconcerting at first, becomes
later, except for brief moments of extraordinary clarity, the sublime order and
composition with which mountain peaks loom against the horizon.

He does not live in New York, his "beloved Manhattan," his "superb-faced"
and "million-footed" Manhattan, where he looks in whenever he wishes to sing a
song of "what I behold Libertad." Cared for by "loving friends," since his books
and lectures provide scarcely enough for his daily bread, he lives in a small house
nestled in a pleasant country nook. From here, in his carriage drawn by the horses
he loves, he goes out to see the "stout young men" at their virile diversions, the
"comrades" who are not afraid to rub elbows with this iconoclast who wants to
establish "the institution of the dear love of comrades"; to view the fields they till,
and the friends who pass by arm-in-arm, singing; and the sweethearts in couples,
cheerful and lively as partridges. He tells of this in his *Calamus,* a very strange
book in which he sings of the love of friends: "Not the pageants of you, not your
shifting tableaus . . . repay me. . . . Not the processions in the streets, nor the bright
windows with goods in them, Nor to converse with learn'd persons . . . ; (but that
as I pass through my Manhattan the eyes I meet offer me love); . . . Lovers,
continual lovers, only repay me." He is like the old men whom he announces
at the end of his censored book, his *Leaves of Grass*: "I announce myriads of
youths, beautiful, gigantic, sweet-blooded; I announce a race of wild and splendid
old men."

He lives in the country, where natural man, in the sunshine that tans his skin,
plows the free earth with his tranquil horses; but not far from the hospitable,
teeming city, with its life noises, its many occupations, its thousand-fold epic, the
dust of its wheels, the smoke of the heavy-breathing factories, the sun looking
down on it all, the workers who talk at lunch on piles of bricks, the ambulance
that speeds along with the hero who has just fallen from a scaffold, the woman
surprised in the midst of a crowd by the august pain of maternity.

But yesterday Whitman came from the country to speak, before a gathering of
loyal friends, an oration on another man of Nature, the great, gentle soul, the
"great dead star of the West," Abraham Lincoln. All literate New York attended
that luminous speech in religious silence, for its sudden grace notes, vibrant
tones, hymnlike fugues, and Olympian familiarity seemed at times the whispering
of stars. Those brought up in the Latin tradition, whether academic or French,
could not perhaps understand that heroic humor. The free and decorous life of
man on a new continent has created a wholesome, robust philosophy that is issuing forth upon the world in athletic epodes. For the largest number of free, indus-

trious men that Earth ever witnessed, a poetry is required that is made of inclusiveness and faith, calming and solemn; poetry that rises, like the sun out of the sea, kindling the clouds, rimming the wave crests with fire, waking the tired flowers and the nests in the prolific forests of the shore. Pollen takes wing, birds exchange kisses; branches make ready; leaves seek the sun; all creation breathes music: with the language of the strong light Whitman spoke of Lincoln.

Perhaps one of the most beautiful products of contemporary poetry is the mystic threnody Whitman composed on the death of Lincoln. All Nature accompanies the sorrowful coffin on its road to the grave. The stars have predicted it. The clouds have been darkening for a month. In the swamp a grey-brown bird sings a song of desolation. With the thought and the knowledge of death the poet goes through the grieving fields as between two companions. With a musician's art he groups, conceals, and reproduces these sad elements in a total twilight harmony. When the poem is done it seems all Earth has been clothed in black and the dead man has covered it from sea to sea. The clouds come, the veiled Moon announcing the catastrophe, the long wings of the grey-brown bird. It is much more beautiful, strange, and profound than Poe's "Raven." The poet carries a sprig of lilacs to the coffin.

His whole work lies in that.

Willows no longer weep over tombs; death is the harvest, the outlet, the great revealer. What is now in existence existed before and will exist again; oppositions and apparent griefs are blended in a solemn, celestial Springtime; a bone is a flower. Close at hand the sound of suns is heard, which with majestic movement seek their definitive station in space; life is a hymn; death is a hidden form of life; the sweat of the brow is holy, and intestinal fauna are holy; men should kiss one another's cheeks in passing; the living should embrace with ineffable love; they should love the grass, animals, air, sea, pain, death; suffering is less intense for souls possessed by love; life has no sorrows for him who understands its meaning soon enough; honey, light, and a kiss are of the same seed. In the darkness that shines peacefully like a dome crowded with stars; to soft music, over worlds asleep like dogs at its feet, a serene, enormous lilac tree rises.

Each social category brings to literature its own mode of expression, in such fashion that the history of peoples could be told in the various phases of literature, with greater truth than in chronicles and annals. There can be no contradictions in Nature; the same human aspiration to find a perfect type of charm and beauty in love, during this existence and in the unknown life after death, shows that in the total life we must rejoicingly fit together the elements which in the portion of life we presently traverse seem disunited and hostile. A literature that announces and spreads the final, happy concert of apparent contradictions; a literature that, as a spontaneous counsel and instruction from Nature, proclaims in a single, overshadowing peace the oneness of the dogmas and rival passions that in the elemental state of peoples divide and plunge them into bloody conflict; a literature that in the timid spirit of men inculcates such a deep-rooted conviction of justice and definitive beauty that the privations and sordidness of existence will not discourage or embitter them; such a literature will not only reveal a social status closer to perfection than any known but also, felicitously joining reason to grace, will provide Humanity, eager for marvels and poetry, with the religion it has been confusedly awaiting ever since it realized the hollowness and insufficiency of its old creeds.

Who is so ignorant as to maintain that poetry is not indispensable to the peoples of the earth? There are persons of such mental myopia that they believe a fruit is finished after the rind. Poetry, which unites or severs, which fortifies or anguishes, which bears up souls or dashes them down, which gives men faith and comfort or takes them away, is more necessary to peoples than industry itself, since the latter bestows the means for subsisting, while poetry gives them desire and strength for life. Where would a society go that had lost the habit of thinking confidently about the meaning and scope of its acts? The best among them, those whom Nature has anointed with the holy desire for the future, would lose, in a silent and sorry annihilation, all incentive to surmount human ugliness; and the common herd, the people of appetites, the multitude, would procreate empty sons without godliness, and would raise to essential function those who ought to serve as mere instruments. With the bustle of an always incomplete prosperity they would bemuse the irremediable melancholy of the soul, which takes pleasure only in beauty and sublimity.

Other considerations to one side, freedom should be blessed, because its enjoyment inspires in modern man — who before its appearance was deprived of the calm, stimulation, and poetry of existence — the supreme peace and religious well-being that the world order produces in those who live in the pride and serenity of their free will. Look to the mountains, O poets whose puerile tears dampen deserted altars!

You think religion lost because it is changing form over your heads. Arise, for you are the priests! Freedom is the definitive religion. And the poetry of freedom is the new form of worship. Such poetry calms and beautifies the present, deduces and illumines the future, explains the ineffable purpose and seductive goodness of the universe.

Hark to what this industrious, satisfied people is singing; hark to Walt Whitman. His exercise of himself raises him into majesty, his tolerance into justice, his sense of order into happiness. He who lives in an aristocratic creed is an oyster in its shell, seeing only the prison that enfolds it, and believing, in the darkness, that this is the world. Freedom lends wings to an oyster. And what inside the shell seems a portentous strife becomes, in the light of day, the natural movement of fluids in the energetic pulse of the world.

The world, to Walt Whitman, was always as it is today. It suffices that a thing exists for one to know that it must have existed before, and when its existence shall not be needed, it will not exist. That which exists no longer, that which is not seen, is proved by that which does exist and is seen; for everything is in the whole, one thing explaining the other; and when that which is now ceases to be, it will be proved in its turn by that which comes later. The infinitesimal collaborates toward the infinite, and every thing is in its place: a tortoise, an ox, birds, "winged purposes." It is as lucky to die as to be born, for the dead are alive; "No array of terms can say how much at peace I am about God and about death." He laughs at what they call dissolution, and he knows the amplitude of time. He accepts time absolutely. All is contained in his person; all of him is in everything else; where one sinks, he sinks; he is the tide, the influx and the efflux; why shall he not be proud of himself, since he feels he is a live and intelligent part of Nature? What does it matter to him if he return to the bosom from whence he came and, in the cool, moist earth, be converted into a useful plant, a beautiful flower? He will nourish men, after having loved them. His duty is to create; the atom that creates is of divine essence; the act in which one creates is exquisite and sacred. Convinced of the identity of the universe, he intones the "Song of Myself." Out of all things he weaves the song of himself: of the creeds that struggle and pass, of man who procreates and labors, of the animals that help him — ah, of the animals! "Not one kneels to another, nor is superior to any other, nor complains." He sees himself as heir to the world.

Nothing is strange to him, and he takes all into account: the creeping snail, the ox that looks at him with its mysterious eyes, the priest who defends a part of the truth as though it were the whole truth. A man should open his arms and clasp all things to his heart, virtue the same as crime, dirtiness the same as cleanliness, ignorance the same as wisdom. He should fuse all things in his heart, as in a furnace; he should drop his white beard over all things. But — mark this well! — "We have had ducking and deprecating about enough." He rebukes the incredulous, the sophists, the garrulous; let them procreate instead of quarrelling, and they will add something to the world! Creating should be done with the same respect as a pious woman's who kisses the altar steps!

He belongs to all castes, creeds, and professions, and in all of them finds justice and poetry. He gauges religions without anger, but he thinks the perfect religion is in Nature. Religion and life are in Nature. If there is a sick man, "Go," he says to the physician and the priest; "I will stay with him. I will open the windows, I will love him, I will speak softly to him. You shall see how he recovers; you are the words and the herbs, but I can do more than you, for I am love." The Creator is "The great Camerado, the lover true"; men are "cameradoes"; and the more they love and believe, the more they are worth, although anything that keeps its peace and its time is worth as much as any other. But let all see the world for themselves, since he, Walt Whitman, who feels within himself the whole of the world since its creation, knows by what the sun and open air teach him that a sunrise reveals more than the best book. He thinks of orbs, and desires women, feels himself possessed by universal, frenzied love. From scenes of creation and the trades of men he hears rising a concert of music to flood him with joy, and when he looks into a river at the moment when shops are closing and the setting sun ignites the water, he feels he has an appointment with the Creator; he recognizes that man is defini-tively good and from his head, reflected in the current, he sees spokes of light diverge.

But what can give an idea of his vast, burning love? This man loves the world with the fire of Sappho. He sees the world as a gigantic bed. A bed is an altar to him. "I will prove illustrious," he says, "the words and ideas that men have prosti-tuted with their stealth and false shame; I sing and consecrate what Egypt conse-crated." One of the sources of his originality is the Herculean force with which he prostrates ideas, as though he were going to violate them, when in reality he is only going to give them a kiss, with the fervor of a saint. Another source is the ma-terial, brutal, fleshly form with which he expresses his most delicate idealities. Such language has seemed lascivious to some who are incapable of understanding its grandeur. There have been imbeciles who, when in *Calamus* he honors love among friends with the warmest images in the human tongue, have felt they saw, as they tittered like naughty school boys, a return to the ignoble yearning of Virgil for Cebetes and of Horace for Gyges and Lysciscus. And when in *Children of Adam* he sings the divine sin, in pictures that dim the most glowing of the *Song of Solomon*, he trembles, he shrinks, he pours himself out and spreads, he goes mad with pride and satisfied virility; and he recalls the god of the Amazon who passes over forests and rivers scattering seeds of life: "My duty is to create!" "I sing the body electric," Whitman says in *Children of Adam*; and you should first read in Hebrew the patriarchal genealogies of Genesis; you should follow the naked, car-nivorous bands of the first men through the trackless jungles, in order to find an appropriate resemblance to the enumeration, full of Satanic might, where like a famished hero licking bloodstained lips he describes the pertinencies of the female body. You say this man is brutal? Listen to this poem which, like many of his, has only two lines: "Beautiful Women."

Women sit or move to and fro, some old, some young,
The young are beautiful — but the old are more beautiful than the young.

And then there is "Mother and Babe":

I see the sleeping babe nestling the breast of its mother,
The sleeping mother and babe — hush'd, I study them long and long.

He foresees that just as virility and gentleness combine to a high degree in men of superior temperament, these two qualities must join in the delightful peace on which life itself rests, with solemnity and joy worthy of the universe; these are the two energies that are needed to continue the task of creation.

If he walks into the grass, he says that the grass caresses him, that "he already feels its joints move," and the most uneasy novice would not find such fiery words to describe the joy of his body, which he looks upon as part of his soul, when it feels itself embraced by the sea. All living things love him: earth, night, and the sea love him: "Penetrate me, oh sea, with your loving moisture." He savors the air. He gives himself to the atmosphere like a tremulous bridegroom. He wants doors with no locks and bodies in their natural beauty; he believes he sanctifies all he touches or that touches him, and he finds virtue in all corporeality; he is

Walt Whitman, a kosmos, of Manhattan the son,
Turbulent, fleshy, sensual, eating, drinking and breeding.
No more nor less than anyone else.

He depicts truth as a frantic lover who invades his body and, eager to possess him, frees him from his clothes. But in the clarity of midnight the soul, free of occupations and books, emerges integral, silent, and meditative from a nobly spent day, and reflects on the themes that please it most: on night, dreams, and death; on the song of the universal for the benefit of the common man; on how it is very sweet "to die advancing on" and to fall at the foot of a primitive tree, holding the ax in one's hands, stung by the last serpent in the woods.

Imagine, then, what a new, strange effect this language, charged with splendid animality, must produce when it extols the passion which will unite men. In one poem of *Calamus* the poet brings together the delights he owes Nature and country; but he finds that only the ocean waves are worthy to chorus by moonlight his joy at seeing by his side, asleep, the friend whom he loves. He loves the humble, the fallen, the wounded, even the evildoer. He does not scorn the great, for to him only the useful are great. He puts his arm around the shoulders of teamsters, sailors, plowmen. He hunts and fishes with them, and at harvest time climbs with them atop of the loaded wagon. More beautiful to him than a triumphant emperor is a brawny Negro who standing on the string-piece behind his Percherons drives his dray calmly along busy Broadway. He understands all virtues, wins all prizes, works at all trades, suffers all pains, feels a heroic pleasure when he stops on the threshold of a smithy and sees that the young men, stripped to the waist, swing their hammers over-hand and each one hits in turn. He is the slave, the prisoner, he who fights, who falls, the beggar. When a slave comes to his door harried and covered with sweat, he fills a tub for him, has him sit at his table; in the corner he has his firelock loaded to defend him; if anyone comes to attack the slave he will kill the pursuer and come back to sit at his table, as though he had killed a snake!

Walt Whitman, then, is satisfied; what pride can sting him when he knows he is standing on a blade of grass or a flower? What pride does a carnation have, or a leaf of salvia, or a honeysuckle vine? Why should he not look on human grief with equanimity when he knows that over all is an endless Being for whom there waits a happy immersion in Nature? What haste shall spur him when he believes all is where it belongs, and the volition of one man cannot change the path of the world? He suffers, it is true; but he considers minor and passing the part of him that suffers, and above toil and misery he feels there is another part that cannot suffer, for it knows universal greatness. It is enough for him to be as he is; and he watches, complacent and amused, the flow of his life, whether in silence or in acclamation. With a single blow he knocks aside romantic lamentation, a useless excrescence. "Not asking the sky to come down to my good will!" And what majesty there is in the phrase where he says that he loves animals "because they do not complain." The truth is that there are already too many who would make cowards of us. There is a pressing need to see what the world is like, in order not to make ants into mountains. Give men strength instead of taking from them with lamentations the little that pain has left them. Do the ulcerated go through the streets showing their sores? Neither doubt nor science disturbs him. "To you the first honours," he says to the scientists, "but science is only a room in my dwelling, it is not my whole dwelling; how poor are subtle reasonings compared to a heroic fact! Long live science, and long live the soul, which is superior to all science." But where his philosophy has completely mastered hate, as the wise men command, is in the phrase—not untinged with the melancholy of defeat—with which he plucks all envy by its roots: "Why should I envy," he says, "any brother of mine who does what I cannot do?" "He that by me spreads a wider breast than my own proves the width of my own." "Let the sun penetrate the Earth, until it is all clear, sweet light, like my blood. Let joy be universal. I sing the eternity of existence, the joy of our life, and the implacable beauty of the universe. I wear calfskin shoes, a side collar, and a cane cut from a branch!"

All this he utters in apocalyptic phrases. Rhymes, stresses? Oh, no! His rhythm lies in the stanzas which, in the midst of an apparent chaos of overlying and convulsed sentences, are nevertheless linked by a wise method of composition that distributes the ideas in large musical groups, as the natural poetic form of a people who do not build stone by stone but by huge masses of stones.

Walt Whitman's language, entirely different from that which poets have used till now, corresponds in its extravagance and drive to his cyclic poetry and to the new humanity congregated on a fertile *continent* under auspices of such magnitude as not to be contained in ditties or coy lyrics. This is not a matter of clandestine amours or of courtly ladies trading old gallants for new, or of sterile complaints by those who lack the energy to master life, or of discretion suitable to cowards. This is not a matter of jingles and boudoir sighings, but of the birth of an era, the dawn of a definitive religion and of the renewal of mankind. It is a matter of a faith to replace the dead one, and it is revealed in the radiance of a redeemed man's proud peace; it is a matter of writing the holy books for a people who, as the world declines, gather from the udders and Cyclopean pomp of wild Nature all the virgin power of liberty. It is a matter of reflecting in words the noise of settling multitudes, of toiling cities, of tamed oceans and enslaved rivers. Should Walt Whitman then match rhymes and put into mild couplets these mountains of merchandise, forests of thorns, towns full of ships, battles where millions of men lay down their lives to insure the laws, and a sun that holds sway over all and pours its limpid fire into the vast landscape?

Oh, no! Walt Whitman speaks in Biblical verses; without apparent music, although after hearing them for a short time one realizes that these sounds ring like the earth's mighty shell when it is trodden by triumphant armies, barefoot and glorious. At times Whitman's language is like the front of a butcher shop hung with beef carcasses; at others it resembles the song of patriarchs seated in a circle, with the sadness of the world at the time of day when smoke loses itself among the clouds. Sometimes it sounds like an abrupt kiss, like a ravishment, like the cracking of leather as it dries in the sun. But never does his utterance lose its rhythmical, wavy motion. He himself tells how he speaks in "prophetical screams." "These," he says, "are a few words indicating the future." That is what his poetry is, an index finger; a sense of the universal pervades the book and gives it, within the surface confusion, a grandiose regularity; but his sentences — disjointed, flagellant, incomplete, unconnected — emit rather than express. "I fling out my fancies toward the white-topt mountains"; "Say, Earth, old top-knot, what do you want?" "I sound my barbaric yawp over the roofs of the world."

He does not set in motion, not he, a beggarly thought, to stumble and creep along under the outward opulence of its regal dress. He is not one to puff up humming birds to resemble eagles; he showers down eagles every time he opens his hand, as a sower broadcasts seeds. One line may have five syllables, the following forty, and the one after that ten. He does not strain comparisons; as a matter of fact, he does not compare at all but says what he sees or remembers with a graphic, incisive complement and, being a confident master of the total impression he is ready to create, he uses his art, which is one of entire concealment, to reproduce the elements of his picture with the same disarray in which he observed them in Nature. Although he may wander off, he does not make discords, for this is the way an unordered or unenslaved mind strays from a subject to its analogues; but then, as though he had only loosened the reins without dropping them altogether, he draws them suddenly tight and with a masterful hand keeps close control over his restive team, while his lines gallop along, swallowing up distances with each movement. Sometimes they whinny eagerly like stud stallions; at other, white and lathered, they set their hoofs on the clouds; and at still others, dark and daring, they plunge inside the earth, and the noise is long to be heard. Whitman sketches, but you would say that he uses a fire-tipped point. In five lines he groups, like a sheaf of freshly gnawed bones, all the horrors of war. An adverb is enough to expand or contract a phrase, and an adjective to sublimate it. His method has to be large, since its effect is; but it might be thought that he proceeds without any method whatsoever, especially in his use of words, which mixes elements with unheard-of audacity, putting the august and almost divine side by side with those which are considered the least appropriate and polite. There are some pictures that he does not paint with epithets—which with him are always lively and profound—but with sounds, which he assembles and disperses with consummate skill, thus, with a succession of procedures, maintaining interest, which the monotony of an exclusive mode would have jeopardized. Through repetitions he draws out melancholia like the savages. His caesura, unexpected and run-on, he changes ceaselessly and without conforming to any rule, although an intelligent arrangement can be detected in its developments, pauses, and grace notes. He finds that accumulation is the best way to describe, and his reasoning never assumes the pedestrian form of argumentation or the high-sounding form of oratory, but instead uses the mystery of suggestion, the fervor of uncertainty, and the flaming word of prophesy.

At every step of the way we find words from our Spanish: *viva, camarada* [*sic*], *libertad, americanos.* But what could better depict his character than the French words with which, in visible ecstasy and as though to expand their meaning, he incrusts his poems: *ami, exalté, accoucheur, nonchalant, ensemble? Ensemble,* especially, charms him, for he sees in it the highest sphere of a people's life or a world's. From the Italian he has taken one word: *bravura!*

Thus, honoring muscle and boldness; inviting passersby to put their hands on him without fear; hearing the song of things, with his palms upturned to the air; surprisedly and delightedly proclaiming gigantic fecundities; gathering up, in epic verse, seeds, battles, and orbs; showing astounded generations the radiant lives of men who on American valleys and mountains reach out to brush the hem of vigilant Liberty's skirt with bee wings; shepherding centuries toward the sheltering bay of eternal calm; thus while at outdoor tables his friends serve him the first catch of Spring fish washed down with champagne, Walt Whitman awaits the happy hour when the material part of him will withdraw, after having revealed to the world a truthful, sonorous and loving man, and when, given over to the purifying air, he will sprout and perfume it, "carefree, triumphant, dead!"

La Nación (Buenos Aires) (April 19, 1887). Translated by Arnold Chapman. Reprinted in José Martí, *Obras completas* (La Habana: Editorial Nacional de Cuba, 1964) and widely reprinted in South America. Martí heard Whitman give his Lincoln lecture in New York on April 19, 1887.

2. RUBÉN DARÍO

"Walt Whitman"

En su país de hierro vive el gran viejo,
Bello como un patriarca, sereno y santo.
Tiene en la arruga olímpica de su entrecejo
Algo que impera y vence con noble encanto.

Su alma del infinito parece espejo;
Son sus cansados hombros dignos del manto;

Y con arpa labrada de un roble añejo,
Como un profeta nuevo canta su canto.

Sacerdote que alienta soplo divino,
Anuncia, en el futuro, tiempo mejor.
Dice al águila: "¡Vuela!"; "¡Boga!", al marino,

Y "¡Trabaja!", al robusto trabajador.
¡ Así va ese poeta por su camino,
Con su soberbio rostro de emperador!

In his land of iron lives the great elder
Beautiful patriarch, serene and holy;
His furrowed brow, of Olympic splendor,
Commands and conquers with noble glory.

His soul, like a mirror, the cosmos evokes,
And his tired shoulders merit the mantle;
With a lyre chiseled from an ancient oak,
As a new prophet he sings his canticles.

A high priest inspired with divine avail
Heralds, in the future, a better spring,
He tells the eagle: "Fly!"; the sailor: "Sail!";

And the robust worker to keep on working.
Thus, the poet passes along his trail,
With the splendid countenance of a king.

Azul, 2d ed. (Guatemala: Imprenta de "La Union," 1890). Translation from Didier Tisdel Jaén, ed., *Homage to Walt Whitman* (University: University of Alabama Press, 1969). Translated by Didier Tisdel Jaén.

3. CEBRÍA MONTOLIÚ

"Walt Whitman's Philosophy"

We consider Whitman's philosophy only a vision or subjective impression, a pure experience of the soul. Indeed, he is pragmatic *par excellence*, for in his conceptions one finds not only the origin but also the spirit itself of that philosophy of efficiency which would not be methodically formulated in his country until years later. This fact is an excellent proof of the autochthonous nature attributed to that doctrine. Whitman's pragmatism, at heart, is nothing but a pure and spontaneous manifestation of his passionate Americanism, a simple expression of his innate and vehement national temperament.

As a good *practical thinker* Whitman systematically avoids formulas. Furthermore, not only does he abhor all formulas and systems but, also, in a most clear and emphatic way, he anticipates those who would deduce a doctrine from his writings and challenges their useless insistence in strong terms.

While Whitman does not formulate, perhaps precisely because he does not formulate, he experiments and believes. His faith is built, as we shall see, on pure experience. There is a certain incompatibility between faith and symbol, just as between experience and doctrine, and this condition makes one of the two disappear when it becomes fused or crystalized in the other. The tragic problem of all life and movement is that they cannot be conceived without being, at the same time, destroyed. Just as we saw Whitman absorb with measureless desire all that was within reach of his hungry senses so we shall see him now absorb, with an equally insatiable instinct, the ideas that were floating in the intellectual atmosphere of his time, and swallow everything, without making distinctions, transforming all into his own substance, even the most contradictory opinions and theories.

We have seen already a sample of this process when we considered the spiritual heritage that our poet received from Emerson. This heritage was so absolutely assimilated that, in his old age, once its narrow limits had been surpassed, Whitman did not even remember having ever used it and digested it at the time of his own personal development. And now we see how by the same means and similar vehicles, Whitman comes into contact with the immense wave of German idealistic subjectivism, then at the climax of its progress. Through the august figure of Carlyle, and by insensible derivations, he reaches this philosophy and permits Fichte and Hegel, especially, to take possession of his spirit to a point where he seems surrounded by their metaphysical eschatologies and rushing towards that hazy goal of a mystic speculation which related the full manifestation of the individual to the apocalyptic predestination of the Germanic country. No wonder then, that driven by the same idealistic whirlwind he gives himself over to the most static levities in Eastern mysticism with which — particularly in its broadest and deepest expression, Hindu theosophy — Whitman seemed to be intimately familiar.

With such antecedents Walt might have become a sort of gymnosophist sleepwalker or a starved and frenzied poet, such as those turned out abundantly by the then fashionable romantic movement. But Walt did not let himself be imprisoned by the subtle threads of this metaphysical net. His spirit, always alert and open to the four corners of the world, absorbs with equal easiness the most ethereal inspirations of the soul and the grossest forms of the material world.

Being an unrepentant sinner, according to his own confession, he declares himself the poet of the body with just as much enthusiasm as he declares himself the poet of the spirit and thinks none of the elements of the surrounding world lacks in divine qualities. It is not strange then to find in his writings — as deeply as the influence of German idealism — the trace left by the opposite and to a certain degree complementary ideologies initiated by Lamarque and Darwin in the field of physical sciences and transplanted by Comte and Spencer to the realm of ethics. Whitman, consistent with his principles, wished to apply to the sacred garden of poetry the method of direct observation, verbal information and objective description which that school had accepted as the only tools worthy of a scientific operation. He was not intimidated by the possibility of being considered prosaic, a charge to which he left himself open because of his didactic tone and particularly because of the long enumerations of objects in some passages of his work. His primordial objective was to live in intimate contact with his country and his epoch and in order to accomplish this he did not spare himself efforts or sacrifices of any kind. Following the recommendations of positive science he availed himself of journalistic information and used it as a source for his poetical work, a fact that is revealed by the piles of clippings which he carefully saved and which were found after his death. The use of New York slang as his main instrument of literary expression, a practice that seemed to revolt some over-scholarly Yankees, should suffice to show how rigidly and completely Whitman attempted to embody the whole configuration of modern thought while pursuing an anti-aesthetic course. Likewise, Whitman, like Christ, wanted to descend to the infernal depths of the brilliant world that supported him, even if it was only to rise with greater strength to the lofty empire of his glorious resurrection. This titanic enterprise left on his work unequivocal signs of his desperate struggle to reconcile the eternal oppositions and to encompass the opposite poles of universal equilibrium. This we must consider a heroic decree of fate. The faults inherent in such an attitude should be viewed with indulgence or, at most, with the charming irony displayed by Emerson when, already an old man, he cast an Olympian glance over the finished work of the poet and said that it seemed to him a strange mixture of the *Bhagavat-Gita* and the *New York Herald*.

Let us not draw erroneous conclusions from our analysis. No matter how deeply the materialistic forces acted on his spirit, and no matter how idolizing and passionate his sensual inclinations might have been, Whitman was still, at the bottom of his heart, the same Quaker poet already described in our account of his life [omitted in this extract]. Although some simple and devout soul may be scandalized by this assertion, the truth is that Whitman, a great Epicurean, appeared to be transfigured by an insatiable thirst for immortality. "He is a God-intoxicated faun," we feel tempted to exclaim when, without prejudice, we contemplate the entirety of his poetic work in a single glance. For the more we penetrate his spirit, the firmer our conviction grows that Whitman is "the poet of the body" in a most absolute way, not only for what the body is in itself, but also for its divine content. The body reveals this in its highest form and Whitman worships it with idolatry. Because this is so we may say, in a profound sense, that we can hardly conceive of him as a whole unless it is as a great mystic poet, certainly one of the greatest in the history of mankind.

So patent is his direct human vocation, as one of his latest commentators has said (Carleton Noyes in *An Approach to Walt Whitman*) that Whitman, the good comrade, seldom appears immediately as a spiritual guide. Those who knew him in life felt irresistibly attracted to him without perhaps discovering the true source of his extraordinary strength and balance. There was more than merely a commanding personal magnetism to distinguish him from the masses. There were unsuspected depths of which his charm was only the overflow and expression. He was endowed with a heroic physique, of great perfection and beauty, and yet the specific essence of his temperament was spiritual. He himself recognized, in a manner allowable only to a few chosen ones, that the central reality of the human being is the soul. The passion and struggle to reach the soul's heritage became the driving force of his life. Once he has cast himself happily into that great adventure, he dares everything, he risks and he suffers all. His happiness lies in the prosecution of this great enterprise. His reward is getting to know God.

In accordance with this mystic vision of the world, Whitman finds the key to life's enigma in death and only in death. But death — and this should be well understood — has for him the mystic significance of a bridge which leads to a new phase of eternal life. Death is not cessation, but change of being; it is not the end but the beginning, and in this transition there is no dissolution of continuity; all life tends towards this development and expansion of itself. In regard to the ill-defined question of "immortality," Whitman wastes no time trying to solve it; he considers it a vain problem and simply affirms his belief in it. The conviction of truth comes to him as an intuition, but in such a vital manner that there is no room for argument. Immortality is the premise of all his life experience and his supreme and unique interpretation of it. This concept determines his way of thinking.

Whitman is, then, a real visionary and however correct Bucke may be in fixing the moment of his life when he had this vision, the truth is that this vision did occur and that it transfigured with the most resplendent celestial aura all the life and work of this heroic personality. Once this is accepted, it is hardly necessary to add what Carleton Noyes says: "Whitman's intimate experience cannot be expressed with words." Only the soul knows God and souls have no words. Whitman's religious experience is so intimate and personal that he can express it in his poems only through symbols extracted from common language by his exuberant imagination. One fact clearly stands out from all others in his life: the sum and essence of Whitman's life is Religion. In a sense both mystical and practical, his supreme desire was to attain union between soul and God. Religion, as he conceives it and lives it, is not merely one part of human experience — indeed, the loftiest — but the totality of existence, giving value to all forms of human activity and making possible that "the whole and its parts fit together."

As is usually the case with Anglo-Saxons, Whitman's mysticism is neither egotistical nor static; it does not gravitate towards itself in the sterile fashion of contemplative lives which rejoice in the stagnant waters of a negative passivity following the spirit of some schools in our midst which have monopolized the realm of the soul. On the contrary, Walt transforms his own revelation into a "message," declaring himself the "prophet of a greater Religion." It is difficult to define this religion in a few words, especially when he himself was not able to define it in his whole life. But we might say to the reader that although he may already consider Whitman a mystic pantheist, he must not let himself be deceived by this term, because Whitman's conception of God has nothing of that dry vagueness so commonly criticized in pantheism. Whitman believes in the divine quality of everything without implying that each thing is God; but rather affirms that God reveals himself in all and each of them. For Whitman *everything is divine*, but if he must choose for his own worship he chooses the human figure as the most divine of all, the true temple of God, as Saint Paul said. What might this God be? This is the mystery. Let us call him, according to Saint Paul, "the unknown God"; let us believe firmly in his revealed work and this will suffice to put us in direct communication with him, although it may be impossible for us to see him. This is precisely what happened to Whitman, according to his own testimony, when he raised a corner of the veil that hides the mystery of his mystic revelation.

Burning in this immense fire of love, in which, as we shall see further on, he is to forge all his ethic and social conception of the world, his religious program is a pure, ample derivation of that brotherly embrace in which he encompasses all beings. He calls it a greater Religion not because he wishes to oppose it to the various religions disputing among each other for the faith of a majority of men, but because he wishes to embrace them all in his powerful arms.

Let us make clear, however, that no eclecticism finds its way into this religious attitude; rather it is the transcendental force itself of his faith which impels him to accept others as approximate instruments for expressing that which in his own faith is essentially inexplicable. The capital center of his mystic apostleship, that which inspired him to write "All is truth" and to search and defend a broader and higher form for his Religion, is found in the profound truth of all things, there, where all divergencies meet.

Such is, in synthesis, Whitman's religious pragmatism. Firmly based on the fundamental findings of his own experience, he always refuses to define the concrete contours of his ideal kingdom so as to allow freedom for every one. However, he was once or twice guilty of attempting definitions. Such is the case of "Chanting the Square Deific," a poem in which Whitman ventures to outline a sort of vast theogonic synthesis coinciding with some commonly accepted formulas and making use of symbols already established by tradition. In this poem, "Chanting . . . ," without failing to recognize the ineffable nature of God, Whitman dares to express in human terms that which he humanly conceives as the ineffable and divine principle of the universe. He draws a symbol magically suggestive of all his gnostic experience.

Four powers or forces compose the Square: law and judgement; love and forgiveness; rebellion and malice; and reconciliation and fusion of all in one. These four powers are personified by Jehovah, Christ, Satan and the Holy Spirit.

Law is the fundamental principle of the universe. Nothing can escape the non-created, fatal norm of its own creation. The decree of compensation by which Law retributes all actions is imperturbable, inexorable and mathematically just. Jehovah is the God-Judge who passes sentence without appeal and executes without scruple.

But this is only the basis of the Square. Interdicting Law and rising against its ruling, Love appears. Christ rises and beholds us, gentle comforter, stretching out his hand to bless us. God is Love and therefore Christ is the most powerful of all gods. Love departs from the Law, but perpetuates it, it does not destroy Law, it only redeems it from its tyranny; Love is the divine grace that bears fruit in the world which is Law's slave, by means of the celestial dew of hope. The individual dies, but Love survives. The Savior passes, but salvation is eternal.

At the extreme opposite of Love, Rebellion rises. The individual affirms himself and his own divine will. This is the domain of Satan, the Anti-Christ, divine and "permanent," the same as any other and as real as any other. Where Law exists, so does transgression of the Law. There is no good without its corresponding evil. In the finite world of human experience the principle of evil is a necessity and will exist as long as its limitations last.

Closing the Square, parallel to Law, satisfying Love, dominating Evil, comes the Holy Spirit. This is the last reality and the only essence of all things, which includes not only the Savior and Satan, but also God himself conceived as a person.

And with the consideration of this brief but superior sketch of theodicy we come to the end of Whitman's bold though really unformulated philosophic conception. We recognize, of course, the grave doubts that the various and startling projections suggested in the course of our brief perusal may have raised in the reader's mind. But, whatever be the absolute value of this amalgamation of the most contradictory ideas and tendencies, one thing is clear and that is that the real tie linking these antitheses is no other than the author's robust personality, a personality which is one of the most dynamic and compact syntheses to have embodied the volatile and multiform human logos. We must not lose sight of Whitman's inaccessible position on an intellectual level superior to the thousand controversies originated by the juxtaposition of those ideas.

In spite of the doubts that we may feel, it is not useless to surmount these intellectual heights since it is in these heights where we shall find the true source of Whitman's specific opinions in the realm of immediate reality. And if from this postulate of "pure reason" we pass on to the examination of his "practical reason," we shall easily deduce the diverse consequences of the application of those superior principles to the uneasy field of ethical, political and aesthetic problems of contemporary life.

Introduction to Montoliú's Catalan translation of *Leaves of Grass* (*Fulles D'Herba*) (Barcelona: Libreria L'Avene, 1909). Translation from the Spanish version, *Walt Whitman, el hombre y su obra* (Buenos Aires: Editorial Poseidón, 1943), by permission of Poseidón. Translated by Fernando Alegría.

4. MIGUEL DE UNAMUNO

"Adamic Song"

It happened one Biblical afternoon, the towers of the city gloriously resting against the sky like giant ears of golden wheat emerging from the greenness that clothes the river. I took up *Leaves of Grass* by Walt Whitman, that American, enormous embryo of a secular poet, about whom Robert Louis Stevenson said that like a shaggy dog, just unchained, went scouring the beaches of the world baying at the moon. I took those leaves and translated some for my friend in the quiet splendor of the golden city.

And my friend said to me: "What a strange impression one gets from those enumerations of peoples and lands, nations, things and plants! . . . Is that poetry?"

And I said to him: "When lyric poetry becomes spiritualized and reaches the sublime it ends in mere enumerations, in uttering dear names with a sigh. The first stanza in the eternal love-dialogue may be "I love you, I love you very much, I love you with all my soul," but the last one, the one that comes with surrender contains only these two words: Romeo! Juliet! Romeo! Juliet! There is no deeper love-sigh than the repetition of the beloved name, relishing it like honey in your mouth. And consider the child. I shall never forget an immortal scene that God put one morning before my eyes. I saw three children hand in hand, standing by a horse, singing nothing but these words in mad delight: A horse! a horse! a horse! They were creating the word as they repeated it. Theirs was a Genesis song.

"How did lyric poety begin?" asked my friend, "which was the first song?"

"Let us turn to legend," I said, "and listen to what the Genesis says in its second chapter: 'So out of the ground the Lord God formed every beast of the field and every bird of the air, and brought them to the man to see what he would call them; and whatever the man called every living creature, that was its name. The man gave names to all cattle, and to the birds of the air, and to every beast of the field; but for the man there was not found a helper fit for him.' This was the first song, the song naming the animals; Adam in ecstasy before them, in the dawn of mankind."

To give a name! To give a name to something is, in a way, to take possession of it spiritually. This same Walt Whitman, whose *Leaves of Grass* we have here, in his "Song At Sunset" said these words: "To breathe the air, how delicious! To speak — to walk — to seize something by the hand!" He could have added: To name things, what a startling miracle!

Upon naming the animals and birds, Adam took possession of them. And note the eighth Psalm: after singing of God's command to man that he be the master of the works created by the divine hands, God having laid everything at his feet — sheep and oxen, beasts of the field, birds of the air, and fishes of the sea, and what-ever passes along the path of the sea, the psalm ends: "O Lord, our Lord, how majestic is thy name in all the earth!" If we knew an appropriate name, a poetic name, a creative name for God, all lyric poetry would be summed up in it as in an eternal flower.

Also in Genesis, verses twenty-four to thirty, chapter thirty-two, we are told how Jacob crossed the ford of Jabbok and, searching for his brother Esau, decided to spend the night outdoors; he was attacked by a stranger, an angel sent by God or perhaps God himself, and during the struggle Jacob, full of anguish, kept inquiring the other's name. In those ancient times a traveler who uttered his name gave away his essential being. Homeric heroes immediately tell us their names.

And these names were not said; they were sung in a surge of enthusiasm and adoration. And I am most certain, reader, that the hymn which most deeply penetrated your heart was that which carried your name, your baptismal name, pure and bare, expressed with a sigh in semi-darkness. That is the crown of lyrical poetry. The litany is perhaps the most exquisite poetic form that a lyrical explosion can offer: a name repeated as in a rosary and each time joined to lively epithets which enhance it. And among these we find the sacred epithet.

In Homeric poems the sacred epithets shine forth: each hero has his own. Achilles is he of the fast feet; Hector, the plume shaker. And in all times and places when someone finds the sacred epithet which poetically fits a man, everyone adopts it and repeats it. And what is true of men is also true of animals, things and ideas. The sly fox, the faithful dog, the noble horse, the patient donkey, the slow ox, the churlish goat, the mild sheep, the timid hare . . . and Providence's intentions, can they be anything but inscrutable?

Singing, then, a name, enhancing it with a sacred epithet is the reflective exaltation of lyric poetry; and the irreflective exaltation, the supreme, is singing the name by itself, bare, without epithet; it is repeating it again and again, as if submerging one's soul in its ideal content. "I am not surprised," I told my friend, "to see that those enumerations affect you in a strange manner, and I confess to you that they may not possess anything poetical at all. Yet, they seem stranger to those of us who, by means of dead words, have reduced lyric poetry to something oratorical, a sort of rhymed eloquence. Remember besides," I added, "that a word has not attained its splendor and purity until it has acquired rhythm and until it has become joined to others through its own cadence: it is like wheat which is not clean and ready for the mill until it has been purified by winnowing on the threshing floor."

"Now I remember," said my friend inserting a whimsical note, "I remember a Yankee joke which goes like this: when Adam was naming the animals and he approached the horse, Eve told her husband, 'This thing that is coming here looks like a horse; so let's call him horse.'"

"The joke is not bad," I said, "but it happens that when Adam named the country-animals and the birds, woman had not yet been created, according to Genesis. Therefore one must conclude that man felt the need of talking even when he was alone, that is to say, talking to himself, which is the same as singing, so that his act of naming the creatures was an act of lyrical purity, perfectly unselfish. He invented the names to enjoy them in ecstasy. But once he created the names and sang them he needed a fellow creature to whom he could communicate these names; after the naming-hymn had resulted from the exuberance of his enthusiasm, he felt the need of an audience, but, according to the text, Adam did not find help around him. And immediately after this, the Biblical narration tells us of the creation of woman, growing her out of a rib of the first man, as though man had felt the need for a companion as a result of having mastered the animals by giving them a name. Man was in need of someone to talk to, and so God made a woman for him. And as soon as the woman appears before him, after he said, 'This is bone of my bone and flesh of my flesh,' the first thing that he does is to give her a name, saying: 'this will be called a woman, because out of man she was created.' But the Spanish *varona* did not prevail. The majority of cultured peoples have a name for woman which comes from a different root and which seems to make out of man and woman two different species."

"Except English," said my friend.

"And some other languages," I added.

And gathering up Walt Whitman's *Leaves of Grass* we left behind the splendor of the city melting into the twilight.

"El canto adánico," in *El espejo de la muerte* (Madrid: Companía Iberoamericana de Publicaciones, 1930). Translated by Fernando Alegría.

5. LEÓN FELIPE

"Habla el Prologo"

¿Es inoportuno, amigos y poetas americanos y españoles, que yo os congregue
    aquí ahora y os traiga conmigo al viejo comarada de Long Island?
No. Ésta es la hora mejor.
Ahora . . .
cuando avanza el trueno para borrar con trilita la palabra libertad, de todos
    los rincones de la tierra,
cuando el hombre ha perdido su airón y su bandera
y todos somos reses marcadas entre vallados y alambradas,
quiero yo presentaros a este poeta de cabaña
sin puerta frente al camino abierto,
a este poeta de halo, de cayada y de mochila;
ahora . . .
cuando reculan frente al odio el amor y la fe
quiero yo presentaros con verbo castellano, y en mi vieja manera de decir,
a este poeta del amor, de la fe y de la rebeldía.
Aquí está. ¡Miradlo!

Se llama Walt.
Así lo nombran
el viento,
los pájaros
y las corrientes de los grandes ríos de su pueblo.
Walt es el diminutivo de Walter (Gualterio en castellano).
Más bien es la poda del patronímico hasta el monosílabo simple,
    onomatopéyico y gutural: Walt.

4
CANTARÁ SU CANCIÓN Y SE IRÁ

No tiene otro título ni rótulo a la puerta.
No es doctor,
ni reverendo
ni maese . . .
No es misionero tampoco.
No viene a repartir catecismos ni reglamentos,
ni a colgarle a nadie una cruz en la solapa.
Ni a juzgar:
ni a premiar
ni a castigar.
Viene sencillamente a cantar una canción.

Cantará su canción y se irá.
Mañana, de madrugada, se irá.
Cuando os desperetéis vosotros, ya con el sol en el cielo, no encontraréis más
    que el recuerdo encendido de su voz.
Pero esta noche será vuestro huésped.
Abridle la puerta,
los brazos,
los oídos
y el corazón de par en par.
Porque es vuestra canción la que vais a escuchar.

"The Prologue Speaks"

Is it inopportune, friends and poets, American or Spanish, that I gather you
    here today and bring to you with me the old comrade from Long Island?
No. This is the best hour.
Now . . .
when the thunder advances to erase with tritium the word freedom from all
    the corners of the earth,
when man has lost his plume and his banner,

and all of us are branded cattle within palings and wire fences,
I want to present to you this poet with a cabin
without door facing the open road,
this poet with a halo, with a cane, and a knapsack;
now . . .
when love and faith are yielding to hatred
I want to present to you in my Castilian words, in my old manner of speaking,
this poet of love, of faith, and rebellion.
Here he is. Behold him!
His name is Walt.
Thus he is called
by the wind,
the birds,
and the currents of the great rivers of his people.
Walt is the diminutive of Walter (Gualterio in Spanish).
It is rather the pruning of the patronymic to the monosyllable, simple,
    onomatopoeic and guttural: Walt.

4

HE SHALL SING HIS SONG AND THEN LEAVE

He has no other title or inscription at his door.
He is not a Doctor,
nor a Reverend,
nor a Master . . .
Neither is he a Missionary.
He does not come to deliver catechisms or laws,
nor to hang a cross on anybody's breast.
Nor to judge
to reward,
or to punish.
He simply comes to sing a song.

He shall sing his song and then leave.
Tomorrow, at dawn, he shall leave.
When you shall awaken, with the sun already up in the sky, you shall find
    nothing but the burning memory of his voice.
But tonight he shall be your guest.
Open your door,
your arms,
your ears,
and your heart fully wide.
For the song you shall hear is your song.

From the verse prologue in *Walt Whitman: Canto a mí mismo* (Buenos Aires: Losada,
1941). Translated by Didier Tisdel Jaén. Reprinted by permission of the translator.

León Felipe [117]

6. PABLO NERUDA

"Oda a Walt Whitman"

Yo no recuerdo
a qué edad,
ni dónde,
si en el gran Sur mojado
o en la costa
temible, bajo el breve
grito de las gaviotas,
toqué una mano y era
la mano de Walt Whitman:
pisé la tierra
con los pies desnudos,
anduve sobre el pasto,
sobre el firme rocío
de Walt Whitman.

Durante
mi juventud
toda
me acompañó esa mano,
ese rocío,
su firmeza de pino patriarca, su extensión de pradera,
y su misión de paz circulatoria.

Sin
desdeñar
los dones
de la tierra,
la copiosa
curva del capitel,
ni la inicial
purpúrea
de la sabiduría,
tú
me enseñaste
a ser americano,
levantaste
mis ojos
a los libros,
hacia

el tesoro
de los cereales:
ancho,
en la claridad
de las llanuras,
me hiciste ver
el alto
monte
tutelar. Del eco
subterráneo,
para mí
recogiste
todo,
todo lo que nacía
cosechaste
galopando en la alfalfa,
cortando para mí las amapolas,
visitando
los ríos,
acudiendo en la tarde
a las cocinas.

Pero no sólo
tierra
sacó a la luz
tu pala:
desenterraste
al hombre,
y el
esclavo
humillado
contigo, balanceando
la negra dignidad de su estatura,
caminó conquistando
la alegría.

Al fogonero,
abajo,
en la caldera,
mandaste
un canastito
de frutillas,
a todas las esquinas de tu pueblo
un verso

tuyo llegó de visita
y era como un trozo
de cuerpo limpio
el verso que llegaba,
como
tu propia barba pescadora
o el solemne camino de tus piernas de acacia.

Pasó entre los soldados
tu silueta
de bardo, de enfermero,
de cuidador nocturno
que conoce
el sonido
de la respiración en la agonía
y espera con la aurora
el silencioso
regreso
de la vida.

Buen panadero!
Primo hermano mayor
de mis raíces,
cúpula
de araucaria,
hace
ya
cien
años
que sobre el pasto tuyo
y sus germinaciones,
el viento
pasa
sin gastar tus ojos.

Nuevos
y crueles años en tu patria:
persecusiones,
lágrimas,
prisiones,
armas envenenadas
y guerras iracundas,
no han aplastado
la hierba de tu libro,
el manantial vital

de su frescura.
Y, ay!
los
que asesinaron
a Lincoln
ahora
se acuestan en su cama,
derribaron
su sitial
de olorosa madera
y erigieron un trono
por desventura y sangre
salpicado.

Pero
canta en
las estaciones
suburbanas
tu voz,
en
los
desembarcaderos
vespertinos
chapotea
como
aqua oscura
tu palabra,
tu pueblo
blanco
y negro,
pueblo
de pobres,
pueblo simple
como
todos
los pueblos,
no olvida
tu campana:
se congrega cantando
bajo
la magnitud
de tu espaciosa vida:
entre los pueblos con tu amor camina
acariciando

el desarrollo puro
de la fraternidad sobre la tierra.

"Ode to Walt Whitman"

I do not remember
at what age
nor where:
in the great damp South
or on the fearsome
coast, beneath the brief
cry of the seagulls,
I touched a hand and it was
the hand of Walt Whitman.
I trod the ground
with bare feet,
I walked on the grass,
on the firm dew
of Walt Whitman.

During
my entire
youth
I had the company of that hand,
that dew,
its firmness of patriarchal pine, its prairie-like expanse,
and its mission of circulatory peace.

Not
disdaining
the gifts
of the earth,
nor the copious
curving of the column's capital,
nor the purple
initial
of wisdom,
you taught me
to be an American,
you raised
my eyes
to books,
towards

the treasure
of the grains:
broad,
in the clarity
of the plains,
you made me see
the high
tutelary
mountain. From subterranean
echoes,
you gathered
for me
everything;
everything that came forth
was harvested by you,
galloping in the alfalfa,
picking poppies for me,
visiting
the rivers,
coming into the kitchens
in the afternoon.

But not only
soil
was brought to light
by your spade:
you unearthed
man,
and the
slave
who was humiliated
with you, balancing
the black dignity of his stature,
walked on, conquering
happiness.

To the fireman
below,
in the stoke-hole,
you sent
a little basket
of strawberries.
To every corner of your town
a verse

of yours arrived for a visit,
and it was like a piece
of clean body,
the verse that arrived,
like
your own fisherman beard
or the solemn tread of your acacia legs.

Your silhouette
passed among the soldiers:
the poet, the wound-dresser,
the night attendant
who knows
the sound
of breathing in mortal agony
and awaits with the dawn
the silent
return
of life.

Good baker!
Elder first cousin
of my roots,
araucaria's
cupola,
it is
now
a hundred
years
that over your grass
and its germinations,
the wind
passes
without wearing out your eyes.

New
and cruel years in your Fatherland:
persecutions,
tears,
prisons,
poisoned weapons
and wrathful wars
have not crushed
the grass of your book;
the vital fountainhead

of its freshness.
And, alas!
those
who murdered
Lincoln
now
lie in his bed.
They felled
his seat of honor
made of fragrant wood,
and raised a throne
spattered
with misfortune and blood.

But
your voice
sings
in the suburban
stations,
in
the
vespertine
wharfs,
your word
splashes
like
dark water.
Your people,
white
and black,
poor
people,
simple people
like
all
people
do not forget
your bell:
They congregate singing
beneath
the magnitude
of your spacious life.
They walk among the peoples with your love
caressing

the pure development
of brotherhood on earth.

Odas elementales (Buenos Aires: Editorial Losada, 1954). Translated by Didier Tisdel Jaén.
Reprinted by permission of the translator.

7. JORGE LUIS BORGES

"Camden, 1892"

El olor del café y de los periódicos.
El domingo y su tedio. La mañana
Y en la entrevista página esa vana
Publicación de versos alegóricos
De una colega feliz. El hombre viejo
Está postrado y blanco en su decente
Habitación de pobre. Ociosamente
Mira su cara en el cansado espejo.
Piensa, ya sin asombro, que esa cara
Es él. La distraída mano toca
La turbia barba y la saqueada boca.
No está lejos el fin. Su voz declara:
Casi no soy, pero mis versos ritman
La vida y su esplendor. Yo fui Walt Whitman.

The smell of coffee and the daily *Times.*
The Sunday morning tedium, once again,
And on the page, unclearly seen, that vain
Publication of allegoric rhymes
By a happy colleague. On his death-bed,
In his decent though humble bedroom,
The man lies white and wasted. With boredom,
He views the tired reflection of his head.
He thinks, no longer amazed, that this face
Is he, and brings his distrait fingertips
To touch his tarnished beard and ravaged lips.
The end is near, and he states his case:
I hardly am, but my verse is rhythmal
To the splendid life. I was Walt Whitman.

Obra poetica (Buenos Aires: Emece, 1966). Translated by Didier Tisdel Jaén. Reprinted by
permission of the translator.

8. JORGE GUILLÉN

My Relationship with Whitman

My dear friend, you ask me to write, as a reader and an author, a few words about my relationship with Walt Whitman. Well, I first took notice of the great poet — I still consider him so — in the twenties, and I read him with interest a little later at Sevilla in the thirties in Léon Bazalgette's translation published by the *Mercure de France* (1922 is the date of my edition). My reading of it — which I pursued in English — was posterior to the impulse which made me write *Cántico*, without any bookish influence — God knows, as we say in Spanish — and as the mere expression of a temperament.

Whitman dazzled me and confirmed my instinctive tendency to look for — or better, to feel for — an immediate contact with life without looking for it. It is strange that man's attachment to life should not be accompanied by a clearer consciousness: the consciousness of the ears which hear, of the eyes which see, of the lungs which breathe. Life and poetry are like a deep breathing. Nothing made me *feel* it so much — from a literary point of view — as Whitman's verse, whose form did not suit my purpose as a poet and whose historical birth took place far away in the United States at a time when it was beginning to grow. But I was attracted by the *élan*, by the lambent light of dawn, by physical health as a potent factor, and the loving embrace; by that manly encounter with a beyond which is this earthly herebelow. And all this without the interference of any theory.

Optimism and pessimism are opinions — nothing more. And a poem does not record opinions, but something which is really experienced by the whole being. Whitman revelled in wonder — like the philosopher according to Socrates. This Spanish reader was — and is — in spite of so many vicissitudes — an admirer. Of what? Of the act of breathing. Like Whitman. For fifty years I have not said — in the foreground of my poems — anything else.

Roger Asselineau and William White, eds., *Walt Whitman in Europe Today* (Detroit: Wayne State University Press, 1972). Translated by Roger Asselineau, from a letter written to the translator by Guillén on April 11, 1971.

MARIA CLARA BONETTI PARO

Whitman in Brazil

In 1889, on the occasion of a republican government replacing a monarchy in Brazil, Walt Whitman sent "a Christmas Greeting" to the South American country, welcoming his "Brazilian brother" into democracy (LG, 548). But not until the twentieth century did the new and rebellious perfume of *Leaves of Grass* reach Brazil, carried by symbolism and the avant-garde movements, mainly futurism and unanimism, which were flourishing in Europe during the first quarter of the century.

Literature in Brazil at the turn of the century was ruled by neo-Parnassians, neo-naturalists, and neo-symbolists, who emphasized rigid obedience to metric rules and Portuguese grammar. Beyond this there flourished an impersonal concept of art for art's sake that had grown artificial and outdated amidst a nationalistic climate that strengthened civic pride and the desire to find a personal voice for Brazilian literature. Even though good poetry had been written, Parnassianism, the dominant school, was incapable of coping with the increasing social, political, and cultural changes of the first decades of the new century that required new forms of expression. "To make rhymes in Brazil is still the best way not to be a poet," wrote poet Carlos Drummond de Andrade (1902–1989) in 1923 (de Andrade, 32). Striving to change the situation, a new generation of writers had to wage long, hard battles that led, eventually, to poetic renovation and to the literary movement known as modernism (1922–1945).

The principal arena in this artistic struggle was the Municipal Theater in São Paulo, where the Modern Art Week Exhibition (the Brazilian equivalent to the American Armory Show) was staged in February 1922. The date had been deliberately chosen to make the overthrow of the archaic aesthetics coincide with the centennial celebration of Brazil's political independence. The period from 1922 to 1930 is correctly called "heroic" because both sides, the "traditionalists" (*passadistas*) and the "futurists" (as the modernists were known at that time), assumed militant and often extreme positions. Consider the following lines by writer and critic Sergio Milliet (1898–1966) regarding the position of those who wanted renovation: "We had to break everything, destroy, kill, bury, cremate. That is what we did from about 1921 to 1932" (Milliet, 240–241). Although *Leaves of Grass* was not well known at that time, Whitman's reputation was strong enough for him to be enlisted in the ranks of Brazilian modernism. Amazingly enough, in the first phase of Brazilian modernism, Whitman came to be respected by both of the opposing groups.

In the early 1920s Whitmanism had reached its greatest peak in France and remained influential throughout the decade (Allen, 287). It is no surprise that there was also a Brazilian "whitmanismo," for in the first decades of the century Brazil was culturally linked to France. Whitman's presence in French literature was then so strong that he was even included in a collection of contemporary French poetry entitled *L'Anthologie de L'Effort*, published in 1912 by Jean-Richard Bloch (Erkkila, 171).

Before the 1920s, Whitman was scarcely mentioned in Brazilian periodicals, and when he was, his name was frequently paired with French and Belgian symbolists. *Leaves of Grass* crossed the Brazilian border with a symbolist literary passport. Pointing out the importance of Belgian symbolism for the study of that movement in Brazil, critic Andrade Murici said that "the powerful Verhaeren prepared the road for a late but numerous Whitmanian seaquake" (Murici, 1: 44). In the 1920s in Brazil, Whitman's spirit, or his gospel, was easily found. He was the welcome spokesman of the modern world, the apostle of renovation in form and content, and one of the poets who could nourish what John Barth called a "literature of replenishment" after the exhaustion of the old aesthetic rules and principles.

References to the singer of the New World became increasingly more frequent in the debates that followed the Week of Modern Art. In an article written in 1934, the essayist Sebastião Sampaio expressed regret about the delay of reciprocal cultural exchange between Brazil and the United States and added that "Whitman came so late that it was in fact Modernism that made his homage to Brooklyn Bridge [*ponte de Brooklyn*] known to the public" (Sampaio, 22). Due to Whitman's literary reputation and "contemporaneity," he was used by the *passadistas* as a shield against the attacks of those who accused them of being behind the times and by the futurists, for whom he was a spear, to encourage Brazilian literature to venture "in paths untrodden" (LG, 112).

Speaking for the *passadista* group, Angelo Guido, in a 1923 article entitled "Futurism," gave his own definition of this avant-garde movement and added that several *passadistas* had done exactly the same (Guido, 376–379). Whitman is included among the *passadistas*. On behalf of the futurists, Murilo Araújo, in the article "Futurismo e Estética Intencional," declared that he took pride in being called a futurist because "Verhaeren, the great, and Walt Whitman, the two best poets in the world, are called futurists by critics nowadays" (Araújo, 314–316).

In those days in Brazil, futurism was very often used in a broad sense. It was an antonym of traditional (*passadista*) and had almost nothing to do with the Italian movement founded in 1909 by Filippo Marinetti (1876–1944). Nevertheless, futurism helped spread Whitman's work when Marinetti mentioned him among six other writers as a forerunner of his aesthetics. Despite the differences between Whitman and Marinetti, in some critical appreciations they were nevertheless paired as literary innovators.

For the embattled modernists who were trying to break down the rigid adherence to metric rules, Whitman offered a model of free verse. At a time when the modernists were trying to turn away from the poetic emphasis on the past, with its cultural allusions to Greek gods and mythology, Whitman was looked upon as the poet of the present and the singer of the common people and the modern world. And when, with nationalistic pride and suffering from an "anxiety of influence," they were trying to do without European models, Whitman was looked upon as a brother and as an escape from European influence. He was someone who, like Poe, had inverted the direction of influence between the Old and the New World, named "notre poete" by Valery Larbaud (Erkkila, 179).

It is not difficult to find extremely appreciative references to Whitman's work in publications of the 1920s. In the article "A literatura em 1920" ("Literature in 1920"), Alceu Amoroso Lima expressed a desire for a Brazilian Whitman: "The world of action can produce a Whitman. We have not had him yet, and our poetry continues to be a place secluded from everyday reality" (Lima, 12). In 1923 critic Tasso da Silveira (1895–1968) expressed the same wish: "I say 'our Whitman' and not just 'our great poet,' because it is a Whitman we long for; it is for a passionate singer who, in gigantic symphonies, would celebrate the new world that we are, the dawning of a new race we represent, the vastness of the place we have been given on the planet, and the multiform uproar of desire and dream which comes from our complex ethnic identity" (Silveira 1923, 151).

Unlike in France, where literary citizenship was conferred on the American poet, in Brazil Whitman was often regarded either as the singer of the New World (encompassing, therefore, the three Americas) or as a North American who could fertilize Brazilian or tropical leaves of grass.

Whitman's idealistic vision of America as a huge Bakhtinean marketplace where a poet-prophet, with cosmic consciousness, could transform everybody into comrades and equals in a "new city of Friends" was especially attractive to the Carioca spiritualist group of the symbolist magazine *Festa*, which published twelve issues in 1927 and 1928. The influence of Jules Romain's unanimism (1905–1914) and more specifically of Emile Verhaeren's poetry is also evident in this utopian vision, and many times Whitman and Verhaeren are mentioned together.

Among the members of *Festa*, Tasso da Silveira is the poet who most clearly embraces Whitman's prophetic gospel. He translated into Portuguese the first poem from *Leaves of Grass* to appear in Brazil: in the fourth issue of *Terra do Sol* (*Land of the Sun*) a Portuguese translation of "Poets to Come" ("Poetas que virão") was published anonymously (Silveira 1924, 35), and later Silveira acknowledged the translation as his. In the same issue, in "Notas e Comentátios," the same poem was presented in three other languages: in French, translated by Léon Bazalgette; in Italian, by Luigi Gamberale; and, in Spanish, by Armando Vasseur. The fact that the original English version was not given is an indication that many Brazilian writers read Whitman's poems in translation before reading them in the original version.

Whitman's impact on *Festa* is unquestionable. He was the only foreign poet represented in the first issue—a translation of Section 3 of "Salut au Monde!" (Silveira 1927, 12). In the fifth issue (February 1928), Sections 18, 21, and 24 of "Song of Myself" were published in anonymous translations again (no doubt also by Silveira) (Silveira 1928).

It is not difficult to see which topic of Whitman's "ensemble" was most cherished by the spiritualist members of *Festa* and by Silveira: the idyllic and optimistic vision of the natural, human, and social world. As for form, Silveira's free verse, which he began writing in 1926, corresponds more closely to the model given by Verhaeren, whose importance in his work and life he acknowledged several times. Although dressed up in Christian array, Whitman's diction is clearly perceived in most of Silveira's poems, from *Alegorias do Homon Novo* (*Allegories of the New Man*) (1926) to *Cantos do Campo de Batalha* (*Battlefield Songs*) (1945), and the latter book contains an overt allusion to Whitman in the poem entitled "Palavras a Whitman" ("Words to Whitman") (Silveira 1962, 204–206). In direct opposition to the misreading of Whitman as singer of all the Americas, Silveira—as an ephebe who tries to "complete" his "truncated precursor"—abounds in "tesserae" (to use Harold Bloom's terminology [Bloom, 49–73]). In his poetic tribute, Silveira calls Whitman the "wonderful incomplete" because, although he exalted the whole world, when he sang America he referred to only one half of the continent:

A outra metade que não advinhaste, não previste,
no fundidouro dos destinos misteriosos
se condensava
e vai surgindo agora
como algum virgem orbe que faltasse
ao equilibrio das constelções . . .

E assim, Poeta-Profeta,
ao lado de teu canto,

erque-se, por integrar-te, um canto novo:
— o canto da alma inquieta
do meu povo! (Silveira 1962, 204)

The other half that you didn't foretell or foresee
was condensing itself
in the melting pot of an unknown destiny
and is becoming visible
as a virgin orb that was missing in the balance of the constellations . . .

And so, Poet-Prophet
Beside your song,
Rising to join it, a new chant:
— the chant of the anxious soul of my people.

In spite of various readings or misreadings of *Leaves of Grass*, what is certain is that Whitman was part of the general literary consciousness in those days in Brazil. Even when references were made to the fact that Whitman was not well known, the tone was always one of regret.

The same high standards by which Whitman was judged in *Festa* are used by the so-called dynamic traditionalists, who gathered around writer and diplomat Graça Aranha (1868–1931). Among the members of that group, Ronald de Carvalho, one of Aranha's favorite disciples, unquestionably became the most Whitmanian writer with *Toda a América* (*All the Americas*), published in 1926. There is no doubt that Carvalho had Whitman in mind when he wrote *Toda a América*. In the general conception of the book, as well as in many of the poems, he echoed the American poet, or "completed" him, in a manner similar to what had been done by Tasso da Silveira. Whitman's "Americanism" was enlarged to include the three Americas. Carvalho's interest in the continent as a whole was not an isolated attitude but a reflection of Brazil's general awakening to a feeling of camaraderie toward its neighboring nations and an increasing interest in strengthening social and cultural ties with them. Brazilian intellectuals wanted to replace — or at least add to — their centuries of gazing across the Atlantic with an actual journey into the backlands of their own country and of the other American countries. They longed for an American discovery of America.

As soon as *Toda a América* was published, many writers would call attention to the similarities between it and *Leaves of Grass*. Although the "Americanisms" in *Leaves of Grass* and in *Toda a América* are different, Whitman's impress is clearly present in several poems. In the poem "Brasil," for example, Carvalho echoes Whitman directly in idea and image and uses a mélange of passages from "Salut au Monde!" and "I Hear America Singing." He delights in cataloging what he hears by transporting his poetic self to different places in the country. Carvalho includes another poem that is connected to "Salut au Monde!," or more precisely to Section 4 of this poem, where Whitman describes what he sees. In "Entre Buenos Aires e

Mendoza," Carvalho again makes use of the Whitmanian catalog and begins his lines with the repetition of "Eu vejo" ("I see").

There is in *Toda a América* another signal of indebtedness to *Leaves of Grass*. Both books have a poem entitled "Broadway." The urban crowd is their common theme, but whereas Whitman regards the passersby with empathy and transcendental interest and inquires into their inner lives, Carvalho focuses on their external attitudes at the same time that he reveals a personal and impressionistic attitude toward them. The street which is taken as a lesson by Whitman remains unlearned in Carvalho's "Broadway."

As far as form is concerned, the two poets are most different, ironically, at precisely the moment when they seem most similar. Although Carvalho uses free verse in a manner that is reminiscent of Whitman, he frequently breaks up his lines, forming several verses; Whitman avoided such enjambment. By breaking up Whitman's end-stopped lines or thought rhythm, Carvalho also moves away from another key feature of Whitman's technique—the caesura. In its formal restraint, Carvalho's free verse is sometimes closer to Apollinaire's model. Nevertheless, when he sets his expansive lines with a relatively fixed initial structure, his verse resembles Whitman's. Just like Whitman's twenty-one-line delay of the main verb in "Out of the Cradle Endlessly Rocking," Carvalho withholds the verb in the first stanza of "Advertência" ("Warning") and writes a poem that clearly sounds Whitmanian:

Europeu!
Nos tabuleiros de xadrez da tua aldeia,
na tua casa de madeira, pequenina, coberta de hera,
na tua casa de pinhões e beirais, vigiada por filas de cercas paralelas, com
    trepadeiras moles balançando e florindo;
na tua sala de jantar, junto do fogão de azulejos, cheirando a resina de
    pinheiros e faia,
na tua sala de jantar, em que os teus avós leram a Bíblia e discutiram casa-
    mentos, colheitas e enterros,
entre as tuas arcas bojudas e pretas, com lãs felpudas e linhos encardidos,
    colares, gravuras papéis graves e moedas roubadas ao inútil maravilhoso;
diante do teu riacho, mais antigo que as Cruzadas, desse teu riacho serviçal,
    que engorda trutas e carpas;
Europeu!
Em frente da tua paisagem, dessa tua paisagem com estradas, quintalejos,
    campanários e burgos, que cabe toda na bola de vidro do teu jardim;
diante dessas tuas árvores que conheces pelo nome — o carvalho do açude, o
    choupo do ferreiro, a tília da ponte — que conheces pelo nome como os
    teus cães, os teus jumentos e as tuas vacas;
Europeu! filho da obediência, da economia e do bom-senso, tu não saves o
    que é ser Americano! (Carvalho, 9–11)

European!

In the chess boards of your village,

in your small, wooden house overgrown with ivy,

in your house with mallow and eaves, guarded by rows of parallel hedges with
    slowly climbing trees that swing and bloom;

in your dining room, close to the tiled stove that smells of pine resin and
    white poplar,

in your dining room, where your grandparents read the Bible and discussed
    weddings, harvests, and burials,

among your black and bulgy chests, full of fluffy wool and stained linen,
    necklaces, engravings, somber sheets of paper and coins stolen from
    useless wonders;

in front of the brook, more venerable than the Cruzadas of your providential
    brook where trouts and carps are fed;

European!

In front of your landscape, your landscape with roads, small backyards,
    steeples and boroughs that fits entirely in the glass ball of your garden;

in front of your trees that you know by the name — the oak by the dam, the
    poplar of the blacksmith, the linden by the bridge — that you know by the
    name just like you know your dogs, your donkey and your cows;

European! child of obedience, economy and common sense, you do not know
    what it is to be an American!

The striking parallels between both poets indicate that Carvalho had Whitman very much in mind when he wrote *Toda a América*. Although Carvalho claimed to be a poet integrated with his land, he never managed to get rid of European manners and taste, and he never became the poet he believed was necessary for America. The times when Carvalho used Whitman's gospel and form were precisely when he strayed from his model. He had not heard Whitman's advice in "Song of Myself" that "he most honors my style who learns under it to destroy the teacher" (LG, 84), and he had not paid attention to Whitman's warning in "By Blue Ontario's Shore" that "rhymes and rhymers, pass away, poems distill'd from poems pass away" (LG, 350).

It was in São Paulo that Whitman's "yawp" was more clearly heard. Mário de Andrade (1893–1945), the most prominent figure in the first phase of the Brazilian modernist movement, was a careful reader of *Leaves of Grass* and a writer who showed interest in Whitman's poetry all his life. The marginal annotations he wrote on his volume of the centennial edition of *Leaves of Grass* reveal his careful reading of Whitman's work. Besides having Whitman's *Complete Prose Works* (1920), he had Léon Bazalgette's translation, *Feuilles d'Herbe* (1922), as well as the two other books the French critic wrote on Whitman: *Le poèm-évangile de Walt Whitman* (*The Poem-Gospel of Walt Whitman*) (1921) and *Walt Whitman: l'homme et son oeuvre* (*Walt Whitman: The Man and His Work*) (1908). He also had two German translations (by Karl Federn [1904] and by Gustav Landauer [1921]) and a

Portuguese translation by Agostinho Veloso da Silva (1943). In a letter to poet Carlos Drummond de Andrade, dated July 23, 1944, Andrade comments that he planned to read Whitman again to see if he might find some suggestions for *Lira Paulistana*, a book he wrote in the year prior to his death (Andrade 1988, 210).

Andrade's interest in Whitman is evident from the beginning of his career. Whitman is mentioned in both of the most important texts in which Andrade, who was considered the "pope of the Modernist Creed," explains his own aesthetic principles and the movement's aims. The first text is the preface to his book of poems *Paulicéia Desvairada* (*Hallucinated City*), published in 1922, and the second is the essay "A Escrava que não é Isaura" ("The Slave That Is Not Isaura"), published in 1925 (Andrade 1972, 195–300). There is only a single reference to Whitman in the preface (which he ironically calls "Prefácio interessantíssimo" ["The most interesting preface"]), suggesting that the reader should know the American poet, but Andrade mentions him four times in *A Escrava*. He calls attention to the effect of simultanity, one of the characteristics of modernist poetry that is already present in *Leaves of Grass* (266–267). He also praises Whitman's thematic freedom and quotes "Starting from Paumanok": "I will make the poems of materials, for I think they are to be the most spiritual poems!" (217). Andrade could have mentioned several artists of the avant-garde movements who defended thematic freedom, but he preferred Whitman because of the spiritual basis of his "materials." Andrade also cherished Whitman's social concern and declared in his literary essay "O Movimento Modernista" that all his work represented a commitment to his time and land (Andrade 1974, 252). Although one can hear echoes of Whitman's work in various poems written by Andrade, he did not imitate the North American poet. To employ T. S. Eliot's terms, Andrade did not "borrow" from Whitman but "stole" whatever he needed, making it his own.

The same thing is true about another great artist, Jorge de Lima (1895–1953), who actually mentions the American bard in some poems, such as "A Minha América," published in *Poemas* (1927) and "Democracia," published in *Poemas Negros* (1947). The dates of these two books illuminate Whitman's literary reception in Brazil. In the 1920s critical and creative responses to his work were frequently found in books and literary periodicals. The same is not true in the 1930s. Political and social changes altered the focus of interest from poetry to prose and from aesthetics to ideology. Nevertheless, a second wave of Whitman enthusiasm began again in the 1940s when his "voice" was heard in Portuguese translations and books and when essays about the poet were published.

Substantial translations of Whitman came late in Brazil. Mário D. Ferreira Santos published *Saudação ao Mundo e outros poemas* (*Salut au Monde and Other Poems*) in 1944, and then in 1946 Oswaldino Marques, a distinguished poet in his own right (who in the same year published his *Poemas quase dissolutos*), published his translation of a few of the shorter poems of *Leaves of Grass, Cantos de Walt Whitman*. Marques's rendering was so fine that some critics said they had the impression of reading the original. Marques's own poetry was inspired by Whitman, especially the social message, but his form definitely remained his own. Another poet, Geir Campos, author of *Rosas dos Rumos*, published a brief selection of translations, *Folhas de Relva* (*Leaves of Grass*), in 1964, and then in 1983 brought out *Folhas das Folhas de Relva* (*Leaves from Leaves of Grass*). This popular book contained a larger selection of Whitman's poems, but only fragments of the longer poems were included. Its original three thousand copies sold so quickly that it was reprinted a second time in the same year and was reissued again in 1984, 1989, and 1990. Paulo Leminski's introduction to Campos's translation tended to radicalize Whitman, presenting him as the poet of the American Revolution and the first beatnik, the forerunner of Mayakowski, Rimbaud, and Marinetti, and a bold pioneer of the same kin as Jack London, Jack Kerouac, Norman Mailer, and Malraux.

Whitman's revolutionary message was also what appealed to Gilberto Freire. In his *O Camarada Whitman*, published in 1948 (see selection 1), he saw Whitman above all as the champion of democracy, standing against not only the feudalism of Europe but also the feudal slaveholding system of the U.S. South as well as the industrial slavery of the North. He praised Whitman's sense of universal comradeship "in a manner at once Franciscan and Hellenic," without any of the "ethnocentric Hebraism that spread from the Hebrews to the Anglo-Saxon Protestants known as Puritans." He regarded the American poet as closer to such Spaniards as San Juan de la Cruz, Cervantes, and Ramon Llull than to his own compatriots. He even claimed that some of Whitman's lines in *Leaves* seemed themselves to have been translated from Spanish or Portuguese. In Freire's eyes, Whitman's Americanism was pan-human, not pan-American, and Whitman was thus on the side of the Argentinean statesman who proposed the generous concept of "America for humanity" rather than on the side of Monroe, who upheld the doctrine of "America for the Americans."

Leaves of Grass continues to attract Whitman's "Brazilian brothers," and books and articles on his work have appeared with some regularity over the past decades—most notably, perhaps, Irineu Monteiro's *Walt Whitman: Profeta da América* in 1984. In spite of the interest in Whitman's work shown by the Brazilian reading public, *Leaves of Grass* ("the permanent revelation," as poet Paulo Leminski calls it [Leminski, 7]) continues to await a complete Portuguese translation.

WORKS CITED

Allen, Gay Wilson. *The New Walt Whitman Handbook*. New York: New York University Press, 1975.

Andrade, Carlos Drummond de. "Na curva do caminho." *Ilustração Brasileira* 38 (October 1923): 32.

Andrade, Mário de. *Obra imatura*. 2d ed. São Paulo: Martins; Brasília: INL, 1972.

———. *Aspectos da literatura brasileira*. 5th ed. São Paulo: Martins, 1974.

———. *A Lição do Amigo: Cartas de Mário de Andrade a Carlos Drummond de Andrade*. 2d ed. Rio de Janeiro: Record, 1988.

Araújo, Murilo. "Futurismo e Estética Intencional." *O Mundo Literário* (Rio de Janeiro) 3 (July 1922): 314–316.

Bloom, Harold. *The Anxiety of Influence: A Theory of Poetry.* New York: Oxford University Press, 1975.

Carvalho, Ronald de. *Toda a América* (com a versão espanhola de Francisco Villaespesa). Rio de Janeiro: Hispano-Brasilena, 1935.

Erkkila, Betsy. *Walt Whitman among the French.* Princeton: Princeton University Press, 1980.

Guido, Angelo. "Futurism." *Revista do Brasil* (São Paulo) 88 (April 1923): 376–379.

Leminski, Paulo. Preface to *Folhas das Folhas de Relva,* trans. Geir Campos. São Paulo: Brasiliense, 1990.

Lima, Alceu Amoroso. "A literatura em 1920." *Revista do Brasil* [São Paulo] 64 (April 1921): 3–15.

Milliet, Sergio. "O meu depoimento." In Edgard Cavalheiro, ed., *Testamento de uma geração: 26 figuras da intelectualidade brasileira prestam o seu depoimento.* Porto Alegre: Globe, 1944.

Murici, Andrade. *Panorama do Movimento Simbolista Brasileiro.* Vol. 1. Rio de Janeiro: Departamento de Imprensa Nacional, 1952.

Sampaio, Sebastião. "Brasil-Estados Unidos: duas nações irmãs." *Revista da Academia Brasileira de Letras* 149 (May 1934): 5–29.

Silveira, Tasso da. "O poeta da profunda tristeza." *O Mundo Literário* (Rio de Janeiro) 20 (December 1923): 131–152.

———. "Poetas que virão." *Terra do Sol* (Rio de Janeiro) 4 (April 1924): 35.

———. "Saudação ao Mundo." *Festa* (Rio de Janeiro) 1 (October 1927): 12.

———. "Traduçoes Anônimas." *Festa* (Rio de Janeiro) 5 (February 1928).

———. "Palavras a Whitman." In *Puro Canto-Poemas Completos.* Rio Janeiro: GRD, 1962, 204–206.

1. GILBERTO FREIRE

"Camerado Whitman"

The man in whom contemporary America [i.e., North and South America] most nearly recognizes its image is good gray Whitman in his open-collared shirt, in his white nurse's smock, in his typesetter's work clothes. Whitman, one of the greatest one-man orchestras of all time, a polyphony, not just one voice. Whitman, full of antagonisms and contradictions, far from coherent, anything but logical; still an adolescent in his adult years, but, at thirty, wearing the hair and beard of any old man; an imperfect, rude, unfinished, and at the same time classic, being; a friend of Emerson and an admirer of Lincoln, and at the same time a man so understandingly human that he never was ashamed to live among "roughs";

the Anglo-American who first celebrated a Negro woman in a poem; an American from the middle class who neither revolted against the middle class nor limited himself, as poet, to a single class, a single race, a single religious creed, a single sex, a single movement, or a single country, but chose to be the comrade of all Americans, of all human beings in search of better, or at least more fraternal, times for America and for humanity.

The one who in this way understood his position as man and as poet, as American and as citizen, and ran the risk of being misunderstood by the sectarians of all sects, by the purists of all purisms, by the orthodox of all orthodoxies, anticipated the Americanism which other progressive Americans are only today beginning to attain: integral, pan-human, pan-democratic Americanism. For in the men of America, of the West, and perhaps of the whole world, Whitman renewed the sentiment, the conception, the ideal of brotherhood—brotherhood as opposed to any kind of despotic paternalism—with a revolutionary and poetic power such as had not existed among men since that other great poet and revolutionary who was likewise above the paternalistic ideals of his time in questions of class and sect, race and sex: Saint Francis of Assisi.

Whitman lived in times particularly inauspicious for democracy in his country. In his eyes the two presidential candidates in the 1856 elections were, in comparison with Emerson, mere dwarfs; perhaps he would have liked to see as president not a common man, but some extraordinary Emerson. He was therefore disgusted by that exhibition of Lilliputians in the electoral battle for the presidency. For it should be noted that, in spite of all his faith in the common man, Whitman always recognized the need, in posts of authority, for the uncommon man. Uncommon not for academic knowledge or the exquisitely literary or aesthetic temperament of a sage or artist divorced from daily life, but for superior capacity for leadership, and at the same time for ability to identify himself with the needs and aspirations of the community. Two of his poems are dedicated to one of those uncommon men who had come from the midst of common men, the son of a woodcutter, in fact—Lincoln. In Lincoln Whitman incarnated his concept of the "redeemer" of the Americans, of the "captain," of the "first-class leader."

His faith in democracy was that of one who saw with a clear eye the whole tremendous storm that democratic institutions were passing through in his country and in his time. But even though the anti-democratic winds blew ever stronger; even though the waves mounted ever more terrible against the democratic effort not only of the common men but also of the Lincolns of the United States; even though the black clouds rose ever blacker against the concept of democratic life held by Jefferson and other prophets of the first days of the Republic—it did not matter. The ship of democracy had not, indeed, been made only for favorable winds, gentle waves, rose-colored clouds:

Ship of the hope of the world—Ship of Promise,
Welcome the storm—welcome the trial,

Why now I shall see what the old ship is made of,
Anybody can sail with a fair wind, or a smooth sea.

Whitman was inspired by a concept of democracy very much in accord with his somewhat Darwinian sense of reality, of life, and of the contradictions of man: a democracy capable of resisting anti-democracy by its own efforts. If it lacked the virility or the capacity to resist the fury of its enemies, then democracy did not deserve to survive.

In his eyes, anti-democracy was embodied not only in absolute monarchy but also in a powerful plutocracy. Not only in the feudal slaveholding system of the South but also in the industrial capitalism of the North with its new kings and barons at the head of banks and privileged business enterprises. That is why Whitman always censured the abolitionists for narrowness of vision: they saw a single social problem, that of the liberation of a race exploited and dominated by agrarian feudalism. No single race or class or region ever seemed to Whitman such a cause as a democrat should fight for. "America" itself seems to have been for him less a physical than a social expanse: the symbol of humanity or of the world of the future which, by "manifest destiny," would have its center in the American continent. In his opinion — that is what his Americanism seems to indicate, an Americanism to which we can perhaps compare the Slavism of modern Russian Stalinists — the American continent was the one most fit to take the lead in the realization of a democracy as nearly complete as possible: social, not merely political; ethnic though he did not emphasize as much as José Bonifácio this aspect of human intercourse, whose democratization seems a characteristically Brazilian contribution to the democratic complex — not merely economic. For Whitman's concept of democracy was a total one, not merely a narrowly political one, much less a mechanically electoral one.

So that, on the approach of the War of Secession, a conflict rather between two antagonistic economic systems than between two regions, Whitman did not let himself be dominated completely by either of the partisan creeds: neither by that of Yankee unionism nor by that of state autonomy defended by the Southern slaveholders. His vision of America — at least of English America — in 1860 was already that of the "indissoluble continent" which today inspires many of us:

With the love of comrades,
With the life-long love of comrades.

One of the most lucid interpreters of Whitman — I refer to Professor Ralph Henry Gabriel — emphasizes what the Civil War meant for the Poet, ever confident in democracy's power of resistance to anti-democratic forces: in 1872 Whitman recalled that those terrible days of conflict showed that "popular democracy, whatever its faults and dangers, practically justifies itself beyond the proudest claims and the wildest dreams of its enthusiasts." Not that, in Whitman's opinion, the Civil War had resulted in the rose-colored triumph of democracy over plutoc-racy. Agrarian slavocracy had been ruined, and abolition had won its small battle for the emancipation of the blacks from agrarian and feudal slavery — that was all. But the war had been democratic because it had brought common men from the two regions into the bitter struggle, over a question of duty democratically con-ceived. And those men had borne themselves valiantly in combat. After the vic-tory of the North over the South, at a time when — as in the sad case of General Grant himself — some of the highest offices of the Republic were held by persons who did not always honor them, those men continued to be the reserve of vitality and of manliness, of honesty and of sense of responsibility, of which the war had revealed the existence among the common people of both North and South. And Whitman's faith in democracy as a process or method of human intercourse rested on his faith in those men.

When he addressed as "comrades" all human beings — not only those of his own economic class or of his own intellectual caste, of his own region or territor-ial area, or of his own race of white-skinned, blond-haired men — there was not in that fraternization of Whitman's with all Americans — or with all human be-ings of his day capable of the same fraternalism — the affected or conventional at-titude of the sectarian of an ideology that, though international, was nevertheless exclusive as to the class, the race, the activity, or the sex of individuals. "Comrade" was his natural way of speaking, in a manner at once Franciscan and Hellenic, to other men free from artificial and preconceived ideas. There was in his attitude al-most no Hebraism, the exclusive, ethnocentric Hebraism that spread from the Hebrews to the Anglo-Saxon Protestants known as Puritans, in whose spirit on occasion was jeopardized the democratic, and at the same time Christian, concep-tion of life and of human relations. "Comrade" was his way of addressing other men who were simply men. Simply men and women. Common men, not super-men in the Nietzschean sense. For it was common men—I repeat—who made possible Whitman's democratic faith. He believed in the future of democracy in an epoch as troubled for American democracy as that in which he lived because he came to know the common man, the average man—the average man, it should be noted, not merely the middle-class man—the simple man of his country; because he saw him at close range with all his defects and all his good qualities; because he became conscious of his basic virtues not only through the eyes of a poet but also through the clinical eyes of a nurse, not to say a doctor. It was through those eyes that he saw, on the naked bodies of the men whom he treated, wounds caused not only by war but also by social malformations of peace time; it was through those eyes that he saw not only the naked bodies of hundreds of common men but also the naked souls or personalities of men near death. Many were the common men — soldiers of the abolitionist North and of the slaveholding South — who died in his fraternal arms as in those of an older brother. Many were the common men who confessed in Whitman's ears their last worldly thoughts.

Perhaps his long white hair made him seem paternal or maternal in the eyes of fatally wounded young men. But he was above all an older brother to the soldiers of both North and South. Perhaps also a sister in a sense parallel to that in which our illustrious Miguel Couto desired to be for his widowed mother rather a daughter than a son.

Whitman was a rough-hewn giant, but it seems that as a nurse to the sick who were closest to death, he could be as gentle as a woman. So fraternal was he in his sense of life and of human relations and so capable of tenderness in those relations — a tenderness which, generally speaking, in the civilizations where the sexes are most intensely differentiated, is accepted only in women — that some of his attitudes and some of his poems have been interpreted as affirmations or sublimations of narcissism and even of homosexuality, which has been confused with bisexualism. It is bisexualism of attitude, not of action, born of empathy, not of vice, that is found in Whitman. For he seems not to have indulged in homosexual practices either in the debauched manner of a Verlaine and an Oscar Wilde, or even in an attempt, difficult but ethically oriented, to tendencies less common than the dominant ones: the tremendous effort, in our day, of an André Gide. He seems principally to have had the courage of great friendships with other men (sometimes, perhaps, with a remote homosexual basis) alongside enthusiasms for "perfect women" — a fact which emphasizes the bisexualism of his attitude; and the "narcissism" of celebrating the beauty of the human body — that of man as well as that of woman — not merely the grace and charm of a woman's body seen through the eyes of a man.

Dugas, in his study on friendship, points out that where friendship was a cult, as in the classical civilizations, relations among friends did not imply the absence or the sacrifice of relations of any of them with the public in general. Walt Whitman, reacting against agrarian feudalism and feudal industrialism, both of them responsible for rigid hierarchies between the sexes and among men—hierarchies hostile to great friendships, which are mostly fraternal ones — restored the cult of friendship without sacrificing to that cult his public spirit: he was a friend to some and a comrade to many. He would have liked to be a comrade to all or nearly all. Hence his democratic solution of the problem: his fraternalism expressed in the feeling of a *comrade*, an extension of the feeling of a *friend*. All of these sentiments were aspects of the same democratic spirit: that of fraternity.

Saint Francis of Assisi, in his poetic rebellion against the Hebraically or feudally paternalistic excesses within the Church, had extended that democratic fraternalism beyond men, applying it to water, to fire, to animals, to trees. All things were his brothers. Whitman, naturalistic, yes, but above all personalistic in the best sense, did not go so far. Nor did he go to the extreme of another type of rude naturalism: that of Thoreau, who seems to have preferred leaning on the branches of New England trees to trusting in the support of human arms, even friendly ones. For Whitman, the term "comrade" included all men able to understand, love, and complete one another through human symbols and human means of integration. Integration of individuals into one another, according to special affinities; and of all persons, fraternally, into the community.

At the same time his conception of friendship was akin to Saint Augustine's as it is revealed in the *Confessions*. There Augustine says that he does not know how he can go on living after losing the friend who in life complemented him to such a degree that the two formed "only one soul." Such is, or seems to be, the meaning of Whitman's famous "Calamus" poems, which belong in the same category as the great Church Father's famous pages, Shakespeare's *Sonnets*, and Tennyson's *In Memoriam*.

That was what overflowed most abundantly from Whitman into his books: a personalistic and fraternalistic sense of life and of the community, a sense so vibrant as to seem at times homosexualism gone mad whereas it was probably only bisexualism sublimated into fraternalism. Whitman was not, as a poet, much less as a writer, impersonal, inhuman, esoteric, cut off from his condition as a man, a person, a citizen. Poet, citizen, and man formed in him a complex of inseparable activities and conditions. In this he was like an Iberian. The Iberians are most likely to be made that way: integral personalities in whom the intellectual, the artist, or the public figure on the one hand and the private citizen on the other are identified to such a degree that it is impossible to distinguish the private individual in them from the writer or the artist, the political figure or the mystic. When Whitman exclaimed very Whitmanesquely one day, characterizing one of his books, "Camerado, this is no book, / Who touches this touches a man," he spoke in an English that seems translated from Spanish or Portuguese. Thus would have spoken Angel Ganivet or Anthero de Quental; Saint Juan de la Cruz or the author of *Don Quixote*; and especially Ramon Llull.

In Whitman the idea of emotional interpenetration of the individual and the masses, of the poet and the community, was a constant. There was no suggestion of what we should today call racism in that interpenetration. His sense of community was, or is, sociological, not biologically ethnic, just as his sense of life and nature was, or is, rather Hellenic than Hebraic although in his mode of expression, in his rhythm, in his poetic breathing there are not lacking clearly biblical, and therefore chiefly Hebraic, echoes. But let us not forget that the Bible that had the greatest influence on Whitman, as a boy and the son of a carpenter, was the Bible interpreted by Quakers; and let us recall that the Quakers are a kind of Franciscans of Protestantism.

Whitman would be amazed at being compared to the Franciscans. There are those who practice Christianity or Franciscanism without realizing that they are Christians or Franciscans — they are sociologically Franciscans, shall we say, in order to accentuate the independence of the theological content from the form, which is the sociological aspect of Franciscanism or of Christianity. Whitman was, to a degree, that type of Franciscan. He was Franciscan in his cult of a simplicity at times dangerously close to simple-mindedness. Franciscan in his pleasure in associating with the uneducated, in delighting in the knowledge of intuitive people, in the spontaneity and the freshness of intelligence even of illiterates, so different from academic and doctoral intelligence, so impregnated with the joy of approaching problems as if man were always an apprentice, never a master; as if he were always, at every moment, beginning to learn, "walking along with life" — as a Minorite has said in defense of his brothers in religion — "in order not to be left behind."

Whitman was a Franciscan also in his taste for always going about dressed in work clothes or wearing an open-collared shirt, just as the other Franciscans, the religious disciples of the Saint, went about in a plain gray habit of coarse and rough cloth. He acted on the theory that clothing makes the man (and to a certain degree it does); that constant wearing of work clothes and systematic repudiation of the bourgeois frock coat, of the conventional businessman's sack coat, of the academic or bureaucratic black swallow-tailed coat, of the bachelor's or doctor's gown, eventually turns the intellectual into the man of the people or brother of the man of the people that he would like to be; that work clothes, worn all the time and not only for a bourgeois stint at painting a wall or repairing a bathroom faucet, eventually become a second skin for the intellectual, a layer or a coat of social flesh over his individual's flesh — and are not the costume of one who might make of his populism or of his proletarianism a kind of masquerade or literary or political carnival.

"I see clearly" wrote Whitman in 1871 — "that the combined foreign world could not beat [America] down." So that if America failed, she would be defeated or prevented from fulfilling her mission, from realizing the American spirit, from spreading what was universal in the American spirit, by enemies within, not without. The "American programme," as he called it, was not addressed, in his opinion, to social classes — neither to the bourgeoisie nor to the proletariat — but to "universal man." Hence the expansionist or universalist character of that program.

When an Argentine statesman proposed, instead of the Monroe doctrine of "America for the Americans," the famous concept of "America for humanity," he was in a sense repeating Whitman. For Whitman's Americanism always aimed at "universal man." Everything in his writings indicates that he always considered the American Revolution more universal than the French Revolution: it was a revolution in favor of man, not only of one group or one class of men. As Whitman respected human personality, he obviously could not conceive of "universal man" reduced to a caricature of American man. He seems to have conceived only that the circumstances of their history had given Americans magnificently ample opportunities to develop democratic forms of human intercourse which, as general forms, though with different ideological content and many peculiarities of national or regional stylization, could and should be extended to the whole world in the interest of so-called "universal man." At least that is how I interpret what can be called the American expansionism or the democratic imperialism that is found in Whitman, a mystical faith to which he gave poetic expression with Messianic vigor.

Although he considered the American democracy of his time "an almost complete failure in its social aspects, and in really grand religious, moral, literary and aesthetic results," Whitman nevertheless kept a belief, a faith, a confidence in an America Messianic in its "programme of culture" for the whole world. He explained it thus: "True, indeed, behind this fantastic farce" — the gaudy materialism of the United States — "solid things and stupendous labors are to be discover'd, existing crudely and going on in the background, to advance and tell themselves in time." It was in order that more should be done for the people, in order that those solid things might grow and those stupendous labors might increase that his prophetic voice was raised more than once in an attempt to attract the most capable and most honest Americans to political activity. America, taken as a whole, was perhaps doing very well in spite of all the depravity of businessmen and all the corruption of bureaucrats who jeopardized the democratic health of the community. It was principally "the dilettantes, and all who shirk their duty" who were not doing well. Hence Whitman's cry: "Enter . . . into politics. I advise every young man to do so." Let everyone inform himself of the facts; let everyone try to act for the best; let everyone vote. He was not enthusiastic for political parties; but he recognized the necessity of parties, of elections, of voting. He addressed himself chiefly to the independents — farmers, clerks, mechanics, laborers: let these, ever vigilant, be the decisive element in elections. It is almost with fury that he insists on condemning the attitude of the dilettantes, in whose minds political activity had become so corrupt in the United States that there was no salvation for American democracy.

Whitman was a personalist. It would not have been easy for him to accept the positivist generalization that it is always the individual who is in ferment and humanity that leads him. He lived too close to the phenomenon represented by Lincoln not to believe that there are moments in which the opposite is true: humanity — or a great part of humanity—is in ferment, and it is a great man who leads it. A man who, when he is really great, does not let himself be moved by his contemporaries' excesses or be dominated by their hatreds for class or race or sect; a man able to place eternal values before those of the moment, to uphold great sentiments over small ones: the passion for justice, for example. Lincoln. All Lincolns. They have not been numerous, those Lincolns, but they have existed. The second Roosevelt was one of them, and we are suffering for lack of him. The really great men are those who attempt or achieve the conciliation of antagonistic points of view instead of incarnating ideals or interests exclusive to one class, one race, one nation, one sect, one creed. Whitman was himself a human orchestra, in whom echoed and by whom were expressed diverse and even contradictory ideals.

That is why he is a poet even more for today than for his own time. It is the American people of today — the people of all the Americas, not only of English America — who are absorbing him today.

For our age, it would seem, is destined to synthesize or integrate values that in the eyes of the men of the nineteenth century were irreconcilable: such diverse values as socialism and personalism, Christianity and Marxism, intellectualism and intuitivism. Whitman was one of the first to develop the concept, the notion of synthesis that is to characterize the world of tomorrow. A champion of the "divine average," he nevertheless upheld, against the democratic principle of the average, the somewhat aristocratic principle of personality — aristocratic in that it puts a special value on quality. It implies creative personality conscious of its creative power, able to synthesize, to interpret differences and antagonisms.

Perhaps it can be said that Whitman's faith in the common man came from the conviction that, if all men were given an equal opportunity for expression and creation, there would arise from among common men some intellectually and aesthetically uncommon men who would benefit from the whole community and its total culture. He was not dreaming of a leveling of all men; but of the opportunity for each one to develop to the full his own personality within a framework of equal opportunities for personal development. Once this integration of the rights of the individual with those of the community is reached, much will have been achieved in the direction of synthesis between the antagonisms that still oppose each other: collectivism represented today chiefly by the incomplete Soviet democracy, and individualism or, in the most advanced milieu, personalism, represented today by the likewise incomplete democracies of the West, of which Whitman's America has become the greatest: the center of a real social and cultural system that can be defined as Euramerican, whereas the collectivist system is, in a way, Eurasian. The "East" and the "West" from which Professor F. S. C. Northrop hopes for a new synthesis, greater, sociologically, than the Thomist or even the Christian synthesis. The greatest efforts of man today should be in the direction of integrating or reconciling those antagonisms. Hence the value of Walt Whitman for our time.

"Camerado" Whitman defined himself almost a hundred years ago by an Americanism that was pan-human in its perspectives, in its meaning, and in its program of cultural expansion. The Orient will, in all certainty, eventually absorb a large part of that Americanism; and at the same time that Americanism will be enriched with Oriental values within the conception outlined in a recent book by Professor Northrop. According to him, it is not economics, so highly touted today by the Anglo-Americans and by the Soviet Russians, that is the key to the humanities; it is the humanities, including the aesthetic factor, that are the key to the solution of the problems of economics.

"Camerado" Whitman loved his neighbor fraternally without disdaining himself: rather he sang his own body—his whole body—to the point that people thought him narcissistic and even obscene. But he was neither narcissistic nor obscene, he was personalistic. An intense personalist—that is what he was. It may be repeated here that in his political ideas he was a passionate personalist, in contrast to those who boast of being superiorly impersonal and coldly dispassionate. For "Camerado" Whitman, political activity was a manner of expressing his moral passion. His passion for social justice. His passion for human solidarity. His passion for the community, embodied in his eyes chiefly by the common man.

If he definitely approached socialism at the end of his life, as one of his most authoritative biographers claims, he always inclined—I repeat—toward ethical, not mechanical or deterministic socialism. Personal, not impersonal, socialism. Pan-human socialism, not narrowly proletarian socialism, which glorifies only manual or mechanical labor and is hostile to intellectual, artistic, freely scientific, superiorly technical work; or hostile to religious activity. The socialism that is ardently interested in moral values, not the socialism that is uninterested in those values because its practitioners or its apologists believe in an absolute economic determinism within any human intervention except that represented by cynically Machiavellian maneuvers destined only to accelerate the solutions.

Though Whitman believed firmly in Science with a capital S, his humanism never lost its fluidity, never hardened into political, economic, or sociological determinism. I do not know to what extent he was familiar with the sociology or the sociologies of his day. In any case it is certain that he foresaw an original sociology born of America; and everything seems to indicate that in that sociology he did not see a new expression of determinism within which there would be no room for Lincolns or Whitmans, for the great men who contain multitudes within themselves instead of being contained by them.

I believe that his faith in science would allow of the anti-scientific restrictions so well expressed in late years by another clear-sighted American — Charles A. Beard — and, more recently, by Northrop. Beard points out that if all human affairs were reduced to law or to a kind of terrestrial mechanics, man's very control over occurrences and actions would become meaningless. And "the past, present, and future would be revealed as fixed and beyond the reach of human choice and will. Men and women would be chained to their destiny as the stars and tides are to their routine."

Meanwhile the sciences of man, far from authorizing us to believe in economic determinism or sociological fatalism, continue to allow plenty of room for the adventurous humanism, the experimental democracy, the life incessantly renewed in various of its aspects by man himself which is constantly found in Whitman's thought, in his democratic spirit, and in his Americanism, always tempered by the most anti-mechanistic, anti-doctrinaire, and anti-deterministic of personalisms.

O Camarada Whitman (Rio de Janeiro: José Olympio, 1948). Translated by Benjamin M. Woodbridge, Jr.

ROGER ASSELINEAU

Whitman in Portugal

With a population of merely 9 million inhabitants, some of them completely illiterate, Portugal has only a very small reading public. Portuguese publishers therefore cannot afford to publish many translations of foreign authors, especially poets. It is for this economic reason, no doubt, that there exists no complete translation of *Leaves of Grass* in Portuguese. The only translation available is that of the "Song of the Open Road" by Luís Cardim, which appeared rather late, in 1947, more than fifty years after Whitman's death. It cannot even be called a book; it is just a small pamphlet of a score of pages. Books of criticism are just as scarce. There is only one: *Walt Whitman: Vida e Pensamento* by Luís Eugénio Ferreira, published in 1970, which contains in an appendix the translation of a selection from *Leaves of Grass* (only a dozen short poems, mainly from "Children of Adam" and "Calamus," plus, to emphasize Whitman's modernity, "To a Locomotive in Winter") and also a translation of "A Backward Glance O'er Travel'd Roads." The book is clearly intended for the general public. It begins with a poorly documented biographical sketch based almost exclusively on Léon Bazalgette's romanticized biography, and the critical study which follows is extremely superficial. It consists of a quick survey of the various themes of *Leaves*, insisting more particularly on the unity of the physical world in Whitman's poetry beyond the chaos and complexity of its appearance. The author also analyzes what he calls the three dimensions of Whitman's self, his conception of democracy, and his vocabulary. He then summarily describes the critical reception of *Leaves* and its ten successive editions. The Portuguese reader thus can gain a fairly accurate if overly succinct and simplified idea of Whitman's poetry.

All this is hardly worth mentioning, and the reception of Whitman in Portugal could be passed over if there had not occurred a kind of miracle: the sudden (and spiritual) encounter of the greatest Portuguese poet of the twentieth century, at the beginning of his career, with Whitman. It took place in 1914, when Fernando Pessoa, who was born in Durban, South Africa, and educated in English there, by chance acquired an English edition of *Leaves of Grass*. He devoured it. He was twenty-six at the time and so far had written poems mostly in English. Some, like *O Marinheiro*, were definitely decadent and deliquescent, based on a sense of the absolute unreality of physical "reality" as well as the unreality of consciousness, which, he suggested, resembles the broken cistern of the Danaides unable to hold the water poured into it. Whitman's poems were a revelation to him, like Dr. Teufelsdröckh's sudden illumination in rue St. Thomas de l'Enfer in Paris. He realized that he could fill up the vacuum of his self by peopling it with several distinct selves, each of them endowed with an imaginary existence and a personality corresponding to one of his own potential personalities. He was not at all influenced by the form of Whitman's poems, and he never lost his independence. *Leaves* acted upon him more like a catalyst. He was sustained by the almost physical presence of the poet in his poems and fed by the rich concreteness of his evocations and invocations, and he extrapolated from there. Under an apparent submission to and admiration for his spiritual guide, he never ceased to be Pessoa.

It was indeed a very strange and quite unexpected case of superposition of two dissimilar poets; the result was a cataclysm which changed the face of contemporary Portuguese poetry—and the face of Whitman, too, for he cannot be read quite in the same way after one has read Pessoa's modernist "Salutation" to him (see selection 1).

The Case of Fernando Pessoa

SUSAN M. BROWN

To address the question of Walt Whitman's effect on Fernando Pessoa is to begin an exploration of the poetic process itself, for the fascinating and complex relationship between the American bard and the Portuguese modernist goes far beyond the superficial and obvious forms of poetic influence. It becomes an investigation into the way in which Whitman was a deep-seated presence, hidden at the base level of the creative process, acting on Pessoa's imaginative powers as a liberating force.

Let's begin by looking at one section of "Saudação a Walt Whitman" ("Salutation to Walt Whitman"). After a long initial stanza in which the poet conjures up both himself and Whitman "walking hand in hand" with the universe "doing a dance" in their souls, he goes on to qualify Whitman in stanzas two and three (see selection 1).

What is so striking in this enumeration of qualities is the resounding emphasis on the Whitmanian "merge," that infinite drive to be personally and sexually involved with all things. This aspect of Whitman caused D. H. Lawrence to explain: "When he is infinite he is still himself. He still has a nose to wipe. The state of infinity is only a state, even if it be the supreme one."[1] While one may be tempted to read the whole of the poem as parody and thus reply that Pessoa, like Lawrence, is suspicious of Whitman's unlimited capacity and indiscriminate desire to mix with (and be) all things, such a temptation diminishes once we understand Pessoa's real need for Whitman. In the light of what Pessoa wrote in other places,[2] it seems more appropriate to read his "Salutation to Walt Whitman" as a highly "sincere" and unusual self-confessional poem in the Pessoa corpus.

The notion of sincerity in reference to Pessoa needs some explanation. Pessoa's sensibility, unlike Whitman's, was shaped by a late-nineteenth-century skepticism about the relevance of any simple concept of personality. Moving through his works, one repeatedly stumbles over the same obsessive concern with the loss of self, the vacuity of the "I," the nothingness of the poetic personality. As he succinctly put it in one of his diary entries: "I've no idea of myself, not even one that consists of a non-idea of myself. I am a nomadic wanderer through my consciousness."[3]

A need for a more complex, less personal "self" eventually led Pessoa to the explosive creation of his heteronymic world. To appreciate this consciously construed poetic project of fictional selves—alternately referred to as his "drama in characters," his "fictions of the interlude," and his "peoplebooks"—Pessoa must be viewed as a modernist struggling within the postromantic condition.[4] This condition can be characterized as an awareness of the "I" as obstacle, a condition shared by most of the early modernists (postromantics). Shared with them as well was his drive to transcend the paralysis of solipsism by gathering and transmuting the fragments of consciousness into a more authentically modern voice. Like the mask theories of Yeats, the dramatic monologues of Eliot's strangely pathetic portraits of the exhausted ego, the various personae of Pound, and the theoretical considerations of Stevens on a supreme fiction and the major man, Pessoa's heteronymic coterie of fictional poets came as a response to a late-nineteenth-century cul-de-sac: the impasse brought on by the excesses of subjectivity. In this respect, Pessoa's letter of January 20, 1935, to his friend Adolfo Casais Monteiro is of special interest:

What I am essentially—behind the involuntary masks of the poet, of the rational thinker and of whatever else there is—is a dramatist. The phenomenon of my instinctive depersonalization to which I alluded in my previous letter, in order to explain the existence of the heteronyms, leads naturally to this definition. Being thus, I do not evolve: I TRAVEL. . . . I keep on changing personalities, I keep on (here there might be some evolution) enriching myself in the capacity of creating new personalities, new types of faking that I understand the world or, better, of faking that it is possible to understand it. That is why I gave this parade of myself as comparable, not to an evolution, but to a trip. . . .[5]

The "parade of myself" is the heteronymic triumvirate consisting of Alberto Caeiro (pastoral poet and keeper of sheep), Álvaro de Campos (engineer poet), and Ricardo Reis (monarchist and poet of classical odes), all of whom were invented in 1914 and in whose names Pessoa continued to write throughout his lifetime. Within this world of invented poets — each of whom wrote distinct bodies of poetry different from the other two (and from the poetry Pessoa himself wrote under his own name) — the presence of Whitman is palpable. Following the lead of Eduardo Lourenço, one of Pessoa's finest critics, I would argue that *Leaves of Grass* is at the very genesis of the heteronyms; more particularly, that Pessoa saw in Whitman two poets — Alberto Caeiro, personifying the self-transcendent part of Whitman that can "witness and wait," and Álvaro de Campos, who, in reenacting Whitman's barbaric yawp, endlessly and frenetically expresses his anxieties and insatiabilities. When seen in the light of the Whitman intertext, these two heteronyms seem personifications of two latent poets within Whitman: poet of the body (Campos) and poet of the soul (Caeiro). Elsewhere I have described this transfiguration of Whitman's body/soul dichotomy as conveyed through the heteronymic drama of Pessoa:

> If Campos is Walt Whitman with Caeiro inside, the principal drama of the heteronymic world resides in the implicit dialogue of two incompatible voices within the consciousness of Campos: the silent voice of the Poet as an all-seeing God, real as dreams are real (Caeiro), and the manic-depressive voice of a dangling consciousness, the voice in the wilderness. Emblematic of the modern poet in a destitute time, Campos searches in vain for traces of the fugitive god, finding nothing but his own dismantled image, his own disbelieving voice. His is the poet's frantic struggle against time to regain the "self-transcending calm" of Pessoa's essential Whitman, the master Caeiro. Campos' condition only begins to make sense in the light of the loss, in the light of his bitter nostalgia for the extinguished Me myself of Alberto Caeiro, the vanished God.[6]

Another way of stating this (transformed) relationship is to say that Caeiro — who represented the ideal (objective) poetic stance — is the most removed from Pessoa's own sensibility. And yet it is through his mediation that Pessoa was able to unleash his truest feelings. In another Pessoa letter to Adolfo Casais Monteiro, this notion is borne out: "Into Caeiro I put all my power of dramatic depersonalization, . . . into Álvaro de Campos, all the emotion that I allow neither in myself nor in my living."[7]

Now, as to the matter of "sincerity" in "Salutation to Walt Whitman," we should note that the poem is written by Álvaro de Campos. We should also note that it all turns on the tension built between the "barbarian"[8] and the overly civilized self within the figure of Pessoa/Campos. As we recall Ezra Pound's words —

"Mentally I am a Walt Whitman who has learned to wear a collar and a dress shirt (although at times inimical to both)"[9] — we also see that "Salutation" begins with a brief self-portrait: "I, with my monocle and tightly buttoned frock coat," and a few lines later, "I, so given to indolence, so easily bored." In the course of the poem this image of the reticent fin de siècle dandy gives way to another self-image of Campos as he moves from being one single man, "slight and civilized," into something larger, more wild and transpersonal. The first step in this transformation comes with the claim that he is Whitman:

> Look at me: you know that I, Álvaro de Campos, ship's engineer,
> Sensationist poet,
> Am not your disciple, am not your friend, am not your singer,
> You know that I am You, and you are happy about it!

With Whitman as passport, Campos spans the universe in a body-rage for the dynamic Whitmanian moment of pure identity with God:

> Open all the doors!
> Because I have to go in!
> My password? Walt Whitman!
> But I don't give any password . . .
> I go in without explaining . . .
> If I must, I'll knock the doors down . . .
> Yes, slight and civilized though I am, I'll knock the doors down,
> Because at this moment I'm not slight or civilized at all,
> I'm ME, a thinking universe of flesh and bone, wanting to get in
> And having to get in by force, because when I want in I am God!

To be consubstantial with God is to be consubstantial with Whitman (and thus with his true self) because Whitman is the solution to the fundamental problem at the heart of nearly all Pessoa's poems: the paralysis of will and the inability to desire. As long as Campos can sustain the illusion of identity with Whitman, he has a self, a will, a purpose.

But the whole character of Álvaro de Campos is rooted in the incessant wavering between Being and Nothingness. At the end of his poem to Whitman he first confesses both his exhaustion and his lucidity — "Now that I'm almost dead and see everything so clearly, / I bow to you Great Liberator" — and he then terminates with the bitter admission: "Maybe I had no mission at all on earth." As a perfect conjunction of Whitman's most positive energies and Pessoa's most negative ones, the Campos persona makes a violent attempt to merge with otherness (being simultaneously both subject and object) and then abruptly falls into impotence and isolation. In the final analysis, Álvaro de Campos represents the defeat of imagination in its effort to expand the self. Ultimately, he is the abstract mechanical man whose *volante* (flywheel) is what generates his imagination and desire, since his soul—personified by Alberto Caeiro and representing the essential Whitman—has been irreversibly severed from him. A failed Whitman? An early-twentieth-century version of Whitman? Certainly he is the "medium of Modern Times" (to borrow Pessoa's expression for Whitman) if we look at the way Pessoa characterized his times:

> As moderns, we act out the exact meaning of that line from Voltaire in which he says, if the worlds are inhabited, the earth is an insane asylum of the Universe. In effect, we're a madhouse, whether other planets are inhabited or not. We live a life that has already lost all notion of normality, and where health only flourishes in lapses between illnesses. We live a chronic illness, a feverish anemia. Our fate is not to die because we have not adjusted ourselves to our condition as perpetual moribunds. How can a spirit of the race of builders, whose soul is child to the great pagan truths, have anything in common with an age like ours? It can't, except by a spontaneous gesture of repulsion and thoughtful disdain. We are thus the only ones to disagree with decadence, and nature compels us to assume a stance, equally decadent. An indifferent attitude is a decadent one, and we're forced to be indifferent by our incapacity to adjust to our surroundings. We don't adapt because healthy men don't adapt to a morbid environment. By not adapting, we're also morbid. It is in this paradox that we pagans live. We've no other hope or remedy.[10]

While other poets as diverse as Ginsberg and Guillén, Lorca and Lawrence, Borges and Berryman, Neruda and Nemerov, Hopkins, Honig, and Hughes have found in Whitman reason for momentary enthusiasms or ejaculatory praise and deep-rooted indebtedness, Pessoa found something more. Through Whitman he discovered his heteronymic world, and through that world he discovered and gave expression to his multiplex personality. One of Whitman's truest disciples, Pessoa has made him a vivid twentieth-century presence. And for us these are two distinctly separate (and inextricably inseparable) poets, both of whose voices are echoes of Whitman's voice and who, together, update and modernize the Whitman Pessoa called "my brother in the Universe."

NOTES

1. D. H. Lawrence, "Whitman," in Jim Perlman, Ed Folsom, and Dan Campion, eds., *Walt Whitman: The Measure of His Song* (Minneapolis: Holy Cow! Press, 1981), 47.

2. Pessoa clearly indicated his debt to Whitman. For his comments on Whitman, see the following works: Fernando Pessoa, *Páginas de Estética e de Teoria e Crítica Literárias*, ed. Georg Rudolf Lind and Jacinto do Prado Coelho (Lisboa: Atica, 1973), 156 (in Portuguese) and 178, 190, 197–198, 272–273 (in English); Fernando Pessoa, *Páginas Intimas e de Auto-Interpretação*, ed. Georg Rudolf Lind and Jacinto do Prado Coelho (Lisboa: Atica, n.d.), 177, 360 (in Portuguese) and 142, 335–343, 368–372 (in English); Fernando Pessoa, "Apontamentos pare uma Estética Não-Aristotélica," in *Obra em Prosa*, ed. Cleonice Berardinelli

(Rio de Janeiro: Nova Aguilar, 1982), 246; Maria Isabel Rocheta and Maria Paula Morão, eds., *Sobre Portugal: Introdução ao Problema Nacional* (Lisboa: Atica, 1978), 224–225.

Furthermore, Pessoa had two copies of Whitman's work in his personal library: one is an undated edition from the Master Library series (Penny Poets XXVII) entitled *Poems of Walt Whitman* (London: Review of Reviewer's Office) and signed Alexander Search (one of his earliest experiments in voice, whose poems were all in English); the other book is entitled *Leaves of Grass* (The People's Library Edition, 1909) and signed Fernando Pessoa with the date "16.5.1916." See Appendixes B and C of my dissertation for all Pessoa's annotations in these two copies of Whitman (Susan M. Brown, "The Poetics of Pessoa's *Drama em Gente*: The Function of Alberto Caeiro and the Role of Walt Whitman" [Ph.D. diss., University of North Carolina, 1987], 365–396).

3. My translation. Fernando Pessoa, *Livro do Desassossego*, ed. Maria Aliete Galhoz and Teresa Sobral Cunha (Lisboa: Atica, 1982), 1:261.

4. Pessoa was nearly four years old when Whitman died in March of 1892, although in his poem to Whitman, Pessoa alters these facts, stating, "And though I never met you, born the same year you died." This span of roughly seventy years between the two poets made an enormous difference in terms of their sensibility. Whereas Whitman is paradigmatic of mid-nineteenth-century American romanticism, Pessoa is an example of the early-twentieth-century's postromantic ambivalence, which hungered for the kind of confidence Whitman exuded.

5. From the letters I am presently translating for publication by Gavea Brown. The original text is in Antonio Quadros, ed., *Obra em Prosa de Fernando Pessoa* (Lisboa: Publicações Europa-America, 1986), 233. The letter can also be found in a collection of Pessoa's letters translated into French (José Blanco, ed., *Pessoa en Personne*, trans. Simone Biberfeld [Paris: Éditions de la Différence, 1986], 309).

6. See Susan M. Brown, "The Whitman/Pessoa Connection," *Walt Whitman Quarterly Review* 9 (Summer 1991): 1–14.

7. Quadros, *Obra em Prosa*, 224–232. This is the famous letter of January 13, 1935. See Blanco, *Pessoa*, 297–307.

8. Pessoa had written in English: "The other element of notoriety called fame is being a barbarian. By being a barbarian I mean coming into civilization from outside it; belonging to it by street number but without the soul to understand why streets were made and numbers put to the old tradition of separate doors." And a bit further: "The essential thing about the barbarian is that he is wholly modern; he is altogether of his times because the race, to which he belongs, has no civilizational time before. He has no ancestors outside biology." And in yet another place, again in English: "A magnificent type of poet who will survive by representativeness is Walt Whitman. Whitman has all modern times in him, from cruelty(?) to engineering, from humanitarian tendencies to the hardness of intellectuality—he has all this in him. He is far more permanent than (Schiller or) Musset, for instance. He is the medium of Modern Times." See Pessoa, *Páginas de Estética*, 197–198, 272–273.

9. Ezra Pound, "What I Feel about Walt Whitman," in Perlman, Folsom, and Campion, *Measure of His Song*, 31.

10. *Poems of Fernando Pessoa*, trans. and ed. Edwin Honig and Susan M. Brown (New York: Ecco Press, 1986), 183.

1. FERNANDO PESSOA

"Salutation to Walt Whitman"

Infinite Portugal, June eleventh, nineteen hundred and fifteen . . .
A-hoy-hoy-hoy-hoy!

From here in Portugal, with all past ages in my brain,
I salute you, Walt, I salute you, my brother in the Universe,
I, with my monocle and tightly buttoned frock coat,
I am not unworthy of you, Walt, as you well know,
I am not unworthy of you, my greeting is enough to make it so . . .
I, so given to indolence, so easily bored,
I am with you, as you well know, and understand you and love you,
And though I never met you, born the same year you died,
I know you loved me too, you knew me, and I am happy.
I know that you knew me, that you considered and explained me,
I know that this is what I am, whether on Brooklyn Ferry ten years before
    I was born
Or strolling up Rua do Ouro thinking about everything that is not Rua do
    Ouro,
And just as you felt everything, so I feel everything, and so here we are
    clasping hands,
Clasping hands, Walt, clasping hands, with the universe doing a dance in our
    soul.

O singer of concrete absolutes, always modern and eternal,
Fiery concubine of the scattered world,
Great pederast brushing up against the diversity of things,
Sexualized by rocks, by trees, by people, by their trades,
Itch for the swiftly passing, for casual encounters, for what's merely observed,
My enthusiast for what's inside everything,
My great hero going straight through Death by leaps and bounds,
Roaring, screaming, bellowing greetings to God!

Singer of wild and gentle brotherhood with everything,
Great epidermic democrat, up close to it all in body and soul,
Carnival of each and every action, bacchanalia of all intentions,
Twin brother of every sudden impulse,
Jean-Jacques Rousseau of the world hell-bent to produce machinery,
Homer of all the *insaisissable* of wavering carnality,
Shakespeare of the sensation on the verge of steam propulsion,
Milton-Shelley of the dawning future of Electricity!
Incubus of all gestures,

Spasm penetrating every object-force,
Souteneur of the whole Universe,
Whore of all solar systems . . .

How often do I kiss your picture!
Wherever you are now (I don't know where it is but it is God)
You feel this, I know you feel it, and my kisses are warmer (flesh and blood)
And you like it that way, old friend, and you thank me from over there —
I know this well, something tells me, some pleasure in my spirit:

Some abstract, slant erection in the depths of my soul.

There was nothing of the *engageant* in you — rather the muscular, the
    cyclopic,
Though in facing the Universe yours was the attitude of a woman,
And every blade of grass, every stone, every man was a Universe for you.

Walt, dearest old man, my great Comrade, *evohë*!
I belong to your bacchic orgy of freed sensations,
I am yours, from the tingling of my toes to the nausea of my dreams,
I am yours, look at me — up there close to God, you see me contrariwise,
From inside out . . . You divine my body, you see my soul —
You see it properly, and through its eyes you take in my body —
Look at me: you know that I, Álvaro de Campos, ship's engineer,
Sensationist poet,
Am not your disciple, am not your friend, am not your singer,
You know that I am You, and you are happy about it!

I can never read through all your poems . . . There's too much feeling
    in them . . .
I go through your lines as through a teeming crowd that brushes past me,
Smelling of sweat, of grease, of human and mechanical activity.
At a given moment, reading your poems, I can't tell if I'm reading or living
    them,
I don't know if my actual place is in the world or in your poems,
I don't know if I'm standing here with both feet on the ground
Or hanging upside down in some sort of workshop,
From the natural ceiling of your stampeding inspiration,
From the center of the ceiling of your unapproachable intensity.

Open all the doors!
Because I have to go in!
My password? Walt Whitman!
But I don't give any password . . .
I go in without explaining . . .
If I must, I'll knock the doors down . . .

Yes, slight and civilized though I am, I'll knock the doors down,
Because at this moment I'm not slight or civilized at all,
I'm ME, a thinking universe of flesh and bone, wanting to get in
And having to get in by force, because when I want in I am God!

Take this garbage out of my way!
Put those emotions away in drawers!
Get out of here, you politicians, literati,
You peaceful businessmen, policemen, whores, *souteneurs*,
All your kind is the letter that kills, not the spirit giving life.
The spirit giving life at this moment is ME!

Let no son of a bitch get in my way!
My path goes through Infinity before reaching its end!
It's not up to you whether I reach this end or not,
It's up to me, up to God — up to what I mean by the word *Infinite* . . .
Onward!
I spur ahead!
I feel the spurs, I am the very horse I mount,
Because I, since I want to be consubstantial with God,
Can be everything, or I can be nothing, or anything,
Just as I please . . . It's nobody's business . . .
Raging madness! Wanting to yelp, jump,
Scream, bray, do handsprings and somersaults, my body yelling,
Cramponner at the car wheels and to go under,
Get inside the whirling whiplash that's about to strike,
Be the bitch to all dogs and they not enough for me,
Be the steering wheel of all machines and their speed too slow for me,
Be the one who's crushed, abandoned, pulled apart, or done for,
Come dance this fury with me, Walt, you there in that other world,
Swing this hoedown with me, knocking at the stars,
Fall exhausted to the ground with me,
Beat the walls with me like mad,
Break down, tear yourself apart with me,
Through everything, in everything, around everything, without anything,
In an abstract body rage that stirs up maelstroms in the soul . . .

Damn it! Get going, I said!
Even if God himself stops us, let's get going . . . it makes no difference . . .
Let's go on and get nowhere . . .
Infinity! Universe! End without end! What's the difference?

(Let me take off my tie, unbutton my collar.
You can't let off steam with civilization looped around your neck . . .)
All right now, we're off to a flying start!

In a great *marche aux flambeaux* of all the cities of Europe,
In a great military parade of industry, trade and leisure,
In a great race, a great incline, a great decline,
Thundering and leaping, and everything with me,
I jump up to salute you,
I yell out to salute you,
I burst loose to salute you, bounding, handstanding, yawping!

This is why I send you
My leaping verses, my bounding verses, my spasmodic verses,
My hysteria-attack verses,
Verses that pull the cart of my nerves.

My crazy tumbling inspires me,
Barely able to breathe, I get to my feet exalted,
For the verses are me not being able to burst from living.

Open all the windows for me!
Throw open all the doors!
Pull the whole house up over me!
I want to live freely, out in the open,
I want to make gestures beyond my body,
To run like the rain streaming down over walls,
To be stepped on like stones down the broad streets,
To sink like heavy weights to the bottom of the sea,
And all this voluptuously, a feeling alien to me now!

I don't want the doors bolted!
I don't want the safes locked!
I want to horn in there, put my nose in, be dragged off,
I want to be somebody else's wounded member,
I want to be spilled from crates,
I want to be thrown in the ocean,
I want them to come looking for me at home with lewd intentions —
Just so I'm not always sitting here quietly,
Just so I'm not simply writing these verses!

I'm against in-between spaces in the world!
I'm for the compenetrated, material contiguity of objects!
I'm for physical bodies commingling like souls,
Not just dynamically but statically too!

I want to fly and fall from way up high!
To be thrown like a hand grenade!
To be brought to a sudden stop . . . To be lifted to . . .
The highest, abstract end-point of me and everything else!

Climax of iron and motors!
Accelerated escalator without any stairs!
Hydraulic pump tearing out my guts and my feeling it!

Put me in chains, just so I can break them,
Just so I can break them with my teeth bleeding,
Bleeding away in spurts, with the masochistic joy of life!

The sailors took me prisoner,
Their hands gripped me in the dark,
I died momentarily from the pain,
My soul went on licking the floor of my private cell
With the whirligig of impossibilities circling my taunt.

Jump, leap, take the bit between your teeth,
Red-hot iron Pegasus of my twitching anxieties,
Wavering parking place of my motorized destiny!

He's called Walt:

Entryway to everything!
Bridge to everything!
Highway to everything!
Your omnivorous soul,
Your soul that's bird, fish, beast, man, woman,
Your soul that's two where two exist,
Your soul that's one becoming two when two are one,
Your soul that's arrow, lightning, space,
Amplex, nexus, sex and Texas, Carolina and New York,
Brooklyn Ferry in the twilight,
Brooklyn Ferry going back and forth,
Libertad! Democracy! The Twentieth Century about to dawn!
Boom! Boom! Boom! Boom! Boom!
BOOM!

You who lived it, you who saw it, you who heard it,
Subject and object, active and passive,
Here, there, everywhere you,
Circle encompassing every possibility of feeling,
Quintessence of all things that might still happen,
God-Terminus of all imaginable objects, and it is you!
You are the Hour,
You the Minute,
You the Second!
You interpolated, liberated, unfurled, sent,
Interpolating, liberating, unfurling, sending,
You, the interpolator, liberator, unfurler, sender,

The seal on all letters,
The name on all addressed envelopes,
Goods delivered, returned, and to follow . . .

Trainful of feelings at so many soul-miles per hour,
Per hour, per minute, per second, BOOM!

Now that I'm almost dead and see everything so clearly,
I bow to you, Great Liberator.

Surely my personality had some purpose.
Surely it meant something, since it expressed itself,
Yet looking back today, only one thing troubles me —
Not to have had your self-transcending calm,
Your liberation like star-clustered Infinite Night.

Maybe I had no mission at all on earth.

That's why I'm calling out
For the ear-splitting privilege of greeting you,
All the ant-swarming humanity in the Universe,
All the ways of expressing all emotions,
All the shapes and patterns of all thoughts,
All the wheels, all the gears, all the pistons of the soul.

That's why I'm crying out
And why, in a parade of Me's to you, they all begin to buzz
In their zeal and metaphysical gibberish,
In the uproar of things going on inside without nexus.

Good-bye, bless you, live forever, O great bastard of Apollo,
Impotent and ardent lover of the nine muses and of the graces,
Cable-car from Olympus to us and from us to Olympus.

"Saudação a Walt Whitman," in *Poems of Fernando Pessoa* (New York: Ecco Press, 1986).
Translated by Edwin Honig and Susan M. Brown. Translation copyright © 1986 by Edwin
Honig and Susan M. Brown. Reprinted by permission.

WALTER GRÜNZWEIG

Whitman in the German-Speaking Countries

Whitman's German reception can neither be separated from its broader European context nor from the center of Whitmanite activities in the United States. From the very beginning, German reception tied in closely with an international literary, artistic, and political avant-garde from which it received important ideas and to which it also contributed a good deal. The Whitman phenomenon in the German-speaking countries, therefore, proves that our understanding of reception processes may be incomplete if we dogmatically apply a bilateral and unidirectional model of cultural transfer. In Whitman's case at least, a multicultural network of relationships seems to be at work, which proves the emergence of an international literary and artistic community. By the same token, the story of Whitman's German reception would be far from complete if limited to the literary realm. Whitman's reception also covers a variety of nonliterary fields such as music, youth and proletarian cultures and subcultures, politics, and sexuality.

This brief overview attempts both to sketch out the richness of the German Whitman tradition and to characterize the selections included in this volume. These reception documents, most of which are original translations, prove that "reception," once taken out of the contemporary theoretical controversy, is still a very real and dynamic part of the evolution of world literature.

GREATER THAN WAGNER?

It is no surprise that the first German to take notice of Whitman, as well as his first translator, was a revolutionary and an exile. It took a revolutionary to appreciate Whitman's poetry and to value its socio-political implications, and it required an exile to discover Whitman in 1868. This was a time when Germany and Austria had just emerged from a nationalistic quarrel about the leadership among the German states, a time of autocratic rule and little democracy, far removed from the discussion of the issues raised by Whitman's poetry.

Ferdinand Freiligrath (1810–1876) was outsider enough to appreciate Whitman, but his ties to Germany were strong enough to enable him to act as mediator. A former friend of Marx and a revolutionary poet, he was repeatedly forced into British exile, where he worked for the London branch of a Swiss bank while keeping up his literary work and especially his literary translations. By the time he became acquainted with Whitman's poetry through William Rossetti's British edition of *Leaves of Grass*, he had already made a name for himself as a translator of serious poetry even in the United States, and it is no surprise that Whitman and his friends hailed Freiligrath's translations as a seminal victory for their cause.

Although Freiligrath's translation of Whitman in the weekend edition of Germany's leading daily, the *Augsburger Allgemeine Zeitung,* consisted of only ten poems, preceded by an introduction, it made a strong impression on the reading public. Freiligrath wanted to proceed with additional Whitman translations but was unable to do so, probably because his friends had managed to secure permission for his return to Germany at just that time. Yet his name remained connected to Whitman's. In the 1970s and 1980s Whitman editions in the German Democratic Republic still stressed the American's connection to a German revolutionary tradition starting with Freiligrath.

The English translation of Freiligrath's introductory essay in the Augsburg paper (selection 1) is historical. It was facilitated by Whitman's friends, probably under the aegis of William D. O'Connor, Whitman's chief propagandist in that period. It was O'Connor who suggested to Whitman that "I write F.F. a letter, (to go with the package) explaining things generally, and making him as far as possible a master of the situation."[1] Freiligrath reports that the letter consisted of thirty-two sheets in which O'Connor outlined the "true" character of Whitman's poetry and mission. This is an example of the many attempts by Whitmanites to further their poet's overseas reception, conforming to Whitman's own dictum that it was important to him to be "admitted to and heard by the Germanic peoples."

While Freiligrath's essay broke ground for Whitman in Germany, it hardly did justice to the essential modernity of the American's works. Freiligrath's selection of poems, mainly from Whitman's Civil War poetry in *Drum-Taps*, reveals that he appreciated Whitman more for his political and social ideas than for his aesthetic program. What Whitman expressed was more important to Freiligrath than the mode of expression, although Whitman's poetry clearly raised aesthetic questions for him as well: "Has the age so much and such serious matter to say, that the old vessels no longer suffice for the new contents? Are we standing before a poetry of the ages to come, just as some years ago a music of the ages to come was announced to us? And is Walt Whitman greater than Richard Wagner?"

GRASHALME

It would be twenty years after Freiligrath's essay until the first book-length German translation appeared — neither in Germany nor in Austria but in Switzerland, which in the later 1880s was a haven for German dissenters from all walks of life. One of the ideological centers of German progressive thinking of this period about which we still know too little was a publishing house in Zürich. Its owner, Jakob Schabelitz (1827–1899), a friend of Freiligrath's during his London years and himself a radical, had published first editions of works by the iconoclastic Viennese poet, critic, and dramatist Hermann Bahr, the naturalist and socialist poets representative of "Youngest Germany," Karl Henckell and Arno Holz, and the Scottish-German anarchist and lyricist John Henry Mackay.

Here, then, was a publisher ideally suited for a first edition of *Leaves of Grass*. The translators were an unlikely team — Thomas William Rolleston (1857–1920) was an Irish nationalist and Karl Knortz (1841–1918) was a German immigrant to the United States. Both men pursued political motivations with their translation. Knortz, an educator and cultural historian, had been working toward the democratic education of Germans throughout his life. In his view, both Germans and Americans of German extraction sorely lacked democratic traditions, and he hoped that Whitman's poetry would be more effective than political tracts in changing the minds of his people. Rolleston had his own agenda. He believed that Ireland would be freed from England only if the British Empire were confronted with a strong Germany. While he considered the German character solid enough, he insisted that Germans needed to be strengthened politically by thorough training in democracy. Both translators were in close touch with Whitman and his friends, and Whitman proudly approved of their activities.

Of the two collaborators, Rolleston had the more sophisticated program. He believed that the Germans had lost their native creativity and ingenuity in British positivistic philosophy and needed to be brought back to their own idealistic philosophical traditions. This, he insisted, could only be achieved through a massive shock to the complacent German bourgeois sensibility, and he believed Whitman's poetry would provide the necessary voltage. With Whitman, Rolleston outlined an aesthetic program with political implications.

Surprisingly, the first German edition of *Leaves of Grass*, published in 1889 and entitled *Grashalme*, was received well enough. While some critics did admit that they were puzzled about poems that looked as though they were copied from an encyclopedia, most admitted that something new had arrived on the German literary scene. The book seemed commensurate with the newness of the New World, which in the minds of most German-speaking Europeans — shaped by the American novels of James Fenimore Cooper and Charles Sealsfield — still had strong mythical dimensions.

THE GERMAN WHITMAN CULT

One of the most avid readers of *Grashalme* was Johannes Schlaf, who would become the leader of the German Whitman cult. Together with Arno Holz and Gerhart Hauptmann, German literary history credits Schlaf with the introduction of "naturalist" literary principles into German literature. However, given the strong subjectivist orientation of German philosophy and literature ever since Kant and the German romantics, this "naturalism" displayed a special quality. In his essay on Whitman (selection 2), a necrologue written in 1892, Schlaf explains how, through the example of Whitman's poetry, he had been able to escape the limitations of naturalism and discover the richness of his innermost self. He celebrates Whitman as a healer and a prophet of a new age of humanity. Deconstructing this rhetoric, however, we find that he read — and imitated — Whitman's poetry as an answer to the ills of modern existence: urbanization, alienation, and even dissociation of the self, all the issues we now consider to be critical in our judgment of modern civilization.

It is characteristic of Whitman's German reception that, while his poetry was applied as therapy to the ills of existence in a modern world, it also accelerated the development of a modernist aesthetic. Although it sometimes promised to do so, Whitman's poetry never actually led back to holistic premodernist times but rather pointed forward to the disintegration of the self. This process, from a traditionalist viewpoint, reduced humans to a bundle of nerve endings. While German readers, aghast at the rapid technological and industrial development of their society, were looking toward the American poet for assistance, the medicine they actually received was an aesthetic correlative to the newly industrialized culture from which they were attempting to escape.

Schlaf seems to have understood the danger, because he celebrated the emergence of a "new humanity" with Walt Whitman, a humanity no longer grounded in the old value system but rather responding to external stimuli. At the same time, he popularized O'Connor's version of the "good gray poet," which became Germany's favorite image of Whitman. In Schlaf's many articles on Whitman, in his translation of Henry Bryan Binns's biography and several other books, he always stressed the superhuman quality of the poet who was destined to deliver humankind. In this endeavor, he was supported by Horace Traubel, Ernest Crosby, and other Whitmanites who warmly approved of his activities. His most important contribution to Whitman's popularity in the German-speaking countries was a widely circulated translation of a representative cross section of *Leaves* published in a cheap, popular edition. It was through this 1907 edition that Whitman's work became the collective property of practically all German-speaking readers, thereby insuring Whitman's astounding popularity.

Given Schlaf's manifold activities relating to Whitman, it comes as no surprise that he was also in contact with French-speaking devotees of the "good gray poet": Emile Verhaeren, the celebrated Belgian poet; Henri Guilbeaux, editor of a French anthology of German literature in which Whitman's name appears frequently and later a collaborator of Romain Rolland's and a friend of Lenin's; and Léon Bazalgette, Whitman's French translator. Bazalgette once even suggested the foundation of a European equivalent to Traubel's Walt Whitman Fellowship International (for Hermann Hesse's disdain for such organizations, see selection 3), a plan that was never realized, probably owing to increasing nationalist tensions in Europe.

PSYCHOPATHOLOGY

With Traubel, Schlaf shared a true partisan devotion to Whitman, which seems exaggerated and almost childish to the modern observer. Yet Schlaf and others did believe it necessary to "defend" Whitman against all negative criticisms: such critics were automatically denounced as "enemies." This echoes Whitman's own paranoia, and it became a permanent feature of the international Whitman movement. One such villain, and Schlaf's archenemy, was Eduard Bertz (1853–1931), a close friend of the British novelist George Gissing. Bertz was an unlikely candidate for Schlaf's wrath. He had come to know Whitman during an early stay in the United States and, after his return, published an article in which he praised Whitman exuberantly. Bertz sent this article, which appeared in 1889, to Whitman, along with the promise that he was going to "reveal" Whitman to the German people. After Schlaf's 1892 article, however, Bertz was forced to face the fact that Johannes Schlaf, not Eduard Bertz, was going to be Whitman's German prophet.

Bertz, originally a socialist, devoted himself to a number of causes. He wrote ethical treatises and a book outlining a philosophy of the bicycle, and most important, he was active in the early German homosexual movement. The aim of the movement, led by Berlin physician Magnus Hirschfeld, was the legal emancipation of homosexuals. A petition to that effect, carrying the signatures of the majority of German and Austrian intellectuals and artists of the period, was submitted to the German government in 1899. Although it was denied, the petition gave the activists around Hirschfeld a chance to argue for their cause. In the same year, they began publishing a journal in which they tried to dispel scientifically the destructive myths about homosexuality. A regular series in this journal featured the contributions of homosexuals to human history. In 1905 Bertz published a long article on Whitman's homoeroticism, referring to him as a sexually inactive homosexual. In the "psychopathological" language of the day, he called him an *Edelurning* (literally translated, a noble homosexual). Although not intended as such, Bertz's article was perceived by Whitman's followers, especially Schlaf, as an attack on the poet. Schlaf wrote a furious pamphlet in which he accused Bertz of slandering Whitman. Bertz misunderstood and believed that Schlaf and the "terrorists" of the heterosexual world wanted to repress Whitman's homosexuality in order to thwart the movement for homosexual emancipation. With ever-increasing paranoia, Bertz wrote two books attempting to prove not only Whitman's homosexuality but also the existence of a plot by Whitmanites around the world to silence him. In fact, he went so far as to suggest there might be a homosexual conspiracy designed to "sell" Whitman's "homosexual ideas" to the world in the guise of "healthy" poetry.

While all this may not seem to make Bertz a gay liberationist, we must remember that, at the time of this quarrel in the first decade of the twentieth century, the possibilities of the gay movement were much more limited than today. Advocates of homosexual emancipation, content with legal progress, considered any aggressive position taken by homosexuals as counterproductive and destructive. The article by Bertz presented here (selection 4) is a late contribution, published in the *Jahrbuch für Sexuelle Zwischenstufen*, the journal of Hirschfeld's organization, in 1922. However, it reflects the arguments brought forth in the quarrel between 1905 and 1907.

SOCIALISM, ANARCHISM, EROTOCRACY

Apart from whatever effect the debate may have had on homosexual emancipation, Schlaf's eventual "victory" was important for Whitman's continued popularity in the German-speaking countries. If Schlaf had not managed to deny Bertz's well-meant allegations, Whitman would probably not have been accepted in the German-speaking countries—the prejudices against homosexuality and homosexuals were too strong in Central Europe at that time. But since Bertz did not manage to convince the public, Whitman's progress was uninhibited. By the end of the first decade of the twentieth century, his significance for the development of German literature and German thinking was taken for granted.

The German expressionists—from Franz Werfel, Johannes R. Becher, Oskar Maria Graf, and Armin T. Wegner to Franz Kafka—reported the enthusiasm with which they welcomed Schlaf's translation of Whitman. This small booklet fit in every pocket and was carried by numerous activists: socialists, who found that Whitman supplied the much-needed spiritual dimension Marx had abolished from their creed; anarchists, who admired Whitman's refusal to follow aesthetic conventions as much as his call for disobedience and moral independence; members of an influential youth movement, the *Wandervögel*, who reacted enthusiastically to Whitman's call to the "Open Road"; even nudists, who took certain passages from Whitman's poetry quite literally. Essays by Landauer and Bahr (selections 5 and 6) provide examples of the ways Whitman was read between the turn of the century and Hitler's takeover in 1933.

Gustav Landauer (1870–1919), a friend of the German philosopher and theologian Martin Buber, is one of the most interesting personalities in the history of German literature and ideas. Throughout his life he attempted to combine a visionary mysticism with his version of anarchist socialism. Unlike the Marxists, Landauer abhorred power and violence as means toward an ideal society. Whereas social democratic ideologues justified their involvement in and support of World War I by quoting Whitman the wound-dresser who, they claimed, believed that participation in war was necessary to alleviate human suffering, Landauer stressed the antimilitaristic and pacifist tendencies in Whitman's poetry. For Landauer, Whitman's democracy consisted in the free association of human beings living together on egalitarian terms and sharing their everyday work. Landauer gave much thought to questions of human alienation and spiritual impoverishment, which the Marxists then believed could be put off until after their predicted decisive revolutionary change in politics and economics had taken place. In his view, spiritual and intellectual changes had to precede a new social order; a society based on traditional thinking could never bring forth the new human relationships toward which socialism aspired.

Whitman's poetry would provide the spirit (*Geist*) Landauer predicted would serve as a guiding light for a new society based on small units of production, self-managed economic enterprises, and a daily routine requiring each member of society to be engaged in both intellectual and manual labor. Already within the capitalist system, small pockets with "new" human beings could develop, people committed not to nationhood but to a new way of living. When Landauer referred to Americans as a new and exemplary type of "nation," he meant they would overcome the old nationalism in a new community comprising all nations.

When Kurt Wolff, a well-known publisher and sponsor of German expressionist authors, asked Landauer in 1916 whether he would be willing to undertake a Whitman translation, Landauer enthusiastically agreed. The poems, and the edition as a whole, were to serve his pacifist politics during the war. Unfortunately, however, the war did not leave him time to complete his excellent translation, and afterward Landauer joined the short-lived Bavarian Soviet Government in Munich (November 1918–May 1919), hoping to implement his humanist ideas in practical politics. When the government fell, Landauer was arrested; shortly thereafter, soldiers killed him inside a prison. In the United States, a contributor to Max Eastman's leftist paper *The Liberator* and an observer of the events in Germany described Landauer: "A poet, a crusader, with the passionate dreaming soul of 1848. A sensitive man, a man whom every one loved; a devoted admirer of Walt Whitman, whose work he made known to Germany. . . . It was Walt Whitman and Tolstoy, never Marx and Lassalle, whom he hoped to realize in a new Bavaria." Landauer's Whitman translations were finally collected and published by Wolff in a slender but beautiful volume in 1922.

Hermann Bahr (1863–1934), an Austrian critic and dramatist, was a man devoted to the avant-garde. A leader of the modernist members of the "Young Vi-enna" group (the term "modernism" in the artistic sense is sometimes attributed to Bahr), he attempted to break ground for any new movement that would fur-ther artistic and aesthetic progress. In a 1908 essay, he welcomed a new "barbar-ianism" in literature which was, in his view, the only adequate answer to the chal-lenges brought about by emerging technological realities. Arts and humanities, he believed, were firmly grounded in old nineteenth-century traditions and thus were unable to cope with these challenges. If a later generation looked to art and literature to explain and interpret his period, only one author could be said to have given expression to this new era—Whitman.

Whitman remained a constant in Bahr's life. The essay reprinted here was writ-ten on the centenary of Whitman's birth. In it Bahr still stresses the fact that Whitman sings the "modern man." But Whitman's message had by now acquired broader meaning and appeal. Both Germany and Austria had become democratic republics, and intellectuals in both countries had to find a new place in their changing societies. What is the artist's place in a democratic society? What is the nature of democratic art? The questions that had so intensely preoccupied Ameri-can romantics in their struggle for a national literature now came to haunt the Eu-ropeans. Related questions of nationalism preoccupied them as well. After the old monarchies fell, Central Europe presented itself as a colorful quilt of dozens of na-tions and nationalities. How would they relate to each other? These issues provide the background against which Bahr's essay must be read. The answers Bahr found in Whitman are original and explain, in part, Whitman's enormous popularity in the years following World War I. The artist would have to be the universal human mediator between individuals, classes, and nations, and a democracy that could solve these problems would have to become an "erotocracy."

A GERMAN CLASSIC

Whitman, Bahr emphasized admiringly, perceived reality through his sensual-ity—he "philosophizes with the phallus." Hans Reisiger (1884–1968), one of the great translators of the twentieth century and to whom German readers owe the "classic" two-volume translation of Whitman's work, expressed it much the same way. Reisiger "encountered" Whitman as early as 1909 and published his first translations in the leftist journal *Das Forum* at the beginning of World War I. Whitman's true significance for his time, however, was not revealed to Reisiger until after the war. In the introduction to his first one-volume edition of Whit-man's works, he emphasizes that only a quasierotic relationship among men and women (but especially men) could actually make German democracy work.

He shared this curious idea, along with his passion for Whitman, with his close friend Thomas Mann. Mann, who publicly welcomed the publication of Reisiger's translation, had been politically conservative. With the breakdown of the Central European monarchies, Mann had to redefine his position, and he did so with the aid of Whitman. Democracy, he now believed, could work only if what used to be a hierarchical order could be replaced by an erotic commonwealth. Eroticism and sexuality—the common denominators of all human beings—could thereby serve as a glue to keep democratic society from disintegrating. Both Reisiger and Mann were aware of Whitman's homoeroticism and discussed it in connection with his poetry, especially the "Calamus" poems. In a series of surprisingly "public" statements, Mann and Reisiger both referred to the attachment of man to man as the "heartbeat of true democracy" and as the "life nerve of communal life of the future in all states and cities" (see selection 8). It is surprising that this openness was no longer cause for indignant outcries and public protests. Fifteen to twenty years following the debate between Schlaf and Bertz, Mann's and Reisiger's interpretation of Whitman was apparently accepted—although we do not know how much of it was actually understood.

With Reisiger's attractive two-volume edition (upon its publication Mann wrote an open letter that appeared on page one of the leading German daily; see selection 7), Whitman had become a "classic." He was now a recognized part of "world literature," a household word—at least in the households of the educated, artists, and intellectuals. This, however, also meant that the reception of his work became less spontaneous and dramatic. While Whitman's passionate rhetoric was much in demand in the turbulences associated with the war (when scores of German poets, mostly "messianic expressionists," imitated Whitman), the post-expressionistic poets of the *Neue Sachlichkeit* (New Objectivity) had much less affinity with the vitality of the American bard.

Obviously, the Nazis had little use for Whitman's poetry. Although there were two or three attempts to enlist Whitman for national-socialist ideology by turning him into a "Germanic bard," he stressed democracy and internationalism too often to be useful to the ideology of the Third Reich. Yet, as Nazi poet Heinrich Lersch slyly observed, if the word "democratic" is exchanged for the word "*völkisch*" (i.e., belonging to the German people), Whitman might be of some use yet. Lersch was part of a group of poets who were Whitman devotees in their early years and who found that some of the rhetoric they had learned from Whitman was applicable in the Nazi context. Some of Whitman's imagery of blood, soil, and even women came fairly close to the Nazis' rhetoric of the German character, the German homeland, the German earth, and the German mother. The Nazis thus preempted the possibility of a wide use of Whitman's poetry for the anti-Nazi struggle waged by German exiles, and they also prevented a true Whitman renaissance after World War II. Although several new volumes of Whitman's works appeared after 1945, including a number of new translations, Whitman's reception since World War II has hardly equaled the enthusiasm of the years between 1889 and 1925.

Whitman's reception in the Soviet-occupied zone of Germany, later the German Democratic Republic (GDR), was a special case. But even the GDR, a country professing a "messianic" ideology, did not attempt to use the powerful appeal of Whitman's rhetoric. The excellent translation by the GDR author Erich

Arendt, who had come to know Whitman during his exile in Latin America, is hardly reminiscent of the passion of the earlier translations. Rather, Whitman seems to have been important as a point of convergence between the interests of mostly young GDR readers and the official cultural policies of the state. Because of the interest shown in Whitman by revolutionaries such as Freiligrath, or the first Soviet commissar of culture, Anatoly Lunacharsky, or especially their own Johannes R. Becher, the soundness and usefulness of Whitman's poetry were guaranteed in the GDR, where it always remained available in cheap, attractive editions. The GDR audience, on the other hand, fascinated by America and American literature, was interested in Whitman as the representative of a foreign culture to which they had little access physically, intellectually, or artistically. In 1985 the first complete German edition of *Specimen Days*, translated by a GDR translator, was expertly edited by Eva Manske, a specialist in American literature from Leipzig, whose open-minded and inspiring afterword already anticipated the later developments in that country.

TALKING BACK TO WHITMAN IN GERMAN

Although the German-speaking literary world has acknowledged Whitman to be a classic author and even though he has become a subject of academic inquiry at German, Austrian, and Swiss universities, Whitman's poetry continues to provoke important reactions on the part of creative writers themselves. Lyrical replies to Whitman have always been a measure of his continuing vitality, and German poets have talked back to him frequently and energetically (see selections 9–20).

Christian Morgenstern (1871–1914), a poet, translator, and journalist, had a number of uses for Whitman's poetry. In *Constructing the German Walt Whitman*, I introduced "The Democratic Song of My Room," Morgenstern's parody of Whitman's poetry, which mocks the reception of Whitman more than it satirizes Whitman's poetry. Here I include a second "Whitman poem" which, in a much more earnest fashion, explores Whitman's internationalist theme, always a favorite among Germans. Morgenstern, with his extreme dislike of the German bourgeois life-style, obviously saw Whitman's globalist poetry and his lyrical America as antidotes to the stuffiness of German life.

Arthur Drey was born in Würzburg, Germany, and shared his birth year — 1890 — with many members of the expressionist generation. In 1910 he went to Berlin, where he became acquainted with Georg Heym, one of the most significant German expressionist poets. In 1911 he moved to Marburg and graduated with a doctorate in law two years later. He lived as a businessman in Frankfurt until 1938, when he was forced to emigrate to the United States. He died in New York in 1965. During Drey's short literary career, he contributed to the important expressionist journals *Der Sturm* and *Die Aktion*. His poem "Walt Whitman" demonstrates the expressionists' exaggerated adoration of Whitman as a human being, a poet, and a God-like giant. The poem not only reflects expressionist enthusiasm for Whitman but is at the same time a measure of the alienation of these poets. Quite obviously, Whitman is the receptacle of the projections designed to compensate for their imagined and real deficits as poets and human beings. Their characterizations of Whitman with terms such as "Titan" or, in the poem by Carl Albert Lange, "Giant" suggest the degree to which the human individual is dwarfed by modern technology and industrial society. The violent emotions they ascribe to Whitman, as exaggerated as comic book characterizations, are indicative of the impossibility of expressing subjectivity in a mechanized and controlled society.

The two poems by Swiss writers Gustav Gamper (1873–1948) and Hans Reinhart (1880–1963) appeared next to each other in a Swiss literary journal in 1919, along with Gamper's woodcut of Whitman. These poems are more constrained and devout, exuding a feeling of religiosity, but otherwise they are very similar to the exaggerated diction of the expressionists. Gamper, a native of Trogen, Switzerland, was a poet, musician, and painter. Whitman was the great experience of his life, a model to follow throughout his career. Gamper is best known for his work *Die Brücke Europas* (*The Bridge of Europe*), a Whitmanesque attempt to create a kind of modern national "epic" devoted to his homeland. *Die Brücke Europas* is prefaced by Gamper's poem to Whitman included here. Reinhart, a friend of Gamper's, was born in Winterthur, Switzerland. Descended from a wealthy family, he studied in Germany, Switzerland, and France and traveled widely. He was influenced by anthroposophy after a trip to India in 1909 and devoted his career to poetry, drama, and prose, as well as to local cultural activities in his hometown. He also translated individual poems by Whitman.

The poem by Carl Albert Lange (1892–1952) seems to be from the same expressionist school as Drey's, although Lange is not usually included with the expressionist movement. He was born in Hamburg as a son of a music teacher. In 1914 he was called to military duty and was a Russian POW from 1915 to 1919; these years in Siberia led him to literature. For the most part, he wrote poetry and prose, but he also translated from several languages. Although his work was repeatedly recognized by several prominent German critics and writers, Lange never established himself as a major twentieth-century voice in German poetry.

Not all Germans, however, were uncritical admirers of Whitman. Already one year before the appearance of Lange's poem, in 1926, Kurt Tucholsky, one of the great German satirists, wrote a parody of "Salut au Monde!" Of the three Whitman parodies he wrote — one as early as 1913 — this one is the most interesting. Tucholsky frequently used "Ignaz Wrobel" as a pseudonym. The "Walt Wrobel" in the poem is Tucholsky turned Whitman — or the other way around. Whitman's spiritualized epistemological optimism is shown to be unfounded; the wealth of all appearances could not possibly be grasped by the five senses. Paradoxically, the senses mediate mainly one thing — pain. Whitman's global panorama is here replaced by ridiculous local observations from the author's everyday life. At the very best, it is slightly humorous — something Whitman's poem is certainly not. In spite of this parody's implicit biting criticism, Tucholsky, like other writers critical of Whitman's optimism, nonetheless admired the American as a great poet. On a poetry manuscript by the young German poet Walter Bauer, he commented, "I am much more interested in your intellectual parents than in your professional aspirations. Just so there are no misunderstandings: this does not change anything, not in the least, about the value of your poems. Their rhymelessness is almost a matter of course . . . and one just cannot avoid Whitman."[2]

The sonnet by Johannes R. Becher (1891–1958) probably was written in the early 1940s when he was in Soviet exile. In his youth and early manhood, Becher was a devout Whitmanite; later he programmatically declared his conversion from Whitman to Marx and Lenin. Yet, like many other Marxists, he continued to admire Whitman, even though the sonnet form of the poem included here suggests that the nature of this admiration had changed. Becher, first minister of culture in the GDR, was an influential, although self-serving, cultural politician, whose interest in Whitman helped to insure the poet's "survival" in the GDR.

Gabriele Eckart (born in 1954) is one of the most gifted lyricists in contemporary German literature. At the time she wrote the poem included here, she was still in high school. Her "search for metres," in the course of which she encountered Whitman, already points to the original poetry she would write in the future. By the mid-1980s, Eckart had become a dissident writer and eventually removed to the United States.

The tradition of critical answers to Whitman started by Tucholsky is taken up by the German writer Jürgen Wellbrock and the German-American writer Hans Sahl, but the criticism has become sharper and more pronounced. The poem by Wellbrock (born in 1949), a Berlin-based writer of poems, short stories, and radio plays, is explicitly critical of Whitman and Whitman's rhetoric, yet it testifies to the power of Whitman's voice and the necessity for every poet to come to terms with it. Wellbrock himself speaks of his "ambivalent" attitude toward Whitman, whose expansiveness and freedom he admires but whose rhetoric and glorification of strength and body offend him. The poem is a clever montage of Whitman quotations that have become famous in Germany; Wellbrock carefully refutes each one. No German poet has "talked back" in a more radical fashion to Whitman than Wellbrock. Sahl's "Schädelstätte Manhattan" ("Calvary Manhattan") (1962) uses biblical motifs, but its rhetoric is Whitman's. It remains unclear whether it is Whitman's belief in progress that is targeted here or whether the poem attempts to show that our plastic era does not do justice to our cultural-humanist legacy, the Bible, or Whitman; both interpretations seem possible. Sahl, born in Dresden in 1902, was one of the most prominent German exiles in the literary field. Since 1945 he has worked as a cultural correspondent for several German-language dailies. He is also a prominent translator of American dramatists (among them Williams, Miller, and Wilder). The poem is the sophisticated product of a truly bicultural mind and deserves an important place in German-American literature.

Roland Kluge is another GDR poet, born in Delitzsch, Germany, in 1944. He became a bookseller, worked as a nurse's assistant, then studied medicine in Leipzig, where he specialized in internal medicine. This part-time poet's direct address to Whitman confronts the frequent attempts to pronounce Whitman dead. Yet, to this poet writing in the "mid-age" years of tranquillity and "maturity," Whitman is still as provocative as ever. Kluge writes that "for somebody who was forced to live in a walled-in country, it can be a revelation to see the upright posture of a human being: self-determination instead of other-directedness, sensuality instead of prudishness, love of truth rather than hypocrisy. . . . To me, Walt Whitman was a great help."[3]

In a country where walls have come down, Whitman's German reception will no doubt develop in new and unsuspected ways as a result of the radical changes in East-Central Europe. Whereas the changes in Eastern and East-Central Europe have muted Marxist voices and thus also Marxist respondents to Whitman, a new kind of response is struck by Rolf Schwendter (pseudonym of Rudolf Schesswendtner), born in 1939 in Vienna. A professor of sociology at the University of Kassel in Germany, Schwendter's academic interests include subcultures, future studies, and research into social and cultural deviancy. His poem "You I Sing, Socialism" was written for the 1990 festival of the Austrian Communist press in Vienna and targets both conservative and Marxist orthodoxies from a libertarian, independently leftist point of view. For the first time, Whitman's pluralist aesthetics have been appreciated by a leftist recipient. While it lacks Whitman's lyrical vision, Schwendter's poem is a programmatic and sophisticated piece of work, and it synthesizes the tradition of German responses to Whitman while it opens up new modes of creative political interpretations of his poetry.

NOTES

1. Horace Traubel, *With Walt Whitman in Camden* (New York: D. Appleton, 1908), 2: 431–432.

2. Kurt Tucholsky to Walter Bauer, December 8, 1930, German Literary Archive, Marbach.

3. Roland Kluge, "Der oft schon totgesagte Geist Walt Whitmans," *Neue Deutsche Literatur* 32 (1984): 105.

1. FERDINAND FREILIGRATH

"Walt Whitman"

Walt Whitman! Who is Walt Whitman?

The answer is, a poet! A new American poet! His admirers say, the first, the only poet America has as yet produced. The only American poet of specific character. No follower in the beaten track of the European muse, but fresh from the prairie and the new settlements, fresh from the coast and the great watercourses, fresh from the thronging humanity of seaports and cities, fresh from the battle-fields of the South, and from the earthy smells in hair and beard and clothing of the soil from which he sprang. A being not yet come to fullness of existence, a person standing firmly and consciously upon his own American feet, an utterer of a gross of great things, though often odd. And his admirers go still further: Walt Whitman is to them the only poet at all, in whom the age, this struggling, eagerly seeking age, in travail with thought and longing, has found its expression; the poet *par excellence.*

Thus, on the one side his admirers, in whose ranks we find even an Emerson. On the other, to be sure, are the critics, those whose business it is to abase aspirants. By the side of unmeasured praise and enthusiastic recognitions of his genius are bitter and biting scorn and injurious abuse.

This, it is true, troubles not the poet. The praise he takes in as his due; to the scorn he opposes scorn of his own. He believes in himself; his self-reliance is unbounded. "He is," says his English publisher, W. M. Rossetti, "to himself above all things the one man who cherishes earnest convictions, and avows that he, both now and hereafter, is the founder of a new poetical literature — a great literature — a literature such as will stand in due relation and proportion to the material grandeur and the incalculable destinies of America. He believes that the Columbus of the continent or the Washington of the States were not more truly founders and builders of this America than he himself will be in time to come. Surely a sublime conviction, and by the poet more than once expressed in stately words — none more so than the poem which begins with the line:

"Come, indivisible will I make this continent."

This sounds haughty. Is the man in his right mind, that he talks thus? Let us step nearer to him! Let us hearken to his life and his works. First of all let us open his book.

Are these verses? The lines are arranged like verses, to be sure, but verses they are not. No metre, no rhyme, no stanzas. Rhythmical prose, ductile verses. At first sight rugged, inflexible, formless; but yet for a more delicate ear, not devoid of euphony. The language homely, hearty, straightforward, naming everything by its true name, shrinking for nothing, sometimes obscure. The tone rhapsodical, like that of a seer, often unequal, the sublime mingled with the trivial even to the point of insipidity. He reminds us sometimes, with all the differences that exist besides, of our own Hamann. Or of Carlyle's oracular wisdom. Or of the *Paroles d'un Croyant.* Through all there sounds out the Bible — its language, not its creed.

And what does the poet propound to us in this form? First of all: Himself, his *I,* Walt Whitman. This *I* however is a part of America, a part of the earth, a part of mankind, a part of the All. As such he is conscious of himself and revolves, knitting the greatest to the least, ever going out from America, and coming back to America ever again (only to a free people does the future belong!) before our view, a vast and magnificent world-panorama. Through this individual Walt Whitman and his Americanism marches, we may say, a *cosmical* procession, such as may be suitable for reflective spirits, who, face to face with eternity, have passed solitary days on the sea-shore, solitary nights under the starry sky of the prairie. He finds himself in all things and all things in himself. He, the one man, Walt Whitman, is mankind and the world. And the world and mankind are to him one great poem. What he sees and hears, what he comes in contact with, whatever approaches him, even the meanest, the most trifling, the most every-day matter—all is to him symbolical of a higher, of a spiritual fact. Or rather, matter and spirit, the real and the ideal are to him one and the same. Thus, produced by himself, he takes his stand; thus he strides along, singing as he goes; thus he opens from his soul, a proud free man, and *only* a man, world-wide, social and political vistas.

A wonderful appearance. We confess that it moves us, disturbs us, will not loose its hold upon us. At the same time, however, we would remark that we are not yet ready with our judgment of it, that we are still biased by our first impression. Meanwhile we, probably the first in Germany to do so, will take at least a provisional view of the scope and tendency of this new energy. It is fitting that our poets and thinkers should have a closer look at this strange new comrade, who threatens to overturn our entire *Ars Poetica* and all our theories and canons on the subject of aesthetics. Indeed, when we have listened to all that is within these earnest pages, when we have grown familiar with the deep, resounding roar of those, as it were, surges of the sea in their unbroken sequence of rhapsodical verses breaking upon us, then will our ordinary verse-making, our system of forcing thought into all sorts of received forms, our playing with ring and sound, our syllable-counting and measure of quantity, our sonnet-writing and construction of strophes and stanzas, seem to us almost childish. Are we really come to the point, when life, even in poetry, calls imperatively for new forms of expression? Has the age so much and such serious matter to say, that the old vessels no longer suffice for the new contents? Are we standing before a poetry of the ages to come, just as some years ago a music of the ages to come was announced to us? And is Walt Whitman greater than Richard Wagner?

As to the person and the life of the poet, we learn that he is a man of almost fifty years. He was born on the 31st May, 1819. His birth-place, the village of West Hills, on Long Island, in the state of New York. His father, in succession, innkeeper, carpenter, and architect, a descendant of English settlers; the mother, Louisa Van Velsor, of Dutch descent. The boy received his first school teaching in Brooklyn, a suburb of New York. Compelled at an early age to rely upon his own exertions, he gained his living first as a printer, and later as a teacher, and a contributor to several New York papers. In the year 1849 we find him established as editor of a newspaper in New Orleans, two years later again a printer in Brooklyn. After this he worked a long time, like his father, as carpenter and architect. In the year 1862, after the breaking out of the great civil war (as an enthusiastic Unionist and anti-slavery man he stood firmly on the side of the North), he undertook, by authority from Lincoln through Emerson's mediation, the care of the wounded in the field. And to be sure, he had it expressly stipulated beforehand, that it was to be without any sort of remuneration. From the spring of 1863 onward, this nursing in the field, and in the hospitals at Washington, was his "only employment by day and by night." Over the measureless self-sacrifice, over the kindness and goodness of heart, which he evinced in this trying work, there rises the unanimous tribute of the soldiers' testimony. Every wounded man, from the North and the South alike, had the same careful and loving attendance at the hands of the poet. At the end of the war, it is said, he must have nursed with his own hands more than 100,000 sick and wounded. For six months he himself lay sick; a hospital fever, the first sickness of his life, had seized him. After the war he obtained a minor office in the Department of the Interior at Washington, but lost it in June, 1865, when the minister, Mr. Harlan, had it brought to his attention, that Whitman was the author of the book, "Leaves of Grass," the coarseness, or as it appeared to Mr. Harlan, the immorality of which filled the ministerial bosom with holy horror. But the poet found soon another post of modest salary in the bureau of the Attorney General at Washington. There he is still living. On Sunday, and sometimes in the week also, he still keeps up his visits to the hospitals.

Whitman is a plain man, a man of few needs. Poor, and, according to his own avowal, without talent for moneymaking. His strength, said he to a visitor, Mr. M. D. Conway, an American living in London, lay in "loafing and writing poems." On bread and water, he has discovered, he can live on the whole delightfully and cheerfully. Conway found him (while yet on Long Island — before the war, indeed), in a temperature of 100 degrees Fahrenheit lying on his back in the grass, and staring at the sun. Just like Diogenes. "With his gray clothing, his blue-gray shirt, his iron-gray hair, his swart, sunburnt face and bare neck, he lay upon the brown-and-white grass, — for the sun had burnt away its greenness, — and was so like the earth upon which he rested, that he seemed almost enough a part of it for one to pass by without recognition." He found it not at all too hot, and confided to Conway that this was one of his favourite places and attitudes for composing poems. His abode Conway found very plain and simple. A small room, poorly furnished, with only one window, which looked out on the sandy solitude of Long Island. Not a single book in the room. But he talked of the Bible, of Homer, and of Shakespeare as of favorite books which he owned. For reading he had two especial study-rooms: one was the top of an omnibus, the other Coney Island, an uninhabited little sand islet far out in the Atlantic Ocean, miles from the coast.

"Well, he looks like a man!" cried Lincoln, when he first saw Whitman. At this, we think of Napoleon's expression about Goethe: "Voilá un homme!"

His writings, up to this time, are the above-named "Leaves of Grass" (first edition 1855, set up and printed by the poet himself; second edition 1856; third edition 1860); then, after the war, "Drum-Taps" (1865) with a "Sequel" in which is a fine rhapsody on the death of Abraham Lincoln; and last year, a complete edition with a supplement called "Songs before Parting." A selection from this complete edition has just been published in London by W. M. Rossetti, one of Whitman's English admirers. The coarse expressions of doubtful propriety which were in the New York original edition have been left out of this; and it is the purpose of the publisher by means of this issue to open a path for the preparation of a complete edition and for its unprejudiced reception in England. We are indebted to Mr. Rossetti's preface to this selection of his for the sketch given above of the poet's life.

With these suggestions we leave the subject for this time, but will soon recur to it, especially to give some translated specimens of the poet's productions. Though it is a dubious business to estimate Whitman from specimens. The principle "*ex pede Herculem*" is hardly quite applicable to him; if in any way a poet, he will be recognised and honored as such in his totality.

Augsburger Allgemeine Zeitung, Wochenausgabe, no. 17 (April 24, 1868): 257–259. Translation from *New Eclectic Magazine* 2 (July 1868): 325–329; translator unknown.

2. JOHANNES SCHLAF

"Walt Whitman"

A little while ago, a few German magazines carried reports on the death of one of the most outstanding North American poets on March 26 of this year, Walt Whitman. He had died in Camden near Philadelphia in the seventy-fourth year of his life. The few data on his life and work that accompanied this report, reminiscent of the laconicism of a literary encyclopedia, were hardly designed to inspire further interest for the deceased.

To inspire such interest, however, is very desirable, because hardly anything relevant has as yet been published on Whitman in German. After all, Whitman is not only the most significant poet of North America, but he belongs to world literature, and that, we believe, with greater justification than his countryman Edgar Poe who is, in a manner of speaking, known to the whole world. . . . Our essay does not make any pretensions. It wants to contribute its modest share to awaken greater interest for Whitman by giving a short picture of the characteristics of the poet as far as we can gather them from the incomplete translation of his *Leaves of Grass*. . . .

In the introduction to their translation, one of the translators, Karl Knortz, calls Whitman an "optimist par excellence." But we have to discard the phrase because we cannot force the whole Whitman into this small box. With such a phrase, little is said about a human being who said of himself with these proudly modest words:

I do not trouble my spirit to vindicate itself or to be understood,
I see that the elementary laws never apologize.

The translators have used these lines as motto for their book and they characterize Whitman better than the dusty phrase of the "optimist par excellence." If these words characterize Whitman, he is more than a pessimist or an optimist, then he defines himself as a force in the living, organic texture of all nature. He can hardly deny his own self and is radically different from the incapacitated romanticism and the christianism from which the "Old World" is presently suffering, with hardly enough breath to throw all kinds of blasphemies against sour grapes.

His "barbaric yawp" sounds "over the roofs of the world" like powerful dithyrambs of a new life and a new strength; they resound in the midst of the funeral hymns of the Old World and announce a new religion, a new art and a new meaning of life. *Whitman is neither optimist nor pessimist: he is strength.*

Whitman was born in 1819 on Long Island where his family owned a large farm whose fields the Whitmans tilled with their own hands. There, in the open countryside, in unspoilt nature, he spent the larger part of his youth. Later, in an American manner, he tried his hand in a variety of professions: he was a printer, teacher, carpenter, journalist, building contractor etc. Although he was on his way to becoming successful and wealthy in a variety of trades, he eventually gave everything up and started to write poetry. In the 60s, just after the *Leaves* had appeared, he spent the Civil War on the battlefield and worked as a nurse in the hospitals. During that time, he earned his living as a newspaper correspondent. For his various services, he received a small job at the Ministry of the Interior which he did not keep for long. He owed his dismissal to the Secretary of the Interior, James Harlan, a former Methodist preacher, who was morally outraged over the *Leaves* published in 1855. His friends procured for him a new position in the office of the Attorney General which he kept until 1873. At that time, he suffered a stroke. His health was shattered as a consequence of the exertions in the war. He improved slowly without ever completely recovering. Later, he managed to make a small, very modest home for himself in Camden and this is where, without bitterness and complaint, he authored his best poetry which shows a "special religious consecration" (I am quoting Rolleston, whose introduction to the translation of the *Leaves* serves me as a source for this short sketch of Whitman's life), "a quiet, transfigured beauty, contrasting with the mood of the earlier poems just as the starry nocturnal heavens contrast with the sunlit earth."

Thus he created his poetry while continuously changing locations, at times in midst of the rich colorful traffic of the American metropolis, among the boldest and most enormous achievements of modern industry, at times in the great outdoors of his continent, always in the midst of battle and tumult of a colorful life. The spirit of his art is as different from the spirit of the middle ages as the medieval spirit was itself different from classical antiquity; it grows as organically out of the middle ages as the medieval spirit grew out of that of classical antiquity.

For today, my work is done. It is growing dusky. Tired and deadened from all my writing I lean out of the window and see how the sunlight at the facade of the high building across from me gradually disappears.

And then, after all the reading and all the work, I feel how constricted our lives are, I understand and sense our misery.

Johannes Schlaf [177]

The street with the jumble and the noise of traffic reaches far down, loses itself in both directions in smoke and in the confusing bustle of the side streets. Above, a narrow, scanty piece of heaven, darkened and polluted by the rising food vapors. Behind the windows on the other side, all the way down the long street, next to me, above and below me, from all sides a pressing, shoving and constriction and confusion between the gray masses of stone. And, like here, this extends in concentric circles for hours, far into the countryside. Far, far away somewhere, nature is alive with its free air of the heavens, and its free stars, with its meadows, fields and forests, with mountains, streams, lakes and seas, far away, unreal like a legend, like a fabulous fairy tale which we read in our children's books. The countless threads through which our life, our feeling, and our perception are connected to infinite mysteries seem to be cut. We are alone, alone with ourselves, with what our discriminating judgment would call "human." We are alone with ourselves, man with man, in the vibrating restlessness of this constriction and its nerve-shattering, confusing pell-mell. Our suffering, our misery and our joys, however, turn into monsters in this all too obvious crowdedness, distorted by a devilish perspective. And all the refinements of our aged culture cannot hide the great, fundamental disease which we have been trying to cure with all kinds of medicines for some time: our lack of religion or, if we want, our lack of energy, the atrophy of our perception.

Our recent ethical endeavors. So many half-hearted attempts to get to the root of our general malaise. But how can we help each other, if we have only an understanding of how we are connected with all things close and far but not a living perception of them? If we have no "religion" from which alone originates love, self-awareness, joy, force, art, ethics, manhood and comprehension of life? How can we get to the root of the thousandfold misery of a metropolis, the distress of the poor, if we cannot even stand looking at it and if it seduces us to blasphemies against the world?

Now let's think about all the pessimism and all the decadence of our European world. Let's think about all its art, its artifice, its artificiality, its refinements, its moral hangover, all its nervous and yearning distress — and then let's listen to the "optimist par excellence," Walt Whitman.

> Starting from fish-shape Paumanok where I was born,
> Well-begotten, and rais'd by a perfect mother,
> After roaming many lands, lover of populous pavements,
> Dweller in Mannahatta my city, or on southern savannas,
> Or a soldier camp'd or carrying my knapsack and gun, or a miner in
>   California,
> Or rude in my home in Dakota's woods, my diet meat, my drink from the
>   spring,
> Or withdrawn to muse and meditate in some deep recess,
> Far from the clank of crowds intervals passing rapt and happy,
> Aware of the fresh free giver the flowing Missouri, aware of mighty Niagara,

Aware of the buffalo herds grazing the plains, the hirsute and strong-breasted
    bull,
Of earth, rocks, Fifth-month flowers experienced, stars, rain, snow, my amaze,
Having studied the mocking-bird's tones and the flight of the mountain-
    hawk,
And heard at dawn the unrivall'd one, the hermit thrush from the swamp-
    cedars,
Solitary, singing in the West, I strike up for a New World.

How do we suddenly feel? — It is as if everything existing miles away in a fabulous distance all of a sudden becomes alive in its fresh beauty, everything we feel to
be in contrast to our life here, which we know, yet do not understand. In free
verses, it appears before us with all of its miracles. With unheard-of sounds and
rhythms which seem like the fresh roaring of the wind, like the sea waves approaching with their vast rolling splendor. Unfamiliar, totally separate from the
refinements from our aged and wizened art.

Victory, union, faith, identity, time,
The indissoluble compacts, riches, mystery,
Eternal progress, the kosmos, and the modern reports.

We are forced to stop. Astonished. This is a child's stammering. Helpless, un-
wieldy, unarticulate, ridiculous to our well-trained thinking and feeling. But we
understand: it is the jubilant helplessness in the face of a new infinite wealth of
penetrating perceptions, the surprised jubilant cry with which a child liberates itself from its sweet burden, joyfully, verifying the data it perceives. There is the
blessed, vigorous turmoil of living growth inside. All of this, then, this whole new
fullness rushing in on us:

This then is life,
Here is what has come to the surface after so many throes and convulsions.

How curious! how real!
Underfoot the divine soil, overhead the sun.

See revolving the globe,
The ancestor-continents away group'd together,
The present and future continents north and south, with the isthmus between.

See, vast trackless spaces,
As in a dream they change, they swiftly fill,
Countless masses debouch upon them,
They are now cover'd with the foremost people, arts, institutions, known.

See, projected through time,
For me an audience interminable.

With firm and regular step they wend, they never stop,
Successions of men, Americanos, a hundred millions,
One generation playing its part and passing on,
Another generation playing its part and passing on in its turn,
With faces turn'd sideways or backward towards me to listen,
With eyes retrospective towards me.

What a language! And when we read on, and the deeper we read into him, the more we are carried away by the power of these old primeval songs. This is the power and the energy of the old Hebrew psalmists and prophets. And yet, everything is so new, so simple and so down-to-earth. No artful devices. Not even one as primitive as that reminiscent of the *parallelismus membrorum* of old Hebrew poetry. This language is as earthly as one can imagine, oftentimes just stating, almost with American soberness, that which is. And yet it has as much passionate rhetoric, overwhelming and entrancing, as ever existed. An infinite rhythm, and an infinite melody. Just as the storm has a rhythm of rising and ebbing and newly rising, just as the sea waves have their rhythm, the air shimmering in the warmth of the sun, the song of the birds, the infinite movement of nature. The power and the warmth of healthy blood, freely and freshly pulsating through the body, an unprecedented energy and original intimacy of perception penetrating distance and closeness and all appearances, surrendering to the movement of its becoming and changing with powerful terror, in which vibrations of the eternally moving atoms tremble, free respiration of healthy lungs, the light power of unspoilt eyes, the haleness and elasticity of unimpaired muscles: all of this gives power to these songs, their passion with which they liberate themselves from everything that they call art and artifice, or they expand to the audacity and the power of the living nature. . . . The naivete of a child perceiving a new object and calling its name ten, twenty, a hundred times in succession without becoming tired, with equal delight over the same activity of its vocal chords and over the properties of the object thus designated. A crowded wealth of impressions, only semi-conscious thoughts, impossible to express them fully in intelligible, measured sequence. They push and hold back in a disorderly race; obscurity, mysticism next to plainness and sober clarity. And by all of this, one feels repelled and attracted, just as nature attracts and repels, surrenders itself and denies itself, transparent and mystical with the eternal rhythm of appearances, monotonous yet of infinite variety.

And what a mood! . . . [Reading Whitman] we have overcome isolation and separation which has confused us and made us afraid. Misery and happiness, poverty and wealth, all the incomprehensible oppositions which tortured us in our narrow life: they can no longer harm us or obscure the connectedness of all things. And yet: Everything is there, everything in its place, ordered and redeemed from all conflict through the powerful rhythm of all occurrences and appearances. Everything dissolves in one large feeling of strength and life emphasizing and enclosing all. All the connections with which the individual, the separate is infinitely connected with all that has happened since the first beginning, seemingly dissolved in the consciousness of life, here becomes apparent again in a powerful mood.

In one place of his *Leaves* it says:

> I find I incorporate gneiss, coal, long-threaded moss, fruits, grains, esculent
> roots,
> And am stucco'd with quadrupeds and birds all over. . . .

This is how powerful the religious mood is in Whitman and with how much energy it expresses itself. . . .

Everything lives in him, in you, in all of us, is contained and enclosed by us: humans, stars, times, animals, plants, stones. "My lovers suffocate me . . . thick in the pores of my skin." Everything is made for his sake, for your sake, for all of our sake. Everything is us and we are everything. What, then, are beginning and end, birth and death? Everything is eternal movement.

> Urge and urge and urge,
> Always the procreant urge of the world.

We are everything there was and everything there will be; there is no difference between these two; everything is one. Nothing is offensive or mean. Copulation is no more offensive than death. Everything is a miracle. The body is something miraculous that must be revered. In this spirit, he transfers the attributes of his body to everything that comes in touch with him. He speaks of broad and muscular fields etc. and yet also transfers attributes of lifeless objects to his body, speaks of "the mix'd tussled hay of the head, beard, brawn" etc. He is in love with his body, with himself, with everything.

> Press close bare-bosom'd night — press close magnetic nourishing night!
> Night of south winds — night of the large few stars!
> Still nodding night — mad naked summer night.

With mad, jubilant desire he throws his naked body against the waves, offers his chest to the storm. He does not utter the complaints heard everywhere in the world, that the months are only empty spaces and the ground is nothing but mud and mire. Everything is alive. Everything forces itself into him and he forces himself into everything. The ages are tormenting themselves by pointing to the best and differentiating it from the bad, but he remains silent, and while they are fighting, he goes swimming and admires himself, well-aware of the perfect state and severity of all things. Although he is surrounded with questions and doubt, they are not his true self which is standing apart from all buffeting and twitching. The days of dispute and of confusion are behind him. He needs neither sarcasm nor proofs. *He is identical with what others are trying to prove.* An immense feeling of strength filling all distances and depths, an intimate feeling of oneness with everything is the foundation of his being and his songs.

This foundation could indeed be called religious, and his themes originate from it: love, democracy, and religion. And his main theme is the sublimity of religion. . . . Science must be respected, to love a man and a woman in abundance is sublime, but there is something else that is *truly* sublime and which unifies everything, provides for everything with tireless hands: religion. Not the cult, the dogma with its imperatives, but the powerful broad awareness of life whose force comprises the cosmos with love and wonder, the religious feeling, the intimate, jubilant consciousness of belonging to everything. He sings his songs only in order "to drop in the earth the germs of a greater religion." Without religion, there is no greatness truly great, no state, no character, no life. He does not pray, does not worship, does not bow and scrape before the eternal laws and does not participate in ceremonies. His worship is the mad desire to come in contact with the atmosphere, to throw himself jubilantly into the powerful movement of life, its becoming and passing, blooming, shining, raging, growing, glowing.

Religion is the powerful feeling which makes him stand admiringly before the revolution of the stars, before the magnificence of the human and the animal body. In one song, "I Sing the Body Electric," he enumerates all parts of the human body, pages of enraptured stammering like a child naming things with a bliss beyond expression and feeling the infinite fullness of life in this continued process of naming. It is religion when he enjoys the naked bodies of bathing youths and their elastic and youthful movements. It is religion when he loves flowers and the grass tenderly. And it is religion when the movement of the solar system, the orbit of the earth reveals itself to him in powerful visions, with all its miracles and its life. Religion allows him to immerse himself in the infinitude of the microcosm, in the immeasurable miracles of the low, the scorned, the despised, and which allows him to see everywhere an identical, eternal movement of universal life, not comprehensible for a measuring, reasoning intellect. Religion allows him to admire the development and passing of human cultures. He is happy when he can touch a human body and when the electric touch communicates to him the life of what he is touching. . . .

His feeling of love or his all-encompassing feeling of strength does not ask or measure "who" or "how much" somebody is. He is drawn to the slave in the cottonfield and he presses the brotherly kiss on his cheek and swears by his soul that he would never deny him. He makes higher claims for those who work with hammer and chisel than for all deific conceptions of past and present. The young workman is closest to him, the backwoodsman, the fieldhand, they will understand him best. In all the people he sees himself, nobody is more, nobody even by a grain of barley less. He advocates the rights of those who are suppressed by others, the misshapen, the foolish, the insignificant, the simple-minded, the despised.

He is the hounded slave, the firefighter with crushed chest. Young men who work with fire hoses and rope ladders are no less to him than the Gods of the old wars:

> The snag-tooth'd hostler with red hair redeeming sins past and to come,
> Selling all he possesses, traveling on foot to fee lawyers for his brother and sit
>   by him while he is tried for forgery. . . .

He is the spokesman of scorned criminals and looks at them with the eyes of kinship, defying all hypocrisy. He is the bard of America and her democratic institutions. In jubilant devotion and love he enumerates the names of all of her states. He wanders through her prairies, her virgin forests, bathes at her sea shores, listens to her male and female orators in the public halls, admires her exhibitions, her cities, her buildings and arts, is at home with all of them and is truly the singer of her spirit:

> No dainty dolce affetuoso I,
> Bearded, sun-burnt, gray-neck'd, forbidding, I have arrived
> To be wrestled with as I pass for the solid prizes of the universe.

He sings social revolutions and the future of democracy, he is a lover of cities. For example in a poem wonderfully translated by Freiligrath, "Rise O Days from Your Fathomless Deeps." For long periods of time he has traveled through the prairies, has listened to the "pouring" of the Niagara, has climbed up the "towering rocks along the Pacific," "sail'd through the storm" and "seen with joy the threatening maws of the waves." Avoiding the cities he searched for certainties, craving for original strength and for the fearlessness of the cosmos, regenerating himself. It was good and he prepared himself well and now he again wanders through the cities, observing a yet greater and more powerful drama than the natural wonders of the prairies, the raging of the storm, the waterfalls and the sea:

> Manhattan rising, advancing with menacing front — Cincinnati, Chicago,
>   unchain'd;
> What was that swell I saw on the ocean? behold what comes here,
> How it climbs with daring feet and hands — how it dashes!
> How the true thunder bellows after the lightning — how bright the flashes of
>   lightning! . . .
> How democracy with desperate vengeful port strides on, shown through the
>   dark by those flashes of lightning! . . .
> Thunder on! stride on, Democracy! strike with vengeful stroke!

More than everything he loves the large cities and his "Manhattan." More than the still shining sun, the foliage, the corn and the wheat, more than solitude and the humming of the bees. Untiringly, he is wandering through her streets and losing himself in her traffic which becomes alive in his lines, containing broad, powerful, colorful shining visions. In countless images endlessly strung together, his loving surprise rushes by us. He does not want to leave anything out, does not want to miss anything. With a sharp, discerning eye he relates this colorful medley and lovingly animates each perception which, sometimes through a singular, extraordinarily vivid and characteristic epitheton, become poems for themselves. This wealth of images he strings together like countless small novels, dramas, lyrical poems, often hardly containing one line, a few words. There are slaves, auctions, soldiers, policemen, firemen, workmen, salespeople etc. etc. He wanders through workshops and warehouses, walks along shore boulevards, through storehouses and construction sites. What is the "supernatural" compared to reality, compared to this reality? There is no supernatural, outside of this reality. Everything is contained in the present and closest reality. The supernatural means nothing compared to a worm, a beetle, against the goings-on here on earth. . . .

This religious, all-encompassing feeling makes him the poet of love, of strength, of beauty and of hope. Men with beautiful, powerful limbs, blossoming in strength and health; beautiful women highly capable of procreation with well-built lively children, the gigantic beauty of a stallion are his desire. He does not grow tired to admire them. He cannot get away from them. Energy, physical and intellectual, physical exercises, gymnastics with a beautiful, elastic play of the muscles are the object of his enthusiastic love. A new, more developed culture is his most cheerful certainty, authenticated by the first beginning and by the development becoming alive in gigantic enormous visions in a poem such as "Passage to India." He finds it authenticated in the eternal movement of the world and of life with which his soul "passes to other spheres," when his soul eventually smiles toward death.

This feeling contains the ever-present compensation for all suffering and imperfection which appear when the world disintegrates as a consequence of our ruminating reasoning. In this feeling, all hopes and prophecies are fulfilled, an Other World beyond all weakness and morbid impotence. The Other World of our imagination is no other than this feeling.

In Whitman, there is not a trace of any of these morbid notions such as God, Other World and supernatural salvation. We deny such notions, fight against them, but frequently, because they are still in our blood, legacy of our ancestors, we behave as though they were something real and not mere fantasy; with a certain bitterness, we sulk in a tragicomical way as though anything at all were to be expected from them. In Whitman, there is not a trace of these notions and of the pessimism which frequently expresses itself in this sulking. A beautiful poem by Paul Verlaine comes to mind:

Vous, dieu de paix, de joie et de bonheur,
Toutes mes peurs, toutes mes ignorances
Vous, dieu de paix, de joie et de bonheur,

Vous connaissez tout cela, tout cela,
Et que je suis plus pauvre que personne,
Vous connaissez tout cela, tout cela
Mais ce que j'ai, mon dieu, je vous le donne.

And, as a sidenote, I recall a saying by Nietzsche in the *Götzendämmerung* [*The Twilight of the False Gods*]: "I believe we will not get rid of God, because we still believe in grammar."

In Whitman we would vainly search for such an empty accusation. No greater contrast between this decadence and Whitman.

All of them, Brahma, Buddha, God, Jehova, Jesus etc. are only objects of his historical consciousness. They are valuable inasfar as behind them, in a continuous development, there is always the same relationship to the world with its strong intimacy. Now, it will emerge and blossom again with new strength and more beautiful clarity with the youth of new generations, new conditions of life and human beings:

Nature and Man shall be disjoin'd and diffused no more,
The true son of God shall absolutely fuse them.
Year at whose wide-flung door I sing!
Year of the purpose accomplish'd!

Whitman has been judged in various ways. Not here, because we do not know him yet. But in his own country he has experienced all kinds of prudishness, all kinds of clericalism, hypocrisy, aesthetic and other forms of narrowmindedness and much misunderstanding. In Europe, a Frenchman has written about him in the *Revue des deux Mondes* (June 1872), Rudolf Schmidt has written an essay, a few Englishmen, and good old Lombroso, in his collection of anecdotes *Genius und Wahnsinn* [*The Man of Genius*], has recently locked him into a cell with God knows how many literary and other world-famous mental patients.

But he has also been overrated, praised excessively. For example when Emerson placed him next to Homer, Shakespeare and the psalmists. In an age such as ours, where everybody is forced to show consideration for, or rather is influenced by, our crippled age of transition, it is difficult to be like one of these greatest of men, even for a genius like Whitman. His overloud enthusiasm, the prophetic reference to his own person and the new force which will turn into a new world, is a "sign of the times." He is not securely and quietly rooted in a finished culture like these great spirits, he is only a carrier, the first finished human being of a newly emerging culture. He has no need to emphasize that the completion and implantation of this culture can be expected from poets, orators, singers and musicians yet to come and justify him. All of his songs are no more and no less than enormous dithyrambs, preludes to a coming new world, a new race, "native, athletic, continental, greater than before known." In his songs, his new world is poetically announced for the first time with roaring, brutal, sweet, mystical and raging zealousness and overzealousness. Before Homer, there may have been great dithyrambic-"Dionysian" poets who were prophets like Whitman, prophesying a greater poet yet to come, "optimistic" in the overabundancy of their visionary intoxication and in the power of their greatly increased awareness of life, like Whitman.

Freie Bühne für den Entwickelungskampf der Zeit 3 (1892): 977–988. Translated by Walter Grünzweig.

3. HERMANN HESSE

"Walt Whitman's *Leaves of Grass*"

Whitman has long been known in Europe but he is not known enough in Germany. But it will not be long until they will build altars for him as well, put wreaths on his picture and call his writings a gospel. Already at present, some people call him all kinds of things that he is not, for example a great philosopher and a prophet of the modern laws of life. Our age, with no culture and thoroughly without philosophy, has no longer a sense for dimensions. Enthusiastically they run after every true or false prophet. What have they made out of Nietzsche, of Emerson, even of Maeterlinck! Posterity will have a good and long laugh. And in this same vein there are already "Whitman communities," and other enterprises of aimless enthusiasm here and there.

The author of *Leaves of Grass* was not the most gifted writer, but he was the greatest of all poets in human terms. Actually, one would have to call him the only or at least the first "American" poet. Because he was the first who did not draw from the treasure (or the junk shop) of the old European cultures. Rather, he was grounded with all his roots in the American soil. He intoned the first hymns coming from the soul of this young people of giants, he sings and rejoices out of a feeling of immense power, he knows nothing ancient, nothing that is behind him, but one single presentient proudly moving present and an immensely happy future. He preaches health and strength, he is the orator of a young, strong people which prefers to dream of her grandchildren and great-grandchildren than her fathers. Therefore his dithyrambs are so frequently reminiscent of the voices of old people, of Moses, for example, and of Homer. But he belongs to today, therefore he preaches the Self, the free creative human being, in a way no less fiery. With the proud joy of the unbroken fully-developed human being he speaks of himself, of his deeds and voyages, of his country. He sings how he, "Well-begotten, and rais'd by a perfect mother," comes from Paumanok, how he passed through the southern savannas and lived in tents as a soldier, how he saw the Niagara and the mountains in California, the primeval forests and the buffalo herds in his country. He devotes his songs thankfully and enthusiastically to the people of America, to his people, which he considers an immense, powerful unity.

Whoever reads in this book at the right moment will find something of the primeval world and something of the high mountains, the sea and the prairie in it. Much will seem flashy and grotesque, but the whole will impress him just as America impresses us — against our own will.

Gesammelte Werke (Frankfurt: Suhrkamp, 1970), 12: 303–304. Translated by Walter Grünzweig. Reprinted with permission of Suhrkamp Verlag.

4. EDUARD BERTZ

"A Lyrical Sex Change in the Poetry of Walt Whitman"

In the first years of his youthful virility, when he was filled with eros, Walt Whitman expressed his homosexuality, which dominated him completely, most passionately. This is proven by the "Calamus" cycle in his poetry which first appeared in 1860, when the poet was forty-one years old. But his fear of the uncomprehending prejudice of public opinion led him to regret his openness. In the later editions he eliminated the most conclusive confessions, which are still missing from the Complete Edition. However, they are not lost to us and I myself have made them available in German translation in my study "Walt Whitman: Ein Charakterbild" (*Jahrbuch für Sexuelle Zwischenstufen*, vol. VII, 1905).

Advanced in age, when eros had departed him, Whitman then attempted to deny the homosexual foundations of his poetry altogether, indeed to hide behind the mask of normal heterosexuality. When the Englishman John Addington Symonds, himself a homosexual, wrote him a letter in an attempt to urge him to comment on his psychosexuality, Whitman resolved to eliminate all suspicions by way of the fairy tale of his six illegitimate children. I have proven the implausibility of this invention by the senile and almost childish poet in my book *Whitman-Mysterien* (Berlin, 1907).

His credulous biographer Henry Bryan Binns, on the other hand, author of *A Life of Walt Whitman* (1905), has uncritically accepted the legend of these six children who never existed and has used them as the starting point of a romance invented by himself. This was done out of the fanatic heterosexual desire to hush up homosexual matters and ignored the obligation to truth on the part of scientific research. He supports his thesis by Whitman's only lyrical poem in which the poet paid homage to love with women. This is the piece "Once I Passed through a Populous City," first published in 1860. In this poem it says:

> Yet now of all that city I remember only a woman I casually met there who
> detain'd me for love of me,
> Day by day and night by night we were together — all else has long been
> forgotten by me,

I remember I say only that woman who passionately clung to me,
Again we wander, we love, we separate again,
Again she holds me by the hand, I must not go,
I see her close beside me with silent lips sad and tremulous.

On this evidence, Binns bases his chapter on "Romance." The loving woman, the alleged mother of his alleged illegitimate children, was supposed to have been an aristocrat in New Orleans, of whose existence, however, we have never had a trace. But for every critical Whitman-researcher, the absurd ridiculousness of this fantastic construction was apparent from the very beginning.

Now, finally, the prudent point of view was unexpectedly confirmed in a most curious way. Last fall, two good-sized volumes entitled *The Uncollected Poetry and Prose of Walt Whitman* were published, edited by Emory Holloway (New York, 1921). And this collection contains the original version of this poem which had so far remained unknown:

But now of all that city I remember only the man who wandered with me
   there, for love of me,
Day by day, and night by night, we were together,
All else has long been forgotten by me — I remember, I say, only one rude and
   ignorant man who, when I departed, long and long held me by the hand,
   with silent lip, sad and tremulous.

Thus, Whitman did not dare to remain faithful to himself, but the truth has now been brought to the light of day nevertheless, and all of the yarn by H. B. Binns is now exposed. The deficiency of a homosexual to admit to his nature, a deficiency which so greatly obstructs the just appreciation and eventual liberation of homosexuals, is only too understandable given the terrorism of the heterosexual society. But a forgery of one's own works as occurred in this lyrical quick-change artistry of the American poet, who fearfully hides behind a woman's apron, is a singular example of its kind. This sex change operation is certainly a first-rate curiosity in the area of biographical psychology.

Incidentally, experiences such as the one mentioned in this poem were not the exception in Whitman's life, but the rule. As evidence, we may use his *Diary in Canada*, which is full of addresses by the same type of "rude and ignorant men" as the one mentioned in the poem, recommendations to kindred spirits which likeminded persons at home had given him for his trip. Whitman loved unsophisticated rustic-type males and found them everywhere he went. The woman, however, whom he forged into the poem, which should actually have been a part of the "Calamus" cycle, is not grounded in the reality of his life. Whitman was purely a homosexual.

Jahrbuch für Sexuelle Zwischenstufen 22 (July/October 1922): 55–58. Translated by Walter Grünzweig.

5. GUSTAV LANDAUER

"Walt Whitman"

The person of the poet Walt Whitman and everything he has written appears as though America, the United States, wanted to reply to Goethe's words "America, thou farest better than our old continent; thou hast no ruined castles and no basalt!" with loud words across the ocean: "Yes, yes, yes, it's true!" Often enough, Whitman himself said of the poets of the Disunited States of Europe, albeit with words of the greatest respect, that they belong to the past and to the age of feudalism — with the exception of one, Goethe, who has a special position because he is a king without a country, a poet without a nation. For Walt Whitman, America is the empire of the future, of a human community that is not yet complete but still growing together, emerging.

To argue against Whitman that such a position shows a dangerous, exaggerated arrogance would amount to dull pedantry, maybe even political jealousy. In order to understand the conception Whitman has of himself and of his people, this sort of politics must be ignored; it is located a few floors below an interpretation of culture from the height of the powerful imagination of the poet.

Although he does not express it in these words, Whitman feels that his people have made a new beginning, that they are barbarians, freshly emerged from the amalgamation of peoples, that they are introducing a new age into history. Just think how the old Germanic tribes, already at the time of Arminius . . . were frequently familiar with the important Greco-Roman culture, and how, especially after the new myth, Christianity, had come over them, they had to start with a completely new, seemingly more primitive culture. Whitman feels a great, savage nature, not refracted through any conventions, within himself. To him, Americans are a newly emerging people, barbarians, at the origin of their development: he wants to help them to create a new, strong belief, the new art which has to be a guiding light for any great nation. His self-awareness is much more a feeling for his people than for himself; one should not get confused by the mystical "Myself" of his verses. He has felt this very clearly and said that he is only a very small beginning, an early precursor of an American-Periclean age. Moreover, he has always stated that it is America's special calling to be just a few steps ahead, but that all peoples of the earth would go the same way.

Which way? He is telling us about it in his "Drum-Taps" which rang forth clearly during the war:

Be not dishearten'd, affection shall solve the problems of freedom yet,
Those who love each other shall become invincible . . .
(Were you looking to be held together by lawyers?
Or by an agreement on a paper? or by arms?
Nay, nor the world, nor any living thing, will so cohere.)

His "Democracy" is a free people of active individuals who have left behind all obstacles related to class prejudice, who have broken with all chimeras of a superannuated past; each on his soil or in his trade, at his machine, a man for himself. Just like Proudhon, to whom he is intellectually related in many ways, Whitman unites the conservative and the revolutionary spirit, individualism and socialism. According to his teachings, his artistic feeling, the love between human beings, which must necessarily be a part of this spirit, is not a vague, generalized blurred love for humanity. Rather, just like the kind of love that is at the foundation of families, it must be animated by the spirit of exclusivity. It is designed to connect certain human beings, men with men, women with women and, of course, also men with women, thereby creating new social groups. This is the context of the comradeship to which Whitman's most beautiful and most intimate poems are devoted, with all his dreams of new human beings and a new people. Faddish pseudo-sciences are vainly attempting to detect something perverse, pathological or even degenerated in these feelings of comradeship. We must learn anew that strong men and strong ages are sentimental, and that weak ages and generations are shying away from dedicating their feelings wholeheartedly and fervently to a beloved wife or an intimately loved male friend or a region or the cosmos. Whitman had this cosmic love and this emotional exuberance. He believes his new people can only emerge out of the chaos and the abyss of intimacy. Although he is not interested in parallels and does not even reflect them, there are obvious reminiscences of the intellectual and spiritual world of that artistic people, the Old Greeks, as well as to their social institutions and customs. Whitman's feeling and perception had a special orientation; to conclude from this a special disposition of his nature should be left to the pathological representatives of psychopathology.

It is characteristic of every creative mind that all feelings and shapes contain eros. If Whitman, like Goethe's Faust, had undertaken to translate the Gospel According to John, his first sentence would probably have been: "In the beginning was the feeling." He stresses the feeling (and with it, poetry, as the beginning of all life and all human community) very consciously because he knows, from which direction Americans are threatened: "What American humanity is most in danger of," he says, "is an overwhelming prosperity, 'business' worldliness, materialism: what is most lacking . . . is a fervid and glowing Nationality and patriotism, cohering all parts into one. Who may fend that danger and fill that lack in the future, but a class of loftiest poets?" Only a great people, he believes, can have great poets; but first it must be poetry that shapes a great people, lending it "artistic character, spirituality, dignity."

The poet projected by Walt Whitman's conception of his self and his task is a priest, a prophet, a creator. It is certain that he has exerted and continues to exert an extraordinary power over his people and the intellectual ability of his people — and on those individuals who, among foreign peoples, belong to "his" people as well. How this story continues, whether his most audacious prophecy will become reality in the way fantasy and desires can be realized by helping to establish a reality which will not exactly look like the original projections, nobody can tell today.

But it is certain that he is America's greatest poet and an intimately strong lyricist for us all, and that he has given our poetry a new form and an enormously large new subject matter — all realities of the physical and intellectual world.

> I believe a leaf of grass is no less than the journey-work of the stars.

Out of this spirit, he has called his first book of poetry *Leaves of Grass* (1855) and into this book, his book, representing his person, he has projected his whole poetic *oeuvre* in ever new editions over thirty years. . . .

At the age of thirty, Whitman acquired his creative power; what he wrote earlier hardly bears comparison to the work which then appeared. He was someone who matured slowly and who was overcome with vehemence suddenly [by the creative impulse]. The 1855 preface accompanying his book combines the maturity of a man who occupies his place as though he had taken root, with the ecstasy of the beginner. "The most affluent man is he that confronts all the shows he sees by equivalents out of the stronger wealth of himself." This is his first discovery. The influences from Fichte and Hegel did not come until later while, as Bertz demonstrates correctly in an otherwise intolerable book, Emerson made himself felt already at an early time: man, in his self, in his intellectuality and spirituality, contains the whole world, the world is merely an infinite wealth of microcosms, a plurality and countless "identities," of self-conscious crossing points of the currents of the world. What he brings to Americans as religion of the feeling of spirituality and universality is a new form of the eternal teachings of the philosophers and mystics from India to the Christian mystics up to the magicians of the renaissance and on to Berkeley and Fichte into our days: the so-called monism of our time, on the other hand, has only a weak semblance to this realization. Whitman's teachings are most closely related to the magical pantheism which came from Nicholas of Cusa to such renaissance minds as Paracelsus, Agrippa von Nettesheim and similar spirits, a pantheism which knows no self-denial but addresses the fullness of life. The superstition pervading much of their writings should not disturb our comparison: it was their natural "science," then just created, just as Whitman revels in our natural "science" and technology. Indeed, even in the form of these magicians of the renaissance, there are relationships with Whitman (who had hardly known them). Agrippa von Nettesheim added a powerful motto to his book *Of the Vanity of Sciences*, which is completely Whitmanesque in both spirit and form. I will quote it here:

> Among Gods, nobody remains untousled by Momus.
> Among Heroes, Hercules hunts after every monster.
> Among Demons, the King of the Nether World, Pluto, rages against all shadows.
> Among Philosophers, Democritus laughs about everything.
> But Heraclitus cries over everything.
> Pyrrho knows nothing about nothing.

Gustav Landauer [191]

And it seems to Aristotle that he knows everything.
Diogenes scorns everything.
Of all this, nothing lacks in Agrippa. (Whitman's Myself, I.)
Scorns, knows, knows not, cries, laughs, rages, hunts, tousles everything.
Himself Philosopher, Demon, Hero, God and the whole world.

But Whitman is also extremely close to the ancient poetry of India. By no means all Indian poets tied the idea that the Self is identical with the world to pessimism or escapism. In America, it was said right away that Whitman's poems were a conglomerate from the Bhagavad-Gita and the *New York Herald*. This was very funny but also very wrong because the Bhagavad-Gita already completely contains what is referred to as the *New York Herald*, i.e., the catalogue-like enumeration of the concrete facts of the whole world. The items, enumerated by the Indian poem in order to express the image of infinite variety, were just as modern as the world of technology, of nature, and of culture, Whitman included in his poems.

When reading his poetry, nothing is as obvious as the feeling of immediacy, the complete and total absence of literary reminiscences or any sort of alexandrianism. Although Whitman read much, he was not an eclectic reader, he only absorbed what was already previously in him. Therefore the parting words to the reader in his *Leaves of Grass* are so very true:

Camerado, this is no book,
Who touches this touches a man. . . .

Just as any true artist, Whitman is fully conscious of his creativity, and of the best things that can be said about him in aesthetic-critical terms he informs us himself. The most characteristic quality of his poetry is its "suggestiveness," through which he has ever new shapes surge back and forth for us, not for the ear but for the eye, like the director of an orchestra. Thereby he gives an "atmosphere of the theme or thought" in which our own imagination can take off. He is a poet of great sensuality and concreteness; he seems to have thought only with his senses and even his abstractions, completely immersed in his inner self, preserve this concrete character. Even when he wants to say the inexpressible, and when he wants to say, even stammer, that it cannot be expressed, he cries out at the beginning of a poem as though coming from deepest consciousness:

There is that in me — I do not know what it is — but I know it is in me . . .

and thereby immediately creates for us the atmosphere of a physical experience. . . .

Since his poetic feeling, his rhythmic transfiguration and his perception are always together, there is nothing in the world which Whitman does not transform into poetry. Therefore he is never forced to refer to the traditional models of literary allegories; rather, new and unusual matter is transformed into images in a truly

Homeric wealth. But is this cohabitation of perception and feeling, of the mind with all objects of the world not identical with what he wants to bring out in human beings—Love? Because whoever walks without love, if only for a hundred meters, walks in a shroud in one's own burial.

Whitman's form is a highly rhythmical structure. It is just as little improvised passionate rhetoric as an impressionist picture, producing the impression of momentariness, is dashed off with a few strokes of the brush. It only recognizes the law of tempo but is not bound by any other poetic traditions. The chaotic, the projection of masses, not presented with objective restraint but, in all concreteness, always a felt experience, an effusion of subjectivity, has led to this form. Its effect is like a gigantic, sweeping verbal segment broken out of experience, more than a small, isolated human self. Rather, it seems to have taken everything that can be found externally out of its own universality.

One day, in the time when he cared for the wounded of the war, Whitman wrote in his diary: "It is curious: when I am present at the most appalling scenes, deaths, operations, sickening wounds (perhaps full of maggots), I keep cool and do not give out or budge, although my sympathies are very much excited; but often, hours afterward, perhaps when I am home, or out walking alone, I feel sick, and actually tremble, when I recall the case again before me." He has just jotted this down in order to record a fact; he thought of nothing that can turn this fact into a symbol. Yet, this passage reveals his whole character and the whole and special greatness of his poetic calling. It is indicative of his imagination, sometimes raised to the level of the visionary, that his experiences, once they are past, return with increased force, that his recollections assail him with the full force of an actual experience. This proves his qualities as a poet as much as his behavior in the midst of action shows his steadfast objectivity, his natural bravery, and his self-possessed love of humanity.

Originally published in the German daily *Vossische Zeitung*, no. 143 (1907), and republished several times. Also appeared as the introduction to Landauer's translation of Whitman published posthumously in 1921. Modern republication in Gustav Landauer, *Der werdende Mensch: Aufsätze zur Literatur*, ed. Gerhard Hendel (Leipzig and Weimar: Kiepenheuer, 1980), 85–97. Translated by Walter Grünzweig.

6. HERMANN BAHR

"Walt Whitman"

On his father's side, Whitman descends from the English Quakers, on his mother's side from Holland. The sect of the Quakers does not accept any church, not even the Holy Bible. To them, truth can nowhere be found but at the bottom of one's own soul, the "inner light" must shine, therefore they like to call themselves "children of light." George Fox, their founder, had come to America in 1672 and when a child, Walt found that the memories of this very pious man were still alive everywhere among the people. In this atmosphere he grew up, himself a "child of the light."

The Whitmans were farmers or working men. Walt's father is reported to have been an immensely tall man, of the quiet kind, turned inward and peaceful, but if he ever became irritated and disturbed, he was seized with a savage, unrestrained rage. His son seems to have inherited this tendency; in his other ways, however, Walt seems to have followed more his mother, a simple woman who had difficulties with reading and writing but who had a wonderful, almost magical power over people.

In the course of growing up, little Walt was a kid hanging around in the streets, a pupil, a writer, a messenger boy with a physician, a printer's devil, later assistant teacher, immediately afterwards editor of a country journal and at the same time its distributor, then again a carpenter like his father, for a while also foreman at construction sites, worked at working men's housing; in between all these jobs, however, he liked to celebrate, loafing, roaming about on the sea shore, in the thicket of the forest or also in the much more profound solitude of the large cities. Love for work and yearning for adventures, calm reason and strong desire, continuity and mobility, diligence and laziness, passion and a certain heaviness mixed strangely in the youth who for a long time did not know himself. Possibly, a faintly admonishing presentiment of his higher mission kept him from simply becoming a busy popular orator and a successful journalist. We hear that he was an avid reader who voraciously and indiscriminately devoured everything he found in the New York libraries and also an eloquent visitor of public assemblies, a figure well-known about the city, also through his friendship with the omnibus drivers to whom he liked to recite from Homer or Julius Caesar high up on the coach with his powerful voice drowning out even the roaring street noise. He remained very young beyond the years of his youth and even as a man kept something of the manners of a child, although he was at the same time deliberate, calm, even displayed an external and internal sluggishness. He was a slow human being, stolid, almost plump, and everything about him was so heavy that he has been compared with an elephant. Although his sensuality was great, his purity was so as well, always joyful, never lecherous; he liked to drink but never got drunk and even without drinking always seemed slightly inebriated. Friendship with men was a necessity for him, he did not avoid women but there was a feeling that for him, women were not much different from men.

He never planned to become a poet. Actually, there is only one single poem he ever wrote: the *Leaves of Grass* are always one and the same poem of which parts always remained on his tongue so that he felt urged to keep writing it anew. Until the end, he was not finished writing it. It was published for the first time in 1855, typeset by himself.

In 1862, his brother was wounded. Walt came to the field hospital and took part in the war as nurse or actually more as comforter and, he once said himself, as "missionary" in his own way. Because it turned out that he had a miraculous power to help and heal through his mere presence. When the large slow man in his gray coat with the loose, soft shirt-collar which showed his broad chest, wearing his fresh shiny clothes, quietly came to the bed of a patient, his mere look, the pressure of his strong hand, the miracle of his closeness was medication. He did not even say much, at best brought some flowers and just sat there, was just there, that soothed the pain and was comforting enough. At that time, Walt discovered his true profession: to be a comrade, a comrade to humanity. The *Leaves of Grass* are really just a written document of this idea.

After the war he worked as a clerk in the Department of the Interior in Washington. An outbreak of moral indignation of the type occasionally instigated everywhere against lonely individuals of the quiet type drove him out of this job. Friends procured another job for him; eventually, he was completely freed from having to work in order to earn his bread. Since then he has been living by himself and, especially after his stroke in 1873, he has become an almost mythical figure. The sunset of his life already mixed with the dawn of his world fame. He was much admired and loved even though most people did not know why. Also today, one-hundred years after his birth, twenty-seven years after his death, people really still do not know. In this way, as well, he is like Goethe: he has become very famous but essentially remained unknown.

Something in him attracted people powerfully and remained unforgettable, but they could not explain it. And he himself seems to have felt no different. Day by day he inquired about himself in a surprised manner, without ever being completely satisfied with the answer. The *Leaves* are a diary of these questions and answers. Here, somebody started to wonder about the phenomenon of his own personality and now he spends his life in order to look at the phenomenon from all sides in order to finally get some access to the problem. Therefore he can say of the *Leaves* with justification: "Camerado, this is no book! Whoever touches this, touches a human being!" Maybe there is no other book that remained so completely human, where no part of the human being was changed in order to be turned into a book, where this human being had cast nothing at all off his own self, not even adjusted his person a little for it. It is artless, actually it only provides the material for a work of art, this is the impression one gets time and again. No book but a live human being, this one human being, but all of this human being, and naked! And whoever reads it can sometimes not help thinking that they commit an indiscretion. The result, finally, is that this book, which is not a book but the touch of a human being, remains just as mysteriously inexplicable and closed as this magnetic human being, Walt Whitman, remained towards his environment during his entire life.

The *Leaves* were immediately felt to be something unique and without precedence. People were shocked over their "lack of form." For readers, form means to be reminded of something that they read once before; in this case readers were not reminded of anything that they had ever seen before. Obviously it was not a poem but rather a local news story with visions. There was a feeling of reading a newspaper whose editor was a psalmist. (It took a long time until people remembered that Homer, too, is at times a local editor and that the *Edda* contains passages that could be from the *New York Herald*.) Moreover, there was the problem that the *Leaves* really always start at the beginning and stop nowhere. It really seemed to be formlessness turned into a constructive principle, indeed the formlessness personified in his own person. And the attraction lay in the fact that the reader could in a way listen to the preparations of the poetic process although the final product was always lacking: the poem, existing on its own and by itself, apart from the poet, assuming a shape of its own. What remained inexplicable was how such a shapeless work could exert such power: whoever has heard only a few lines from Whitman is able to recognize his poetry after hearing just one verse; his voice has an unforgettable sound. And while he is called formless for good reason, there is just as much justification to say that possibly no poet since Shakespeare has so much real form, that every sentence, indeed every word of his poem is completely penetrated by him, that he has created his own highly personal language (oftentimes from the most common material). But form in this case is no cover, no ready-made case in which everybody could put their completed thoughts or impressions. Rather, it produces itself, it grows out of his interior, together with the idea, at the same time as the feeling, its form is skin. And he could not have changed this form, as little as the color of his eyes. Often enough, one notices his own surprise over it. Basically, the *Leaves* are nothing but the increasing astonishment of a person over himself, who daily discovers yet another new surprise, who every day rises like the sun and then spends the whole day rejoicing over sunrise.

He always starts out with an immense ego. "One's Self I sing, a simple separate person," announces the first verse of the *Leaves*. He calls himself a "Chanter of personality," he is driven to communicating his own splendor. At first he is all physical: "I find no sweeter fat than sticks to my own bones." "I exist as I am, that is enough, If no other in the world be aware I sit content." Prophecy of the self, glorification of the self, gratification of the self! And he can easily rest with a feeling of satisfaction because inside himself he is sitting in the center of the world: "To me the converging objects of the universe perpetually flow." All rays of the cosmos flow towards him, flow onto him, flow into him, until he, overflown, overflowing himself, calls out: "Walt Whitman, a kosmos!" And he immediately returns like for like: he himself radiates his own self back into the world. In this way he becomes conscious that if he wants to unfold his self, he needs something outside himself, a contrast, a non-self, from which he can differentiate himself, towards which he can present himself: this makes him creative. In order to be special, "a single separate person," there must be another who is different; the more others there are and the more different they are, the better his own pure self can emerge in comparison with them, can emerge through them: His urge to present himself to the world makes him recognize the rest of the world. Whitman, the cosmos, needs a second cosmos outside him in order to demonstrate his own, his love comes from his egotism! The miracle he feels in himself he now feels in all creatures, the glorification of his self becomes a glorification of the world. This is not a glorification of the "whole" in a monistic haze but the glorification of each individual creature, however powerful or inconspicuous it may be, grass leaf or course of the stars, far or close, friend or enemy, good or bad—all these notions shrink before his loud affirmation of the whole world, not just of the sum total of it, no, also of each of its countless individuations! "I will not have a single person slighted or left away . . . pleas'd with the native and pleas'd with the foreign, pleas'd with the new and old. . . . The insignificant is as big to me as any. . . . In all people I see my self, none more and not one a barley-corn less, and the good or bad I say of myself I say of them." But when his affirmation does not differentiate, when it recognizes even evil, when he says that to his meal, the prostitute, the free-loader and the thief are also invited, when he also calls to himself the losers, those unfit for life ("Vivat to those who have failed!"), when he actually calls himself "the poet of wickedness," this is not a desire for evil, Baudelaire's satanism. In the end, it is not a moral but an epistemological category: Even satan is included in God's creation. "All Is Truth" he calls a poem which concludes with the assertion "that all is truth without exception; and henceforth I will go celebrate any thing I see or am, and sing and laugh and deny nothing." Everything is true, "in its place." Because everything that is in a place enables something else to stand in another place, each thing balances another thing and this balance of weight and counter-weight balances the world: everything is true, because it is merely a reply, creation is continuous answering of everybody to everybody, the choir pauses, indeed wa-vers, if just one voice in it comes in too late! But this is no great discovery for him, none at all, because every appearance discovers it, everybody knows it just as everybody always knows what is true: "These are really the thoughts of all men in all ages and lands, they are not original with me: If they are not yours as much as mine, they are nothing, or next to nothing."

To display his ego not merely for the sake of himself but also for every other creature, not merely to "tolerate" the other in others but to enjoy the other in oth-ers out of self-interest. Even more: to demand the otherness of the others because one requires it for oneself, because one becomes what one is oneself only because the others are different, because one only reaches one's own fulfillment through others. Since the beginning of humanity, everybody has in some way experienced this, although it always remains unconscious to most, and all thinkers, all poets, have somehow felt it, from the oldest times until our present time, where Beer-Hofmann has his Jaákob say to his *feindliche* brother: "God needs me in this way—and in a different way you! Only because you are Edom—I may be Jaákob!" But this central human experience, repeating itself over the times from people to people, now receives Whitman's very personal accent, first of all, because he expe-riences everything through his senses; then also, because he is not satisfied to par-take in the other intellectually because he wants more, he wants to experience the other in his own person because his need for transforming his self is indigenous to his personality. Walt's perception always starts as a sensual experience, he thinks with his eyes and ears, he is one of the sensual supra-sensuous suitors who philoso-phize with the phallus, his caritas is preceded by eros and when he uses the strange phrase "amorous love," he betrays his ultimate secret: his love for the world is based on his love for all creatures, a sensual love; therefore he was mistaken by all those whose love remains in the area of the sensual; his sensuality always turned into immediate spirituality. And just as his senses immediately turn into the spiritual, every spirit immediately turns sensual: he becomes whatever he thinks of, and every activity of his soul is immediately joined by his body, he is a born actor. When he sees somebody suffer, he does not only suffer with that person but he becomes, suffering along with that person, himself that person; with the suffering he assumes the person of the sufferer. "I am the man, I suffer'd, I was there . . . I do not ask the wounded person how he feels, I myself become the wounded person, / My hurts turn livid upon me as I lean on a cane and observe" ("Song of Myself," 33). In the end, it is nothing but the typical experience of the actor, brought down to an elementary level, back to the primitive condition of the Dionysian principle, yet intensified to a cosmic state, flooding into all creation and flooding himself with everything that is created, transforming everything, in the end shaping even what is unshaped, voracious for masks until reaching the whole naked truth.

In a love first grasped by his senses, then immediately alarming the soul with all her forces, but never completely denying the sensual beginning, in this love he recognizes "the base and finalé too for all metaphysics": he looks back to all the Sages, to all the Saints of the past and the original source of all their wisdom and all their saintliness is to him "the dear love of man for his comrade, the attraction of friend to friend." Through love, he experiences that everything, everything is as inexhaustible a miracle as he himself: the comrade, the other, every other, every human being, and not just human beings, but every creature, animal, plant, rock, air, sea, star. And he finds that he contains every creature, the possibility of every creature, in himself. In his poems we can eavesdrop on this experience step by step: first it is purely sensual, he sees everything, hears everything, absorbs everything through his senses, but by partaking in creation with his senses, by feeling with all creation, he transforms himself into all creation, he transforms himself into the other. In such diastoles (to use Goethe's diction) he is no longer himself, nothing is left of him, he is the other, he is everything other (the long catalogues of everything he then becomes are almost comical!), he is no longer "contain'd between my hat and boots," he reaches beyond himself into the cosmos, gives himself up to everything, enters everything, lives with everything and thereby brings back the certainty that in this wealth of appearances there are no two appearances that are the same, but that each is good, each is equally good! Not just out of compassion then, but also out of shared joy, knowing that he himself is a "cosmos," but not just he, but every leaf of grass as well, and that each such cosmos, each such leaf of grass, needs the singularity and uniqueness of the others in order to be able to completely feel the miracle of its own singularity. And this his very own experience—that he can identify with everything, transform himself into everything thereby containing the whole of humanity, and also the sun, the moon and the stars, just as they, on the other hand, contain him—this he considers to be something characteristically American, and characteristic for America's mission: to be ahead of the others in that, and, through his example, to lead all others there as well. "All truths wait in all things," everywhere the same truth awaits you, God is looking at you from everything! But this has nothing to do with pantheism; not with the pantheism of the meadows and the woods of our monistic Gymnasium teachers, and also not with any deification of the self in which the self as well as God finally become extinct. Here, out of the exuberant feelings of one's own individuation, the sum total of all possible other individuations are affirmed as well, indeed demanded. As Friedlaender would express it, there is a counterweight for every weight, and exactly out of the "oppositional character of the world" an Other, "contrasting," World emerges; the creator can no longer be rejected. And it has also nothing to do with Buddhism because the Buddhists of all types finally reach the extinction of God with the extinction of the self. Walt does not want to overcome the created world as appearance but he wants to recognize the living truth in every appearance: the eye of God, in order to return from this sight confidently into himself, to his work in earthly life. "The thoughtful merge of myself, and the outlet again" he calls it once and the secret of mystical vision could not be expressed more simply: "merge" means getting rid of the self, overcoming the difference, immersing oneself, in Friedlaender's diction, "the absolute zero on the scale of the differentiation of the world." "Outlet again" is the systolic after the diastolic, inspiration after exhalation, the return to the self, to action, into the world, into the transformation, into the difference, to the split between Yes and No, the balance of which alone is meaning and instinct, suffering and desire, earnestness and play of all life. And in this return, in this return from the depth to the surface, for which those emerging feel a completely new tenderness never known before, there is something of the great human beings of the Baroque, Bernini for example, when he, every morning, went from the Holiest of the Sacraments to his workshop, returned to the lovely iridescence of the earthly dream which can only be really dreamed by those who have been beyond, by the awakened.

Whitman's relationship to his time, to his people, to his country, is just as his relationship to himself. "The Modern Man I sing!" he immediately announces in his first poem, full of pride in his time, but from his time reaching out to all times, the past as well as the present with the same loving reverence. "I will not sing with reference to a day, but with reference to all days." Because just as his own self needs the contrast in the form of the other for the development of its variety, each period receives its specific character out of the character of all other periods. And when he loves his people, his country more than everything, it is just this love that then teaches him to love every other people and country with its special character. Indeed, he will desire this foreign character, because all of these characteristics only emerge together and they can only continue to exist together. He is a nationalist, but especially out of this nationalism he needs for his nation the counterweight of the other nations, whose otherness alone can reveal the meaning of his own. And in this way he becomes a cosmopolitan out of nationalism, a cosmopolitanism not of the washed-out and blurring kind but one that recognizes an identical validity for all special characteristics and their necessity for each other. "Salut au Monde!" is the title of his most powerful poem, indeed, a kiss to the whole world, with a Beethoven-like instrumentation. "Within me latitude widens, longitude lengthens," in him are zones, seas, waterfalls, forests, volcanos, masses, he hears the pulsation of the cosmos, he searches the globe with his looks, he greets all inhabitants of the earth, whoever they may be, he calls them all, one after the other, from the daughter or the son of England to the Czechs, the Hungarian, the Styrian farmer, the workman from the Rhine, the wandering Jew, the pilgrim to Mecca, Chinese, Japanese up to the farthest islands, to the wooly-haired hordes, to the scorned brute-like human being and to all, all he calls:

> Health to you! good will to you all, from me and America sent!
> Each of us inevitable,
> Each of us limitless — each of us with his or her right upon the earth,
> Each of us allow'd the eternal purports of the earth,
> Each of us as divinely as any is here.

And no people, however far back in the development of humanity, should be excluded, because for each the hour will come eventually! "I do not prefer others so very much before you either, / I do not say one word against you, away back there where you stand, / (You will come forward in due time to my side.) . . . / My spirit has pass'd in compassion and determination around the whole earth, / I have look'd for equals and lovers and found them ready for me in all lands, / I think some divine rapport has equalized me with them. . . . *Salut au monde!* / What cities the light and warmth penetrates I penetrate those cities myself, / All islands to which birds wing their way I wing my way myself. / Toward you all, in America's name, / I raise high the perpendicular hand, I make the signal, / To remain after me in sight forever, For all the haunts and the homes of men."

This is the democracy in which he feels America's mission, out of which he hopes for "the continent indissoluble," "the most splendid race the sun ever shone upon," the "divine magnetic lands," from which he watches blossoming "inseparable cities with their arms about each other's necks," the democracy which he calls "ma femme!" with a half sensual, half childlike tenderness. Democracy to him is nothing other than the application of love, the "life-long manly love of comrades." It has nothing to do with external forms and institutions. "I hear it was charged against me that I sought to destroy institutions, But really I am neither for nor against institutions. . . . Only I will establish . . . the institution of the dear love of comrades." His democracy does not consist of laws, it comes out of the heart. This democracy requires a type of human being that is not very common as yet, mindful of each creature, indeed sharing in each creature, intensified up to a transformation of the self, not a moral law, not an "ideal demand," but an immediate experience, starting from the senses, permeating the whole human being with spirit and soul! His democracy passes on an age-old word of humanity which has never completely faded away but which has also never been completely revealed in actuality:

I speak the pass-word primeval, I give the sign of democracy.

His democracy is really an erotocracy.

Die neue Rundschau 30 (1919): 555–564. Translated by Walter Grünzweig. *Die neue Rundschau* was, and still is, one of Germany's most important literary and cultural magazines.

7. THOMAS MANN

Letter to Hans Reisiger

I am delighted to have your Whitman book and cannot thank you enough for this great, important, indeed holy gift; for that matter, the German public, it seems to me, can not be grateful enough either. Since I have received the two volumes, I have opened them again and again, reading here and there. I have read the biographical introduction from end to end and consider it a little masterpiece of love. It is really a great achievement on your part that after years of devotion and enthusiasm you have brought close to us this powerful spirit, this exuberant, profound new personification of humanity. We Germans who are old and immature at one and the same time can benefit from contact with this personality, symbol of the future of humanity, if we are willing to accept him. To me personally, who has been striving for so many years, in my own laborious way, after the idea of humanity, convinced that no task is more urgent for Germany than to give a new meaning to this idea—which has become a mere empty shell, a mere school phrase—to me this work of yours is a real gift from God, for I see what Walt Whitman calls "Democracy" is essentially nothing else than what we, in a more old-fashioned way, call "Humanity." I see, too, that to awaken the feelings of the new humanity has not been accomplished by Goethe alone, but that a dose of Whitman is needed; and this all the more so because these two have a good deal in common, these two ancestors of ours, especially as regards sensuality, "Calamus," and sympathy with the organic. . . . In short, your deed—this word is not too big nor too strong—can be of immeasurable influence. . . .

Frankfurter Zeitung, April 16, 1922. Translated by Horst Frenz. Mann sent this letter to Reisiger in thanks for a copy of Reisiger's translation of Whitman.

8. HANS REISIGER

"The Heartbeat of True Democracy"

Walt Whitman was one of those particularly gifted human beings who from childhood into old age remained secure in the strength and warmth of a maternal world. In the midst of all the visions and passions of a world free and multiform, seizing his lonely breast, there remained with him, at all times, the invisible smile of a child belonging to the essence out of which it had been born. Again and again he would have only had to recall this essence in order to return to it like a little child, in spite of the wrinkles on his forehead and the grey hair and beard. The genuine ardor of his spirited prophesy as to a race beautiful, proud, "athletic" and "electric" — a race chaste, tender, compassionate and "fluctuating along with na-ture" — in itself originates in the maternal womb out of which he had been de-livered into this life: "well-born and brought up by a perfect mother." Mothers give birth to men; thus, it is the prime task of a new race to bring forth mothers of spiritual and physical perfection. The maternal womb serves as the threshold to which innumerable germs throng for new sowings. Forever and ever, birth, fol-lowing after birth and re-birth, labors to achieve new essence out of the maternal spheres.

In the eyes of a mother, small things may grow important, and the large and world-wide things may become simple and as natural as a glance or a kiss. Part of this strength — strength with the help of which Whitman comprehends every-thing, small as well as large, in this world uniting and equalizing all with the aid of love — perhaps arises from the fortunate equipoise of all facets — thoughts and acts — of his nature in the presence of maternal love. And his rejection of all cow-ardice and shame in the souls of men was determined quiescently, for throughout his life, he had never felt a need to feel remorseful, timid and pale about his own emotions, reactions which are detrimental to continued growth. For in the pres-ence of his mother's understanding and ennobling glance, everything had always been open and clearly perceptible. Although but very few of his psalm-like stanzas are addressed to his mother personally, his entire work is permeated by the con-cept of pure and noble motherhood to an extent which would justify its clas-sification as one continuous invocation to the one "that is giving birth," to the "harmonious image of the earth, to the fulfillment beyond which philosophy never reaches nor intends to reach, to the very mother of men."

It is inherent in Walt Whitman's nature that the pale, magic translucence of childhood, the radiance of the first blissful awareness of existence, never faded al-together in him. Never, in his soul, did those portals close which take most people by surprise when one fine morning they fall shut with the jarring sound of daily routine, locking out the domain of childhood and making prisoners of them in a disenchanted world in which things shrivel under the influence of the inexorable power of habit and in which the soul rushes or creeps, dumbfounded, from moment to moment. In the midst of existence, which should make us tremble with genuine wonderment as the hours pass, this sacred power struggles forth from the abused souls only with difficulty. They will no longer be able to recapture that primal splendor in which, once upon a time, appeared to them flower and bird, wind and calmness, closeness and distance, the living cosmos surrounding them and their Ego. The power of wonderment, apex of the human soul and source of all religious activity and creation, grew unimpaired and unrestrained out of the nature of Walt Whitman's childhood into the nature of his mature age: that wonderment of the heart which denotes repose and trust in the incomprehensible as the power to which one is eternally bound.

Thus, from all sides of Walt Whitman's poetry, unrefracted rays shoot forth, back to the dim beginnings of his youth — the inexplicable tears of a child, shed in experiencing the lonely impact of the night and of the dark and boundless ocean, in listening to the half-understood lamentations of the thrush singing of love and death, sparkle like dewdrops on the songs of this man.

Profound, rich and passionate, such is the imagination of every child; and if, later in his life, it is not quenched by the consuming sterility of daily routine, it will continue to pulsate in the blood until death overcomes it. It is idle to ask the conventional question, "If even then?" or the like. If I feel able to talk eloquently about the days of my childhood, I myself have retained the child while becoming a man, one continuous, incarnate soul.

One could hardly express more convincingly and more plainly the continuous unity of the wondrous awe pervading all life than do the last lines of this song ["There Was a Child Went Forth"]. Man's vision extends beyond that of childhood, comprehends the whole earth and all the spheres in which different suns and plants revolve, and embraces infinity whose secret pervades and transports the visible. Yet the soul behind this power of vision remains unchanged, and the commonest things, the things within our closest reach, do not lose their magic but become ever more deeply immersed in the miracle of existence. The same mysterious breath which lingers over the brownish cloud banks in the clear blue sky enwraps the dead who appear to the poet in his reveries of pulsating life. It is the same breath of God which enfolds the burning bodies of man and wife uniting in the ecstacy of procreation.

Many kindred traits began to vibrate in him [Whitman] as so many unconscious, magnetic currents, traits that in his maturity and old age manifested themselves as essentials of his own nature. Later in his life, he enjoyed emphasizing the Quaker element in himself. The "inner light," spiritual intuition, became for him the guiding star in thought and action. Self-respect, and arising from it, respect for his fellow-creatures, constituted the foundation of life, the very air which he breathed. The fact that this elevation and the visionary solitude did not lead him to isolation, but to a warm-hearted, effluent community spirit, to that comradery glowing with spiritualized Eros and to the idea of true democracy — democracy as a free society of self-reliant and self-controlled individuals, of the "divine average" (a *leitmotif* throughout his poetry) — gives evidence of his affinity to the ancient doctrine of Quakerism, i.e., the doctrine of spiritual union and brotherhood of all those who have entered into the consciousness of God.

Even in his personal character and behavior appeared the racial communion with old "friends," for every ethos bears the features of its own race. His honesty and simplicity, his composure and discretion, his friendliness toward everybody, his indifference to established rules of social behavior — all those were true characteristics of Quakerism. After having poured the volcanic fire of his mature age into powerful songs, his genius became more and more dominated by a milder spirit. It should be pointed out here that we would commit a grave error in assuming that Whitman, even during the time of his most passionate and daring productivity, was anything like a man of violence. The most profound element of his unrestraint is calmness; yet he was able to express even the most ruthless things because in his language and voice forever vibrates the timbre of mystic tenderness denoting the soul's communion with itself. Every strong creed originates in the domain of silence and awe. Emerson's famous words which he sent to Carlyle together with a copy of the second edition of *Leaves of Grass* (1856): "One book . . . a nondescript monster which yet had terrible eyes and buffalo strength," point out only one element in the writing most congenial to Emerson's concern with what is fit for "good" society. Actually, even the most sweeping lines of those songs are full of that fervor that has helped to tear them loose from the quiescence of a profound, tender, chaste and pious nature; in between them, again and again, a strange, leisurely smile breaks forth, the shadow of a gesture signifying the words: Why do we speak at all? What are words? Do we not hear the transcendent language of the Unspeakable pervading them?

Whitman himself, at the end of his "Song of Myself," speaks of his "barbaric yawp" sounding over the roofs of the world, and uses this poetic picture as the finale of this powerful rhapsody. At the very climax of his perception of life and death, he falls short of breath; he stands, his voice faltering, at the edge of the sunset in which the physical and the spiritual, the finite and the infinite seem to dissolve in the flaky and fiery shreds of cloud. Then, in the very depth of his soul a cry rings out, lonely, sad, and yet rapturous, similar to that of the nocturnal cry of a falcon. (It reminds me of the last line of Gottfried Keller's wonderful poem: "Far off, wild and sad the falcons' voices sounded.") Whitman's relentlessness is not forced, superimposed or abrupt; it is the natural progression in the process of naming and interpreting all objects and all feelings. In particular his songs devoted to the love of both sexes and the glorification of sex — so widely and so often attacked — are radiant with loneliness, calmness and purity. By speaking out, by realizing them through the medium of a virile and chaste voice all those feelings are purified, sanctified and uplifted into the sphere of existence in which everything is natural. A fragrance is about them as fresh as that issuing forth from his mother's clothes when he touched them as a boy.

All his actions were marked by a certain lassitude, the composure that comes to those whose best qualities mature not through activity but by absorbing tranquility. Whatever attracted him and tempted him to linger, he enjoyed with the quiet repose of the growing vegetative life. The myriad tongues of metropolitan life murmured in his soul like the rush of reeds or the roaring of the sea of our soul, a choir perpetually one with all existence. In his "Democratic Vistas," he explicitly took a stand against the separation of "nature" and "city." His senses are never dulled or strained to excitement by the hubbub of the streets, but take it in with the same alacrity as they do sea, air, and woods.

The pulse beat of this ruthlessly expanding twin city [New York–Brooklyn] was not in the least a slow or peaceful one. Everything there seemed animated with an apprehension of the future. At that time, New York had a population of 200,000 and was growing from year to year. People of different races kept moving into this most opportune of harbors, mixing with the stock of the early English immigrants. The blazing summer sun glared and the icy winter chill blew through the streets of this city full of contrasts. Broadway swarmed with thousands of vehicles, stagecoaches, buses, carriages, and horsemen, altogether more colorful and livelier than in our time. All classes of society participated in the activities that Broadway offered. As yet, the huge grey stone buildings and giant-shaped skyscrapers were not there; instead, the brick houses — looking more colorful and gayer. Even catastrophes, now and then caused by the forces opposed to man's habitation, assumed the character of sombre festivities. The fire alarm, with its tinkling of bells and blowing of bugles, summoned thousands of people to the burning scene where firemen — clad in red and entangled with the intestines of fire hoses, ladders, hooks, and ropes — did their work defying death. In December, 1835, within three days, 13 acres of old buildings burnt down completely. In more than one passage of Whitman's poetry we are aware of the ringing of the fire alarm. In the evening, theaters opened up. In the huge bowery, for instance, holding 3,000 spectators, famous English guest stars played to an audience of raving, roaring workers and craftsmen enthusiastically applauding. There played the famous Booth, whom the 15-year-old Whitman had a first chance to see as Richard III. Whitman for the first time in his life was thrilled by the impact of the artistic expression, the spoken word, the inspired gesture. In retrospect only are we able to grasp the intense emotion which was thus stirred up in the boy. We can imagine how he must have been impressed by the living word, he who, until late in his life, believed in his vocation as an orator as well as a poet, a great popular orator who with his powerful voice would lead the American people, would master them.

The more there grew in Whitman the feeling of belonging to the race of his New World and the old frontier spirit, now transformed into the psychic-human element, the feeling to discover and conquer with this race on a giant virgin continent the new country of men; to produce, out of this rich and polymorphous clay, perfect sons and daughters of this New World—and thus of the whole earth—the more he felt tempted to acquaint himself with that part of his native America so different in many ways: the southern states of the Union.

The more Whitman's capacity to marvel at all things transformed the material world around him into a symbolic world made translucent with spiritual infinity—in other words, the more profound his love for the world of phenomena grew because of their miraculous existence, the more essences and objects gained for him colorful, comprehensible, mobile, pathetic and joyous reality while enclosed in the eternal, univocal reality of the invisible—the more he was to be impressed with every step further into this world of phenomena, into that part of the earth revealing to him its treasure of lavish creative splendor, displaying new colors and fragrances, new harmonies, gestures and symbols, intense brightness and procreative power.

The southern United States presented a picture so radically different from that of the north, as countries bordering the southern Mediterranean do from the northern part of Germany, if not more so. Whitman left the still uncouth winter region to approach a most luxuriant spring.

There is no need to tell with what strange feelings a man, being used to account for geographic relations and the daily as well as annual rotation of our globe, would start out on a journey across a part of this earth he does not know. Following the Ohio River along the newly settled states of Ohio, Indiana, Kentucky and Illinois, still breathing forth and exhaling the fragrance of unexplored backwoods, he came upon the "Father of Waters," the Mississippi, seeing the whole life of this gigantic stream spread out before his eyes. This river, which together with its tributaries supplies half of the arable land of the United States, he held to be the very artery of the New World around which the innermost life of a splendid future would pulsate. This great land called forth, at first mysteriously and impellingly, a similar greatness, spiritual and poetic, something completely new, immediate and challenging; something to continue, to fulfill all older cultures, or at least something equally significant.

To say that he hated earning a living, and, in order to keep faith with poverty, stopped working as a carpenter, seems to apply—as many of his overly enthusiastic admirers do—standards of interpretation apt to glorify his case. It is true, however, that, as the years went by, he came to neglect this profitable craft for the sake of his higher interests; true also that he gave in, unconcerned with gain or loss, at all times to leisure and independent life, not always to the liking of his worried and somewhat embittered father.

This interest consisted in nothing less than the firm decision to give expression, poetically and spiritually, to the manifold ways and varied thoughts of the American people with which he had become intimately acquainted during his journey—an expression which would do justice to their peculiar and original strength, so as to constitute what one may call the Bible of a truly modern, democratic human race. With all his might he directed his powers, during the seven years prior to the publication of the *Leaves of Grass*, to this goal.

Each time a wooden structure had been completed, Whitman went on a vacation which often lasted for weeks. He retired to nature to roam about the island, to take a sunbath on the beach, to swim, to read and to recite. Here, against nature's background, he first tried out his songs. In them he sought to recapture a rhythm corresponding to that of the sea.

Even when working, he carried a book, a magazine or newspaper in his pocket. Throughout his life he remained an ardent reader of newspapers. They communicated to him the feeling of manifold reality, of actual events; through them he heard the sombre roaring of the masses and their interaction of which he was so fond, the "en masse" to which he devoted his life and his poetry. He read the classical authors, Aeschylus and Sophocles, Plato, Dante, Shakespeare and Ossian, *Don Quixote* and the *Song of the Nibelungs*, and whatever else he could lay his hands on. From his early youth he loved and knew well *A Thousand and One Nights* and Scott's ballads. He himself has told us that when he was young he was a book fiend who devoured everything.

The "Consuming Fire" of which he is possessed does not urge him to construct a philosophical system, but rather to give expression to his very being with a mystic force in which reality, the living dream of being pulsates. Within him lives the miracle of identity, the miracle of the absolute, the true self in the individual self, the miracle of the finite and the infinite intertwined; it throbs with the heartbeat of each second, sees, hears, feels, smells, thinks, rejoices, suffers with him in all his senses. The words for which he is grasping are mere suggestions for the eternal, unspoken, forever true words. Each of them he tries to steep in the essence and wonder of his own existence, in order to invoke, through them and their passionate thronging or through their tender, trembling loneliness in some whispered phrase, that power which alone enables us to understand what he really means: the power of a profoundly natural ecstasy—that ecstasy which should make every one of us hold our breath every day and every hour, whilst we perceive the fabulous wonder of our existence. Thus the indifference accompanying everyday life, the unconcerned tranquility which we display in our dubious familiarity with to-day and tomorrow, should be looked upon as the greatest and most extraordinary phenomenon.

This is the reason readers of Whitman are so frequently reminded of the difference between what he really is and what his readers imagine him to be. Why is it that he escapes them continually, with every single word, and yet waits for them, somewhere, calmly and leisurely? By "waiting for them" is meant precisely that natural and mystic awareness of the self which exists in the reader as well as in Whitman himself. To lead his readers to that awareness is the real and innermost purpose of his poetry. Therefore it is so difficult to make any statements about Whitman outside of the sphere which he himself has only now created, a sphere which makes perceptible his meaning. That is why his words are so transparent, why they have such exceptional appeal, a singular quality. Hence, too, the intense power of the word "love," ringing throughout all his songs. Love is but the feeling of attachment, of belonging to a living image hovering in the infinite and permeated by it, a feeling which finds its consummation in the tender intensity of comradeship. The well-known English critic John A. Symonds once said: "Whitman, indeed, is extremely baffling to criticism. I have already said in print that 'speaking about him is like speaking about the universe.' . . . Not merely because he is large and comprehensive, but because he is intangible, elusive, at first sight self-contradictory, and in some sense formless, does Whitman resemble the universe and defy critical analysis." (*Walt Whitman*, page 33.) He would like best to have the reader, the lover, the friend carry his book with him in his coat pocket, to have it rest on his hip, very close to him; for it is not just a book: "Who touches this touches a man." It is not contained in time. The course of centenniums and millenniums forever rolling along is nothing in the face of the eternal tides of truth.

His penchant toward the organic — seen from a general human point of view — is not only directed to the receptive female "you" but also to the male, the camerado in "the Garden the World." With him, too, one walks hand in hand or with the arm around the shoulder. Only more "ethereal," "as bodiless," in a way experiencing one's own self in the Adamic brother, a creation identical to oneself. Males exchanging the "token of manhood," with each other, embodied in the symbol of the calamus collected in the forest shade next to a pond, a vegetative phallic symbol (from the family of the araceae which have been considered as phallic from time immemorial). Different from the female desire to conceive and her feeling of bliss as a result of conception, the erotic dream stirs in the comrade, the comprehension of spirituality, of loneliness in spite of community, of the silent emotion of male thought eternally winding about the mystery of being.

Therefore those of Whitman's songs inscribed with the sign of Calamus blossom in a sphere marked by a most chaste loneliness. They sound as though coming from the curved lips of a Pan-like god, whispered to the bushes and to the flowers in the high glowing heat of the summer. To deny the eros of these poems would mean to sin against them. Eros vibrates through them just as the quiet air of the afternoon before the gates of Athens, where Socrates talked with Phaidrus under the tree next to the brook. And yet differently. Because here in this new "Garden the World," a man is speaking who has just celebrated procreation and woman with words of purest naturalness and directness. Out of the midst of these Calamus songs, he passionately salutes the "fast-anchor'd eternal" to women, the overwhelming desire for the "Bride" ("more resistless than I can tell, the thought of you!"). There is no greater pride for him than the "token of manhood untainted": His own songs are like "offspring of my loins": "jetting the stuff of far more arrogant republics." He has glorified the woman as mother like no one before him.

Only at this point can we feel the true meaning of these Calamus songs, when we realize that in them the singer wants to get something out of the stillness of the Pan-like forest destined to become the life nerve of the community life of the future, the heartbeat of true democracy, electrically playing between all, freeing each individual from cramped egotism, prejudice, maliciousness and dullness. As he proclaims in his *Democratic Vistas*: "Intense and loving comradeship, the personal and passionate attachment of man to man—which, hard to define, underlies the lessons and ideals of the profound saviours of every land and age, and which seems to promise, when thoroughly develop'd, cultivated and recognized in manners and literature, the most substantial hope and safety of the future of these States, will then be fully express'd. It is to the development, identification, and general prevalence of that fervid comradeship, (the adhesive love, at least rivaling the amative love hitherto possessing imaginative literature, if not going beyond it,) that I look for the counterbalance and offset of our materialistic and vulgar American democracy, and for the spiritualization thereof."

Introduction to *Walt Whitman's Werk* (Berlin: S. Fischer, 1922). Translated by Horst Frenz and Walter Grünzweig.

9. CHRISTIAN MORGENSTERN
"Ein Gesang Walt Whitmans"

(Frater, peccavi?)

Ich sitze, den Blick auf meine Weltkarte gerichtet.
Ich besinge das Weltmeer, die Mutter der Erde.
Schwärzlich türmt es sich auf, fürchterlich brüllt es einher, wie ein fließendes Gebirge, unberechenbar, schrecklich, ein Spiel der Stürme.
Blau liegt es da, wie eine Verheißung vielfältigen Glücks.
Weltteile, völkertragende, steigen aus seinem Schaum empor.
Fünf, sechs Venusse tauchen aus ihm empor, ungeheure, liebes- und lebensdurstige, nach der Sonne verlangende und den Küssen der tausend Myriaden Sterne.
Asia, die unergründliche, den Kamm des Himalaja im Haar, an der Brust die Rose von Schiras, ihr Herz Indien, die Mutter der Menschen.
Europa, die blasse, bewegliche, den Kopf voller Träume und Launen, die Französin unter den Fünfen, die Aristokratin, die Freundin der Wahrheit, die Mutter der Kunst.

Afrika, die riesige gelbe Kuh, faul in allzuviel Sonne lagernd, der Pyramiden unfruchtbare Brüste starrend im heißen Samum, mit der schwarzen üppigen Flechte des Nils.

Amerika, die jugendlichste, unreifste, mit den vierundvierzig Herzkammern und noch keiner rechten Seele, begehrlich, erfinderisch, voll übersprudelnder Kraft, weltklug mit überlegenen Allüren, Demokratin (bis auf weiteres), nur des richtigen Mannes bedürftig, um vielleicht einst die Erste der Fünfe zu werden.

Australia, die Blutarme, umgeben von pausbäckigen Amoretten.

Grönland, die Venus der Eisbären, ihr Herz Island mit den heißen Quellen der Sagen.

Sechsfach öffnet sich so der unendliche Meeresschoß, sechsmal birst so die tiefblaue wallende Decke, — und auftauchen die sechs beherrschenden Göttinnen, liebes- und lebensdurstige, nach der Sonne verlangende und den Küssen der tausend Myriaden Sterne.

A Song by Walt Whitman

(Brother, have I sinned?)

I sit, my gaze directed to my world map.

I sing the ocean, the mother of the earth.

Blackish it towers up, horribly it roars, like flowing mountains, unpredictable, terribly, a game of the storms.

It is blue, like a promise of manifold fortune.

Continents, carrying peoples, emerge from it.

Five, six Venuses emerge, immense, thirsty for love and life, yearning for the sun and the kisses of the thousands of myriads of stars.

Asia, the unfathomable, with the Himalaya in her hair, at her chest the rose of Shiraz, her heart India, the mother of humankind.

Europe, pale, mobile, her head full of dreams and moods, the Frenchwoman among the five, the aristocrat, the friend of truth, the mother of art.

Africa, the giant yellow cow, lazily resting, too much sun, the infertile breasts of the pyramids staring in the hot simoom, with the black, luxuriant braid of the Nile.

America, the most youthful, most immature, with forty-four chambers of the heart, but no real soul as yet, greedy, inventive, full of effervescent power, worldly with superior manners, a democrat (for the time being), merely requiring the right man to possibly become the first of these five.

Australia, the anemic, surrounded by chubby-faced amorettos.

Greenland, the venus of ice bears, her heart Iceland with the hot springs of legends.

Sixfold opens the infinite womb of the sea, sixfold the deep-blue bubbling ceiling bursts, — and the six ruling Goddesses emerge, thirsty for love and life, yearning for the sun and the kisses of the thousands of myriads of stars.

Die Schallmühle: Grotesken und Parodien (München: Piper, 1928), 64–65. Translated by Walter Grünzweig. Reprinted by permission of Piper Verlag.

10. ARTHUR DREY

"Walt Whitman"

Fackelschwinger! Lodernder Titan des keuschen Urwalds!
Deine Augen küssen die Welt, und traumschmeichelnd
Fließt die weiße Sonne deiner Haare über das Meer —
Weltmensch!

Dein Herz ist zwischen den streitenden Blöcken Liebe
In aufgerissener Brust blutenden Brudergefühls —
Kinder knien augenmüde vor deiner Jünglingsseele —
Traum!

Aus deinen bleichen Tränen blinkt warmer Friede,
Und Blumen sind deiner lieben Lippen Worte —
Die wir trinken, heilenden Quell —
Wunder!

Dein Urgebäude wächst, wilderndes Gold . . .
Es breiten fromme Länder ihre grauen Hände
Zum Fang — Einsam stehst du am Saume der Welt —
Prophet!

"Walt Whitman"

Swinger of the torch! Blazing titan of virgin primeval forest!
Your eyes kiss the world, and dream-caressing
The white sun of your hair flows over the sea —
Universal man!

Your heart lies between struggling blocks of love
In the torn-open breast of bleeding brotherhood —
Children kneel down eye-tired before your youthful soul —
Dream!

From out of your pale tears warm peace gleams,
And to your dear lips flowers are words,
Which we drink, healing spring —
Miracle!

Your ancient edifice grows, wild gold . . .
Pious lands spread out their gray hands
For the capture — Lonely, you stand on the brink of the world —
Prophet!

Die Aktion 1 (1911): col. 907. Translation from *Walt Whitman Review* 20 (September 1974): 105; translated by John M. Gogol.

11. GUSTAV GAMPER

"Bekenntnis zu Walt Whitman"

Auf meiner Seele Pfad begegnet' ich dem Meister,
und wir entboten uns den Wandergruß.
Oh, daß ich es erkannt, des greisen Camerado Antlitz,
das leuchtend, lächelnd prüft und mahnt und schenkt!
Wann jetzt ein Wipfel rauscht, so rauscht er mir
vom Wanderer Walt Whitman.
Wann See und Fruchtgeländ' und Schneegebirg erblühn in meiner Heimat,
ist's wie seines Geistes Blühn.
Und nehm' ich Anteil an dreifacher Hoheit,
zu welcher sein Gesang uns aufgerufen:
an Liebe, Demokratie, an Religion!
Oh, so betret' ich schon das Wunderreich der Gnade
und lebe wahr,
lebe mit meinem Volk und allen Völkern
aus der Kraft des Herzens, heilbewußt.

"Homage to Walt Whitman"

On the path of my soul I encountered the master
and we greeted each other as wanderers.
Oh, to have recognized the face of the aged Camerado,
examining, admonishing, giving, with sparkles and smiles!
When a treetop now whispers, it whispers to me
from Walt Whitman, the wanderer.

When lake and fruit-bearing fields and snowy mountains bloom in my
    country,
it's like the blooming of his spirit.
And I partake in the threefold sovereignty,
to which his song has called us:
to Love, Democracy, and Religion!
Oh, so I am already entering the fabulous empire of grace
living truly
living with my people and all peoples
out of the power of my heart, confident of salvation.

Jahrbuch der literarischen Vereinigung Winterthur (1919): 166. Translated by Walter
Grünzweig.

12. HANS REINHART

"Weihegruss an Walt Whitman"

Gleich dem Felsenhaupte,
Heilig erhobnen Gebirges,
Festlich gekrönt
Vom Schimmer des ewigen Schnees,
Also ragst du mächtig empor,
Weltherrlicher,
Sänger glühender Lieder,
Gottes ewige Stimme du,
Odem des Weltalls,
Adams edelster Sohn,
Du Held und Hüter der Erde:
Walt Whitman!

"Holy Dedication to Walt Whitman"

Akin to the rocky head
Of a holy raised peak,
Festively crowned
By the gleam of eternal snow,
You loom powerfully,
Glorious man of the world,
Singer of glowing songs,
You, God's eternal voice,
Breath of the cosmos,

Most noble son of Adam,
You hero and guardian of the earth:
Walt Whitman.

Jahrbuch der literarischen Vereinigung Winterthur (1919): 166. Translated by Walter Grünzweig.

13. CARL ALBERT LANGE

"Whitman"

Eines Riesen Schattenbild
wächst herauf dort schwarz am Himmel
und von Büffeln braun und wild
ihm zu Füßen ein Gewimmel.

Seiner Worte hohe Herde,
die er mit verzückten Armen
aus des Mantelschwungs Erbarmen
hinauswirft auf die weite Erde.

All die Dinge, all die Namen
zwischen Zeit und Ewigkeit
und in allen aller Samen
kosmische Verbundenheit.

Was für Schatten! Welch ein Wesen
von erhabenstem Gebilde
dieser Weise, dieser Wilde
in den Bartes Urwaldbesen!

Tierhaft horchend hochgezogen
und gefräst wie aus Granit
überm müd geschliffnen Lid
schmerzen ihn die Augenbogen.

Und die Stirne voller Zeichen,
voller Runen ohnegleichen
spürt er durch die letzten Wände
wie im Traum schon Gottes Hände.

"Whitman"

The shadow image of a giant
rises up there black on the horizon

and brown and wild buffaloes
crowd around his feet.

The lofty flocks of his words
which he throws across
the wide earth with ecstatic arms
out of the compassion breaking forth from his cloak.

All the things, all the names
between time and eternity
and in all of them the seed to everything
cosmic connectedness.

What a shadow! What a being
of loftiest shape
this sage, this savage
in the forest's broom of his beard!

Listening like animals
cut like granite
above the tired eyelid
with raised eyebrow is hurting.

And his forehead full of signs,
full of runes never seen before
he feels through the last walls
already God's hands, like in a dream.

Weltbühne 22 (1926): 492. Translated by Walter Grünzweig.

14. KURT TUCHOLSKY

"Die Fünf Sinne"

Fünf Sinne hat mir Gott, der Herr, verliehen, mit denen ich mich
zurechtfinden darf hienieden:
Fünf blanke Laternen, die mir den dunkeln Weg beleuchten;
bald leuchtet die eine, bald die andre —
niemals sind alle fünf auf dasselbe Ding gerichtet . . .
Gebt Licht, Laternen — !

Was siehst du, Walt Wrobel — ? . . .

ich sehe neben dem unfreundlichen Mann am Schalter die kleine schmutzige
   Kaffeekanne, aus der er ab und zu einen Zivilschluck genehmigt . . .

ich sehe den ehrenwerten Herrn Appleton aus Janesville (Wisconsin) auf der
   Terrasse des Boulevard-Cafés sitzen, lachende Kokotten bewerfen ihn mit
   Bällchen, er aber steckt seinen hölzernen Unterkiefer hart in die Luft; . . .
Das sieht mein Gesicht.

Was hörst du, Walt Wrobel —?

Ich höre den Küchenchef in der französischen Restaurantküche rufen: 'Ils
   marchent: deux bifteks aux pommes! Une sole meunière!' Und vier Stim-
   men unter den hohen weißen Mützen antworten: 'Et c'est bon!' . . .
Das hört mein Gehör.

Was schmeckst du, Walt Wrobel —?

Ich schmecke die untere Kruste der Obsttorte, die meine Tante gebacken hat;
   was die Torte anbetrifft, so hat sie unten ein Paar schwarze Plättchen, da ist
   der Teig angebrannt, das knirscht im Mund wie Sand . . .
Das schmeckt mein Geschmack. . . .

Fünf Sinne hat mir Gott, der Herr, verliehen, mit denen ich mich
   zurechtfinden darf hiernieden:
Gesicht, Gehör, Geschmack, Geruch, Gefühl.
Fünf Sinne für die Unermeßlichkeit aller Erscheinungen.
Unvollkommenheit ist diese Welt, unvollkommen ihre Beleuchtung. . . .

Gebt Licht, Laternen!
Stolpernd sucht mein Fuß den Weg, es blitzen die Laternen.
Mit allen fünf Sinnen nehm ich auf, die können nichts dafür:
   meist ist es
      Schmerz.

"The Five Senses"

Five senses God, the Lord, has given me, in order to find my way around here
   on earth:
Five shining lanterns lighting the dark way;
sometimes one shines, sometimes the other —
never are all five directed to one and the same thing . . .
Shine, lanterns —!

What do you see, Walt Wrobel —? . . .

I see, next to the unfriendly man behind the office window, the dirty little coffee pot, from which he takes a civilian sip every once in a while . . .
I see the honorable Mr. Appleton from Janesville (Wisconsin) on the terrace
   of the Boulevard-Café, laughing cocottes throwing little balls at him, but
   he sticks his wooden lower jaw hard into the air; . . .
This is what my sight sees.

What do you hear, Walt Wrobel — ?

I hear the chef in the kitchen of the French restaurant calling: "Ils marchent:
    deux bifteks aux pommes! Une sole meunière!" And four voices under the
    high white hats reply: "Et c'est bon!" . . .
This is what my hearing hears.

What do you taste, Walt Wrobel — ?

I taste the lower crust of the fruit tart which my aunt has baked; regarding the
    tart, it is a bit blackened below, this is where the dough got burnt, it
    crunches in the mouth like sand . . .
This what my taste tastes. . . .

Five senses God, the Lord, has given me, in order to find my
    way around here on earth:
Sight, hearing, taste, smell, touch.
Five senses for the immensity of all phenomena.
This world is imperfection, her lighting is imperfect. . . .

Shine, lanterns!
Stumbling, my foot is searching for the way, the lanterns are
    flashing.
With all five senses I take it in, and it is not their fault:
    mostly it is
        pain.

Theobald Tiger [pseud.], *Weltbühne* 35 (September 15, 1925). Excerpted and translated by
Walter Grünzweig.

15. JOHANNES R. BECHER
"Walt Whitman"

In seiner Rhythmen hochgespannten Brücken
— Satzweiten dehnten sich wie Prärien —
War er der Freiheit hymnisches Entzücken,
Geist eines Lincoln atmete durch ihn.

Er trug ein Weltall hoch auf seinem Rücken,
Kraft eines Herakles war ihm verliehn,
So schritt er aufrecht, ohne sich zu bücken,
Wenn oft die Last auch unerträglich schien.

Er aber wurde selber hochgetragen,
Als er auf seines Volkes Fundament
Das Reich der Menschenfreiheit kommen sah.

Er sah DIE Zukunft vor sich aufgeschlagen.
Das Sternenbanner war sein Firmament.
O welch ein Glanz lag auf Amerika!

"Walt Whitman"

In the high-flung bridges of his rhythms
— The expanses of the sentences drawn out like prairies —
He was the enraptured hymn of freedom,
Lincoln's spirit breathed through him.

He carried a cosmos high on his back,
The strength of Heracles he was given,
And he walked upright, without bending,
Even if the burden often seemed unbearable.

But he himself was lifted,
When he saw the world of human freedom
Built on his people's foundation.

He saw THE future opened like a book.
The star spangled banner was his sky.
O what a luster was on America! . . .

Aufbau 1 (1945): 286. Translated by Walter Grünzweig. Reprinted by permission of Aufbau
Verlag, Berlin.

16. GABRIELE ECKART

"An Walt Whitman"

auf der suche nach metren bin ich dir
                begegnet, Walt Whitman.
ich weiß, lebtest du heute und hier,
du würdest singen in endloser erstaunung—
die gigantischen themen in hymnen
                erschließen,
du würdest

singen von den wogenden zügen, die die
                  städte durchschreiten,
     jubelnd im beifall der hellen fassaden,
singen von den millionen gesichtern,
      gerötet von begeisterung
    hoch darüber fahnen vom blute
             gefallener Kämpfer,
singen von den riesigen kombines, die wie
         silbervögel
    über die Ackerfurchen eilen,
singen von den studenten auf den bänken
     der endlosen kastanienallee,
     die nächsten hundert jahre berechnend,
singen vom lila flieder, der die kinder
           beschattet,
    sie kennen nicht Lincoln, doch bauen
         im sande
    raketen und schlösser, die keine
          illusionen bleiben,
singen vom atmen der städte,
    die ins all hineinwachsen,
singen von den menschen auf ihren flachen dächern
    hoch oben, die der sonne winken mit roten tüchern,
singen von den blumenüberfluteten wiesen,
    die die liebenden tragen.
doch du bist tot, Walt Whitman,
deshalb sei mein Lehrer; lehr mich deine rhythmen!
ich singe statt deiner!

"To Walt Whitman"

searching for meters I met you,
          Walt Whitman.
I know, if you lived today and here,
you would sing with endless astonishment —
reveal the gigantic themes
       in hymns,
you would
   sing of the surging crowds
          passing through the cities,
    rejoicing in the applause of the light facades,
   sing of the millions of faces,

flushed with enthusiasm
      high above banners of the blood
of fallen fighters,
sing of the gigantic combines,
    hurrying across the furrows
      like silver birds,
sing of the students on the benches
    of the endless chestnut avenue,
    calculating the coming hundred years,
sing of the lilac, giving shade to the
        children,
    they know not Lincoln but build
    sand castles and rockets that do not
      remain illusions,
sing of the breathing of cities,
    growing into the cosmos,
sing of the people on their flat roofs
    high above, waving to the sun with red scarves,
sing of the meadows flooded with flowers,
    carrying the lovers.
but you are dead, Walt Whitman,
therefore be my teacher; teach me your meters!
    I will sing instead of you!

Bernd Jentzsch, ed., *Ich nenn euch mein Problem. Gedichte der Nachgeborenen* (Wuppertal: Peter Hammer, 1971), 154–155. Translated by Walter Grünzweig. Reprinted by permission of the author.

17. JÜRGEN WELLBROCK

"Dein Selbst Kann Ich Nicht Singen"

(*Für Walt Whitman*)

Du singst das Selbst, du Sänger und vollkommner Krieger,
und dein Gesang, unadressiert, trifft einen Toten.
    Töne, die sich verfangen
in deinen zartesten Halmen,
verknoten sich nicht im alten Widerspruch,
den du, Präriegras kauend, geknüpft hast
aus Eile und Gebein.

SCHREIBEN spottet der Technik deines Handgelenks:
im Goldenen Schnitt hast du nie gesungen.
Wer dich heut berührt, berührt ein Buch,
das sich bewegt in den Händen rühriger Leichen.

"Demokratisch" spreche ich, wenn du willst, gelassen aus,
aber meine Physiologie hat keine Sohle.
    Stattdessen schieße ich schon wieder,
und der Knall, der entsteht, ist der Gesang
auf die Krümmung deines schreibenden Fingers
    (o wie er mir schmeichelt).
Dasselbe alte Lachen.

Verkünde nicht, was nach dir kommt:
dein eignes Finale ertrank in den Akkorden.
Wissen, was es heißt, schlecht zu sein,
macht uns nicht besser.

Sänger, Du hast Blasen an den Lippen!

"I Can't Sing Your Self"

(*For Walt Whitman*)

You sing yourself, you singer and perfect soldier,
and your song, carrying no address, meets a corpse.
    Sounds that are caught
in your frailest leaves,
knotted not in the old knot of contrariety,
which you, chewing prairie-grass, have knotted
from haste and bones.

WRITING mocks the technique of your wrist:
you never sang the divine average.
Whoever touches you these days, touches a book,
moving in the hands of busy corpses.

The word "Democratic" I utter, if you will, calmly,
but my physiology has no boot-soles.
    Instead I am shooting again,
and the resulting crack is the song
to the curvature of your writing-finger
    (o how it's flattering me).

The same old laughter.

Do not announce what comes after you:
your own finale drowned in the chords.
To know what it is to be evil,
does not make us better.

Singer, you have blisters on your lips!

Hermann Peter Piwit and Peter Rühmkorf, eds., *Literaturmagazin 5. Das Vergehen von Hören und Sehen. Aspekte der Kulturvernichtung* (Reinbek: Rowohlt, 1976), 136. Translated by Walter Grünzweig. Reprinted with permission of the author.

18. HANS SAHL

"Schädelstätte Manhattan"

Golgatha der Antennen.
Wo sind deine Märtyrer,
die den Essigschwamm
der Commercials tranken,
deine Religionsstifter,
ans Kreuz geschlagen
von ABC, CBS, NBC?

Übrig blieb nur
das Flackern auf dem Bildschirm
und die Störversuche
benachbarter Toaströster,
in denen der Leib des Herrn
rauchend verkohlte.
(Sogar das Brot nahmen sie uns
und machten es ruchlos.)

Laßt den Papierbecher kreisen,
bevor er verbrennt,
Füllt ihn mit dem Abendmahlwein
künstlich besonnter Frühlesen.

Ich singe das Lied vom Untergang der Dinge,
von Beschaffenheiten, die nicht mehr sind,
was sie scheinen, von Nylon, Perlon, Fornicon,
Ich singe das Lied vom Kunststoff Mensch,
geboren in einer Polyester-Krippe
mit synthetischem Heu,
zu Grabe getragen in einem Plastik-Sarg,

unter dem Verstärkergeläut
eines (eingeblendeten)
Jüngsten Gerichts.

Ich singe das Lied von der Unzerstörbarkeit
alles Organischen, von Koralle und Fisch
und vom guten Indianer Squanto, der seine
die Friedenspfeife mit dem weißen Mann
rauchte und nicht an Lungenkrebs starb,
obwohl statistisch dazu ermächtigt.

Ich singe das Lied einer Magnolie,
die gepflanzt wurde im 15.Stock
eines Penthauses und aufblühte,
aufblühte
unter einem unermeßlich blauen
Kohlenstaubhimmel.

"Calvary Manhattan"

Golgotha of antennas,
what became of your martyrs,
who drank the vinegar sponge
of the commercials,
what of your founders of religions,
nailed to the cross
by ABC, NBC, and CBS?

What remained of them—
only the flickering on the TV screen
and the jamming attempts
by nearby toasters,
in which the body of the Lord
charked away
in smoke.
(Even the bread they took away from us
made it stale and odorless.)

Friends, pass around the paper cup,
before it burns;
fill it with the Holy Communion wine
of vintages prematurely ripened by electric suns.

I sing the song of the end of things,
of materials that no longer are

Hans Sahl [223]

what they once pretended to be, of Nylon, Perlon, Fornicon,
I sing the song of man made of plastic
born in a polyester crib
with synthetic hay,
carried to his grave in a plastic coffin,
with the ringing of the amplified computer bells
of a Last Judgment
(faded in).

I sing the song of organic things
undestroyable, of coral and fish and
of Squanto, the good Indian, who
smoked the pipe of peace with
the white man and did not die of lung cancer
although entitled to do so by statistics.

I sing the song of a magnolia,
planted on the 15th floor of
a penthouse and blossomed out,
blossomed out
under an immensely blue sky
full of coal dust.

This version of the poem, written in 1962, is published here for the first time. A later version was published in Gerhard Friesen, ed., *Nachrichten aus den Staaten: Deutsche Literatur in den USA* (Zurich: Hildesheim; New York: Olms, 1983), 112–113. Translated by Walter Grünzweig.

19. ROLAND KLUGE

"Der Oft Schon Totgesagte Geist Walt Whitmans"

In diesen mittleren Jahren   diesen
Jahren der Reife
Da unerschöpflich zu sein scheint die
Zeit
Und wie in Berge von Weizenkörnern
Meine Hände in sie hineingreifen

Traf ich auf dich   auf deine
Stimme traf ich   unzähmbare
Dort
Wo der Rauch ist und das Rollen der

Städte
Wo Menschen aneinanderstreifen
Tauschend ihre Elektrizität

Masse liebst du   Substanz
Zwischen Zähnen zu kauen   zu erschmecken
Körper   zu umschlingen mit tiefsten
Atemzügen   Glänzender
Anwalt unserer Fähigkeiten zu lieben
Ein Niagara   nicht zu überschreien oder
Niederzuzischen

Wie mit Donner erfüllen die Herden der Bisons
Amerikas Ebenen
Ergreifst du den Kontinent von Küste zu
Küste   Geist
Umbrandet die Kapitolinischen Hügel
In entfernteste Zitadellen der Macht
Schmettern die Ozeane
Gischt deiner Worte

Den Kosmos begreifend als Großen
Camerado
Im namenlosen Grashalm wie im
Unerschöpflichen Sperma der
Galaxis vernehmend den gleichen
Gesang
Quillst du noch aus der abgerissenen
Pflanze
Unbesiegliche Wolfsmilch

"Walt Whitman's Spirit, So Often Pronounced Dead"

In these middle-age years   these
Years of maturity
When time seems to be
Inexhaustible
And my hands dive into it
As into mountains of grains of wheat

I encountered you   encountered
Your voice   indomitable
There
Where there is smoke and the rolling of the
Cities

Where humans touch each other
Exchanging their electricity

You love masses   substance
To chew between teeth   to taste
Bodies   to clasp with deepest
Breaths   Splendid
Counsel of our capability to love
A Niagara   not to be shouted down or
Hissed down

The herds of the buffalos
Fill America's plains as if with thunder
You seize the continent from coast to
Coast   spirit
Foaming around the Capitoline hills
In the remotest citadels of power
Dashing the oceans
Foam of your words

Comprehending the Cosmos as Great
Camerado
Perceiving the same
Song
In the nameless leaf of grass
As in the inexhaustible semen
Of the galaxy
Are you still trickling forth
From the broken plant
Invincible wolf's-milk

Neue Deutsche Literatur 32 (May 1984): 105–106. Translated by Walter Grünzweig.
Reprinted with permission of the author.

20. ROLF SCHWENDTER

"Dich Singe Ich, Sozialismus"

Dich singe ich, Sozialismus,
jetzt erst recht, auf dieser Straße der Leistung,
von den Börsenkursen der reichen Leute mit Wegweisern versehen,
wo die Effizienz der Kosten-Nutzen-Kiste verschenkt
Gerechtigkeit und Geschwisterlichkeit.

Dich singe ich, Sozialismus,
altmodisch, unmodern, anachronistisch, überhaupt
keinem Zeitgeist entsprechend, wie ich,
seh' ich die Skyline der großen Banken Frankfurts am Main,
seh' ich die elektronischen Gadgets von Osaka, Tokio, Las Vegas,
es nun gern einmal bin.

Dich singe ich, Sozialismus,
hungrig, wie gesagt, hysterisch, immer noch nackt, wenn auch die
Stimme heiser geworden vom Geheul
der zweiten Generation, wenigstens noch nicht taub
von den Pressenhallen und Discotheken, wenigstens
noch nicht blind von den Bildschirmtextarbeitsplätzen,
unendlich müde zwar, doch nicht müd' genug zu vergessen mein Lied.

Dich singe ich, Sozialismus,
singe Dich gegen multinationale Zusammenballung von Geld und Macht,
singe Dich gegen die Bilder des Kriegs — was können die armen
Hyänen dafür? —, und gegen die Bilder der Folter,
singe Dich gegen die Pappendeckelwohnungen unter
Waterloo-Bridge im England Frau Thatchers,
singe Gemeinsamkeit an, wo es geht, gegen die Konkurrenzen,
ein Minderheitenprogramm derzeit, wie ich weiß.

Dich singe ich, Sozialismus,
singe Dich, wie ich sehn muß, in einem Mosaik aus Scherben,
in einer Klassenanalyse nämlich Mann gegen Mann, und Frau gegen Frau,
von den Einkäuferscharen beständig schwarz retouchiert,
und skizziert vom Willen derer da, die nicht mehr hungern.

Dich singe ich, Sozialismus,
singe Dich auch gegen die Ermordung all der Bauern Machnos,
aller Trotzkis und Bucharins, gegen die Geständnisse,
die erzwungenen, aller Arthur Londons, gegen alle zerschlagenen
Räte in Csepel, gegen alle Ljubljanas
und Bautzens, singe Dich gegen Stasi, GPU, Securitate,
wie auch, selbstredend, gegen Verfassungsschutz, CIA und Staatspolizei.

Dich singe ich, Sozialismus, und wenn es auf einer feuchten Wiese geschieht,
benannt nach päpstlichen Dienern, betreten, vormals (wie ich hoffe)
von Dienern auch, betreten nun, zuweilen päpstlicher als die
Päpste. Der Du entstehen magst in den Farben des Regenbogens: die
rote zwar keineswegs zu vergessen,
doch auch nicht die violette, etwa.

Dich singe ich, Sozialismus,
fragmentarisch, noch nichtmals vernetzt, hinterfragbar,

vorbei an den Gewerkschaften und Kammern, vorbei an den Parteien,
vorbei selbst auch noch, es schmerzt mich an den blauen Blumen
des Prinzips Hoffnung. Auffindbar erst mikrologisch,
wie ein Schreiber der Fugger und Welser geträumt haben mag
vom dereinst weltspannenden Kapital.
Singe Dich, und dies seit Jahrzehnten, gegen Ausgrenzung und Armut,
und jeder Ort, wo es Armut und Ausgrenzung gab und gibt,
mag sich betroffen fühlen, wo immer er lag und liegt.

Dich singe ich, Sozialismus, der Du langsam aufwachen magst nach 70 Jahren
    Schlaf,
im Baikal-See wohl, dem gestorbenen, die veränderte Welt zu
verändern, auch wenn die anderen verändert sie haben, eine
Verkehrsform, noch kaum hinaus über den Anfang, neugierig wär' ich,
wie Einübung sich vollzieht
in Jahrhunderten, leider leb' ich nicht so lang.

Dich singe ich, Sozialismus,
Pessimismus des Wissens, Optimismus des Handelns,
herauszufinden in Spuren, vom Mindestlöhner und -rentner etwa,
von Grundsicherungen, von Urabstimmungen der Basis,
selbst noch von Aktiengesellschaften, wie bei Friedrich Engels,
vereinzelt sogar, vielleicht, von verstaatlichten Betrieben;
herauszufinden in Solidaritäten und gegenseitigen Hilfen,
des Alltagslebens zumal, in genossenschaftlichem Leben . . .
Die sechs Minuten sind um.

Dich singe ich, Sozialismus,
jetzt erst recht.

"You I Sing, Socialism"

You I sing, Socialism,
now more than ever, on this road of competition,
with signposts put up by the share prices of the rich,
where the efficiency of the cost-effective thing gives up on
Justice, Brother- and Sisterhood.

You I sing, Socialism,
old-fashioned, outdated, anachronistic, completely
contradicting any Zeitgeist, just like myself,
I see the skyline of the large banks in Frankfurt on the river Main,
I see the electronic gadgets of Osaka, Tokyo, Las Vegas,
it's just how I like to be.

You I sing, Socialism,
hungry, hysterical, still naked,
even if the voice has become hoarse from the yells
of the second generation, at least not yet deaf
from all the press conferences and discotheques, at least
not blind yet from the jobs behind monitors,
infinitely tired though, but not tired enough
to forget my song.

You I sing, Socialism,
I sing you against multinational concentration of money and power,
I sing you against the images of war — it's not the fault of the poor
hyenas — and against the images of torture,
I sing against cardboard box quarters under Waterloo Bridge in Mrs.
    Thatcher's England,
I sing community, wherever possible, against competitions,
a program for a small minority, at present, indeed, I know.

You I sing, Socialism,
I sing you, as I am forced to recognize, in a mosaic of broken pieces,
in a class analysis of men against men, of women against women,
constantly retouched black by the swarms of shoppers,
and sketched out by the interests of those, who are no longer starving.

You I sing, Socialism,
I sing you against the killing of Makhno's farmers,
against all the Trotskys and Bukharins, against all the forced
confessions, all the Arthur Londons, against all the smashed
commissars in Csepel, against all Ljubljanas and Bautzens, I
sing you against Stasi, GPU, Securitate,
but, of course, also against Verfassungsschutz, CIA and
Staatspolizei.

You I sing, Socialism, even on moist grass,
named after the servants of the pope,
formerly tread upon (I hope) also by servants,
rather embarrassed, at times holier than the pope.
May you emerge in rainbow colors: not leaving out red,
but also not purple.

You I sing, Socialism,
fragmentary, not part of a network, open to questioning,
beyond unions and chambers, and parties,
beyond even itself, the Blue Flower of the hope principle pains
me. To be found only micrologically,
the way a writer of the Fugger and Welser may have dreamt

Rolf Schwendter [229]

of future capitalism spanning the globe.
I sing you, have done so for decades, against exclusion and poverty,
and every place where exclusion and poverty have existed and still do exist,
should feel embarrassed, wherever it was or is.

You I sing, Socialism,
you may slowly awaken after a seventy years' sleep,
in Lake Baikal, which has died,
to change a changed world, even if the others have changed it,
a way of communicating, still in its infancy, I'd be curious
to know how it develops with practice,
over centuries, unfortunately I will not live that long.

You I sing, Socialism,
pessimism of knowledge, optimism of action,
to be found in traces, among those paid minimum wage and those receiving
    minimum pensions,
in basic securities, ballots at the grassroots,
even of stock corporations as in the works of Frederick Engels,
at times even, maybe, of nationalized industry;
to be found in solidarities and mutual assistance,
in every day life, in cooperative life . . .
My six minutes are up.

You I sing, Socialism,
now more than ever.

Volksstimme (Vienna) (October 19, 1990). Translated by Walter Grünzweig. Reprinted by permission of the author.

GAY WILSON ALLEN

Whitman in the Netherlands

Since Walt Whitman often emphasized his Dutch heritage (the Van Velsor family on his mother's side, what he called his "far back Netherlands stock on the maternal side"),[1] it seems worth a brief note to suggest the poet's reputation in his ancestral land.

One man, Maurits Wagenvoort, was responsible for a flurry of interest in Whitman in Holland in the 1890s and early twentieth century. He visited the United States in 1892 and became fascinated by *Leaves of Grass*. After returning, he translated fifteen poems, which he published in 1898 as *Natuurleven*. In his introduction he declared:

> It seems to me that these poems epitomize all the admirable, awe-inspiring, and perplexing things I have seen in America; they are a small scale of the enormous Republic, of American life purified by the love and the intellect of a universal poet . . . [and] seen through the eyes of an American who will be accorded a permanent place among the noblest of all time.[2]

One other author, W. G. van Nouhuys, tried to stir up interest in Whitman in Holland through several magazine articles and reviews; but he did not like Wagenvoort's translations and said "he constantly confuses himself with the American poet."[3] Another critic in *De Hollandische Review* wrote, "Although W. G. van Nouhuys has introduced us to Walt Whitman in a number of articles in *De Gids*,

Whitman's poetry has never become popular in the Netherlands." This critic pronounced van Nouhuys's own translations a failure and wondered if Wagenvoort would succeed (apparently the critic had not yet read his translations), but went on to say, "He may succeed, despite his introduction, which is full of the silliest remarks, with too much emphasis on Whitman the martyr."[4] Another reviewer, "F.L.," in *Elsevier's Geillustreerd Maandschift* in 1900, said Wagenvoort's translation was "not suitable for the drawing room" because he had refused to expurgate the sexual words and descriptions.

An obituary of Whitman in *De Amsterdammer* observed that "Walt Whitman never intended to become a poet for the few; what he wanted was to write for and be understood by the people, to sing about his longing for health, natural life, and his indestructible hope for the future."[5]

Throughout the 1890s both Wagenvoort (under the pseudonym Vasmeer de Soie) and van Nouhuys continued to sing Whitman's praise in numerous articles. In 1893 van Nouhuys collected his essays in a book with the simple title *Walt Whitman* (The Hague: Nijhoff). The defense of Whitman by his ardent German admirer Karl Federn was also publicized in Holland. And in 1917 Wagenvoort published a full translation of *Leaves of Grass* with the Germanic title *Grashalmen* (Amsterdam: Werieldbibliotheek).

Since World War I Dutch interest in the half-Dutch poet has been nearly nonexistent. In a letter to me, dated February 23, 1990, Dr. Hans Bak, of the Faculteit du Letteren in Katholeeke Universeteit in Nijmegen wrote: "I am not aware that any important criticism of Whitman has been published in the Netherlands, either by a Dutch writer, or an academic specialist in American literature."[6]

NOTES

1. Justin Kaplan, ed., *Complete Poetry and Collected Prose* (New York: Library of America, 1982), 690.

2. *Natuurleven* (1898).

3. *Nederlandsche Spectator* (April 1899).

4. *De Hollandische Review* 3 (1898): 829.

5. *De Amsterdammer* 15 (1892): 2–3.

6. For information on the reputation of American authors in the Netherlands, see J. G. Riewald and J. Bakker, *The Critical Reception of American Literature in the Netherlands, 1824–1900: A Documentary Conspectus from Contemporary Periodicals* (Amsterdam: Rodopi, 1982).

ROGER ASSELINEAU

Whitman in France and Belgium

As early as 1860 the *Saturday Press* reprinted (or so it is claimed) an article published in Paris in the *Bibliographie Impériale* (which never existed) announcing the imminent publication of a French translation of *Leaves of Grass* by one V.H. (Victor Hugo? Who knows?). After praising the eccentric aesthetics of the American poet, the article quoted samples of the forthcoming translation, but sooner or later readers could not help but realize that what they were reading was not a true translation but a comic parody, especially when they came to such lines as:

> O mère! O fils!
> O troupeau continental! . . .
> O toi-même! O Dieu! O moyen divin!
> O forts de la Halle barbus!
> O poètes! O dormeurs!
> Eau de Javelle!

The last line with the pun on "O" was particularly satirical, and the exclamation point, which had a lyrical value in the text, had become a *point d'ironie*.

The whole article was a joke.[1] Actually, the first serious translation of some of Whitman's poems (preceded by a brief introduction) appeared only one year later in 1861. It was by Louis Etienne and was published in *La Revue Européenne* (November 1, 1861) under the title "Walt Whitman, poète, philosophe et 'rowdy.'" It was a severe indictment. Whitman was represented as "lawless" and embodying "American turbulence." He was "one more pantheist and St. Simonian in the land of emigration, . . . that republic which is not a state . . . but a still chaotic world." He practices "the religion of the flesh," Etienne also said, and "justifies crime and unreservedly lauds vice." Etienne, moreover, attacked the formlessness and incoherence of Whitman's poetry. Such a reaction was to be expected at a time when, under Napoléon III's rule, all liberal ideas were banned and democracy was regarded as synonymous with disorder and anarchy. Though Victor Hugo claimed he had put the red Phrygian cap on the dictionary in the 1830s and abolished all distinctions between "noble" and common words, French poets still wrote in a literary and ornate language, obeyed strict prosodical rules, and danced with their chains, as Voltaire had put it a century earlier, though he was no innovator himself. French readers therefore could only be horrified by Whitman's vocabulary and the lack of rhymes and set patterns in his poems. How could he dare speak of "the handkerchief of the Lord" when in translations of *Othello*, even Desdemona's handkerchief was chastely replaced by a diamond necklace. Whitman was definitely vulgar. The only acceptable American poet, in the opinion of French connoisseurs, was Edgar Allan Poe. Baudelaire had translated "The Raven" and "The Philosophy of Composition" two years before. Compared to Poe, Whitman was a savage and a "rowdy."

Things did not change radically after the fall of Napoléon III. In 1872 an influential critic, well-read in English literature, Mme. Blanc (Thérèse Bentzon) could still write in the *Revue des Deux Mondes* (June 1, 1872) an article entitled "Un poète américain, Walt Whitman: 'Muscle and Pluck Forever.'" She condemned him for the crudity and bad taste of his naturalism and for combining the worst excesses of Victor Hugo with "the most poisonous compositions of Baudelaire." (She must have been thinking of the six poems that a tribunal obliged Baudelaire to remove from *Les Fleurs du mal* in 1867.)

In 1877 Henry Cochin, the brother of the famous surgeon, still traumatized by the horrors of the Commune, violently protested in *Le Correspondant* against the dangerous anarchism and immorality of "To a Foil'd Revolter or Revoltress." This, he said, is "Democracy run wild, a form of insanity and megalomania." He also criticized the excessive length of some of Whitman's lines. He counted 101 syllables in one of them, whereas there were only 12 in the traditional alexandrine. It was really too much, he thought.

There were some signs of change, however. In the very year when Mme. Blanc published her attack, a more liberal and open-minded critic, Henri Blémont, came to Whitman's defense in a series of three articles in *La Renaissance Littéraire et Artistique* (June 8, July 6, 13, 1872). "He is not Art," Blémont wrote, "he is much more than that, he is life. He is eminently personal, but he includes the whole world in his personality. . . . He is Lucretius's ideal poet. Not only nothing human, but also nothing superhuman or even subhuman is alien to him." It was a dithyrambic eulogy based on the reactions of a number of English poets whose names Blémont mentioned in his article: W. M. Rossetti, Robert Buchanan, Moncure Conway, Roden Noel, and Swinburne, but it had no appreciable effect on French opinion, because apparently French readers were already discouraged by Whitman's lack of art and taste. This is the reason Leo Quesnel gave in an article in the *Revue Bleue* twelve years later (February 16, 1884), and, to his mind, *Leaves of Grass* would never be as popular in France as in Great Britain because Whitman's poetry was untranslatable. "How could one manage to naturalize it?" he asked. "When translated, Whitman is no longer Whitman: his free and rich language . . . cannot be poured into the narrow and pure mould of romance languages."

Despite this pessimistic affirmation, Quesnel himself translated "With Antecedents" for the *Bibliothèque Universelle et Revue Suisse* in February 1886, and a very gifted young poet, Jules Laforgue, in the same year very successfully translated several "*Brins d'herbe*" from that "astonishing American poet, Walt Whitman," as he said. They appeared in three issues of *La Vogue* (June 28, July 5, August 2, 1886), a little magazine edited by the symbolist poet Gustave Kahn and devoted exclusively to poetry. Whitman was now launched. After this, he was officially recognized and adopted by the symbolists. Further translations and laudatory articles about him multiplied and appeared in quick succession. There were some good translations in particular by Francis Vielé-Griffin, a French symbolist who was born in America, and by Teodor de Wyzewa, who was of Polish descent. Vielé-Griffin translated "Faces" and "A Locomotive in Winter" (to stress Whitman's modernity) in *La Revue Indépendante* (November 1888), and Teodor de Wyzewa translated a fragment of "Salut au Monde!" for the *Revue Politique et Littéraire* (April 1892).[2] Unfortunately, Jules Laforgue could not continue his translations. He died the following year, but he was succeeded by Léon Bazalgette two decades later.

In the meantime, as P. Mansell Jones has shown, Whitman's poetry and aesthetics seeped into the works of some of the symbolists, who like him, wanted to suggest meaning (particularly through music), rather than state it explicitly and who believed in being indirect rather than direct.[3] He was therefore regarded as a bold forerunner by Teodor de Wyzewa.[4] And indeed, there seems to have been a kind of preestablished harmony between Whitman and French symbolism. The two American-born French symbolists, Stuart Merrill and Francis Vielé-Griffin, who could read *Leaves of Grass* in the original text, were especially susceptible to his influence.[5] Their poems echo his ideas and themes, though they remained faithful to the rules of French prosody. Two Belgian poets were bolder: Emile Verhaeren and Maurice Maeterlinck. The former, in his later works, *Les Villes tentaculaires* (1895), *Les Visages de la vie* (1899), *Les Forces tumultueuses* (1902), and *La Multiple Splendeur* (1906), broke with the traditional stanzaic patterns and used long lines somewhat reminiscent of Whitman's free verse. He also, contrary to the French symbolists, sang modern industry and large cities, as Whitman had done, but in a pessimistic mode. He rejected, he said, "accepted rules and official parodies" and preferred to translate "what affected his whole being, his bones, his muscles, his nerves, thanks to an infectious emotion which passed from exterior things to his soul . . . a commotion . . . a deep interior upsurge which supplied him with the rhythm of his verse."[6] The influence of Whitman on Maeterlinck was still stronger. In his *Serres chaudes* (1889), he imitated Whitman's repetitions of words and phrases, gave up rhyme and regularity, and created a variety of vers libre. In the poem entitled "Regards," he even closely followed "Faces" as translated by Vielé-Griffin.

Vers libre caught on very slowly in France, but it definitely had its origin in *Leaves of Grass*. The earliest examples were two poems in Arthur Rimbaud's *Illuminations* (1886), "Marine" and "Mouvement," and Rimbaud may very well have read the translations of Whitman published in *La Renaissance Littéraire* in 1872. Édouard Dujardin says so in his "Les premiers poètes du vers libre," in the *Mercure de France* (March 1921), though he quibbled about the difference between French vers libre and Whitman's *verset*. Anyway, it was in vers libre that Francis Jammes wrote his nature poetry, *De l'Angélus de l'aube à l'Angélus du soir* (1898) and *Vivre en Dieu* (1910), and Paul Fort his innumerable *Ballades françaises* (1897–1937). Valéry Larbaud, a rich cosmopolite who could read *Leaves of Grass* in English, adopted a technique reminiscent of Whitman's in *A. O. Barnabooth—ses poésies* (1908), but the tone he used was humorous, and he did Whitman *à la blague*.

An important factor in the growth of Whitman's reputation in France at the end of the nineteenth century was a critical essay by Gabriel Sarrazin in *La Nouvelle Revue* (May 1, 1888).[7] It began with an extremely sympathetic study of Whitman's pantheism. Sarrazin equated *Leaves of Grass* with the writings of the great Oriental mystics and also detected Hegelian traits in the poet's philosophy. Whereas Whitman had so often been described as an illiterate "rough," a wild "rowdy," Sarrazin emphasized his culture. "He had read everything we have read ourselves," he concluded, and he praised his art and the breadth of his thought which reconciles "Jesus and Spinoza, the Brahmins and the Encyclopaedists, Lucretius and Fichte, Darwin and Plato." Whitman's disciples were delighted with such an enthusiastic and well-balanced tribute from a European.

As symbolism gradually lost its impetus, readers and writers became less sensitive to Whitman's art than to the content of his poems—to such an extent that the fragmentary translations by Daniel Halévy and Henry Davray, which appeared after 1910, were no longer in verse but in prose.[8] Halévy even tended to concentrate exclusively on Whitman's political message, and in his "Chants démocratiques" he rendered "A Song for Occupations" by "Aux Ouvriers." A few years later, Elsie Masson, who also translated some of Whitman's poems (in free verse), characteristically entitled an article on the poet in the *Mercure de France* (August 1, 1907) "Whitman, ouvrier et poète."

In the second decade of the twentieth century, Whitman suddenly ceased to be the cult-object of small coteries of aesthetes or leftist intellectuals. His reputation spread in the general public thanks to the almost simultaneous publication of his biography and a complete translation of *Leaves of Grass* by Léon Bazalgette. The biography appeared first in 1908: *Walt Whitman: l'homme et son oeuvre*, in two volumes. It was published by an important publishing firm, le Mercure de France, which helped its diffusion. Bazalgette was an unconditional admirer of Whitman, and his book was a hagiography in the tradition of R. M. Bucke and Horace Traubel rather than an impartial biography. He had a tendency to speak through his heart as some people speak through their noses (to take up a phrase which André Gide applied to someone else). His Whitman was a supernatural figure, an inspired prophet rather than a mere poet, the founder of a new religion. As for Bazalgette's translation of *Leaves of Grass*, it was similarly idealized but extremely awkward and flat, for he was no poet and was attracted to Whitman only by his religious and political themes. It followed the text too closely, and, though it rendered the poems verse by verse rather than in prose, it had no rhythm whatever. Yet, as it was the first time French readers had a chance to read the whole of *Leaves of Grass*, it was extremely popular and was reprinted several times.

Bazalgette's translation appeared at a time when a movement called *unanimisme* founded by Jules Romains was developing. Fernand Baldensperger defined its aim as "a sort of pantheistic and pansocial vision where the poor individual is more or less absorbed."[9] There were undeniable echoes of *Leaves of Grass* in Jules Romains's *La Vie unanime* (1908), which celebrated the collective soul of large city crowds, and in the poems of other members of the group (sometimes called "L'Abbaye" [de Créteil]), Georges Duhamel and Georges Chennevière, who were also, like Whitman, "lyricists of the body."

But Whitman did not remain the exclusive property of those who felt a transcendental presence behind material appearances and/or believed in Man-en-Masse. The aesthetes were not long in reacting. They were grouped around the *Nouvelle Revue Française* (NRF), a literary magazine founded in 1905, which soon became very influential. They championed a new form of purified and rationalized symbolism, and André Gide was their leading spirit. He strongly objected to Bazalgette's translation, which he thought both inartistic and "prettified"— "prettified" because, in particular, it completely censored Whitman's homosexuality. (Bazalgette systematically translated "love" as "affection.") It gave a distorted and idealized image of the poet. Gide therefore welcomed with enthusiasm the introduction that he had invited Valéry Larbaud to write for a collection of translations of *Leaves of Grass* which he planned to publish as early as 1914 and which was eventually published in 1918 under the title of *Walt Whitman: Oeuvres Choisies* (see selection 1).[10] Larbaud completely destroyed the legend built around Whitman by his American admirers, denying, to begin with, that Whitman ever was a workman. He was a typographer who became a journalist, a great solitary, not a "great camerado," and Bazalgette's biography was, in Larbaud's opinion, the work of a disciple rather than a critic. He explained the growth of Whitman's philosophy by the triple influence of the German idealists (and more particularly, Hegel), the formation of the American nation before his very eyes, and Emerson's *Essays*. He did not especially care for Whitman's ethics and politics and attached much more importance to the tone of *Leaves of Grass*, to what he called "expression" and "effusion." He concluded that, though the doctrine it contained would sooner or later be considered mere deadwood like Dante's theological niceties, Whitman's poetry would be saved by its original rhythm and its style, which replaced the eighteenth-century "poetic diction" for which Wordsworth had in vain tried to find a substitute.

Besides Larbaud's introduction, the 1918 *Oeuvres Choisies* contained Laforgue's and Vielé-Griffin's translations, as well as new ones by Louis Fabulet, André Gide, and Larbaud himself.[11] It was for several decades the best translation available and the most influential, though, by a strange aberration, "Song of Myself" was hardly represented at all.

In the years immediately preceding World War I, more and more people were becoming interested in Whitman. They saw him as a "teacher of energy" (Maurice Barrès's phrase). Philéas Lebesque in particular proclaimed: "We have had enough of depressing pessimists!" He saw above all in Whitman a prophet, the author of new Vedas and a Nordic poet like himself.[12] He contributed with Paul Fort, Chennevière, Jules Romains, and Bazalgette to a review called *L'Effort*. A little later, Henri Guilbeaux founded a movement along the same lines, "Le Dynamisme," which took over *L'Effort*, now called *L'Effort libre*. The Swiss adventurer Blaise Cendrars obeyed Whitman's call, *allons!*, and sang with verve his journey across Asia in his *Prose du Transsibérien* (1913), which actually was not in prose but in free verse. Like Whitman, he thought that "merely existing is true happiness."

During the Great War, which was a "European Civil War," Whitman once again served as a comforter, just as he had during the American Civil War. Bazalgette translated *The Wound-Dresser* (*Le Panseur de Plaies*) (1917). Georges Duhamel, then an army doctor, bore it in mind when he wrote *La Vie des martyrs* (1917). Like Whitman, he healed some men "by talking to them in a low voice, smiling at them or stroking their foreheads."

Thanks to the combined influence of the Bazalgette and NRF translations, reinforced in 1926 by a translation of *Specimen Days* (*Pages de journal*) by Bazalgette, Whitman's influence reached its peak after the war in the 1920s. Only one author resisted it, Paul Claudel, who strongly disapproved of Gide's and Whitman's homosexuality and, for this reason, declined Gide's invitation to contribute to the NRF translation. Yet, his lyric poems, notably his *Cinq grandes odes* (1900–1908), were written in free verse akin to Whitman's. He probably had bought a copy of *Leaves of Grass* at the time of his first stay in the United States as French consul in New York and Boston. He said himself that he admired Whitman's cosmic inspiration, but he vigorously denied that he had ever been influenced by him as regards his ideas or his technique, which he claimed was wholly instinctive and personal.[13]

Claudel was all the more shocked by Whitman's homosexuality when on April 1, 1913 (All Fools Day!), Guillaume Apollinaire published in the *Mercure de France* a description of Whitman's funeral, which, according to what an eyewitness told him, he said, had been an orgy, a pretext for sexual perverts to drink and make merry in the cemetery until dawn. This was strongly denied by Stuart Merrill and led to a polemic in which even Eduard Bertz, the German critic, took part.

Despite this, Bazalgette became a more and more fervid worshiper of Whitman. In *Le Poème-Evangile de Walt Whitman* (1921) he nearly deified him and interpreted *Leaves of Grass* as a new Gospel. His friend Marcel Martinet, the literary editor of *L'Humanité*, the Communist daily, and one of the contributors to *L'Effort*, greeted its publication with the following words on July 13, 1922: "Dear Walt! . . . he re-opened to me the Paradise of the world. The words of dear Walt! They are not the words of a writer, but truly revolutionary words which can raise a dispirited man to his feet. . . ." Martinet was a poet himself, and his *Eux et Moi: Chants d'identité* in blank verse often reads like a serious parody of Whitman.[14]

André Gide composed a new version of his rather decadent *Les Nourritures terrestres* (1897). Under Whitman's influence it became *Les Nouvelles nourritures* (1935). Instead of calling the young man for whom he was supposedly writing Nathanaël — "too plaintive" a name, he said — he now called him "comrade" and considered himself a "new Adam born for happiness."[15] The Provençal novelist Jean Giono, who hated large cities, admired Whitman's cosmic poems. "I think of Whitman and of Paumanok, the fish-shaped island," he wrote in *Présentation de Pan* in 1930. He still thought of him a few years later when he put *Le Serpent d'étoiles* under the aegis of a line from *Leaves of Grass*.[16]

By this time the existence of an autonomous American literature had at last been recognized by French academics, and in 1929 Jean Catel published his searching study of the genesis and growth of the first edition of *Leaves of Grass* under the title of *Walt Whitman: La naissance du poète* (see selection 2). The following year Catel, a poet and a musician, devoted a second (slimmer) volume to *Rythme et langage dans la première édition des "Leaves of Grass."* Both books were pioneer work of the finest quality. Unfortunately, they have never been translated into English, which is why a sample of the first one is included here.

After World War II there was a renewal of interest in American literature, and in 1948 Paul Jamati published a small book on Whitman in the very popular series of Pierre Seghers's "Poètes d'Aujourd'hui." It contained a fairly long biographical introduction in which he tried to put the clock back to Bazalgette's time. He saw in "Calamus" simply a celebration of brotherly love and in Whitman primarily the poet of Man-en-Masse. He consequently denounced as subverters of democracy all the critics who were attracted mainly to Whitman's art and personality. In the rest of the volume, he merely reprinted Bazalgette's translation of some of Whitman's poems.

In fact, this simplistic and ideologically oriented book had little influence. It was as a poet that writers continued to celebrate Whitman, as a number of them did in the 1960s and 1970s. Jules Romains thus declared in 1972: "Walt Whitman's poems are indeed poems in which the human soul reveals itself with simplicity and vigor (quite different in this respect from Edgar Allan Poe whose importance and greatness I do recognize)" (see selection 3). Jean Guéhenno, a member of the

French Academy, an essayist, and a fervent admirer of Rousseau, saw in *Leaves of Grass* "the most intimate, the most carnal of books," like Montaigne's *Essays*, and celebrated Whitman as "the greatest bard of Democracy that ever was." [17] Another Academician, Maurice Genevoix, whose novels about forests and poachers had made him famous, in *Un Jour* (written when he was eighty-six) deliberately illustrated Whitman's "Enough to merely be!" [18] Jean-Marie Le Clézio, a much younger writer and the author of poetical novels, wrote (directly in English, as he is a Mauritian): "Whitman is still among us. His eye and his voice still invent our shapes and our words. He is even the most alive of us all." [19]

Since the end of World War II, Whitman's works have never ceased to be translated and studied. Thus in 1951 Pierre Messiaen published *Walt Whitman: Choix de poèmes*, which contained a sensible introduction, but the translation was spoiled by several blunders. In 1954 my own *L'Evolution de Walt Whitman après la première édition des "Feuilles d'herbe"* offered to the French public a well-balanced biography of the poet and a thorough critical study of his works based on materials gathered in America during a three-year stay. It was later translated and published in two volumes by Harvard University Press (1960–1962). I also translated a selection from *Leaves of Grass* which went through several editions in the form of a bilingual anthology. It was declared the best translation of *Leaves of Grass* to date by Alain Bosquet, a distinguished poet, novelist, and critic. Bosquet himself wrote a brilliant introductory book about the poet, *Whitman* (1959), which contained several of his own translations.

In the course of a 1989 televised interview, Henri Thomas, a novelist and essayist born during World War I, lamented: "Whitman is now forgotten. Ah! how beautiful forgotten things are in retrospect!" This was much exaggerated, but it is true that Whitman's poetry has lost part of its appeal and power. Whitman is no longer regarded as a prophet of democracy and a revolutionary — through no fault of his own but simply because the word "democracy" has become devalued and now often leaves people cold. All its poetry has evaporated. It is too often synonymous in Western Europe with corruption, moral laxity, the oppression of minorities, and distrust of elites. It is no longer based on virtue, as Montesquieu believed, but on jealousy. It is now considered a necessary evil rather than an inspiring ideal and the supreme good. Whitman's faith in science and progress is similarly out of date at a time when people feel threatened by the atom bomb, holes in the ozone, and acid rain.

But Whitman's prestige, nonetheless, remains as great as ever among lovers of poetry and students of American literature, to whom he still gives the same shock of discovery and the same thrill as he did to Emerson in 1855. Two recent facts tend to prove it. First, in 1987 Claudette Fillard defended at the Sorbonne a doctoral dissertation which was both very interesting (qualitatively) and quite impressive (quantitatively) on "Walt Whitman, poète des éléments." In eight hundred finely written pages, she methodically and exhaustively followed the role played by the four elements (fire, water, air, and earth) in *Leaves of Grass*. She based her study on the analysis of Gaston Bachelard and Gilberd Durand and thus produced a very original dissertation, which unfortunately has not yet been published. The second event was the publication in 1989 of a new translation of *Leaves of Grass* (a selection; only Bazalgette translated the whole of it). The translator, Jacques Barras, is a poet as well as a professor of English literature, and his translation is sonorous and colorful and of course technically impeccable. (It has been hailed with enthusiasm by reviewers, though it is less faithful to the text than my own.)

Despite the pollution of the atmosphere and the current distaste for democracy, *Leaves of Grass* is thus as green as ever in contemporary France. French poets and connoisseurs of poetry prefer the fluidity of Whitman's free verse to the mineral rigidity of Poe's poems. After all, the essential quiddity of *Leaves of Grass* is its liquidity.

BELGIUM

Ever since obtaining political independence in 1831, Belgium has led an independent literary life. Even when they write in French, Belgian authors have a somewhat different voice from their French neighbors. It must not be forgotten that their country is the confluence of two worlds and is torn between Latin and Germanic cultures. A large part of the population speaks Flemish rather than French, and cultivated Belgians are at least trilingual. They speak the two national languages, plus English and/or German. They are open to French culture if their native language is French and to German culture if their native language is Flemish.

Naturally, under such conditions, Whitman's influence was felt in Belgium as well as in France and Germany. It was felt both directly through (partial) translations of *Leaves of Grass* and indirectly through French poets, like Jules Laforgue and Gustave Kahn, who had themselves been liberated from prosodic traditions by Whitman's example.[20] It can be found in particular in the works of Maurice Maeterlinck (1862–1949) of the Flemish name. Maeterlinck was mostly a poet in prose, but he had published in 1889 a collection of poems entitled *Serres chaudes*. Though most of the pieces were written in conventional form, some of them were in free verse cut up so as to look like traditional verse, such as "Regards" and "Visages." There was a kind of preestablished harmony between Whitman and him. He was fundamentally a mystic, too, and had in 1891 translated from the Flemish "L'Ornement des noces spirituelles de Ruysbroeck l'Admirable"; like Whitman, he was interested in all the old religions of India, Egypt, and Persia. In *Le grand secret*, he wrote these lines, to which Whitman would have fully subscribed: "The great secret, the only secret is that everything is secret . . . everything is God . . . everything is in Him and must end there in happiness, and the only Godhead we can hope to know is in our deepest self."[21] Like Whitman, too, he believed in democracy, in liberty and equality, and he said so in prose in *Le Double Jardin* (1921): "Yes, it is the duty of all those whose thoughts precede the unconscious masses to destroy all that interferes with the liberty of men, as if all men deserved to be free."[22] He also believed that all things have souls, including the "brown ants in the little wells" mentioned in "Song of Myself" (LG, 33), and he devoted three books to ants, termites, and bees, describing (almost singing) in prose their wonderful intelligence.[23]

But the Belgian poet who was closest to Whitman was Emile Verhaeren (1855–1916) (who also had a Flemish name). His first collections of poems—*Les Soirs, Les Débâcles, Les Flambeaux noirs*—were, as the titles suggest, dark, pessimistic, and full of spleen, but he was saved from his decadent despair by a happy marriage, by his conversion to socialism, and perhaps, too, by his discovery of *Leaves of Grass*. From 1892 on, the tone of his poetry changed completely. His symbolism, contrary to that of the French symbolists, became social, dynamic, and energetic instead of languorous and melancholy. In *Les Villes tentaculaires* (1895), *Les Forces tumultueuses* (1902), *La Multiple Splendeur* (1906), and *Les Rythmes souverains* (1910), he sang in free verse and in strong rhythms the tumultuous life of large cities and the power of modern industry, with even more vigor and optimism than Whitman and with such realism that one French critic complained of the rattle made by so much scrap iron in his verse.[24]

Verhaeren denied that he had been influenced by Whitman, since *Leaves of Grass* had not yet been translated into French by Léon Bazalgette, but he was not wholly unacquainted with his poetry, for he was in close touch with French writers who admired Whitman and who in some cases had even translated some of his poems: Vielé-Griffin and Stuart Merrill (both of American origin), Marcel Schwob, and André Gide.

Whitman's example also encouraged a Belgian poet of the next generation to break with tradition. Robert Goffin (1898–1984) at first wrote conventional poetry, but in the 1930s, under the influence of Cendrars and Claudel—and through them of Whitman—he began composing lines with as many as thirty syllables (instead of the traditional twelve of the alexandrine) and with a few rhymes thrown in here and there, however, as in "Table rase," written in 1934.[25] He celebrated in this poem the immensity of the "Kosmos," the billions of stars, the mystery of life and love. Like Whitman, he used a demotic language and did not distinguish between "poetical" and "unpoetical" words. He even occasionally resorted to slang—*nénés, partouzes*—and to medical terms like *hémorroides*. He had complete faith in humanity and, despite the atomic bomb, believed in infinite progress. Existentialism left him cold, and he sang with wonder and fervor the history of our planet in "Sablier pour une cosmogonie" ("Sand-glass for a Cosmogony"). After he visited the United States in 1939, he sang America with the same enthusiasm in "Amérique" (1944)—a poem which reads at times like a Whitmanian catalog.[26] Following the example of Maeterlinck and for the same reasons, he devoted a trilogy to too often unjustly despised creatures:

Le Roman des anguilles (1936), *Le Roman des rats* (1937), and *Le Roman des araignées* (1938).

Flemish speakers also welcomed Whitman with great enthusiasm as soon as they discovered his poetry.[27] In 1908 Auguste Vermeylen (1872–1945), a militant defender of the Flemish language and editor of a magazine called *Van nu en straks* (*From Now On*), translated and published some of Whitman's poems and later, in 1914, delivered a public lecture about him. At that time Paul Van Ostnijen (1896–1928), one of the greatest Flemish poets, who believed both in the irresistible power of the life-force and in collective life, absorbed Whitman's poetry as well as that of the French unanimists (themselves influenced by Whitman). The result was *Music-Hall* (1916), which vehemently evoked in free verse the life of a large city. Afterward, under the influence of German expressionism, his poetry became more and more experimental and dadaist.

In recent decades, Whitman's impact on Belgian poets has been negligible. Interest in his poetry tends to be purely academic, and his influence is now more diffuse and difficult to pinpoint.

NOTES

1. See Charles Cestre, "Un intermède de la renommée de Walt Whitman en France," *Revue Anglo-Américaine* (December 1935): 136–140; and Ezra Greenspan, "The Earliest French Review of Walt Whitman," *Walt Whitman Quarterly Review* 6 (Winter 1989): 109–116.

2. Francis Vielé-Griffin would have liked to publish a complete translation of *Leaves*. He was even ready to do so without royalties, but the publisher whom he approached declined his offer because, he said, Whitman was not sufficiently known in France. Nevertheless, he translated "There Was a Child Went Forth" for *La Cravache Parisienne* (June 1889), "To a Foil'd European Revolutionaire" for *Les Entretien Politiques et Littéraires* (November 1892), and "Song of the Broad-Axe" for *L'Ermitage* (April 1899).

3. P. Mansell Jones, "Influence of Whitman on the Origin of 'Vers-Libre,'" *Modern Language Review* 11 (April 1916): 186–194.

4. Teodor de Wyzewa, "Walt Whitman," *Revue Bleue*, or *Revue Politique et Littéraire* 49 (April 1892): 513–519.

5. On Whitman and Stuart Merrill, see Marjorie Louisse Henry, "Walt Whitman et Le Vagabond," in *Stuart Merrill* (Paris: Champion, 1927), 165–173. On Vielé-Griffin, see Henry de Paysac, *Francis Vielé-Griffin: Poète Symboliste* (Paris: Nizet, 1976).

6. From a letter sent by Verhaeren to G. G. Walch, editor of *Anthologie des poètes français contemporains* (Paris: Delagrave, 1932) 2: 221. See also P. Mansell Jones, "Walt Whitman and Verhaeren," *Aberystwyth Studies* (Aberystwyth University College) 2 (1914): 82–83.

7. Gabriel Sarrazin included this essay in *La Renaissance de la Poésie Anglaise, 1778–1889* (Paris: Perrin, 1889), 235–279. It was translated into English by Harrison S. Morris and published in Horace Traubel et al., eds., *In Re Walt Whitman* (Philadelphia: David McKay), 159–194.

8. Daniel Halévy in *Pages Libres* 2 (1901): 75–80; and Henry Davray in *La Plume* (April 1901) and *L'Ermitage* 2 (December 1902): 401–419. Davray also translated extracts from *Specimen Days* (in the January, February, and March 1903 issues).

9. Fernand Baldensperger, "Walt Whitman and France," *Columbia University Quarterly* 21 (October 1919): 298–309.

10. See *Cahiers André Gide*, no. 14, *Correspondance André Gide–Valéry Larbaud*, Françoise Lioure, ed. (Paris: Gallimard, 1989), 162, 296–297.

11. Fabulet's translations were originally published in *L'Ermitage* (March 1904 and December 1905).

12. Philéas Lebesque, *Essai d'expansion d'une esthétique* (Le Havre, Lyon, Bordeaux: Editions de la Province, 1911).

13. See his letter to Henry Saunders dated April 21, 1916, in volume 42 of his *Whitmaniana* in the Brown University Library.

14. See Roger Asselineau and William White, eds., *Walt Whitman in Europe Today* (Detroit: Wayne State University Press, 1972), 17.

15. See André Gide, *Récits et Soties: Oeuvres lyriques* (Paris: Gallimard [Pléiade series], 1958), 299.

16. "Can your performance face the open fields and the seaside?" From "By Blue Ontario's Shore" (LG, 350).

17. See Asselineau and White, *Walt Whitman*, 18–19.

18. William White, ed., *The Bicentennial Walt Whitman* (Detroit: Wayne State University Press, 1976), 14.

19. Asselineau and White, *Walt Whitman*, 19.

20. Gustave Kahn was the editor of a very influential small magazine called *La Vogue*, which published in particular Jules Laforgue's translations of Whitman and some of his own poems in free verse.

21. "Le grand secret, le seul secret, c'est que tout est secret . . . tout est Dieu . . . tout est en lui et doit y aboutir dans le bonheur et la seule divinité que nous puissions espérer connaître, c'est au plus profond de nous-même qu'il faut la chercher." Quoted by G. Walch, *Anthologie des poètes français* (Paris: Delagrave, 1932), 2: 456.

22. "Oui, il est du devoir de tous ceux dont les pensées précèdent la masse inconsciente de détruire tout ce qui entrave la liberté des hommes, comme sitous les hommes méritaient d'être libres." "Le Suffrage universel," in *Le Double Jardin* (Paris: Bibliothèque Charpentier, 1921), 99.

23. Maeterlinck also sang the intelligence of flowers in *L'Intelligence des fleurs* (Paris: E. Fasquelle, 1907). André Gide perfidiously noted in his *Journal, 1889–1939*: "When I see Maeterlinck in such rapture, I find it rather difficult to find him as intelligent as his flowers" (Paris: La Nouvelle revue française [Pléiade edition], 1939), 808.

24. Henri Clouard, *Histoire de la littérature française* (Paris: Albin Michel, 1947), 1: 114.

25. See Alain Bosquet, *Robert Goffin* (Paris: Pierre Seghers, 1966), 60–62. This book is an anthology with a critical introduction.

26. Ibid., 38, 68–70.

27. See Guillaume Toebosch, "Walt Whitman in Belgium," in Asselineau and White, *Walt Whitman*, 15–16.

1. VALÉRY LARBAUD

"Development of the Poet"

[After a brief sketch of Whitman's youth and
early career, Valéry Larbaud studies the crucial
years between 1850–1855, during which the poet
was composing *Leaves of Grass* and at the same
time writing "barrels of lectures," in the words of
his brother George.]

What were those lectures? What did Whitman want to speak about? Some biographers are amazed at Whitman's capacity for work, because one has found, after his death, registers in which he had classified and pasted a good many magazine articles, pages torn from books, etc., on all kinds of subjects. On the other
hand, in view of this cheap scholarship some people have a little too quickly
jumped to the conclusion that Whitman was self-taught. We are all self-taught.
No matter how ideas and knowledge are gained, what really matters is how this
knowledge has been understood, criticized, assimilated. As a matter of fact we
have a fairly long fragment from the project of a lecture by Whitman on romantic
philosophy—based on elementary text-books. It would probably be necessary to
make a close study of all the other fragments and go through Whitman's registers
to appraise the amount of knowledge he had gained and weigh with precision the
part which this knowledge played in the development of his genius. But here is a
hypothesis based on the indications given by the "papers" contained in the Camden Edition:

Between 1848 and 1850, under the threefold influence of German idealistic philosophy, the spectacle which the U.S. offered him and the reading of Emerson's
essays, Whitman felt called upon to assume a lofty civic and religious mission,
namely to give an ideal, a philosophy, a religion to the American people then in
the making. The Christian dogmas seemed to him outworn. He felt, or fancied he
felt, possessed of great truths, all brand new. And he wrote: "the priest is on the
way out, the divine literatus comes."[1]

First, let us consider the influence of German philosophy. Out of all that came
from Europe—and all that came from the spirit which originated in Europe—
fairly early, apparently, Whitman chose Hegelianism for his spiritual fare. Only a
specialist could say what Whitman's work owes to German philosophy and in
particular to Hegelianism. But it undoubtedly owes much to them. He was descended from a long line of militant Christians and had even received a sort of
Christian education. Above all, he needed a universal doctrine (If I fight against
the churches, it is because I love the Church) and finding nothing satisfactory in
the theology of the different sects whose moral corruption shocked him (The
whole ideal of the church is low, repugnant, horrible), he spontaneously adhered

to the great idealistic systems which issued from Germany. In his theoretical self-ishness, one might find a reflection of Fichte's "Ich"; one may see in his aesthetic ideas a more or less deep mark of Schelling's doctrines. But Hegel took his fancy above all the others. The synthesis of opposites, the philosophical concept considered as logical, universal and concrete, the very "triadism" for which Hegel was so much criticized but thanks to which it has been possible to say that the dogma of the Trinity had been rationally reconstructed (cf. A. Véra, *Introduction à la philosophie de Hegel*, where this point is discussed); the God-Idea ceaselessly materializing in nature; evil as a necessary negation; nature and history as an odyssey of the spirit; the universe understood and unreservedly accepted; indefinite liberty and progress; such is the simplified and elementary form of Hegelianism with which Whitman became intoxicated just as he became intoxicated with the French and Italian operas that he frequently attended in New York. "Only Hegel," he wrote, "is fit for America, is large enough and free enough."[2] He also calls him the beloved doctor of his mind and soul. . . . To idealistic doctrines, Whitman paid the same deep, earnest, eager and uncritical attention as his ancestors had done to Christian doctrines. With him everything originates in the intellectual life of the mind, not in the so-called sentimental life. Everything has its source in the ethical activity and moral earnestness of this son and great-grandson of Protestant dissenters. The objection that one may raise — that he has never read the works of Hegel and knew them only through text-books[3] — throws the better into relief this mystic character of Whitman's Hegelianism: how many of the first martyrs had read the Gospel? (And how many Hegelians are there not unaware that they are Hegelians? And how many triads one meets unexpectedly here and there!)

Let us note at this point that none of the great European poets of the nineteenth century has had such a broad philosophical basis or such a faith as a starting point for his aesthetic activity. (Christian writers were either sentimentalists or polemists, or both.) It may be said that Whitman's poetry has been, in the field of art, the continuation of the German philosophical revolution and that his work is a sort of Gospel of the Hegelian revelation. . . . But let us note too that Hegelianism — as Benedetto Croce has shown it — is so vast and contains so many apparent, if not real, contradictions that immediately after the master's death the disciples split into two groups:[4] Hegelians of the right (such as, to some extent, Carlyle, one of Whitman's masters) and Hegelians of the left whose first act was to publish the *Communist Manifesto*.[5] Does Whitman as a Hegelian belong to the right or to the left of the movement? A specialist alone could solve the problem. But it does seem that the contradictions of the Hegelian doctrine are to be found again in Whitman's works and thought. It is more correct to say that Hegel acts as a stimulant to Whitman's thought and consequently to his works. (It could be interesting to know when and how the poet has been acquainted with the Hegelian doctrine and with romantic philosophy in general.) Before this man whose mind was so firmly settled on a broad basis of beliefs, and to demonstrate, as it were, that indefinite liberation and progress in which he believed, there was then taking place one of the most extraordinary events in history: the making of the American nation. It was the time when the growth of the U.S. was most rapid. The immense reservoir was filling. In a few years, the Western border, being constantly pushed back, had reached the Pacific, and the Southern border extended to the shores of the Gulf of Mexico. The population of the towns had tripled and quadrupled in a short time. Ever more numerous immigrants were coming in and completely new living conditions awaited them in this brand-new country. To this, one should add the unrest which preceded the great crisis of the Union: two civilizations at strife in the bosom of the same nation.

It has been said of Henry James, and perhaps of many other American writers, that they have seen Europe as Americans and America as Europeans. Is it not strange that it should also be possible to apply this criticism to the great national poet of the United States? But skim through the volume of "Preparatory Thoughts and Readings": his idea of Europe is naive, and makes one smile. In a note, he wonders whether the European working class is not, even nowadays, such as Shakespeare depicted it. In another he says: "The definite history of the world cannot go farther than Egypt and in the most important particulars the average spirit of man, except in These States, has not gone forward of the spirit of Ancient Egypt." [6] And again: "The English masses . . . in comparison with the masses of the United States are at least two hundred years behind us." [7] Of course he had heard of the Holy Alliance; he knew that Poland had been parcelled out, Italy enslaved and that reactionary monarchism triumphed even in England where it was welcomed by the poets (Southey and Wordsworth — he reproached them for having betrayed the cause of freedom); above all . . . he had never gone to Europe. He believed that this lack of political liberty entailed a corresponding degradation of character, a sort of servility, an unfitness for modern life. A queer illusion, which the partial or apparent failure of the European revolutions (1830–1848) still reinforced. He despaired of Europe and like some of our revolutionaries, he regarded the United States as a virgin land where the human plant, cramped by the restraint of "feudal Europe," would at last grow freely and bear fruit. But then what about slavery in the Southern States? What about the moral barbarity whose effects he was soon to feel when his so-called sexual poems would be threatened by Puritan persecution?

But this state of mind explains why, in Whitman's works, the words "America," "These States," "Democracy," dissolve into the one word "Future." He acknowledges it in *Democratic Vistas*. He acknowledges it when he says that Longfellow *is* the poet who at the present time is the most suitable for the United States. It is precisely the people to *whom* he wants to give an ideal, that will be "America," "Democracy," etc. We have the raw material, man, the transplanted European. Let us help him to liberate himself and grow. Let us create great personalities; it is the function of the poet: "It is not that he gives his country great poems, it is that he gives his country the spirit which makes the greatest poems and the greatest material for poems. . . ." [8]

And, what carries us still farther into the future, he has in mind the whole of America. In a list of the States he claims to be addressing, we read: Nicaragua, and long before Ruben Darío had written *Los Cisnes* in which the poet asks anxiously:

"Tantos millones de hombres hablaremos inglés?" [9] Whitman, addressing the three Americas, cried:

"Americanos! conquerors! . . ." [10]

(His frequent use of French and Spanish words may be another sign of this intention: he wants to speak *in lingua trina*: French, English, Spanish: the three languages of North America.)

To put the matter into a nutshell, America is for him the place where a Society in the making is to work out a new millennium. His error has been to believe that America alone would have the intellectual, moral, etc., primacy over the rest of the world. And thus he may have failed to realize that when singing for his people, he was singing for all the white race, for all mankind.

Such was, roughly speaking, the part which the spectacle of the making of the modern United States played in the growth of the poet. We shall see later the part played by this same spectacle in the growth of the poem.

At the point we have now reached, namely the time when Whitman was writing "barrels" of lectures in his Brooklyn attic, we see a Whitman dedicated to the logical life and engrossed in his ethical preoccupations.

At no other time perhaps was he farther from his vocation as a poet. It is even alarming. Roughly speaking the whole tradition of the New England Christian preachers from the Mathers to Elias Hicks culminates in him. Is the poet in him going to be sacrificed to the preacher? It is a pity that we should not possess two or three complete lectures. At least we have the notes which relate to the lectures he had planned. They are very naive and rather vague. They could have been written ten years earlier by the young schoolmaster-journalist of Long Island. In one of them he advises himself to make gestures; in another he speaks of a voluntary unpaid orator who would interrupt the politicians at the Capital and accost the President in the open street to remonstrate with him, etc. Elsewhere one gathers that his lectures would merely have been summaries of his magazine clippings and reading. Lastly, the impression left by all the notes and information relating to the lectures is that Whitman had no precise doctrine composed of simple elements to teach his people. He was not lacking in the gifts that make good orators (see his lecture on Lincoln's death and the little speech he delivered on Emerson's grave). But what he wanted to express could not be held within the limits and form of a speech. Several critics have noticed that certain fragments of the lectures resemble poems and announce *Leaves of Grass*. This is the greatest discovery of Whitman criticism. Yes, almost all Whitman's prose pieces tend to become poems.

Like plates in anatomy textbooks on which you see the development of the embryo at the different stages of its gestation, the notes, fragments, prose pieces of Whitman show the growth of the poem. See for instance "The White House by moonlight" in *Specimen Days* and compare especially the Preface to the 1855 edition with the poem entitled "By Blue Ontario's Shore."

It is undeniably therefore this tendency towards poetry, this unrecognized and repressed aesthetic activity which eventually ruined the great preaching project conceived by Whitman. He realized at last that he possessed a more sensitive, delicate and receptive faculty than his intelligence and logical faculty. Rising from the innermost recesses of his moral life, through the superposed layers of his intellectual life, the great lyrical source had at last come to the surface and reached the light of consciousness. He did not stubbornly resist this incursion of an unreasonable and undisciplined element — his indolence, his yielding, "absorbing" nature once more stood him in good stead. Besides, his doctrine was vast enough to accept an outburst of lyricism. Whitman immediately understood that the best way to preach his ideal was to give himself unreservedly. Now literary creation and poetry alone could be the channel of this gift, or rather they were this gift itself. Thus he did not misunderstand his genius to the point of considering it merely as a means; he considered it both as a means and as an end; the moral preoccupation remained, but poetry was saved.

This event was probably hastened by his reading Emerson's *Essays*. One should read in R. W. Emerson's *Essays*, the one entitled "The Poet." It is almost the portrait of the poet as Whitman was to conceive him; it is very nearly Whitman's own portrait. "I was simmering," Whitman said, "Emerson brought me to a boil." We can take his word for it. But the main thing is that the poet having come of age at last should have entered into his inheritance. (As a result, his lecture on the "poet" was left unfinished.)

The 1855 edition, printed in Brooklyn by the author's own hands, appeared — with its volcanic "Preface," rather bad as a preamble and manifesto because, in fact, it was a poem in the making. It was followed by the first poems, with their immense titles,[11] the mastodons and iguanodons of Whitman's creation.

So far we have seen how the poet was formed, took shape and developed in Whitman; and we have tried to show the influences which were responsible for this development. Let us now see the elements and influences which were to determine the development of his poetry.

First of all, we find the intellectual activity. Basil de Sélincourt has a felicitous phrase for this: Whitman, he says in as many words, was or tried to be the first conscious poet. We think every great artist is a conscious one and that in every great work of art the part played by the critical faculty is considerable. But it is certain that Whitman appears especially conscious. And this comes from the fact that, more than any other poet of his time, he has lived on two planes: the ethical and the aesthetic. And he is capable at any given moment of passing from one to the other. His whole mind seems to work at the same time, and one thus gets at once the most inspired and the most voluntary poems. Thus the outline of the work, the title of the work (the idea of growth dominating the poem) were found immediately and never changed. Everything concurs in the same result: statement of a doctrine, revelation of a personality, civic teaching. And the unity of the poem is undeniable. Thus it is, then, that 10 years after Edgar Allan Poe had proclaimed in his lecture on "The Poetic Principle" that it was impossible to write long poems, epic and didactic poems, etc., there appeared precisely in America the longest of the great didactic poems ever to be written.

But this very consciousness, this will is also that which harms the poem more than anything else. When the constructions of the ethical or logical activity do not find an aesthetic expression, whenever the thought fails to transmute itself into poetry, we get merely that "doctrine in its crudest form" [12] as Swinburne said. These are the times when Whitman forgets that his method can only be that of the philosopher. Hence the catalogues, almost all of them unsuccessful, which will never take another meaning than the one they have, whatever H. Bryan Binns may think, and will never be, whatever Miguel de Unamuno may say, the supreme culmination of lyricism, but rather the result of an impotence to express. Hence also horrible lapses into allegory. It is then indeed that Whitman is "above art" or beneath, or beside it: for the poet cannot free himself from art, which is his very freedom. He simply loses his way in philosophy, which is not his field. It might have been preferable for him to persist in writing the other "athletic book"; the lectures would have been derivatives for his doctrine . . . and we should not have been obliged to read them.

Let us note this, but let us not underrate the importance of Whitman's doctrine in his poem. It is the great motive force in his works. It threw him out of the so-called normal path, and tore him away from a career — without any interest or profit for us — as a journalist and popular or well-advertised writer. It put him on *his* path, the path to immortality. And it remained the great stimulant to the artist: a synthesis of opposites, the glorification of democracy (which is less the exaltation of the common man than that of the essential man). America, These States, such are the fetish-words which rouse his inspiration and awake the muse of the New World. In a word, such is Whitman's religion. This is the deep source of his naivety (in the double meaning of the word): the virtue which made him rediscover on his own account the reason, the function, the dignity and the scope of art; and also the simplicity which gave him the courage to undertake, in spite of everything he lacked (and he lacked a lot!) the exploitation of the vast province which he had discovered.

The other great factor — an exciter, too — was the spectacle offered by the United States then in the making. (Living in New York was enough: it was like feeling the pulse of the land.) B. de Sélincourt almost reproaches Whitman for being the poet of an "unfinished nation." But it was precisely Whitman's luck to be the poet of a nation in the making; at least, this is what an Hegelian for whom history is nothing but the history of the indefinite development of liberty, must have thought. The United States in the nineteenth century laid the very image of this development under Whitman's eyes and thus encouraged him to write the poem of the pioneers, projected towards the future, the songs of the forward march, the momentary retreat and the renewed advance. Lastly, his nation at work and at war gave him without the help of any philosophy, the feeling of modern life and made him discover the poetry of the work and wealth of man.

HISTORY OF *LEAVES OF GRASS*

The appearance of *Leaves of Grass* was no more noticed than the appearance of any collection of society verse in the European tradition published in the same year of 1855.[13] But at the end of the summer, Whitman received the famous letter by which Emerson recognized him and inducted him. Until now it is the finest thing that ever took place in America. Through Emerson the good news was announced to Europe and the whole world: "Americans abroad, may now come home: unto us a man is born." [14]

It seems that at this point, assured of ultimate success, Whitman had nothing to do but devote himself to the construction of his poem, a rather absorbing task. A European poet like Wordsworth for instance, once assured that his success does not depend on a coterie, but is guaranteed to him by a certain correspondence between his poetry and the taste of an élite, keeps quiet. He will even be accused of lagging behind to the best of his ability once he is famous. But Whitman identified himself with his poem, and his poem is his doctrine, the salvation of his people and of Democracy. If he had had a fortune, he would have spent it in advertisements to make people read his poem. At least he printed a second edition of it on the back of which he engraved a sentence from Emerson's letter: "I greet you at the beginning of a great career." A big blunder; and he was to make others. For he was not intelligent in the vulgar sense of the word. For the first time he took the offensive. But he did not know how to set about it. What he carried in him, that poetry which has given us such pleasure, deafened him, made him incapable of any social success; he merely succeeded in passing for the most impudent of climbers. His importunity met with silence. And when at last he found followers, he incited them so much to praise him that self-respecting critics, though favorable to Whitman, refused to join "the ignoble fray" (J. A. Symonds).[15] Abroad, he passed for a simpleton, hungry for fame; a European critic wrote: "the mere mention of his name in a newspaper made him cry for joy."

While carrying on this ill-fated war, without losing his calm, he pursued his work. And lo! scandal and slander were added to incomprehension and hatred. The intervention of Europe was necessary to make America respect this great son of civilization. In the meantime it merely rejected his work into thicker obscurity. ... But neither public opinion nor Emerson's arguments, nor the very interest of his book, drew a single concession from Whitman. He was too much the man of God, he was too attentive to the "still small voice" to compromise with the world.

In a poem written in his old age, he compared himself to Christopher Columbus, the most illustrious of great men known for their stubbornness.

From then on [after the Civil War] his life and work are better known to us. So far we have hardly caught sight of him. And even after he was surrounded by friends capable of telling us about him, in Washington, a part of his life — the part which he devoted to his young friend Peter Doyle — remains obscure. However, he appears to us as a humble public servant whose external life was almost as regular as that of Kant. Of course his whole life was directed towards his poem. It was because of his father that he remained a bachelor. (An instinct has impelled me to form no ties. . . .) One must say so: he was a man of letters; such was his trade, his main concern and that since 1850, if not since the beginning. And what is more, it is only because he was a man of letters that we are interested in him.

Another trait appears. We must renounce seeing Whitman as a hearty comrade, an unceremonious "pal," a good fellow, etc. Someone has been aware of his reserve and has even used the word aloofness which implies distance and almost a haughty reserve. . . . Let us beware: maybe this poet who claimed to live intensely has lived above all with and in his book; maybe the "great comrade" has been a great solitaire. . . . (The poem ending with: ". . . filled with the bitterest envy," might be a confession.)

This reserve may have accounted for something of the ascendency which Whitman soon exercised over his friends in Washington and later in Camden after his second stroke (summer of 1873). This second stroke turned him into an old man.

There he is, in Camden. But his friends, his admirers take good care of him. It is a noble sight.

All these good people should be mentioned by name. Let us merely mention the most faithful and the best known of them: John Burroughs, W. D. O'Connor, E. C. Stedman, Anne Gilchrist, Dr. R. M. Bucke and his first young admirer Miss Mary Whitall Smith (now Mrs. Berenson).

Illness, destitution, old age; he said so himself, such are the conditions under which he completed the poem so triumphantly begun in 1850. But the picture was not so dark as he chose to see it. He had always been satisfied with little and he lacked nothing. It was even at this time of his life that he made his longest journeys and had the most leisure. Above all, he was famous, and he knew it. He was famous . . . in Europe and as a consequence he was beginning to be recognized in America. It was the time when he overworked the cameras. He was taking his revenge: the reporters who had split their sides with laughter over an old copy of the 1855 edition that strayed into a newspaper office, now came from New York to Philadelphia to take down in shorthand the statements of the "good gray poet." Yet he was not satisfied. He still urged that people should read his poem and he could not bear criticism. He had never ceased to see in *Leaves of Grass* the remedy, the book which was to give America "the spirit which makes great poems." A mixture of scandal, curiosity, gossip — in short, of nothing but noise — his personal fame was not worth anything in his eyes unless it might help the poem. But how disappointing! He had thought he would be read, understood, absorbed by that American people, that American working class which he had sung, and lo, it was the *literati* of Europe who were reading him and if any readers were to be found in America, they were millionaire Quakers from Philadelphia, and Mr. Andrew Carnegie!

But he kept his illusions. Bliss Perry has written that, in the last years of his life, Whitman was no longer in touch with the spirit of his age. But on the contrary Whitman had every reason to believe that it was his age that had drifted away from him. (It was the eclipse of idealism; it was scientism, the time which has been called philosophical barbarism.)

"I do not think," wrote John Burroughs to W. D. O'Connor, "that either you or I are the custodians of Whitman's fame or that it lies in our power to make or un-make it." We may be confident that this truly expresses what all Whitman's friends thought, the small group, the small court at Camden. That is probably why they had no scruples in collecting so many — indeed too many — of Whitman's words.

He was evidently declining, physically and intellectually. Certain habits force themselves upon him, almost monomanias. He is more and more preoccupied with the immediate success of his work (as though he had not known success for a long time). There he is in his old age:

"Old age land-lock'd within its winter bay," [16] and there he is alone — his "many tearing passions," [17] the life of streets and ports which he had "absorbed" with vacant eyes and hand on hip — alone with the book, which falls heavily upon him. Everything has reference to it. They tell him about Wagner's music and he thinks of the music of *Leaves of Grass*. He judges the writers of his time according to their opinion of *Leaves of Grass*. It was then — and only then — that he was the "great literary egotist" whom Bliss Perry compared to Montaigne (one wonders why). Shall we go so far as to say that he finally admired in himself the author of *Leaves of Grass*? What does it matter to us?

THE RESULTS

Criticism has once and for all done away with its custom of distributing white or black balls. Its function is to follow the development of literary history, which is the history of Expression, and to examine its failures and successes. Great works are those which mark the main stages of this history. It is thus perfectly useless to discuss their merit. But they have their own particular history: failures and suc-cesses in pure expression, a mortal part and a living part.

Mortal Parts

Whitman has placed himself with all those who, for the sake of convenience, come under the heading "Men of '48." Gross simplification of problems: lack of culture, function of the poet warped, extended to a field (social or religious) where its action is necessarily very limited. Hence the didactic (and consequently archaic and at first sight unprepossessing) character of his work, and all the dead weight of doctrine which his lyricism carries along with it. Belief in the impending advent of the "people." Hence his appeal to the American "masses." This has been flatly belied by facts: even nowadays his poetry is meant only for the highest and most exclusive of aristocracies: the happy few.

This leads us to the question of Whitman's and of all artists' nationality. A delicate question — but solved — and so well! — by the author of a preface to a German anthology who wrote — to our joy: "Der französische (aber deutsch fühlende) echte Lyriker Verlaine." (So let us not ponder over this: we should come to the conclusion that Whitman was Dutch . . . or German.)

Yes, he was American, but it is because we smell in the living part of his work a certain undefinable odor which we also find in Hawthorne, Thoreau, a novel by H. K. Viélé and three short stories by G. W. Cable. But he is not American because he was the self-appointed poet of America. Here, too, facts have given him the lie: he was as unappreciated in the United States as Stendhal in Grenoble or Cézanne in Aix. His doctrine is German and his masters are English; as regards his purely intellectual life he was a European living in America. But most of the happy few live in Europe. Thus it was in Europe only that he could be, and was, recognized.

Another question to be examined. It is also out of the more transient part of the work that there have grown all the political parasites (anarchists, sentimental socialists) who have contributed to spread the name of Whitman and obscure the critical study of his works. A careful examination shows that in reality Whitman (who, indeed, presents himself to European revolutionaries with the red flag in his hand) is connected with anarchistic doctrines, etc., only through Hegelianism, and that he is even more conservative than most Hegelians of the left. It is certain that, to his mind, individual property is an indispensable form of liberty. So there you are.

Living Elements

He also had all the qualities that we attribute to the "men of '48": faith in life and in man, enthusiasm, etc. Hence the choice of his doctrine and all the consequences that follow from it. Hence, above all, the virtue which makes him give himself and celebrate throughout his poem the free gift of the individual to society. Such *is* this love, this passionate friendship that he sings. His egoism is nothing less sensual than his sexual poems and nothing less impersonal than his selfishness. But in reality this aspect is the culmination of a movement which originates in the whole inner life of the poet (ideas and feelings, characteristics), and which remains all impregnated with it. Thus, he exalts as a means of republican cohesion, as the unshakeable basis of the modern nation what he calls "manly love," a sort of Achillean friendship, but at the same time it *is* this love, this passionate friendship that he sings. His egoism is really the cultivation and development of the "ego," but this cultivation and development are turned towards social and human service. Such was his discovery and it is entirely his own: a poetry of the self purged from egoism in the narrow meaning of the word, of the self ennobled by everything that it repudiates; of the self that gives up sulking in a corner or taking good care of itself, or cultivating its idiosyncrasies or worshipping itself, but lives in contact with the other egos, lives "en masse." This is precisely what gives him, in his age, that importance, those colossal dimensions which make him resemble, in the middle of the poets of his time, a transatlantic liner in the middle of a flotilla of sailing-ships. Neither his genius nor the volume of his work would give him so much importance. It comes from this discovery: the claiming and taking possession of a vast poetic province: all the social man. The religious man and the "divine" man, he shares with all the European writers of the first half of the nineteenth century.

But the doctrine, however broad it may be, will become antiquated. The province he has annexed will in the end be completely settled. What will remain of the work then?

In the last analysis: pure expression. Whatever those who see works of art through political prejudices may think, it is there that the step forward has been taken, and the blow for the "good old cause" struck; it is in the expression itself that there has been an increase in human liberty. This is the core of Whitman, his poetry, recognizable by that tone which Basil de Sélincourt has called the "conversational tone," but to which it would be better to apply the word Jacques Rivière recently used with reference to the poetry of Paul Claudel: "effusion" (Wordsworth in hatred of the poetic diction of the eighteenth century had looked for it; Whitman has found it).

What does it matter if the doctrine becomes antiquated? The theological subtleties which Dante's verse was merely meant to clothe, do not touch us any more, but his stanza can still tell us:

"Ponete mente almen com' io son bella." [18]

(We have not tried to define Walt Whitman's poetry. We have merely wished to conduct our investigation along the line where the poet and the poem meet. But we have no analysis of rhythm or style, no formula to offer. We have been satisfied with reconnoitering the great earthen socle which serves as a basis and matrix for the beautiful pure rock. Let others try to climb it. But we know at least that beyond the point we have reached, there is nothing but bare stone, and the sky.)

May, 1914

NOTES

1. "Democratic Vistas," *Complete Writings*, vol. 5, p. 54.

2. *Complete Writings*, vol. 9, p. 168.

3. And this has not been proved: Whitman's library (i.e., the books he had read) is not known to us with sufficient precision.

4. B. Croce, "Ce qui est vivant et ce qui est mort de la philosophie de Hegel." Trad. Henri Buriot.

5. Cf. Jean Jaurès's Latin thesis, chap. 4.

6. *Notes and Fragments*, p. 101 (60).

7. *Notes and Fragments*, p. 80 (14).

8. *Notes and Fragments*, p. 68 (49).

9. "Shall we, so many millions of men, speak English?"

10. "Starting from Paumanok," §3, *Inclusive Edition*, p. 13.

11. Such titles appeared only in the 1856 edition. In the first edition the poems had no titles at all (translator's note).

12. In *Under the Microscope*, 1872.

13. The appearance of Longfellow's *Hiawatha* was for the contemporaries the great poetic event of the year.

14. In a letter to Moncure Conway.

15. J. A. Symonds, *Walt Whitman*, p. 3.

16. "Of that blithe throat of thine," *Inclusive Edition*, p. 430.

17. "My 71st Year," Ibid., p. 445.

18. "Bear at least in mind that I am beautiful."

"Etude," in *Walt Whitman: Oeuvres Choisies* (Paris, 1918), 24–32, 34–45. Translated by Roger Asselineau.

2. JEAN CATEL

"Whitman's Symbolism"

In Whitman's own words, "the expression of the American poet is to be . . . *indirect* and not direct or descriptive and epic. . . . Let the age and wars of other nations be chanted and their eras and characters be illustrated . . . not so the great psalm of the republic. Here the theme is creative and has vista."[1] It will suffice to put side by side with these words a few verse and prose passages which will throw light on each other:

> . . . spring-time is here! the summer is here! and what is this in it and from it?
> Thou, soul, unloosen'd — the restlessness after I know not what;
> Come let us lag here no longer, let us be up and away!
> O if I could fly like a bird!
> O to escape, to sail forth as in a ship!
> To glide with thee O soul, o'er all, in all as a ship over the waters;
> Gathering these hints, the preludes, the blue sky, the grass, the morning drops of dew,
> The lilac-scent, the bushes with dark green heart-shaped leaves,
> Wood-violets, the little delicate pale blossoms called innocence;
> Sample and sorts not for themselves alone, but for their *atmosphere*,

To grace the bush I love — to sing with the birds,
A warble for joy of lilac-time, returning in reminiscence.[2]

All this concerns lilacs which Whitman from childhood associated with his most intimate memories:

There was a child went forth every day . . .
The early lilacs became part of this child,
And grass and white and red morning-glories, and white and red clover, and
the song of the phoebe-bird . . .[3]

Nature, the outside world have become part of his soul, ("To glide with thee O soul, o'er all, in all . . .")[4] to such an extent that flowers, trees, brooks, animals have become his very soul, reflections of its inner light, forms of its progressive life. Nature has become "le milieu coloré" (the colored medium) of which Baudelaire speaks[5] where artistic composition takes place, that is to say in Whitman's case: the Soul. This is what Whitman repeatedly expresses. Let us quote a text recently published by Emory Holloway in *The American Mercury* for December 1924:

The kernel of every object that can be seen, felt or thought of, has its relations to the soul, and is significant of something there. He who can tear off all husks and skins and pierce straight through every stratagem of concealment —[6]

Let us again quote Baudelaire:

Tout l'univers visible n'est qu'un magasin d'images et de signes auxquels l'imagination donnera une place et une valeur relatives; c'est une espèce de pâture que l'imagination doit digérer et transformer . . .[7]

Of course, it was something new in France when Baudelaire was thus laying the foundations of Symbolism. But, on close inspection, one realizes that this theory was common practice in English poetry. For Spenser, Keats, Shelley and even for Donne, the outside world had been nothing but a "shop of images and signs."

Whitman frequently reverts to the theory that true poetry is "indirect."

"Something ecstatic and undemonstrable"[8] which underlies life, this alone can be the object of a poem. The subject (if it is necessary that there be a subject) is merely a pretext; the matter, the suggestion or, as Whitman says, the "indirection" of it is eternal. He is convinced that this attitude is new. He throws back into the shadows of the past all the European poets who have been "descriptive" and "epic," "the expression of the American poet is to be transcendent and new."[9]

Whitman thus states the very principle of Symbolism and it could not be otherwise. For, let us remember that Whitman communicates to the reader what is most unreal in him and yet is most powerful. A dream, but a dream on which all life depends. A shade of color, but a shade which tinges all the days and nights of a man. In short, Whitman "celebrates his soul." Now, the very definition implies it, the unconscious is ineffable. In every age and in every place, mystics have professed themselves powerless to express their ecstasies in intelligible terms. They can give us only pale reflections of them. In the same manner, a poet of Whitman's temper will succeed in communicating with us only through "suggestions" and "preludes," to use terms familiar to Whitman. He suggested the ineffable and wrote preludes to the great themes of life and death; such was his attitude. Such was to be presently the attitude of the French symbolists.

The originality of Whitman lies in this, that through him we pass imperceptibly from realism to surrealism, that is to say from a state of clear consciousness in which images have distinct outlines to the unconscious, the soul, in which images are fused in that "atmosphere" — we should rather say that emotional state — in which the poet will transmit it, still warm with life. No one has known better than he how to fuse the objective outline and the inner image in such a way that everywhere reality unifies the soul while the soul animates reality. It will suffice to indicate the fusion of the two elements in the course of our study.

FUNDAMENTAL IMAGES

One cannot insist too much on the importance of the first edition, which is really the key to all the images that will follow. It gives the note, as it were. So it is necessary to isolate the thematic images of this work and sort them so as to bring out the gamut of the whole hymn.

I. *Creation*: It is the theme of the former life of the soul, so to speak. For Whitman fancies that the soul has a past, and this past is the theme of creation.

Whitman expresses it first of all by means of a manifest sign: the germ, the sprout which he has observed in fields and gardens.

The smallest sprout shows there is really no death.[10]

Between the idea of immortality and the image supplied by the sprout which turns green again every year, the poet draws a logical connection which is expressed here by the verb "shows." So this is not yet symbolism proper. To reach it, the poet must suppress the grammatical link. For instance:

Walt, you understand enough . . . why don't you let it out then?
Come now, I will not be tantalized . . . you conceive too much of articulation.
Do you not know how the buds beneath are folded?
Waiting in gloom, protected by frost,
The dirt receding before my prophetical screams,
I underlying causes to balance them at last.[11]

This is pure Whitman. It will be noticed how he passes from the objective image: "Do you not know how the buds beneath are folded?" to the symbolic image which represents him identified with the germ, first in winter, then in spring, when the germ forces its way towards the light. A detailed analysis would show that each word includes a double meaning: that of the objective image, that of the symbol, for instance: "The dirt receding before my prophetical screams" is related both to the image of the seed emerging from the ground and to the notion of the errors which the poet dispels with his work. The identification is perfect. To such a degree that the image of the seed loses its reality and becomes in the next time the abstract idea of "Cause," which possesses enough universality to embrace the real and the spiritual. Hence the apparently metaphysical statement: "I underlying causes," in which one can recognize a memory of the theories of substance, but in which the main thing is the imaginative content.

Another line shows the same process: "All truths wait in all things,"[12] a formula whose imaginative content cannot be understood unless we compare it to the preceding passages in which the word "wait" already occurs: "Waiting in gloom."

Just as the poet waits in solitude and silence for the fatal moment when he will sing, the germ of truth waits for the moment which will certainly come, for "They neither hasten their own delivery nor resist it."[13]

Whitman here adds an image, superimposed upon that of the waiting germ, the image of childbirth; it logically leads up to the line: "They do not need the obstetric forceps of the surgeon."

Now, curiously enough from the point of view of the question that occupies us at present, these lines follow a short passage in which Whitman again symbolizes the notion of creation in the form of a germ. The passage in question is one of the erotic passages of *Leaves of Grass*. The sensual origin of the images cannot be doubted:

I am given up by traitors;
I talk wildly . . . I have lost my wits . . .
I and nobody else am the greatest traitor . . .
You villain touch, what are you doing . . . my breath is tight in its throat;
Unclench your floodgates; you are too much for me.
Blind living wrestling touch, sheath'd hooded sharp-tooth'd touch.
Did it make you ache so leaving me?
Parting track'd by arriving . . . perpetual payment of perpetual loan,
Rich showering rain, and recompense richer afterwards.
Sprouts take and accumulate . . . stand by the curb prolific and vital,
Landscapes projected masculine, full-sized and golden.[14]

Whatever one may think of the chaotic accumulation of images, Whitman's instinctive mastery over words has to be recognized. A short analysis will help to understand the very clever use our poet makes of the symbolic image.

The theme is that of creation — of procreation, for Whitman does not distinguish them.

"Parting track'd by arriving" indicates by means of a familiar image the continuity of life in sexual intercourse. This idea is *immediately* (that is to say without any intermediary of any kind) expressed by a new image: "perpetual payment of perpetual loan," whose obscurity is cleared up only by the context (a further proof) that Whitman builds the whole and each image as merely an "indirection." The ideas of richness potentially contained in this image are taken up again in the next line: "Rich showering[15] and recompense richer afterwards."

Whitman was not so averse to figures of speech as he claimed since we catch him here indulging in a chiasmus, thanks to which moreover he goes on to the notion of fecundation. For the richer recompense which follows the sexual act is, to the poet's mind, the propagation of life.

We should hesitate to extract this meaning from a word obscured by its place in a lyrical context, if the theme of propagation were not familiar to our poet; so familiar that one has sometimes the impression that Whitman wrote *Leaves of Grass* merely to celebrate childbirth. Here is the way Whitman's imagination describes this "richer recompense":

Sprouts take and accumulate . . . stand by the curb prolific and vital,
Landscapes projected masculine, full-sized and golden.

We have already encountered and explained the notion of germination. This time, the image is extended; it is no longer a spear of grass or even a plant or tree which germinates and grows. It is "a landscape," a synthesis of lines and colors; it is the world of external things with its splendor and power: "Landscapes projected masculine, full-sized and golden. . . ."

Rarely has Whitman's ecstasy reached such fullness and vividness. Rarely has sensual intoxication found such proud expression. For the poet's aim in this line is nothing less than a suggestion of the recreation of the world through the sexual act.

One sees how Whitman's symbolism develops. "Whoever has power in his writings to draw bold startling images and strange pictures, the power to embody in language original and beautiful and quaint ideas — is a true son of song."[16] These words which Whitman wrote in 1846 can be applied to himself. He then expressed consciously what under the influence of his "surrealistic" attitude he was to practice unconsciously in his work in 1855. After the theme of creation comes that of existence.

II. *Existence*: It is evident that whenever Whitman wants to express the mere existence of his ego, he has to do so in "indirect" terms. Whitman's ego was beyond the real, that is to say beyond words; consequently his expression can only be symbolic.

Yet, there are places where Whitman has tried to define himself directly. Let us transcribe them in the order in which they appear and see what they can teach us.

"I am the mate and companion of people," [17] which must be put side by side with an identical definition which occurs farther on: "I am a free companion . . . I bivouac by invading watchfires." [18]

On page 20 (of the 1855 edition) there occurs a definition which corresponds more exactly to the artist: "In me the caresser of life wherever moving." [19]

At times the image is suggested rather than described in detail, as when Whitman depicts himself as an orchestra:

> I play not marches for accepted victors only, I play marches for conquer'd and
>   slain persons.
> I sound triumphal drums for the dead — I fling through my embouchures the
>   loudest and gayest music to them . . .[20]

Sometimes the definition of Whitman's ego requires more delicacy and pervasive sweetness. The most significant example is to be found on page 27, when the ego of the poet is changed into an ethereal being, a spirit or ghost, a presence which only the sweetness of evening can make us feel. "I am he that walks with the tender and growing night." [21]

One might say that in this example, Whitman's ego is dissolved in an emotion. In the example which follows it resolves itself into a vital principle:

> Evil propels me and reform of evil propels me . . .
> I stand indifferent,
> I moisten the roots of all that has grown.[22]

A prophetic definition of the potentialities of the ego is to be found on page 45, where Whitman writes: "I am he bringing help for the sick as they pant on their backs." [23]

How many future poems will be nothing but the unfolding of secondary images already contained in this definition!

It seems that we might attribute the same prophetic character to the following definition: "I am the teacher of athletes." [24]

Like the former, it was grounded on the most reliable reality of the ego and, consequently, projects into the future possibilities which naturally came true.

Thus in 1856, that is to say, shortly after the appearance of the first edition of *Leaves of Grass*, Whitman composed for the young men of America a speech full of that energetic determination which, according to him, was to prepare a race of athletes for the United States.[25]

Many a passage of *Leaves of Grass* shows that his ego wanted to lead men along a new road towards truth and beauty:

> I am a dance . . .
> I am the ever-laughing . . . it is new moon and twilight,
> I see the hiding of douceurs . . . I see nimble ghosts whichever way I look,

Cache and cache again deep in the ground and sea, and where it is neither
    ground nor sea . . .
Only from me can they hide nothing; and would not if they could;
I reckon I am their boss and they make me a pet besides . . .
Onward we move, a gay gang of blackguards with mirth-shouting music and
    wild flapping pennants of joy.[26]

It is only when reaching the last stroke of this picture where there throbs a wild
"joie de vivre," that we understand the definition of the beginning:

I am a dance . . .
I am the ever-laughing . . .

This symbol developed by a rich imagination probably indicates better than an
analysis how Whitman became conscious of his deeper self. A dance, a laugh . . .
that is to say what reveals to the senses the rhythm and enthusiasm of physical life.
For it is through the ecstasy that comes from the mere fact of living freely that
Whitman's ego best reveals itself. That is why his imagery becomes most original
and significant whenever, instead of defining his ego, Whitman depicts it in action, so to speak.

III. *Action*: Action is in itself a symbol of the ego. With Whitman, of course, action should not be understood in the social sense of the word. If this kind of action is included in *Leaves of Grass*, we know that it is merely a residue of his public life. But this kind of activity does not represent the true action of the deeper
self. Let us bear in mind the fact that the latter has definitely deserted the realm of
clear consciousness. Whitman's ego no longer knows the meaning of good, evil,
heaven and hell. It is indifferent.[27] Its field of action is the unconscious. There it
lives intensely an immense and throbbing life. It is this action alone that interests
us here; it is the only one that allowed of symbolic treatment.

Yet, even in the realm of unconscious imagination, there are several planes. We
can distinguish two when examining *Leaves of Grass* from the point of view of
symbolism.

a) The passages where Whitman's ego tries to assert its supremacy. The imagery is borrowed from war and army life, for the poet wants to impart to the
reader the idea and emotion of a struggle. . . .[28]

The page in which, in reminiscent ecstasy, Whitman sings the voluptuous as-
cendancy of the sea and the night over his soul, is quite significant of his *defeat*:

I am he that walks with the tender and growing night,
I call to the earth and sea half-held by the night.
Press close bare-bosom'd night . . .
You sea, I resign myself to you also . . .[29]

We have here the action of the ego, but, as it were, its negative action, which is quite characteristic of the nature of Whitman. The night, the sea, two infinite mediums in which his soul dilates in sterile exaltation, sterile as regards practical life, but on the contrary productive of beauty. As a matter of fact, this page is the most transposed of all in the 1855 edition of *Leaves of Grass*. It is one of the most characteristic of Whitman. Never has the imagery been more revealing than in this passage. One may say that Night and the Sea are the symbols in which Whitman has best expressed his soul. Wrapped up in them, his soul has conquered its supremacy.

b) When Whitman considers himself no longer as a defeated person, but as possessing all his combative power, the imagery will thrive on fresh air, the "splendid sun" and the open road. Night is all right for hiding our quiet ecstasies (which are nothing but preparations, as for a rush forward). Broad daylight is necessary for true action. . . .

All that symbolizes the notion of a free and spontaneous impulse in Whitman's eyes, flows naturally from his pen.

He sings the horse:

The gigantic beauty of a stallion . . .
Limbs glossy and supple, tail dusting the ground,
Eyes . . .[30]

But it does not seem to him so fast as his soul:

Swift wind: Space! My soul! . . .
My ties and ballasts leave me . . . I travel, I sail.[31]

c) We are thus led up to the symbols which were bound to tempt Whitman's imagination, those of the ship and the bird which have always in all languages provided poets with a convenient means of expressing the irresistible and infinite yearning of their souls:

I anchor my ship for a little while only
My messengers continually cruise away . . .[32]

lines which were immediately preceded by this one: "I fly those flights of a fluid and swallowing soul."

These two symbols recur with most frequency in the poems which followed the first edition. . . .

Creation, Existence, Action . . . such are the modes of Whitman's hymn. Can there be broader ones? They contain potentially all the poetic variations of mankind.

We have reached the end of our exploration. The inner workings of the mind which lead a poet one day to express in rhythms and images the anxiety that haunts him, begins as soon as the imagination awakens. The one who wishes to catch them, must neglect nothing. As it is impossible for us really to follow the first steps of the mind and senses, we have to consult with great attention the early writings, when there are any, in which these first proceedings were disclosed. In the case of Whitman, there is no lack of these writings at the present day after the patient researches which have brought them to light.

While the young artist tries to express the first gropings of his dreams, he comes into contact with reality, persons and things. It is the time when a sort of struggle begins between the soul of the poet and society, a hidden struggle, which the latter, being a blind force, does not notice, and of which the former, still unaccustomed to thought, is only dimly aware.

We have tried to show that the historical juncture was such that it called for all Whitman's will, but that owing to a natural bent which his manner of life strengthened, something in him kept him away from it and isolated him in a nation in which dreamy solitude was a crime. Hence in Whitman the perpetual sense of a lack of balance between society and his soul, a lack of balance that begets evil.

We have shown that this sense of evil is rooted in the inmost heart of the poet of *Leaves of Grass* and it is probably to this sense that we owe the poetical works of 1855. Sensing the germ of evil deep in his soul, Whitman has naturally dreamed of a pure and healthy life.

If Whitman has told this to the public, he has kept to himself his inner anxiety. It is on a slip found in his personal papers (the date of which seems to be 1868–1870; Whitman was then 51) that Whitman makes this disclosure: "It is imperative that I obviate and remove myself (and my orbit) at all *hazards* (away from) this incessant enormous . . . perturbation."[33]

What Whitman may have suffered in his flesh and in his soul on account of this "perturbation" which isolated him, we shall probably never know. But how much more human the man and the poet now become! How far we are from the prophet satisfied with himself and the world whom his blind friends insisted on seeing in Whitman. It is not in disparagement of him that we tear away the veils that a patient friendship had woven round his face. Here are his infinitely soft and sad eyes, but they are true eyes with the glint of life in them. Here is his skin, with the marks left by caresses, those of the sun and sea air, but also those of human hands and lips. Here is his whole person "that attracts and repels at the same time." His voice sings, stops on the verge of confidence. A sort of shame envelops it. And a great pride.

"We did not like his hat," said Bucke. Yet, it was the sign of his manly pride. His friends would have liked to violate Whitman's solitude. To some extent, their desire was legitimate. But there was a limit which they never overstepped. This

Quaker hat always on his head in the Quaker fashion meant that Whitman would recognize no other will than his own. This will plunged its roots into the very flesh of his being. And there it drew a sap which, if it produced the poetical flowers that we admire, nevertheless separated Whitman from his fellow men forever. The penalty of genius probably.

But what an extraordinary undertaking! Here we have a work meant to draw all men together, and it has its source in a heart's loneliness.

> . . . the yearning and swelling heart,
> Affection that will not be gainsay'd, the sense of what is real, the thought if
>   after all it should prove unreal,
> The doubts of day-time and the doubts of night-time . . .[34]

Who would not hear in such words the murmurings of a heart? It is there rather than in the hymns that the truth lies.

The work he had dreamed of is not complete: the *Leaves of Grass* of 1855 are only a "prelude," as he said. The love he felt for man, the self-pity he transferred to the others; his enthusiasm for physical life, the workings of existence, all this he thought he had sufficiently expressed. He realized he had reached a poetic form which was his own. He said so in his Preface: "The expression of the American poet is . . . indirect and not direct or descriptive or epic . . . the theme is creative and has vista." [35] We have shown that this is poetic symbolism and that herein lies both the strength and novelty of Whitman. Here also lay, for the poet, the solution of the problem of his own existence.

We trust that in the measure that "the ineffable grace of dying days" [36] came to him, Whitman forgot his sufferings. Of his childhood and adolescence, there remained nothing but sweet reminiscences and beautiful images. Death would merge the disharmonies of his days, Death with "the beautiful touch," [37] the Death he had so often called upon with all the unconscious forces of his being, for in death the "health" and "silence" for which he had craved all his life would at last be realized.

NOTES

1. Preface to 1855 Edition, *Leaves of Grass, Inclusive Edition*, p. 491.

2. "Warble for Lilac-Time," Ibid., pp. 318–319.

3. Ibid., p. 306.

4. "Warble for Lilac-Time," Ibid., p. 318.

5. *L'art romantique*, p. 11.

6. E. Holloway, "Whitman Manuscript," *American Mercury*, vol. 3, pp. 475–480, Dec. 1924.

7. "The whole visible universe is nothing but a shop of images and signs to which imagination will assign a relative place and value; it is a sort of food which imagination must digest and transform . . ." *L'art romantique*, p. 14.

8. "Starting from Paumanok," §19, *Inclusive Edition*, p. 23.

9. Preface to 1855 Edition, Ibid., p. 491.

10. "Song of Myself," §6, Ibid., p. 29.

11. "Song of Myself," §25, Ibid., p. 46.

12. "Song of Myself," §30, 1.1, Ibid., p. 49.

13. "Song of Myself," §30, Ibid., p. 49.

14. "Song of Myself," §28, 29, Ibid., p. 49.

15. "Showering": Whitman makes rather too frequent use of this image.

16. *Brooklyn Eagle*, June 13, 1846.

17. "Song of Myself," §7, *Inclusive Edition*, p. 29.

18. "Song of Myself," §33, Ibid., p. 55.

19. "Song of Myself," §13, Ibid., p. 33.

20. "Song of Myself," §18, Ibid., pp. 38, 561.

21. "Song of Myself," §21, Ibid., p. 41.

22. "Song of Myself," §22, Ibid., p. 42.

23. "Song of Myself," §41, 1.1, Ibid., p. 63.

24. "Song of Myself," §47, 1.1, Ibid., p. 71.

25. *The Eighteenth Presidency.*

26. "The Sleepers," §1, *Inclusive Edition*, p. 356.

27. "I stand indifferent," "Song of Myself."

28. Cf. "Song of Myself," §28, *Inclusive Edition*, pp. 48–49.

29. "Song of Myself," §21, 22, Ibid., pp. 41–42.

30. "Song of Myself," §32, Ibid., p. 51.

31. "Song of Myself," §33, Ibid., pp. 51, 571.

32. "Song of Myself," §33, Ibid., p. 55.

33. *Uncollected Poetry and Prose of Walt Whitman*, vol. 2, p. 95.

34. "There Was a Child Went Forth," *Inclusive Edition*, p. 307.

35. Preface to 1855 Edition, *Complete Writings*, vol. 5, p. 163.

36. "Song of Myself," §45, *Inclusive Edition*, p. 69.

37. "A Song of Joy," Ibid., p. 140.

Walt Whitman, *La naissance du poète* (Paris: Editions Rieder, 1929), 439–452, 466–469. Translated by Roger Asselineau.

3. JULES ROMAINS

Statement about Whitman

I remember the time when my friends and I — we were still very young — discovered *Leaves of Grass* in Bazalgette's translation. (I was not to read the original text until much later.) I must add that we were quite prepared to welcome this book, for we had read some time before the substantial study which Bazalgette had devoted to Whitman. Our enthusiasm was aroused by the fact that the American poet renewed the relationship between poetry and man, a relationship which so many poets in recent times had done their very best to break. Walt Whitman's poems are indeed the poems in which the human soul reveals itself with simplicity and vigor (quite different in this respect from Edgar Allan Poe, whose importance and greatness I do recognize, however).

Later, when I became acquainted with the United States — and I became very well acquainted with it indeed, I assure you — I admired the way this great poet was the poet of that land and people, and the way he succeeded in singing of their essential qualities. Besides, I discovered with pleasure, thanks to the many conversations I had there at quite different times, that for most American intellectuals, even those who represented entirely different tendencies, Walt Whitman remained specifically the greatest American poet.

Once, however, I was somewhat disappointed and shocked. The city of New York had organized an exhibition devoted to Whitman. I visited it, but I discovered that I was distressingly alone as I went through the various rooms. Maybe I had chosen the wrong moment and, if I had gone at a different time, I would have had the joy of seeing American crowds pressing in front of all those mementoes of the poet who knew so well how to sing of them.

Roger Asselineau and William White, eds., *Walt Whitman in Europe Today* (Detroit: Wayne State University Press, 1972). Translated by Roger Asselineau.

ROGER ASSELINEAU

Whitman in Italy

Italian critics and scholars became aware of the existence of
Leaves of Grass later than their French counterparts, since the first article about
Whitman appeared in Italy only on December 7, 1879. Published in *Fanfulla della
Domenica*, the article was written by Enrico Nencioni, a lover of English poetry.
But, like Louis Etienne, Nencioni disapproved of Whitman's rejection of traditional patterns and accused him of not really writing in verse, an "enormous defect" in his eyes. He nonetheless admired the "divine afflatus" of the American
poet, his "infinite vision" and "humanitarian enthusiasm." In short, he wished
Whitman had written like Poe, but he recognized his greatness and went on writing about him every few years through 1891 in *Fanfulla della Domenica* and even
later in *Nuova Antologia*. He praised in particular Whitman's vigorous virility, his
simplicity, and his naturalness as opposed to the overrefined "boudoir poetry"
which was being written by Italian poets. "Here is truth, here is poetry," he concluded in 1881. He preferred this to his compatriots' debilitating "opium." He
wanted to open new horizons to them, and as years went by he tended more and
more to emphasize Whitman's democratic message. In one 1884 article, he even
associated Whitman and Mazzini, the republican patriot. He praised their common democratic ideal and dreamed of a new Dante who would sing like Whitman
of the New World and the titanic achievements of modern men and women. He
also celebrated "the poet of the American War," the "wound-dresser," the singer

of "the heroic joy of individual life," but recalled that "for Whitman, the universe is something sacred, vital, symbolical and worthy of worship. His contemplation of it is more often mystical than scientific."

Nencioni's articles launched Whitman in Italy. The two greatest Italian poets of the time, Giosuè Carducci and D'Annunzio, were enthusiastic and congratulated him. "Italy has need to cleanse herself," Carducci told him. Above all, Nencioni's campaign encouraged Luigi Gamberale to translate *Leaves of Grass*. The first volume of the *Selected Poems of Walt Whitman*, translated and introduced by Gamberale, appeared in 1887 and the second volume, which contained a translation of the 1855 and 1872 prefaces and even extracts from *Specimen Days*, three years later. They were very successful and had to be reprinted. Encouraged, Gamberale persevered and published in 1907 a complete translation which was very well received by critics as well as by Carducci, D'Annunzio, Pascoli, and later Papini. He had corrected the errors and removed the archaisms that were indeed contrary to the spirit of Whitman's poems. His work therefore remained the standard translation of *Leaves of Grass* until the appearance in 1950 of Enzo Giachino's, which is closer to the original text, less "literary," cleaner in the sense in which the *Ossi di seppia*, the "cuttle-bones" of Eugenio Montale, are clean.[1] Mariolina Meliadò-Freeth, who herself excellently translated *Specimen Days* in 1968, considered Giachino's translation "beautiful."[2] It certainly is, but tastes keep changing, and his successful translation, reprinted several times in diverse forms, now has a rival which may displace it. Appearing in 1988, nearly forty years after Giachino's translation, it was done by Ariodante Marianni and was appositely introduced by a well-known scholar in the field of American studies, Biancamaria Tedeschini-Lalli. It is the third complete translation of *Leaves of Grass* into Italian — as is fitting, almost one per generation.

This proliferation of translations (for there were other incomplete ones, which can be passed over) shows how popular Whitman's poetry has been in Italy from the start. But, for all his popularity with the general poetry-loving public (if there is such a thing), Whitman has also been in Italy a poets' poet and a critics' poet.

At first, as we have seen, the critical response to *Leaves of Grass* was hesitant and ambiguous. His form — or rather his apparent lack of form — shocked readers inured to the strict rules of Greek, Latin, and Italian prosody. The more conservative critics rejected him or refused to take him seriously: G. Strafforello, in *Letteratura Americana* (1884), regarded him as a humorist or, "if not properly speaking a humorist, at least a baroque and bohemian [*scapigliato*] poet." But the more open and enlightened writers welcomed him as a liberator letting a breath of fresh air into the stuffy room of Italian poetry. Thus F. Chimenti, in *Note di Letteratura Americana* (1894), praised Whitman's sense of rhythm ("the natural measure . . . of the idea expressed"). Whitman, he said, by "freeing himself of all conventional chains and of the shackles of rhyme and measure, replacing them by the rhythmical movement of prose . . . obtains marvelous effects."[3] This technique and these effects were meticulously described and analyzed by Pasquale Jannacone in his book *The Poetry of Walt Whitman and the Evolution of Rhythmi-*

cal Forms (1898). It was a complete rehabilitation of Whitman's revolutionary prosody. Jannacone showed that Whitman's work was a perfectly justified return to primitive modes of poetic expression, which the similarity of themes rendered necessary. The psychic structure of Whitman's rhythms was also determined, he claimed, by the "incoercibility" of his thought, which could not be poured red-hot into ready-made molds. Even if one might disagree with some of his specific analyses, Jannacone nonetheless incontrovertibly proved that there was method in Whitman's madness. A few years later the poet Giovanni Pascoli, though protesting against the danger of confusing poetry with prose, recognized the existence of a certain rhythm in Whitman's "formless" poems, the very rhythm that could be found in the Old Testament. It did not seem necessary to him, however, to adopt this rhythm in Italy. To his mind, the native hendecasyllabic line was amply sufficient and afforded enough liberty to poets. There was thus a strong resistance to vers libre, which never struck roots in the land of Dante, despite Marinetti's later efforts.[4]

The debate about Whitman's prosody was not, in any case, the fundamental question in Italy. Critics preferred to discuss the contents of his poems or, if they were politically committed, his ideology. Thus Ulisse Ortensi stressed the "evangelical" quality of Whitman's humanitarianism (and incidentally pointed out that Whitman, like Wagner, had replaced melody with harmony).[5] Giulio Pisa, in Studi Letterari (1899), greeted Whitman as the prophet of a new world and considered him much superior to his master Emerson on account of the "impulso vitale" which he sang with such vigor.

Luigi Gamberale, who had studied Whitman's poetry minutely in order to translate it, criticized Leaves of Grass more searchingly than did his predecessors. For him, Whitman was not a mere singer of natural beauties: rather, Whitman identified himself with nature, literally became nature: "He and Nature, he and mankind became one thing. No poet is more subjective and none is, really, more objective. The illusion comes from the fact that object and subject are fused into one and cannot be separated. . . . His is a case of 'impersonal personality.'" Nemi, for his part, examined Whitman's mysticism and very appropriately noted that it was of a strange kind, since Whitman was a "mystical Materialist." The "body electric" was the channel through which the "Superior Soul" invaded him, and Nemi also showed how the American poet idealized the "normal and mediocre man" of his experience into "the divine average." In 1908, G. Rabizzani gave these analyses a romantic twist. Whitman's democracy, according to him, was based on "individualism and identity," because his self mysteriously coincided with everyone's self. He regarded Whitman as "a seer who knew, whereas the masses did not, not a mere being, but a symbol, not a man, but mankind."[6]

In the same year, Giovanni Papini went still further and turned Whitman into a myth. "The soul of Whitman," he said, "is as vast as the world, it is ample, generous, and contains all." And he exhorted Italian poets to follow Whitman's example, to leave their houses and cities, to touch and love things directly, whether clean or dirty, barbarity being a necessary antidote to an excess of civilization (see selection 1).

During the troubled postwar years, when Italy was torn by factions and party strife, politics took precedence over poetry, and Whitman was enlisted in support of various causes. His democratic message was appropriated by Communist leaders, such as Antonio Gramsci and Palmiro Togliatti, but later fascist critics, such as Giuseppe Lesca, found the message of *Leaves of Grass* equally compatible with their own views. The tug-of-war went on, and when Enzo Giachino published his translation of *Leaves of Grass*, Mario Alicata, a Marxist, launched a savage attack on Whitman. He branded him as the champion of a petty bourgeois society and even accused him of failing to understand the evolution of the United States after the Civil War, for, he said, "liberty now only meant the realization of the pioneers' Americanism."[7]

Though he belonged for a time to the Communist Party, Cesare Pavese wore no such blinkers and wrote in 1933 a very fine essay on Whitman. He was interested in *Leaves of Grass* exclusively as a work of art. He started reading it when he was still an adolescent and wrote his doctoral thesis on Whitman while at the University of Turin. He had discovered American literature after the claustrophobic years of fascism and World War II, and its freedom and vitality filled him with wonder and enthusiasm. He loved imaginative writing and wrote fiction and poetry of his own. The American poet who impressed him most was Whitman. He did not imitate the form of his poems, however, and deliberately ignored both his prosody and his homosexuality — "eternal bagatelles," he called them. What attracted him above all was the poet's bold self-confidence, his passion for individualism, and his vital acceptance of modern life, which contrasted with Pavese's own lassitude and despair. In his 1933 essay, he insisted on Whitman's complexity and rejected "the uncritical canonization of the 'seer.'" Whitman, was, in his eyes, an idler who let his thoughts drift and grow, but he was also a conscious artist. He dreamed of writing a primitive poem but could not in the nineteenth century, and so he wrote instead "the poem of that dream." "He made poetry out of this very design, . . . he wrote poetry out of poetry-writing." Hence the subtitle of Pavese's essay: "Poesia del far poesia." Consequently, he praised "Song of Myself" above all and rightly found a difference in kind between Whitman's prose and poetry (see selection 2).

This lucid and passionately sincere piece was very influential. It stimulated such critics as Carlo Bo and Glauco Cambon, encouraging them to write about Whitman.[8] Carlo Bo, who was a specialist in French symbolism and a contributor to avant-garde periodicals, believed that Baudelaire's concept of "correspondences" could help elucidate Whitman's oneness with the physical world. He recommended a "hermetic" or purely subjective reading of *Leaves of Grass*, which alone, he thought, could enable people to seize "the unspoken meanings of the earth," the "truths [that] wait in all things" (LG, 224, 58), as Whitman put it. He thus concluded that *Leaves of Grass* is poetry in the making, constantly to be reinterpreted. This reinterpretation in Italy proceeded with the publication of excellent essays in the 1950s and 1960s, especially by academic critics such as Glauco Cambon and Sergio Perosa, who ignored the political message of Whitman and preferred to concentrate on his style and his language as the dynamic expression of a reality in a perpetual state of flux, "unstable, tense, explosive and chaotic."[9]

Some Italian academic critics have published very thorough studies of certain aspects of *Leaves of Grass*, like Francesca Orestano Vanni, who distilled the essence of her doctoral dissertation in a short essay entitled "Song of Myself 1855–1892: la prima e l'ultima stesura a confronto," in which she compares the first and the final versions of "Song of Myself." Her disciple, Giuseppina Calò, has explored in her 1990 dissertation, "La Poesia Americana e Walt Whitman nelle Reviste Letterarie Siciliane dell'Ottocento," a field which Italian researchers had until then neglected: Sicilian reactions to *Leaves of Grass*. By going through the files of forgotten periodicals, she has brought to light an interesting polygraph, Girolamo Ragusa Molet, who championed Whitman, criticized Nencioni, encouraged Gamberale, and illustrated his articles with translations by one Virginia Bonafede (otherwise unknown), who boldly used a kind of poetic prose, whereas her Sicilian predecessors, Sebastian Ajello and Francesco Contaldi, tried to remain faithful to traditional prosody, even (in Ajello's case) to rhyme. This shows the reluctance of Italian poets "to dance without shackles" (to borrow Voltaire's phrase), and it demonstrates how difficult it was to obtain *sprovincializzazione*, i.e., the deprovincialization of Italy after it had at last obtained its unity.

More recently, Marina Camboni, a disciple of Biancamaria Tedeschini Lalli, published in 1990 an eighty-eight-page essay entitled "Il Corpo dell'America: *Leaves of Grass* 1855 — Introduzione all'Opera di Walt Whitman," a well-written and carefully documented study of the first edition of *Leaves of Grass*, based in particular on Edward Grier's edition of Whitman's notebooks and unpublished prose manuscripts. The author brilliantly comments in turn on the cover, the poet's portrait, the preface, and the three constituent elements of the initial line of "Song of Myself": "I celebrate myself." The preface and the poems are interpreted as embodying Whitman's "isomorphic" vision of an American man, land, and literature characterized by their superlative qualities and the poet's sense of the infinity of space and time. According to Camboni, *Leaves of Grass* thus celebrates a self breaking all internal and external boundaries in order to be born; metaphors of birth give it its thematic unity. Fortunately, Camboni does not carry out her promise — or threat — to study *Leaves of Grass* as "an ideological colloquium on a large scale or a romantic 'semiosphere.'" Other essays on Whitman by Camboni and Tedeschini Lalli are included in *Utopia in the Present Tense: Walt Whitman and the Language of the New World* (1994), a collection of essays edited by Camboni, gathering the papers delivered at a 1992 international Whitman conference in Macerata.

It is easier to inventory the writings of critics on Whitman than to assess his influence on poets. When Nencioni introduced him to the Italian public, both Carducci and D'Annunzio wrote to Nencioni to express their enthusiasm. Carducci did not cease to consider Homer, Shakespeare, and Dante unsurpassable, but he nevertheless deeply appreciated the "immediacy and originality" of the

American poet. It is symptomatic that he thought of translating some of Whitman's poems into Homeric hexameters. For D'Annunzio, Whitman's undoubted greatness contrasted with the "littleness" of contemporary Italian art. Each poet credited himself with creating a precedent, and each felt encouraged to innovate, but classical tradition was too strong and their revolt remained very timid. Besides, their themes were different, and their language never had the demotic raciness of Whitman's. Mariolina Meliadò found a number of reminiscences of *Leaves of Grass* in some of D'Annunzio's poems.[10] Mario Praz, for his part, thinks that "Maia" and "Laus Vitae" could not have been written if "Song of Myself" had not existed.[11] The same thing is true of Cesare Pavese's *Lavorare Stanca*; as a poet, he could not forget what he had read and written as a critic. Meliadò has also shown the influence of Whitman on Giovanni Pascoli, whose "Il fanciullino" somewhat resembles "Out of the Cradle Endlessly Rocking."[12] But the Italian poet who was most influenced by Whitman belonged to a later generation: Dino Campana (1885–1932), whose *Canti Orfici* (1914) sings in a mixture of prose and verse the spiritual adventures of a frantic Whitman on the open roads of the world.[13] Many later developments in Italian poetry could probably not have occurred if Italian poets had not read *Leaves of Grass* in English or Italian.

NOTES

1. For a comparison of the two translations, see Grazia Sotis, "A Study of the Two Complete Translations of Walt Whitman's *Leaves of Grass* into Italian" (Ph.D. diss., University of Connecticut, 1981), summarized in *Dissertation Abstracts International* 42 (1982): 39991A–39992A. See also Grazia Sotis, *Walt Whitman in Italia: La traduzione Gamberale e la traduzione Giachino di "Leaves of Grass"* (Naples: Società Editrice Napoletana, 1982).

2. Mariolina Meliadò-Freeth, "Walt Whitman in Italy," in Roger Asselineau and William White, eds., *Walt Whitman in Europe Today* (Detroit: Wayne State University Press, 1972), 20.

3. G. Stafforello, *Letteratura Americana* (Milan: Hoepli, 1884), chapter 7, 144–145; F. Chimenti, "Walt Whitman," in *Note di Letteratura Americana* (Bari: Pansini, 1894), 21–36.

4. See Filippo Marinetti, *Enquête Internationale sur le vers libre et Manifeste du Futurisme* (Milan: Poesia, 1909).

5. Ulisse Ortensi, "Letterati Contemporanei: Walt Whitman," *Emporium* 8 (July 1898).

6. Luigi Gamberale, "La Vita e le Opere di Walt Whitman," *Rivista d'Italia* 6 (February 1903): 181–207; G. Rabizzani, "Il Mondo Poetico di Walt Whitman," *Nuova Rassegna di Letterature Moderne* 6 (1908): 113–120.

7. For Togilatti, see "A un rivoluzionario Europeo vinto," *Ordine Nuovo* 1 (December 6–13, 1919) (a translation of "To a Foil'd European Revolutionaire"), and "Europe," *Rinascita* 5, no. 8 (1948): 310; Giuseppe Lesca, "Carducci lettore di Whitman," *Bolletino della Comunale di Bologna* 32 (1937): 64–73, and *Giornale d'Italia* (May 18, 1937); Mario Alicata, "Note su Whitman," *Rinascita* 8 (May 1951): 249–254.

8. It must be added, to Pavese's credit, that he encouraged Enzo Giachino to translate

Leaves of Grass. He revised the manuscript of the translation during the week preceding his suicide, and Giachino recognized his debt in his introduction.

9. Sergio Perosa, "Quando nacque la grande American," *Il Resto del Carlino* (February 26, 1969): 11.

10. See Charles S. Grippi, "The Reputation of Walt Whitman in Italy" (Ph.D. diss., New York University, 1971), pp. 89–90.

11. "Walt Whitman," *Enciclopedia Italiana* (Rome) (1949) 35: 734.

12. See Grippi, "Walt Whitman in Italy," 137.

13. See Robert Coppini, "Su Dino Campana," *Revue des Langues Romanes* 89 (1985): 137–156.

1. GIOVANNI PAPINI

"Whitman"

I must confess that I, a Tuscan, an Italian, a Latin, have not felt what poetry really means through Vergil or Dante — and still less thanks to Petrarch or Tasso, luxury poets and consequently men of letters rather than poets — but on the contrary through the childish enumerations and impassioned invocations of the kindly harvester of *Leaves of Grass....*

We must inject into the dried up veins of the dilettantish, effeminate and well-scrubbed town-dwellers that we are, some of the healthy red blood of the peasants, of the mountaineers, of the divine mob. It is not enough to open the windows, as Giulio Orsini used to say. We must leave our houses, leave the cities and feel and love things directly, the most delicate as well as the most repugnant things, and express our love without paying attention to anyone, without resorting to sweetish euphemisms or metrical subtleties, without respecting too much the sacred traditions, honest conventions and stupid rules of good society. We must, to some extent, become barbarians again — toughs even — if we are to rediscover poetry.

Nuova Antologia (June 16, 1908): 696–711. Translated by Roger Asselineau.

2. CESARE PAVESE

"Whitman — Poetry of Poetry Writing"

Too often, it seems to me, the image of Walt Whitman which commentators have before their eyes is that of a bearded centenarian intent on contemplating a butterfly and gathering into his mild eyes the final serenity of all the joys and miseries of the universe. It may be the fault of the photograph which all the definitive editions of *Leaves of Grass* authorized by Bucke, Harned, and Traubel, his literary executors, bear on the frontispiece; or of the myth of a stately prophet, almost a thaumaturge, which his enthusiastic disciples have created; or of his being considered as the unconscious third member of the triad Tolstoy-Hugo-Whitman which for a time obsessed all minds. Though definitively destroyed by the works mainly of English and French critics,[1] the legend of Walt Whitman as a seer, an illuminee, the founder of new religions, the image of Walt Whitman as a handsome white-bearded old man has persisted and unconsciously influences the preferences of readers—and thus the opinion is too widespread nowadays[2] that the true, the great Walt is, if not exactly the personality of the last effete sections of *Leaves of Grass* ("Sands at Seventy"; "Goodbye, My Fancy"; "Old Age Echoes"), at least the man who wrote the short pieces on friendship ("Calamus"), the vigorous and tender war-vignettes entitled "Drum-Taps" and the fugitive visions contained in "Whispers of Heavenly Death." The comparison of a white-bearded Walt Whitman with the poems of "Calamus," composed between thirty-five and forty, which vibrate with such youthful health and self-confidence, will seem strange. And it is well known that poetry is neither youth nor old age; it is simply poetry. But I am not speaking of these sections of *Leaves of Grass* precisely in this way to disparage them. I am only saying that the commentators of Whitman who tend to reduce all his works *merely* to these pages devoted to impressions or vignettes run the risk of falsifying and minimizing to no inconsiderable extent the unique originality of the poet and even ultimately the vignettes themselves. For, in this way, the poetry of mature inspiration, even though it has produced the short poems of "Calamus," has also given rise after all to something like the long Songs which constellate the first two editions of *Leaves of Grass*. These should not be judged by the same standard as the effete and disconnected garrulity (the judgment is Walt Whitman's own)[3] of an old age which, we may now say, was not quite Olympian.

Indeed, people frequently forget something which is quite obvious: that when the "sage of Camden" gave the definitive form to the book of his whole life in the 1881 edition—the seventh one—he was merely verifying and concluding at seventy-two years of age the results of a work which he had conceived dimly for the first time at thirty and already completed for the greater part at forty-eight in the 1867 edition—the fourth one. And what Walt Whitman's superb manhood was, the manhood during which he meditated and translated his book into actions, whoever has not understood it through his poems, may realize it by looking at the photograph which Whitman himself, when he was not yet the "sage of Camden," placed at the beginning of the future "Song of Myself" in 1855, in the first edition of *Leaves of Grass*. A giant with a worker's shirt open at the neck and a thick beard; all his life is concentrated in two mysterious eyes which at times really look quite tender—I believe someone has called this photograph that of a "rowdy." But, whether we like it or not, the Walt Whitman of almost all the *Leaves of Grass* that counts, is this one—at least for those who can understand him.

In spite of the skepticism that has become widespread as the result of a legitimate reaction against the uncritical canonization of the "seer," it can be maintained with good arguments that Walt Whitman has always worked consciously, with a clear critical sense. And it is only natural, for it would be necessary otherwise to turn Walt Whitman, an earthly minded man and a keen user of the file if ever there was one, into the antipathetic figure of an ecstatic idler into whose ears from time to time a demon whispers his songs. *The Magnificent Idler* is precisely the title of a lively biography in novel form, devoted to him by Cameron Rogers, the scholar who to date, I think, has best understood the poet, precisely because he has not attempted to dissert in a rhetorical manner about the catalogues and vignettes, the psychic and internal rhymes, his homosexuality or his magnetism and such trifles, but has soundly recreated his man, attributing to him gestures, words, moods, which any unassuming reader can glimpse in the poems. And an idler Walt Whitman truly was in the sense in which every poet is an idler when instead of working he prefers to go for a walk, ruminating and twisting in his mind his future lines or "verses" with much fatigue and the rare joys which compensate for that fatigue. An idler [he was] as regards ordinary kinds of work, because he had other work to do which robbed him of all other interests and perhaps even of some of his sleep. But these things Valéry-Larbaud has already said and very well indeed.

Instead of this, it is important to emphasize that Walt Whitman knew what he was doing and that, when all is said and done — like every artist who achieves something, Walt Whitman ruminated, twisted, lived, *willed* his something, and that, if some of his theoretical pretensions have proved wrong or ill-founded in the long run in the light of our present age, the same thing has happened and keeps happening not only to all artists, but also to all men. And if before such a sentence as: "Isolated advantages in any rank or grace or fortune — the direct or indirect threads of all the poetry of the past — are in my opinion distasteful to the republican genius and offer no foundation for its fitting verse,"[4] anyone will observe that these are things which should not be said, even in jest, we can answer that it was above all by means of thoughts of this kind that Walt Whitman managed to clarify and delimit the proper "poetic matter" and that in any case, immediately after this heretical sentence, he takes pleasure in relating an anecdote he had read in his youth — which anecdote will also show how in the old days when theoreticians were still disputing on *genres* and schools, artists knew where they stood regarding all these things. Rubens said to his students before a picture of uncertain authorship: "I do not believe the artist, unknown and perhaps no longer living, who has given the world this legacy, ever belonged to any school, or ever painted anything but this one picture, which is a personal affair — a piece out of a man's life."[5] And, reporting these words when almost seventy, Walt Whitman knew what he was saying — knew, if ever any man in America did, what was a work made out of the whole existence of one man.

It would be easy, however, by compiling a list of gnomic passages gleaned from the numerous prefaces, explanations, glosses and memoirs with which the volume of his *Prose Works* is crowded, to throw a paradoxical light on many aspects

chosen among the gaudiest of Whitman's predications, and unsuspected consequences would result from it — consequences unsuspected not only by the author.

Walt Whitman said: "Our fundamental want today in the United States, with
closest, amplest reference to present conditions, and to the future, is of a class, of
native authors, literatuses, far different, far higher in grade than any yet known,
sacerdotal, modern, fit to cope with our occasions, lands, permeating the whole
mass of American mentality, taste, belief, breathing into it a new breath of life . . .
affecting politics far more than the popular superficial suffrage, with results inside
and underneath the elections of Presidents or Congresses — radiating, begetting
appropriate teachers, schools, manners, and, as its grandest result, accomplishing
. . . a religious and moral character beneath the political and productive and intellectual bases of the States."[6] It should be noted that this is one of his great obsessions; there are traces of it at the very beginning of the volume of his *Prose Works.*
If then we put side by side with it the companion obsession whose singularity nobody has yet noticed: the story of the world seen only through its supreme literary
manifestations, through the great national poems, and if we recall his naturalistic
habit of declaiming in the open air, which frightened the seagulls of Coney Island,
as he has described it himself, or entertained the omnibus-drivers of Broadway at
the expense of Homer, Shakespeare, Aeschylus, Ossian and other immortals, we
shall find it easy to build up on documents such a paradoxical theory of the Whitman phenomenon as we mentioned above. To the aforesaid poems — the contemporaries, Walter Scott and Alfred Tennyson were counted, like Ossian, as great
national poets — we must add the numerous magazines of the time, Emerson,
natural history books, encyclopaedias, melodramas, and we shall have all the apparent, exterior culture of Walt Whitman.

And then, in conclusion, we shall say that Walt Whitman wanted to do for
America what the various national poets have done in their day for their own
people. Walt Whitman is quite obsessed with this romantic idea which he was the
first to transplant to America; he sees America and the world only in relation to
the poem which will express them in the XIXth century and in comparison with
this nothing else matters. He it is, the great primitive, the fierce enemy of all literature that deprives nature of its spontaneity — he it is who, in a supreme lament
on the extinction of the red race, has said: "(No picture, poem, statement passing
them to the future) . . ."[7]

Walt Whitman lived out the idea of this mission so intensely that, though not
avoiding the fatal failure of such a design, he yet avoided through it the failure of
his work. He did not write the primitive poem of which he dreamed, but the poem
of that dream. He did not succeed in his absurd attempt to create a poetry
adapted to the democratic and republican world and to the character of the newly
discovered land — because poetry is one — but as he spent his life repeating this
design in various forms, he made poetry out of this very design, the poetry of the
discovery of a world new in history and of the singing of it. To put the apparent
paradox in a nutshell, he wrote poetry out of poetry-writing.

But we have said, Walt Whitman worked consciously and with a certain critical sense. And it would seem from this essay on poetic art that he certainly was not the best historian of his own work. The case is complex at this stage. Walt Whitman deceived himself about the scope, the effects, and the meaning of *Leaves of Grass*; we might even say that he raved about such matters. But it is quite another matter with the essence and nature of his book and I cannot bring myself to believe that a poet, and especially a poet like Walt Whitman, who undertakes to renovate the expression and the spirit of the taste of his time, if he succeeds in producing something vital, should fail to know afterwards how it is done, in other words that he should fail to know why he has written in this way rather than in that way and on this rather than on that. Especially Walt Whitman, I repeat, who has not even the ambiguous halo of a very young poet to protect himself, but at thirty, after trying various trades, after pitiful attempts at short-story writing and journalism, put together a hundred pages or so after working at it for at least four years, and slowly evolved, developed, enriched, modified it in an indefatigable search for a better expression of his thought. Anyone reflecting upon it without knowing the work would find it quite natural for Walt Whitman to have indulged in doctrinal idiosyncrasies. But there remains the problem that while none of those who shared his culture has been able to draw from it anything but collections of medieval ballads or hymns to progress, Walt Whitman has worked the miracle of *Leaves of Grass*, through it or in spite of it.

And anyone who knows how to read will soon discover in the *Prose Works* certain protests, certain assertions, certain intuitions (for lack of a better word) which are definitely among the best passages of all Whitman's erratic critical essays. Let us think, for instance, of the serenity with which the poet analyzes the reasons and motives of his book in the already quoted "A Backward Glance O'er Travel'd Roads." The first thing he says about it is this: ". . . a feeling or ambition to articulate and faithfully express in literary or poetic form, and uncompromisingly, my own physical, emotional, moral, intellectual, and aesthetic Personality in the midst of, and tallying, the momentous spirit and facts of its immediate days, and of current America — and to exploit that Personality, identified with place and date, in a far more candid and comprehensive sense than any hitherto poem or book." [8] At bottom, after the usual absurd expositions of the truly democratic nature of *Leaves of Grass,* there recurs as a conclusion the idea that the book is not the expression of an imaginary world, or a gallery of detached figures (the vignettes), but a Person, a sensibility, living in the real world. "*Leaves of Grass* indeed (I cannot too often reiterate) has mainly been the outcropping of my own emotional and other personal nature — an attempt, from first to last, to put *a Person,* a human being (myself in the latter half of the Nineteenth Century, in America) freely, fully and truly on record." [9] This idea, besides its critical bearing on Walt Whitman's work, is of singular historical importance, because there appeared with it for the first time in America the problem which in the twentieth century all American artists have again tried to solve. However one may define it, there is something eternal and ever new about this problem. While a European artist, belonging to the Old World, will maintain that the secret of art is to build up a more or less imaginary world, to deny reality in order to replace it by a much more significant one, an American of the recent generations will tell you that his ideal is to reach the true nature of things, to see things with virgin eyes, to attain that "ultimate grip of reality"[10] which alone is worth acquiring. A kind of conscious adaptation of the self to the world and to America. It is therefore fair to recognize that Walt Whitman has not only been the first to evince in his work this tendency of the national culture, but has also discovered it within himself and formulated it with a great critical clarity that few of his commentators have been able to attain.

If I do not believe that the *form* of Walt Whitman's poetry consists of a series of small pictures remarkable for their gracefulness, as many commentators have declared or suggested, I do not believe either that the architecture of the whole book is in any way effective, contrary to what Walt and his disciples always thought.

The small pictures, or vignettes, would be those short impressionistic poems — or fragments of poems — in which a figure, a scene, a thought or a landscape is fixed in its essential lines: and they also had the defect of multiplying pitilessly as he grew older on account of the half-ridiculous, half-pitiful mania of the "sage of Camden" for seeing in every small thing the symbol of his vast system and to express it in a parallel, an image, or a description. Yet, in a nature like his, which had a tendency to prophesy, the vignette, in which he was generally so skilled, rather took the form of an apologue or exemplification justified by the whole of his doctrine and of his book. But more recent critics who have rightly rejected his prophetic pretensions, have merely deprived the vignettes of their support and meaning, reducing them to miserable fragments, and completely destroying the perspective, because it has naturally become the fashion to consider best among the vignettes the more melodramatic of them, like "O Captain! My Captain!," "Come up from the Fields, Father," and "The Singer in Prison."

The extreme justification of the vignettes, which consisted of the architectural design of *Leaves of Grass*, represents — as all may see — the translation into art of the prophetic impulse, the practical purpose of the book, in the same way as the bold architecture of the *Divine Comedy*. Yet, as the architecture of *Leaves of Grass* is made up of less appreciated philosophical material, or as it bears little resemblance to a cathedral, or for some other reason, there has been less hostility towards it than towards that of the *Divine Comedy*, and the boldest are finally those who accept it, claiming as an excuse that, all things considered, the order of the poems is in its essential lines the chronological order of their composition,[11] and so the matter ceases to be worth examining.

Thus we must dismiss the vignettes — the effete or modest impressions as well as the descriptive passages of the long "Songs" — and the structure of the book — a useless hierarchy imposed on identical pages of argument or passion — but where then shall we find Walt Whitman's form?

Let us pause to consider a poem, a long poem I should say, the hardest piece of

Leaves of Grass, the "Song of Myself." As early as the first edition this "Song" stood out as the main poem of the book though without a title as yet, and it shared the fortune of the rest of the book, undergoing changes, corrections, suppressions and additions of all kinds. In 1881 we find it in its definitive form, with fifty-two sections, enormous even by comparison with the poems of the first brood "aux titres immenses, les mastodontes et les iguanodons de la création whitmanienne." [12] This "Song of Myself" is, as it were, the quintessence of *Leaves of Grass:* one can find in it all the themes, the profound with the simple, contained in Whitman's poetry.

One of the interesting points about it is that just as the whole book is worthless as far as the structure is concerned, so this poem could bear, without any harmful consequences, long suppressions or additions or transfers, which is precisely what the author has done or would have gone on doing if he had not been prevented by the accidental occurrence of old age and death. Do we mean by this that the worth of the poem lies in the fragmentary pictures in which some realistic description holds the attention? Not at all, though there are in it passages which can be neglected and others which can be counted among the one hundred best pages of the poetry of all times.

Let us begin with the meter. It is a waste of time — and I have wasted a lot myself — to go through the *Prose Works* of the good gray poet with the hope of extracting from *Specimen Days,* from his experiences as a wound-dresser during the Civil War and his happy holidays as a nudist in the solitude of Timber Creek, pages, fragments, vignettes comparable to similar themes in *Leaves of Grass* and apt to show conclusively that there is no difference between his prose and his poetry. No one admires more than I do the artistic prose of Walt Whitman, but it is further necessary to point out that it was almost all written after the Civil War, during his illness, when his beard was already at least grizzly. I have already shown how, from then on, Walt Whitman brooded rather long over his poems and, though he discovered the new vein which we might call "contemplative" [cf. all *Leaves of Grass* from *Autumn Rivulets* (1881) to *Old Age Echoes* (posthumous)], yet in that Indian summer of the impressions, thoughts, revealing comparisons and endless flowering of his vignettes, in spite of numerous new qualities, there is lacking the vigor and the thrill which transfigured even the most allegorical or dogmatic pages of the first *Leaves of Grass.* Almost all his poems from *Autumn Rivulets* (which he began to compose as early as 1865) to his death, would gain in immediacy, clarity, and power by being written in prose. And the prose passages which accompany them, are indeed undoubtedly preferable. On the contrary, in what he wrote before *Whispers of Heavenly Death* (1871), who wants to read, or even remembers nowadays, his few prose writings? There are therefore two parts in Whitman's work: his poetry and his prose, and there is between his poetry and his prose a fundamental difference which cannot be ignored, for it would amount to confounding, among other things, what Walt Whitman himself differentiated with such care.

1. Bliss Perry, Basil de Sélincourt, Valéry Larbaud, H. B. Binns, Régis Michaud, among others.

2. For a recent example cf. Lidia Rho Servi, *Intorno a Walt Whitman* (About Walt Whitman) (Turin, 1933).

3. Cf. "Queries to my Seventieth Year," *Leaves of Grass, Inclusive Edition*, edited by Emory Holloway (Garden City, 1926), p. 422. (Hereafter referred to as *Inclusive Edition*.)

4. "A Backward Glance O'er Travel'd Roads," *Inclusive Edition*, p. 535.

5. Ibid.

6. "Democratic Vistas," *The Complete Poetry and Prose of Walt Whitman*, Vol. 2, p. 210.

7. "Yonnondio," *Inclusive Edition*, p. 433.

8. Ibid., pp. 523–524.

9. Ibid., p. 535.

10. The phrase is Sherwood Anderson's in *Dark Laughter*, but the general idea can be verified only by studying extensively all the vast field of North American experiments in poetry during the last thirty years.

11. Basil de Sélincourt, *Walt Whitman — A Critical Study*, 1914. Cf. all the chapter entitled "Plan."

12. ". . . of the immense titles, the mastodons and iguanodons of Whitman's creations," Valéry Larbaud, *Oeuvres Choisies de Walt Whitman*, 1930, p. 32.

"Whitman — Poesia del far poesia," in *La Letteratura Americana e Altri Saggi* (Turin: Einaudi, 1951). Translated by Roger Asselineau.

ARTHUR GOLDEN & MARIJA GOLDEN

Whitman in the Former Yugoslavia

Though no translation of the entire *Leaves of Grass* has yet appeared in the former Yugoslavia, Whitman has nevertheless been well represented
since 1900 in translations of individual poems, in journals, in editions of selected
works, and in various influence studies. Stephen Stepanchev has noted that the
earliest Yugoslavian translation of Whitman was the 1912 appearance of a poem
called "Mine Is a Powerful Music," translated by "I.A.," in the magazine *Srpski
Knjizevni Glasnik* (*Serbian Book Herald*), the same periodical that in 1920 printed
other Whitman translations by Svet. Stefanovich. Such eminent literary figures as
the Nobel laureate Ivo Andrić, Ljubo Wiesner, Borivoj Jevtić, Tin Ujević, and Oton
Župančič have over the years written perceptively on Whitman or have translated
selections from *Leaves of Grass*. Ujević's edition of Whitman's poems, *Vlati Trave*
(*Leaves of Grass*), was the first book-length collection to appear in Yugoslavia, and
it was not issued until 1951, after Tito established his regime. More recently, Whitman has been well served by the publication of various volumes containing translations by a single hand of representative selections from *Leaves*.[1]

Several languages, of course, are spoken in the territory that used to be known
as Yugoslavia: Slovenian in Slovenia; Serbo-Croatian in Croatia, Serbia, Bosnia
and Herzegovina, and Montenegro; Macedonian in Macedonia; and Albanian in
the territory of Kosovo. This essay focuses on Whitman's reception in Slovenian
and Serbo-Croatian, with brief comments on the Macedonian and Albanian re-

sponse. The responses of various ethnic minorities, such as the Italians, Hungarians, and Germans, are not dealt with here.

In a Slovene edition of *Travne bilke* (*Leaves of Grass*) (Ljubljana, 1962), Peter Levec provides a thorough twelve-page general introduction on Whitman's career and influence, along with skillful translations of twenty-eight poems from *Leaves* that span the poet's thirty-seven-year career. Levec includes selections from such longer poems as "Song of Myself," "Salut au Monde!," "Starting from Paumanok," "I Sing the Body Electric," and "Song of the Open Road," but "Crossing Brooklyn Ferry" and "Out of the Cradle Endlessly Rocking" are given complete, along with "One Hour to Madness and Joy," "I Hear It Was Charged Against Me," several of the "Drum-Taps" poems, "There Was a Child Went Forth," "Miracles," and others.[2]

In *Walt Whitman* (Ljubljana, 1989), Uroš Mozetič offers the most recent Slovene translation of twenty-nine poems from *Leaves*, along with a chronology and useful checklist of Whitman in Slovene translations from 1925 to 1986.[3] Mozetič gives selections from such longer poems as "Song of Myself," "Song of the Open Road," "Salut au Monde!," "Song of the Broad-Axe," and "Passage to India," but "When Lilacs Last in the Dooryard Bloom'd" is given complete, as are such poems as "This Compost," "I Sit and Look Out," "The Mystic Trumpeter," "For You O Democracy," "A Woman Waits for Me," "Whoever You Are Holding Me Now in Hand," "I Saw in Louisiana a Live-Oak Growing," along with several "Drum-Taps" poems. Like Levec, Mozetič has skillfully caught Whitman's rhythms, but his twenty-three-page introduction, "Walt Whitman — enfant terrible in prerok nove Amerike" ("Walt Whitman — Enfant Terrible and Prophet of New America"), is simply pedestrian when not pretentious, and in one instance it is simply inaccurate, as when he says that "in order to safeguard public morality in most of the States, American cultural circles succeeded in prohibiting the printing and, among other things, distribution of *Leaves of Grass*."[4] And a lapse in the chronology for 1865 would leave the reader wondering how Whitman managed after he was summarily fired from his clerkship in the Interior Department; no mention is made of his being hired the next day as a clerk in the Attorney General's Office, where he remained until 1873.

Volt Vitmen: Vlati trave: Izabrane pesme (*Walt Whitman: Leaves of Grass: Selected Poems*) (Belgrade, 1985), the noted poet Ivan V. Lalić's translation of selected poems from *Leaves of Grass* into Serbo-Croatian, is work of a different order.[5] In a wide-ranging thirty-page introduction informed by impeccable scholarship, Lalić places Whitman in the forefront of the world's poets and defines his influence as a "pioneer in modern poetry." Lalić perceptively discusses Baudelaire, Eliot, Frost, Swinburne, and others, in relation to Whitman's achievements. He is also at ease with contemporary Whitman criticism and draws to advantage on such critics as Roger Asselineau, Mark Van Doren, Richard Chase, Roy Harvey Pearce, D. Mirsky, Randall Jarrell, Malcolm Cowley, and Leslie Fiedler.

Along the way, Lalić refutes what he terms the only overall negative assessment of Whitman in Serbo-Croatian, Bogdan Popović's rehearsal of familiar anti-

Whitman sentiments in the 1925 article "Volt Vitmen i Svinbern" ("Walt Whitman and Swinburne"): "[Whitman was] a man without culture or taste. Such people with such talents and education cannot become Shakespeares, Miltons, or even Swinburnes. Such people become Whitmans, primitive people with primitive brains. One hundred lines constitute his best work. The rest is a long, boring prosaic procession of words without thought, with an individual spark here and there lost among the mass."[6] Lalić effectively counters this argument, and his summary statement that Whitman is "one of the classics of modern poetry" is, on the evidence, inarguable.

Lalić has ambitiously opted to translate poems from *Leaves* in their entirety. Among the thirty-four poems he has selected, the major works are well represented: "Song of Myself," "Crossing Brooklyn Ferry," "The Sleepers," "Out of the Cradle Endlessly Rocking," and "When Lilacs Last in the Dooryard Bloom'd." He also includes such representative works as "This Compost," "I Hear America Singing," "Shut Not Your Doors," "Darest Thou Now O Soul," "A Noiseless Patient Spider," several "Calamus" and "Children of Adam" poems, and five "Drum-Taps" poems, among them "Come Up from the Fields Father." Lalić skillfully captures the variety and vigor of Whitman's lines. Checklists of "Translations of Whitman Poems in Serbo-Croatian, 1900–65" and "Articles on Whitman, 1922–55," compiled by Mara Čurčić, and imaginative Dali-esque line drawings by Radomir Relijić round out this excellent volume.

In *Walt Whitman: Vlati travi (Leaves of Grass/Respondez!)* (Sarajevo, 1988), Hamdija Demirović provides another translation of Whitman into Serbo-Croatian.[7] This volume approaches Whitman's career from several angles. Dmirović introduces his expert translations of sixty-one poems from *Leaves* with the essay "Walt Whitman: Pjesnik ljubavi za život" ("The Poet of Love of Life"), which traces Whitman's influence on William Carlos Williams, Wallace Stevens, Robert Frost, and others. His discussion of Whitman's career is well handled, but elsewhere Demirović tries to cover too much ground in so short an essay on Whitman's influence. Often he is elliptical. Demirović certainly knows his subject well, but for some reason he does not explore the full implications of his (brief) assessments.

Selections are given from such longer poems as "Song of Myself," "Starting from Paumanok," "I Sing the Body Electric," "The Sleepers" (two lines), and "When Lilacs Last in the Dooryard Bloom'd." He omits "Passage to India." However, "Crossing Brooklyn Ferry" is given complete, as are such poems as "This Compost," "To a Common Prostitute," "Miracles," and "A Noiseless Patient Spider." Otherwise he draws on the full range of Whitman's poetry from 1855 to 1881 and concludes with several selections from the 1891 annex *Good-Bye My Fancy*. Such important clusters as "Children of Adam," "Calamus," and "Drum-Taps" are well represented. The supporting apparatus is comprehensive. A brief selection of Whitman's prose writings includes one of his anonymous reviews of the first edition of *Leaves*. This is followed by a selection of excerpts and includes the text of Emerson's letter to Whitman on the first edition, with additional commentary by Algernon Swinburne, Gerard Manley Hopkins, John Jay Chapman,

George Santayana, Ezra Pound, D. H. Lawrence, T. S. Eliot, Amy Lowell, F. O. Matthiessen, and Randall Jarrell. A final section, "Whitman in Our Country," offers brief commentaries on Whitman's career by Ivo Andrić, Antun Branko Simić, and Miroslav Krleža. There is also a suggestive concluding note by Miodrag Pavlović on Whitman's "apocalyptic vision" in "Respondez!," a poem that Whitman dropped from the final 1881 edition. Demirović's notes to the poems are knowledgeable and concise.

In a Macedonian edition of *Volt Vitman Poezija* (*Walt Whitman Poetry*) (Skopje, 1974) — transliterated from the Cyrillic — Ivanka Koviloska-Poposka offers a brief six-page introduction outlining Whitman's career and reception, a chronology, and translation of thirty-two poems from *Leaves of Grass*. The first line of each poem is given in English below the Cyrillic title. Excerpts are given from "Song of Myself," but otherwise the poems are complete. The selections cover a wide range of Whitman's poetry: "I Sing the Body Electric," "Crossing Brooklyn Ferry," "When Lilacs Last in the Dooryard Bloom'd," "Passage to India," "I Saw in Louisiana a Live-Oak Growing," "Sometimes with One I Love," "A Woman Waits for Me," "For You O Democracy," "To a Common Prostitute," "I Sit and Look Out," "The Dalliance of the Eagles," several "Drum-Taps" poems, "A Noiseless Patient Spider," "A Farm Picture," "Beautiful Women," and others.

In an Albanian edition entitled *Vollt Vitman Fije bari: Pjese te zgjedhura* (*Walt Whitman Leaves of Grass: Selections*) (Prishtine, 1971), Skënder Luarasi provides an eleven-page introduction and a translation of thirty-one poems. Selections are given from "Salut au Monde!," but otherwise the poems are complete and various: "Song of Myself," "Song of the Broad-Axe," "Song of Joys," "Song of the Open Road," "Me Imperturbe," "I Sit and Look Out," "For You O Democracy," "The Dalliance of the Eagles," "The Base of All Metaphysics," "To a Common Prostitute," "On the Beach at Night Alone," "Tears," "When I Read the Book," "To a Foil'd European Revolutionaire," and others. Luarasi also includes two early 1850 poems taken from *Specimen Days and Collect* (1882) and not included in *Leaves*: "Wounded in the House of Friends," a political protest poem, and "Blood Money," an attack on Daniel Webster for supporting the proposed Fugitive Slave Law.[8]

The attention given to Whitman's works from 1900 on in the various republics of the former Yugoslavia through translations of his poetry and prose and through the publication of critical articles about him offers every reason to believe that Whitman will continue to be an important figure in the cultural life of this area of Europe.

WHITMAN IN CROATIA

Croatians were the first Slavs to write about Whitman. The initial attraction to Whitman in Croatia was political, as Antun Nizeteo suggests: "He was the bard to those generations of Croatian patriots who, subjugated to the Austro-Hungarian monarch, were dreaming of freedom and democracy. It was Whitman . . . who was the most attractive voice for those who wanted, in Croatia and in the whole world, national, social, and revolutionary changes."[9] Vladoje Dukat (1861–1944) was the first figure in Croatian literature to write about Whitman; in *Slike iz povijesti engleske književnosti* (*Pictures from the History of English Literature*) (Zagreb, 1904), he declared that "Whitman stands for the principle of complete freedom, and he is convinced (as was Wordsworth) that the language of a poem must not be different from the everyday speech of the common people. Accordingly, his poems usually recognize neither rhythm nor metrics; his description is thoroughly naturalistic, and the accumulation of unimportant details in order to magnify his effect, strikes the European reader as superfluous and annoying. Despite all this, Whitman is a very original phenomenon on the American Parnassus."[10] In 1908 Nikola Andrić published "The American Poet Walt Whitman" in the Zagreb journal *Narodne Novine*. By this time, an anonymous translation of part of Whitman's "Song of the Broad-Axe" had already appeared (in 1900) in *Svjetlo* (*Light*) (the translator complained about Whitman's "strange rhythm" and "irregular lines"), and in 1912 Ivo Andrić, Ljubo Wiesner, and Slavko Cihlar published selections from several Whitman poems, including "Song of Myself," in *Plamen*.[11] Andrić, Cihlar, and two other translators—Marko Nani and Živko Verkarić—added other Croatian translations of Whitman's poems before World War II.

Although several critics and authors wrote about Whitman before 1950, their reactions pale in comparison to Tin Ujević's powerful response to the American poet.[12] Ujević (1891–1955) first read Whitman's work in high school in Split, but his real encounter with Whitman came while he lived in France (1913–1919), where Whitman, Verhaeren, and Rimbaud all became powerful influences. His admiration for Whitman was enhanced by the unanimists' (and especially Jules Romains's) high regard for the American bard. The French response to Whitman sanctioned Ujević's own growing interest in the poet.

Over the years, Ujević internalized his admiration for Whitman. He affectionately characterized Whitman's poetry as "barking" and referred to "Whitman's spoutings, the violent elemental nature of a living primeval forest, vigorous and savage," all qualities that Ujević would seek to capture in his own work: he sought to become a "paroxyst," a poet who would write in free verse and express himself fully and freely, in a paroxysm of wrath and emotion. He thus worshipped Whitman for taking poetry beyond symbolism: "The monstrous was needed. Nietzsche and Whitman became acquainted with the *Bible* and the *Upanishads*." Whitman, he believed, drew us back to the primitive, "the past, the lakes in which antedeluvian monsters were revived." Ujević also found in Whitman the key to the growing Americanization of Europe; in 1939 he wrote that the "rhythmic effects of the real Walt Whitman are translated into a hearty, sometimes inspired, visionary prose" that makes "perfectly clear" that "*Americanization has started in the world! On the Rhine, on the Danube, on the Volga the new Americans are born.*" Some of this Americanization was troubling—Ujević worried that "Whitman frequently is not far removed from the commercial spirit, or even from the mentality of a shopkeeper"—but the Americanization also imported more attractive ideas, like Whitman's notions of brotherhood, faith in science, progress, and material prosperity. Nizeteo notes that "although Ujević occasionally doubt[ed] Whitman's originality, he [was] never in doubt about his greatness" and "always considered Whitman to be *the* outstanding name in American literature."[13]

Ujević did most of his translations of Whitman in the 1930s but did not publish a volume of them until 1951, when Communist authorities relaxed publication standards. Antun Branko Šimić, a friend of Ujević and also an admirer of Whitman, referred to Ujević in 1954 as "of the Whitmanesque tribe."[14]

Whitman in Slovenia

IGOR MAVER

American poetry is poorly represented in Slovene translations in the first half of the twentieth century. Many important American poets were completely unknown in Slovenia, but this was not the case with Whitman, for the Slovene poets who had even minimal knowledge of American literature admired his work.[15] He was then considered the epitome of a new democratic America that had convulsively emerged after the Civil War, but to what extent did his poetry in translation influence Slovene literary, political, social, cultural, and artistic imagination by forging the myth of America in Slovene literary consciousness? How much did his work help in the making of Slovene national/literary identity in the first half of the twentieth century?

There were various internal and external factors—political, economic, and ideological—that determined which American poetry would be rendered into Slovene. Slovenian translators looked for writers who could offer support for greater national independence and who would encourage democracy.[16] The first translations from America appeared only at the turn of this century with Andrej Smrekar's (1868–1913) renderings of Longfellow and Bryant (1898), and the period between the two world wars saw a substantial body of Whitman's poems enter Slovene. The paucity of Slovene translations from American poetry is a result of several factors: American literature was considered by many Slovene poets and translators as simply derivative of the more worthy European "high" and "traditional" culture. Also, the general cultural orientation of Slovenia at the turn of the century was toward the neighboring German-, Italian-, and French-speaking countries and their respective cultures.

Whitman's literary fortunes in Europe begin with his reception in Germany, France, and, to a lesser extent, in Italy. In nineteenth-century Europe, French and German were far more widely used than English. Therefore, Whitman's reception in Germany and France influenced his reputation among the Slavic nations, including Slovenia. The German, French, and Italian connections are all the more important, given the socio-political circumstances in Slovenia—its inclusion in the Austro-Hungarian empire prior to the First World War and in the kingdom of

Yugoslavia until the beginning of the Second World War. In Germany, Whitman had been accepted as a poet of revolutionary social democracy, while in France his fame was assured by the symbolists and socialists; his poetry reached Italy by way of French critics.

Upon arriving in Slovenia, Whitman's poetry, in addition to its aesthetic appeal and value, had a strong ideological and political impact. He was the bard of generations of Slavic poets who dreamed of freedom and democracy. The interest in Whitman thus coincides with nationalist movements, socio-political reforms, and the rise of the idea of spiritual liberty in the struggle against any kind of oppression.

The Slovenian response to Whitman's poetry roughly falls into two literary periods: the so-called modern period (1899–1918) and the expressionist phase (particularly the 1920s and into the 1930s). The Slovene modern period includes the literary opus of Ivan Cankar, Oton Župančič, Dragotin and Jusip Murn, who during their studies in Vienna became acquainted with the decadent movement and symbolism. They were rebels, rejecting narrow bourgeois liberalism as well as moralistic Catholic literary criticism.[17] These representatives of the modern had no definite literary-ideological tenets, which is why they never published in the major Slovene literary magazine *Ljubljanski zvon* (*The Ljubljana Bell*). Rather, they submitted their works to Croatian-Slovene magazines (*Nova nada, Mladost,* etc.), where Whitman's name first appears in Slovene.

The very first Slovenian mention of Whitman is in 1897 in *Nova nada* (*New Hope*), edited in Vienna by Vladimir Jelovšek. The unknown author of this informative article saw *Leaves of Grass* as a poetic realization of Emerson's essays. In the same year we find two more articles by Arthur Schneider in *Nova nada*; they view Whitman's work in the context of the newly emerging symbolism in France. Albin Ogris in 1912 wrote an article in *Omladina* (*Youth*) which presented Whitman in some detail, and he even translated a few stanzas to illustrate his points.[18] Ogris praises Whitman for his "cosmic Poem of spacelessness and timelessness" and laments the fact that "between the Drava and the Kolpa rivers there is no proper selection of his poetry," and he pleads for a greater diversity of poetic translations into the Slovene language.

Whitman, therefore, was brought into the Slovene cultural environment by the younger generation of Slovene and Croatian students living in Vienna, who set Whitman alongside Emerson's transcendentalism and European symbolism. Although the question of Whitman's relation to symbolism is still debatable, it is nonetheless clear that Whitman's poetry emerged on the Slovene literary scene from German and Austrian cultural backgrounds.[19] The youngest Slovene literary generation of the period wanted to establish Whitman's fame in Slovenia, and it is safe to say that its two most significant representatives — the writer Ivan Cankar (1876–1918) and the poet Oton Župančič (1878–1949) — were familiar with Whitman's poetry.[20] However, their outlooks on the world and their aesthetic concerns were radically different: Cankar was essentially a pessimist and Župančič an optimist, which is why the latter was attracted by Whitman's enthusiastic descriptions of nature, his unchallenged faith in the future, and his inexhaustible optimism, while Cankar was more drawn to Whitman's descriptions of social and moral injustice.[21]

The tenets of the French philosopher Henri Bergson (1859–1941) brought Župančič in close intertextual contact with Whitman's verse through the intermediary role of Verhaeren, particularly in his early "Whitmanesque" phase after his return from Paris (1905–6), where he had attended the lectures delivered by Bergson at Collège de France.[22] This can best be illustrated by Župančič's famous patriotic poem "Duma" ("Meditation"), which he wrote in 1906 when Whitman's star was ascendent in France, especially owing to the unanimists (Romains, Claudel, etc.). Whitman's influence on Župančič is clear when we compare "Duma" to a poem like "Salut au Monde!" Župančič was reading Whitman's poetry while staying in Paris in 1905. Textual evidence suggests that "Duma" was composed sometime between 1903 and 1907 and published for the first time in the collection *Samogovori* (*Monologues*) in 1908.

A talk with Oton Župančič, recorded by Izidor Cankar, is the only direct evidence that Župančič did know Whitman: "I was trying to compose in free verse already in high school, but I am not influenced by a thing, unless I actually experience it. Then my experience coincides with what someone else had already found out. Recently I have been reading Verhaeren and Whitman."[23] The first part of "Duma" is a complex case of literary borrowing, perhaps demonstrating an affinity to — more than a direct influence from — Whitman's "Salut au Monde!":[24]

I hear the workman singing and the farmer's wife singing,
I hear in the distance the sounds of children and of animals early in the day, . . .

I see male and female everywhere,
I see the serene brotherhood of philosophs,
I see the constructiveness of my race,
I see the results of perseverance and industry of my race, . . .
And I salute all the inhabitants of the earth. (LG, 138, 145)

The anaphoras of the first-person verbs ("I see," "I hear"), the inconsistent rhythm and rhyme (vers libre, in keeping with Bergson's idea of élan vital), and a number of other formal features are likewise found in "Duma":

I heard a song and singing voice,
A male voice as if answering a female voice,
I heard how the heart sang.

You stand in the *fields* and you sing me a song, all green,
A song of *wind* and branches and *grass* and the sun on the *grass*,
A song of breaking and a song of placid *waves*,
A song of silver and a song of golden *waves*—
A song of *streams* and a song of *wheats*. (my translation)

In "Duma," the characteristic Whitmanesque natural elements emerge as transcendental presences (wind, grass, sun, waves, wheats): "What rivers are these? what forests and fruits are these?" (LG, 137). There is almost a direct parallel between Župančič's "I love to hear the telegraph pole / the motionless messenger that sings and sings" and Whitman's "I see the electric telegraphs of the earth," while Župančič's "The rhythm of railway tracks, identical under the stars" echoes Whitman's "I see the tracks of the railroads of the earth" (LG, 141); in both cases, the telegraph poles and railway tracks signify an extension into eternity. Župančič's poem "Kovaska" ("A Blacksmith's Song") is also heavily indebted to Whitman's style, revolutionary spirit, and verse technique, although it relies far less on Whitman's typical romantic, subject-oriented presentation.

In 1920 *Ameriški družinski koledar* (edited in Chicago by American Slovenes Etbin Kristan and Frank Zaitz) published a twelve-page essay by Frank Harris called "Walt Whitman," in which Whitman is described as "the greatest and most original American poet." Harris argues that Emerson is much too "literary and puritanical in his views," which is why Whitman has to be cherished more. Still, despite his very positive attitude toward Whitman, Harris denigrates Whitman's borrowings from foreign languages, as well as his "provincialism and shallow optimism."[25] In 1925 the major Slovene literary magazine of the period, *Ljubljanski zvon* (*The Ljubljana Bell*), published Giovanni Papini's article on Whitman in Slovene translation; Papini viewed Whitman as a predecessor to Nietzsche, for both had faith in some "higher human tribe" and were extremely self-confident.[26] This essay provided the most complete information about the American poet in Slovenia in the 1920s.

In 1926 Karlo Kocijančič published an essay entitled "Walt Whitman to His Mother" in the magazine *Ženski svet* (*Woman's World*).[27] This magazine was edited in Trieste, Italy, one of the key centers of the Slovene minority living outside Slovene state borders. The special 1926 issue of the magazine is dedicated to the mothers of famous Slovene and foreign men. Kocijančič is the only translator of Whitman into Slovene in the 1920s. He points out in the article that in Whitman's "democracy" women are considered equal to men, and he praises Whitman's cycle of poems "Songs of Parting," which in his view reaches the artistic stature of a Ivan Cankar's worshipful, idolatrous attitude toward motherhood. In 1927 Kocijančič's translations from Whitman's *Children of Adam* appeared in the same magazine.[28] It is significant that the poem "This Is the Female Form" ("To je podoba žene") is in the original nine lines longer than in the translation, for the translator deliberately left out those lines he thought lewd and offensive to public morals. Kocijančič's own poems — the collection *Večna plamenica* (*Eternal Torch*) (Ljubljana, 1923) — reveal Whitman's influence in both form and content. Nevertheless, his selections of Whitman's poems for translation is consonant with the then prevailing interpretations of the American poet: critics tended to stress his boundless joy of life and nature and not the sensual nature of his verse.

Generally, there was no systematic approach to Whitman's poetry, and the translations were usually occasional pieces.[29] The first real translation of Whitman into Slovene was by the well-known poet and writer Tone Seliškar, who in 1926 published in the American Slovene press in Cleveland "A Dissonant Poem."[30] Slovene immigrants in the United States were important mediators between American and Slovene literature. A large number of translations from African American poetry and a generally revived interest in American poetry was, for instance, triggered in the 1930s by the well-known American Slovene Louis Adamic's (1898–1951) first visit since his childhood to his native Slovenia. Many translations from American poetry appeared in 1932 in *Ljubljanski zvon*, because Adamic suggested some of the possible texts for translation.

Miran Jarc (1900–1942), a poet, fiction writer, dramatist, and critic, essentially toed the line of the expressionist movement and was interested in the "cosmic issues" — human anguish at the confrontation with the mysteries of the hostile cosmos. In the novel *Novo mesto*, Jarc describes the protagonist walking in the park with a copy of Whitman's *Leaves of Grass* in his hands. Suddenly he is stopped by a young woman, who is clearly surprised to find someone in "this small town" reading the "internationally famous" Walt Whitman. This passage indicates that in the 1920s Whitman's poetry was still unknown to the average Slovene: "When he turned his head a surprised woman's voice enquired: 'You read Whitman?'. . . 'What is so strange about my reading Whitman?' he blushed. 'This is very unusual in such a small town nowadays.'" The emphasis on "such a small town" only confirmed his assumption that the beautiful foreign woman was "a real cosmopolitan."

It was only in 1932, the crucial year of Louis Adamic's visit to Slovenia, eighty years after its original publication, that Slovenes got a more comprehensive selection of poems from *Leaves of Grass*. Janez Žagar (Lojze Šegula) in his verse translations succeeded in creating a smoothly flowing free verse or, more precisely, a special kind of rhythmical prose in which it is indeed hard to find any kind of recurring metrical pattern: "I Hear America Singing" ("Čujem pesem Amerike"), "Gods" ("Bogovi"), "Beat! Beat! Drums!" ("Bojna"), "Mother and Child" ("Mati in otrok"), and "A Clear Midnight" ("Samotni drozg in svetla polnoč").[31] His translations faithfully follow the original and show a fairly good command of English.

In the period of expressionism, Anton Podbevšek translated a body of Whitman's verse (1939) to celebrate the 120th anniversary of Whitman's birth. His translations reflect his determination to search for visually well-constructed lines and stanzas, similar to his own original typographic poetry in which verse and prose sections alternate. Among Podbevšek's translations are "When I Read the Book," "Poets to Come," "A Woman Waits for Me," "I Am He that Aches with Love," "Once I Pass'd through a Populous City" and "To a Western Boy." Podbevšek was one of the progressive minds in the late 1930s in Slovenia and tried to introduce into Slovene literature modernist trends, especially futuristic and surrealistic elements (as in *The Man with Bombs* [1925]); later he developed a special kind of Slovene expressionism. His early poetry is particularly characterized by such things as long Whitmanesque sentences, effusive expressions, and lack of stanzaic forms, in order to capture "the chaos of time." The young Slovene generation of the period, which had gone through the horrors of World War I, felt it was time for a change, for a new humanity and a new world.

Their artistic search was thus directed toward new values and the modernist ego available in expressionism. The parallelism between Whitman's post–Civil War period and the emergence of Whitman's poetry in Slovene translations after the First World War is therefore not entirely out of order. Whitman's verse left visible traces on Slovene expressionist poets (Oton Župančič, Miran Jarc, Karlo Kocijančič, Anton Podbevšek, Tone Seliškar), who, except for Župančič and Jarc, all published Slovene translations from his verse. It is true, however, that Whitman's influence was limited to poetic form during the modern period, whereas Podbevšek's expressionist phase shows a growing thematic interest in the "new Man" and nation. Župančič and Jarc, however, confirm the assumption that Whitman was a well-known and appreciated poet, who also exerted an influence on many Slovene poets of the period. Since the Slovenes were then still to a large extent dependent on the mediating role of the German language, it is very likely that the first articles, mentions, and even translations of Whitman's poems were based on the notices and translations in foreign newspapers and periodicals, while later on, as communication links with the United States were improved, translators relied almost exclusively on the originals that had been forwarded to them by the cultural workers among the Slovene immigrants across the Atlantic.

In tracing literary influence via verse translations across national or linguistic borders, we can easily fall into the reductionist trap of a simple reception model: in the context of intercultural influence, the intertextual approach (including literary mediation) should supersede the rather reductive notion of influence. There were many factors that promoted, impeded, or otherwise affected the processes of transmission of American verse to Slovenia, but Whitman was clearly the major translated poet in the period between the two world wars. The translations of Whitman's poetry entailed not merely textual but also personal encounters between American Slovenes and Slovene cultural figures (e.g., Louis Adamic, Etbin Kristan, Ivan Zorman). Despite a rather low level of Slovene interest in the cultural developments in America, a translation policy that favored translations from German and Slavic languages, and obstructive censorship and publishing procedures, Whitman's "barbaric yawp" was nevertheless highly valued.

NOTES

1. All translations in the first section of this essay are by Marija Golden. For a concise overview of Whitman's reception in Yugoslavia, see Sonja Bašić, "Walt Whitman in Yugoslavia," in Roger Asselineau and William White, eds., *Walt Whitman in Europe Today* (Detroit: Wayne State University Press, 1972), 24–26; and Stephen Stepanchev, "Whitman in Other Slavic Countries," in Gay Wilson Allen, ed., *Walt Whitman Abroad* (Syracuse: Syracuse University Press, 1955), 156–158.

2. Levec includes a translation of "Give Me the Splendid Silent Sun" by the noted poet

Janez Menart. Interestingly, this volume appeared in a series of world classics and was included in the reading list of secondary school (gymnasium) students, as was Hamdija Demirović's *Walt Whitman: Vlati trave / Respondez!* (Sarajevo: Svjetlost, 1988).

3. Translations of "Out of the Cradle" and two shorter poems had appeared initially in Peter Levec, *Travne bilke* (Ljubljana: Mladinska, 1962).

4. In the chronology for 1881 he indicates that, under pressure from the district attorney in Boston, publisher James R. Osgood "stops the distribution" of the newly published sixth (1881) edition of *Leaves* (not the "seventh," as he states). But this is not quite the same as the kind of broad censorship he is suggesting. In 1882, using the same 1881 Osgood plates, a different publisher reissued *Leaves*. Whatever its critical reception over the years, the various editions of *Leaves*, with this one brief and localized exception, were issued without incident.

5. An earlier edition by Lalić appeared in 1974.

6. Bogdan Popović, "Volt Vitmen i Svinbern," *Srpski Književni Glasnik* (*Serbian Book Herald*) (January 1925): 34.

7. This attractive volume, with a reproduction of a Salvador Dali painting on the front cover, is included on the reading list for secondary school pupils in Bosnia and Herzegovina. For a brief review of this book by Arthur Golden and Marija Bolta, see *Walt Whitman Quarterly Review* 7 (Summer 1989): 36–37.

8. See Thomas Brasher, ed., *Walt Whitman: The Early Poems and Fiction* (New York: New York University Press, 1963), 36–37, 47–48. Whitman is also represented in the Serbo-Croatian *Moderno svetsko pseništvo* (*Modern World Poetry*), edited by R. Luvada et al. (Belgrade, 1983). A recent translation into Serbo-Croatian of Whitman's letter to Emerson appended to the 1856 edition of *Leaves* appears in Zvonimir Radeljković, ed., *Ralf Voldo Emerson, Društvo is osama: Izbor iz dnevnika i eseja/Volt Vitmen: Pismo Emersonu* (*Ralph Waldo Emerson, Society and Loneliness: Selections from the Journals and Essays/Walt Whitman: Letter to Emerson*) (Sarajevo, 1987), 229–240. Oddly, Emerson's celebrated letter to Whitman about the 1855 edition of *Leaves* is not included.

9. Antun Nizeteo, "Whitman in Croatia: Tin Ujević and Walt Whitman," *Journal of Croatian Studies* 11–12 (1970–71): 107. Nizeteo's essay offers a full and rich examination of Whitman's presence in Croatia and his influence on Ujević; this essay is indebted to Nizeteo's work.

10. Ibid., 109.

11. Sonja Bašić, "Walt Whitman in Yugoslavia," 25.

12. See Nizeteo, "Whitman in Croatia," 105–133, for a detailed examination of the relationship between the two poets. Nizeteo appends to his essay Ujević's excellent translations into Serbo-Croatian of five poems from *Leaves*: three sections of "Song of Myself" and all of "Prayer of Columbus," "That Music Always Round Me," "Manahatta," and "To Him That Was Crucified."

13. Ibid., 130, 127, 131, 129.

14. Ibid., 121.

15. See Janez Stanonik, "Ameriško-slovenski odnosi" ("American-Slovene Relations"), *Enciklopedija Slovenije* (Ljubljana: Mladinska Knjiga, 1987), 69–73; and Igor Maver, "The Possibilities of Verse Translation: The Reception of American Poetry in Slovenia between Two Wars," *Acta Neophilologica* (Ljubljana) 21 (1988–89): 31–37.

16. See Igor Maver, "The Question of Literary Transmission and Mediation: Aesthetic, Linguistic and Social Aspects of Slovene Translations from American Verse until 1945," forthcoming in *Slovene Studies.*

17. See Anton Ocvirk, "Slovenska moderna in evropski simbolizem" ("The Slovene Modern and European Symbolism"), *Naša sodobnost* (1955): 195.

18. Albin Ogris, "Walt Whitman," *Omladina* (Prague) 9 (1912–13): 13–16.

19. See Dusan Pirjevec, *Ivan Cankar in evropska literatura* (Ljubljana: Cankarjeva Za-ložba, 1964), 87.

20. For detailed examinations of the Whitman-Župančič relationship, see Henry R. Cooper, Jr., "Influence and Affinity: Walt Whitman's *Leaves of Grass* and the Early Poetry of Oton Župančič," in *Obdobje simbolizma v slovenskem jeziku, književnosti in kulturi* (18 seminar, Prvi del, Mednarodni simpozij v Ljubljani od 1. do 4. julija 1982, Univerza Edvarda Kardelja v Ljubljani, Filozofska fakulteta, Ljubljana, 1983): 267–276.

21. Dušan Pirjevec, "Ivan Cankar in Oton Župančič," *Slavistična revija* (1959–60): 57.

22. See Andrej Capuder, "Bergson in Župančič," *Obdobje simbolizma v slovenskem jeziku*: 255–266.

23. Ivan Cankar, *Dom in svet* (1911): 75–77.

24. For a more extensive analysis, see Cooper, "Influence and Anxiety," 267–276.

25. Frank Harris, "Walt Whitman, k 31. maju 1919," *Ameriški družinski koledar* (Chicago) 6 (1920): 127. See also the short notice on Whitman by Vladimir Martelanc, "Walt Whitman," *Učiteljski list* 3 (1922): 76–77, 85.

26. Giovanni Papini, "Walt Whitman," trans. Karlo Kocijančič, *Ljubljana zvon* 45 (1925): 551–555, 625–629, 686–691, 750–754.

27. Karlo Kocijančič, "Walt Whitman svoji materi" ("Walt Whitman to His Mother"), *Ženski svet* (Trieste, Italy) 4 (1926): 365.

28. Karlo Kocijančič, "To je podoba žene" (from *Children of Adam*), *Ženski svet* (Trieste, Italy) 5 (1927). Kocijančič was, during the period between the two world wars, active in the fields of literature, painting, music, and philosophy; after the Second World War, he worked almost exclusively as a photographer. For more about his life and work, see Sergej Premru, "Umrl je Karlo Kocijančič" ("Upon the Death of Karlo Kocijančič"), *Jadranski kodedar* (Trieste, Italy) (1971): 113.

29. "Iz lirike Walta Whitmana" ("From Walt Whitman's Poetry"), trans. Anton Pod-bevšek, *Modra ptica* 10 (1938–39): 359–361.

30. Walt Whitman, "Disonančna pesem" ("A Dissonant Poem"), trans. Tone Seliškar, *Ameriški družinski koledar* (Chicago) 12 (1926): 94.

31. Walt Whitman, "Iz *Travnih bilk*" ("From *Leaves of Grass*"), trans. Janez Žagar, *Modra ptica* 4 (1932–33): 213–215.

F. LYRA

Whitman in Poland

TEXTS

Whitman's presence in Polish literary culture has developed erratically: from reluctant recognition in the 1870s and 1880s through a long period of salient and eager acceptance; then an interval of near oblivion in the late 1930s until the early 1950s; an eruption of celebratory attention in 1955 that solidified his fame but did not immediately produce any important critical or scholarly studies or translations until 1966, when two collections of his poetry appeared followed by a third in 1971, also the year of the publication of the first book-length biography of Whitman in Poland. During the 1970s and 1980s, interest in Whitman declined again; his presence was kept alive through periodicals which occasionally published translations of new poems or reprinted older ones. In 1988 the volume began to increase, mainly due to Andrzej Szuba's translation activity, capped by an attractive bilingual edition of sixty-two poems in 1991. Over half of them appear in *Piesn o sobie* (*Song of Myself*), published in 1992 — the most extensive selection of *Leaves of Grass* ever published in Polish.[1]

With three collections to his credit and a fourth on the way, Szuba has emerged as the leading Polish translator of Whitman. In the entire history of Polish-American literary relations, over fifty translators—including such luminaries as Czeslaw Milosz, Julian Tuwim, Ludmila Marjanska, Wiktor Woroszylski, and Zygmunt Kubiak — have tested their talents against his poetry, but no litterateur's commitment to Whitman in Poland can match that of Kornei Chukovski's in Russia.

The impressive number of translators belies a fundamental shortcoming in Whitman's Polish reception: absence of the whole *Leaves of Grass*. Reasons for this deficiency elude hard evidence, since no Polish translators have divulged their criteria of selection; nor have they accounted for the fragmentary versions of some major poems or sections. "Song of Myself" — if my inquiry is correct — has in various degrees enticed twelve translators, but the following sections of the poem have yet to appear in Polish: 15, 25, 27–29, 38, 40–43, 46, 48. Whitman scholars will quickly perceive that most of these deal with the erotic and egotistic sides of human nature. On the other hand, masterpieces such as "The Sleepers," "Crossing Brooklyn Ferry," "Out of the Cradle Endlessly Rocking," "As I Ebb'd with the Ocean of Life," and "When Lilacs Last in the Dooryard Bloom'd" have each had several Polish renditions, while "Song of the Exposition," "Song of the Redwood-Tree," "A Song for Occupations," "By Blue Ontario's Shore," and "Proud Music of the Storm" — among others — remain unknown.

Whitman's prose has been served poorly, though as early as 1901 and 1902 two of his stories — "The Last Loyalist" and "Death in the School-Room" — were published in a newspaper, and in 1912 a weekly introduced a sample of *Specimen Days* ("Hours for the Soul"), but there was no follow-up until Juliusz Zulawski's 1966 book, which contained Polish versions of "Origins of Attempted Secession," fragments of correspondence, and extensive extracts from *Specimen Days*, "Preface 1855," "Preface 1876," "Whitman to Emerson, 1856," "Democratic Vistas," "A Backward Glance O'er Travel'd Roads," "Poetry To-Day in America — Shakspere — The Future," and *November Boughs* ("New Orleans in 1848").

RECEPTION

With no evidence to the contrary, it must be assumed that from the beginning Polish translations of Whitman were carried out directly from the original; initially, however, knowledge about Whitman was accumulated through the mediation of France, Germany, and Russia. Critical recognition was slow in coming, and the earliest estimations reflect a mixture of Emersonian and Whittierian attitudes. For Seweryna Duchinska, the first to introduce Whitman in Poland in 1872, Whitman was "a garroter of poetic ideals"; his egocentrism, naturalism, refusal to differentiate between good and evil, between the spiritual and the material realms, "made up a preposterous morality." Puzzled by Emerson's high praise, she chafed at the erotic passages "unfit for repetition" and found "Chants Democratic" "most horrible." Nevertheless, in her eyes Whitman redeemed himself as a poet with *Drum-Taps*, their "thick naturalism" notwithstanding. Duchinska was able to relate to these poems existentially as a patriot who had been conspiratorially involved in organizing aid for families whose men were fighting the Russians in the January Uprising (1863–1864). Posing as a prophet, she predicted that Whitman's poetry would find no followers or imitators. She proved to be right for half a century. In the meantime, Zenon Przesmycki, an editor and critic of increasing authority and a Parnassian poet, learned about Whitman through Ferdinand Freiligrath in the eighties. He commended the German poet for having first introduced Whitman and Bret Harte to Europe, but judged Harte "a better writer than Whitman."

By the end of the century, however, the American poet had become known to other prominent literati of diverse literary and ideological provenance who realized that his poetry yielded to a wide range of interpretation. In time, it gained recognition among the neo-romantics (e.g., Antoni Lange), the futurists (e.g., Jerzy Jankowski), professors of Nietzscheanism (e.g., Jozef Jedlicz), expressionists (e.g., Jan Stur), and folklorists (e.g., Stanislaw Zdzierski); Whitman also attracted Marxist critics as early as 1893 (e.g., Leon Winiarski). In fact, the first extensive study, published as a pamphlet (1921), was written by Antonina Sokolicz, a member of the Polish Socialist Party. Marxist criticism, however, generated little resonance in Whitman's overall Polish reception; Marxism lacked the sanction of creative talents and gifted translators who embraced causes and ideologies more in line with Polish cultural traditions. Above all, Whitman's work elicited great enthusiasm among poets and intellectuals associated with the eclectic *Skamander*, which began appearing in 1920 — notably Julian Tuwim, Kazimierz Wierzynski, Stefan Napierski, and Jaroslaw Iwaszkiewicz, who in 1921 familiarized Polish readers with Léon Bazalgette's work on Whitman.[2] In the same year in which Antonina Sokolicz published her pamphlet, Stanislaw Vincenz preceded his little collection with an introduction in which he stressed the religious element in Whitman's poetry.

The last to become involved in the reception were the academics, chiefly Roman Dyboski and Stanislaw Helsztynski, who through their historical knowledge of American literature were able to present Whitman in a wider diachronic perspective of American literary culture. In an extensive study (1945), reprinted in his valuable book *Wielcy pisarze amerykanscy* (*Great American Writers*) (1958), Dyboski incisively analyzed the complex relationship between Whitman and the transcendentalists. Helsztynski's pleasurable readings, published in textbooks, remained for many years the authoritative source of knowledge about Whitman for students. Polish academics' interest in Whitman culminated in Agnieszka Salska's *The Poetry of Central Consciousness: Whitman and Dickinson* (1982).[3]

The ceremonious commemoration of the centennial of *Leaves*, ideologically sponsored by the World Council of Peace, which declared 1955 a Whitman year, occasioned an unprecedented dissemination of knowledge about him through numerous journalist publications and radio programs. They extended the mythmaking and expanded the carpenter legend by adding a couple of new humble professions to the biography. For a short time, Whitman became a household name in Poland, for the commemoration had all the attributes of a propaganda campaign which, typically, generated no significant critical or scholarly contributions or important translations. He was celebrated not as an artist but rather as a poet of social consciousness. The requisite rhetoric was best exemplified in the comparison of his "grass" with the proletariat: "grass is the proletariat in the world of plants."

Except for Viola Sachs's articles, no serious work appeared between 1955 and 1971, when Juliusz Zulawski published *Wielka podroz Walta Whitmana* (*Walt Whitman's Great Journey*).[4] Zulawski successfully draws his artistic and moral profile directly from insight into Whitman's work and imposes no biased interpretation. The numerous reviews of the biography, the first of its kind in Polish, failed, however, to generate much critical interest, one exception being Zbigniew Bienkowki's stimulating essay (1973), which compares Whitman's religious beliefs to Paul Claudel's Catholicism. Underscoring the lack of Polish criticism, a translation of Jorge Luis Borges's essay on Whitman was published in the periodical *Poezja* (1977), but it appeared only as filler—the reader looked in vain for information about the original source.

INFLUENCE

Whitman's impact on Polish creative writers has yet to be explored. Whatever is known so far about their relations to his work is limited to what they themselves have chosen to reveal. A few of them have also been his translators—for instance, Mikolaj Bieszczadowski and Czeslaw Milosz, or Ludmila Marjanska, whose trip to the United States inspired her to write a poem entitled "Pojmujac wreszcie rozlewnosc, bujnosc i koniecznosc powtorzen Walta Whitmana" ("Finally Understanding the Prolixity, Exuberance and Necessity of Whitman's Repetitions") (1977).

Whitman's work conspicuously affected the young *Skamanders*, some of whom emerged as the nation's best-known poets: Julian Tuwim, Kazimierz Wierzynski, and Antoni Slonimski. Tuwim and Wierzynski declared him their master and made his poetry their program. The former raised his work to a worldview and a cognitive method. Whitman would have been pleased with Wierzynski's poetic celebration of his memory in "Miasta i ludzie" ("Cities and People") in language reminiscent of his "barbaric yawp." Jozef Czechowicz, a major poet between the two world wars and an ardent opponent of the *Skamander* group, may have drawn inspiration from Whitman in his celebration of homosexual love. Whitman tantalized the completely forgotten Roman R. D. Emanowicz, who at the age of twenty was killed in the Polish-Bolshevik war in 1920. One of Poland's greatest novelists, Stefan Zeromski, out of sheer admiration for Whitman, made an attempt at translating him, but only his version of "For You O Democracy" is extant. Joseph Wittlin, an expressionist poet turned novelist who has been acclaimed in both the United States and Europe, turned to Whitman for stylistic effects.

Surely the overdue study of Whitman's influence on Polish literature—if ever written—will demonstrate that Whitman has touched Poland's poets beyond the present level of recognition.

1. The history of Whitman in Poland includes seven collections of poems: *Trzy poematy* (*Three Poems*), trans. Stanislaw Vincenz (Warszawa: Ignis, 1921), a slim volume containing translations of "When Lilacs Last in the Dooryard Bloom'd," "Out of the Cradle Endlessly Rocking," and "Passage to India"; *75 Poematow* (*75 Poems*), trans. Stefan Napierski (Warszawa: J. Mortkowicz, 1934); *Zdzbla Trawy* (*Leaves of Grass*) (Warszawa: Panstwowy Instytut Wydawniczy, 1966), a highly select edition of translations by various people, prepared by Juliusz Zulawski; *Liscie Traw* (fragmenty) (*Leaves of Grass* [fragments]), trans. Jadwiga Lipinska (London: Poets' and Painters' Publishers, 1966); *Poezje Wybrane* (*Selected Poems*) (Warszawa: Ludowa Spoldzielnia Wydawnicza, 1971), edited by Hieronim Michalski and including the work of several translators; *Kobieta Czeka Na Mnie* (*A Woman Waits for Me*), trans. Andrzej Szuba (Kraków: Wydawnictwo M, 1991); *Piesn o Sobie* (*Song of Myself*), trans. Andrzej Szuba (Kraków: Wydawnictwo Literackie, 1992); and *Slysze Spiew Ameryki* (*I Hear America Singing*), trans. Andrzej Szuba (Kraków: Wydawnictwo Miniatura, 1995).

2. Teresa Kieniewicz, "Walt Whitman i Skamandryci" ("Walt Whitman and the Skamandrysts"), *Przeglad Humanistyczny* 3 (1972): 97–104.

3. Salska's study was republished as *Walt Whitman and Emily Dickinson: Poetry of the Central Consciousness* (Philadelphia: University of Pennsylvania Press, 1985).

4. Viola Sachs, "Poetyka Walta Whitmana" ("Walt Whitman's Poetics"), *Przeglad Humanistyczny* 3 (1962): 45–67; and "Walt Whitman and the Orientals," *Kwartalnik Neofilologiczny* 9 (1962): 147–160.

STEPHEN STEPANCHEV

Whitman in Russia

It would be difficult to overestimate the importance of Walt Whitman in the history of twentieth-century Russian letters.[1] His audience, reputation, and influence have been enormous. Kornei Chukovsky's translations from *Leaves of Grass* were published in editions of ten, twenty, and fifty thousand copies; Soviet critics have for decades honored the poet as a high priest of democratic idealism and as a saint of the Revolution of 1917; and his influence on the practice of Russian poets, especially in the 1910s and 1920s, was felt both in choice of subject matter and in verse technique. Rightly or wrongly, the Russians have identified Whitman with their own revolutionary struggle; in his emphasis on a democratic future, his optimism, and his sense of equality and essential divinity of all people, they have recognized the tone of their own convictions and aspirations.

In view of this identification, it is not surprising that Whitman should have come into prominence in Russia in the early years of the century, when the social malaise and ferment of the times (expressed so admirably in the work of Chekhov) led to the abortive revolution of 1905. Indeed, interest in Whitman before 1900 was tentative and sporadic, kept alive in literary circles by the intriguing fact that government censorship forbade any reference to him and the fact that he was achieving considerable fame in Western Europe.

The first mention of Whitman in Russia came in 1861, the year after the publication of the third American edition of *Leaves of Grass*. An anonymous reviewer of foreign novels for *Otechestvenniye Zapiski* (*Annals of the Fatherland*) mistook the poet's work for a novel and, in commenting on the furor that *Leaves of Grass* had created in England, remarked:

> The attacks are concerned with the moral aspect of the novel. "He should be printed on dirty paper, as is appropriate for a book intended chiefly for police scrutiny," said one critic. "This is the emancipation of the flesh!" exclaimed another.

This amusing Russian echo of gentility's battle against Whitman received no reinforcement, however. More than twenty years passed before the poet was again called to the attention of the reading public, this time by way of John Swinton's lecture on American literature. A translation of it appeared in *Zagranichnyi Vestnik* (*Foreign Herald*) in 1882. Then, in March 1883, N. Popov published an article on "Uolt Guitman" in *Zagranichnyi Vestnik*, which was the first Russian estimate of the American poet and a rhapsodic tribute:

> Who is this Walt Whitman? He is the spirit of revolt and pride, Milton's Satan. He is Goethe's Faust, but a happier one. It seems to him that he has solved the riddle of life; he is drunk with life, such as it is; he extols birth equally with death because he sees, knows, senses immortality. This inquiring naturalist arrives at rapture through the lessons of putrid corpses as much as through a vision of fragrant flowers. "Every life is composed of thousands of corpses!" he exclaimed.

The censors found this commentary alarmingly decadent, put the author in prison, and suspended the magazine for the rest of the year.

The year before Popov's article, Whitman had received a letter from an Irishman living in Dresden, Dr. John Fitzgerald Lee, asking permission to translate *Leaves of Grass* into Russian. How well Dr. Lee knew Russian is unknown, and the translation was never made, but the proposal excited Whitman, partly because he believed he had been ignored in his own country. Whitman replied by giving his blessing to the proposal along with a greeting to the Russian people:

> As my dearest dream is for an internationality of poems and poets binding the lands of the earth closer than all treaties and diplomacy — As the purpose beneath the rest in my book is such hearty comradeship, for individuals to begin with, and for all the nations of the earth as a result — how happy I should be to get the hearing and emotional contact of the great Russian people.[2]

Whitman, of course, had addressed the first edition of *Leaves* to an American audience, confidently ending his preface with the assertion that "the proof of a poet is that his country absorbs him as affectionately as he has absorbed it" (LG, 729). Having failed that test, he now fantasized an international audience, and his fantasy began with Russia.

Despite the state censorship, Whitman had some Russian readers during this period. Ivan Turgenev was so moved by Whitman's poems that he offered to translate a few of them for E. Ragozin, editor of *Nedeli* (*The Week*). In a letter to his friend P. V. Annenkov, he wrote: "To Ragozin, together with portions of *Sketches of a Sportsman*, I am sending some translated verses of the astonishing American poet Walt Whitman (have you heard of him?) with a short introduction." He was particularly excited by "Beat! Beat! Drums!" and tried to translate it. The manuscript still survives in the Bibliothèque Nationale in Paris, and both Chukovsky and I. Christova have commented on Turgenev's mistakes.[3] Chukovsky says Turgenev misunderstood some of Whitman's words, but the task was almost impossible anyway. For example, "Beat! beat! drums! blow! bugles! blow!" contains seven syllables in all, and they "ring energetically and courageously." But in Turgenev's translation there are sixteen syllables: "That is slow and flabby." In his own translation, Chukovsky used eleven syllables, but he admits that they do not closely approximate the English: the prolixity of the Russian language is a real barrier to the effective translation of Whitman.

Turgenev put his work on Whitman aside, and the non-English reading public had to wait until 1907 for a book of translations from *Leaves of Grass*. That Turgenev continued to be interested in Whitman, however, is clear from the fact that he spoke of him to an American writer (possibly Henry James) in Paris in 1874, remarking that although there was a great deal of chaff in the poet's work there was also good grain.

Another one of Whitman's readers was Leo Tolstoy, whose reactions were likewise mixed. On receiving a gift copy of *Leaves of Grass* in 1889, he wrote in his diary: "Received book: Whitman — ugly verses." But later, when R. W. Collins, an Irish admirer, sent Tolstoy a copy of an Irish edition and suggested that there were similarities between his ideas and Whitman's, Tolstoy took the trouble to read the book and found a number of admirable poems to underline, such as "I Dreamed in a Dream" in the "Calamus" section. In his diary he remarked that Whitman was empty much of the time, but that now and then he was good. By 1890 he was clearly interested in winning a Russian audience for the poet, as in that year he wrote to Leo Nikiforov, the translator, that Whitman "is already very famous in Europe, but among us he is virtually unknown. And an essay about him with a selection of translated poems would, I think, be acceptable to every journal, to *Russkaya Mysl* [*Russian Thought*], I believe." Unhappily, Nikiforov failed to respond to this suggestion. But Tolstoy's continuing ambivalence toward Whitman is apparent when his remark to Aylmer Maude, his English translator, that Whitman lacked a philosophy of his life is combined with his later listing of the poet (in 1900) among those American authors who were important to world literature.

After N. Popov's unhappy experience with the czarist censorship in 1883, there was no public notice of Whitman until 1892, the year of his death. In that year obituaries appeared in at least three Russian periodicals: *Nablyudatel'* (*The Observer*), *Bibliograficheskiya Zapiski* (*Bibliographic Annals*), and *Knizhki Nedeli* (*Book Week*). The last-mentioned journal characterized Whitman as "the American Tolstoy" and as "the most remarkable of North American poets." But in the same year an article in the *Brockhaus-Efron Entsiklopedicheski Slovar* (*Brockhaus-*

Efron Encyclopedic Dictionary) attacked him for his "chaotic unfamiliarity with thought" and his "anti-artistic methods." Later in the decade, in 1896 and 1898, Whitman received the favorable attention of Dioneo (pseudonym of Isaac Shklovsky), a correspondent in England who wrote articles on English and American literature for Russian magazines. He spoke of the wide audience that Whitman had won in England, America, and Australia, of his "classical talent," of his superiority over Nietzsche, and of his altruistic democracy. "Whitman speaks of the widest, universal altruism," he said.

Notwithstanding all these indications of interest, the fact remains that Whitman was little known and little read in Russia during the nineteenth century. Then, during the first decade of the twentieth, he was swept up in literary and political currents as Russia's great revolutionary generation discovered its war slogans. Whitman's emphasis on pioneering, on building a new democratic future, on brotherhood and equality elicited a warm response both from youthful Marxists and from partisans of a gentler, more middle-class orientation. Numerous writers and journals assisted in relating Whitman to the Russian zeitgeist, in making him a contemporary Russian poet, but the two more avid publicists were Konstantin Bal'mont, himself a distinguished symbolist poet, and Kornei Chukovsky, a devoted Whitman scholar who saw his translations from *Leaves of Grass* go through twelve editions before his death in 1969.

Konstantin Bal'mont began his translations from Whitman in 1903 and completed them in 1905 to the sound of revolutionary guns, as he said. He published them in the literary magazines *Vessy* (*The Scales*) and *Pereval* (*Mountain Pass*), together with commentaries in which he tried to elucidate Whitman's ideas and technique. In 1911 the poems were collected and published under the title of *Pobegi Travy* (*Shoots of Grass*) in an edition of fifteen hundred copies. The book was prefaced by an enthusiastic, Whitmanesque essay, "Polarity," which Bal'mont had printed in *Sovremenny Mir* (*Contemporary World*) in 1910.

In his articles on Whitman, Bal'mont tried, on the one hand, to explain the American poet's neglect in Russia and, on the other, to justify a much greater measure of interest in him. In "The Bard of Individuality and Life," an essay that appeared in *Vessy* in July 1904, he pointed out that Whitman was unread because of his indifference to European literary forms and because of the absence from his work of conventional elements of "beauty." He also noted that many purely American details and local color provided a barrier to understanding. But he insisted that Whitman was even more worthy of Russian attention than his "aristocratic" compatriot, Edgar Allan Poe, of whom the Russian public was very fond. In comparison with Poe, Whitman might be chaotic and undisciplined, but

> he takes us to the morning of world-making and gives us a sense of the tremendous creative expanse of earth and sea. . . . He sings of freedom, of his young country chaotically moving toward the building of new forms of life. Sensing himself new, he rejects the old, and, above all, being a poet of the future, he rejects old forms of verse. . . . He sings the simple, powerful ego of a young race.

... Whitman's democracy shows itself in great part not as a political manifestation, but, rather, as a form of religious enthusiasm. . . . He is a poet of individuality, of unlimited life, and a harmonious joining of all separate personalities with the Universal One.

In the preface to his *Pobegi Travy*, Bal'mont pursued these ideas but gave them a more explicitly political formation when he said that the poet was "a part, and a strong part, of that future which is swiftly coming toward us, which is, indeed, already being made in the present. Ideal Democracy. Full Sovereignty of the People. . . . Whitman spoke of it."

Bal'mont's contemporaries did not question these sentiments, but some of them, notably his rival, Kornei Chukovsky, objected to his translations. The chief charge leveled against them was that they were too literary, too pretty, too full of symbolist embellishment that contradicted Whitman's simplicity of phrase and rhythm. Chukovsky pointed out that Bal'mont's fear of simplicity can be seen in the very title of the book, which is *Pobegi Travy* (*Shoots of Grass*) instead of *List'ya Travy* (*Leaves of Grass*). The second charge leveled at him was that his knowledge of English was so rudimentary that he made inexcusable errors in translation. Bal'mont had remarked in the preface of his book that he had observed the most scrupulous exactitude in his labors, "having recourse to paraphrase only where my literary perception was absolutely necessary," but Chukovsky noted that Bal'mont had translated "lilacs" as "lilies" and "a column of figures" as "figures on columns." He showed, too, that Whitman's line about women, "they are ultimate in their own rights," was incorrectly rendered as "they know how to issue ultimatums." "These are not women," Chukovsky said wryly, "but diplomats of enemy countries." Chukovsky's third charge against Bal'mont was that he sometimes substituted a generality for the concreteness of the original text. Where Whitman had written "my Mississippi" or "prairies in Illinois" or "my prairies on the Missouri," Bal'mont had preferred some all-inclusive phrase, such as "rivers and fields and dales."

That there is much justification for Chukovsky's strictures on Bal'mont's work is clear to any impartial reader, and it should be noted that Soviet encyclopedias and literary histories echo the opinion that the symbolist poet's translations were "unsuccessful." However, in the first decade of the century, Bal'mont had his champions, and when Chukovsky attacked him in an article in the October 1906 issue of *Vessy*, he drew a long and vehement reply from an outraged reader, Elena T. Their correspondence was published in the December issue of the magazine. Bal'mont had another defender in M. Nevedomsky, a writer for *Sovremenny Mir*, who asserted in an article "On the Art of Our Days and the Art of the Future" (in the April 1909 issue) that Bal'mont's translations were "more reliable" than Chukovsky's.

It is undeniable, however, that Kornei Chukovsky was the foremost Whitman scholar in Russia and that his translations and articles in the crucial first decade of the century helped to establish Whitman in his high position in Russian letters. In his 1969 essay in *Sputnik* (see selection 3), Chukovsky explained how he discovered *Leaves of Grass* purely by chance. He says that at the time he bought a copy of Whitman's poems he was alienated from his parents (his father had abandoned the family, and his mother supported her children as a laundress) and was working as a day laborer on the docks of Odessa. Chukovsky was only seventeen when he bought a copy of *Leaves of Grass* from a sailor in Odessa; he had never heard of the author's name. By this time, though self-educated, he had gained considerable facility in reading English. When he began reading Whitman's poems, he thought the author must be an inspired madman: this poet could transcend space, and, even better, he identified with everyone — for him there was no inequality. Chukovsky's "youthful heart eagerly responded to his ecstatic call for human brotherhood, and to the radiant hymns he sang to labor, equality and democracy, to the joy he took in the simple things of everyday life and to his daring glorification of emancipated flesh."

Because Chukovsky wanted to share this "emancipation" with others, he began trying to translate the poems into Russian. In the preface to his sixth (1923) edition of *Uot Uitmen i Ego List'ya Travy: Poeziya Gryadushchei Demokratii* (*Walt Whitman and His Leaves of Grass: Poetry of the Future Democracy*), Chukovsky described the first years of his campaign in behalf of Whitman:

> When I began to publicize Walt Whitman in Russia one of the newspapers declared that there had never been such a poet and that I had simply thought him up. The article indeed began in this way: "Chukovsky invented Walt Whitman." The name of the American bard was known only to a narrow circle of readers, chiefly esthetes-symbolists. The form of his verses seemed so slovenly and awkward that at first not a single journal would agree to print my translations.

Chukovsky confessed that, in his eagerness to win an audience for Whitman, he resorted to bowdlerization: he corrected Whitman's verses and added rhymes and, in general, misrepresented the poet to a far greater degree than Bal'mont ever did. A few of these mistranslations can be found in the old magazine *Nive* (*Fields*). The scholar indicated, too, that he had had some trouble with the censorship, particularly in 1905, but declared that

> I continued to preach the gospel of Whitman everywhere, and there was no publication, it seemed, in which I did not print an article about him or translations from *Leaves of Grass*. I wrote about him for the journal *Odesskie Novosti* [*Odessa News*] (1904), the almanac *Mayak* [*The Lighthouse*] (1906), the journal *Vessy* (1906), the gazette *Rech'* [*Speech*] (1909, 1911), the gazette *Russkoe Slovo* [*The Russian Word*] (1913), the journal *Russkaya Mysl'* [*Russian Thought*], the gazette *Navodnyi Vestnik* [*The People's Messenger*] and, it seems, in tens of others.

But Chukovsky's chief contribution to Whitman scholarship during the early 1900s was his 1907 edition of *Leaves of Grass*, the first in Russia. The work was called *Poeziya Gryadushchei Demokratii: Uot Uitmen* (*Poetry of the Future Democracy: Walt Whitman*).[4] It was reviewed favorably by Yuly Eichenwald in the August 1907 issue of *Russkaya Mysl'*, though the reviewer brushed aside Chukovsky's characterization of Whitman as an apostle of democracy and made him an advocate of anarchism instead. Eichenwald saw Whitman as a great, free, titanic father-figure:

> Above us, who are exhausted by doubts, who are growing small through our petty labor and worry, above us, Lilliputian souls, rises the masterful self-confidence of a great man. And when one finds himself near him, one wants to talk not in his ordinary, quiet voice, but louder and louder; he wishes to imitate his energetic speech, which is without redundance and connectives, without disgusting softness. . . . Huge, loud, titanic, he differs from us in that we feel ourselves children, that our view of the world is childish, submissive, and Whitman is the father.

During the second decade of the century, a turbulent time of world war and successful revolution, public interest in Whitman was so great that three new editions of Chukovsky's translations from *Leaves of Grass* appeared. In 1914, three thousand copies were printed of the improved second edition of *Poeziya Gryadushchei Demokratii: Uot Uitmen*, with an introduction by I. E. Repin, the painter; this edition was seized by the czar's censors (see selection 1). The third edition, of five thousand copies, was published in Petrograd in 1918 with an epilogue by the Marxist critic A. Lunacharsky. And in the following year the Petrograd Soviet of Workers and Red Army Deputies issued fifty thousand copies of the fourth edition. With this huge printing, it can be said that Whitman had finally achieved an audience in Russia.

It should be added that several pamphlets and broadsides containing Whitman's verses were published between 1918 and 1923. Some of these were distributed to Red Army troops and workers in the trenches and at the barricades. Among them was a translation by "M.S.," *Pionery* (*Pioneers*), issued as a four-page pamphlet in Petrograd in an edition of one thousand copies. Another was a broadside, *V Boi Pospeshim My Skorei* (*We Shall Hurry to Battle*), printed in an edition of one thousand copies in Tot'ma, a town in northern Russia on the route to the Archangel revolutionary front.

In these years, though Whitman was enlisted in the revolutionary struggle, there was no consistent view of his political and social thought. Some critics, like M. Nevedomsky and Yuly Eichenwald in the first decade, saw him as an anarcho-socialist; others, like Chukovsky, his most careful student, described him as a democratic individualist; still others, like I. E. Repin, emphasized his Christianity. Repin's point of view was, briefly, this: "I do not believe that this religion of brotherhood, unity, equality, is so new, indeed, as K. I. Chukovsky imagines; it was manifested to the whole world nearly twenty hundred years ago." Repin saw Whitman as counteracting the malignant influence of Nietzsche's cult of "selfishness." Individualism among the Russians, according to Repin, was characterized by rowdyism, rapine, and suicide, and he expected Whitman to give the deathblow to this kind of individualism, "for he is the poet of union, brotherhood, love."

But the most common view was essentially Marxist. In the eyes of the socialists and Communists, Whitman was, as Vladimit Friche put it, "the singer of equal value and equal rights of men, of international solidarity"; he "sang the big city, the hurly-burly of its streets, the ceaseless labor of machines, the working people and the folk mass, the busy life of an industrial-democratic society." Maxim Gorky went even further, however, maintaining that Whitman, after his disillusionment with bourgeois democracy in the 1870s, advocated revolution: Whitman "began with individualism and quietism" and then "came over to socialism, to the preaching of activism." A. Lunacharsky, too, made an effort to draw the poet into the Communist fold:

Whitman is a man with an open heart. Many will be like him when they break out of their one-man prisons, the prisons of individualism and possessions. . . . Communism carries a radiance with it. . . . Communism puts a man in his place. Man awakes and happily realizes his destiny—he is a being conscious and immortal, completing the universal architecture. Immortal. Man is immortal. Though the individual dies. He who does not understand this does not understand Whitman either. In the sphere of politics and economics communism is a struggle against private property with all its hereditary governmental, ecclesiastical, and cultural superstructure. And in the realm of the spirit it is an effort to discard the pitiful envelope "I" and discover a being who is winged with love, immortal, fearless, like Whitman — possessing the shape of a great, all-embracing man.[5]

It was during this period of war rumors, war, and revolution that Whitman exerted his first influence on the practice of Russian poets. He had been greatly admired by the symbolists, particularly by Bal'mont, but he had had very little effect on their poetry. Now, in the second decade of the century, he was taken up by Moscow and St. Petersburg circles of futurists, who strongly opposed the conventional aesthetic of the past and espoused a rough, masculine, even coarse verse line. They hailed Whitman for his loud, brash, swaggering poetry, "the poetry of the future," and did him the honor of imitating him. Among these futurists was Velemir Hlebnikov, whose poem "Sad" ("The Garden") shows Whitman's influence. According to Chukovsky, Hlebnikov liked to listen to Whitman's poems read in English, "even though he did not fully understand the English language." Two other luminaries wearing Whitman's cloak at this time were Mihail Larionov, who regarded Whitman as his collaborator in undermining the bases of traditional aesthetics, and Ivan Oredezh, a St. Petersburg Whitmanian who at times parodied the master.

Preeminent among the futurists was Vladimir Mayakovsky, who in the years immediately succeeding the revolution became a major Russian poet. In his formative years he liked and imitated Whitman; he was impressed by Whitman's "spirited vulgarity," the free, rather conversational language, the phrasing of the average person. His poem "Chelovek" ("Man") comes closest to Whitman's rhythms and diction, according to Chukovsky, who introduced the poet to Whitman's work in 1913. But Mayakovsky was not wholly satisfied with the poems of the American, for he once told Chukovsky that some of his lines were flabbily made and, on another occasion, that Whitman was not true to himself in his struggle to achieve a revolutionary form of art. It seems that Mayakovsky regarded himself as the more masculine and powerful of the two. He developed an idiom and a voice of his own, but most Russian critics are quick to agree that Whitman played no small part in that development. Yassen Zassoursky, for example, claims that "Whitman is perceived in our poetry mostly through the eyes of Mayakovsky," and he goes on to suggest that Mayakovsky's poems "play an essential role in linking Russian poetry and Whitman":

> [Mayakovsky's] poem "Vladimir Mayakovsky" was written on the pattern of Whitman's "Song of Myself." It was in fact almost a translation of Whitman's poem. While Mayakovsky's use of rhyme and his rhythm differed from those of Whitman, Mayakovsky's approach to life, his imagery, his sense of the greatness of the world, and his cosmic vision were close to Whitman's. . . . Mayakovsky mentioned Whitman several times in his poems when he spoke about democratic America. One of his famous poems ["150 Millions"] . . . includes the line, "I am a free American citizen. The earth is full of various Lincolns, Whitmans, Edisons." In another poem, "The Fifth International," Mayakovsky stressed the international brotherhood of democrats and poets. There he mentioned Whitman the democrat. In his poetry, which in its urban and global approach to life was very close to that of Whitman, Mayakovsky lived up to the legacy of the American poet.[6]

In the 1920s, years of construction and reconstruction in Russia, Whitman maintained his hold on the reading public. The fifth edition of Chukovsky's translations from *Leaves of Grass*, in a printing of four thousand copies, was published in 1922 under the title of *List'ya Travy. Proza* (*Leaves of Grass. Prose*). In this edition, selected passages from *Democratic Vistas* and other prose writings of Whitman were included for the first time. In the following year, the sixth edition, in a printing of five thousand copies, made its appearance; it was entitled *Uot Uitmen i Ego List'ya Travy: Poeziya Gryadushchei Demokratii* (*Walt Whitman and His Leaves of Grass: Poetry of the Future Democracy*). It should be noted that, in addition to these two editions, copies of older editions were still available to the public in bookstores and libraries. Indicative of popular interest in Whitman was the fact that he was quoted frequently in the newspapers and that his verses were published in various anthologies of poems for recitation by schoolchildren. Interesting, too, is the fact that "actors of the proletarian culture" in Archangel dramatized and acted his poem "Europe." William Parry reports that in Baku poems by Whitman were distributed as morale builders to oil workers engaged in reconstructing the oil industry. In 1921–22 the Bureau of Public Engagement issued large, brightly colored calendars (twenty by thirty inches in size) in the style of those previously distributed by mail-order firms or by periodicals. These calendars had formerly displayed a large Pietà surrounded by various saints, martyrs, and angels. The Soviet version had a large likeness of Lenin in the center and a border of portraits of men and women whose writings had contributed to revolutionary thought. Marx sat directly above Lenin, just as the Holy Ghost had wavered above Christ in the old pictures. Among the influential men in the border area were Carlyle, Lincoln, Paine, and Whitman.

Russia's poets were active during this era of revolutionary triumph and experimentation, and among them Whitman was a god. They liked the brash, proletarian flavor of his verse and his free-ranging subject matter. Through him they learned that they could write about anything; there was no "poetic" subject matter or diction. The Whitman influence was so sweeping, indeed, that, in his comments on the poet in the sixth edition of his translation, Chukovsky remarked that

> the poetry of Whitman has emerged from the covers of his small book and become an air that many poets in Russia breathe. . . . In recent years, since the Revolution, the influence of Whitman has spread so widely that it is impossible (and, indeed, unnecessary) to point to individual poets who are not under his influence.

And, as in the prewar period, students and poets began to organize literary circles in his name.

In the years after 1929 and the implementation of the first Five Year Plan, the Russian literary scene was shaken by controversies over "content" and "form" and "socialist realism." One group maintained that writers should be allowed to experiment with form and content as much as they pleased, while another group, and the dominant one, insisted that writers should reject the "formalism" of the past and concentrate on realist reporting of the Five Year Plan and the emerging Soviet social order. Throughout these battles, Whitman maintained his position of esteem, and in 1931, at the height of the controversy over "formalism," Chukovsky's *List'ya Travy* (*Leaves of Grass*) was issued in an edition of 20,000 copies. In the following year, the eighth edition, *Uot Uitmen: Izbrannye Stihotvoreniya* (*Walt Whitman: Selected Poems*), was issued in 3,000 copies, with an introduction by A. Lunacharsky, now a commissar of education. The ninth edition, *List'ya Travy: Izbrannye Stihi i Poemy* (*Leaves of Grass: Selected Poems*), was published in 1935 in a printing of 10,300 copies.

Chukovsky, however, refused to use Whitman for Communist propaganda. He continued to translate and admire him, but one sign that he may have begun a reevaluation is that in the 1935 edition he used Count D. S. Mirsky's essay, "Poet of American Democracy," as a preface (see selection 2); Mirsky's essay also appeared in an English edition of *Leaves of Grass* published in 1936, in a printing of twenty-five hundred copies, by the Cooperative Publishing Society of Foreign Workers in the U.S.S.R. Mirsky did not think that Whitman anticipated Communism; in fact, he called him "the last great poet of the bourgeois era of humanity, the last in the line that began with Dante." Although Whitman tried to be "the poet of democracy" before the Civil War, he had to admit in the 1870s that America had not attained democracy, although he still hoped that might be possible in future "Vistas."

The settled Russian view of Whitman during the 1930s and 1940s was that he was the greatest American poet and a remarkable product of American middle-class democracy of the nineteenth century. Marxist critics saw his contradictions as reflecting the contradictions of his age, as stemming from the impossibility of joining democratic idealism to a capitalist order bent on destroying democracy. An expression of this view can be found in volume 2 of the Soviet *Literaturnaya Entsiklopediya* (*Literary Encyclopedia*), edited by P. I. Lebedev-Polyansky and I. M. Nusinov:

> That book [*Leaves of Grass*], the intellectual-artistic credo of Whitman, was created in an epoch that was unusually stormy and rich in social movements. It was the poetic prelude to the civil war of North and South, which cleared the path for capitalist expansion. But that expansion also limited the democracy of the American bourgeoisie in the 1950s.
>
> The work of Whitman — the poet of the petty bourgeois democracy of that epoch — expresses unprecedented progress in the technical power of the bourgeoisie, its conquest of the forces of nature, and, at the same time, the illusions of the American democracy. . . .
>
> The realism of his poetry does not exclude a deep inner contradiction in his world view. Whitman himself did not know where humanity called him: to the big cities of stone and steel or to the solitude of nature. . . .
>
> And although Whitman, of course, was not a Socialist, the sense of collectivism is expressed with such power in his poetry that we can count him with us in our epoch of struggle for the classless society; the progressive ideas of Whitman, such as his affirmation of labor, cannot but find a response in the Soviet reader.

A similar view was expressed in 1942 by the anonymous authors of *Luchshie Predstaviteli Angliiskoi i Amerikanskoi Literatury* (*The Best Representatives of English and American Literature*):

> Whitman expressed the pathos and optimism of the American radical democracy in the middle of the nineteenth century. Toward the end of his life Whitman was disillusioned about the possibility of universal brotherhood within the framework of capitalist society.

Throughout the commentary on Whitman in the 1930s and 1940s one can also find a note of genuine affection for a poet who had played so important a role in Russian cultural history during the days of the revolution. A feeling of nostalgia crept into articles written in 1939 to commemorate the 120th anniversary of the poet's birth, a feeling one can find underlining much of what Chukovsky had to say in an essay on Whitman that appeared in the *Literaturnaya Gazeta* (*Literary Gazette*) of June 10, 1939. Chukovsky gave his readers an impression of Whitman's great role in Russian literary history in the 1910s and 1920s, noted his fame and popularity (as M. Zverev did, too, in the *Moscow News* of June 5, 1939), and named him comrade in the antifascist crusade.

The tenth and last edition of Chukovsky's translations from Whitman was announced for publication as early as 1939, but it made its appearance as *Uolt Uitman: Izbrannye Stihotvorenniya i Proza* (*Walt Whitman: Selected Poetry and Prose*) only in 1944, toward the end of the Second World War, when relations with the United States were especially cordial. The work was issued in an edition of ten thousand copies. Unfortunately, as the title indicates, the book contained only selections from Walt Whitman; it was not complete. It still remains for some writer in Russia to give the reading public a complete translation of *Leaves of Grass*.

In the 1940s Chukovsky's loyalty to a Communist state was severely tested and undermined by attacks on him; he was a victim of the Soviet psychology, and Lenin's widow censured him for defending fairy tales for children and writing poems for them which had no obvious utilitarian value.[7] He survived the attacks and miraculously escaped Stalin's purges, perhaps partly because he shifted his literary criticism to interpretations of the great nineteenth-century Russian authors, whom even the Communists still revered. Ironically, he may have been partly protected also by the popularity of his books for children, the very books he had been attacked for, which every Russian family possessed and which most adored. But some of his best friends were not so lucky, notably Isaac Babel, Osip Mandelstam, Boris Pasternak, and Andrei Sakharov, who were imprisoned and tortured. He further exposed himself to danger by trying to help and defend these men.[8]

During the relaxation of state persecution of dissenters during Kruschev's leadership, Chukovsky was awarded the Lenin Prize, and Oxford University gave him an honorary D.Lit. degree for his translations of British and American authors. Michael Scammell, Solzhenitsyn's biographer, says Chukovsky survived Stalinism "physically intact and morally uncompromised." Chukovsky gave a speech at the 1955 centennial celebration of the first edition of *Leaves of Grass*, sponsored by the Academy of the Soviet Union (other speeches were given by the secretary of the Union of Soviet Writers and by Maurice Mendelson, the second most prominent interpreter of Whitman in Russia). But Chukovsky lost favor again with the Soviet government when he defended Pasternak after he won the Nobel Prize in 1958 and was forbidden to receive it and again two years later when he praised Pasternak at his funeral (Pasternak, a great admirer of Whitman, once addressed a poem to Chukovsky that ended with "a bear hug / For your gift of Whitman" — see selection 3).[9] Chukovsky was still out of official favor when he died in 1969. In 1980 an edition of his letters was sabotaged in a government printing office.

One might think that Whitman would flourish in Russia under *glasnost*. But it is very difficult to obtain information about his reception during the late 1980s. Chukovsky published his *My Walt Whitman* in 1966, and Maurice Mendelson's *Life and Work of Walt Whitman: A Soviet View* came out in 1976. This latter book has much valuable critical and bibliographical information about Whitman in

Russia, but it has the Soviet "spin"—Whitman is viewed as a proletarian poet (see selection 4). In 1986 Yassen Zassoursky, dean of the School of Journalism at Moscow State University, ended an essay on "Whitman's Reception and Influence in the Soviet Union" with the prediction: "In view of the Soviet Union's long-standing interest in Whitman we can safely predict a prolonged life for Whitman in the Russian language, in Russian literature, and in our Soviet culture." However, by 1990 visitors to Russia could not find a single copy of Chukovsky's translations in any bookstore in Leningrad.

Zassoursky suggested in 1986 some of the ways *glasnost* writers were reconstructing Whitman, and he described the growing popularity of Whitman in the Soviet Union in the 1980s:

> Recent Soviet critics have tried to revise the view that Whitman was a realist, saying that he was a Romantic. Also, better translations of Whitman have appeared. Twenty poets were invited to collaborate on a complete translation of Whitman's *Leaves of Grass*. The book, published in 1982, contributed greatly to the popularity of Whitman. All in all, since the 1917 revolution, twenty-eight editions of Walt Whitman have been published in our country. . . . Whitman has been translated into twelve languages besides Russian. Our country is a multinational country, and we have a lot of literatures; we have about one hundred languages. Although we have a long way to go to make Whitman read by all the ethnic groups in our country, Whitman is now available to most people in the Soviet Union.[10]

Paradoxically, though, as Russians attain more freedom, they seem to have less use for the American "poet of freedom," though this may be partly because the Communists praised him and he is therefore suspect. Evidently Whitman's future in Russia depends upon the outcome of the political struggle—and possibly upon a new anti-Communist (or post-Communist) translator. Still, given his influence on generations of Russian poets, it is not an exaggeration to say that Whitman is now a Russian as well as an American author.

NOTES

1. This essay originally appeared in Gay Wilson Allen, ed., *Walt Whitman Abroad* (Syracuse: Syracuse University Press, 1955), 144–155. It has been updated and expanded by Gay Wilson Allen.

2. Walt Whitman, "Two Letters," in *Complete Poetry and Collected Prose* (New York: Library of America, 1982), 1049.

3. Kornei I. Chukovsky, "Turgenev i Whitman, *Literatura Rossiya* 2 (July 28, 1967): 17; I. Christova, "Turgenev i Whitman," *Russkaya literatura* 2 (1966): 196–199.

4. Since Latvia was at this time a part of the Russian Empire, it should be noted that a Lettish translation of Whitman by Roberts Skarga, *Sahlu Steebri* (*Leaves of Grass*), was issued in Riga in 1908.

5. A. Lunacharsky, "Whitman i Demokratia" ("Whitman and Democracy"), in Kornei I. Chukovsky, *Poeziya Gryadushchei Demokratii* (*The Poetry of the Future Democracy*) (Petrograd, 1918), 150–153.

6. Yassen Zassoursky, "Whitman's Reception and Influence in the Soviet Union," in Geoffrey Sill, ed., *Walt Whitman of Mickle Street* (Knoxville: University of Tennessee Press, 1994), 286, 289.

7. Lydia Chukovskaya, *To the Memory of Childhood* (Evanston: Northwestern University Press, 1988), 151.

8. Chukovskaya, *Memory of Childhood*, 154. Lydia Chukovskaya, Chukovsky's daughter, suffered more than her father for defending persecuted writers. Her organized support for Joseph Brodsky helped him gain release from a Soviet state farm, but she could not prevent his deportation. She also aided the great poet Anna Akhmatova, whose son was killed in prison and whose husband was tortured to death. Chukovskaya's novel about this experience, *Going Under*, was smuggled out of the country and published in the West but was banned in Russia until 1988. In a postscript to her memoir of her father, Chukovskaya reported that in 1988 she was still battling with the Soviet Union of Writers for control of the museum in Peredelkino, where her father's library is preserved.

9. For more on Chukovsky, see Gay Wilson Allen, "Kornei Chukovsky, Whitman's Russian Translator," in Sill, *Walt Whitman*, 276–282.

10. Zassoursky, "*Whitman's Reception*," 288–289.

1. ANONYMOUS REVIEW

"The Poet of Democracy: Walt Whitman"

In his book *Poetry of the Future Democracy*, K. Chukovsky provides a brilliant characterization of the work of Walt Whitman, the American poet, who commands enthusiastic followers in Western Europe and little fame among us.

"I believe that my book is timely," writes K. Chukovsky in the introduction. "We can dislike Walt Whitman, if we choose, but we must, at any rate, know him. Europe has already made use of him. Without him the history of world literature would be incomplete. In France, especially, there has been in recent years a strengthening of the cult of his spirit. . . . All poetry has turned in the direction pointed out by the American poet.

"I believe it is inevitable that the American bard will play an important role in our poetry too. Unfortunately, my efforts to make his works known in Russia have had little success up to now. Perhaps this small book will finally win a response."

We cite some of the most striking passages from K. Chukovsky's beautiful book:

"Regardless of our wishes, one of these days, if not today then tomorrow, we shall be forced to face the problem of democracy and cope with it in some way. In Europe, as in America, the springs of inspiration had dried up. Classical antiquity and medieval romanticism could no longer nourish contemporary art. Literature and art, if they were to maintain their position, had to adapt themselves to new, to changing conditions. They were compelled to find a new faith—not in an esthetic, a style, a rhythm, but in their mission, their destiny: to give concrete and forceful embodiment to the new life, to its religion and essence, and to do so as powerfully as the Greek sculptors expressed paganism and the Italian artists medieval Catholicism."

Whitman undertook to accomplish this grandiose task, asserts the author of the cited book. He was the first to understand and to declare that in our renascent world it is necessary that democracy have a religious pathos, a religious ecstasy of its own—even though in secret—and he boldly announced himself the first priest of that universal religion. That secret faith was for him the road that democracy must take, and when, at times, he saw, with amazement, that despite enormous successes in the achievement of purely material prosperity democracy failed to realize its religious potentialities, he was prepared to turn his back on it. "It is as if someone had given us an enormous body and a small soul or none at all," he wrote in such a moment. The tremendous struggle of workers for better wages left him indifferent: their meetings, parties, proclamations, and strikes were not mirrored in his book. "According to you, dear friend," he wrote in one of his manifestoes, "democracy is achieved if there are elections, politics, various party slogans, and nothing else. As for myself, I believe that the present role of democracy begins only when she goes farther and farther. . . . Her real and permanent grandeur is her religion; otherwise she has no grandeur."

Just as the people contain all, assimilating all nations, climates, ages, points of view, natures, religions, so the democratic bard rejects nothing and no one in the world:

I left no one at the door, I invited all;
The thief, the parasite, the mistress—these above all I called—
I invited the slave with flabby lips
And invited the syphilitic!

In former ages no one ever dreamed of such mindless expansiveness. "I am both white and black, and belong to every caste—mine is every faith—I am a farmer, gentleman, mechanic, artist, sailor, Quaker, criminal, visionary, brawler, lawyer, priest, and physician. . . ." This sense of one's multiplicity, this identification with everyone—here we have the first great expression of the personality of the democratic bard.

He never forgot, even for a moment, that around him were myriads of worlds and behind him were myriads of centuries. In each drop he saw the ocean; in each second he sensed eternity. Nothing petty, nothing small! He had a soul like a telescope: he knew only the far and the wide. "I am only a period, only an atom in the floating desert of the world"—such was his inexhaustible sense of things. . . .

There is neither better nor worse—no hierarchy!—all things, all acts, all feelings are equal and right, and a cow, dully chewing her cud, is as beautiful as the

Venus of Melos; and a small leaf of grass is no less than the ways of the sky's planets; and to see a pod of peas transcends the wisdom of the ages; and the soul is not more than the body, and the body not more than the soul; and one may pray to the bug and to manure: they are as worthy of prayer as the very holiest of holies. Everything is divine and everything is equal:

I'm glad for all the weeds that grow; I'm ready to water them!

Or do you say that the laws of the universe are wrong and must be changed?

A frog is a masterpiece; there can be none greater! And a mouse is a miracle
    which can stagger sextillions of infidels!

I do not call the turtle evil because it is only a turtle.

Because you are greasy or pimpled, or were once drunk, or a thief,
Or that you are diseas'd, or rheumatic, or a prostitute,
Or from frivolity or impotence, or that you are no scholar and never saw your
    name in print,
Do you give in that you are any less immortal?

Life is as beautiful as death; honor as good as dishonor. Victory and defeat are one. "Have you heard that it is good to win and to conquer? I tell you that defeat is good too! It is all the same: to destroy or to be destroyed!"

Universal equality, identity! And science, toward which every microbe and vibrio contributes as much as the greatest among us in this universal life, and according to which the metals and gases under my feet are he same as those on the farthest suns, and even the erratic comet moves by the same laws as the ball of a playing girl — science strengthens, broadens the contemporary spirit's democratic feeling of equality.

For the poet it has come to this, that he speaks for whatever he sees: and this is I! — and here we have no scheme, no formula, but the living human sensibility. He feels in every nerve his equality with everything and everyone. . . .

"I have no amorous stanzas for women with stomach aches! Away with the sweetness of meter!" shouted the American bard — and spent several years cutting out of his work all the effects and embellishments of ordinary verse, seeing them as servants of a dead feudal culture, the heritage of an aristocratic world.

"We have in America such mad storms, such mighty men, such tremendous events; we have the largest oceans, the highest mountains, limitless prairies — how, then, can we tolerate these soft, pretty dolls, made with flabby fingers! . . ." he said of American letters. "The awakening of the people and the destruction of social barriers served as a call to contemporary poetry, and unconsciously I answered it."

In the name of democracy he rejected the heroes of the old balladry, all former themes, the old esthetic:

"Muse, migrate from Greece, give up Ionia, the stories of Troy; stop singing of

Achilles' wrath, of the wanderings of Odysseus and Aeneas! Affix this placard on Parnassus: *Removed. To Let.*

"My purpose is to invest the gray masses of America with that shining greatness and heroism with which the Greek and feudal poets invested their gods and heroes."

Traditional poetry was nailed up in a coffin. "The locomotive has its own rhythm, the streets of Chicago resound differently from the ancient pastures of Arcadia." Whitman regarded himself as the greatest reformer of versification, "the Richard Wagner of poetry," and it is indeed remarkable that the finest esthetes, traditionalists, guardians of classic canons now speak enthusiastically of his daring rebellion against standards of traditional beauty.

But I fear that the singer of the gray multitude, among whom everyone is equal, among whom all are as one and one as all, does not see or distinguish *separate* human beings.

If he regards Hamlet as identical with Chichikov and Shakespeare as Smerdyakov's twin, then we are dealing not with Shakespeare or Hamlet or personalities but with some sort of statistics or algebra that is both horrible and oppressive.

If the poetry of the future is to be found in this depersonalized personality, then I do not want either poetry or the future!

I would not give up even the nose of Cyrano de Bergerac, the famous fundamental nose without which Bergerac is not Bergerac, or even the hunchback of Quasimodo, or the scent of Petrouchka, for these are distinguishing traits — and I find it painful to read poems dedicated to the First Met.

"I celebrate each one and everyone and love anyone!" the poet reiterates continually, and he does not look at the person whom he celebrates. Why should he look, if everyone is alike? The First Met, some depersonalized personality, is the new Aeneas, the Ulysses of the future democratic epoch, and all we know about him is that he is like a million others. . . . But no, he is not a single person:

He is not alone!
He is the father of those who themselves become fathers!
A many-peopled kingdom flourishes inside him, proud, rich republics,
And do you know who stems from the descendants of his descendants?

And the woman whom he praises is a general woman, everybody's woman, and not this one or that one, marked by a mole, who has the most distinctive and peculiar gait in the world. He sees her as a productive womb, but does not sense the fascination of her personality.

"I pour myself into you!" he declares to his lovers: "For thousands and thousands of years I shall be incarnated through you!" We hear of thousands more, of ages and ages as yet unknown; will Juliet or even the latest "doll" consent to serve her Romeo for all these nameless, incarnate centuries?

When you love—how powerfully, how keenly, you sense the individuality of the loved one, her singularity, her "inequality with anyone":

This hair-line running to the left
Is the only one in the world;
This childish, wistful glance
Is singular and best.

But can one discern anything *singular* in these crowds, legions, billions of the loving, compassionate poet? Here he is blind, and hopelessly blind. "Out of the ocean of humanity, out of the roaring sea a droplet splashed and whispered: I love you"—this is his experience of love.

From the world turn to the ocean, my love;
I, too, am but a drop in the ocean. . . .

And, characteristically, when he wished to mourn the death of President Lincoln, he mourned for all those who are dead, for every death, and the personality of the great warrior found no place at all in his majestic poem. He is the wholesale poet of the herd! And the enemies of democracy exult: what else can one expect of poets of the crowd, of the commonplace and the ordinary!

"O divine average! O divine banality, platitude!" he shouts defiantly, and because of his scorn for individuality many are led to speculate as to the failure and bankruptcy of democratic taste.

Now these many, happily enough, are in error, and I am as wrong as they are. The poetry of democracy is especially the poetry of personality! Never before has personality been expressed so impetuously, so enchantingly, as in this bard of the gray, undistinguished mass! And the first personality that he celebrates is himself:

I celebrate myself, I sing myself!

I am divine both inside and outside; I look into a mirror, and I see God before me (even though the mirror reveals a disheveled man, without a neck-tie, with a swollen neck).

Isn't this the revolt of personality, unbridled, satanic, Promethean? The poet falls before the mirror and kisses his reflection as the image of God.

I too work wonders.

I am not the enemy of revelation and the Bible: the smallest hair on my hands is a revelation and a Bible.

He is ready to build himself a shrine and perform his own liturgy and cry out on every side that all the universe is one and that he is the center of all worldviews: "It is for me, earth, that you have set forth these flowering apple trees which now perfume the air. . . ."

Ascending sun, blindingly bright, how soon you would have destroyed me,
If the sun inside me had not ascended to meet you!

He has bought up all the gods, they are in his pocket, and on every altar before which people worship he sits sacrilegiously in order to banter with the gray, equal multitude which he has just sanctified. . . . He is not false to them; he does not betray.

You are side by side with me on the throne — we are one, whoever you are,
    and if you glance into the mirror you, too, will see God there.

Now what if one sees mean little eyes in the mirror, the face of a syphilitic, a hangman, or an idiot? Is this indeed God? It is! Psalms and exaltation are due to the most abominable among us! Odes! Hymns!

You do not know of yourself how great you are!

Oh, I do not celebrate anyone in my poems, not even God, if I do not cele-
    brate you!
No one has so fine a gift that you do not possess it too, or such beauty, or such
    goodness as you already have!

"These measureless prairies! These boundless rivers! You are measureless and boundless like them!" he assures everyone: the first met, the idiot, the hangman, the syphilitic. And soon not a single human being is left on earth: all have been transformed into gods. The old ikon painters placed a golden crown on one Head and left all others dark and uncrowned; on the poet's ikonostasis there are numberless crowds of heads, and each has a golden halo. The former God-man has been replaced with a throng of man-gods; they swarm on the street, in the stores, on the Exchange, and each of them is a messiah, each has come from heaven to work miracles, and each is himself a wonder incarnate. In this, then, lies the triumph of democracy, that she considers every man Unique, that she not only does not scorn personality but, indeed, brings it out and sanctifies it. The wails of the fearful have been meaningless:

Huns! Vandals! Save yourselves, those who can: run. They are crushing,
    destroying us!

Well, the Huns came, and they not only failed to crush anyone, but — according to their poet — they said to all: you are divine. It is precisely for that reason that the poet joins Derzhimord, Schiller, Smerdyakov, and Hamlet under the same crown: he senses, he plainly sees, that at the root, in their mystic essence—under deceptive covers—their souls are equal, alike, similarly divine, immortal, and beautiful; and he denies that the envelope of the soul distinguishes Smerdyakov from Schiller. Remove the shell, the husk, dispel the mirage, and only then will you see their authentic, eternal personalities. Only then will you realize that the famous nose of Bergerac and the scent of Petrouchka and the mole of Karamazov's Grushenka and the genius of great men and the vulgarity of the vulgar are not aspects of personality, the expression of personality, but masks behind which it hides. Our individuality begins where our particular traits end, and through checkered and many-imaged veils the poet sees everyone's unique soul:

> Whoever you are, I fear you are walking the walks of dreams,
> I fear these supposed realities are to melt from under your feet and hands,
> Even now your features, joys, speech, house, trade, manners, troubles, follies,
>   costume, crimes, dissipate away from you,
> Your true soul and body appear before me,
>
> They stand forth out of affairs, out of commerce, shops, work, farms, clothes,
>   the house, buying, selling, eating, drinking, suffering, dying. . . .
> The mockeries are not you,
> Underneath them and within them I see you lurk,
> I pursue you where none else has pursued you.

In these magnificent words the poet gives us the eternal, granite basis for the development of democratic equality: a belief in the mystic essence of man's immortal ego—so that democracy might "with flower, fruit, radiance, and divinity achieve true humanity" and strengthen the new religion of universal divinity.

Democracy has given mankind a new word: comrade. The sense that we are the soldiery of some Great Army which goes from victory to victory without Napoleons and marshals has sprouted in the people who fill the public squares, theaters, banks, universities, restaurants, cinemas, street-cars of today's teeming cities.

Now this wonderful sense which, as we know, the poet felt so strongly that it drew him to the wounded and dying in hospitals, wards for infectious diseases, fields washed by blood—this sense has not yet found full expression in contemporary poetry. The chivalrous adoration of woman, proper to the Middle Ages, the cult of the Beautiful Lady which ennobled sexual love and achieved social refinement, is now insufficient: the future of humanity needs a cult, too—the cult of the comrade, the cult of democratic union, for a new tenderness suffuses the hearts of men, a love of the fellow warrior, co-worker, fellow traveler, of him who journeys with us shoulder to shoulder and takes part in the general movement; it is this still weak feeling, this embryo or beginning of feeling, that the poet strengthened in his gigantic soul, brought to flame, to passion, to that all-encompassing, grand emotion with which, as he believed, he transfigured himself in a vision of the world triumph of democracy.

He anticipated the future even in this. And if today his odes to comrades, to those whom he called *camerado*, seem unreal, strange, and remind one of serenades to a lover — they are excessively pleading and flamingly affectionate — that is so because the days have not yet come when our hearts, too, can flame with such magnificent passion.

There is a whole anthology of these strange love poems in his book.

Words have not yet been found for such a feeling. The formal word *comradeship* does not express it. This is a burning, stormy, almost alarming love of man for man, and without it, as the poet believed, democracy is only a shadow, an illusion.

"These lovers will have full freedom, these comrades will have full equality. Or do you ask that some public official join you as comrades? Or do you wish some sort of agreement on paper? Or force? No, no one in the whole world or in the universe can bind you so."

Now it is clear why the fratricide and bloodshed of Europe drew this request from the bard:

I'd like a poem from over the sea:
You, heart of free hearts!

More than all contemporary poets he is the singer of joy, the hopeful messenger of future happiness; and what do we tired, impoverished, degenerate souls need today if not this new gospel of universal divinity, universal beauty, and universal happiness?

Review of *Poeziya Gryadushchei Demokratii: Uot Uitmen*, 2d ed., trans. Kornei I. Chukovsky, *Biulleteni Literaturi i Zhizni* (*Bulletins of Literature and Life*) 22 (July 1914): 1253–1258. Translated by Stephen Stepanchev.

2. D. S. MIRSKY

"Poet of American Democracy"

I

Walt Whitman is the last great poet of the bourgeois era of humanity, the last in the line that began with Dante. Just as the appearance of Dante marked the birth of a new, freer, more progressive age in that country which was the first to start breaking from its feudal prison, so did Whitman's appearance in the youngest of the great capitalistic nations mark the latest historic moment at which it was possible still to believe in the triumph of bourgeois ideals of humankind and, strong in such a faith, to discover the soil for a great poetry. . . .

II

Whitman is the poet of American democracy of the fifties and sixties, in all of its organic strength. He gives poetic voice to democracy's illusion that a new humanity has already been born, one that has but to grow and develop normally; his is the highest expression that we have of such illusions. But with all of his genius, he bears the indelible brand of that democracy's anti-revolutionary and provincial character.

The individual quality of Whitman's poetry derives in good part from the strange and even weird combination that we find in it of originality and inspired daring, in a choice of themes never before treated by poets, with a provincial naïveté that is utterly incapable of beholding itself through the eyes of others. Out of this provincialism comes a break with the culture of the past and the poet's obstinate depiction of himself as prophet and preacher. Such a provincialism, obviously tinged by and akin to religious sectarianism, enabled Whitman to build up out of the illusions of American democracy a system which to him presented the same appearance as had that historic order which was based upon the religions of the past. If on the one hand Whitman is a brother spirit to Dante and Goethe, his other affinities would include such individuals as Brigham Young, leader of the Mormon sect, and the founder of "Christian Science," Mrs. Eddy.

Being a systematization of far-flung illusions, pointing to a luminous future to be evolved out of a present that was bubbling with life and energy, Whitman's ideology was a reasoned admixture of materialistic and mystical elements. Taking an environment that was ready at hand, in the fullness of its sweep and scope, with all of its material and practical implications, as a high and authentic reality, Whitman was unable to grasp that reality in its true revolutionary unfoldment. His optimism was not based upon a correct and active comprehension of what lay wrapped up in all this energy, and so, had need of a "higher" strength by way of support. While his point of departure was materialism, he could not avoid falling back upon mystic pantheism. He felt the need of an imminent god, the "soul" of matter. This soul was in the nature of a pledge, to the effect that all was making for a brighter future, that all was right with the world and moving in a necessary direction, one that would assure a better order of things. Whitman's mystical pantheism was an expression not alone of that illusory character of his ideals, but of their anti-revolutionary character as well. Animate nature might be left to see to the progress of her off-spring.

At the same time, however, it is Whitman's democratic pantheism, which underlying that cult of the common man, constitutes the fundamental pathos of his poetry. In his pantheism, he is not highly original, nor does he stand alone among democratic (and pseudo-democratic) ideologists of the nineteenth and twentieth centuries. Optimistic in outlook, this pantheism is sharply inimical to the old dogmatic religions; but it is nonetheless definitely religious in mental attitude and definitely mystical in world-view; in substance, it is above all a popularization of the philosophy of bourgeois democracy. The kernel is from the contemplative

D. S. Mirsky [321]

Rousseau, while Hugo, in his historiosophic poems, supplies an embodiment which in poetic strength is second only to Whitman's own. A plain traveler, this, in that stream of petty bourgeois thought that gravitates toward socialism, one which, in our own time, was to be given a notably vulgarized, though for a wide circle of the petty bourgeoisie, an extremely effective expression in the Saint Joan of Bernard Shaw.

The mystical basis of Whitman's system will be found set forth with the utmost clarity in the fifth section of the poem "Walt Whitman," in a language which is quite familiar to all who possess an acquaintance with the "classics" of mysticism.

Whitman's mysticism, however, was not uprooted from materialism; just as democratic illusions regarding the future still had their roots in the reality of present-day democracy. It was a spontaneous, idealistic outgrowth of materialistic premises that were true enough, even as the illusions were swift-growing, optimistic offshoots of real conditions. Whitman very definitely extols science and that knowledge of the world which it affords. But science was not sufficient. In addition to it, there must be a "higher knowledge": in the Foreword to the edition of 1876, he wrote:

> Only (for me, at any rate, in all my prose and poetry) joyfully accepting modern science, and loyally following it without the slightest hesitation, there remains ever recognized still a higher flight, a higher fact, the eternal soul of man (of all else too) the spiritual, the religious. . . .

One can no more shut his eyes to the anti-revolutionary character of Whitman's ideology than one can to his mysticism. His position in American democracy was not on the extreme Left. If a man like John Brown, striving with a handful of companions to stage a slave uprising, is an exceptional and well-nigh solitary figure, the Whitman of before the war stands definitely apart, not only from a John Brown, but from the abolition movement of the world, which was fighting to do away with slavery by legal means.

Whitman's democracy, organically and in deepest essence, was nationalistic. Democracy for him was something specifically American. He accepted it as something already existent in the nature of the American people and needing only to be brought to light. At the beginning, he believed — as a present-day prophet — that the publication of *Leaves of Grass* would be the signal for the discovery of a true democracy. Later on, in the seventies, he had to confess that America of the present was yet far from the ideal; but all the same, he continued to assert that

> . . . the morbid facts of American politics and society everywhere are but passing incidents and flanges of our unbounded impetus of growth . . . weeds, annuals, of the rank, rich soil—not central, enduring, perennial things. . . .

At the same time, he had learned that

> . . . the true growth-characteristics of the democracy of the New World are henceforth to radiate in superior literary, artistic and religious expressions, far more than in its republican forms, universal suffrage and frequent elections. . . .

Thus it was, Whitman was led to that assertion of the inferiority of politics, its lack of worth as compared to "higher values," which is to be met with in Shelley, and which is so characteristic for the whole of non-democratic humanism. His historic world-view will be found expressed, in extremely concise form, in the following verses, bearing the curious subtitle "After Reading Hegel" (the title is "Roaming in Thought"):

Roaming in thought over the Universe, I saw the little that is Good steadily
    hastening toward immortality,
And the vast all that is call'd Evil I saw hastening to merge itself and become
    lost and dead.

In America, the "little that is Good" was already at work and might be left to complete its task to the fullest extent. As for other peoples, Whitman, like American democracy as a whole, sympathized with them in their struggle with kings and feudal barons. He occasionally sings the praises of the French Revolution, and he extends greetings to the émigré rebel of 1848 (for Whitman, "The 72d and 73d Years of These States"). But his sympathy is purely a passive one, and the class war never comes within the range of Whitman's themes. If the Southern slaveholders were his enemies, it was not because they were slaveholders, but for the reason that they had wanted to cease being Americans.

Human brotherhood meant for Whitman, depending upon the direction it took, two very different things. In the one case, it was something wholly concrete and related to life, an emotional brotherhood with the "mass" of "average" Americans round about him. In the other case, it was a pantheistic feeling of fraternal sympathy with each and every human being, and—what is more—with every living creature and with all matter. This latter sentiment is thoroughly passive, and is unaccompanied by any arduous desire to struggle for a real, democratic brotherhood of peoples. It is measurably nearer to Christian brotherhood than it is to a communistic solidarity of workers. If there was in Whitman, in relation to his brother Americans, an active "love of comrades," one that is given an inspired lyric expression in his verse and a practical application in his hospital work during the years 1861–1865, his feeling of brotherhood, on the other hand, toward mankind in general, toward men of another race or class than his own (e.g., the slave), was no more than a "survival," no more than an "inner experience." He is conscious of a fraternal, pantheistic identity with the fugitive slave; indeed, he migrates into the slave's body and soul ("Song of Myself," section 99); and the verses he has given us on this subject are among the strongest that we have from his pen.[1] Yet, earlier in this same poem (section 16), speaking of his sense of universal identity, he is equally one with the slaveholder: "A southerner soon as a northerner—a planter nonchalant and hospitable; down by the Oconee I live." In his no less inspired "I Sing the Body Electric," he speaks thus of the sale of a slave at auction:

A man's body at auction;
I help the auctioneer—the sloven does not half know his business.

Gentlemen, look on this wonder!
Whatever the bids of the bidders, they cannot be high enough for it. . . .

Back of man's vileness and degradation, Whitman beholds his native grandeur, but in such a manner that the vileness and degradation are skimmed off, as an inferior and unauthentic reality, and so, ceasing to exist, are no longer an occasion for struggle. This is precisely the path followed by Christian thought, which announces that "there is neither slave nor free man, Greek nor Jew, but that all are children of the heavenly father and the partakers of his glory."

It is not possible to disavow or gloss over these aspects of Whitman's as being the inconsistencies and contradictions of an insufficiently thought out system of reasoning. For Whitman's ideology is fully thought out and rounded. Its contradictions are the organic and unavoidable ones to be found in all bourgeois thinking. It is one that is still held, in the full force of its implications, by all social idealists and left-revolutionists. We are, accordingly, obliged to adopt a critical attitude toward it. For it would be a gross distortion to attempt to cover over its anti-revolutionary and mystical aspects, and to behold in Whitman a seer with the brain of a proletarian revolutionist, looking forward to a classless society of the future. If his ideology is a democratic one, his brand of democracy is thoroughly bourgeois.

However, we do not judge writers and thinkers of the past by their ideologies, nor by that element of the ephemeral and the nationalistic which is inevitably to be met within each of them; we judge them rather by what is progressive and enduring in their work.[2] This progressive and enduring element in the case of Whitman is his poetry.

III

The basis of Whitman's art lies in a vanquishing of Romanticism upon its own ground, that of "exalted" poetry. Arising out of a protest against the realistic path taken by the French Revolution and by capitalism in its development, Romanticism affirmed a break between knowledge and the ideal. Leading poetry out of the concrete real of today, it proceeded to confer upon it a heavenly-incorporal or retrospective character. This attitude was a widespread one; it is to be found not merely in a few Romanticists, but throughout the whole of nineteenth-century poetry in Europe. The contemporary scene — political, economic, and technological — might make its way into the poet's pages only when symbolically transmuted, only when trigged out in a more or less precapitalistic garb. Even where, as in Faust, poetry was an expression of underlying forces at work in the present, its gaze was turned aside from the element of concrete falsity inherent in those forces. Only in the field of satire did it remain realistic in style, preserving a bond of union with the prose of the literary realists. In Russia, Whitman's contemporary, Nekrasov, was at work here, broadening the scope of satire and creating a new poetry.

But satire as a whole was looked down upon, as being of a lower order; and even when they sympathized with its ideas, Nekrasov's countrymen deemed his work of little value from the poetic point of view, holding it to be nothing more than "prose in verse." This orientation of poetry in the direction of realistic prose was marked by a repudiation of the great philosophic themes dealt with by bards of a more exalted kind, and by an abandonment of free lyricism.

In this orientation lay, too, an avowal of the triumph of prose over poetry, of the poet's subdual by capitalistic reality. Don Juan and Germania were not capitulations to a "century hostile to poetry"; they represented a forced understanding to the effect that the century in question was to be combated on its own field, that of prose.

Whitman, breaking sharply with all nineteenth-century poetry, brought a new affirmation of reality, by creating a lofty, lyric interpretation of the present. This it is which is basic and central in his work, rendering it a forerunner of the poetry of socialism. And this affirmation, needless to say, is inseparably bound up with the poet's democratic illusions, with his system of thought. These twin phases of Whitman are wholly different in value. His system provided a logically complete, abstract generalization of environing reality and that future which was reared upon it. His poetry afforded a true and concrete reflection of that same reality. The system put a false estimate upon the internal tendencies of bourgeois democracy. The poems laid bare in the bourgeois-democratic consciousness that humanity which could come to full bloom only under socialism. And that which was false when given an abstract-theoretic generalization thanks to the saving concreteness of art was left standing as a truth.

That reality which Whitman affirmed was a bourgeois reality. But in this affirmation, the poet stressed not that which was essentially bourgeois, but that which was creative and progressive. This spark of the creatively progressive was one that he fanned and nursed; and if in his system the result was a crude distortion of perspectives, in his poetry the sane impulse went to enrich a hyperbolism that is legitimately and organically present in the domain of science.

Whitman keeps telling us, over and over again, that "I celebrate myself." One of his bold and original "sorties" is the calling of himself by his full name in the course of a sustained lyric poem ("Song of Myself"). But in essence, Whitman is as genuine a specimen as any that there is of the impersonal type of poet; the poet in this case is no "lyric hero"; he is without lyric biography; he but gives "choric" expression to feelings and ideas that are not dependent upon any personal destiny. Another especially good example of such a poet in modern times is Schiller; but in contrast to him, Whitman stands out brilliantly by reason of his originality and his innovations. The contemporary scene enters into Schiller's poetry after it has been abstractly purged of its concrete aspect. In Whitman's it is all there, with all of its everyday, prosaic topicality, in all its grime and mire. It is lifted and generalized into poetry, not through any process of abstraction or catharsis, but by means of a symbolic expansion, predicating the importance of the discovery of types and their significance in the scene's lowest and most trivial elements.

Whitman's poetry is profoundly realistic. And like all enduring art of the kind, it is based upon a disclosure of the typical in the individual. Whitman's realism, however, does not consist in an unfoldment of plots and characters such as we know from our reading of the classic realities in the form of the novel.

This is a realism that is achieved by separate strokes, with subjects and incidents neither described nor depicted, but simply and swiftly listed, listed with a definitive concreteness. From the conjunction of these strokes springs Whitman's essential, generalized poetic form — which is, at the same time, that of American democracy.

The quality of Whitman's verse is very uneven. When the poet loses his realistic concreteness, it degenerates into a noisy rhetoric, crude and monotonous in rhythm and yet cruder and more monotonous in its tone, which is like a prolonged, continuous shout. Here belong many declamatory lines which come not so much from the poet as from the prophet and system-builder. Under this head are those verses where Whitman, striving to remain concrete, is led to speak of things that he knows nothing about, inasmuch as they exceed the bounds of his American horizon. Such clumsily rhetorical passages are sometimes redeemed by their unconscious humor. This, for example, may be said to be true of the celebrated poem, "Salut au Monde!," constructed in accordance with his favorite method, that of cataloguing. Whitman's provincialism and lack of cultural background are here evidenced in a fortuitous piling up of appellations for objects and incidents taken from a popular geography and compelled to yield a grandiose and vulgarized picture of present-day humanity in the bulk.

The core of Whitman's work, its rock-bottom, so to speak, will bear comparison with the best poetry that the world has produced. One may mention here such poems as "Song of Myself," "I Sing the Body Electric," "The Sleepers," "Crossing Brooklyn Ferry," "Song of the Broad-Axe," "Out of the Cradle Endlessly Rocking," "Pioneers! O Pioneers!," "When Lilacs Last in the Dooryard Bloom'd" (on the death of president Lincoln), and a whole series of shorter poems, including one so notable for its lyric qualities as "Tears" (from the group "Sea-Drift"), and "Drum-Taps," which is almost a whole collection dealing with the Civil War, 1860–1866. All the pieces mentioned belong to the fifties and sixties, which witnessed the simultaneous dawn of American democracy and of democracy's great poet. In 1873, Whitman suffered a paralytic stroke, which definitely shattered his health. This coincided with America's rapid capitalistic decline and the crushing of that objective optimism which had marked the preceding decades. It was in this period of depression that Whitman's work made its appearance. The last two decades of his life added little to the substance of that work, although those years do include so surprising a poem as "The Dalliance of the Eagles," which contains, it may be, the concentrated essence of his genius, of all that he wrote.

The "Walt Whitman" whom Whitman "celebrated" was not an individual endowed with a definite biography, a definite personality differentiating him from others; he was a metonymical type, the average man, the average American, bringing from out of the American masses the sum and substance of the contemporary scene. The individuality that Whitman hymns is crystallized with precision in the opening lines of the first poem (first in the final group) of his collected verse, "One's Self I Sing." This untranslatable blending of an impersonal "one" with a recurring "self" might be rendered as "the self of everyman," or "everyman's self"; it has a light to throw upon bourgeois democracy, and upon democracy's poet.

The pathos of Whitman's poetry is the pathos of union, equality, human dignity and progress. The artistic expression of these themes in verse is not to be identified with their theoretic development in the ideologic system; the former is not to be viewed in the light of the latter. In thinking out, intellectually, the subjects that he took for his verse, Whitman was led to abandon a poetic concreteness of imagery for a false and one-sided process of abstract generalization which comes as a break in the true pathos of his work. It is Whitman the prophet acting as self-interpreter for Whitman the poet. Inasmuch as it is difficult to demarcate one from the other with exactitude, we should proceed from the premise that the prophet's interpretations not only are not binding upon us, but that they actually interfere with a proper understanding of the poet.

Thus, in connection with the theme of unity, there is no need for us to accept, naively and unquestioningly, the "prophetic" explanation of it, as pantheism. The sentiment of unity with respect to the nation, humanity, the world order is in Whitman a direct lyric expansion of the vital sympathy he felt for the democratic masses. It receives an incarnation in the form of a feeling for the political unity of "These States," as expressed in the war poems, in a concrete feeling of brotherhood with the American who is one of the people — in the theme of "comradeship," as democracy's basic cement. As for the theme of unity as a common link embracing all humanity, while it is given a glowing expression in certain isolated instances (the fugitive slave in "Song of Myself," the episode of the mother and the Indian squaw in "The Sleepers"), it is in general set forth in verses that are abstract rather than realistic. But at the other pole, the theme unfolds in an opulent lyric bloom, in the form of verses on the oneness of nature, the sea and the universe. This motive, indeed, that of a union with material nature, is accorded in Whitman a simpler, more direct and immediately lyric treatment than in any other poet of modern times.

The idea of an actual union with the whole of things attains a highly original peak in the theme of death. In the Whitmanic acceptation, death is a "cool" and happy fusion with the material universe, a conception in which there is no room for weariness or decay. It is a thoroughly optimistic feeling, this, and one that springs from an animating sense of identity of direction, the feeling that each man is traveling a path along which others will continue after him — the classic sense of succession and survival. Nor is it strange if the theme in question stands out with especial clarity in the notable poem written on the death of Abraham Lincoln, leader and hero of American democracy, "When Lilacs Last in the Dooryard Bloom'd" (in particular, the song of the hermit thrush).

D. S. Mirsky [327]

The theme of equality, likewise, enters into Whitman's poetry, as one of its organic and organizing constituents. This it is which at bottom explains the poet's passion for bestowing an exalted lyric treatment upon everything which up to his time had been looked upon as vile and "unworthy of the Muse." Closely related to this are Whitman's realistic innovations and his cataloguing, a method of which he is so fond. With him, the sentiment of equality is especially directed against unilateral affirmation of the "spiritual" man at the expense of the flesh-and-blood being. This theme comes, accordingly, to be closely interwoven with the exaltation of the body, which lends itself to the development of another, broader motive, the forceful revelation and assertion of human dignity. One of the nodal passages in all Whitman's poetry is the famous ninth section of "I Sing the Body Electric," where he applies his inventory method to the parts of the body, from the head to the lower organs, all the way down to the heels, by way of affirming their equal worth with the human consciousness or "soul."

In this dignifying of humankind through the human body, Whitman aligns himself with the followers of Saint-Simon, bent upon a "rehabilitation of the flesh." But in working out the idea poetically, Whitman displays a maximum of originality. The rehabilitation of the flesh, as a counterpoise to Christian repression, had already been brilliantly dealt with by Goethe. Goethe, however, was unable to get along without stylization. Just as in Faust he had need of a Renaissance dress, so in his Roman Elegies and other erotic verse, he still was unable to dispense with antiquity. Like the men of the French Revolution, he felt the necessity of justifying and fortifying himself with the authority of the ancients. In essence, his eroticism comes close to the practical materialism of the Southern slaveholder. A woman for him is above all an object of enjoyment and possession. There is here, as well, a trace of that art for art's sake, all exaggerated development of which is to be seen in Théophile Gautier and — carried further yet — in Rémy de Gourmont. Whitman is free at once of artiness and of stylistic tricks. Beauty to the latter is merely the complete unfoldment of man's nature, one mode of realizing human dignity to the utmost. Of the very warp and woof of Whitman's eroticism is the merging of the physical passions with a sentiment of equality and respect toward womankind, something that is absolutely new in world poetry, even though, ideologically speaking, the Saint-Simonians are the precursors here.[3] Hung upon a lovely poetic thread in "I Sing the Body Electric," this theme is expressed with a definitive concision and in a truly inspired manner in that pearl among poems, "The Dalliance of the Eagles."

And then, finally, there is Whitman's fourth theme, that of the inorganic possibilities unfolding to man's view through a conquest of nature, the theme of democratic expansion and democratic construction, the principal embodiment of which is to be found in the "Song of the Broad-Axe" and in "Pioneers! O Pioneers!" (1856 and 1865, respectively).

One cannot but be struck by the parallel between this motive and our own socialist construction. There are, needless to say, sharp contrasts which are equally striking. Not to speak of the fact that American democratic expansion was essentially predatory, so far as Indians and Mexicans were concerned (a circumstance of which, naturally, no notice is taken in Whitman's poetry), democratic construction, both in reality and in the pages of its bard, was an elementary, one-man affair. But for all of that, in his handling of the theme, Whitman is undoubted forerunner of the poetry of socialism. The chief thing that goes to make him such a harbinger is the fact that he was the first to introduce the theme of labor into poetry, in the form of a creative, lyric statement. Amid all his work, Whitman's poems on the subject of democratic construction come the nearest of all to the ode form. But these are odes of an utterly new kind.

It is not the idea of labor, not labor in general, that finds a place in Whitman's verse, but rather, labor's realistic, concrete, and technical processes. The "Song of the Broad-Axe" may be compared to Schiller's "Song of the Bells," one of the rare instances in bourgeois poetry where such processes are treated in the concrete. In the first place, Schiller singles out work as a theme for the reason that it bears, to begin with, the stamp of religious approval in this case — the labor of casting the bells; in the second place, work is here, in a special sense, precapitalistic, being closely associated with the guild organizations; and lastly, the work of the bell-founders is no more than an allegory, symbolizing a prudent bourgeois progress that knows how to ward off revolutions.

In place of one traditional process, Whitman takes the work of construction in all its range, all the infinite variety of its applications, processes and products. There is no allegory within. No antithesis between the construction of the material object, on the one hand, and, on the other hand, the social construction of democracy. Out of isolated fragmentary images, the "Song of the Broad-Axe" is built up, an endless succession of images, metaphors, instances, fashioned out of the same stuff as constructive democracy. Inventoried with the greatest conciseness and the utmost concreteness, objects and incidents form an impressive generalized image of the whole of democratic America.[4]

Based upon the favored Whitman method, of inventory and catalogue, the poem consists of a number of successive strophes of a cumulative intensity. Following a lyric introduction, the third section serves as a sort of index, being made up of a series of nouns (alluding to objects or actions) with their attributive definitions. This is done in such a way, creatively, that objects and actions stand out in a delimiting sharpness, as if they were parts of a poetic encyclopedia of carpentry that is to function as a symbol of democratic construction in America.

This is followed by a fresh catalogue of objects created by the broad-axe. The construction here is a parallel and again a cumulative one, ranging verbally from monosyllabic nouns like "hut" and "tent" to lengthy adjectives, and ideationally, from the same hut and tent to "Manhattan steamboats and clippers, taking the measure of all seas."

In a third movement, we have the enumeration of no end of objects having to do with the builder's trade, saturated, all of them, with a complex and elevated social content. Starting from simple terms ("factories, arsenals"), the poet goes on to build up a picture out of objects taken as points of departure for incidents replete with social meaning—

> The shape of the step-ladder for the convicted and sentenced murderer, the
> murderer with haggard face and pinion'd arms, . . .
> The door whence the son left home, confident and puff'd up;
> The door he enter'd again from a long and scandalous absence, diseas'd,
> broken down, without innocence, without means.

This movement is rounded off with the significant and unifying "shapes" that mark the national scene—American democracy and its accompaniments.

And thus is constructed a new and unprecedented type of realistic ode, one springing out of an everyday and prosaic reality and catching up the myriad artistic threads of a highly variegated American life.

On the side of form, Whitman shows himself to be a thoroughgoing innovator, breaking completely with an older poetry of a "feudal" Europe and Asia (and its American imitators) and building up a new poetic art from the very beginning. Assuredly, in all the history of art there is no other case of so absolute a break; we shall have to acknowledge that Whitman was a truly great innovator, the greatest that the world of poetry has known.

His innovations in form are directly derived from his novelty of content. This is a fundamental point, involving a liquidation of the dignity of the disparity between the conventional, stylized and retrospective idiom of elevated poetry and the language of the present. Whitman's language is that of the prosaic and democratic scene about him. His democratic speech, however, is of a different order from that of a Mayakovsky[5] or—to stay within Anglo-American precincts—of a Kipling or a Vachel Lindsay. The prose idiom that Whitman employed in bringing new life to poetry was not the colloquial tongue of the street, the factory or the barracks; it was, rather, the language of printed prose, of newspapers and of popular science. Today, when American colloquial speech is at so very far a remove from that of literature, and when, at the same time, it is making such enormous gains in the literary field, the difference between Whitman's poetic vocabulary and that of his contemporaries, such as Emerson and Longfellow, is less noticeable. The truth is, Whitman avoided not only jargon and slang, but, in general, any tendency to colloquial syntax. The linguistic novelty of his poems springs from a new store of themes; the new words that we find there are for the most part the names of objects which up to his time had been held to be unpoetic.

To a considerably less degree dependent upon novelty of content is another fundamental tenet of Whitman's stylistic credo, namely, the avoidance of rhyme and metrics for the sake of rhythm and cadence. The poet's contempt for such "feudal playthings" is an immediate result of the one-sided character of the bond that held him to the democratic masses. Whitman gave expression to the masses, but he did not speak for them. He spoke in their name, but not to them. This was because he failed to realize that poetry written for the masses must first of all be easy-flowing, readily memorizable, and that therefore it must possess a rhythmic transparency of form. Now, in the English language (as in the vast majority of contemporary European tongues, including the Russian), this calls for rhyme. But Whitman — in his own eyes — was first of all a prophet. The important thing was not that the masses should memorize the words of his poems, but that they should adopt his teachings. He was writing, not songs, but books of sermons, scriptures. . . .

IV

In connection with Whitman, we are vividly reminded of what Marx had to say of the capitalistic era's hostility to poetry. Here, we have a poet of genius, bringing us a veracious, substantial, deep-rooted expression of American bourgeois democracy; yet that same democracy did not take him in. He himself, of course, was in part to blame for this, in so far as his poetic form was distinctly anti-popular. But though Whitman may have grievously erred on this question, despite the fact that he was possessed of a profound and structural acquaintance with, and understanding of, the society in which he lived, this but serves to cast into deeper relief the fact that, on all questions save that of poetry, he spoke the same language as democracy's self.

Bourgeois democracy could not accept a poetics such as his. Poetry for it meant "fine" poetry, of the sort purveyed by a Longfellow. Of great poetry, a poetry related to life, it felt no slightest need.

If the unpopularity of Whitman's poetic form was but the fruit of a thoroughly anti-poetic attitude on the part of the bourgeois-democratic masses, this was not any the less of an obstacle to its acceptance by the proletariat. A popular proletarian poet Whitman was not. Instead, he was the favorite of a sufficiently wide circle of the petty bourgeois intelligentsia. His enormous growth in popularity and influence at the close of the nineteenth and the beginning of the twentieth century was closely associated with the growth of those democratic illusions that marked the rise of imperialism.

Notwithstanding all the really new elements that he brought into poetry, it was not possible to appraise Whitman at the start of the new era. As for the history of poetry after Whitman, it is one of degeneration and decline. Verhaeren stands to Whitman in the same relation that European democracy of the imperialistic epoch does to American democracy of the Civil War years. Whitman's direct descendants — the Unanimists in France, Carl Sandburg in America — have taken above all the weaker sides of his poetry, the rhetoric and abstraction of his worst pieces; they have carried these phases still further and have given to the Whitmanic form, yet more of an unpopular character. Whitman is for them Whitman the prophet, not Whitman the poet.

These abstract and rhetorical blemishes go to explain the place that Whitman occupies in proletarian poetry. He is integrally a part of an earlier stage of that poetry's development, when abstractions alike rule with regard to the revolution and to the cosmic process, a view of the world dependent for expression upon a rhetorical form. He was not able to open up a new poetic era in bourgeois society, for the very good reason that, in such a society, there could be no such new era. Down to this day, he does not succeed in reaching the proletariat, inasmuch as he is handed to the masses by petty bourgeois disciples who have taken from him precisely that which is of least worth.

If Whitman did not succeed in inaugurating a new era, he did create a poetry containing much that is not to be found in any of the classic bards of old, and which, without a doubt, brings him near to the proletariat and to socialist man. It was through a statement of environing reality that he did this; and if that reality, as stated by him, is a bourgeois one, he for all of that selected what was most worthwhile and progressive in it — democracy, labor, the conquest of nature. He brought to poetry a new concreteness, a new feeling for the material object, not as an owner aesthetically sensing it, but as the man who works with his hands and who has an interest in the product of his labor. He it was who created the poetry of human dignity, a practical vision of that full man whose fullness is only to be realized under socialism.

It is not as to a prophet with a system that we should come to Whitman, but as to an artist. The important thing is not his views, with their resulting false and theoretic concatenation of ideas, but rather those concrete forms to which he brought all the depth and strength of his emotion, all that he as an artist had learned from the American scene. This is the Whitman who occupies an honorable place with the great poets of the past, who have afforded us — I repeat — a vision of that full man who in reality is only able to exist as, at once, the builder and the creator of constructive socialism.

NOTES

1. The point is to be stressed that Whitman was not a nationalist in practice. The European immigrant was as much a brother to him as was the "hundred per cent" Yankee.

2. See Engels' letter to Schmidt, July 1, 1891.

3. The erotic theme in Whitman's poetry, as developed abstractly and theoretically, attains a similar degree of distortion, serving as it does as a locus for that sexual mysticism which is typical of a new line of decadents, and of the founder of that line, who was an immediate disciple of Whitman, the theosophical "socialist," Edward Carpenter.

4. The woodsman's axe serves Whitman as a symbol of construction. It is to be kept in mind that, in 1855, the "iron age" was just beginning (up to that time, America, outside the central sections of large cities, had been nine-tenths rural). Democratic construction was, in fact, construction in the rural districts.

5. Whitman's influence on Mayakovsky . . . was ideologic rather than poetic. It shows most clearly in connection with the Utopian-humanistic stage of Mayakovsky's work.

Introduction to Kornei I. Chukovsky's translation of *Leaves of Grass*, 9th ed., 1935. Translated by Samuel Putnam.

3. KORNEI I. CHUKOVSKY

"Many Thanks, Walt Whitman!"

It all began with my buying, quite unexpectedly, a self-tutor of English from a secondhand bookstall on Odessa. I intended to buy Flammarion's *Astronomy*. When this book could not be found on the stall, I bought the English textbook as a mark of gratitude to the bookseller, who had rummaged through all his stock for the Flammarion.

The English textbook was much the worse for wear; certain pages were missing, and it bore a generous spattering of ink and grease stains. Despite these deficiencies it had taught me, even before I got back to my attic, that "ink" means *chernila*, "dog" means *sobaka* and "spoon" means *lazhka*. I was so delighted at this invaluable information that I did not part with the book for a whole year. By the end of that time I was able to read without too much effort Longfellow's *Evangeline* and Poe's "The Raven."

In those days I had not so much as set eyes on an Englishman. A lonely, ever-hungry teenager, I had been thrown out of school and kept body and soul together by doing odd jobs such as sticking up theatre bills, working on the Odessa docks, and reading psalms at funerals. All my free time was devoted to memorizing the self-tutor as if this were my sole salvation.

I was then almost seventeen. Passers-by must have been startled by the sight of me: long, lanky, pale-faced, uncommunicative, with the clothes fairly falling off my back.

I read voraciously and without system. A conglomeration of Darwin, Schopenhauer, Dostoievsky and Pisarev left my mind in utter confusion. Out of this confusion I constructed a fantastic philosophy which was to defy all the Kants in the world and bring about the regeneration of mankind. Like most seventeen-year-old Russian youths, my nights were made sleepless by ruminations upon the origin of the universe, the mystery of life and the hereafter.

In the winter, when work on the docks was slack, I spent whole days in the snug and comfortable municipal library. It was there I discovered Carlyle's *Heroes and Hero-Worship*, a book I revere to this day.

Another year went by like this. I had broken completely with my family.

One day when I was working on the docks a foreign sailor beckoned to me and thrust a thick book into my hands, demanding 25 kopeks for it. He glanced furtively about him as he did so, as if the book were a banned one. Sailors on foreign ships often brought forbidden literature into Tsarist Russia.

That evening after work I took my book to the lighthouse at the end of the jetty. It was a book of poetry written by a certain Walt Whitman, whose name I had never heard before.

I opened at random and read:

My ties and ballasts leave me, my elbows rest in sea-gaps,
I skirt sierras, my palms cover continents,
I am afoot with my vision . . .
Under Niagara, the cataract falling like a veil over my countenance . . .
Walking the old hills of Judea with the beautiful gentle God by my side,
Speeding through space, speeding through heaven and the stars . . .
I visit the orchards of spheres and look at the product,
And look at quintillions ripen'd and look at quintillions green . . .

Never before had I read anything like this. Clearly it had been written by an inspired madman who, in a state of trance of delirium, fancied himself absolutely free of the illusions of time and space. The distant past was to him identical with the present moment and his native Niagara Falls was neighbor to the millions of suns whirling in the void of the universe.

I was shaken by these poems as much as by some epoch-making event. The chaos of my emotions at that time was in perfect harmony with the chaotic composition of the poetry. I seemed to have climbed to dizzying heights from which I looked down upon the ant-hill of human life and activities.

But other poems followed, poems written from within the very heart of this human ant-hill and dealing with the commonplaces of ant-hill life. The poet appeared to have forgotten his cosmic ecstasy in the midst of the poor realities of every day. People and things falling haphazardly within his range of vision passed in endless procession:

The lunatic is carried at last to the asylum a confirm'd case,
(He will never sleep any more as he did in the cot in his mother's bedroom),
The jour printer with gray head and gaunt jaws works at his case,
He turns his quid of tobacco while his eyes blur with the manuscript . . .
As the deck hands make fast the steamboat the plank is thrown for the shore-
    going passengers . . .
The floor-men are laying the floor, the tinners are tinning the roof, the ma-
    sons are calling for mortar . . .

Many-peopled is this poem. It would remain in my memory as a vast collection of unrelated sketches drawn from life were it not for the wonderful concluding lines which give unity to the whole and deep meaning to each of its parts:

And these tend inward to me, and I tend outward to them,
And such as it is to be of these more or less I am,
And of these one and all I weave the song of myself.

Today it is hard for me to understand why I should have been so overwhelmed by this poem. No doubt the poet's ability to renounce the personal in himself and identify his own existence with that of every other individual completely answered my own spiritual urgings at the time, even though I myself was unaware of them. I felt that these lines were addressed directly to me.

For months thereafter Walt Whitman and I were inseparable companions. I took him with me to the docks and to the beach where I helped blind fisherman Simmelidi mend his nets. There were passages in the book I did not understand, there were others I found dull and trite, but when I came upon such treasures as "When Lilacs Last in the Dooryard Bloom'd" I felt I was rich.

By the coming of the winter my kinship with Whitman was complete. My youthful heart eagerly responded to his ecstatic call for human brotherhood, to the radiant hymns he sang to labor, equality and democracy, to the joy he took in the simple things of everyday life, and to his daring glorification of emancipated flesh.

Young readers have a marvellous facility for molding their lives according to the dictates of a book that has deeply impressed them. That was what happened with me. I began to see the world through the eyes of Walt Whitman and was, in a way, transformed into him. All that I saw about me, all people, all things, every manifestation of nature, was seen against the background of countless centuries, illuminated by a million suns.

It was only natural that I should want to share the happiness I had discovered with others. That is why, in 1901, I undertook the translation of those pages of *Leaves of Grass* which most delighted me.

But alas! I turned out to be a wretched translator. My translations were heavy, clumsy, uninspired. Whitman's lines lost all their force and vigour in my rendering. Since Russian words are nearly three times as long as English ones, my incompetent pen turned out flaccid, bloodless lines that a reader found tedious.

To overcome this tediousness I resorted to an expedient proscribed by all laws of translation: I transformed Whitman's free verse into lines with regular rhythm and ornamented by striking rhymes. I am even now ashamed to acknowledge so heinous (if unintentional) a crime, but one must remember that I was a lonely self-taught youth without the faintest idea of how literary translations ought to be done.

Of course I had not dared to hope my Russian version of Whitman would ever see the printed page. It was only in 1907, when I moved to the capital and began being published in St. Petersburg journals, that the student Youth Circle of the St. Petersburg University brought out a small edition of my translations of the American poet. The translations, I repeat, were bad; even so, the little book was a great success. After its appearance Whitman's name was met again and again in Russian literary magazines.

But this success brought me little satisfaction. I suffered from a guilty conscience. I loathed the beastly book and tried to redeem myself in Whitman's eyes by making a new translation.

In 1914 this new translation, which was far better, was published in Moscow. The book was destroyed by the Tsarist censor and never reached the public. I managed to obtain one copy of it.

Readers, however, insisted on having *Leaves of Grass*, and after the Revolution it was brought out and went through one edition after another (1918, 1919, 1922, 1923, 1931, 1932, etc.). I revised each one again and again.

In 1944, not long before the end of World War II, the tenth edition came out. This year, 1969, which marks the 150th anniversary of Whitman's birth, will see the twelfth edition, also revised and partly rewritten.

Whitman's poetry has exerted a powerful influence on many Soviet poets. A poem addressed to me by Boris Pasternak in the thirties ends with:

> *. . . and a big bear hug*
> *For your gift of Whitman.*

I have never limited myself to merely translating Whitman; in extensive critical articles introducing every volume of his poems I have tried to interpret him and reveal his significance to the reader. In these articles I point out Whitman lines which in one way or another are reflected in the poetry of Mayakovsky and Khlebnikov.

The appearance of fundamental works on Whitman by the Frenchman Roger Asselineau and the American Gay Wilson Allen helped me to a better understanding of the poet's life and work. Today I know a thousand times more about him than I did in 1901 when, as an unsophisticated youth, I read the *Song of Myself* in the Black Sea port. But I cannot deceive myself into thinking that Whitman evokes the same fiery response in me today as he did then. Try as I will, I cannot feel my heart lift with joy as I did when I first beheld the whole world through the inspired eyes of Walt Whitman.

And it seems to me it is not the scholars and critics who truly understand poetry, but rather it is the youthful readers, who absorb this poetry into their very life's blood and draw from it such rich nourishment for the spirit.

Yet even today, with my ninetieth birthday in the offing, I am full of gratitude to the poet whose book so deeply influenced my anxious and unsettled youth.

Sputnik (June 1969): 30–39. This essay was published on the 150th anniversary of Whitman's birth.

4. MAURICE MENDELSON

Life and Work of Walt Whitman: A Soviet View

In the mid-1850s there appeared in the United States a new party of national importance, the Republican Party. This was a bourgeois party, but among the Republicans there were a great many honest champions of democracy and genuine enemies of slavery. The Republicans adopted several slogans from the Free Soilers. On the eve of the war the Republican Party nominated Abraham Lincoln for president, and millions of working people gave it support. At that very time the ideas of Marxism, the teachings of scientific socialism began to penetrate the country. Whitman could scarcely have known of them, but like thousands of other Americans he had certainly been acquainted with utopian socialist ideas.

Walt was five years old when Robert Owen twice addressed the American legislators, once by invitation of the House of Representatives, and once by invitation of the president. In his speeches this utopian socialist expressed his hope for the foundation of a society which would guarantee the happiness of every man.

The utopian colony founded by Owen in America in 1825 ("The New Harmony") had dissolved long before Whitman was consciously aware of what was going on in the world around him. But the American followers of Fourier were quite active by the time Whitman was fully grown. The Fourierist Albert Brisbane published his book *Social Destiny of Man* in 1840. In it he described the world of the future as a kingdom of culture and beauty. In Brisbane's opinion it would be easiest of all in America to put Fourier's ideas into practice. Another outstanding Fourierist was Park Godwin, the son-in-law of the poet Bryant. In the mid-forties he published a book in which he protested against the division of contemporary society into two classes, one of which possessed everything, and the other nothing.

In 1841 the Brook Farm colony was founded, based on a rather original interpretation of Fourierist principles (several notable American writers took part in the venture, including Nathaniel Hawthorne). The colony, whose members strove to combine physical labor with spiritual development and moral improvement, lasted only a few years, but it attracted a great deal of interest. During these years several dozen other colonies were founded in the USA, all by people trying in some way to follow Fourier's teaching.

An active writer like Whitman, of course, could not bypass utopian socialism. There is no doubt that he read the *New York Tribune*, in which Fourierist articles appeared, and even the journal which was published by the members of the Brook Farm colony.

At times the poet offered sober criticism of some of the more vulnerable features of Fourierism. On some occasions Whitman was taken in by the philistine interpretation of this social teaching. In any case an article which the poet wrote while in New Orleans contains the following: ". . . but to us it seems a great objection [against Fourierism] that nobody, as far as we learn from the system, is to do anything but *be happy*. Now who would peel potatoes and scrub the floors?"

Nevertheless, Whitman's ideas about "a great city," the city "of the faithfullest friends," ran along approximately the same lines as the dreams of both Owen and Fourier. Most probably the ideas of Marx were quite unknown to Whitman before the war, despite the fact that several American friends of the poet not only knew Marx's work, but Marx himself personally.

One of the participants in the Brook Farm experiment was Charles A. Dana, who later edited the *New York Tribune* together with Horace Greeley. Dana, who was a warm friend of the poet, visited Marx, together with Brisbane, in 1848. Describing the experience, Brisbane characterized the author of the *Communist Manifesto* as the leader of a movement of the people, and wrote that in Marx he felt "the passionate fire of a daring spirit." Soon Dana invited Marx to write for the *New York Tribune*, and Marx's articles appeared in the paper for many years. It is impossible to say for certain whether Whitman read them; we know only that the poet followed the *New York Tribune* with great interest. Some of his own poems were published in it.

A significant part of Whitman's publicistic writing in the fifties advocated the deepening of bourgeois democracy. He continued to fight the institution of slavery, but the pages of the newspapers were usually closed to his abolitionist articles. . . .

[In the 1870s] Whitman drew even closer to John Swinton. When he fell ill once, the poet asked Swinton to visit him. Whitman joyfully informed O'Connor that Swinton spoke very kindly of *Leaves of Grass*. Swinton more than once commented favorably on Whitman's work in the press. Incidentally, he authored one of the first articles about *Leaves of Grass* to appear in the Russian press. In 1880 John Swinton made the personal acquaintance of Karl Marx. In the *New York Sun* he called Marx "one of the most remarkable men of the day." Marx was a man who for forty years had played "an inscrutable but puissant part in the revolutionary politics." His mind, wrote Swinton, is "strong, broad, elevated," and his dialogue is "so free, so sweeping, so creative, so incisive, so genuine." Since Whitman always followed the New York press closely, it is quite possible that he read his friend's article. . . .

But the person who was closest of all to Whitman in the last years of his life was Horace Traubel. Traubel was fifteen years old when he began to chat occasionally with the white-bearded old poet on the streets of Camden. Later the young bank clerk, a convinced socialist who in secret wrote poetry similar to Whitman's, became wholeheartedly devoted to the poet. . . . Horace Traubel was in some ways a link between Whitman and that part of American twentieth-century literature which was inspired, to a greater or lesser degree, by socialist ideas. In the second decade of the century, and up to his death, Traubel wrote for the journals the *Masses* and the *Liberator*. . . .

As early as 1868 Ferdinand Freiligrath introduced Whitman's work to the German reading public by printing an article on the American poet in a German newspaper. It was one of the first critical works on Whitman to appear in the continental press. There is some evidence (the accuracy of which is, however, disputed) that Karl Marx became acquainted with Whitman's work at about this time. In his book about the life and work of Marx, first published in English in 1910, John Spargo affirms that when Marx heard of the "Good Gray Poet" he immediately became interested. According to Spargo, he would even quote sections from "Song of Myself" and the poem "Pioneers."

(Moscow: Progress Publishers, 1976), 99–101, 298–299, 310.

CARL L. ANDERSON

Whitman in Sweden

Whitman's poetry received little more than sporadic attention in Sweden and Swedish communities in Finland in the early years of this century, but it developed into a principal source of inspiration and example to poets coming into print there after the First World War. They were of the "new generation," as they were soon named, and had no patience with the genteel complacencies still dominant in Swedish poetry in their time despite the many tumultuous social and political changes then under way. Whitman's democratic vigor inspired the ambition of these new poets to give untrammeled expression to the energies buried in the inner life of even the common person. They cherished Whitman's robust forthrightness and sought to capture it in translations of selected portions of *Leaves of Grass* but, more important, to rise to its demands in their own poetry. In time, they succeeded in providing the shock of modernism that was to alter the course of poetry in Swedish.

The earliest references to Whitman in Sweden — beginning with a passing reference in 1895 — had been more or less isolated events. Ellen Key, the famous proto-feminist and a convinced Emersonian, had briefly commended Whitman's renewal of "the new spirit of the west" in her *Lifslinler* (*Lifelines*) (1903–1906). Emilia Fogelklou, theologically trained and a distinguished commentator on contemporary issues, had emphasized a few years later Whitman's message of "Joy" (Fleisher 1957, 20–21; Åhnebrink, 43). In 1905 a third woman, Andrea Butenschön, published in what was then Sweden's leading journal of literature and the arts a long, warmly appreciative essay on Whitman. It included in its twenty-one double-columned pages her translation of "Proud Music of the Storm," as well as numerous extracts from other poems.

Butenschön's father was a Norwegian who had lived for many years in America. The home he later provided his family was situated in western Sweden, but at that time Norway and Sweden were still in union, and Oslo (then Christiania) remained the family's cultural center. Andrea Butenschön had literary ambitions and might well have had her attention first directed to Whitman's poetry through the admiring lectures and essays of the Norwegians Kristofer Janson and Hans Tambs Lyche, but it was her longstanding interest in India that came most distinctively into play in her Whitman essay. She had moved in literary circles during a year's travels in India in 1890–91, and she subsequently undertook Sanskrit studies in England and at the Sorbonne and at Kiel; in 1902 she published her translation of the Katha Upanishad, and in 1913, the year Rabindranath Tagore received the Nobel Prize in literature, she anticipated the award with a translation of his *Gitanjali.* In India, Tagore regularly gave readings of Whitman's poetry; his nephew, Kshitindranath Tagore, published an essay on Whitman in Bengali in 1891. The latter's endorsement of the view then prominent of Whitman as the poet of freedom and democracy was shared by Butenschön, but in her essay she also gave a more personal response: "I thought that in Whitman I had at last found what I longed for: a singer steeped in Wisdom but without dogmas and theories which everyone must accept; who sang because he could not do otherwise and bore witness with the force of his native strength to life's root meaning [*urtanke*]." She accepted the sexual frankness of the poems as being a necessary, serious consequence of Whitman's insistence on the spirituality of all aspects of life. "He is the only one I know who has succeeded in creating a personal, living philosophy of religion practiced in his own time from the heart of the wisdom of the Indian prophets — whether he obtained his wisdom from India or not."

Whatever interest Butenschön's essay may have held for her readers in 1905, it was in quite different terms that Whitman became, little more than a decade later, an almost legendary figure for young poets and critics anxious to break away from the Swedish equivalent of Edwardian decorum and to give full expression to the unruliness of people's inner life. German expressionism had been pointing the way, in metaphysical terms at first, but then more broadly to include advocacy of a reconstituted social order in accord with broad principles of the human camaraderie and the common good. In this context, Whitman was hailed readily enough as the truthsayer who sang in new poetic forms "of Life immense in passion, pulse, and power," yet uttering "the word Democratic, the word En-Masse" (LG, 1).

Many developments converged to create this act of homage by writers in Swedish — both in Sweden itself and in Finland, where Swedish communities remained more or less intact following the seven centuries that Finland had been a Swedish province (before Russian annexation in 1809). Substantial if mixed benefits from industrialization had not begun to be fully realized until the 1870s in either country, but soon significant shifts in population occurred from rural areas into the towns and cities. At the same time, political affiliations also underwent drastic realignment so that, for example, by 1932 the Social Democrats in Sweden would be voted into power, there to remain for many decades. Finland experienced even more drastic political change, including a bloody revolution in 1918 in the course of cutting its ties with Russia and declaring itself an independent republic for the first time in its history.[1]

It was obvious enough that the stratified social order of the past was dissolving and was moving uncertainly and fitfully toward a new, more democratic—or socialist, or perhaps Communist—political arrangement. With few exceptions, the new poets in Sweden and Finland were visibly in sympathy with this drift as they combined a strain of anti-intellectual Nietzschean expressionism with a more activist tendency that looked toward the dedication of one's divinely conferred inner life to enlarged social ends. Whitman's poetry was enlisted in support of both strains in a context derived from many sources: Bergson's concept of the élan vital, Kandinsky's argument that genuine art is created only through some inner necessity, and supplementary or parallel ideas from even earlier sources like Baudelaire, Dostoyevsky, Strindberg, and, not least, van Gogh, who had himself been influenced by Whitman (Schwind, 1).

Leaves of Grass was regarded in this context as one of the founts of modern poetry: transcendental yet realistic, life-affirming, democratic in spirit, and forthright in its presentation of the inner person. In addition, it had by that time garnered sufficient authority in the European community to legitimate the abandonment of meter. Meter was a straitjacket, it was now argued, from which poetry must escape in order to achieve artistic autonomy in the twentieth century without dependence on "artificial" aids. Later, Carl Sandburg, Edgar Lee Masters, and Vachel Lindsay were for similar reasons indiscriminately placed in Whitman's long shadow; by the late 1930s they in turn would be succeeded by Eliot and Pound.

One of the first of the modernist poets writing in Swedish and perhaps the one most thoroughly conversant with the new literature appearing on the continent was the Finland-Swedish poet Elmer Diktonius. He had grown up in parlous times of war and revolution. He taught music and at one time harbored an ambition to become a composer under the tutelage of Arnold Schoenberg. He wrote defiantly of the need for poetry to redefine the self under radically altered social and political conditions. In this, he had been encouraged by his close friend and former student, Otto Vihelmovich Kuusinen, who fled Finland after the defeat of the Reds and later rose in the ranks of the Communist Party in Soviet Russia to become secretary of its Central Committee.

Diktonius was already known for his letters from London and Paris, published in the Communist *Stormklockan*, when his first volume, a collection of aphorisms entitled *Min dikt* (*My Poem*) (Stockholm, 1921), appeared. There followed in 1922 the publication of his explosive *Hårda sånger* (*Hard Songs*), marking a new, radical phase in Swedish poetry. In the course of writing these poems, Diktonius had begun reading Whitman, first in Franz Blei's translation, *Hymnen für die Erde*, and later in English (Romefors, 48; Espmark 1977, 98 n.38). His commitment to radical change had led him to Whitman, it has been suggested, essentially for "his social universality, revolutionary fervor, bold overthrow of tradition." However, if Whitman was at one pole, Nietzsche was at the other, violent and refractory — qualities that appealed strongly to Diktonius. *Hårda sånger* rejected the "sentimentality" of speaking of "the rich" and "the poor"; rather "I say: the strong and the weak." In this and his other writings, Diktonius stated that his primary commitment was not to art but to life; his purpose was to "beget art in order to slay art — to create what is human" (O. Enckell 1946, 123, 124, 171).[2]

Diktonius was quickly enrolled as a contributor to *Ultra*, a short-lived bilingual (Swedish and Finnish) magazine of the modernists. Its first issue in September 1922 included translations of poetry by Franz Werfel (himself a translator of Whitman) and commentary on Proust, the new music of Scriabin, Stravinsky, and Prokofiev, the art of van Gogh, the theater of Pär Lagerkvist, and the poems of another new Finland-Swedish poet, Edith Södergran. Diktonius published in its pages a free translation of Whitman's "Poets to Come" (R. Enckell, 47) and others (Romefors, 116 n.76). In Louis Untermeyer's popular anthology of American poetry, he discovered Carl Sandburg and Edgar Lee Masters, both sharply sensitive to social inequality and injustice. He wrote appreciatively about *Chicago Poems* and in 1925 followed this up with *Ungt hav* (*Young Sea*, named after a poem of Sandburg's about the sea that "pounds on the shore / Restless as a young heart"), a collection that included translations of both Sandburg and Masters as well as Ezra Pound (136). This poetry, a reviewer suggested at the time, would surely displace the English-manorhouse-and-landscape strain in Swedish poetry and admit in its stead "a perhaps somewhat barbaric but youthful and powerfully vital poetry" coming out of America (Espmark 1964, 31).

It was not until Diktonius had published *Hårda sånger* in 1922 that he understood what considerable advances had already been made by his compatriot Edith Södergran. Working quietly on her own, she had preceded him with *Dikter* (*Poems*) in 1916, followed by four other volumes that soon established her as the first of the "new generation," as they were later designated. In a newspaper article in 1924, Diktonius conceded Södergran's indebtedness to her Swedish forebears despite her dazzling originality, then added that without Whitman, nevertheless, none of the entire "new generation" of poets would have been possible (Romefors, 12). Diktonius's poetry itself bears little or no resemblance to Whitman's; nor, for that matter, does Södergran's. The former is too blunt, violent, or explosive for that; the latter is too quietly and intensely insistent on inner meanings in a cosmic setting. Yet as Diktonius intimated, both may have drawn some indefinable support from Whitman in their efforts to express a powerful sense of "Life" inherent in the self and, as Diktonius wrote in a newspaper article in 1923, of "the fire, the glow, the passion — the revolutionary [spirit] which alone gives the poet the right to create his own forms, the power to create them" (15).[3]

In 1925 the agenda of these new poets was rehearsed by the propagandist of the group, Hagar Olsson, in *Ny generation* (*New Generation*), a gathering of previously published essays. In the first of these she recalled that "the pervasive aristocratic tone which the nineties had contrived to confer upon poetry had plunged it into an isolation like nothing so much as death. . . . Poetry had lost all touch with the greater whole: with community, belief, an ideal." It relied instead, in its "veneration of dead beauty," upon "the wisdom of disillusioned old men." "It was a poetry for connoisseurs and sybarites," not for living, breathing people. The "profane intruders" of expressionism were the first to crash into the holy domain, "followed by the masses close on their heels." But a vision of a paradise on earth rather than in heaven could already be glimpsed, Olsson exclaimed, "in the Whitmanian landscape" (Olsson, 7–9, 11–13). The day of romantic lyricism was irretrievably past, while that of modern poetry was at hand — realistic in expression, closely resembling the "prose" of Masters's "epitaphs" and Whitman's poetry.

In another essay, Olsson described Whitman as an innovator with a flaming vision of the future, a pioneer for those who are, in her emphasis, "destructively creative" (Olsson, 22, 23). Lurking in that phrase may have been her recollection of reading about Martin Eden's tortuous struggle to become an author. In any case, Whitman appeared again in the role of hard-hitting visionary in her third essay, "Walt Whitman Foregångaren" ("Walt Whitman, Forerunner"), previously published in *Ultra* in 1922. It extolled the breadth and spontaneity of his poetry; Whitman was an evangelist, a revolutionary: "He was a true democrat *sans peur et sans reproche*: freedom, equality, brotherhood were for him the cornerstones on which all that is human rests, and he abided by these principles in his own life and poetry" (28). The sources of Olsson's elevation of Whitman to the role of visionary and hero-poet of democracy can, of course, be found plentifully enough in *Leaves of Grass*, but the social and political volatility of the times added extra fervor. The new poetry was to have a place in a new age, and Whitman was enrolled in the great cause of reshaping literary tradition in a transformed world.

Curiously, Whitman's imminent significance had been foreseen with a certain degree of uneasiness as early as 1908 in a review in *Finsk tidskrift* of Frank Norris's fiction. The reviewer, Sigurd Frosterus, regarded Norris's novels as examples of a new kind of literature — "let us call it Americanism" — in which the forces of nature are once again raised romantically to godlike status but are cast by "Yankee imagination" in new, contemporary forms. "The architects of Americanism are Edgar Allan Poe and Walt Whitman. No European . . . has expressed so strikingly a sense of infinitude as have these two men, natives of the boundless land in the west where . . . all life pulsates in a faster and rhythmically more vigorous tempo." In this light Whitman was "the first great pagan in the post-classical world of literature, the first to sever ties with the mythological and historical concepts of civilized nations, the naive creator of a new and rough-hewn and powerfully triumphant view of life. . . . His poetry is scarcely to be called verse, but even less so prose." Frosterus recalled recent criticism in Europe of American culture, in particular by Scandinavians like Johannes V. Jensen, Knut Hamsun, and Henning Berger, "all telling in different voices and languages about a world not like ours, a world which increasingly penetrates ours and thrusts it aside." Thus a novel like Norris's *Octopus* should be read as "a synthesis of motley America's contradictory elements" (Frosterus, 80, 81, 82).[4]

The Finland-Swedish poets were heavily promoted in *Ultra* and in *Quosego*, its short-lived (1928–29) but influential successor. Their aggressiveness at first baffled or angered the reviewers in mainland Sweden who were unprepared for them, but it heartened aspiring writers already persuaded of the need to express, in undisguised form, the intensity of their innermost feelings and perceptions. One of the contributors to *Quosego* was Artur Lundkvist in Stockholm; he, too, was a Whitman enthusiast. While in Copenhagen in 1925, he had come upon Johannes V. Jensen's translation of "A Song of Joy" in his novel *Hjulet* (*The Wheel*) (1905); he copied the poem, having received, he later wrote, such a "decisive impression" that he had to keep it with him (Lundkvist 1966, 34). He may also have seen a volume of Whitman's poems in the translation by Jensen and Otto Gelsted that appeared in 1919.

Copenhagen had offered the excitement of a metropolis for the first time to the nineteen-year-old Lundkvist, who had left his parents' impoverished one-horse farm to work, no more happily, in industry. Feeling that he belonged neither on a farm nor in industry, yet sympathizing with workers in both places, he bridged the gap by calling himself a "proletarian of the soil." He found an outlet for his writing in radical journals and papers, but he was put off, he later said, by their unimaginative equating of happiness with a full stomach. He replied to a critic of his poem "Revolution" (1928) by defending his ambiguous position; at the same time, he revealed the activist spirit in which he had been reading Whitman: "I believe in the unrequitable song of the blood, in the turmoil and unceasing hunger of the soul. I am not a communist but a revolutionary! . . . I want to get to the heart of naked pure beautiful life and the same also of people." To Elmer Diktonius in Finland he wrote that he was a revolutionary only insofar as he was fundamentally opposed to the "life-maiming" nature of society as it was then constituted (Espmark 1964, 81–84, 89).

At first Lundkvist adopted in his own poems Diktonius's hard-hitting expressionistic manner: "My ideal then was that words should fall brutally direct, to be felt like chips of stone, punches of the fist" (Lundkvist 1966, 51). He wrote approvingly of Diktonius as an "expressionist-revolutionary" in the radical *Stormklockan* and welcomed enthusiastically the American poets included in Diktonius's *Ungt hav*. Lundkvist's own debut as a poet in 1928 with *Glöd* (*Smolder*) and his leadership in bringing together the following year four other like-minded aspiring Swedish authors in an anthology entitled *Fem unga* (*Five Young Men*) mark pivotal moments in Swedish literature. In *Glöd*, Diktonius's blunt protest against staleness and sterility in society and art had undergone a sea change, but the por-tent was the same: a new generation had arrived also in mainland Sweden. Diktonius praised *Glöd* but had reservations about the undue American influence that contributed to what he considered to be Lundkvist's diffuseness. Lundkvist confessed that, compared to Diktonius's "splintered, angular, monosyllabic" poems, his own were "entirely too drawn out and wordy. Too much of Whitman — not a stylistic ideal yet I have fallen for it nevertheless." In fact, Whitman's expansiveness and vigorous long lines had permanently left their mark on Lundkvist's sensibilities. He continued to fit this new freedom to his own expressive needs with great distinction for the rest of his career (Espmark 1964, 65–69, 70–72).

In the course of the next three years, Lundkvist published an additional three volumes of poetry and prepared essays on contemporary American poets for a volume to which he had given, he said, the "neutral" title of *Atlantvind* (*Atlantic Wind*) (1932) rather than the "forbidding" but more accurate one of *Dynamic Modernism*. What was the prospect for "dynamic modernism" in a Swedish culture that had become "a museum of discarded and dead forms"?

> Life goes on, always, ceaselessly on. Life is a constant protest against all those stratified forms that inhibit, paralyze, stultify. And surely the task of the poet is precisely this: to interpose himself in the dynamics of events by maintaining constant creativity in opposition to the destructive attitude fostered by rigid outworn forms. (Espmark 1964, 53)

This was Lundkvist's clearest declaration of his modernist, "vitalist" principles. Here and elsewhere in *Atlantvind* he focused on the concept of *livsdyrkan* (literally, life-worship) that would govern his literary career thenceforth: "an attempt to find new, living forms organically related to the times, containers for the new way of life that is evolving." The poor and the hungry would at last have a place given them, for modernism was a program that "emanates from the deeply felt need of so many people in our time to shape life in keeping with its inherent preconditions and from the need to secure the necessities of life in accordance with the old revolutionary slogan: bread and freedom for all" (Lundkvist 1932, 191, 221). Despite the jargon, this was a writer's visionary ideology rather than a political or social program. It had its roots in the poverty of his childhood, but its full articulation owed more than a little to Whitman; it prepared the way for Lundkvist's highly individualistic confrontation with books over a long lifetime, among them the works of a score of American poets and novelists (Espmark 1964, 24).

Whitman dominated the opening essay in *Atlantvind*: "Manhattan's son with the broad proletarian chest, cosmos-lover, and evangelist in a slouch hat." Of the two poets America was said (once again) to have rejected, Poe and Whitman, the latter was "the real American, shaped and fulfilled by America, a pioneer and a pathbreaker, enamored of his vast virgin land, intoxicated by his visions of its thronging life." The source of Whitman's creativity lay within: "the free, proletarian man who lives life fully and earthily, identifies himself with nature, with the cosmos, abandoning himself to its inherent powers and his own instincts with total confidence" (Lundkvist 1932, 10).

Lundkvist had already paid tribute to Whitman in the same tones three years earlier in "Porträtt: Whitman," a poem first published in May 1929 in the radical student paper *Clarté* and reprinted as "Whitman" later that year in a volume entitled *Naket liv* (*Naked Life*) (see selection 1). "Whitman" was a celebration of "Life" in the context of comradeship that embraces all experience, signifying therefore some undefined ultimate purpose. The poem concluded:

And your song lingers still among the heights, echoes across the oceans;
Your footprints remain, deep, indelible in the soil,
     showing THE WAY,
And light blooms up from them.

In *Atlantvind*, Lundkvist likened Whitman's poetry to "swollen rivers, mighty streams of direct impressions and feelings" unimpeded by conventions of form: "No problems of verse form existed for him. He broke spontaneously through the walls of form; no artificial dams could impede his poetic flow" (Lundkvist 1932, 11). Lundkvist had no more than this to say about the art of *Leaves of Grass*; his emphasis was wholly on Whitman as full-fledged mystical modernist.

Lundkvist's *Naket liv*, containing his poem to Whitman, came in for a drubbing by the young poet Johannes Edfelt, who, schooled in classical verse, remained unpersuaded of the virtues of free verse until late in his own career. In a review in 1930 of ten recent volumes of poetry, including *Naket liv*, Edfelt warned Lundkvist that "this hybrid of verse and prose, which he cultivates so assiduously, is scarcely *le dernier cri* any longer." Edfelt named the influence responsible: "Lundkvist's poetry follows the line laid down in modern times principally by Whitman. It would not be surprising if, after becoming acquainted with many of that poet's intellectual progeny — and they are legion — one were to mumble something like bastard [hybrid] or call to mind an old saying which is a true saying: *Quod licet Iovi, non licet bovi*" (quoted in Landgren, 14). Ironically, aestheticism and lack of originality were the underlying faults Edfelt found in the poetry Lundkvist had written precisely as a modernist protest against those very failings. But Edfelt preferred British poets like Rupert Brooke, A. E. Housman, and Yeats, among others; he believed the obligation of poetry was to strive for universality and permanence through the power of metaphor, an ambition distinctly at odds with the modernists (Landgren, 87, 185; Ekman, 65). In later years, he modified his complaint against the Lundkvist generation and, following the lead originally given him by Franz Werfel, translated several of Whitman's short poems himself.[5]

Another member of the *Fem unga* group was Harry Martinson, recipient of the Nobel Prize in 1974. Thrown on his own at an early age, he had spent several years at sea as a coal stoker. Lundkvist was impressed by this new voice, even though it was still too strongly colored by Jack London's prose. Just as modernism had released Lundkvist's own poetic energies, it catapulted Martinson decisively within a few years into the independence he needed to proceed on his own (Espmark 1970, 11–12). In a statement prepared for publication in 1931, Martinson characterized modernism in a deliberate paradox as "dynamically irrational, self-centeredly world-encompassing" (quoted in Espmark 1970, 22). He had read American poets from this perspective, beginning in 1927 with Carl Sandburg, first as represented in Diktonius's anthology *Ungt hav* and then in separate volumes. He turned next to Masters; only later did he relive Lundkvist's delight in Whitman through reading the Danish translations included in Jensen's *Hjulet*. Martinson wrote for a maritime magazine, *Sjömannen* (*The Seaman*) (December 1930), a piece entitled "Valt Vhitman — universalisten," but, like Diktonius, he thought Whitman wordy, preferring Sandburg's matter-of-fact presentation of an everyday reality that retained awareness of the universal (Espmark 1970, 26, 39, 59–68). Whitman may have reinforced the "cosmic perspective" of Martinson's poetry (177–179) but either too late or perhaps too grandly to have served as a "forerunner" as he had for the Finland-Swedish poets and Artur Lundkvist. The following generation of poets had no inclination for the cosmic and visionary pretensions of prophetic poets. Even Lundkvist published a poem in 1937 in which he saw himself ironically as "the wandering singer looking for a lost myth but finding only statues of stone." Eliot's arid spiritual landscape was to set the scene for the 1940s (Algulin, 8–9, 11).

In 1976 Lundkvist openly rejected Whitman, at least as a prophet, in an issue of the poetry magazine *Lyrikvännen* devoted entirely to Whitman's life and works. America's failure to fulfill the promise delineated in Whitman's vision was the subject of a long "essay-poem" by Lundkvist, "Försenad hyllning till Whitman" ("Belated Homage to Whitman") (see selection 2). It faulted Whitman's failure to divert or mitigate the corruption and harm that America had thrust upon the world. The guilt was no less Whitman's than America's for having dared to nurture hopes that had proved so vulnerable and so futile. Lundkvist's essay-poem, seeking to recapture the oracular quality that he had admired in Whitman, contained allusions to and echoes from moments in "Song of Myself" and the poems on Lincoln's death, but Lundkvist considered the American poet's vision flawed by its very excess, for it was of a dreamland where "strong young men of the West advance with plow and axe . . . without the curse of slavery," of a world that "will work indefatigably for the idea of brotherhood," and where "man is free and from the very beginning has been saved, and Christ who has never been crucified will wander as a vagabond through these states." This dream had been blasted by the horrors of contemporary civilization, which have their source in none other than Whitman's native land. Lundkvist followed with a litany of America's deceits and failings, the obverse of the paean in the first part. The wonders Whitman had promised earlier were replaced by images of sterility and destructiveness: skyscrapers, city pavements, cash registers, computers, atom bombs. "Alas, too late, too late on earth, Walt Whitman, you sower in vain of the seeds of hope." The bitterness of this inverted homage was obviously a measure of the depth of Lundkvist's devotion to the modernist dream engendered nearly fifty years earlier when he read Whitman's poems in the charged atmosphere of the late 1920s and early 1930s. He beheld then in the poems what he wanted to see (to paraphrase Whitman's "To Foreign Lands"), but little more.

Reasonably complete Swedish translations of *Leaves of Grass* have yet to appear. Andrea Butenschön sprinkled her 1905 essay with translated fragments in addition to a complete version (save for a few lines) of "Proud Music of the Storm." All "barbaric yawps" were suppressed in favor of lofty, antiquated diction supposedly suited to Whitman as a singer steeped in wisdom.[6] Diktonius's translations have already been described; Artur Lundkvist contributed four to radical papers in the late 1920s.[7] A promising essay on Whitman by Roland Fridholm appeared in 1934 but was unaccompanied by translations. Fridholm's thesis, derived from Jean Catel's psychoanalytical *Walt Whitman*, was that Whitman's frustration as a secret homosexual was no doubt the source of his celebration of friendship, comradeship, "adhesiveness," and ultimately of "democracy." Whitman yearned for the great "Camerado" as the symbol of everything he longed for in life; disarming frankness was his way of thwarting potential criticism.

A volume of translations by Karl Alfred Svensson, a librarian in Halsingborg, using the deathbed edition as his text, appeared as *Strån av gräs* (*Leaves of Grass*) in 1935. It included an introductory biography based on Hans Reisiger's introduction to his monumental German translations, as well as other biographies. "Song of Myself" and "When Lilacs Last in the Dooryard Bloom'd" appeared in complete versions in this collection; the remaining sixty-five selections were short poems or excerpts from longer ones. Dutifully accurate, the translations resorted on the other hand to a standard of poetic diction that Whitman-inspired modernists had already effectively discarded in their own poetry. In 1937 Erik Blomberg, well known as a poet and as art critic for *Social-Demokraten*, the organ of the Social Democratic Party, included a complete version of "When Lilacs Last in the Dooryard Bloom'd," extracts rearranged from "Song of Myself," and eight short poems in a section on Whitman in *Modern amerikansk lyrik från Walt Whitman till våra dagar* (*Modern American Poetry from Walt Whitman to Our Days*), a selection of twenty-eight poets from Untermeyer's voluminous anthology. Again, the translations were accurate enough, if uninspired and at times reductive and misleading; in "What Think You I Take My Pen in Hand" Whitman's "two simple men" who kiss and embrace publicly "parting the parting of dear friends" became in Blomberg's translation "two simple people [*människor*]" who kiss "while he [*han*] who was about to depart clasped her [*henne*] tightly in his arms" (Blomberg, 37).

The 1976 issue of *Lyrikvännen* containing Lundkvist's bitter "belated homage" also included a brief up-to-date biographical sketch of Whitman by the editor, Rolf Aggestam, a portion of the 1855 Preface, and excerpts from eight poems as well as complete translations of two short poems and "Out of the Cradle Endlessly Rocking." These attempted to use fresh diction and phrasing comparable in effect to the original; a strenuous effort was made to avoid words and tones reminiscent of high romanticism in Swedish poetry or the emollient tendencies of previous Whitman translations by Svensson and Blomberg. Aggestam, himself a poet, published his translation of "Song of Myself" (1855 version) in *Sången om Mig*

Själv in 1983. To recapture the ambience of the original, the book was printed in a format only slightly smaller than that of the first edition of *Leaves of Grass* and in similar type. The questions to which this volume gave rise were not those associated with revolutionary efforts to change the course of Swedish poetry or modern society, but with the meaning and effectiveness of an important poem with an important history that nevertheless continues to speak to all. In addition to embellishments by the translator, the usual recalcitrant difficulties in discovering equivalents of structure, syntax, meaning, and connotation in another language and in another cultural setting persisted inevitably also in this labor of love, fully dedicated to the translator's purpose of keeping Whitman's poetry strikingly alive for a new generation of Swedish readers and poets.

NOTES

1. "For many Finns the 1918 war was the war when [Western] culture was victorious over [Eastern] barbarism, when the Whites and the Germans joined together against the Reds and the Russians" (Willner, 8, quoting Gunnar Castren in *Nya Argus*, 1918). The use in Finland of the Swedish language had been placed on equal legal footing with the use of Finnish early in the century, but Swedish-speaking Finns had grown nervously defensive of their heritage. That accounted in part for the coolness or disdain with which they at first greeted the deliberately unconventional language and themes of their young poets. Holmqvist (13–22) notes the conflicting forces in play among Finland-Swedes at this time: their persistent sense of being Swedish even while joining in the rising spirit of Finnish nationalism; hence their uneasiness concerning their possible provincialism, which might be corrected through their growing internationalism, including increased awareness of the many literary currents abroad—symbolism, expressionism, futurism, etc.

2. This precept also underlay Diktonius's activity as critic from 1922 to 1934 on *Arbetarbladet*, under the editorship of a prominent member of the Social Democratic Party. The appeal of Carl Sandburg and Edgar Lee Masters lay, he would argue, in their revelation of the shortcomings of middle-class pretensions and the plight of the masses under industrialized capitalism.

3. In reply to criticism of her poems, Södergran wrote that they would have achieved their purpose if but one reader attained through them a vision of the transcendent and the urge to find self-fulfillment (Wrede, 45–46). Her reading of Whitman may have lent breadth to this purpose even while it fostered the inclusion of unpretentious details, and it has been suggested that by his example she cast her poems in long lines employing anaphora (Tideström, 83, 95–96, 101); similar practice, it must be noted, was being followed in expressionist poetry elsewhere, and there is no external evidence she ever read Whitman in English or in any of the several languages familiar to her in which translations of Whitman had already appeared (Brunner, 37–40, 281). A large part of the value of her poems to her contemporaries seems to have lain in her unrelenting distrust of ossified poeticism. "Take them for what they are" but not as "literature," Hagar Olsson later said of Södergran's poems, though scarcely in Whitman's sense given in "A Backward Glance O'er

Travel'd Roads" — "varicolored, brilliant sparks from the anvil where a life of suffering and madness was forged into a nugget of truth" (Södergran, 14). (Diktonius's poems also were to be read not as "literature," he asserted, but as moments in "the ceaseless flux of *life*," a view paralleling Whitman's about his own poetry.) Olof Enckell (1949, 141–151) proposed "side-impulses" from Whitman in Södergran's poetry that on examination become scarcely distinguishable from influences from other sources.

4. In an earlier review of a Danish adventure novel in *Argus*, Frosterus had suggested that, being typical of the new century, it might well have been entitled "Intense Life" (Roosevelt's words in English). It was the very intensity of life projected in Whitman's distinctly "American" poetry that was to suit perfectly the aims of the Finland-Swedish poets. In this context belongs Bertel Gripenberg's positive review in the same year of Jack London's extraordinarily popular *The Call of the Wild*, a work much favored, like all of London's writings, by social democrats and frequently reprinted.

5. "How Solemn as One by One" in *Hymner och visor* (Stockholm: Bonniers, 1942); "Come Up from the Fields, Father" and "O Tan-Faced Prairie-Boy" in *Joker* 2, no. 9 (1944): 20–21, reprinted in *Nya tolkningar* (Stockholm: Bonniers, 1945); "I Hear It Was Charged against Me" in *Sanning, dikt, tro* (Stockholm: Bonniers, 1968) and again in *Synkrets* (Stockholm: Bonniers, 1974); and "By the Roadside: A Farm Picture," also in *Synkrets*. They were all reprinted in *Följeslagare:: Dikttolkningar från sex decennier* (Stockholm: Bonniers, 1989). I am grateful to Dr. Edfelt for this information.

6. For example, the roundly rhetorical opening stanza of "Proud Music of the Storm" concludes in the original with the poignant simplicity of "why have you seiz'd me?" Butenschön's translation lost this effect by pitching the question in a lofty, consciously antiquated form: "hvi hafven I gripit mig?"

7. In *Nya Dagligt Allehanda*, November 23, 1930 ("All moderns sång"), and January 4, 1931 ("Ned mäktig musik"); *Fönstret*, December 27, 1930 ("De badande"); and *Frihet*, June 1, 1931 ("Gräs").

WORKS CITED

Åhnebrink, Lars. "Whitman and Sweden." *Walt Whitman Review* 6 (1960): 43–44.

Algulin, Ingemar. *Den orfiska reträtten. Studier i svensk 40-talslyrik och dess litterära bakgrund* (Stockholm: Almqvist & Wiksell, 1977). Stockholm Series in History of Literature 18.

Blomberg, Erik. *Modern amerikansk lyrik från Walt Whitman till våra dagar* (Stockholm: Bonniers, 1937).

Brunner, Ernst. *Till fots genom solsytemen. En studie i Edith Södergrans expressionism* (Stockholm: Bonniers, 1985).

Ekman, Hans. "Från Gryningsröster till Aftonunderhållning. Studier i Johannes Edfelts ungdomsdiktning." *Samlaren* 88 (1967): 56–83.

Enckell, Olof. *Den unge Diktonius* (Stockholm: Wahlstrom & Widstrand, 1946).

———. *Esteticism och nietzscheanism i Edith Södergrans lyrik*. Helsingfors: Svenska Litteratursällskapet i Finland, 1949.

Enckell, Rabbe. "Inledning," in Rabbe Enckell, ed., *Modärn Finlandssvensk lyrik i urval* (Helsingfors: Söderström, 1934), 5–117.

Espmark, Kjell. *Livsdyrkaren Artur Lundkvist. Studier i hans lyrik till och med Vit man* (Stockholm: Bonniers, 1964).

———. *Harry Martinson erövrar sitt språk. En studie i hans lyriska metod 1927–1934* (Stockholm: Bonniers, 1970).

———. *Själen i bild: En huvudlinje i modern svensk poesi* (Stockholm: Norstedt, 1977).

Fleisher, Fredric. "Walt Whitman's Swedish Reception." *Walt Whitman Newsletter* 3 (1957): 19–22, 44–47, 58–62.

Frosterus, Sigurd. "Frank Norris och den amerikanska romanen." *Finsk Tidskrift* 65 (1908): 67–83.

Holmqvist, Bengt. *Modern Finlandssvensk litteratur* (Stockholm: Natur och Kultur, 1951).

Landgren, Bengt. *De fyra elementer: Studier i Johannes Edfelts diktning från Högmässa till Bråddjupt eko* (Stockholm: Almqvist & Wiksell, 1979).

Lundkvist, Artur. *Atlantvind* (Stockholm: Bonniers, 1932).

———. *Självporträtt av en drömmare med öppna ögon* (Stockholm: Bonniers, 1966).

Olsson, Hagar. *Ny generation* (Helsingfors: Schildt, 1925).

Romefors, Bill. *Expressionisten Elmer Diktonius. En studie i hans lyrik 1921–1930* (Helsingfors: Svenska litteratursällskapet i Finland, 1978).

Schwind, Jean. "Van Gogh's 'Starry Night' and Whitman: A Study in Source." *Walt Whitman Quarterly Review* 3 (1985): 1–15.

Södergran, Edith. *Samlade dikter*, ed. Gunnar Tideström (Stockholm: Wahlström & Widstrand, 1949), 9–38.

Tideström, Gunnar. *Edith Södergran*, 2d ed. (Stockholm: Aldus, 1963).

Willner, Sven. *Dikt och politik* (Helsingfors: Söderström, 1968).

Wrede, Johan. "Den finlandssvenska modernismens genombrott. En studie i idéernas sociala dynamik," in Sven Linnér, ed., *Från dagdrivare till feminister. Studier i finlandssvensk 1900-talslitteratur* (Helsingfors: Svenska litteratursällskapet i Finland, 1986), 41–70.

1. ARTUR LUNDKVIST

"Porträtt: Walt Whitman"

Du allas broder,
du man med det stora hjärtat,
du starke vandrare i livets storm.

Du glömde aldrig dessa morgnar från din ungdom
då du var med kamraterna i en båt på havet och fiskade:
     doften av tång, stämningen över vattnet
     med rop mellan båtar
     och blå rökstrimmor ur kajutor —
å, detta starka sköna kamratskap mellan män!

Du livets älskare,
för dig var dagarna som svala gröna böljor:
    hängiven, vällustfylld
lät du dem skölja över dig, uppbära dig, lyfta dig,
    slunga dig framåt —

Morgonvandrare,
du gick genom världen
i en stor oknäppt fladdrande kappa
och efter dig blev en virvlande vind;
du sjöng
och din sång dröjer ännu mellan höjderna, ekar över oceanerna;
dina fotspår står djupa, outplånliga i marken,
    visande VÄGEN,
och ljus blommar ur dem.

"Portrait: Walt Whitman"

You, brother of us all,
you, big-hearted man,
you, strong wanderer in the storm of life.

You never forgot those mornings from your youth
when you went fishing with comrades in a boat on the sea:
    the scent of seaweed, the mood created on the water
    with shouts between boats
    and blue smoke streaming out of the cabins —
oh, that strong fine comradeship between men!

You, lover of life,
for you the days were like cool green waves:
    consecrated, sensuous
you let them lave over you, buoy you, lift you, hurl
    you forward —

Morning-wanderer,
you walked through the world
in a great unbuttoned, flapping coat
and after you there came a whirling wind;
you sang
and your song lingers still among the heights, echoes across the oceans;
your footprints remain, deep, indelible in the soil,
    showing THE WAY,
and light blooms up from them.

Clarté no. 4–5 (May 1929): 12; reprinted as "Walt Whitman," in *Naket liv* (Stockholm: Bonniers, 1929), 64–65. Translated by Carl L. Anderson.

2. ARTUR LUNDKVIST

"Belated Homage to Whitman (An Essay-Poem)"

Two of the nineteenth century's most world-renowned beards belonged to Marx (the prophet) and Whitman (the poet),

they were practically contemporaries and in their later years came to resemble dandelions (that most folk-like of flowers) past blooming but bristling with seed, scattering seed:

of the two I can picture Walt Whitman strolling like some Neptune along the seashore, droplets of water glistening in his beard

or like some Adam in a new creation, a newly conquered continent (these United States),

and his eyes are moist like a deer's, moist with unexpended tenderness and prodigal compassion,

at the same time luminous to the point of blindness, reminiscent of the hyper-sensitive air bubble in a spirit level,

Whitman, brotherly but perhaps still more fatherly and motherly, with milk-filled breasts and nipples red as rose-hips,

not unlike the Egyptian river god seen lying in the fertile ooze with countless infants sprawling over him.

He awakens with the morning star while the sea is still milky in the dawn, stands there on the threshold between the Moon's night and the Sun's day,

himself belonging to both, a soul united with a body, in reconciliation of the old oppositions, possessed of God from his crown to the soles of his feet,

just as every mite and crumb is possessed of God, every creature and being exalted in its own sacredness, yet also partaking of the whole:

Whitman bathes by the shore, solitary White Man cradled in the arms of brother Ocean who is also mother Atlantis,

before once again indoors he whets a bread knife on his thigh and greedily drinks newly caught oysters,

groping about with his tongue in the slippery-rough bowl as in a womb (seeking the pearl?),

he sits with a darning needle held between lightly trembling fingers in order to cover a hole in his stocking with a web of wool,

perhaps he discovers also that a button is missing on his fly, but is distracted by a wild duck which he espies brooding eggs in its nest or a horse with rider approaching from the edge of the forest, horse and rider equally handsome

yet not the ultimate centaur he continues to await.

He walks barefoot now, his trousers turned up, his suspenders sweat-marked over the worn knit sweater, his hands large like a workman's but womanly soft inside,

he carries with him the Book, presses it close, his evergrowing book of Creation, flesh of his flesh,

like a living body to be touched, like a comrade clad only in his warm skin.

And there he sits between bare wooden walls, the door open to the ocean, and thus he writes like the ocean waves rolling in, endlessly, endlessly, in the smell of the rancid ink and into the night from the light of the lightly smoking kerosene lamp:

the whole world exists to be named, to be felt, to be made human, thing after thing, creature after creature,

so vastly much that awaits his words of deliverance, his enkindling finger:

nothing is too slight and nothing too great for him, he enters everything and everyone without partiality,

he is countless tongues singing the praises of creation, celebrating himself in others and others in himself.

Never can creation be praised enough nor the Creator, present in the progress of all things toward fulfillment,

mankind sprung up through natural selection for a destiny in whose fulfillment it itself participates,

thus it is that Whitman sings praises of all that he sees or envisages: logger and statesman, soldier and harlot,

locomotive and river barge, wheat and the farmer, spider's web and bird's nest, coal miner and cotton-picking Negro,

the bullet and the wound, cradle and cannon, eel and lark, the toes and the boot, the scythe in the reeds and the cricket in the tree:

sings praises, sings praises, endlessly, fervently, in the rhythms of sex and of the ocean's ground swells, free of the measured metronome,

with the smell of newspaper ink, wood shavings, and seaweed brought together in the poem.

On the wall behind him hangs a musty knapsack, a memento of the war when he changed dressings for the wounded and gave comfort like fresh spring water,

confronting in brotherhood pain and death among ten thousand men, as dear to him as his own life,

but now sorrow attends the lilacs in the midst of their blooming, lilacs with clusters like heavy white tears:

America is fatherless and the States are adrift like a disabled flotilla, the war between brothers has left behind a bloody divide which new growth is slow to cover over,

the green growth which Whitman sees as the ultimate victor, the endless, indefatigable armies of grass, forests trunk by trunk thrusting upward their community of rustling crowns,

the grass and the trees which will overcome all resistance, propitiate, unite,
cover all graves and the whole earth's wounds.

Oh, the seas will wash the feet of the cities, the wind disperse the clouds and
smoke, industries will remain negligible stains in nature,

the Hudson River will continue to issue forth from the womb of the forests, a
mighty stream of invincible freshness,

the strong young men of the West will advance with plow and axe, under the
peaceful sign of a spear of wheat, without the curse of slavery,

the bee will protect the sunflower and the ant will crawl up one's leg in com-
panionable intimacy,

the world will work tirelessly for the realization of brotherhood, no backsliding
and no innate depravity will stand in the way,

mankind is free and redeemed from the very beginning, and Christ who has
never been crucified will wander like a vagabond through these States,

sorrowless, in a slouch hat dripping with rain, deceptively like a dreamy white-
bearded poet,

and America will be a resurrected Atlantis where snakes twist like jewelry
around one's wrist and wild beasts follow after in ancient devotion.

But alas, who bellows like wounded sea-elephants from out in the ocean, what is
that acrid smoke rolling across the land,

what is that face displayed in the moon over the forests, blackened with soot
and streaked with blood,

what are the stars and stripes that resemble sparks expiring in grime and the
smear of bloody hands,

what can that tremor be reaching him from the America to come, the earth-
quake from the tremendous, heaped up forces?

Alas, too late, too late has it become on earth, trustful Whitman,

your affirmation of everything has twisted around on itself and returns as
negation,

brotherly democracy never realized but turned into parody,

all that you dreamed of sullied and ravaged in a flood of machines and ruins
throughout the world,

in an unrestrained flutter of the dollar's fake green, sweeping ahead like a hur-
ricane over nations and peoples,

alas, the overpopulated loneliness of skyscrapers, the elevators rising and sink-
ing like mercury columns in barometers of angst,

the forsakenness felt by the surging and whirling rivers of humanity, the omi-
nous swishing of millions of shoe soles on asphalt and the snakelike hissing of
rubber tires,

the outrage that distorts black faces into frightening beauty, ready to burst into flame like oil slicks on water,

alas, the Imperium's floundering presidents with their yellow goat's-eyes of greed and wide-open crocodile jaws,

all those gilded colossi calculating humanity's drops of sweat in cash registers chiming as though measuring energy,

the blind computers with their faces of numbers and their networks of electronic nerves,

the atomic explosions' thunder above and below ground and the white temples of the power stations brooding over their fearful secrets,

the fanatical brotherhood of researchers seeking life in death under the all-seeing eye of global surveillance, in the service of the new inquisition.

Alas, Whitman, Whitman! sprawled across the continent, lowered into the earth, you, interred father, overgrown with oilwells and silos, driven over millions of times a minute,

your red flesh cut into pieces for a sacrament that no one accepts any longer by mouth,

the voice rising out of your throat stifled, your message drowned in the clamor of the media echoing back from the satellites,

among waitresses with breasts like wax fruits, without milk and unnaturally hard as stone from paraffin injections,

moods from the time of infancy reawakened, a lingering hunger that cannot be appeased,

reeking excretions are presented on golden plates at banquets given at the highest level, while virgins shriek of rape under the tables,

and poisonous dreams in technicolor inflame the senses like gangrene left unchecked, in place of the visions of prophets and poets.

Whitman, your disciples on the open road rushing ahead like howling demons, dazed from sheer haste,

in a revolt with no outcome, solely the greedily licking tongue seeking its outlets, the new love member,

and you like a fleeting, hazy phantom, a puff of air across the face as from a human breath, a sudden tear in the corner of the eye,

you with the neglected bluebell in the corner of your mouth, a whitened hair that has landed in the bread, a childish knee that has struck itself on a stone,

a grizzled flag over a tower of brittle wood, a sun-dazzled seal resting on a rock in the sea, an albino-white tapir searching for ant hills,

alas, too late, too late on earth, sowing the seed of hope in vain, Walt Whitman!

"Försenad hyllning till Whitman," *Lyrikvännen* (1976): 6–9. Translated by Carl L. Anderson.

GAY WILSON ALLEN

Whitman in Denmark and Norway

Walt Whitman was discovered almost simultaneously by Rudolf Schmidt in Denmark and by Bjørnstjerne Bjørnson in Norway. Both were
associate editors of the Scandinavian magazine *For Idé og Virkelighed* (*For Idea
and Reality*) and shared the same ideas of social and political reform in a modern,
Darwinian world. Schmidt was the last of the German intellectual school, despised
by Georg Brandes, the leading critic and literary historian of Scandinavia, who belonged to the school of French realism. In 1872 Schmidt published in the magazine
an enthusiastic article on "Walt Whitman: The Poet of American Democracy." As
a result of this article, a correspondence developed between Schmidt and Whitman and the poet's most loyal supporters in the United States, Dr. R. M. Bucke
and W. D. O'Connor. In his article, Schmidt declared: "In the poem 'Walt Whitman' [retitled "Song of Myself" in 1881] is drawn the bold outline of a new departure in humanity — a man vigorous, with warm blood and fruitful brain, strong
muscle, wealth of imagination healthily rooted in sensuous organic nature, and at
the same time with a power of spiritual flight — able to attain the highest thoughts
of the human mind." Two years later Schmidt published a translation of *Democratic Vistas* (*Demokratiske Fremblik*), only one year after the American publication and the first to appear in Europe.

Bjørnson was famous for his stories of rural life and his social-problem plays,
for which he would be awarded the Nobel Prize in 1903. What he thought of Whit-

man and *Democratic Vistas* has been preserved in a record of a visit to him by Rasmus Anderson, who taught the Norwegian language at the University of Wisconsin. During Anderson's visit in 1872, Bjørnson received a letter and photograph from Walt Whitman and a copy of the latest edition of *Leaves of Grass*. Bjørnson asked Anderson what he thought of Whitman. Anderson had never heard of the poet but tried to stall by saying opinion on him was divided. Bjørnson detected the bluff: ". . . he became wild; he got up and paced the floor like a raging lion. . . . He said that we Americans did not appreciate our greatest men; that we let our most gifted poets starve." And he kept muttering something that sounded to Anderson like "Democratic wits." After returning home, Anderson finally discovered that the book was *Democratic Vistas*, which Bjørnson had read in Schmidt's translation.

Another Norwegian, a Unitarian minister named Kristofer Janson, was pastor of a church in Minneapolis, Minnesota, from 1881 to 1892. At the end of his first year, he published a book in Copenhagen on American culture called *Amerikanske Forholde*, in which he devoted most of his first chapter to Whitman, declaring emphatically:

> The most original poetic mind America has at present is undeniably Walt Whitman. Intentionally I say poetic mind; for he has not yet become a poet and he is an old, afflicted man. But I am certain that sometime in America's saga, he will be named as a pioneer in new forms, like a prophet who, along with all prophets, is not accepted in his own land. It is Walt Whitman's strange fate to be better known and respected in Europe . . . than in America. In America they laugh at him and call him a crazy old man.

But the enthusiasm of Schmidt, Bjørnson, and Janson was not shared by another Norwegian author, Knut Hamsun, who would win international fame with his realistic novel *Hunger* (1890; English translation 1899) and would win a Nobel Prize in 1920 after publishing *Growth of the Soil* (1917). He made two trips to the United States, the first from 1882 to 1884 and another from 1886 to 1888. During the second visit, he worked in the wheat fields in North Dakota and as a streetcar conductor in Chicago. He strongly disliked America because of the industrial-urban life he observed there and the "radicals" who advocated social welfare and women's rights. In fact, he detested democracy, and during World War II he supported the Nazi invasion of Norway, for which he would be censured and fined in 1948.

In 1889 Hamsun gave a vituperative speech in the Student Union in Copenhagen on Walt Whitman, which he later published in *Fra det moderne Amerikas Aandsliv* (*The Cultural Life of Modern America*) (see selection 1). Hamsun called Whitman "somewhat of an Indian both in his language and emotions." It is doubtful that Hamsun knew much about American Indians, but he was convinced that Whitman was an ignorant savage. The nearest he ever comes to praise is when he says that "the innate primitiveness of his nature, the barbaric Indian feeling of kinship with the elements about him, is expressed everywhere in his book and often bursts into brilliant flame." There are some glimmerings of insight in a few of Hamsun's condemnations, as when he notes how Whitman sought magic in his chanting of names or that his style echoed the Old Testament. Some of his comments on the poet are almost epigrammatic: "It requires at least twice as much inspiration to read such verse as it does to write it"; "If he had been born in a land of culture and had been intelligently educated, he might possibly have been a little Wagner"; "He is rather an exuberant man than a talented poet. Walt Whitman certainly cannot write. But he can feel."

The enthusiasm of Schmidt and Bjørnson and the indignation of Hamsun for Whitman did not, however, influence any other writer in Norway or Denmark, except the Danish poet and philologist Niels Møller. In 1888 Møller published translations of seven of Whitman's old-age poems in his youthful collection called *Efteraar* (*Autumn*), though in *Walt Whitman* (1933), Frederik Schyberg says Møller translated these poems into "a remarkably archaic, intricate, and obscure rhythmic diction which showed a lack of understanding of Whitman's poetic language." But the greatest barrier to the reception of Whitman in Denmark and Norway was the influential Georg Brandes, who completely ignored him. Schyberg attributes this, at least in part, to his having been "'discovered,' not by him, but by his opponent and arch-enemy, 'the insignificant' Rudolf Schmidt."

But a change came early in the new century. When Johannes V. Jensen, a new and original voice in Denmark, visited the United States in 1902–03, "he proclaimed," says Schyberg, "the New World as the new refuge of civilization, the place of regeneration and expansion," and he anointed Walt Whitman its spokesman. In Jensen's novel set in Chicago, *Hjulet* (*The Wheel*), he included translations of three of Whitman's poems ("Starting from Paumanok," "A Song of Joys," "When I Heard at the Close of the Day") which, again in Schyberg's words, "caused the greatest sensation by their frankness of language and the complete break with Danish lyrical traditions." Later, in 1919, these poems and others translated by Otto Gelsted were published in Copenhagen as *Walt Whitman: Digte* (*Walt Whitman: Poems*), along with a remarkable introduction in which Jensen calls Whitman "a guidepost to the West" (see selection 2).

In *Hjulet*, Jensen created two characters who personify two possibilities in Whitman's influence, one a genuine "poet of democracy" and the other a demagogue or "false prophet." Schyberg says further that in "Jensen's work may be traced a direct Whitman influence, both in his early radical lyrics and in many of the story-essays he called *Myter* (*Myths*) (1907–1944): a mixture of half-fables, half-essays, reminiscences, meditations, nature-observations, and pure fiction. The conclusion of a myth entitled 'Hjertet' ['The Heart'] (1916) seems to be written on the Whitmanian theme of the pulse beats of Europe and America."

Whitman's influence is also very strong in Jensen's masterpiece, *Den lange Rejse* (*The Long Journey*), for which he was awarded the Nobel Prize in 1944. He had published this epic in six volumes between 1908 and 1922; a partial translation first appeared in the United States in 1923. Whitman's influence is especially noticeable in *Christofer Columbus* (1921), the final book, with its lyrical descriptions of the American "pioneers":

> Here, in the new soil and for a long time unnoticed, liberty grew up, which had become homeless in Europe, the ancient independence of the peasants.
>
> And when it was strong enough it was able to turn back to the old world and show its light there; when the Republic, the pristine natural form of the West, was reintroduced to France, the infection came from the young American Union.

Schyberg mentions a dozen Danish authors of the First World War generation who were influenced by Whitman through Jensen's and Gelsted's translations, including Thøger Larsen, Otto Gelsted, Emil Bønnelycke, Tom Kristensen, Svend Borberg, Arne Sørensen, and Aage Berntsen. In Harald Bergstedt's poems, writes Schyberg, "not only the Whitmanesque sentiment but also the Whitmanesque expressions are repeated with striking accord." However, Bergstedt also illustrates the demagogic use of Whitman, for he thought he saw in Hitler's *Volksgemeinschaft* a realization of Whitman's type of democracy.

In 1919 the hundredth anniversary of Whitman's birth was observed in Denmark by the publication of several translations of individual poems and a biographical article by Ingrid de Lorange in *Illustreret Tidende*. Ten years later, Børge Houmann published a translation of "Song of Myself" and "When Lilacs Last in the Dooryard Bloom'd"—Houmann's best, according to Schyberg. In 1926 Helge Rode in *Det store Ja* (*The Great Affirmative*) had praised Whitman as a religious prophet and "one of the healthy-minded great."

In 1933 Schyberg himself published a small book of translations of Whitman's poems, including several from *Drum-Taps* and "Calamus." But Schyberg's great contribution was his biographical-critical study called simply *Walt Whitman* (1933). In tracing Whitman's development through all the editions of *Leaves of Grass* and in writing an epoch-making chapter on "Whitman in World Literature," he made a major contribution to Whitman scholarship. By focusing on the four decades in which Whitman had assiduously revised, retitled, and rearranged his poems, Schyberg was able to trace not only the growth of his art but also his changing psychology.

Schyberg thought that in world literature actual sources and influences were less important than similarities in mood, ideas, and styles: "In the relationships of literary history the influence of one author on another is only half the story, and often the least interesting. . . ." For his epigraph, Schyberg quoted these verses from Whitman's 1860 "Proto-Leaf":

> O strain musical, flowing through ages—now reaching hither,
> I take to your reckless and composite chords—I add to them, and cheerfully
>   pass them forward.

Schyberg claimed that, although Whitman did not know it, there had been poets before him who wrote Whitmanesque poems, and some contemporaries of Whitman might be accused of imitating him if they had known his work. Some examples mentioned by Schyberg are the Persian Rūmī (1207–1273), the German mystic Angelus Silesius (1656–1674), the Dane Jens Baggesen (1764–1826), and the Swedes Thomas Thorild (1759–1808), F. C. Sibbern (1785–1872), and C. J. L. Almqvist (1793–1866). Comparisons between Whitman and England's William Blake have often been made, but Whitman did not read him until the similarities were called to his attention. Kjell Krogvig suggested that, for Norwegian readers, their great epic poet Henrik Wergeland (1808–1845) provided the best approach to Whitman, though neither knew of the other's existence (see selection 3).

My own summaries of Schyberg's interpretations in my *Walt Whitman Handbook* caused Lionel Trilling to urge the Columbia University Press to publish a translation. With the cooperation of Schyberg, Evie Allison Allen made a translation which was published in 1951. But soon after correcting final proofs, Schyberg died—a great loss to literary criticism.

In 1947 the Norwegian poet Per Arneberg translated "Song of Myself" (*Sangen om meg selv*) into *nynorsk* (New Norwegian), a language based on native dialects which seems to be congenial to Whitman's innovative diction and rhythms. Sigmund Skard, in his splendid introduction (see selection 4), says that Arneberg accomplished "one of the most masterly translations ever made in Norway." Whitman predicted that no one would ever be able to translate his "barbaric yawp." But in the opinion of Skard, a renowned Scandinavian scholar of American literature, "Arneberg has managed to do so, without letting the reader see how great the difficulties must sometimes have been." It may be that *nynorsk*, with its robust German accent, is more congenial to Whitman's "language experiment," as he once called *Leaves of Grass*, than Danish, with its glottal stops, or Swedish, with its remnants of pitch stress.

Though no other Scandinavian translation of Whitman can compare with Per Arneberg's, Danes have not forgotten him. In 1950 P. E. Seeberg published a selection from *Specimen Days* (*Fuldkomne Dage*). One of the most interesting translations of Whitman's poems in Danish was Poul Borum's 1976 bilingual edition, *Fremtidens Historie* (*The History of the Future*), containing two dozen shorter poems from *Leaves* and selections from longer poems, including "Starting from Paumanok," "Song of Myself," and "When Lilacs Last in the Dooryard Bloom'd." In his preface, Borum explains why he made the translation:

Whitman and Baudelaire, the two giants at the beginning of modern literature, of Modernism, can still be read today as if they were writing today. Modernism is something we are still in the middle of, and Whitman and Baudelaire are our contemporaries. That's why the future they both write about is still our future. . . . The purpose of this selection is to introduce a contemporary poet who was born in 1819 and died in 1892. . . . Of great current interest and promising for the future I find the gigantic freedom of the body in these poems—not only the metaphors continually alluding to all-pervading sexuality, but also the bodily rhythms and corporeal syntax, which the translator has been very eager to recreate in Danish. And Whitman's democracy is a democracy of bodies. Also, his political message should be heard in a period which demands such messages.

In 1991 Annette Mester published a complete translation of *Democratic Vistas* (*Demokratiske Visioner*), which has been warmly praised by Danish critics. In translating Whitman's title, she preferred the connotation of a "vision" to Rudolf Schmidt's *"fremblik"*; this perhaps implies a prediction or glance into the future. Whitman's *Vistas* is ambiguous, but considering the state of American society at the time he composed the work, his "vision" was indeed an optimistic ideal. Mester has made a subtle choice of title.

Using Villy Sørensen's essay as an introduction to *Demokratiske Visioner* was also an excellent idea, raising the question of whether poetry can be "democratic." Whitman's role as "poet of democracy" has always been paradoxical. It was his greatest ambition to be that poet, and this was his designation in his first introduction to Denmark and Norway, as well as many other foreign countries. Certainly no one believed more strongly in the Jefferson-Jackson theory of democracy than he did. He came from the "common people" and wanted *them* for his audience, not "elitist" artists, musicians, and scholars. But common people, beginning with members of his own family, could not understand his poems. No one can doubt Whitman's sincerity or that in his own character and conduct he was a genuine "democrat." He wanted to be a "public poet," but he was actually a "private poet"—as are all lyric poets. Of course he said that "myself" included all selves, but his inspiration was his own emotions. And in his best poems he was an artist *lui-même*. At any rate, Sørensen raises a question of vital importance in Whitman criticism.

It should be noted that today most Danes and Norwegians can read Whitman in English, for in both countries schoolchildren begin the study of English in grammar school.

1. KNUT HAMSUN

"The Primitive Poet, Walt Whitman"

In 1885 [*sic*] a book was published in Boston which evoked a letter from Emerson, a reprint in London and an essay by Rudolf Schmidt. The book was called *Leaves of Grass* and the author, Walt Whitman. When this book appeared Whitman was thirty-six years old.

The author called the work poetry; Rudolf Schmidt also called it poetry; Emerson, on the contrary, had plainly not been able to hit on any designation for this work with its extremely weak system of thought. In reality it is not poetry at all; no more than the multiplication tables are poetry. It is composed in pure prose, without meter or rhyme. The only way in which it resembles verse is that one line may have one, two, or three words, the next twenty-eight, thirty-five, or literally up to forty-three words.

The author called himself a "cosmos"; Rudolf Schmidt called him a "cosmos." I, on the other hand, can only with difficulty find any connection with a term so extremely comprehensive, so that for my part he could equally well be a cosmos, a pigeon-hole, or anything else. I will modestly and simply call Walt Whitman a savage. He is a voice of nature in an uncultivated, primitive land.

He is somewhat of an Indian both in his language and emotions; and, accordingly, he celebrates the sea, the air, the earth, the grass, the mountains, the rivers, in brief, the natural elements. He always calls Long Island, his birthplace, by its Indian name, Paumanok; he constantly uses the Indian term *maize* instead of the English *corn*. Again and again he refers to American places — even whole states by Indian names; in his poetry there are entire stanzas of American aboriginal names. He feels so moved by the primitive music of these places that he crams long series of them in to passages where they have no connection whatever with the text; often he mentions a score of state names in a row without saying a word about the states. It is a pretentious game with savage words. One of his poems goes thus:

From Paumanok starting I fly like a bird,
Around and around to soar to sing the idea of all,
To the north betaking myself to sing there arctic songs,
To Kanada till I absorb Kanada in myself, to Michigan then,
To Wisconsin, Iowa, Minnesota, to sing their songs, (they are inimitable;)
Then to Ohio and Indiana to sing theirs, to Missouri and Kansas and
    Arkansas to sing theirs,
To Tennessee and Kentucky, to the Carolinas and Georgia to sing theirs,
To Texas and so along up toward California, to roam accepted everywhere;
To sing first (to the tap of the war-drum if need be).
The idea of all, of the Western world one and inseparable,
And then the song of each member of these States.

The innate primitiveness of his nature, the barbaric Indian feeling of kinship with the elements about him, is expressed everywhere in his book and often bursts into brilliant flame. When the wind whispers or an animal howls, it seems to him that he hears a group of Indian names. He says:

animals in the woods, syllabled to us for names,
Okonee, Koosa, Ottawa, Monongahela, Sauk, Natchez, Chattahoochee,
    Kaqueta, Oronoco,
Wabash, Miami, Saginaw, Chippewa, Oshkosh, Walla-Walla,

Leaving such to the States they melt, they depart, charging the water and the
land with names.

It requires at least twice as much inspiration to read such verse as it does to write it.

His style is not English: his style belongs to no culture. His style is the difficult
Indian picture-writing, without the pictures, influenced by the ponderous and
hard to comprehend Old Testament. His language rolls heavily and confusedly
over the pages of his book, roaring along with columns of words, regiments of
words, each one of which makes the poem more unintelligible than the other. He
has poems which are completely grandiose in their unreadableness. . . .

O'Connor said that one must have seen Whitman to understand his book;
Bucke, Conway, and Rhys also say that one must have seen him first to be able to
understand his book. But it seems to me that the impression of dream-like bar-
barianism one gets from reading *Leaves of Grass* would be strengthened rather
than weakened by seeing the author. He is certainly the last specimen of a modern
man who was born a savage.

Thirty or forty years ago people in New York, Boston, New Orleans, and later
Washington met on the streets a man of unusually powerful physique, a large,
serene man of somewhat crude appearance, always dressed in careless fashion, re-
minding one of a mechanic, or a sailor, or some other workman. He almost always went without a coat, often without a hat; in warm weather he kept to the
sunny side of the street and let the sun beat down on his great head. His features
were large but handsome; he had at once a proud and benign expression; his blue
eyes were gentle. He frequently spoke to passersby whether he knew them or not;
sometimes tapped strange men on the shoulder. He never laughed; usually he
wore gray clothes, which were always clean but often lacked buttons; he wore colored shirts and a white paper collar about his neck. Such was the appearance of
Whitman at that time.

Now he is a sick old man of seventy years. I have seen a picture of him taken a
few years ago. As usual he is in shirt-sleeves; as usual he inappropriately has on his
hat. His face is large and handsome, his thick hair and beard, which he never cut,
cascade over his shoulders and chest. On the forefinger of his extended hand he
holds an artificial butterfly with wings outstretched; he sits and observes it.

These portraits of Whitman do not civilize his book; as a literary production it
is a poetic desecration. Some people have wanted to regard him as the American
folk-poet. This can only be considered ironical. He lacks all the unity and simplicity of a folk-poet. His primitive emotions antedate those of the people. And his
language is not calm but raucous power; it mounts now and then to high orchestral outbursts, frightful shouts of victory which remind the stunned reader of Indian war dances. And everywhere, on closer inspection, we find it is only a wild
carnival of words. The author made a great effort to express something in his
poems but he could not get it said for the words. He has poems which consist of
almost nothing except names. . . .

It is heresy to say it, perhaps almost blasphemy, but I confess that in the darkness of night when I could not sleep and yielded to the impulse to think of writing poetry, it has happened that I had to grit my teeth in order not to say frankly: I could write poetry like that too!

What did Whitman want? Did he want to abolish the slave trade in Africa or forbid the use of walking sticks? Did he want to build a new school house in Wyoming or introduce woolen hunting jackets? No one knows! In the art of talking much and saying absolutely nothing I have never met his equal. His words are warm; they glow; there is passion, power, enthusiasm in his verse. One hears this desperate word music and feels his breast heave. But one does not know why he is enthusiastic. Thunder rolls through the whole book and lightning flashes; but the spark never comes. One reads page after page and is not able to find the meaning of anything. One is confused or intoxicated by these enthusiastic wordtables; one is paralyzed; crushed to earth in stupid hopelessness; their eternal unending monotony finally affects the reader's understanding. By the time one has read the last poem one cannot count to four. One really stands before the author who strains an ordinary person's mentality. The poet merely went along the road ("Song of the Open Road") and felt himself overcome by ecstasy—"the road shall be more to me than my poems"—and afterwards as he wandered on this often-mentioned road, he found "divine things well envelp'd." He was like the man of the desert who waked one morning at an oasis and fell into a revery as he looked at the grass. "I swear to you there are divine things more beautiful than words can tell," he exclaims constantly in regard to this road which he mentions over and over again. But he never expresses the divine things, so does not make the reader any wiser.

Even with the author's own picture vividly before his eyes, *Leaves of Grass* is still like "unspeakable" darkness for the poor reader, like a book without pictures. It is perhaps highly doubtful whether one could understand the poems better if one actually knew the poet. At most he personally might explain what he meant by his various catalogues; however, they were not expressed in understandable words but remain in writing which supposedly contains "songs." Moreover, according to his own and his biographer's account, Whitman meant to celebrate Democracy in his book. He is "the poet of Democracy." Furthermore, he is also, according to Rhys, the "Poet of the Universe"; so one must presume the singer is a highly gifted man. One does not fail to observe that at times he must have had difficult problems with his catalogues.

How is he "the poet of Democracy"? In "I Hear America Singing," which is a program-poem, he is the poet of democracy in the following manner and fashion:

I hear America singing, the varied carols I hear,
Those of mechanics, each one singing his as it should be blithe and strong,
The carpenter singing his as he measures his plank or beam,
The mason singing his as he makes ready for work, or leaves off work,
The boatman singing what belongs to him in his boat, the deckhand singing
  on the steamboat deck,

The shoemaker singing as he sits on his bench, the hatter singing as he stands,
The wood-cutter's song, the ploughboy's on his way in the morning, or at the
   noon intermission or at sundown,
The delicious singing of the mother, or of the young wife at work, or of the
   girl sewing or washing,
Each singing what belongs to him or her and to none else,
The day what belongs to the day — at night the party of young fellows, robust,
   friendly,
Singing with open mouths their strong melodious songs.

In this poem he forgot, if meter means anything, to count at all; and if verse
is all-inclusive, he forgot to hear saddlers or street-car conductors, or general
managers sing! If a poet of democracy here at home wrote such a poem —
whether it was about a shoemaker who sings as he sits on his bench or a hatter
who sings as he stands — and brought it to a newspaper or the Danish editor of an
almanac, I venture to believe that they would want to feel the singer's pulse and
maybe offer him a glass of water. If he refused to admit that he was ill, one would
at least feel that he jested very crudely. . . .

If he had been born in a land of culture and had been intelligently educated, he
might possibly have been a little Wagner; his spirit is sensitive and his disposition
musical; but born in America, that remote corner of the world where he could always shout Hurrah and where the only recognized talent is salesmanship, he had
to be a changeling, a mixture of primitive being and modern man. "In our country," says the American author, Nathaniel Hawthorne, "there is no shadow, no antiquity, no mystery, no picturesque and gloomy wrong." For an original primitive
like Whitman his innate inclination is to do more or less primitive reading; thus
for him reading the Bible is the highest poetic enjoyment; in this way he undoubtedly developed his savage tendencies more than he repressed them. Everywhere in
his poetry the language and the imagery of the Bible reappear; in places the similarity to the Bible is so striking that we must almost marvel at the completeness
with which he has been able to assimilate such a peculiar form. In "Song of the
Answerer" he says:

A young man comes to me bearing a message from his brother,
How shall the young man know the whether and when of his brother?
Tell him to send me the signs.
And I stand before the young man face to face, and take his right hand in my
   left hand and his left hand in my right hand,
And I answer for his brother and for men, and I answer for him that answers
   for all, and send these signs . . .

Doesn't that read like an excerpt from one of the Old Testament writers? Whitman's constant study of biblical poetry has certainly increased his literary bold-

ness, so that he frankly mentions things that are taboo. He is modern in so far as he always writes brutally with the intense literalness felt and thought by uncultivated minds. But it is scarcely because of any conscious feeling of artistic courage that he has poeticised Reality; it is much more the result of the naivete of a child of nature. The section of erotic poems in *Leaves of Grass* for which he has been censured and about which supercilious Bostonians shouted to heaven, in reality contains nothing more than can be said with impunity in any literature; it is another matter entirely that the audaciousness is rather crudely, illiterately spoken, as it certainly is. With somewhat less naivete and a little less biblical influence, one could say twice as much as he says and give it double the literary value merely by a superficial use of literary dexterity, such as shifting a word here, revising another there, deleting a vulgarity and replacing it with an acceptable term. The language in Whitman's poetry is by far the boldest and warmest in all literature, but in the main it is naive and lacking in taste.

Walt Whitman's naivete is so incongruously great that it can actually be captivating, and now and then the reader can put up with it. It is this strange naivete which has won him a few disciples among men of letters. His catalogues, those impossible reiterations of persons, states, household furniture, tools, articles of dress are certainly the most naive poetry with which a literature has yet been augmented, and had it not been sung from a naive heart, it would certainly never have been read, because it shows not a vestige of talent. When Whitman celebrates something he says so in the first line, then mentions another thing in the second line and a third in the next line, without celebrating any of them except by mentioning them. He knows no more of things than the names, but he knows many names, hence all the enthusiastic name-calling. . . .

Among the poems which Whitman has collected under the title of "Calamus" are to be found the best in the book. Here he sings of the love for men which beats strongly in his good warm breast and occasionally finds an echo in others. Through "love of Comrades" he will rejuvenate the corrupt American democracy; by it he will "make the continent indissoluble"; "make inseparable cities with their arms about each other's necks"; "make the most splendid race the sun ever shone upon"; "plant companionship thick as trees along all the rivers." There occur isolated coherent passages in these poems; they stand out therefore as strange exceptions in his book. His primitively unrestrained emotional nature is here expressed in somewhat civilized English, which is thus intelligible even to his compatriots. In a poem entitled "Sometimes With One I Love" he is so extraordinarily clear that, in surprise, one supposes these two or three lines must have been written by his mother or some other intelligent person:

> Sometimes with one I love I fill myself with rage for fear I effuse unreturn'd love,
> But now I think there is no unreturn'd love, the pay is certain one way or another,

(I love a certain person ardently and my love was not return'd,
Yet out of that I have written these songs.)

Here—if we overlook the author's break in rhythm in the first and second lines—we can find a comprehensive thought expressed in intelligible language—actually in language which, remembering that it is lyrical, is used legitimately; but he cannot restrain himself long; a few lines further he is again the incomprehensible savage. . . .

Whitman is a very genial person, a man of native capacity, born too late. In "Song of the Open Road" he plainly reveals what a benevolent disposition he has, mingled with all the naivete of his ideas. If his verse were written in a little more regular style, much of it would be poetry; on the other hand, it is novel for an author to continually hinder the understanding of his poetry because of the incomprehensible word-mechanism he uses. He cannot say a thing once emphatically; he is incapable of making a point. He says a thing five times and always in the same grand but meaningless way. He does not control his material, he lets it control him; that is evident in his colossal form which accumulates and overwhelms him. In all this song of the highway his heart is warmer than his brain is cool; therefore he can neither describe nor celebrate; he can only exult—exult in wild outbursts over everything and nothing. One feels a heart beating violently in the pages of his book, but one seeks in vain for a probable reason why that heart has been so strongly moved. One cannot conceive that a mere road could make a heart palpitate so. Whitman is intoxicated by it; his bosom heaving with emotion, he says frankly: "I think I could stop here myself and do miracles."

How his great joyous heart leads him astray: "I think whatever I shall meet on the road I shall like, and whoever beholds me shall like me." He says in his strange inaccurate language:

Whoever denies me it shall not trouble me,
Whoever accepts me he or she shall be blessed and shall bless me.

He is impressive, very impressive. At times his great goodness astonishes even himself, so that the naive and simple soul goes on to sing:

I am larger, better than I thought,
I did not know I held so much goodness.

He is rather an exuberant man than a talented poet. Walt Whitman certainly cannot write. But he can feel. He lives an emotional life. If he had not received that letter from Emerson his book would have failed, as it deserved to fail.

This essay is an expansion of an address Hamsun gave in the Copenhagen Student Union during the winter of 1889 and was published in *Fra det moderne Amerikas Aandsliv* (Copenhagen, 1889), 63–85. Translated by Evie Allison Allen.

"Walt Whitman"

Had Walt Whitman lived to be a hundred years old—and it would have been like him, since he had something of the longevity of Drakenberg, Ashaserrus, and all other vagabonds—he would have encountered an enormous growth in his reputation such as he could scarcely have dreamed of but which was inherent in his poetry. Briefly, the universal was Whitman's passion and an age which seeks the universal seeks Walt Whitman. At the moment [1919] he is assiduously imitated in France, a phenomenon that is not easily explained; the war has drawn France and America closer together, and since two incommensurable entities must take something from each other, France has taken Whitman. In Germany he is imitated, and the explanation is obvious; he has been taken over as another novelty, not from America but from France, just as Naturalism, Impressionism, and more recently the Negroid style have been in turn. For this latest brilliant cultural borrowing the Germans have invented the term Expressionism, which gives a very good idea of the lightning speed with which people express themselves when they are fortunate enough to get both the tempo and form from others. Whitman was introduced into this country [Denmark] as early as the Rudolf Schmidt-Rosenberg period [1870s] without attracting any attention except as a curiosity. In due course I translated some of his poems which appear in this collection, supplemented by Otto Gelsted's translations. But I must be permitted to comment that these poems originally appeared in a novel [*Hjulet* (1905)] with an American motif and consequently a peculiarly American atmosphere; thus they have a relative value. If it is of any interest, I might say in this connection that the poems I have written in free verse have not been in any way inspired by Whitman. In fact, I used Goethe's "Wanderer's Storm Song" and Heine's "North Sea" as models. I have studied Whitman but one should look for the influence in my prose. As early as 1900 I wrote about machines in the spirit of Whitman, but did not use his verse form. It occurred to me even then that what Whitman stood for and what he taught is this: Express your own age in the language of your own time. It should be obvious that to follow Whitman one does not begin by imitating his poetry, since both the period and the people are different from the nineteenth-century America. Nevertheless, most people do not interpret him in this way; they Whitmanize in many tongues, happy to escape from the bondage of rhyme until it has become a sort of horse-measure, probably similar to that in which the Houyhnhnms once whinnied. Many who do not have anything to say in prose and lack the capacity for a purely lyrical expression try to find a so-lution in an extravagant strophe form which at least typographically suggests Whitman.

Yet Whitman should not be held responsible for the sins of his disciples; what innovator has not had a troop of followers who copied all the obvious literary eccentricities, the trademarks, and yet remained innocently unaware of their master's philosophy of life.

If we compare Whitman's work with that of the other American and English writers of his day, his achievement is tremendous, unique, an outburst of originality such as not every century sees; a very special state of mind turned this ordinary artisan into a vital artistic force, impervious to the prevailing contemporary literary forms. The whole basis of his aesthetic is an atavistic memory and a lusty, phenomenal joy. He began by turning his back on all literature and literary circles and started alone in the street. He did not reform or re-make current poetic style; he threw it aside and simply put Whitman in its place. His rhythm is made up of things themselves, of sounds; to him a series of names is poetry — and it is poetry, an invocation, an ecstatic proclamation of the things he loves.

If one should try to find the origin of the Whitmanesque style I believe he could point to two sources, the American press and the Bible. The American newspaper style, the exclamatory, telegrammatic style, the banked headlines, the explosive conglomeration of details all remind us of Whitman; the content of any American newspaper suggests Whitman's famous catalogues and grows in the imagination in the same way. He began his career as a printer, and in the printing office he could have received a permanent visual impression of the identity of language and objects which he afterwards developed into his strophe. The free verse of Goethe and Heine undoubtedly came down from Pindar and Greek chorus, but the actual form is found in the Eskimo incantation. The primeval source is the ecstatically delivered prose of the shaman. Whitman's free rhythms are like the Greeks, but otherwise he is entirely non-Greek, non-academic. The complete lack of classical form alone makes Whitman a modern. He is solemn and direct as the prophets, his style recalls the strophe divisions of the biblical prose, with the ponderous movement resulting from the translation of the original Hebraic poetry into the prose of another language. In a certain sense the Bible is more modern than the Greeks, it is more elemental, more savage, has more of our own Darwinian age; each person determines its meaning for himself.

The form that Whitman evolved was his own, a piece of nature. With all the power of his lungs he proclaimed America. When one considers the poetic literature of the period, with its English primness and decorum, in which roses conversed with lilies, and poesy fed on poesy, Whitman's effect is that of an avalanche of matter, things, substance. *Leaves of Grass* is an immense collection of material, an experimental register of America's realities. It does not go beyond that; it is a colossal inventory, but to accomplish this enumeration is an intellectual achievement. It is easy to see now that America of that period should have been more openminded, but the majority failed to see what *Leaves of Grass* stood for. It was a period of great immigration, a folk-blending took place on a scale hitherto unheard of. Travel was in its infancy, and though the actual, athletic America had arisen so recently, yet it had not won a very desirable name for itself. The word "American" had come to mean gigantic, fabulous, and could be characterized in no other way than by the robust, money-made practical joker personified in the concept of a Yankee. Only recently had people begun to take America seriously, but they thought her crack-brained. In France the superficial wits still considered American a term of opprobrium. Heine called America a land of boors. In the '90s Henrik Cavling had the same amused but respectful attitude toward America which one might assume toward a vast carnival. Hamsun attacked America as the "dollar-land" it is, and he was especially blind to Whitman's importance. Yet it was from America that Hamsun brought back the linguistic innovations which afterwards turned back the French inundation. Understanding of America was slow in coming; Americans did not understand themselves but wavered between Cooper's colorful Indian country and Mark Twain's buffoonery. In reality Whitman was the only one with a clear vision. He saw the real America, and now we are beginning to see it with his eyes. He had the insight to see with his own eyes, and now the two worlds, the old and the new, are beginning to agree on what he saw.

Whitman's significance should be sought in the glory he throws over America; he is a guidepost to the West. His personality does not repay the curious for a closer look. Neither his own autobiographical contributions nor the accounts of others are of special interest. The pathological nature which he could not conceal restricted his private life to a sphere which is familiar ground to those who suffer from the same malady and is a closed world to others; but the nature of his impulses need not diminish the artistic value of his work. It often happens in nature that disease leads to momentous development in other fields. It is a mistake to be interested only in the cause of illness. An ethical evaluation should be avoided. America has not yet offered to gather around Whitman as a national intellectual leader; presumably that is not to be considered. He towers among the great eccentrics, but not among the harmonious greats such as Björnson.

In one respect the abnormal in Whitman's nature is of purely aesthetic interest to the student of pathology. For example, Whitman's emotions, as expressed in many passages of his writings, seem to me to reveal the dark secrets of feminine psychology. Women cannot and will not go into it, and those who have done so have not been real women. Whitman's erotic confession sounds as if it came from an instrument tuned in the womanly key; like a girl's, his soul is just beneath the skin, everywhere and nowhere. He is vasomotorly prompted whether in the bath or before the fire; like a woman he feels the tension in all sorts of places. Beauty is present, as always when we meet femininity, so long as you forget while you read that it was a big, bearded, lubberly fellow who wrote it.

When we look at Whitman from this point of view, we realize he should be comprehended in many different ways if we are to benefit from his work, and that one view does not exclude the other.

At the moment his influence is scarcely fruitful. I see that some rejoice in his doctrine that the Libido shall rule unchecked, without regard to sex, a world of nothing but "Camerados," which would certainly be a snug monkey-cage. His irresponsible vagrancy, vagabondage, the baring of his soul, which made him akin to the Russians and Verlaine, seems to attract many, a symptom of a decadent period.

Yet as a prophet he is of outstanding significance. If instead of making use of his idiom we would use his method, the world would be the gainer. He is more than a perplexing individual about whom critics and biographers give us information, more than a soothsayer or monotonous shaman; rather he is a Prince of Words and a gateway to America. America is a huge book and *Leaves of Grass* is the key to it.

Introduction to Johannes V. Jensen and Otto Gelsted, *Walt Whitman: Digte* (Copenhagen: Nyt Dorsisk Forlag, 1919). Translated by Evie Allison Allen.

3. KJELL KROGVIG

"Approach to Whitman through Wergeland"

His love of humanity is all-embracing, but his perspective on the human race is often cool and distant, even bitter. Compassionate by nature, and with a capacity for sympathy of unique depth, he often has touches that are gruesome and at times he is brutal in treatment. He eulogizes life and immortality but pictures corruption and annihilation with a wealth of detail which approaches obsession. He is possessed by faith and doubt in equal proportions and is at the same time arrogant and proud, vain and humble. In his soul the clay struggles with the spirit, the shadow with the sunshine, earthy amorousness with heavenly purity, anxious sighs with an eternity of peace. And, though according to his own words, he was a mere poet, he entered wholeheartedly into all the affairs of his day.

These words, which so strikingly point up the contrasts in Henrik Wergeland's rich mind, are taken from an essay by Anders Wyller on Wergeland's poem "Fölg kallet" ("Follow the Calling"). This essay is found in Wyller's posthumous collection of articles and speeches entitled "Kjempende humanisme" ("Humanism at War"). But all the foregoing might equally well have been said about the Walt Whitman whom we learn to know in "Song of Myself," which just this year [1948] appeared in Per Arneberg's translation. And if one places these two giants side by side, it is perfectly obvious to any Norwegian that the way to an understanding of this remarkable American is through an understanding of our great Norwegian poet. The similarity between the two goes much deeper than the spiritual affinity naturally existing between two men of genius, and if one did not know it to be an impossibility, one might be tempted to speak of direct influences. In a search for the underlying reasons for this similarity we must examine the purposes of these two poets and the place of each in his own milieu.

They were practically contemporaries, with a difference of only eleven years in their ages. To be sure, their environments were radically different. Wergeland was the son of a preacher and belonged to the upper class, while Whitman was the son of a poor farmer and carpenter. Wergeland died young and Whitman became an old man. But each of them worked on his own particular masterpiece which neither completed to his own satisfaction. Whitman published the first edition of *Leaves of Grass* in 1855 when he was thirty-seven, and up to the time of his death he continued with revisions on this work. Wergeland brought out *Skabelsen, Mennesket, og Messias* (*The Creation, Man, and Messiah*) in 1830, at the age of twenty-two, and like Whitman, he never finished revising his work to his complete satisfaction. Much of what he wrote afterwards is a repetition and an extension of his central work, which he finally revised on his death-bed.

There was perhaps no great similarity in their outward lives, but their poetic inspiration was dipped from the same spring. Both Wergeland and Whitman stepped forth from young struggling nations, and each one felt in his veins the coursing vigor of his own people. These two nations were at this time the freest and most democratic in the entire world, and this freedom gave the two poets an overweening strength and a wild courage to maintain the human rights which their people had won. Their faith in the evolutionary process had no bounds; in liberty and democracy they envisioned boundless possibilities for human development, and each one looked upon himself as a standard-bearer in the struggle to defend the liberties his youthful nation had won. Whitman championed his red and black brothers; Wergeland fought for the Norwegian constitution and Norwegian nationalism.

Their own periods found difficulty in following these two in their wild flights and in their apocalyptic visions; their compeers, who had more than enough with the daily struggle, could sense their deep human warmth. Posterity, too, has found them hard to understand because they both indulged in the careless imagery of genius; yet each one has been in his own particular country the foundation for later literature, and each has been a creative force in shaping the independent culture of his own young nation.

From the religious standpoint there is superficially much to distinguish Wergeland and Whitman, but a closer view reveals that the differences lie more especially in the milieu and background. Wergeland made his debut in a young nation and in an old tradition-bound society. Whitman did not have this dead weight to struggle with; he had no strong roots either in faith or in tradition; he stood absolutely independent in his relationship to God and to society. He did not view God as creator and omnipotent ruler of the universe; to Whitman God did not reveal himself outside of nature and of the human spirit. And man himself could become deity because man is a spirit which embraces all. For Wergeland, nature and the human spirit were also of God, even if only a small fragment of Him; God Himself ranked considerably higher as the ruling power in the universe. In the term "God," Wergeland included the Christian God, while Whitman also included the God of the Indians and of the Negro. Among the wild primitive children of nature Whitman found the uncorrupted spirit and the liberated human being, who, in effect, is God. Whitman had lived in direct contact with primitive people and had discovered that their stronger feelings for nature, for the supernatural, and for the forces of nature made them more receptive and responsive to everything that surrounded them. Wergeland attempted to find this same primitivism in the peasant and the laborer and he recognized and extolled their simple child-like faith; but he did not delve into their intimate pagan contact with nature. But even if the two had varying concepts of God, there is a close agreement in their concepts of nature and in their worship of everything from the smallest blade of grass to the myriads of stars in the heavenly dome.

Also in form and imagery, Wergeland was bound by tradition, while Whitman stood untrammeled. It was not the spirits which spoke through Whitman but rather nature directly. It is for this reason that Wergeland could never give such a frank testimony as the one Walt Whitman gives in the opening lines of "Song of Myself." Here Whitman is humanity as a whole; that is to say, sheer primitive humanity, the child of nature; and it is nature herself which speaks through primitive humanity. Wergeland also was the mouthpiece of the universe but he had to speak through the spirits of God and of the Messiah. It is the elements themselves which through man's awakened senses bring nature to Walt Whitman; these elements fill him full and he warbles forth the song of nature to humanity. Those who follow him in his song will experience the great all-embracing miracle, not through Walt Whitman but through his inmost being, for nothing is greater than the human being. In addition, he says, we must always remember that instinct is everything. This instinct we must accept as we are, primitive, clean, and naked in body and in soul. At this point, thinking will not avail; speculation is useless, for nothing is large or small; there is no beginning or end; nothing new or old. All is now and all is eternal.

If we go with him further into the poem we discover that it is thus also that he regards his own soul, liberated from the daily humdrum of existence and surrendering itself to the contemplation of the miracles of nature. The soul has nothing to do with this daily humdrum but is bound to nature, through which it arrives at a mood full of peace and knowledge of "all the arguments of earth." Then the soul is at peace both with humanity and with the spirit of God.

Wergeland was not able to go quite this far in a blending of nature, spirit, and humanity, but when these two poets seek God in nature, they again stand on the same ground. The child, the human seed, the grass of the field, the lowliest thing alive is a revelation of God, and death exists for none of them. Everything continues onward; nothing is annihilated or disappears.

But at this point Walt Whitman is forced one step further; he admits that the spirit is more than this; it is beyond birth and death. Like Wergeland, he places goodness and love above the earthly, goodness for both the fortunate and the unfortunate. To the spirit nothing is damned or beyond redemption; the spirit represents love, fertility, desire, fulfillment, and happiness. It is this which takes possession of Whitman and gives him inspiration, and in this poem he exults in jubilant praise for this gift of nature. All of life is perfect, he says further, the groping love-life and ecstasy, the life of the child of nature and of the laborer and of the Negro in his bodily perfection. The essence of the life is spirit; even the humblest life is of greater consequence than all the eloquence of the world can express. Spirit and nature are, nevertheless, not quite the same, but the spirit understands the voice of nature, knows its place in the universe and is subject to the same laws; it is the "common air that bathes the globe."

Both Wergeland and Whitman understand their own particular genius and both suffer from the knowledge that they cannot gain the entire world as audience. Wergeland was bitter over being born in a small country and being able to reach so few with his poetry, he who had both a European and a universal viewpoint. Whitman had the advantage of writing in a world language but had the disadvantage of living in pioneer society which had little appreciation or taste for his universality. He loved and eulogized this country and its rich natural resources and he realized its enormous potentialities. He sang for his strong primitive people about their great future, and was tortured by their refusal to take the time to listen to him. They both possessed boundless self-confidence and each felt within himself the limitless potentialities of his own spirit. But within his own limitations, each one ranged free and unconfined.

If we continue further in this poem ["Song of Myself"] we hear Whitman say that his spirit is deathless and limitless because he himself is a part of primitive nature. He is the earth itself as well as the loved one who on the night of nights shall come and create the passionate life of the mystic. It is quite natural for him to be at the same time materialist and realist. But it is time alone which makes everything come to pass and everything perfect, and the eternal gives freedom and liberation. But the great wonder in his soul would slay him unless he could give utterance to it and sing it forth to humanity at large.

In his poetic impulses and creative joy, Whitman can be as crude and as barbaric as Wergeland, but like him he reveals at the same time a tender compassion for everything frail, pure, and innocent. But when he expounds his naturalism, nothing can stop him, least of all calm reason, practical advice, and narrow criticism. He probably has only partial control over what the spirit has to communicate to him, but he knows that what he has to say is of the spirit and is therefore the truth. And thus a transmutation is created in him; the spirit talks through him to humanity and humanity in turn sings its songs in his songs and poses to him the great riddle "that we call being." And his answer is: "Only he who knows all, feels all, can really know what Being is." Wergeland, too, must be able to identify himself with other human beings, express himself, give of his own strength, give all in human content, and fulfill the law of fertility. The progress of life is like the free flight of birds; Whitman himself is one with the animals and birds because, like them, he has no consciousness of evil. Love is the only thing he can assimilate because he himself loves everything from the lowest creeping thing and the most depraved human being up to the deathlessness of his own soul. Not until he has eliminated the self does he know for a certainty that he really exists. Not until then has he become a part of nature and of the life and emotions of humanity.

When he has thus become filled with this love, he feels drunk with joy and begins to celebrate all of humanity and its life. Now he wants to liberate humanity as a whole, and in accomplishing this he must absorb all evil, the terrors of war, and all the sufferings of humanity. But all of this becomes at length too heavy to carry. In the face of evil he is forced to surrender. Whitman, like Wergeland, can assimilate only pure love and neither has any weapon against evil, which must be met with new evil instead of with love. For this reason Whitman looks in anticipation toward death and after death toward the resurrection, after which he hopes to be reincarnated as a pure and innocent child of nature. At this point, where he attempts to absorb into himself the emotions of the entire world regarding good and evil, he reaches the dramatic climax of the song of himself.

When he has been reincarnated as a child of nature, a slightly more peaceful happiness steals over him as he again begins to reconstruct humanity and to embrace it in its entirety with greater strength for the final miracle. He would sweep aside all ancient views of the universe, melt together all ancient religions and all of life and shape everything anew. Unlike Wergeland he does not believe in original sin nor in demoniac possession; by means of his ideal nature-child he hopes to accomplish his goal. Again he begins singing his triumphal chant, for now everything in spirit and in nature is approaching perfection. Again he commences celebrating life. Now he will arouse humanity. He insists that humanity must realize that the all-important thing is man himself and the spirit of man. God lives on through human immortality and for this reason Whitman is not afraid of death; all is form, unity, design, eternal life, and spiritual bliss. This is his gospel, and his own liberated spirit is but one expression of nature's versatility. Those who will search will find what they are looking for; and if some suppose that he contradicts himself, then the contradiction is merely proof of how all-embracing he is.

And if one goes to Walt Whitman with an open and receptive mind and good resolution, one will discover what his message is for every single human being and will be swept up by his passionate worship. One will feel his strong happiness or deep Weltschmerz, or his powerful love for humanity or his stormy joy in nature. There will always be some place where Walt Whitman will speak to one — so many-sided is he, so rich is his interpretation, so big in his thinking. It is for this reason that posterity has been able to dip into Whitman as we have dipped into Henrik Wergeland's rich spirit.

And because everyone finds something for himself in his poetry and everyone reads him according to his own particular needs and moods, every reader will interpret him according to his own ideas. To translate a poem like Walt Whitman's "Song of Myself" is, therefore, a hopeless task even for the most sensitive poet. If one were to penetrate to the uttermost limit of his visions, the inmost emotions of his soul, one could go on and analyze him in large erudite tomes, after which there would hardly be anything left of Walt Whitman, the poet.

Per Arneberg has done the only thing possible; he has employed Walt Whitman's own formula; he has filled himself with the poet's moods, visions, and images, and has given them out again in the way that they have touched his own mind. It is quite natural that he should have taken on this almost impossible task. He himself is the latest flowering of the long Wergeland tradition in our literature. He has surely sensed his relationship to this great American mind, and for this reason his interpretation will be the most faithful that is possible. Fortunately he has not reduced Walt Whitman to easy reading; here [in this translation as in the original English] we must follow the words of the poet, approach him with an open mind, must receive and experience the miracle.

"Till Whitman Gjennem Wergeland," *Samtiden* 57 Aarg., Heft 3 (1948): 196–202. Translated by Sigrid Moe.

4. SIGMUND SKARD

Walt Whitman and His Book

Ever since Walt Whitman found his first readers in Norway about a century ago, he has been compared to the Norwegian poet Henrik Wergeland, and for good reasons. In their genius, in their emotional worlds, and in their literary form, these poets are close to each other. The similarities in their work would lead one to suspect plagiarism if we did not know that they never read each other.

Both poets were subjects of dispute in their lifetimes and after their deaths. As late as the 1940s, I met aging professors of literature in the United States who hesitated mentioning Whitman's name in decent company. But principally the two poets resemble each other in their historical positions. Norwegians justly see the figure of Wergeland in the very portal to the modern history of their nation. Whitman holds the same central position in the literature of the United States.

The intellectual history of America naturally falls into two periods. Until the Civil War, literature was in the hands of the cultivated class of citizens in the old settlements along the East Coast. In their traditions they were still Europeans and were determined to remain so. But beneath this European crust America was changing radically. Every year ever larger crowds of immigrants surged ashore in the harbors of the New World and streamed westward across the plains by rail and in covered wagons. Every year new areas of American land, as large as medium-sized kingdoms in Europe, came under cultivation.

And the plough was followed by the railroad tracks and the speculators. The acquisition of land released an economic struggle for life more immense in its dimensions and more brutal in its forms than anything seen anywhere before. This America no longer was a European colony. It was nothing but itself, wildly fantastic and unbelievably crude, the home of dizzy dreams and the most realistic prose.

To give voice to this new country, its wonders of nature and its new masses of population, was the immense task of an emerging American literature. Walt Whitman pointed to the problem and started solving it. He is the first American poet who could only have been American.

In his long life (1819 to 1892), he attempted to gather the entire country into his own self. He grew up in the home of an artisan in Brooklyn, a suburb of New York; forest and grassland were across his garden fence, a metropolis across the river. He was never ground smooth by ordinary school attendance but rather was allowed to mature by his own impressions. He was born omnivorous, greedy alike for nature and for man; and he was given to satisfy himself with both. He dabbled in many trades but mainly worked as a journalist and reporter, a tireless and systematic idler along rivers and ocean shores and in the teeming humanity of Broadway. He travelled both in the South and in the new lands of the American West. Everywhere he was absorbing impressions, with a scope and sensitivity of impression hardly equalled in any other poet.

But in Whitman, as in Wergeland, his real genius was in the heart. He did not record coldly what he experienced. Everything — man, animal, dead things — he met with the same all-embracing power of love. In both poets this was a part of their own openness of mind which allowed them to confront the entire register of life, from the ethereal to fullblooded sensuality. In Whitman, though, the scope was perhaps even wider, because his sexuality embraced more than the normal range. To say that he was "homosexual" is a distorting simplification. Rather, he seems to have belonged to a kind of intermediate type: that demarcation which the ordinary human being draws between the two sexes was, for Whitman, fluid. He faced everything in life with the same profound and erotically colored sympathy, a feeling which drew its power from the deepest wells within himself.

Around 1850, these elementary forces suddenly, like the breach of a dam, made their appearance in Whitman, and in the course of a few years they turned the quite commonplace small-town journalist into one of the great poets of world literature. But he was no sentimental dreamer. His love of man had its solid foundation in the ideas of the Age of Enlightenment about liberty and human rights. Advancing in years he became ever more radical. And he gradually supplemented his views with the new theories of evolution.

At the center of his thought were the American people, struggling to build their new democratic life. He would be the poet of these wordless masses. Like Wergeland, he demonstrated his position by dressing plainly and "popularly": homewoven clothes (with the neck-opening giving a glimpse of a red undershirt), high boots, and a sailor's hat. But he gathered his creative power around what he hoped would become the National Poem of America: the volume of verse without rhyme called *Leaves of Grass*. It appeared in 1855 and became Whitman's life work. He enlarged and rewrote it again and again. When the final edition appeared in the year of his death, the number of pages had increased tenfold.

Even today, *Leaves of Grass* remains a "strange" book. One can imagine how it must have appeared to readers in the 1850s. To Norwegians, it calls to memory some of the "wild" poems from Wergeland's youth—and in many ways Whitman remained at that early stage of development. He never became a reliable judge of his own work; many of his poems drown in their monotonous stream of words. Also, he had less intellectual stamina than his Norwegian counterpart. Curiously, his poems sometimes seem to lack a skeleton. The images have little clear distinction, and the ideas become frayed at the edge.

But the patient reader of Whitman finds his reward. When the poet is at his best, he safely takes his place at Wergeland's side. He has something of the same overwhelming power of imagination, and he uses it on a new and huge subject. The book has wonderful cosmic visions. Nature is experienced intensively. There are glimpses of a surprising power of psychological penetration. But what moves the reader most profoundly are the pictures of man: the American nation itself, in its most violently formless period of creation. They are all there. The hunter sleeps in the wild woods behind the canvas of his tent. The omnibus is wagging heavily through the crowded streets of the big city. The child dozes in the buzzing sunshine with fly-netting over its face. The compositor chews his quid of tobacco over his box of types, the letters disappearing in a haze before his eyes. A groaning woman hurries homeward in order to give birth to a baby. The hayload rolls toward the barn in soft jolts, through a smell of rocks and hot flowers. Once in a while the pictures flicker as in a movie. At other times, the light comes to a stop and falls clearly and quietly over a face, revealing a human fate.

Through all of it moves a feeling of awe before the vast dimensions of life and of the human mind. The poems are blood-warm and near. But there is also a bridge to eternity: the gospel of the senses ends in God. There is about these poems something strangely primeval. Here paints a poet who clearly is able to make grandiose errors, but who in his best hours gives words to his visions with a sovereign power. He certainly may be lacking in clarity, but frequently that is just because he is seeking his way toward unknown depths. His free verse carries the reader with a rhythmic movement similar to that of the ocean itself.

Through his entire work, Whitman speaks in the first person. In a way, his book is almost crazily egocentric. But the reader soon discovers that the "I" who expresses himself is only the symbol and representative of the countless crowds speaking through him. It is this almost primitive feeling of human identification that makes this profoundly romantic book so pivotal in the history of American poetry.

One cannot say that Whitman has many "pupils." Imitations of his poems are a little too easily discovered. But the first sprouts—both good and bad—of the entire spiritual future of America are in his book. It foreshadows the courage to go on in a new society without ignoring that society's shallow optimism. The book is carried by a deep trust in humanity; sometimes it sounds magnificent, at other times just naive. Here speaks a noble love of liberty and faith in brotherhood, along with an unruly worship of self which directly denies those ideals. There is in Whitman a deep humaneness; at the same time, there is also a mass effect, something ascribing value to quantity itself, which points to one of the basic dangers in modern society, not least in the United States. There is a genuine warmheartedness and, at the same time, a touch of the boastful, the bombastic, and the empty. The book is in the same breath realistic and symbolic. And all of this belongs to the United States. In its very unrestrained, fleeting form, *Leaves* reminds the reader of America itself. But at the same time, it is this superabundance of contrasts which gives *Leaves* its character of victorious vitality. With all its flaws it is still a modern book. How much of the literature of the 1850s deserves that kind of praise today?

The center of Whitman's work is the great poem about himself. It appears already in the first edition and can perhaps be called the culmination of his creation. It has the dewish freshness of the first experience; at the same time, it contains all the most important ideas that the poet was to take up later in his life. It is the best introduction available to that world which he was going to create. Per Arneberg translated "Song of Myself" into Norwegian in 1947. His book is regarded as one of the most masterly translations ever made in Norway. Recreating Whitman in another language is difficult, to put it mildly. The poet may be verbose and vague in one line, concentrated like a rock crystal in the next. Whitman himself warned that no one would ever be able to translate his "barbaric yawp." Arneberg has managed to do so without letting the reader see how great the difficulties must sometimes have been.

Arneberg points out, justly, that a translation of Whitman is inevitably bound to be an interpretation. Therefore his translation often is more clear than the original; this is hardly a loss to the reader, who will travel a straighter road ahead. The reader is thus able to yield more freely to the billowing rhythm in ideas and cadence, finally acknowledging what Whitman himself once said about his work: "This is no book, / Who touches this touches a man."

Preface to Walt Whitman, *Sangen om meg selv*, trans. Per Arneberg (Oslo: Den norske Bokklubben, 1973). Translated by the author.

NIILO PELTOLA

Whitman in Finland

The process that makes a poet well known in a foreign country usually comprises three stages: translation, criticism, and influence on the country's native poetry. Generally speaking, this is also true of the reception of Walt Whitman in Finland. The main process, however, was preceded by preliminary flashes on the Finnish literary scene. The first was a short item on Whitman in the general history of the literature of the world written in Finnish by O. A. Kallio in 1905.[1] The book was intended for the general public, not for professionals. Kallio pays attention to Whitman's free verse meter, dismissing it as "formless and defying all rules," but he also speaks about "his strongly statured songs echoing the spirit of a big and free republic."[2] The first full-scale article on Whitman to be published in a Finnish periodical was written in Danish by Paul Harboe. He was surprisingly well versed in his subject, but his influence on Finnish poetry and criticism was minimal. The same is true of the first article on Whitman which was written in Finnish.[3] It was published in 1917 in a respected literary periodical, but because the author was relatively unknown, readers tended to disregard his opinion despite his evident enthusiasm for the subject.

It was not until the interwar period that Whitman really emerged as an influence in Finnish poetry, first in the Swedish-speaking literary circles of the country. Three poets were of major importance here: Elmer Diktonius, Hagar Olsson, and Edith Södergran; all three were internationally oriented, unprejudiced, and interested in experimentation. Diktonius and Olsson were bilingual and wrote partly in Finnish. Their influence on Finnish poets was considerable. They both contributed to the bilingual literary periodical *Ultra* (1922), which launched Whitman into the consciousness of Finnish poets. There Olsson published her article "Walt Whitman, föregångaren" ("Walt Whitman, the Pioneer"). The style of her article is highly poetical, and she tries to portray an all-embracing vision of Whitman: "With out-stretched arms he stood there; with nothing beside him, nothing behind him, everything before him. . . . This man saw further into the future than many of the youngest had done. He dreamed about the golden age of brotherhood which was to become the ideal of the new generation emerging from amidst the atrocities of the war."[4] The article is followed by Diktonius's Swedish translation of Whitman's poems, including "Poets to Come." Thus Whitman's poetry made its first appearance in the Finnish literary world.

More important for the rise of the Whitman cult was the publication of Södergran's modern type of verse, first in Swedish and then in the 1920s in Finnish. Her tragic fate appealed to the Finnish poets, but even more striking were her passionate, visionary fervor and her free, rhymeless meter, unprecedented in Finnish poetry. The poet admitted to her friends that part of her inspiration came from Whitman. It has been pointed out that "in many of her poems she used Whitman's enumerative style with non-rhyming lines of varying length. The enumerative 'I' style which she often used in her poetry is clearly an echo from 'Song of Myself.'"[5]

The year 1928 saw the publication in Finnish in a respected literary periodical (*Jousimies*) of a full-scale biographical and critical essay on Whitman, Oskari Nousiainen's "Walt Whitman, Amerikan suurin runoilija" ("Walt Whitman, the Greatest American Poet"). It contained a translation of "Proud Music of the Storm." The article clearly shows that the author was not ignorant of Whitman's importance for American poetry and for the literature of the world; he was, however, a journalist and a translator rather than a serious critic or poet, and for that reason the article attracted little attention. But the work of Södergran, Olsson, and Diktonius did have an impact; it influenced a number of young poets writing in Finnish who called themselves *Tulenkantajat* (Torch-bearers). For them, Whitman was a pioneer of democracy and what they called modernism. Whitmanesque echoes are to be found in the rhymeless verse of such poets as Katri Vala, Arvo Turtiainen, and Viljo Kajava, writing partly under the banner of socialism. It seems that in Finland Whitman's position among literary circles had established itself by the end of the 1930s,[6] but his image was still somewhat vague, as is evident in Kajava's poem "Kevät" ("Spring"), where Whitman is included among poets who had been victims of "persecution":

He saw those who had spoken about life
and those who had spoken against destruction and slavery
like Whitman, Heine, Ossietzky.

From the middle of the 1930s we also have Turtiainen's comment on modern trends in Finnish poetry: "Long ago we would have needed, here in these back-woods, a great poet of life and reality like Walt Whitman." Turtiainen is even more explicit about a quarter of a century later: "Modernism has age-old tradi-tions in the history of literature. Two of its greatest names in lyric poetry are Whitman and Mayakovsky."[7]

It was not until after the Second World War that a kind of Whitman boom made itself felt among Finnish-speaking poets, critics, and scholars. There are ev-ident reasons for this boom: better English-Finnish dictionaries, an improved knowledge of the language and literature of the English-speaking countries, grants for studying at American universities, and visiting professors of American lit-erature at Finnish universities. The primary instigator, however, was the then-approaching centenary celebration of the first edition of *Leaves of Grass*. This led in 1954 to the publication of the first comprehensive Finnish translation of Whit-man's poems, *Ruohonlehtiä* (*Leaves of Grass*), by Viljo Laitinen, a university stu-dent who was only twenty-two years old and who published the poems at his own expense. Considering his age, Laitinen's achievement was an impressive one. He had a sharp ear for Whitman's rhythmic flow, and his diction is clear. But the trans-lation is devoid of subtlety in the choice of words, and there are downright mis-takes in the translation of single items: "the drunkard's stagger" ("Song of the Open Road"), for example, refers in Laitinen's version to a way of speaking rather than a way of walking, and when he comes to the phrase "music rolls, but not from the or-gan" ("Song of Myself"), the translator does not think of organ as a musical instru-ment but rather as part of the body! Laitinen had a tendency to make omissions, as for instance in the long enumerations of "Starting from Paumanok," Section 16.

Literary criticism followed in the tracks of the translation. Lauri Viljanen, one of the leading literary critics in Finland, published a review of Laitinen's transla-tion and also extended his sympathetic attention to Whitman. He applies the ex-pression "portal figure" to both Whitman and Baudelaire because, as he points out, "their production gives rise to new highways leading far ahead." His explana-tion of Whitman's enumerative style is also worthy of note: "Enumeration [in Whitman] does not express subsequence, not even traveling, as is the case with Baudelaire and Rimbaud, for instance, but a powerful experience of simultaneity. In reading the poems 'Salut au Monde!' and 'Crossing Brooklyn Ferry,' time and space do not mean anything; all continents and all races live in Walt Whitman when he gives expression to his mystical feeling of unity and vocation."[8]

The centenary celebration of *Leaves of Grass* also prompted a translation and literary assessment of Whitman by Ville Repo, who had been studying at Emory University in Georgia in 1948–49. He had already distinguished himself as a trans-lator of Elizabeth Bowen, Tennessee Williams, W. B. Yeats, and T. S. Eliot before his work on Whitman. In 1956 he published a comprehensive article on Whitman together with his translation of "Crossing Brooklyn Ferry."[9] This was a poem which Laitinen had already rendered into Finnish, but Repo was a more experienced translator, more adept at solving typically Whitmanesque verbal problems. In his article, Repo took a partly biographical and partly psychiatric approach, which led him to naive moral lecturing. In reading Whitman's poems in praise of democracy and a healthy life, Repo tended to see masks where others saw Whitman's own face. He also thought he had found the source of Whitman's style: the King James Bible, not the poet's own creative mind.

The 1950s saw a deepening interest in Whitman not only in translations but also in scholarly studies. Harry Järv, in his 1955 article on Whitman as the poet of democracy, analyzed the characteristic features of Whitman's style and his achievement as a verbal master. I myself have discussed Whitman's poems from a narrow stylistic point of view in *The Compound Epithet in American Poetry* (1956).[10]

In the next decade we again meet the most outstanding Finnish Whitman enthusiast, Arvo Turtiainen (1904–1980), poet and translator, who published his first collections of poems in the 1930s. Before starting his work on Whitman he had produced a translation of *Spoon River Anthology* (1947), which instantly became very popular in Finland. He was unable to publish his Whitman translation by 1955, as he had probably planned; when it was finally printed in 1965, it was still not a complete edition but nevertheless was clearly a more comprehensive and more mature translation than Laitinen's. Turtiainen seems to have known his predecessor's work and observes a kind of division of labor: although both of them translated "Song of Myself," "Song of the Open Road," and "Out of the Cradle Endlessly Rocking," only Laitinen translated "Starting from Paumanok," "Crossing Brooklyn Ferry," "Song of the Redwood-Tree," and "The Sleepers," whereas only Turtiainen translated "Children of Adam," "Calamus" and *Drum-Taps*.[11] Turtiainen was deeply conscious of the obligation and also the difficulty involved in his Whitman translation. In his preface, he expressed the opinion that a good Whitman translation would require as many years as Whitman himself had spent on the writing of his poetry. Unfortunately, Turtiainen was unable to produce a complete Finnish edition of Whitman's poems before his death, and the work remains unfinished.

Turtiainen's translation attracted a great deal of attention and critical discussion of Whitman. Hannu Launonen wrote a good introduction to Whitman's poetry and to Turtiainen's translation of it in one of the major newspapers, *Uusi Suomi*. His contribution was to place Whitman against a historical and cultural background: "Democracy in Whitman's America had critics and exponents but no voice of its own; Whitman wanted to be that voice." He sees "Song of Myself" as "the first attack against Victorian abstinence in America," and so he relates Whitman to D. H. Lawrence in Britain. Launonen appreciates the enthusiastic and congenial attitude of the translator toward his poet. He notices, however, that Turtiainen's work is often an interpretation rather than a translation and proceeds to point out a few mistakes. Another review, written by Harry Forsblom, is more reserved in its praise of Whitman. The critic seems to empathize with both the admirers and the antagonists of the poet. He, too, comments on errors in Turtiainen's translation.[12]

Last but not least, Rafael Koskimies, the leading Finnish literary critic of the mid-twentieth century, has shown a deep understanding of Whitman's poetry and its significance for world literature. He considers Whitman the father of free verse meter and of "much more that was later called symbolistic and expressionistic poetry." He points out that Whitman had a predecessor in the Norwegian poet Henrik Wergeland: "They both found their most intimate way of expression in unrestrained verse." Accurate knowledge was not important for Whitman: "He wanted to depict and outline a popular ideal, his own type of Americanism, which clearly differed from the structure of European class society." [13]

Once Whitman's status in world literature had been clearly defined in Finland by the end of the 1960s, he became canonized, as it were, at Finnish universities and in literary circles. Whitman is no longer a strange bird that attracts mere curiosity. He is duly recognized in academic surveys of world literature, and Finnish radio has made him familiar to the general public. [14]

NOTES

1. For this reference and many others, I am deeply indebted to Sirkka Heiskanen-Mäkelä, Department of Literature, University of Jyväskylä, and to Urpo Kovala, who is in charge of a computer-based bibliography of translations of Anglo-American literature in the same department.

2. All translations from Finnish and Swedish into English are my own, unless otherwise noted.

3. Valvanne Väinö, "Walt Whitman," *Sunnuntai* (1917): 3.

4. Hagar Olsson, "Walt Whitman, föregångaren," *Ultra* (1922): 46.

5. See F. Fleischer, "Walt Whitman i svenskspråkig litteratur," *Nordisk tidskrift för vetenskap, konst och industri* 38 (1962): 136.

6. See Viljo Kajava's biographical and critical sketch of Whitman, "The First American Poet," *Kirjallisuuslehti* (1935): 336–342; and translations of Whitman's poems, mainly from *Drum-Taps*, by Katri Vala and Elias Siippainen in *Talenkantajat* no. 40 (1933), nos. 51–52 (1936), no. 53 (1937).

7. Arvo Turtiainen, "Itsetuholla suuruuteen," *Kirjallisuuslehti* (1936): 22–24; and *Tilanne* 1 (1961): 31.

8. Lauri Viljanen, "Walt Whitmania suomeksi," *Parnasso* 6 (1954): 278–280.

9. Ville Repo, "Crossing Brooklyn Ferry," *Parnasso* 5 (1956): 195–205.

10. Niilo Peltola, *The Compound Epithet in American Poetry* (Helsinki, 1956).

11. See Walt Whitman, *Ruohoa* (*Leaves of Grass*), trans. Arvo Turtiainen (Helsinki: Kustannusosakeyhtiö Tammi, 1965).

12. Harry Forsblom, "Laulu itsestään," *Helsingin Sanomat* (January 30, 1966).

13. Rafael Koskimies, *Maailman kirjallisuus IV* (Helsinki: Otava, 1965), 126–130.

14. See, for instance, *Kansojen kirjallisuus* 8 (1976): 504–522; and *Helsingin Sanomat* (July 1, 1976).

EZRA GREENSPAN

Whitman in Israel

The most remarkable aspect of the phenomenon of Whitman's reception in Israel has been, and still remains, the very fact of the phenomenon itself: the absorption of the greatest poet of the New World into the life and language of the "new world" of Israel. For all the cultural differences between Whitman—whether it be his individuality, eroticism, or Christianity—and traditional Jewish and/or Israeli customs, the fact remains that Whitman has exerted an important influence on the cultural life of modern Israel.

The central word of this phenomenon, as I understand it, is "absorption." A favorite word of Whitman's, it is also, in a very different way, a central word of the modern Jewish state, which has seen as its mission the ingathering of the Jewish people from centuries, or even millennia, of exile around the world and which has established a system of absorption centers throughout the country to expedite the process of assimilation. One of the most important aspects of the process conducted at these centers is, of course, the instruction of the Hebrew language. But while devoting a considerable amount of its material resources and energies to absorbing immigrants into the society, Israel has also sought to open itself to the outside world. Culturally speaking, that has meant absorbing the great works of foreign cultures into modern Hebrew, itself as new (or, if you will, as old) as the renascent nation.

The absorption of a foreign writer into a culture is always a complicated phe-

nomenon, one whose difficulties often transcend the literal problems of translation. But the absorption of foreign writers into Hebrew has presented an especially complicated set of challenges and difficulties, since the language was (and,
to a certain extent, still is) both so established and yet so unestablished, so historically and morphologically disconnected from the languages and cultures of the
West and yet so open to their influence. Because the revival of Hebrew was an integral part of the revival of the nation, Israelis feel an enormous pride in their language and a vital stake in its development. In this context, the translation of an
important writer into modern Hebrew has often been a genuine cultural event,
one of a magnitude not easily comprehensible to a person born to English. One
thinks, for instance, of the widespread importance accorded at the time to the
translation into Hebrew of Shakespeare by the poet Avraham Shlonsky or of
Homer by the poet Saul Tschernichowsky.

Understood in this context, the translation of Whitman into Hebrew would
naturally have been the single most significant event in his reception in Israel, as
in fact the Hebrew translation quickly became upon its appearance. But even before Whitman became directly accessible to Hebrew readers in the early 1950s, his
work had already begun to have an influence on a scattering of writers and intellectuals aware of his poetry in English and other European languages. In fact,
Whitman had long been a particular favorite among Jewish writers and intellectuals in the United States and in Eastern and Western Europe. Many of them were
affiliated with the political Left and readily identified the voice of his poetry with
the cause of the working masses or that of urban democracy. In the United States,
he was even translated into Yiddish by Louis Miller, whose *Poems from "Leaves of
Grass"* was published in New York in 1940.

Actually, as early as the appearance in 1929 of the essay manifesto *Kelape
Tish'im Vetish'ah (Against Ninety-Nine)* by the fine young Hebrew poet Uri Tsvi
Greenberg, Whitman's importance in the cultural world of the Jewish *yishuv* in
Palestine was well established. Greenberg's manifesto was a literary call to arms, in
many ways reminiscent of Whitman's 1855 Preface to *Leaves of Grass*. Greenberg
called for a revitalized Jewish national literature incorporating the same kind of
energizing spirit that Whitman had brought three generations earlier to American
literature. Like Whitman, Greenberg was an outsider to the literary establishment
of his time who saw the current literary productions as too tame and pusillani-
mous to suit the urgent needs of his nation. The "ninety-nine" of his title, to
whom he addresses himself with an iconoclastic self-assurance worthy of the
young Whitman, are the Hebrew writers against whom he positions himself and
his ideas of the requirements incumbent upon the new national literature. Whatever may have been his personal aspirations, the young Greenberg conceived unreservedly of his as the voice of the historic moment. While belittling his generation of Hebrew poets for contenting themselves with their "little songs" and
"polished rhymes," he called for a revolutionary poetry befitting the citizens of a
reborn people and a reborn language.

At the same time, Greenberg would never have accepted the Whitmanian distinction between the individual and the collective; on the contrary, as a Jew he saw no necessary incongruity between the existence of the individual and that of the collective: "In the redemption of the Hebraic mass here in this land is the redemption of the individual in Israel. Beyond the circle of this redemptionary vision there is no reward for the Israeli individual."[1] Furthermore, Greenberg was acutely aware of the abnormal nature of the Jewish national experience and therefore of the specific conditions for its literature. For him, the necessary distinction for the modern Jewish writers was linguistic: to write either in Yiddish (the language of the diaspora into which he was born) or in Hebrew (the language of his adopted homeland). Having made that choice, he declares that Yiddish is literally "jargon," an impoverished language of a deracinated people and a language for which, even before the imminent threat of Naziism, he predicts a speedy death. By contrast, he speaks of Hebrew as a language possessing a virtually mystical significance, just as he ascribes to Hebrew writers a mission virtually religious in nature: to lead their people to a new — or, more exactly, to a renewed — homeland in language.

At the end of this remarkable manifesto, Greenberg surveyed the landscape of his land, and what he saw left him with a mixture of sorrow and hope:

> Days of famine and sorrow are upon us, the nation rebuilders. The kingdom of the aching spirit reigns over the material world, which walks around on the soil of the Land of Israel in the element of its familiar hunger and poverty. Tuberculosis and fever accompany it. I eat and drink from the Bible. And in my reflections, I pass overseas to America. And in my contemplation of America, there comes to my mind . . . Longfellow. "Hiawatha." But in the end, I stumble upon Walt Whitman, the universal sea wall, the giant. Upon the celebrating man of flesh and blood who raises the worldly to the level of the divine, inspiring action. And I think that Whitman should have written in Hebrew, since he is moulded from the same substance as a Hebraic prophet. He did not know Hebrew as I do, and what a pity! And as I think so, another idea comes to me: oh, would Whitman have been in trouble had he written such "poems" as his among us in Hebrew! Such a traitor against art: he thunders in his baritone and prevents people from sleeping, as though it weren't already enough that he refuses to sing lullabies for overgrown babies:

> Here, this is the city and I am one of the citizens!
> What interests the others — interests me, too.
> Politics, wars, markets, newspapers, schools,
> Mayor and city councils, banks, tariffs, steamships,
> Factories, stocks, warehouses —
> Etc. (thus far I quote from memory)

> The nine muses [of the non-Jewish world] blush with sorrow and humiliation from such poetry, and the gods on Olympus cry. But my ancient, ances-

tral, Hebraic God Almighty tore open his heavens before the voice of the giant of the American shore.

In my "visionary leap," I transfer, as you know, Vilna, a city so like Jerusalem, from the soil of Poland and position it securely near Tiberias. Afterward, I also transport Walt Whitman to the living Land of Israel.

Rise up, our Hebraic Walt Whitman, rise up![2]

Greenberg's manifesto helped to establish Whitman's name and reputation in his society; thereafter, it was only a matter of time before Whitman became accessible to the Hebrew reader. His eventual translator, the poet and teacher Shimon Halkin, was fully aware of the cultural significance of his undertaking, as his long and devoted essay accompanying the translation reveals.[3] Halkin, who had lived for a period of years in America before the establishment of the State of Israel in 1948, had become familiar with the physical and social background of Whitman's world and had developed a respect for American democracy. He saw Whitman as a major poet and one extraordinarily useful in expanding the range of Hebrew poetry. But even apart from ideological or cultural considerations, one can sense the exciting challenge presented to Halkin in taking Whitman's poetics, so often remarked upon by commentators as being analogous to and perhaps even influenced by biblical poetics, and putting them into Hebrew verse.

Freed from the narrow necessity of inventing Hebrew rhymes and formal metrical equivalents to match the English, Halkin was able to concentrate on rendering the free rhythms of Whitman's verse in Hebrew. This he managed far better than he did in finding a stylistic equivalent to Whitman's colloquialisms.[4] In fact, the most remarkable achievement of Halkin's masterful translation is the degree of correspondence he achieves between the rhythms of the original and those of Hebrew, a feat that has not been universally possible in other languages, Western and non-Western alike. While not directly touching on the question of the possible correspondence between Whitman's poetics and those of the King James Bible, Halkin's translation does persuasively establish a structural and linguistic (if not cultural) congruity between Whitman and modern and biblical Hebrew.

In the foreword to the translation, Halkin speaks of the primary criterion governing his selection of Whitman's poems as being his desire to "stand the world of Walt Whitman's poetry before the eyes of the Hebrew reader in the fullest possible circumference within the dimensions of this volume."[5] The dimensions of that volume, if falling somewhat short of encompassing the full text of *Leaves of Grass*, are nevertheless generously inclusive. All in all, he included about 60 percent of the 1881–82 poems, but that figure includes nearly all the major poems of length, as well as most of the shorter poems valued then and now. Furthermore, some of the serious omissions, such as of "As I Ebb'd with the Ocean of Life," were corrected in the revised edition. In making and organizing his translations, Halkin followed the text and format of the 1881–82 edition, a decision that, in his later years, he would regret and correct in the expanded translation he published in 1984, which concluded with selections taken from the two annexes of the

1891–92 text. Handsomely printed and bound, the resulting volume makes — as Whitman himself would have been quick to appreciate — an impressive duodecimo presentation of his work.

In the same year that Halkin's translation was published there also appeared in Hebrew translation an unusually perceptive analysis of Whitman and his poetry in the literary supplement to one of the country's socialist daily newspapers. Originally written in Russian in the 1930s by the great literary historian D. S. Mirsky as the introduction to a Russian translation of *Leaves of Grass*, this essay is most immediately relevant for my purposes because of what it reveals about the climate of Israeli literary opinion on Whitman in the 1950s.[6]

Its angle of analysis becomes clear with its opening sentence: "Walt Whitman is the last great poet of the bourgeois era of humanity, the last in the line that begins with Dante." Mirsky then goes on to give a far-reaching Marxist reading of Whitman that places him along the historical continuum of great Western poetry of the pre-Bolshevik era and gives a perceptive account of Whitman's peculiarly tangled relations with his contemporaries: "But though Whitman may have grievously erred on this question [of popularity], despite the fact that he was possessed of a profound and structural acquaintance with, and understanding of, the society in which he lived, this but serves to cast into deeper relief the fact that, on all questions save that of poetry, he spoke the same language as democracy's self."[7] It is not hard to see why the editors of an Israeli socialist paper would choose to reprint Mirsky's article, since they could safely have assumed that a poet who, to use Mirsky's distinction, spoke for, if not to, the masses was a poet as eminently relevant to Israeli society in the years immediately following independence as he had been in the previous generation to Greenberg and others. At a time when the founding socialist ideology of the nation still pervaded the labor movement, health care system, reigning political party, and the kibbutz and moshav movement, and when ties of birth and culture still held many Israelis to the Soviet Union and Eastern Europe (a statement that applies to much of the Israeli intelligentsia of Greenberg and Halkin's generation), Mirsky's article would have accorded at least loosely with the general ideological thinking then current. In fact, it is hard to imagine any American literary figure who would have been more relevant to this generation of Israelis than was Whitman.

Of the Israeli writers who came to maturity with the establishment of the nation, the story of Moshe Shamir and his interest in Whitman is particularly interesting. Shamir was the son of an American Jew who had served as a volunteer in the British brigade fighting in the Middle East in World War I and who had remained in Palestine after the overthrow of Turkish power. Not long after having established himself there, he received a letter from a fellow member of the brigade who had returned home to Philadelphia after the war, in which the friend had inscribed a greeting composed of lines taken from *Leaves of Grass*. Later, that same friend sent over a thick, green copy of *Leaves*, which the young Shamir remembered from his earliest years as sitting on the family bookshelf. Years later, he

would become so enamored of Whitman as to try his hand at occasional translations of individual poems.

Upon receiving the Neuman Prize in 1981 in Jerusalem from New York University's Institute of Hebrew Culture and Education, Shamir reminisced about his
longstanding admiration for Whitman. As he did so before an audience that included the president of Israel, numerous leading Israeli writers, and literary scholars from both America and Israel, he spoke about the complicated relationship
("the love-hate-envy affair") between the U.S. and Israel and even more so between the Jewish community of America and the Jewish people of Israel.[8] Against
this context, he spoke of Whitman as serving as a sustaining tie between the two
sides of the ocean. Perhaps for this reason, he then went on to make remarks,
presumably directed to the American and Israeli scholars in attendance, about the
necessity of further inquiry into Whitman's influence on contemporary Israeli
writing:

> To the researchers of our literature on both sides of the ocean, I would suggest
> that they investigate and summarize the influence of Walt Whitman on mod-
> ern Hebrew poetry—and not less on Israeli prose. The most famous example
> is, of course, Uri Tsvi Greenberg, who wrote about Whitman not only in admi-
> ration but moreover in an open invitation to an uprising within ourselves, in
> his manifesto *Against Ninety-Nine*. But I would suggest that researchers inves-
> tigate especially among our younger poets—[Amir] Gilboa, [A.] Hillel—and
> yet without ignoring our fiction writers.[9]

Another of the leading Israeli intellectuals drawn to Whitman was the distinguished scholar Gershom Scholem. Scholem, who devoted his extraordinarily
productive life to the study of the field of Jewish mysticism, which he had virtually
created himself, introduced a strain of thought into the reception of Whitman I
have not yet mentioned, one that has assumed an increasingly central role in the
life and thought of Israel in the last twenty years: religion. In surveying the status
of Israel as it neared the end of its first generation, Scholem was left with the distinct impression that this was a "generation in crisis."[10] Knowing that mysticism
had historically been most attractive to peoples in times of crisis, he wondered
openly about the likelihood of a new mysticism appearing in contemporary Israel.
But on that possibility Scholem cast a tough skepticism, one based on his belief
that, at least as far as traditional Jewish theology was concerned, his contemporaries were "anarchists" unable to accept its tight, binding structure.

At the same time, Scholem was unwilling to yield the field of ideology to secular Zionism. He had been compelled to locate the borders of the secular and the
religious in his own life, once insisting to an interviewer that "my secularism is
not secular"; likewise, he gave serious thought in his scholarly work to those borders in the life of the nation.[11] In a country in which that dividing line had never
been defined precisely, leaving the society with a vaguely and precariously situated
religious establishment, Scholem was treading one of the most problematic and,

as recent Israeli history has shown, sensitive lines in the life of the country. Even before the religious sector began to expand its power base in the country following the wars of 1967 and 1973, Scholem was pondering the possibility of finding a viable solution to the integration of the secular and religious in contemporary Israeli society. More specifically, Scholem wondered whether experiences essentially religious in nature could be expressed or manifested in our time in terms essentially secular. As he searched for an analogy to what he desired, he brought into his discussion the remote figure of Whitman as an example of someone who had been able to negotiate this fine line of modernity:

> We do not have for this purpose an outstanding example of our own (if we do not wish to mention the teachings of A. D. Gordon in this context). But we, who operate as Jews in the Land of Israel, have a deep interest in a certain text: the book of poems by Walt Whitman, who a hundred years ago sang the song of America out of a feeling of absolute sanctity within the realm of absolute secularism. Whitman is a most prominent representative of this phenomenon, which had many spokesmen in the last three generations. These people saw that the mystical experiences might continue to sprout in people, for this is a deep-rooted human experience connected to the sheer essence of the human being as long as humankind exists.

After Whitman, he immediately moved to a mention of Richard Maurice Bucke, whom he saw as the author of "the classic book on secular mysticism, as an extreme expression of the thoughts I have mentioned here." [12]

During the last three decades, institutions of higher learning have spread throughout Israel, and with the expansion of formal learning has come a considerable growth in literary scholarship. For so small a population — but one avid in its respect for literature, especially poetry — Israel has an unusually large number of literary journals supporting both academic and creative writing. And as the country has gradually moved from its early admiration for Soviet society and culture to a far-reaching absorption in American culture, with English well established as its second language and its lifeline to the world, it is not surprising that one can readily find articles about major American writers in these journals, as well as in the literary sections of the Hebrew press.

While it is difficult to generalize about the academic scholarship on Whitman in Israel, in recent years there has been a tendency to move away from the ideologically based readings of earlier decades to more technical approaches toward Whitman's work. This may be a sign that Whitman no longer presents as ready an ideological brother to the post-1967 generation as he once did to the earlier pioneering generation or to that closer to socialist ideology. In fact, given the renewed encounter the post-1973 generation has made with the memory of the Holocaust and the enormous pressure it has felt concerning its physical security, Whitman may have come to seem a more foreign voice than he once was. At the same time, much of the leading Israeli literary scholarship of the last generation has tended to eschew affiliated political ideology of any sort as it has eagerly turned to the new critical theories which have revolutionized scholarship through-out the West. In fact, one of the people who turned their attention to Whitman the writer, rather than to Whitman the man or the ideologue, was a founder of Tel Aviv University's Porter Institute for Poetics and Semiotics, Benjamin Hrushovski (or Benjamin Harshav, as he has called himself in recent years).

In the opening issue of the fine academic literary journal he edited, *Hasifrut*, Hrushovski gave one of the first purely stylistic readings that Whitman's verse had received.[13] He did this in the context of an extended, searching analysis of the ex-pressionist poetics of Uri Tsvi Greenberg, to which he saw an analog in the poetry of Mayakovsky and Whitman. In all three, he noted a free verse style characterized by its reliance on long poetic lines comprised of elementary units defined by syn-tax or rhythm. But while Greenberg and Mayakovsky accepted limitations in the form either of their elementary unit or of their line, Whitman was less strictly re-stricted by either. Hrushovski expatiated on this point by quoting a long excerpt from the catalog of Section 33 of "Song of Myself," which he used as the basis of his remarks about the kinds, as well as the limits, of the freedoms Whitman took in composing his poetry. He described Whitman's poetry there as an ongoing flow, moving "wave after wave" in lines given structure by their parallelism and anaphora and concluding only with the closure of the full sentence-strophe. But although he called Whitman's verses "unmetrical" in any conventional sense, Hrushovski did see Whitman as relying heavily on syntactical parallelism within as well as at the beginning of lines in order to structure his verse. This practice, he pointed out, distinguished Whitman's kind of parallelism from the Bible's, which did not break up verse lines into smaller structural units. He also pointed out that, just as Whitman's structural freedom had its limits, so, too, did his rhythmic free-dom; a typical Whitman line was organized into a given number (usually two or three) of word groups for the reception of rhythmic emphasis.[14]

A survey of the reception of Whitman in Israel would not be complete without mention of the fact that Israel has been blessed with possession of two of the finest Whitman collections in existence outside of the United States. The larger of the two is the Feinberg Collection at the National and University Library of the He-brew University of Jerusalem. Not only the greatest but also the most philan-thropic of Whitman collectors, Charles Feinberg had amassed multiple copies of a number of original editions of Whitman and Whitman-related works and do-nated many of them over the years to various university libraries. In fact, one can go through the card catalogs of libraries at Jewish universities in the United States and Israel and be reasonably confident in interpreting their thick bunches of rare Whitman volumes as evidence that Feinberg had passed through them. In 1967, at a time when the Hebrew University and its library were still the major center of English-language literary scholarship in Israel, Feinberg gave the university a fine set of Whitman books, proof sheets, and related material. His collection includes copies of a number of original editions of *Leaves of Grass*, including the 1855, 1860, 1867, 1872, 1876, and 1882 texts, as well as original editions of *Franklin Evans* (as an "extra" from the *New World* of November 1842), *Democratic Vistas, Passage to In-*

dia, Memoranda During the War, Two Rivulets, Specimen Days and Collect, November Boughs, the 1888 *Complete Poems and Prose of Walt Whitman,* the 1892 *Complete Prose Works,* and Richard Maurice Bucke's *Notes and Fragments.* It also contains proof sheets of a number of Whitman's poems, of his reading book, and of the first page of "A Backward Glance on My Own Road"; a copy of "Shakspere–Bacon's Cipher" with autograph corrections; a ticket to Whitman's seventieth birthday party and the accompanying menu and program; and a collection of Whitman pictures.

The other major Whitman collection is the Freedman Collection at the Sourasky Library of Tel Aviv University, which was donated in 1987 by the Whitman scholar Florence Bernstein Freedman. Freedman, a student of Emory Holloway, was a longtime patroness of Alfred Goldsmith's rare-books store in New York and gradually assembled a small but choice collection of Whitman books and memorabilia. The Freedman Collection includes original editions of *Leaves of Grass* from 1860 (as well as its look-alike pirated version of several decades later), 1867, 1872, and 1881–82 (the suppressed Osgood edition, with a note in the hand of John Burroughs), supplemented by William Michael Rossetti's 1868 London edition of *Poems of Walt Whitman, After All, Not to Create Only, Two Rivulets, Specimen Days and Collect, November Boughs,* the Maynard edition of *Calamus,* and Bucke's *The Wound Dresser.* The collection also includes many Whitman-related works of compilation and scholarship, some quite rare, which appeared in the generation or two after Whitman's death, as well as much of the more current academic scholarship. Among its curiosities are several quarto pages of the 1855 Preface excised from a first edition of *Leaves,* which Freedman had mounted and framed behind double glass, and a homemade album of Whitman pictures assembled from the pictures collected by Henry Saunders for the edition of Whitman photographs he privately published in 1946.

Taken all in all, Whitman's reception in Israel, of which I have been able to discuss only a small—but, I hope, representative—portion, has been a remarkably rich and dynamic one. It has embraced the poles of modern Israeli society, from the socialist Left to the nationalist Right, from the secular to the religious, from the academic to the journalistic. Given the strength and diversity of Whitman's appeal to Israeli readers so far, the one safe prognostication about his future reception in Israel seems to be that, however Israeli society may evolve, Whitman's richness and breadth will allow him to remain a continuing source of attraction to future generations of Israeli readers.

NOTES

1. Uri Tsvi Greenberg, *Kelape Tish'im Vetish'ah* (Tel Aviv: Sadan, 1928), 26.

2. Ibid., 35. Greenberg quotes here from Section 42 of "Song of Myself," and very nearly exactly.

3. Halkin called his translation *Ale Esev* (Tel Aviv: Sifriat Poalim, 1952) and followed

it with a long, learned essay on Whitman and his poetry, divided into four chapters: "The Problem: Walt Whitman," "Life of Walt Whitman," "Guiding Lines in Whitman's Poems," and "America in the Work of Walt Whitman." The essay was reissued in Hebrew as a separate volume accompanying the publication of the revised (1984) edition of Halkin's translation.

4. For instance, the important poem of farewell "So Long!" is called "Shalom" by Halkin.

5. Halkin, *Ale Esev*, 9.

6. According to an accompanying headnote, the article was being translated into Hebrew from the text of an English translation. This English translation, though not mentioned here, was presumably the one that appeared in the short-lived New York socialist journal *Dialectics* (1937), although a better translation was done by Samuel Putnam for Gay Wilson Allen, ed., *Walt Whitman Abroad* (Syracuse: Syracuse University Press, 1955), 169–186. The Hebrew version is called "Walt Whitman — Poet of American Democracy," and appeared in *Masa* (May 1952): 4–5; and (August 1952): 3, 8, 9, 11. Beneath the text of the first page of Mirsky's article is printed an original poem by Hanoch Bar-Tov entitled "Poem to Walt Whitman," one of the many first-person, return-direct-address poems that Whitman's poetry has inspired over the years.

7. Allen, *Walt Whitman*, 169, 184.

8. Moshe Shamir, "At the Wells of the Water of Life," *B'Tsaron* 3 (November 1981): 6 (in Hebrew).

9. Ibid., 8.

10. Gershom Scholem, "Reflections on the Possibility of Jewish Mysticism in Our Day," *Emot* 8 (September/October 1964) (in Hebrew). This essay was republished by Scholem in a book of essays, *D'Varim B'Go* (Tel Aviv: Am Oved, 1975), 74.

11. The quotation comes from a 1975 interview, "With Gershom Scholem: An Interview," in Werner J. Dannhauser, ed., *On Jews and Judaism in Crisis* (New York: Schocken Books, 1976), 46.

12. Scholem, *D'Varim B'Go*, 82.

13. Benjamin Hrushovski, "The Theory and Practice of Rhythm in the Expressionist Poetry of U. Z. Grinberg," *Hasifrut* 1 (Spring 1968): 176–205 (in Hebrew).

14. Ibid., 197.

V. K. CHARI

Whitman in India

Although Whitman left no visible mark on the literatures of modern India, and interest in him has been confined to the English-educated writers and scholars, he has always had a special appeal to the Indian people, together with Emerson and Thoreau. Indian readers have been quick to perceive affinities between Whitman's "Songs" of the self and the mystic utterances of the Gita and the Upanishads. We learn from Romain Rolland's *Prophets of New India* (1930) that Vivekananda called him "the Sannyasin of India." Rabindranath Tagore, according to Emory Holloway, declared that "no American had caught the Oriental spirit of mysticism so well as [Whitman]." [1] William Norman Guthrie, himself impressed by the Vedantic parallels in Whitman, in 1897 quoted an Indian as saying that Whitman "must have studied the *Bhagavad Gita*, for in *Leaves of Grass* one finds the teachings of Vedanta; the Song of Myself is but an echo of the sayings of Krishna." [2] Later, Ananda Coomaraswamy, in his *Buddha and the Gospel of Buddhism* (1916), pointed out many parallels in "Song of Myself" to Buddhist ideas. Sri Aurobindo, the sage of Pondicherry, compared Whitman to the "old Indian seers": "That which the old Indian seers called the *mahan atma*, the Great Self, the Great Spirit, which is seen through the vast strain of cosmic thought and cosmic life, is the subject of some of his strains" — strains in which "one of the seers of old time reborn in ours might have expressed himself." [3] Sri Chinmoy, another spiritual leader of our time, also thinks of Whitman as a seer who "peers into Truth . . . dynamically fronting . . . Reality."[4]

In addition to Rabindranath Tagore and Aurobindo, there were three early regional Indian writers who were impressed by Whitman's poetry. Kshitindranath Tagore (1869–1937), a noted Bengali essayist and thinker and a member of the Tagore family, was inspired by *Leaves of Grass* to write an essay on Whitman in Bengali in 1891.[5] However, he saw Whitman's value as a prophet of democracy rather than as a mystic. The Tamil national poet Bharati (1880–1921) wrote an essay in Tamil praising Whitman for liberating verse from conventional prosody and for developing an all-embracing vision of the world. Himself a Vedantist of sorts, Bharati also noticed the similarities between Whitman and Vedantic thought. V. Sachithanandan's *Whitman and Bharati: A Comparative Study* (1978) examines the affinities between the two writers in terms of their theistic, rather than nondualistic, Vedantic thought, and their erotic mysticism, which he calls "bridal mysticism." The Punjabi poet Puran Singh also wrote in praise of Whitman in his *The Spirit of Oriental Poetry* (1926), remarking on his "immensity" and his "cosmic consciousness."

Thus it is the spiritual aspect of Whitman's poetry that attracted most Indian thinkers of the early generations and that still continues to engage the attention of Indian academics, rather than his democratic or purely humanitarian message or his futuristic vision of the New World apparent in poems such as "Passage to India." It is also noteworthy that none of those features of his poetry, such as his egocentrism (which struck his contemporaries as insane or eccentric and provoked the bitterest attacks upon him), ever bothered Indian readers, for they could readily absorb such elements, including his erotic ecstasies, into one or another of their own mystical traditions. These very elements seem to have evoked the most sympathetic response in them.

This perception of Whitman as a sage and a mystic is by no means confined to Indian readers. Even the early commentators, friends, and reviewers of Whitman were struck by the parallels to Oriental literature in his poetry. It was this mystical strain in him that, one suspects, inspired Emerson's initial enthusiasm for his poems. When Thoreau received a copy from Whitman of his 1856 edition, he remarked that certain poems, specifically "Song of Myself" and "Crossing Brooklyn Ferry," were "wonderfully like the Orientals" (meaning the Hindu poems). Whitman's work reminded Edward Carpenter of "the subtle and profound passages" in the Upanishads, and he remarked that the poet "seems to *liberate* the good tidings and give it democratic scope and worldwide application unknown in the older prophets, even in the sayings of Buddha."[6] More recently, Malcolm Cowley, in his introduction to the reissue of the 1855 *Leaves*, not only hailed "Song of Myself" as a great mystical poem and Whitman's "miracle" but asserted that it is best understood when studied in relation to the mystical philosophies of the world, especially those expounded in the Bhagavad Gita and the Upanishads. Henry Miller, in an insightful remark, said that "Whitman is closer to the Upanishads, Dostoevsky to the New Testament."[7]

However, the question of what Whitman owed to Hindu sources and whether he read them at all during the preparatory stages of the 1855 *Leaves* remains an enigma. Whitman's own statements on the question are contradictory. When Thoreau asked him in 1856 if he had read the Hindu poems, Whitman replied, "No, tell me about them." But strangely enough, years later, in "A Backward Glance O'er Travel'd Road" (1888), he mentioned "the ancient Hindoo poems" among the "embryonic facts" of *Leaves of Grass* (LG, 569). Another problem is that, unlike Emerson or Thoreau, Whitman's references to Indian books are superficial; his remarks indicate his familiarity with them but do not show that his thought was deeply impressed by them. Despite this, his review of Emerson's poem "Brahma" in 1857 suggests that he had a sure grasp of Vedantic thought. He is known to have owned a copy of W. R. Alger's book *The Poetry of the East* (presumably acquired in 1860) and a copy of an 1855 translation of the Gita, presented to him in 1875, which he read and annotated, but we do not know if he had any previous acquaintance with it. Therefore, most studies of Whitman and India have been content to review the generally accepted canon of transcendentalism and the influential role that Orientalism played in it, and then proceed with the business of comparison.

The first extensive investigation of Whitman and Indian thought was Dorothy Mercer's "*Leaves of Grass* and the Bhagavad Gita: A Comparative Study," portions of which appeared in the late 1940s in a series of articles in *Vedanta and the West*.[8] Mercer explores parallels in ideas such as God and self, love, Yoga, and reincarnation, and suggests points of agreement and difference between Whitman and the philosophical ideas of the Gita. The next systematic study was my own *Whitman in the Light of Vedantic Mysticism: An Interpretation* (1964).[9] This book, with its logical and philosophical approach, attempts a consistent explanation of Whitman's meanings in the light of the Vedantic concept of self and argues that the "I" of Whitman's poems is no other than his ego freed from the false identifications of time, place, and person so as to come into its own true nature as "kosmos." Cosmic consciousness is the immediate apprehension or "intuitional sense" of the unity of all things in the self. It breaks through the subject-object barriers and releases in the poet a limitless dynamism which expresses itself in his cosmic voyages and dramas of identification. Further, I try to show that all of Whitman's fundamental ideas — his democratic philosophy, his notion of universal brotherhood, and his attitude toward sin and evil — follow as corollaries from this central concept of the self. This self is not, however, an occult matter merely, but is implied in all human consciousness.

There have been a number of studies in subsequent years — both books and articles — further substantiating Whitman's Vedantism. K. Srinivasa Sastry's *Whitman's 'Song of Myself' and Advaita* (1982) develops my emphasis on Whitman's affinities to the nondualistic thought of Vedanta and offers further illustrations of his ideas of self and identity and of time as a continuum. Sastry states: "Thus projecting himself into the universe and its multitudinous beings and objects, and projecting the universe into himself, Whitman experiences the vastness, all-pervasiveness, and imperishability of Self in 'Song of Myself.'"[10] Sudhir Kumar's

"The Gita and Walt Whitman's Mysticism" is another general exposition of Whitman's philosophical stance in the light of the monistic thought of the Gita. Mohan Lal Sharma states in his article "Whitman, Tagore, Iqbal" that all the three poets shared the same "spinal idea," namely, the transcendental concept of selfhood. V. John Matthew, in "Self in 'Song of Myself': A Defence of Whitman's Egoism," observes that all inconsistencies, polarities, and irrationalities of the self in Whitman's poem — his sexuality, materialism, and his enigmatic assertion that he is God himself — will be justified when studied in the light of Hinduism. Thakur Guru Prasad, in "The Orient in Whitman's 'Passage to India,'" interprets Whitman's "passage" as his spiritual journey to Indian thought. Raman K. Singh, in "Whitman: Avatar of Sri Krishna?," compares Whitman's attitude toward love and sex with Krishna's sermon in the Gita teaching the sublimity and spirituality of the body. Singh observes that sex is seen in Hindu philosophy as a means to achieving spiritual freedom. Whitman's hedonistic experience is ascetic and spiritual because it frees the poet from earthly ties. O. P. Sharma, in "Walt Whitman and the Doctrine of Karma," finds in Whitman a striking restatement of the Hindu theory of Karma.[11]

Indian interpretations have received support also from recent Western scholars. Beongcheon Yu, in his *The Great Circle: American Writers and the Orient*, surveys the literature on Whitman and India and adds that, although the question of influence remains uncertain, Whitman nonetheless "knew a great deal more about the Orient than he pretended." The Orient played an important part in his creative life and "in all probability, helped Whitman define his own self and assured him of the authenticity and universality of his personal life." Yu argues further that "Passage to India," discounted by previous critics because of its more traditional, devotional tone, best expresses Whitman's attraction to India: "as the cradle of mystic wisdom, India represented all religious aspiration." Arnold Mersch, in "Cosmic Contrast: Whitman and the Hindu Philosophy," says that throughout his poetry "Whitman unintentionally reflects and projects some of the basic tenets of the Hindu philosophy concerning the unity of life, the nature of reality, man's place in the universe, the idea of caste and duty, and man's goals." Ward Welty's "The Persona as Cosmos in 'Song of Myself'" develops my earlier view that the concept of the cosmic self offers the best characterization of the "I" of the poem. Harold M. Hurwitz, in "Whitman, Tagore, and 'Passage to India,'" finds striking similarities between Tagore's *Gitanjali* and Whitman's poem, which serve "to underscore the fact that Whitman had accurately recaptured and reflected the Indian spirit in his poem."[12]

O. K. Nambiar's two books, *Walt Whitman and Yoga* (1966) and *Maha Yogi Walt Whitman: New Light on Yoga* (1978), add another dimension to the study of Whitman's mysticism. While the other mystical studies derive their interpretations from Whitman's notion of the self, Nambiar connects him to the esoteric experience of Tantric Yoga — a type of supernormal consciousness marked by the awakening of psycho-physical energy and resulting in the dissolution of the barriers between matter and spirit, the self and the universal. "Yoga" means the union of these opposite principles. When awakened, this bio-psychic energy, called the "serpent power" or "Kundalini" — which lies dormant in every person — is said to ascend from the root of the spine up along the spinal axis to the cerebrum, piercing the various force centers; in this movement the consciousness of the world is dissolved. The passage of the energy current is accompanied by audio-tactual sensations such as pressure, motion, humming, or hissing. It then descends down the same steps, returning the consciousness to world experience, but with the psyche and the senses totally transformed, so that the mind experiences a vision of unity. It "sees in every particle divine miracle and beauty; in every face, a god; in every event, plan and purpose. . . . Adam is restored to his primeval innocence, and heaven lies about him once again." [13]

Nambiar applies this account of Yogic experience to Section 5 of "Song of Myself" (which he calls Whitman's "core poem"), a key passage which has puzzled many readers. He traces there a stage-by-stage ascent and descent of the serpent power; in his reading, this section describes the onset of the mystical experience and the resultant expansion of consciousness that were to characterize Whitman's cosmic celebrations:

> Whitman's "we" stands for the body and the soul. The sensations felt in and by the body are apparently what he has set forth in these lines. The sensation starts from a point or source situated "athwart the hips," where he feels the beginning of an ascending movement. The line "How you settled your head athwart my hips and gently turned upon me," describes an axial rotatory movement. This is followed by a sensation of chill ascending along the body. As a consequence he feels a sense of physical exposure as if his shirt is being stript off his bosom. When the movement reaches the region of the heart he has another vivid tactual experience. Here he experiences the sensation and what could possibly arise out of it, the vision of a tongue plunged deep into his heart — a very definite, unmistakable, physical pressure. From this point the sensation moves upward to the region of his throat ("until you felt my beard"). This is followed by a descending movement reaching down to the lower extremity of the body, "till you held my feet."
>
> After this comes the swift transformation, the profound experience of peace and love which filled him, as it were, from head to foot. [14]

Although the vagueness of Whitman's description may lend itself to a more literal interpretation on the auto- or homoerotic level, Nambiar believes that with the "Tantric key" a satisfactory interpretation is possible: one that is supported by the case histories of Indian mystics such as Sri Ramakrishna or Western mystics such as St. Teresa and St. John of the Cross. This kind of experience is not, Nambiar shows, confined to the Indian tradition alone but is a universal psychic phenomenon. Nambiar's approach also illuminates many other passages in "Song of Myself" and other poems.

Nambiar's Yogic reading might appear to be different from the Vedantic interpretation, but the two approaches are in essence the same because both seek to explain Whitman's cosmic consciousness, although Nambiar does not make the connection. Nor is there an essential difference between Vedanta and Yoga, if we disregard their doctrinal origins: one dwells on the bliss resulting from self-knowledge; the other deals with the psychological mechanism (tantra) of its attainment.

A more recent article by R. S. Mishra, "Whitman's Sex: A Reading of 'Children of Adam,'" addresses specifically Whitman's conception of sex in the light of the Tantric philosophy of self. Since the goal of Indian mysticism is the "unselving of objects" — dissolving the individual and his or her world of separate things — sex, too, is seen as a nondualistic, "liquid" experience in which the distinctions of gender and person are dislocated or dissolved. "When the self is experienced as a process," says Mishra, "sexual acts can no longer be sexually defined and isolated" as homo or hetero. Whitman "dislocates the sexual act from the sexual context when he says 'Touch Me, touch the palm of your hand to my body.'"[15]

While none of these comparative studies sheds fresh light on the question of Whitman's indebtedness to Indian sources (in fact, they seem not to be bothered by it), T. R. Rajasekharaiah's provocative and brilliantly written *The Roots of Whitman's Grass* (1970) sets out to answer it.[16] Convinced of fundamental resemblances between Whitman and Hindu philosophical thought, Rajasekharaiah examines the numerous Indian sources — translations, expositions, and commentaries — that were available to Whitman in the New York libraries and in periodicals during the gestation of his first *Leaves*. A close comparative analysis of these sources with Whitman's writings convinces Rajasekharaiah that the poet had more than a casual understanding of the nature and quality of India's philosophies, even during his formative years, and that the entire philosophical material of his poems could have been derived from these sources. Since there is no documentary evidence that Whitman actually read them, however, the author bases his conclusions on the presumptive evidence of parallels in thought, echoes, and remote verbal correspondences, which he discovers in astonishing number. But in his enthusiasm to trace almost every idea or sentiment in *Leaves* to an Indian source, Rajasekharaiah does not consider the possibility that some of Whitman's ideas, such as reincarnation or the immortality of the soul, could have come from Western sources. Neither does Rajasekharaiah give credit to Whitman for having any experiences of his own or for being able to express them in his own words. Whitman's adoration of the "body electric," after all, did not necessarily come from Ward's account of Tantric worship, nor was the experience of Section 5 of "Song of Myself" drawn from the *Vishnu Purana*, although it is possible that Whitman confirmed his intuitions when he encountered these works.

Rajasekharaiah rejects the mystic revelation theory of Whitman's poetic genesis, the view that Whitman had a transforming mystical illumination, to argue instead that his poems were wholly of Indian derivation. In such an account, when the poet told Thoreau he had no knowledge of the Indian books, he was simply trying to cover his tracks and pose as an original genius and god-inspired man. Rajasekharaiah argues that Whitman had no genuine philosophic vision of his own to express, and his first poems (unlike some later lyrics, like "Out of the Cradle") therefore did not spring from the pressure of an urgent emotion or deep cogitation; they were an assemblage of unassimilated bits of knowledge gathered from Indian philosophical literature. Hence, Rajasekharaiah believes that they do not present an integrated conception of the self. The entire *Leaves of Grass*, he says, is "one complex 'Song of Myself,'" but the self that is celebrated in the book is an incongruous combination of different identities: a metaphysical self borrowed from Sankhya, Vedanta, and Yoga, an assumed role as an American bard, and Whitman's own private self. Such a self is hardly the cosmic self of the Gita and the Upanishads.

The Vedantist would not see any such incongruity in the conception of the self presented in poems like "Song of Myself." The all-inclusive self of the poet can absorb other identities, including the private person, since in terms of Vedantic logic, the individual is the whole of the cosmos. Therefore, Whitman is able to write: "Walt Whitman, a kosmos, of Manhattan the son." But it would not be correct to apply this Vedantic concept to the entire *Leaves of Grass*, because poems written in different periods and under different psychological circumstances cannot be expected to maintain a strict consistency of thought or tone. The Vedantic interpretations previously mentioned recognize this and generally restrict study to the early poems. Although Rajasekharaiah does not appreciate the remarkable unity of conception and visionary power of poems like "Crossing Brooklyn Ferry," his work nonetheless makes a valuable contribution: it carries the discussion of Whitman's debt to India beyond the facile assumptions of earlier scholars by establishing that a surer context exists for a comparative study of Whitman and Indian thought than was previously known.

Interestingly, there have been skeptical voices among the Indian responses to Whitman. R. K. DasGupta, in "Indian Response to Walt Whitman," decides that Whitman's experience "is not really Vedantic experience." On the other hand, he declares that Whitman's democratic spirit, which of course owed nothing to India but had its roots in American life, constitutes the essence of Whitman's message. The educated individual of colonial India "was yet to grasp the mystique of the word Democratic," and even today he or she has not fully realized it. This, DasGupta thinks, may be one reason why Whitman's influence has never been an active element in the development of modern Indian literatures. Sisir Ghose, in "Chari, Whitman, and the Vedantic Self: A Note," questions the claims made for Whitman as a Vedantic mystic. He says that Whitman was hardly the wise man of the Upanishads: "His announcements . . . are remarkable for their cocksure superficiality." Ghose questions the justification for the Indian comparisons and asks: "Why should we drag the spiritual classics to elevate, in every case, Whitman's status?" Instead, Ghose sees Whitman's importance as a radical poet and individualist.[17]

Similar doubts have been expressed by Western critics concerning the legitimacy of comparing Whitman's ideas to Indian thought. Joseph Benevento, in "Whitman and the Eastern Mystic Fallacy," asks: "Is Eastern philosophy needed to explain and validate Whitman? Is he incoherent unless viewed in terms of this philosophy?" While it is true that many of Whitman's ideas are compatible with key concepts in Indian philosophy, it is nonetheless fair to question whether there is any need to import Indian ideas if Whitman's thought can be understood in terms of his own culture and the American democratic faith. Americanism is what prompted Whitman's muse, as it did Emerson's. But for both Emerson and Whitman, the deeper foundations of that idea lay in a spiritual center, in a unitive conception of the self and the world. Whitman's idea of democracy, as Lawrence Buell puts it, "is but one specific deduction" from his mystic awareness of cosmic unity-in-diversity, and eastern mysticism presents the clearest and most eloquent expression of this unity. G. S. Amur, in "Whitman's Song of Man: A Humanistic Approach to 'Song of Myself,'" calls Whitman a humanist but says that his type of humanism is not irreconcilable with religion in its wider sense: it is a "religious humanism." Again, Whitman's glorification of the body and sex need not be explained only in pathological terms. As Nambiar points out, sex for Whitman is a "cosmic, procreant principle." [18] Therefore, a proper understanding of it may require turning to other models of experience, such as Tantric mysticism.

Once again, it is the joyful, celebratory aspect of Whitman's poetry that most Indian readers have been attracted to and in which they see his message. But this has led to the canonizing of Whitman's "songs" of the self at the expense of his other beautiful lyrics and elegiac poems. Gay Wilson Allen asks pertinently: "The question is, how much meaning is added or left out by interpreting *Leaves of Grass* in the context of Vedantic mysticism?" [19] Admittedly, there is much in Whitman's poetry that the Hindu readings cannot account for. Most critics would no doubt agree with the Indian view that the self in *Leaves of Grass* is crucial to our understanding of the work. But one objection to the Vedantic model is that it does not recognize the problematic nature of Whitman's search for identity but assumes identity is fixed and realized. As Malcolm Cowley has pointed out, Whitman's notion of the self changed in the course of his career and passed through many crises. The exultant vision of "Song of Myself" is no longer present in the "Calamus" poems or poems of the later editions — some of which are direct antitheses to "Song of Myself." But in the early poems there is a strong projection of the cosmic self, and the Vedantic interpretation gives a most satisfactory explanation of this experience.

The most intriguing problem in understanding *Leaves* is deciphering some passages which, because of their obscure references, have invited the application of diverse, and sometimes mutually opposing, explanatory models. The famous fifth section of "Song of Myself" is a case in point. When it is read as a description of a homosexual or pathological experience, the mystical interpretations — Yogic or other — would seem completely off the track. But here as in other poems, the Indian models give a consistent interpretation of Whitman's meanings. A comparative study is justified if it clarifies the text it is studying and if it establishes a general context for the comparison. Although some Indian studies have been overzealous in trying to prove influences or in searching for parallels, they do not invalidate all comparisons. They show that comparisons of Whitman and Eastern philosophies are neither totally irrelevant nor alien.

It is no exaggeration to say that Indian readers have found in Whitman a kindred spirit to whom they can respond with uninhibited sympathy. In the 1950s the Sahitya Akademi (India's national academy) began translating *Leaves of Grass* into the eighteen major literary languages of India. That this is the only project of its kind to be undertaken by that august body is a mark of the affection with which Indian scholars and thinkers have always held Whitman and a tribute to his stature as "the poet of the kosmos."

NOTES

1. Emory Holloway, *Walt Whitman: An Interpretation in Narrative* (New York: Knopf, 1926), 156.

2. William N. Guthrie, *Walt Whitman, Camden Sage* (Cincinnati: Robert Clark Co., 1897), 25.

3. Sri Aurobindo, *The Future Poetry* (Pondicherry, 1917–1920), 253–257.

4. Sri Chinmoy, "Walt Whitman," in *America in Her Depths* (Hollis, N.Y.: Vishma Press, 1973), 21–25.

5. See *Walt Whitman Review* 19 (1973): 3–11 for a translation, by R. K. DasGupta, of this essay. Besides hailing Whitman as an apostle of democracy and freedom, Kshitindranath Tagore also defends Whitman's prose rhythms. The translator informs us in a footnote that Rabindranath Tagore, too, wrote in Bengali justifying Whitman's prose poetry. One detects in Tagore's English version of *Gitanjali* similarities to Whitman in rhythmic organization as well as in sentiment. Aurobindo and the Tamil poet Bharati were also impressed by Whitman's prosodic freedom.

6. Henry David Thoreau, Letter to Harrison Blake, 1856, in Edwin H. Miller, ed., *A Century of Whitman Criticism* (Bloomington: Indiana University Press, 1969), 4–6; Edward Carpenter, *Days with Walt Whitman* (London: George Allen, 1906), 76–78.

7. Malcolm Cowley, ed., *Walt Whitman's "Leaves of Grass": The First (1855) Edition* (New York: Viking Press, 1959); Henry Miller, Letter to Pierre Lesdain, in Miller, *A Century of Whitman Criticism*, 196.

8. Dorothy F. Mercer, "*Leaves of Grass* and the Bhagavad Gita: A Comparative Study" (Ph.D. diss., University of California, 1933); see also *Vedanta and the West*, vols. 9–12.

9. V. K. Chari, *Whitman in the Light of Vedantic Mysticism: An Interpretation* (Lincoln: University of Nebraska Press, 1964).

10. K. Srinivasa Sastry, *Whitman's "Song of Myself" and Advaita: An Essay in Criticism* (Delhi: Doaba House, 1982), 63.

11. Sudhir Kumar, "The Gita and Walt Whitman's Mysticism," in Abhai Maurya, ed., *India and World Literature* (New Delhi: Indian Council for Cultural Relations, 1990); Mo-

han Lal Sharma, "Whitman, Tagore, Iqbal: Whitmanated, Under-Whitmanated, and Over-Whitmanated Singers of Self," *Walt Whitman Review* 15 (1969): 230–237; V. John Matthew, "Self in 'Song of Myself': A Defence of Whitman's Egoism," *Walt Whitman Review* 15 (1969): 102–107; Thakur Guru Prasad, "The Orient in Whitman's 'Pasage to India,'" *Calamus* 17 (1979): 4–9; Raman K. Singh, "Whitman: Avatar of Shri Krishna?" *Walt Whitman Review* 15 (1969): 97–102; Om Prakash Sharma, "Walt Whitman and the Doctrine of Karma," *Philosophy East and West* 20 (1970): 169–174.

12. Beongchen Yu, *The Great Circle: American Writers and the Orient* (Detroit: Wayne State University Press, 1983), 62, 71; Arnold Mersch, "Cosmic Contrast: Whitman and the Hindu Philosophy," *Walt Whitman Review* 19 (1973): 49–63; Ward Welty, "The Persona as Komos in 'Song of Myself,'" *Walt Whitman Review* 25 (1979): 98–105; Harold M. Hurwitz, "Whitman, Tagore, and 'Passage to India,'" *Walt Whitman Review* 13 (1967): 56–60.

13. O. K. Nambiar, *Walt Whitman and Yoga* (Bangalore: Jeevan Publications, 1966), 22.

14. Ibid., 42.

15. R. S. Mishra, "Whitman's Sex: A Reading of 'Children of Adam,'" *Calamus* 23 (1983): 19–25.

16. T. R. Rajasekharaiah, *The Roots of Whitman's Grass* (Rutherford N.J.: Fairleigh Dickinson University Press, 1970).

17. R. K. DasGupta, "Indian Response to Walt Whitman," *Revue de Litterature Comparee* 47 (1973): 58–70; Sisir Ghose, "Chari, Whitman, and the Vedantic Self: A Note," *Calamus* 4 (1970): 9–20.

18. Joseph Benevento, "Whitman and the Eastern Mystic Fallacy," *Calamus* 22 (1981): 12–23; Lawrence Buell, *Literary Transcendentalism* (Ithaca: Cornell Unversity Press, 1973), 168–169; G. S. Amur, "Whitman's Song of Man: A Humanistic Approach to 'Song of Myself,'" *Walt Whitman Review* 18 (1972): 50–56; Nambiar, *Walt Whitman*, 104.

19. Gay Wilson Allen, *A Reader's Guide to Walt Whitman* (New York: Farrar, Straus, & Giroux, 1970), 149.

GUIYOU HUANG

Whitman in China

Leaves of Grass first influenced China in the early decades of the twentieth century when Whitman's work was welcomed by a limited number of writers and critics. Since then his reception has reached three peaks: the first was during the 1920s and 1930s when China was undergoing a literary revolution characterized by vernacular literature; the second was during the 1940s and mid-1950s, a period notable for the founding of the People's Republic; and the third was during the open door policy since the late 1970s, an important phase in modern Chinese history, when a great demand for democracy and freedom and an increasing desire to know the outside world burst open the heavy Chinese door.

It is often difficult to investigate the Chinese reception of literary figures. The nation is so vast, so varied, and so different linguistically from Western countries that minor international figures are most often absorbed without discernibly marking Chinese literature or thought. To study a giant figure — Shakespeare, Cervantes, Tolstoy, or Whitman — is considerably easier but still can be problematic because of drastic and anomalous changes in Chinese politics over the past decades. Until 1978, because of the political nature of modern China, the so-called progressive foreign writers have been the ones most likely to receive attention and favorable treatment: Gorky and Fadeyev of Russia, Dreiser and London of the United States, Milton and Shelley of Great Britain, Doudèt and Stendhal of France, to name only a few. In the Chinese judgment, Whitman, though inevitably exhibiting the limitations of his time, belongs to the group of progressives. These writers — including Shakespeare, Dickens, Thackeray, Shaw, Twain, Steinbeck, and others — form the largest number of all foreign writers who are studied from either a political or literary perspective. Depending on the political climate, Whitman may be defined at one moment as a good writer and at another moment as less praiseworthy. In China, of all the major American writers, perhaps the best known are Twain, Dreiser, Whitman, Stowe, and Hemingway, with Whitman being the only poet. That these writers are the most discussed — rather than, say, Ezra Pound or Edith Wharton or Frederick Douglass — may seem absurd to Americans, but the fact that people of different political ideologies do have different criteria in appreciating literature is hardly deniable.

China's favorite literary "isms" in the past fifty years (dating from 1942, when Mao Zedong gave his *Talks at the Yan'an Forum on Literature and Art*) may very well be socialist realism and critical realism.[1] Writers are instructed to follow socialist realist doctrine in literary activities; in judging foreign literature, critical realism is applied as a guiding principle, because Western writers of this school are said to write in a realist manner criticizing capitalist society, which is why Twain and Stowe are popular. Dreiser's reputation (*Sister Carrie* in particular) resulted from his being an American Communist Party member. Hemingway's antiwar writings, such as *A Farewell to Arms*, appeal to the Chinese; his *The Old Man and the Sea*, seen as a reflection of humanity's struggle against nature, has particular attraction because Mao teaches that humans can conquer nature, and this spirit is found in Hemingway's work. Whitman is different both because he is a poet and because he is of the "common people," a phrase taken to be synonymous with the working class (or the proletariat). In China, Whitman's greatest contributions have been to the literary revolution of the second and third decades of this century and to the spirit of freedom and democracy that encouraged the Chinese people to fight for their own liberation from Japan in the 1940s.

Since Whitman was first introduced to China in 1919, coinciding with the May Fourth Movement and the hundredth anniversary of his birth, this critical history will cover the period from 1919 to the present, with emphasis on three peaks of influence. I will deal with three interrelated issues — Whitman's influence on Chinese writers, his role in Chinese literature, and the criticism written about him in China.

THE FIRST PEAK

In 1988 at an international conference on "Whitman and the World," Geoffrey Sill put his finger on an interesting and paradoxical phenomenon concerning the influential American bard:

Walt Whitman and his works have been absorbed more affectionately by the rest of the world than he has been by his own country. In France, China, the

Soviet Union, and many South American countries, he is regarded as the spokesman for that romantic impulse through which the individual self declares its liberty, or (somewhat paradoxically) affirms its solidarity with its comrades, regardless of time, race, or national identity.[2]

China is mentioned because it has indeed appreciated Whitman for seventy years, albeit with an interruption of two decades. The 1911 bourgeois revolution led by Sun Yat-sen ended the long history of Chinese feudalism, and all China was awakened. October 1917 witnessed the Bolshevik victory in the Russian revolution led by Lenin; and to the Chinese Communist Party (CCP), the October Revolution ushered in Marxism-Leninism and signaled the dawn of Chinese revolution. In 1919 the Versailles Conference held in Paris offended China by favoring Japan's demand for possession of China's Shandong from Germany, an event that led to the breakout of the May Fourth Movement. Then the movement developed into one of antiforeign aggression and antifeudalism, demanding the downfall of Confucianism and the introduction of democracy and science. At the same time, the New Culture Movement—initiated by Chen Duxiu of Peking University, editor of "the leading journal of Chinese intellectuals," *The New Youth*, and Hu Shi— broke out and soon swept the whole country.[3] A little later the movement was joined by Lu Xun, Guo Moruo, Mao Zedong, and many other enthusiastic young people.[4] *The Young China*, a radical journal like *The New Youth*, at this juncture published Tian Han's article, "Commemorating the Centenary of the Birth of Whitman—the Poet of the Common People."[5] About half a year later in Japan, Guo Moruo wrote to Tian that he had read and admired his long article about Whitman. For the first time Whitman was heard, but via Japan, where study of foreign literature was more advanced and where Guo and Tian read and translated the American poet whom they valued so much.

Interestingly, the major initiators of the New Literature Movement that took place on the mainland lived elsewhere. While Tian, Guo, and Lu were in Japan, Hu Shi was in New York. Achilles Fang states, not without exaggeration, that "the so-called Chinese literary revolution of 1917 was actually launched by a single man a few months earlier from New York with a formidable program and a neat poem."[6] According to Fang, the program for literary revolution was inspired by American imagism as advanced by Ezra Pound and Amy Lowell. Hu's program contains eight points (the gist of which is pushing for the use of vernacular Chinese instead of the classical), and his poem "The Butterflies" consists of eight short lines of vernacular Chinese, written in the vein of imagist poetry. Yet when Fang further notes that "Ezra Pound was the god-father, and Amy Lowell the god-mother, of the Chinese literary revolution of 1917," his claim is somewhat far-fetched, because Hu's method for reviving Chinese poetry eventually failed.[7] Chinese poets did not, over the long term, find imagism appealing. In the stormy 1920s a new source of inspiration was necessary, a source more open and expansive and conforming better to the spirit of the time. This source was Whitman, whose influence suddenly came to the fore through Tian Han's high praises and

Guo Moruo's own poetry. Yet Hu Shi's efforts cannot be ignored, since they succeeded in encouraging poets to write poems in vernacular Chinese; the effort was continued by Guo, "the apostle of Chinese Whitmanism," though in a considerably different political direction.[8]

Guo Moruo (1892–1978), a leading figure in modern Chinese literary history, was an outstanding poet and dramatist in addition to being a historian and paleographer. Guo's best poems were written in the 1920s, and many of them bear witness to Whitman's influence.[9] After studying the early poems of Guo in connection with *Leaves of Grass*, Fang points out the superficial resemblances between "I Am a Worshipper of Idols" and "So Long!" He also observes that the characteristics marking Guo's poetry are "humorless sincerity, death-seriousness, even deadly dullness — traits one seldom finds in traditional Chinese poetry."[10] But Zhu Ziqing, in a more appreciative reading, notes the originality of Guo's pantheism and a rebellious spirit new to the Chinese literary tradition.[11] Whitman's *Leaves of Grass* had inspired Guo so much that "immediately he proceeded to translate Whitman's poems and to write Whitmanesque poems of his own."[12] The result is a collection of poems entitled *The Goddesses* (1921). The prefatory poem written in May 1920 is noteworthy:

> I am a proletarian:
> Because except for my naked self,
> I possess nothing else.
> *The Goddesses* is my own creation,
> And may be said to be my private property,
> Yet I want to be a Communist,
> Therefore I make her public to all.
>
> *Goddesses!*
> Go and find the one with the same vibrations as me,
> Go and find the one with as many kindling points as myself.
> Go and strike the heartstrings
> In the breasts of my dear young brothers and sisters,
> And kindle the light of their wisdom![13]

In this poem, Guo proclaims himself a proletarian and Communist, though the CCP was not founded until a year later in July 1921. It is an important poem making clear Guo's political stance and charting his future as a Communist-oriented poet with Whitmanian individualistic characteristics.

Guo, like Whitman, uses poetry as "an outlet for relieving himself of irrepressible egotism and eleutheromania, two things most solicitously suppressed by all traditionalists."[14] Whitman's influence in Guo's "Good Morning!," "Hymn to the Rebels," "Globe, My Mother," and "Three Pantheists" is distinctly recognizable. Recent Chinese critics regard this influence as positive (see, for example, Wang Yao and Huang Suyi). But Guo's contemporaries seemed skeptical of his style and content. In *Yesterday, Today, and Tomorrow of China's New Poetry* (1929), Cao-chuan Weiyu (apparently a pseudonym) denigrates Guo's Whitmanesque poems, claiming that *The Goddesses* is a failure for two main reasons: abstractness and verbosity. Taking "Nirvana of the Feng and Huang" for example, Caochuan comments:

> Unfortunately, after reading it, we get nothing but abstraction, concept. . . . For instance, the fourth stanza of the "Song of the Feng" is cursing the universe with all power: it is this, it is that. . . . Flying west, east, south, and north for half a day, but what is the real sense? The end says: "We are born into such a world, that we cannot but learn to weep like the sea." Clamoring for half a day only to learn to weep like the sea! OK, go ahead and weep. . . . The last fourteen stanzas are not poetry, they are fourteen stanzas of geometric formulas:
>
> Light are you, Light am I!
> Light is he, Light is fire!
> Fire are you! Fire am I!
> Fire is he! Fire is fire!
>
> Thus you, I, he, and fire linked together, and he insists that they are one; that is, A is B, A is C, A is D, therefore A, B, C, D are all equal. It is abstract to the extent of being unintelligible. . . . "The Sky Dog" is even more fantastic: "I am I! The I of I is about to explode!" OK, go ahead and explode.[15]

Though he stops short of identifying Guo with Whitman, Caochuan seems to criticize Whitman indirectly. Nevertheless, as a result of Guo's efforts, Whitman-ism — instead of American imagism as preached and practiced by Hu Shi — did take root in China. But this does not necessarily mean that traditionalism was entirely rejected. Fang believes too readily that Guo ended traditionalism in Chinese poetry;[16] Julia Lin counterargues that Guo "introduced a much-needed element, vitality, into the new verse, but he did not bring down the curtain on tradition. Traditionalism continued to play a meaningful part not only in Kuo's [Guo's] poetry but in the poetry that followed."[17] The most obvious case is Mao, with whom Guo used to discuss poetry. Mao continued to write traditional poetry into the 1960s in the form of "ci," a classical form with strict rhymes, meters, and a set number of words.[18]

The 1920s and the first half of the 1930s were a time of various literary experiments, a very rare scene almost comparable to the period of Warring States between 500 and 300 B.C., when indeed "one hundred flowers were in blossom and one hundred schools contended."[19] Such a scene has not appeared again in the past fifty years. Almost all the major modern writers were educated and reached their full powers at this time. Literary groups like the Literary Studies Society, the Sunk Bell Society, the Creation Society (where Guo was leader), the Small Talk Society, the Crescent Moon Society (publishing on English and American literature), and the League of Leftist Writers (with Lu as leader), all engaged in continuous disputes, and "on many issues the coteries were hostile to each other. Nevertheless, Whitman seemed to be accorded a warm reception by all the major literary societies. . . . Because the Chinese new poets believed that Whitman offered both the spirit and the form of expression they had been looking for, they considered themselves to be part of a world movement pioneered by Whitman." [20] The influences on Guo were multifaceted: he had translated and written in the manners of Turgenev, Mayakovsky, and Tolstoy in Russia; of Goethe and Heine in Germany; of Matthew Arnold in England; and, most important of all, of Whitman. He publicly acknowledged two major influences: "More than many other foreign writers, Walter Scott influenced me tremendously; it was almost a secret of mine," and "Whitman's unconventional style was particularly in line with the storming spirit of the May Fourth Movement. I was entranced by his unrestrained, powerful tone." [21] Of the two influences, Whitman is probably the more important, since Guo is a poet rather than a novelist.

Although Whitman is vast and varied, Guo Moruo is, if anything, an even more complicated figure because of his greater range of expertise. Outside of China he is best known as a poet, but in China he is recognized as an outstanding archaeologist, a foremost playwright, and a successful politician. Guo's scholastic and political career is to some extent an epitome of Chinese society from 1920 to 1978. Born in the year that Whitman died (1892), he succeeded the American bard on the eastern side of the Pacific. As the Chinese apostle of Whitman, he helped to create the first peak of the American's reception and then witnessed the second, though not the third. Mao's death and the downfall of the Gang of Four (which Guo celebrated in a short poem) in 1976 marked the end of the notorious ten-year Cultural Revolution. For political reasons, the years 1976 to 1978 were a literary vacuum. Guo died in June 1978, just as China was about to resume its studies of foreign literature, important signs of which were the publication in Chinese of the complete works of Shakespeare and republication of Chu Tunan's translation of *Selections from Leaves of Grass*, both by the prestigious People's Literature Press. Guo very likely read the first publication of Chu's version in 1955, since both Guo and Chu held important positions in the CCP's propaganda departments, and both were scholars of English and American literature.

Guo himself translated a number of Whitman's poems while studying in Japan, but unfortunately almost all of them were lost. Li Yeguang, a Chinese poet and Whitman scholar, mentions that Guo translated "The Song of the Open Road," but it was lost in the mail he sent to Zong Baihua, then editor of *The Young China*, which published the first article on Whitman by Tian Han. [22] In fact, it was not lost: Guo only translated the first eight lines of the poem in his March 3, 1920, letter to Zong. In May of the same year the fragmentary translation was published amidst a collection of letters by Guo, Tian, and Zong, appropriately entitled *Three Leaves of Grass*. [23] Guo's translation is very faithful, though he dropped the seventh line, "Done with indoor complaints, libraries, querulous criticisms." A reader without knowledge of English, however, is unlikely to miss the lost line because Guo's translation flows so smoothly. [24] But Guo, for all his talents, was not a major translator of Whitman. Until 1980, the major translator, without question, was Chu Tunan, who sometimes used Gao Han as his pen name. Chu started his translation as early as 1930, a fact that surprised Gay Wilson Allen, who wondered if there were people interested in Whitman that early in China.[25] He would have been more surprised had he learned that as early as 1919 Tian and Guo were reading, translating, and imitating Whitman.

The reception of Whitman reached the second peak when the Sino-Japanese War broke out in the late 1930s on Chinese soil. The American poet again became a source of inspiration and a symbol of freedom as China was plundered by Japan. Whitman was read politically during the war and the founding of the People's Republic. Xilao Li points out that "modern Chinese poetry underwent tremendous changes as China waged her war against Japanese aggressors in 1937," and Whitman's poetry certainly played a role in this just cause.[26] His spirit encouraged young people to fight for their country's freedom. Poet Mu Mutian was heard saying, "Aren't we now in need of poets such as Du Fu, Milton, Whitman, Hugo and Shelley?" — a slogan reminiscent of Wordsworth's "Milton, England hath need of thee!" when England feared external aggression.[27] Whitman was now a fighting poet on the Chinese soil; his "battle ground was not on university platforms, but in the cultural and literary circles."[28] During this time, translators concentrated on Whitman's poems that displayed a militant spirit, and the sole purpose of these translations was to call on the Chinese people to stand up heroically against Japanese invaders. In the 1941 Yan'an, headquarters of the CCP, Whitman was more welcome than any other foreign writer. Poet Xiao San brought to Yan'an from the USSR a 1936 Russian edition of *Leaves of Grass*, and soon translations of "I Sit and Look Out" and "O Captain! My Captain!" appeared in *New Poetry*, and other translations surfaced in *Poetry*. Writer and party official Zhou Yang together with his comrades even set up a journal called *Leaves of Grass*, publishing progressive writings, including one of Zhou's own articles comparing Whitman and Guo Moruo. Thus Whitman became better known among the progressive anti-Japanese forces than among others.

The Chinese victory over Japan in 1945 coincided with the beginning of the Second Civil War, during which Whitman was still read and studied. In 1948 Tu An published his translation of *Drum-Taps* (fifty-two poems); Chen Shihuai did "The Singer in the Prison" (thirty-one poems) around this time, though the publisher remains unknown. In March 1949 Chenguang Press brought out Chu Tunan's *Selections from Leaves of Grass* (fifty-eight poems).[29] In October 1949 the People's Republic was founded, and China entered an important and relatively stable phase. Then the Korean War, involving both China and the United States, broke out in 1951 and lasted through 1953. Two years later, in 1955 (coinciding with the hundredth anniversary of the first publication of *Leaves*), the American bard made a conspicuous appearance on the occasion of the World Peace Council held in Beijing, which was to show the world that Chinese people, like Whitman, were peace-loving and war-abhorring; at the same time, "a number of articles, memoirs, and critical biographies by Chinese poets and translators as well as by Soviet Russian and Eastern European critics were published" to celebrate the occasion.[30]

The same year saw the publication of Chu Tunan's *Selections from Whitman's Leaves of Grass*, a revised edition of the Chenguang publication, this time brought out by the People's Literature Press. It was not until September 1958, however, that Angela Chih-Ying Jung Palandri's review of this work appeared in the *Walt Whitman Newsletter*. Palandri, after welcoming the translation in "Red China," questioned some lines that seemed "consciously" rendered to conform to the current Chinese political scene. She complained about the difficulties in translation: "Many great poems of the West have turned commonplace in Chinese simply because of limitations of Chinese poetic forms."[31] (This statement unfortunately misrepresents the capacities of Chinese, a more implicit language than English, especially in poetry. If a translation falls flat, the problem almost invariably rests with the translator rather than anything intrinsic to Chinese poetic forms.) Chu adopted vernacular Chinese as advocated by Hu Shi and used simplified ideograms introduced by the CCP, and his style was "half prose and half verse."[32] Chu's selection of poems was based on a political standard, so Whitman's poems on the Civil War and the liberation of slaves were given the most attention. To the Chinese, Whitman's popularity among common people is inseparable from President Lincoln's, since they regard the wartime president as from the lower class (like Mao, a farm boy), someone who sought liberation and happiness for the working class. So poems dedicated to Lincoln, the working man and emancipator of the slaves, were included in the volume (e.g., "When Lilacs Last in the Dooryard Bloom'd"). It goes without saying that the reviewer saw this translation primarily as a political instrument. Because of the "red" nature of China, Palandri indicated her interest in the reception of the translation, hoping that "the seeds of freedom and democracy of the *Leaves of Grass* may be sown in the heart of Chinese readers and bear fruit eventually."[33] Her wish was well meant, though it sometimes takes longer for an idea to take root than it does for a tree to bear fruit in an exotic land.

Whitman studies were flourishing when they experienced a sudden decline in 1959: Ho Ch'i-fang (He Qifang) published an article criticizing Guo for adopting the dangerous aspects of Whitman's poetry, and his criticism contributed to a curbing of Whitman studies in China.[34] Ho was a famous poet and literary critic, and his criticism was influential. Mark Cohen reports that, according to Ho's judgment,

> Whitman reflected the rise of American capitalism as well as the spirit of democracy. Although Whitman was politically somewhat progressive, as a poet he was often not economical in his diction, too abstract in his ideas, and too confused in his thinking. Thus Ho concludes — after reading Whitman in translation — the poorer aspects of Kuo Mo-jo's poetry most likely came from

Whitman. The good points of Kuo's poetry came from being a reflection of a revolutionary period in early 20th-century China.[35]

As noted earlier, Guo had been criticized by Caochuan in the 1920s. What is striking is the similarity of Ho's criticism to Caochuan's three decades earlier. In talking about Guo's effort to express romantic feelings, Caochuan says, "Guo's poetical expression of this spirit is a total failure . . . first because he adopts an abstract style; secondly, because he is not economical in his art."[36] In other words, Guo's weaknesses are similar to Whitman's.[37] Seen from this perspective, Guo is even faithful to Whitman's shortcomings. Nevertheless, Cohen accuses Ho of ignoring the idea that the spirit of this revolutionary period was similar to the spirit of Whitman: "One cannot easily separate what is the spirit of the time and what is the spirit of Whitman."[38] In fact, Cohen only sees one side of Ho's criticism: Ho's commendation of Whitman was more than high. Acknowledging his own indebtedness to Whitman's free verse, he then recognizes Whitman's weak points, such as the accumulation of too many nouns and the use of abstract ideas.

Li Yeguang praises Ho's criticism as pertinent analyses that are "rarely found at least before the Cultural Revolution."[39] There is no justification in saying, as Cohen once argued, that Ho's criticism "signalled the beginning of a twenty-year silence on Whitman studies in China," since silence on almost all foreign writers was ushered in when political movements set in one after another from 1958 to 1978, a choking silence of twenty long years, during which the Palandris, Allens, and Cohens, like Whitman before them, had to wait for "the seeds of freedom and democracy of the *Leaves of Grass*" to be sown "in the heart of Chinese readers and bear fruit eventually."

Cohen's review of Chu's republished version of *Leaves* came twenty-two years after Palandri's notice of the same book. As indicated earlier, Chu's version of *Leaves of Grass* was republished in 1978 when the revival of foreign studies began in China. In 1980, a year after the establishment of Sino-U.S. relations, Cohen published "Whitman in China: A Revisitation," with the purpose of assessing an earlier reviewer's prediction about Whitman's imminent absorption into Chinese culture: "Viewed from a twenty-four-year-old panorama we can say that *Leaves* has borne a limited fruit. Until recently, however, the harvest has been bitter." Perhaps more patience is needed, and a foreign scholar like Cohen would have had a difficult time understanding thoroughly what was going on in the Chinese literary world around 1980. But he was absolutely right in pointing out that "traditionally Communist China's translation and appreciation of foreign literature has been greatly influenced by her foreign relations."[40]

This is precisely the situation with Sino-British, Sino-Soviet, and Sino-U.S. relations since 1949. America's containment policy and China's "leaning to one side" policy (toward the Soviet Union) mutually contributed to the international Cold War. The Sino-Soviet split, however, caused people to give up learning Russian and to pick up English instead (British English, of course, since the U.S. was still China's archenemy). Then detente reduced tension between China and the

U.S. The thaw finally came in 1979 when the normalization of bilateral relations was realized, and Whitman reemerged in China. On this occasion, Huang Zhen, former head of the Chinese Liaison Office in Washington and then Minister of Culture, published his "My Days in Washington" in the English language weekly *Beijing Review*. Toward the end he writes:

> I would like to end with a quote from the American poet Walt Whitman, who wrote in "The Song of the Open Road":
> Allons! . . .
> The goal that was named cannot be countermanded.
> Allons! the road is before us.
> We Chinese people and the American people will march on from generation to generation along this road to friendship![41]

Huang's quotation of these lines is not for a literary purpose, but it does tell the American and Chinese peoples that China has now indeed opened its door to the West.

THE THIRD PEAK

American critics have been concerned about the fruit borne by *Leaves of Grass*, ever since its translation and publication in the People's Republic in 1955. To Cohen, for example, the fruit is limited and the harvest bitter; to Chinese critics, however, it is otherwise. Xilao Li records that a young Chinese poet was reading Whitman one morning in 1983 when the American bard's voice "dropped right from the sky and hit hard upon me. . . . For a whole day, I listened to the dropping of the rain." He goes on to conclude, "What a striking similarity between this new poet's feeling and that of Guo Moruo sixty years ago when the two came into contact with Whitman! How deeply rooted the seeds Whitman cast in the soil of the Chinese mind have become today!"[42] A whole decade has passed since Cohen reviewed Chu's translation of *Leaves of Grass*, and now it is time again to examine how the seeds are growing and what fruit they are bearing.

It is the wish of all that Chu Tunan should not be forgotten because he "made the greatest contribution in introducing Whitman and his ideas and poetry to China."[43] But David Kuebrich wrote in 1983 that "Chu's important pioneering effort is now being superseded by a new translation by Chao Lo-jui [Zhao Luorui], an experienced translator and one of China's foremost scholars of American literature."[44] Both Guo Moruo and Chu Tunan were CCP members and were politically oriented scholars: Guo used to have personal contact with Mao and held various important positions; Chu was the chairman of the League of Democracy and was elected vice chairman of the Standing Committee of the People's Congress in 1988. Unlike Guo and Chu, Zhao Luoruo is a scholar through and through. In the late 1940s she received both her Master's and Ph.D. degrees in English at the University of Chicago, with emphasis on nineteenth-century American literature. She returned to China in 1949 and since then has been teaching comparative and foreign literature at Peking University, except for an interruption of ten years because of the Cultural Revolution when she had to "reform" herself like all other intellectuals in China. Zhao has devoted herself to the study of such figures as Henry James, T. S. Eliot, the Brontë sisters, and Whitman, whom she admires the most.

Kuebrich's brief article, "Whitman in China," is really about Whitman and Zhao Luorui; except for a passing mention of Chu's translation, the essay is based on Kuebrich's personal interviews with Zhao. According to Kuebrich, Zhao began work on Whitman in 1963, but nothing came of it because of the political tumult. In 1980 she turned with fresh energy to the task of translating *Leaves of Grass* in its entirety, "without sacrificing accuracy." Zhao's effort in translating Whitman aroused American attention; a sample of her work was published in the *New York Times* in Chinese *pinyin*. As a professional scholar, Zhao (unlike Chu) does not have to be so concerned about politics and is not afraid to try her hand at the sensitive pieces in Whitman's opus, such as "I Sing the Body Electric." Besides, Zhao's era is drastically different from Chu's in the 1950s, when politics dominated literary studies and one would be held responsible for anything construed to be politically unsound. Sexuality and religion are surely sensitive issues to the Chinese people. "I Sing the Body Electric" is very likely to be regarded as indecent; parts of stanza 5 may even risk the danger of being labeled pornographic. When Zhao rendered the "more controversial" poems, it was decidedly an act of courage, foresight, and sagacity.[45]

"Song of Myself" may be the best-known piece of Whitman's poetry in China, and it has been translated by at least six hands; Zhao published her version in a single volume in 1987.[46] The striking title of the poem, the unaffected style, and the fresh content produce a newness that appeals to the Chinese audience. China is basically a nonreligious country; religion is often identified with superstition and therefore rejected. Whitman's religious outlook is inoffensive to both the traditional secularism and antireligious Communism of the Chinese because, like them, he stresses a human-centered universe. He chants in Section 44:

It is time to explain myself—let us stand up.
What is known I strip away,
I launch all men and women forward with me into the Unknown. (LG, 80)

And in Section 48:

I have said that the soul is not more than the body,
And I have said that the body is not more than the soul,
And nothing, not God, is greater to one than one's self is. . . .

And I say to mankind, Be not curious about God,
For I who am curious about each am not curious about God,

(No array of terms can say how much I am at peace about God and about
  death.) (LG, 86)

To a Chinese reader this sounds pagan and pantheistic. Compare Guo Moruo's
"Three Pantheists" (1919):

I love my country's Chuang Tzu
Because I love his pantheism,
Because I love his making straw sandals for a living.

I love Holland's Spinoza
Because I love his pantheism,
Because I love his grinding lenses for a living.

I love India's Kabir
Because I love his pantheism,
Because I love his making fishnets for a living.[47]

Whitman and Guo Moruo meet in a pantheism which leads to the love of everything in nature and which in turn produces ebullient feelings in the poet.

Translation has always been an important but difficult business, and translating poetry is especially tricky. Linguistic differences between Chinese ideograms
and English alphabetical spellings often frustrate translators. Despite these problems, China, as has already been suggested, has done much in this field. Shakespeare perhaps enjoys the largest number of translations in Chinese despite the
syntactical difficulty of Elizabethan English; Whitman is widely read but seems to
have had only two major translators, Chu Tunan and Zhao Luorui, though individual poems have been rendered and published in a scattered manner. Zhao
is undoubtedly a serious, responsible, faithful, and qualified Whitman translator, who emphasizes "a judicious blend of accuracy, fluency, and what she speaks
of as 'idiomatic grasp,'" though at the same time she thinks translating him is
impossible.[48]

What is Whitman's status in China today? It is perhaps only partially true
when Kuebrich says that, "unlike such American writers as Twain or Jack London, Whitman is not widely known in China today [1983], even among students
of American literature."[49] Huang Suyi, a research fellow of foreign literature at
the Chinese Academy of Social Sciences, remarks: "Except for Whitman and
Dreiser, nearly all the important writers, such as Nathaniel Hawthorne, Herman
Melville, Mark Twain, Harriet Beecher Stowe, Jack London, O. Henry, Ernest
Hemingway and William Faulkner, only received brief mentions in some short articles or in the prefaces and postscripts to the Chinese translations of their
works."[50] This observation, like Kuebrich's, is not entirely true. Wang Yao, a well-
known historian of Chinese literature, in talking about foreign influences on
modern Chinese literature, stresses Whitman's role in the New Poetry, though he

is more aware of Russian literary influence.[51] That Kuebrich mentions Twain and Huang cites Whitman indicates that there is disagreement about the reputation and reception of American writers in China. I believe Twain is better known than Whitman because his "Running for Governor" was translated and filtered down into the high school textbooks throughout the country as a model piece of critical realism that exposes the so-called false democracy in a capitalist country. In other words, all high school graduates know who Mark Twain is. Other than Twain, Whitman and Hemingway are no doubt at the very front of a long list of American writers. Since the open door policy was implemented, young people's minds have opened up, and they are losing interest in those like Dreiser and London who used to be labeled progressive writers.

Since 1980, China's Ministry of Culture has done a great deal in international cultural exchange. To continue the open door policy, it is important for China to have cultural leaders with knowledge of one or more foreign languages, since such people are often more open-minded and less prejudiced against foreign cultures. Huang Zhen knows English well and, as was noted, quoted Whitman in a political speech. Wang Meng, Huang's successor as cultural minister in the late 1980s, was once a victim of the Anti-Rightist Movement and the Cultural Revolution. As one of the leading Chinese novelists today, he writes in the stream-of-consciousness style and is a very Western-oriented writer. Wang's associate minister, Ying Ruocheng, is another versatile figure: well-known actor, reputable theater director, and experienced translator of English and American literature, who translated, directed, and played the lead in Herman Wouk's *The Caine Mutiny*, Arthur Miller's *Death of a Salesman*, and Shakespeare's *Measure for Measure*. After reading Huang's memoirs of his Washington days, Cohen, like Palandri, wonders, "Will China's cultural minister lead the country down a literary road that has been countermanded?"[52] The road traveled by Whitman in China has been tortuous, but these cultural leaders did try to lead the country down a literary road that has been countermanded through their efforts to promote cultural exchanges and through their own writings and performances partially shaped by Western influences. Because of all this, fruit stemming from foreign literary seeds (including Whitman's, of course) has developed, despite the hard fact that both Wang and Ying were removed from their positions after Tian'anmen in 1989.

The winter of 1986 witnessed a large-scale but failed student movement demanding more democracy and freedom of speech. This movement was officially recognized as the result of the influence of Western bourgeois liberalization, in which foreign literature played a conspicuous part. To avoid the tragedy of the Cultural Revolution, not all foreign literature was declared unhealthy (only works by Jean-Paul Sartre and Sigmund Freud). But the whole Anti-"Spiritual Pollution" Campaign was aborted, and in effect Sartre and Freud became even more popular for a time. The Anti-Anti-"Spiritual Pollution" Campaign reached its climax in the outbreak of the mass movement in the spring of 1989, which ended in tragedy. These two movements are sweet and bitter fruits of the open door policy characterized by learning from the West, in which democratic ideas and the spirit of freedom as expressed by Whitman and his comrades play a major role. Of course, this is not to accuse them of misleading Chinese intellectuals. On the contrary, the Whitmanian spirit encouraged them to seek their own values in a monolithic state.

The third peak of Whitman's reception was reached when numerous important publications on Whitman poured forth during the late 1980s. In 1986 Zhang Yujiu selected and translated thirty-nine of Whitman's essays and published them under the title *Selected Prose Works of Whitman*. In 1987 Li Yeguang completed his translation of *Leaves of Grass* based on Chu's earlier work (433 poems and five essays); the same year saw Tu An and Chu's translation of 56 poems entitled "I Dream'd in a Dream." Early in 1988 Li Shiqi translated and annotated *Selected Poems of Whitman*. In August of the same year two important publications appeared: Li Yeguang's *Critical Biography of Whitman*, the only book of its kind, which the author calls "a new effort" in Chinese scholarship on Whitman, and his edition of *Studies in Whitman*, a selection of translated British and American critical essays written between 1855 and 1980.[53] Li Yeguang's work on Whitman has been prolific; his 1981 poem "To Whitman" reveals the intensity and intimacy of his response to Whitman and is one of many such poems written to Whitman by contemporary Chinese poets (see selection 1).

Interestingly, unlike the years before 1978 when works on Whitman were published only in Beijing and Shanghai, the two leading cultural cities of China, recent works of and on Whitman have been published in provincial capitals such as Taiyuan, Changsha, and Guilin (the capital of a southern province where there are more minority people than Chinese). The spread of Whitman's fame suggests that he has gained more popularity and is more widely read than at any time since he was introduced to China in 1919.

In May 1990, about a year after Tian'anmen, Peking University Press brought out a massive *Companion to Masterpieces in World Poetry*, which includes forty-six American poets. Whitman's "When Lilacs Last in the Dooryard Bloom'd" and a large fragment of "Song of Myself" are included. The editors again adopted Chu Tunan's version of "Lilacs," the version Palandri spoke of as "half prose and half verse";[54] I would characterize it as highly poetical and musical — Chu's is a very proper way of rendering Whitman's poetry — free but harmonious, unrhymed but rhythmical. Following are the first three lines both in the English original and Chinese *pinyin* to give the reader a flavor of Chu's rendition:

When lilacs last in the dooryard bloom'd,
And the great star early droop'd in the western sky in the night,
I mourn'd, and yet shall mourn with ever-returning spring. (LG, 328)

Dang zidingxiang zuijin zai tingyuan zhong kaifang de shihou,
Nake shuoda de xingxing zai xifang de yekong yunluole,
Wo aidaozhe, bing jiang suizhe yinianyidu de chunguang yongyuan de
    aidaozhe.[55]

Chu not only retains the original structure of the poem, he even retains most of its punctuation marks, though at times he reorganizes certain sentences to conform to Chinese syntax or grammar and to make them idiomatic.

Not long ago, Zhao Luorui completed her translation of the complete *Leaves* and submitted it to the publisher. Whitman scholars, teachers, and students are looking forward to its appearance with an enthusiastic hope that her translation will be refreshing and entertaining in terms of poetical quality, as well as accurate and faithful in terms of understanding and interpretation. As the efforts made by Chu, Zhao, Li Yeguang, and many others have shown, Whitman, as an original poet and democratic symbol, has to be studied in depth; if he is, the fruit will both be great and sweet.

NOTES

1. Mao delivered his *Talks* in Yan'an on May 23, 1942, when the Anti-Japanese War was at a critical moment. The influence of this long speech has been enormous; even today writers in China are urged to study it. To commemorate the forty-ninth anniversary of its publication, the vice president of China, Wang Zhen, delivered a speech at the National Conference of Young Writers on May 23, 1991, in which he pointed out that the *Talks* "nurtured thousands upon thousands of writers and artists generation after generation. Its fundamental tenets will never be outdated, always guiding the healthy development of our nation's socialist literature and art." See Wang's "The Spirit of the *Talks* Shines Forever," *People's Daily* (May 24, 1991).

2. Geoffrey M. Sill, introduction to "Whitman and the World," *Mickle Street Review* 9 (1988).

3. Wong Yoon Wah, *Essays on Chinese Literature: A Comparative Approach* (Singapore: Singapore University Press, 1988), 39.

4. Chen Duxiu was editor of *The New Youth* in Beijing, the most influential journal of the time in China, established in the mid-1910s; he then became the first general secretary of the CCP when it was founded in July 1921. Hu Shi was in the United States from 1910 to 1917, pursuing his Ph.D degree; he later became the president of Peking University and the Nationalist Chinese Ambassador to the U.S. Lu Xun was and still is modern China's "standard-bearer"—which in Chinese means the foremost leader in literature; Guo Moruo was another standard-bearer after Lu. Guo was studying medicine in Japan during the May Fourth Movement of 1919 and Lu had returned to China earlier, but later both became leading Chinese writers. Mao Zedong at this time was a library assistant at Peking University.

5. The journal was published in Shanghai; its editor was Zong Baihua. Tian Han's article is in the inaugural issue of July 1919.

6. Achilles Fang, "From Imagism to Whitmanism in Recent Chinese Poetry: A Search for Poetics That Failed," in Horst Frenz and G. L. Anderson, eds., *Indiana University Conference on Oriental-Western Literary Relations* (Chapel Hill: University of North Carolina Press, 1955), 177.

7. Ibid., 181.

8. Ibid., 185.

9. Guo's poems written in the 1920s, *The Goddesses* in particular, have won the most critical attention since then.

10. Fang, "From Imagism to Whitmanism," 186.

11. Zhu Ziqing, "Introduction to Modern Poetry," in Cai Yuan-pei et al., eds., *Collection of Introductions to the Corpus of Chinese New Literature* (Shanghai: Liangyou-Fuxing Book Company, 1940), 353 (in Chinese).

12. Fang, "From Imagism to Whitmanism," 187.

13. My translation. For the Chinese original, see Guo Moruo, *The Goddesses* (Beijing: People's Literature Press, 1985).

14. Fang, "From Imagism to Whitmanism," 186.

15. Caochuan Weiyu, *Yesterday, Today, and Tomorrow of China's New Poetry* (Peiping [Beijing]: Haiyin Publishing House, 1929), 63–65 (in Chinese).

16. Fang, "From Imagism to Whitmanism," 186.

17. Julia C. Lin, *Modern Chinese Poetry: An Introduction* (Seattle: University of Washington Press, 1972), 198.

18. For a discussion of Mao's traditionalist poetry, see Douwe Wessel Fokkema, *Literary Doctrine in China and Soviet Influence: 1956–1960* (The Hague: Mouton, 1965), 105–106.

19. Feng Youan, *A History of Chinese Philosophy* (Beijing: Peking University Press, 1985), 39 ff. Originally published in English by the University of Pennsylvania Press, translated into Chinese by Tu Youguang.

20. Xilao Li, "Whitman in China," *Mickle Street Review* 9 (1988): 69.

21. Quoted in Wang Yao, "The Relations between Modern Chinese Literature and Foreign Literature," trans. Hu Zhihui, *Chinese Literature* 8 (1988): 151, 155.

22. Li Yeguang, "Whitman in China," in Li Yeguang, ed., *Studies in Whitman* (Guilin: Li River Press, 1988), 568 (in Chinese).

23. Tian Han, Zong Baihua, and Guo Moruo, *Three Leaves of Grass* (Shanghai: Oriental Book Company, 1920) (in Chinese). The title is derived from a German term, *kleeblatt*. This is a small collection of letters, and today's readers are unlikely to notice it because of its age and small size.

24. Guo translated poetry beautifully, as can also be seen in his handling of Matthew Arnold's "Dover Beach," Goethe's *Faustus*, and even some Japanese poems.

25. Gay Wilson Allen, *The New Walt Whitman Handbook* (New York: New York University Press, 1975), 98.

26. Xilao Li, "Walt Whitman in China," *Walt Whitman Quarterly Review* 3 (Spring 1988): 3.

27. Quoted in Xilao Li, "Walt Whitman," 69.

28. Li Yeguang, "Whitman in China," 578.

29. The author thanks Li Yeguang for providing this information.

30. Xilao Li, "Walt Whitman," 5.

31. Angela Chih-Ying Jung Palandri, "Whitman in Red China," *Walt Whitman Newsletter* 4 (September 1958): 95.

32. Ibid.

33. Ibid., 97.

34. Mark Cohen, "Whitman in China: A Revisitation," *Walt Whitman Review* 26 (March 1980): 34–35.

35. Ibid., 34.

36. Caochuan, *Yesterday*, 63.

37. The same charges have, of course, been leveled at Whitman: Mark Van Doren held that *Leaves of Grass* "gains with most readers when it is cut. Much of it is repetition, and much of it is bad." See the introduction to *The Portable Walt Whitman* (New York: Viking, 1977), xviii.

38. Cohen, "Whitman," 34.

39. Li Yeguang, "Whitman in China," 574–575.

40. Cohen, "Whitman," 39.

41. Huang Zhen, "My Days in Washington," *Beijing Review* 4 (January 26, 1979): 16.

42. Xilao Li, "Walt Whitman," 73.

43. Ibid.

44. David Kuebrich, "Whitman in China," *Walt Whitman Quarterly Review* 1 (September 1983): 33.

45. Ibid., 34.

46. These translators are Xu Zhimo, Chu Tunan, Gong Mu, Li Shiqi, Zhao Luorui, and Li Yeguang.

47. Julia C. Lin's translation.

48. Kuebrich, "Whitman in China," 34.

49. Ibid.

50. Huang Suyi, "English and American Literature in China," trans. Hu Zhihui, *Chinese Literature* 9 (1982): 109.

51. Wang Yao, "Modern Chinese Literature," passim.

52. Cohen, "Whitman," 35.

53. This Chinese biography of Whitman was published by Shanghai Literature & Art Press in 1988; Li's own comment on it is in "Whitman in China," 583.

54. Palandri, "Whitman in Red China," 95.

55. For a full translation of the poem, see Gu Zhengkun, Guiyou Huang, et al., eds., *A Companion to Masterpieces in World Poetry* (Beijing: Peking University Press, 1990), 624–627.

1. LI YEGUANG

"To Whitman"

Are you the sea, Whitman?
Why do I hear from your songs of yonder years
The roaring of the seas,

Standing on the sea-cliffs today,
But see not your grey and proud face?
Perhaps the sea-waves, the powder-faced waves,
Are your later-year beard and hair, like flying mist,
And the profound heaven of an autumn night,
Pervades your eye-ridges and frontal eminence,
Like the low but broad brim of your hat;
Perhaps you are raising your head,
To observe which of those mysterious stars
Is portending the changes of America's tomorrow. . . .

O, you are muttering, meditating,
Conceiving of a new prophecy.
Democracy — hangs the star-sparkled banner on the waist,
Liberty — decays from the soul to the thighs,
Equality, fraternity — only remains a colored shirt.
Even railways connecting continents, cables under the ocean,
Have already given way to rockets
Flying through space into the Milky Way.
If the globe must sink into an earthen bowl,
And America can grasp an ear-ring thereof,
Or compete with powerful rivals, or,
Altogether, throw the bowl down into an evil hole,
If the people still entrust their fate
In the vast sea of dust, and the shining light of stars. . . .

Then, of all your songs?
The drum-beats, like rain-drops
That strike the northern land,
And the petals of lilacs that are weeping
Sorrowfully in the mourning-hall of the White House,
When your federation is tottering on surging waves,
When the triumphant banner just leapt up on the mast,
When your captain —
The wood-cutters who have felled thousands of trunks!
Left their steering-wheel and broad axes
Beside themselves. . . .

Ah! Whitman,
My "good grey old man,"
How solitary you were then!
The bunches of leaves from your masculine strong poetry
Sprang up on the wasteland of the new continent,
Like myriads of swords pointing upward toward the sky, yet,
The respectable tiger-painters on the American literary arena

With spittle, dirty mud, and dictionaries
Resisted the challenging whistle-arrows —
An awakening string on the soul of the cosmos!

O, you compared yourself to the sea,
That carried the first cloud-sail:
The sea's breadth, the cloud's imagination,
And the inspiration swift as water tides,
Drove your heart toward the people,
With hope, love, and convincing eloquence,
Yet, the world blocked you, and blocked you,
You could not but stand on the sea shore alone,
Calling to the sea without a break!

Now it has been ninety years, Whitman,
I seem to behold you steering a wheel-chair,
Sauntering on the solitary seabeach.
You did not wield a saw or axe to make a building,
But opening the windows to meet the storms of the time,
Or inviting those friends of yours,
Seamen, horse-cart drivers, wounded soldiers, and tramps,
Although Mrs. G——
Wearing that mystery ring of yours in melancholy
Pulled down the curtain on the other side of the ocean. . . .

Ah, your poetical thought meanders, murmurs,
When you descended the last step of your life,
With "so long!" repeated again and again
That's not nostalgic of Egyptian hieroglyphs,
Nor cherishing the memory of ancient Roman athletes,
Nor of India's folk song, magic dance,
Homer, Dante, and Shakespeare's splendor,
All these are no more than a shadow and echo of history,
Which once made turns in your midnight thought,
Just as Longfellow's low-voiced chants
That stirred no vast surges in the Ontario Lake. . . .

True, you laid open history and folded it again,
Like a roll of yellow silk on your desk.
You said: this is not me, this is not the America at the foot of Columbus or in
    my heart!
Therefore you searched, measuring virgin lands,
Just as a long train of ox-pulled carts
Pouring into the vast wasteland of the west,
But the wasteland of human life can never reach an end.
Aloud to the thundering drum beats with your head high,

(But not a row of small piano-keys!)
You sang of life, of the "self,"
Of one point of inspiration between heaven and earth—
The expression that flashes in the eyes of black slaves
And the bloody bile burning in France,
That which is in every grit, every colorful cloud,
From every natural phenomenon to the infinite time and space—
That is your poetry, your poetry!
Beating its wings of love and beauty, onward, and on. . . .

And thus, Whitman,
In the autumn night of airy sky and misty seas,
I come to seek your splendor and songs of older days,
Clouds floating and stars twinkling, winds far but sonorous,
As if history were drifting right before my eyes—
Clusters of joys and sorrows, countless number of nightmares,
While the cosmos is painfully and loudly pulsing,
With tonight, tomorrow morn, and faith,
This moment I seem to have embraced life,
Hearing it so eagerly crying out:
"Myself," no longer a solitary one,
Belonging not to the barren seabeach!
I am a wave, jumping, racing, laughing,
Rushing forward—toward the verdant horizon. . . .

— September–November 1981, Beidaihe-Beijing

The Poetry Journal (1983; in Chinese). Translated by Guiyou Huang. "Tiger-painters" is a classical Chinese allusion to those painters who try to paint a tiger but end up with a dog.

2. LI YEGUANG

"Walt Whitman in China"

Walt Whitman is one of the first American writers introduced to China and is the American poet who has the greatest influence over China's new poetry movement. He appeared in China almost simultaneously with the May Fourth Movement, which upheld the banner of "Democracy and Science." . . .

Ai Qing (1910–), the best-known contemporary Chinese poet and a persistent forerunner in Chinese poetry from the 1930s to the 1940s, is a good example of how poets from China absorb Whitman's influence and achieve great success. He began to read Whitman as well as Verhaeren and Mayakovsky in the early 1930s in France and was immediately attracted to their work. He said the main reason why he was fond of these poets was that "they have brought poetry to a higher realm" ("The Prosaic Beauty of Poetry" [1939]). In his programmatic work, "On Poetry," he offered many Whitman-inspired ideas: he said that "poetry is the information which mankind sends to the future"; "the top theory or declaration is always a piece of a poem"; "a poem is a personality and should be made sublime and perfect"; "the melody of poetry is the melody of life"; "it is better to be naked than to be suffocated by illfitting clothes." Even Ai Qing's expressions are similar to Whitman's. His "Peace Letters to Pablo Neruda," written in 1952, declared that "no one would forget the American war of independence and freedom, no one would forget Lincoln the carpenter's broad bosom, no one would forget Whitman as a tall oak tree standing ingenuously on the earth and roaring night and day."

In his "Sixty Years of Chinese New Poetry," published in 1980, Ai Qing indicated right from the beginning that "the 'Goddess,' published in August 1921, accepted Whitman's influence, courageously breaking through the fetters of formalities, singing of the great nature, the earth, the ocean, the sun, the modern metropolis, the motherland, and the power." A commentator who has kept communication with Ai Qing since the 1930s once said, "Ai Qing writes about the wide road, the ocean, about their broadness and openness, in ways that remind us of Whitman, and sometimes he uses long Whitmanlike verses." Indeed, Whitman's style can be felt even in Ai Qing's first famous poem, "The Da Yan River, My Nanny," which came out in 1933, and in a series of fine later pieces, such as "Snow Falls on the Land of China" (1937), "The Bugler" (1939), "Lamenting for Paris" (1940), "Times" (1941), and "The Prairie Fire" (1942). All these pieces bear the same free and unrestrained style and vigorous and luxurious fragrance as *Leaves of Grass*. But Whitman's influence on Ai Qing goes far beyond artistic characteristics. Ai Qing sings in his "Towards the Sun" (1938) that "Whitman / inspired by the sun / with broadness of the ocean / composed poems with the same broadness." Is Ai Qing himself not singing of his nation and his era with such "broadness" and such "inspiration" as Whitman did? . . .

With the founding of the People's Republic, Whitman entered a new historical period in China. On November 25, 1955, a conference to commemorate the centenary of the publication of *Leaves of Grass* was held in Beijing. Zhou Yang (1908–1989) made a speech at the conference and said, "In Whitman's poetry, democracy, freedom, and equality are his fundamental ideas. . . . Victory and happiness are his persistent beliefs which mankind will eventually achieve" (*Wenyibao* 22 [November 1955]). In the same month, a forum on the same topic was held in Shanghai where Ba Jin (1904–) said that "Whitman's poetry is still a great inspiring impetus to the Chinese people who are marching towards socialism today" (*Liberation Daily* [December 4, 1955]). Centering on this commemoration, more than twenty articles written by well-known poets, writers, or commentators, as well as some of Whitman's poems, were published in different newspapers or magazines all over the country, and the revised edition of the *Selections of "Leaves of Grass"* came out from the People's Literature Publishing House. In addition, Maurice Mendelssohn's Russian *On Whitman*, A. Capek's *Critical Biography of*

Whitman, and Edward Carpenter's *Days with Walt Whitman* were translated and published in Beijing and Shanghai. During this commemoration period, Xu Chi made a speech at a public meeting entitled "On *Leaves of Grass*." Although he commented on Whitman mainly from political and social points of view, he still ardently praised "Calamus." He had selected and translated this series of poems and found therein his own artistic views. In fact, an attentive reader is able to find the "Calamus" message in Xu Chi's early experiments of poetry. . . .

According to rough statistics, about 110 new translations of Whitman's poems and 80 articles about Whitman appeared in different Chinese newspapers or periodicals from 1979 to 1988. In addition, we often read poems addressed to or singing about Whitman, composed by Chinese poets — "The Friendship Pine — Chatting with Whitman" by Li Yourong in 1979; "A Cluster of Lilac for You" by Zou Difan in 1980; "To Walt Whitman" by Li Yeguang in 1983; "Looking at the Manuscripts of Whitman's Poems" by Li Ying in 1985; "On Reading Whitman" by Lu Yuan in 1985; and "Long Island" by Tu An in 1986. These poets are all Whitman admirers, and some of them are specialists both in translating and studying Whitman.

When commenting on or recommending Whitman, Chinese translators and scholars are unavoidably marked with the influence of the times and the society they live in, as well as their own personal preferences. However, the condition is improving. Especially in recent years, the goal of "Letting a hundred flowers blossom and a hundred schools of thought contend" has begun to be realized. What is encouraging is that Whitman's Chinese translators are all conscientious and serious, trying to be true to the original and under no circumstances intentionally deleting or distorting Whitman's work.

Of course, because of the abstruseness and subtlety of Whitman's poetry, and what with the translators' different faculties of comprehension or different abilities in commanding their own language, the various translations are rather diversified and bring about different effects. This problem has aroused controversy recently. Some translators, particularly the younger ones, have begun to query and dispute each other, and some have raised critical objections to the translations of well-known scholars. So discussions have been organized in translation and publication circles to take advantage of this new trend. The "Forum on Literary Translation," held in August 1991 in Beijing, was a successful attempt in this field.

Whitman's appearance in China seems a bit later than in many other countries, and yet, in terms of the historical mission, he arrived in time after all. His seventy-year hard and rough journey in China can be divided into two historical periods. In the thirty years before the founding of the People's Republic, those who appreciated and introduced Whitman to China were mainly poets, and most of them advocated and persisted in writing free verse, while some worked for the creation of new metrical patterns for many years and still others became famous for their classical poetic compositions. They belonged to different schools in different times, including the Crescent School, Modernist School, July School, and so on, and they also embraced different trends, like romanticism, realism, or symbolism. Their perspectives on Whitman varied, but they all respected him and benefited from his works in differing ways. Few of them reacted to him passively, just as we would expect given the historical development in China. Since the May Fourth Movement, the task confronting the Chinese literature revolution has been one of opposing imperialistic and traditional feudalistic cultures with democratic and scientific spirit in order to build a new national democratic literature. Whitman's completely new democratic ideas and his urgent demand for an independent national literature for the New World aim in the same direction. Secondly, the advocates of Chinese new poetry eagerly aspire to create a free verse or a new metrical poetry to keep pace with the new era, and Whitman, as the radical revolutionist in poetic patterns and the true creator of free verse in the world history, meets the needs of all schools of new poetry in China. Therefore, throughout the democratic revolution in China, under the new condition when writers were exploring and creating in the field of poetic art, Whitman became all the more valuable to them. What Whitman brought to the Chinese new poetry movement in this period, as pointed out by Professor Wang Zuoliang, was the upsurge and development of the bold and unconstrained poetic style after Guo Moruo. This influence is felt in the spirit, in the force, and in the style. So it can be said that Whitman's influence permeates the very blood as well as the external features of the Chinese new poetry.

In socialist China, particularly during the past decade, the study of Whitman has been more and more widely undertaken by younger translators and scholars. Nevertheless, Whitman's influence on Chinese poets continues to grow, and his poetry — which sings of democracy, freedom, modern civilization, and love of mankind — along with his incessant exploration in the ideological field and his bold creation and experience in poetic art are still gaining popularity and depth, still inspiring and encouraging. The poet Shao Yanxiang wrote after reading the first complete translation of *Leaves of Grass* that, as a "cosmic poet," Whitman appeals for the "acceptance, integration and renovation" of the alien culture and proposes to "shape it with our own character," a message that is close to us Chinese who are opening extensively to the outside world today ("The Evergreen Leaves of Grass" [*People's Daily*, September 26, 1987]). I am sure Shao Yanxiang's feelings are to a certain degree representative of most Chinese poets, including myself.

Li Yeguang, ed., *Studies in Whitman* (Guilin: Li River Press, 1988). Translated by the author and updated in 1992 for this volume.

TAKASHI KODAIRA & ALFRED H. MARKS

Whitman in Japan

Whitman welcomed Japan more than thirty years before Japan welcomed him. On June 16, 1860, the poet watched a parade on Broadway that included the members of the first mission from Japan to the United States, sent to Washington to deliver ratified copies of the Treaty of Commerce of 1858. Whitman believed their appearance to be a transcendental omen and expressed that and much more in his poem "The Errand-Bearers," which appeared in the *New York Times* on June 27. He planned to include the poem in the volume *Banner at Daybreak*; when that collection failed to find a publisher, he revised the poem and included it in *Drum-Taps* (1865) as "A Broadway Pageant," the title it still bears. His revisions show that Whitman did some research on Japan and the diplomatic mission, because he substituted the word "nobles" for "princes" in several places. The envoys were not princes.

Whitman's introduction in Japan did not come until 1892, the year of his death, but the circumstances of that introduction made a lasting impression. The person who first wrote of the poet was none other than Sôseki Natsume, one of the greatest writers of modern Japan. Although he had not yet established his reputation and his essay on Whitman was unsigned, his powerful prose made a deep impression that grew stronger with the years as his fame increased. Titled "On the Poems of Walt Whitman: The Representative of Equality in the Literary World," the essay was published in the *Journal of Philosophy* (*Tetsugaku Zasshi*) in October of 1892. Sôseki was then about twenty-four and a student at Tokyo University. Many of his ideas on Whitman were derived from Edward Dowden's essay, "The Poetry of Democracy: Walt Whitman," published in the *Westminster Review* in 1871. A glance at Sôseki's first few pages is illuminating:

> The French worked out how to pursue revolution in politics. The British showed it in literature. Those who have read through Burns know what it is like to be imbued with a concern for equality. Shelley did not waste words. The first act of *Prometheus Unbound* shows his view well enough. Byron's *Childe Harold* fired off a charge of wholehearted dissatisfaction, repeated in *Don Juan*. England's poets, fairly calm and traditional even while claiming that pent-up rage boiled in every pore, provided the past with a clean face. In America, where, amid all the advocacy of this thinking, a republican government was established on the strange basis that men would stand up and die for this principle, and where universal brotherhood was preached, there was not one man who stood up and shouted: "I am the poet of the republic."
>
> Longfellow was a poet, but his thinking reflected the Middle Ages and not the new world of America. Irving was a fine author, but his taste did not rest entirely with his native land, but instead leaned toward the European continent. We may look for authors to compare with these in England, but we will not find them. There are also Bryant and Hawthorne — distinctive authors of the first water, without question. And yet the new poet worthy of representing the never-before-seen republic known as the United States had not appeared.
>
> Then, at the appropriate time, a giant descended from the heavens, exhaling great flames on behalf of the United States, creating wildly extravagant poems, with the power of the buffalo that roams the prairies. His voice skimmed the waves to the other side of the Atlantic, and the doctrine it preached surpassed that of Byron and Shelley, becoming what one must declare as truly the happiest event of recent years.
>
> That poet was named Walt Whitman.[1]

As may be inferred from this quotation, Whitman studies in Japan have been linked to democratic, even socialist, politics, and thus have flourished or declined depending on the shifts of official political opinion during the past hundred years. These shifts have been dramatic in the three imperial eras that have elapsed since the Japanese discovered Whitman in 1892: Meiji (1868–1911), Taishô (1912–1924), and Shôwa (1925–1989). The Meiji era was expansive and filled with a sense of discovery. The Taishô era continued that spirit, taking it further and higher. Whitman scholarship during these two eras and translation of his poetry into Japanese grew accordingly. The Shôwa era, during which the military took control until the end of World War II, was marked in the early years by repression, and attention to Whitman became dangerous. Since the end of the war (in the twentieth year of Shôwa), democracy has been present in Japan as never before, and attention to Whitman has flourished without restriction.

Japanese Whitman studies could have been strengthened by Lafcadio Hearn, who wrote about the poet in the *New Orleans Post-Democrat* as early as 1882. Hearn carried on a long and cordial correspondence with Whitman's friend and admirer William D. O'Connor and gave a number of lectures on Whitman during his tenure as professor at Tokyo Imperial University from 1896 to 1903. His 1882 article, however, was not favorable, and in spite of Hearn's confessions to O'Connor that some of his voiced disaffection with Whitman stemmed from the pressures of writing for a family newspaper, the tone of his university lectures was no better. In fact, Hearn went so far as to warn his Japanese students against using Whitman as a model for their writing, whether poetry or prose.

Although Hearn chose to disparage Whitman, his negative opinions were only minimally influential. As early as 1895, the critic Umaji Kaneko had been elevating Whitman to the status of one of the world's literary giants. Though his views appear to have been shaped by Havelock Ellis, Kaneko's assessments of Whitman influenced a number of important authors. Then, in 1898, Rintaro Takayama, later known by the penname Chogy, wrote in the magazine *Taiyô* (*Sun*) an unforgettable short passage on Whitman:

> While our countrymen were reviling the new poetic forms of Dr. Sotoyama, Americans were welcoming Walt Whitman. Today we wonder what our literary scholars are thinking as they read his collection of poetry.
>
> His poems don't follow the sound of the letters but the reverberations of the soul. In this world of pride and hypocrisy, who is there to sing of this stark naked human being? Rather than do it for 100,000 imposters, I would do it for this one forthright Whitman.

When pressed on what he meant by "imposters," Chogy made a proclamation that sounds like a mixture of Whitman and Nietzsche, whom he also revered:

> What are false poets? Those who set themselves up as poets without any poetic gifts. . . .
>
> We immediately get enough of their creative weeping, their creative laughter. What we crave is the voice of the spirit. What does it matter that the voice has a stammer? We all have a soul in us that answers that voice. Only spirit can recognize spirit.
>
> Depart, false poets — imposters who attempt to fashion poems out of archaic words and grammar. This is the time of the poetic revolution.[2]

Chogy was twenty-six at this time, and he would die only four years later, in 1902, but before his death he established a reputation like that of John Keats — a short-lived, intense romantic who had a tremendous effect on his contemporaries. His critical response to Whitman was clearly philosophical and even religious, but in these years, less than a half century after the opening of Japan, Japanese intellectuals were desperately searching for ways to accommodate the new ideas — particularly Christianity — pouring in from the outside, yet they were restrained by the strictures of Buddhism, Shintô, and, above all, neo-Confucianism. Whitman, the iconoclast, held out his hand to them from a middle course. Chogy's response was further complicated by a fervent nationalism and a Nietzscheism that led him to search for heroes in a manner now associated with the Germans of many decades later.

Three men who were learning to read Whitman in English at the turn of the century would dominate Whitman studies for the rest of the Taishô era. They were Kanzô Uchimura, Takeo Arishima, and Yonejirô Noguchi, the last better known as Yone Noguchi, a poet in English and Japanese and the father of the sculptor Isamu Noguchi.

Uchimura (1861–1930) attended the Sapporo College of Agriculture (now Hokkaido University), where instruction was largely in English. He was profoundly affected by William Smith Clark, the Amherst, Massachusetts, educator who was in Japan for only eight months in 1876 and 1877 and refused to teach any students who were not Christian. Uchimura was one of the large numbers of students who were baptized and whose lives were significantly changed by Clark. After a number of years at Amherst College and Hartford Theological Seminary, Uchimura returned to Japan and became, like Ralph Waldo Emerson in America, an unordained heterodox-Christian theologian as well as an influential literary and social critic. Uchimura was conspicuous for his pacifism and social protest during Japan's slow march back into the thought control and militarism that culminated in World War II. An important part of his theology of *mukyôkai,* or "churchless religion," was the thinking of Walt Whitman, whom he began to champion in 1898.

Takeo Arishima (1878–1923) attended Sapporo College of Agriculture long after Uchimura, but after a period of living in the home of Uchimura's classmate Inazô Nitobe and meeting Uchimura himself in Tokyo, Arishima began to shape a philosophy that eventually blended Christianity with the ideas of Whitman, Ibsen, Tolstoy, and Kropotkin. After spending three and a half years at Haverford and at Harvard (where he enjoyed most the lectures of Paul Elmer More), he returned to Japan and became a novelist and important figure in the Shirakabaha, or White Birch branch of Japanese naturalism. Before he left Japan, Arishima was aware of Uchimura's interest in Whitman and immersed himself in *Leaves of Grass* while he was abroad. It was an immersion that would continue to deepen as long as he lived. His principal writings on Whitman were published between 1919 and 1924 and included five volumes of translations into Japanese of the poems in *Leaves of Grass.*

Yone Noguchi (1875–1947) went to the United States in 1893 and stayed until 1903. He spent three years of that time in the home of the poet Joaquin Miller in the mountains of California. While in the United States, he honed his skills in the English language and published his first volume of poems in English in London in 1903. Titled *From the Eastern Sea,* it caught the attention of no less than Austin Dobson, Thomas Hardy, George Meredith, and Andrew Lang. Naguchi wrote much on Whitman in Japanese and devoted a chapter to Whitman in his book *Japan and America*, also written in English. In the first chapter of that book, "Japan Today," he had this to say about the importance of Whitman and his associates for the development of democracy in Japan:

> It was only natural that we turned our heads to Whitman and read *Leaves of Grass* to be encouraged and strengthened in our own new belief. Those who were not vigorous and healthy enough to embrace the Good Grey Poet went to Edward Carpenter, this poetical backwoodsman by deliberation and choice, and talked with him on the worth of a real life and the harmony of seemingly conflicting elements. Some people who were craving good-naturedly and even madly for a copious and close comradeship of men tried to introduce even the name of Horace Traubel.[3]

None other than Horace Traubel was a force in the career of Shigetaka Naganuma as a scholar and translator of Whitman. The two met in 1920, while Naganuma was living in the United States, and they toured some of the Whitman haunts together. At the time, Naganuma was considering translating Traubel's poems, but Traubel advised him to translate Whitman instead. When Naganuma returned to Japan, he started the translations that eventually became the complete *Leaves of Grass* in Japanese. Despite accusations by late Taishô and early Shôwa proletarian poets and critics who complained of what they saw as Whitman's ties to American capitalism in the Gilded Age, Naganuma persevered and brought out his first volume of translations in 1932. The complete translation was published in 1950, and it has gone through several editions since then. Its appearance after World War II, thirty strife-torn years after Naganuma's visit with Traubel, is a testimony to the translator's persistence and his importance in the history of Whitman studies.

Three men stand beside Naganuma to form a bridge between the prewar studies of Whitman in Japan and those of the postwar period: Seigo Shiratori, Yoshinori Yoshitake, and Takashi Sugiki. Shiratori, born in 1890, was a poet of the White Birch School that included Takeo Arishima. In 1914 he published what appears to have been Japan's first biographical essay on Whitman, entitled "Whitman no Seikatsu" ("The Life of Whitman"); he continued to write about Whitman into the 1960s. Yoshitake, born in 1900 in the thirty-third year of Meiji, began publishing articles on Whitman in the early 1930s and as recently as 1980 brought out the fine volume *Whitman Juyô no Hyakunen* (*One Hundred Years of Whitman Reception*). He was the first president of the Walt Whitman Society of Japan, founded in 1964. Sugiki published the biography *Whitman* in 1937 and has continued publishing Whitman essays and translations ever since. He collaborated with Norihiro Nabeshima and Masayuki Sakamoto in the first volume of their three-volume translation of *Leaves of Grass*, a work which has been reprinted at least ten times. Nabeshima was the second president of the Walt Whitman Society of Japan.[4]

The emphasis in Whitman studies today in Japan is different from those early years of the Meiji and Taishô eras, when young Japanese were looking to the West for spiritual guidance and for direction into the future for themselves and their nation. Whitman is studied in Japan now much as he is in the United States: as an important poet who must be reckoned with by college faculty and students in any nineteenth-century American literature curriculum. He has become a favorite thesis subject for senior undergraduate students. Many American professors, including Gay Wilson Allen, have lectured on Whitman in Japan. Japanese professors — notably Saburô Ota and Rikutarô Fukuda (Whitman translator and fourth president of the Walt Whitman Society of Japan) — lecture in the United States on Whitman-related subjects. Ota's 1959 paper, "Walt Whitman and Japanese Literature," delivered at Indiana University, is still a classic. William L. Moore, of Tokyo's International Christian University, has taught courses on Whitman and published for his students a heavily annotated text of *Walt Whitman's Poems*, including "Song of Myself" and "By Blue Ontario's Shore."[5]

This essay is indebted to four monumental studies on Whitman written in Japanese: Shunsuke Kamei's *Walt Whitman in Modern Literature: A Comparative Study of Japanese and Western Appreciations* (1973); Shigenobu Sadoya's *Walt Whitman in Japan: His Influence in Modern Japan* (1969); Norihiro Nabeshima's *A Study of Whitman* (1959); and Yoshinori Yoshitake's previously mentioned *One Hundred Years of Whitman Reception* (1979).[6] The concluding paragraph of Saburo Ota's 1959 essay, not greatly changed by the intervening thirty years, provides the best summation of Whitman's influence in Japan:

> When we trace back the sixty years since the introduction of Walt Whitman to Japan we see that Whitman has been understood from various sides, according to both the conditions of the time and society and to the individuality of each person concerned. His readers had sometimes mutual and sometimes differing understandings of him. However, the social and cultural conditions of Japan may have been an important factor in the introduction of Whitman. First, the attention of literary critics was attracted by Whitman's concept of humanity and by the idea of literature of and by the common people. Then, men of letters reached out to Whitman with their hearts and minds, and built their literature on a new idea of humanity. When the consciousness of democracy developed in Japan, the democratic thought of Whitman entered Japanese poetry, and at the same time the significance of free verse was realized. The democratic thought, the free verse style, and the movement of colloquialism in poetry — these three were combined when men of letters opened their eyes to the liberation of human beings. This was an achievement of the Minshu-shi-ha [defined earlier by Ota as "poets of the common people"] school of the 1910s. After that, Whitman lost contact with Japanese literature and became the object only of scholarly investigation. The case of Walt Whitman may be one pattern of the fate of writers in foreign countries.[7]

1. Sôseki Natsume, "Bundan ni Okeru Byôdô Shugi no Daihyôsha Walt Whitman no Shi ni Tsuite" ("On the Poems of Walt Whitman, Representative of Equality in the Literary World"), *Tetsugaku Zasshi* 10 (October 5, 1892): 93–109.

2. Rintaro Takayama, *Taiyô* (1898).

3. Yone Noguchi, *Japan and America* (New York: Orientalia, 1921).

4. Yoshinori Yoshitake, ed., *Whitman Juyô no Hyakunen* (Tokyo: Kyôiku Shuppan Center, 1979); Takashi Sugiki, *Whitman* (Tokyo: Kenkyûsha, 1937); Walt Whitman, *Kusa no Ha*, 3 vols., trans. Norihiro Nabeshima, Masayuki Sakamoto, and Takashi Sugiki (Tokyo: Iwanami Bookstore, 1976).

5. Walt Whitman, *Walt Whitman's Poems*, ed. William L. Moore (Tokyo: Kenkyûsha, 1957).

6. Shunsuke Kamei, *Kindai Bungaku ni Okeru Whitman no Unmei* (Tokyo: Kenkyûsha, 1973); Shigenobu Sadoya, *Nihon ni Okeru Whitman* (Fukuoka, Japan: Seinan Gakuin University, 1969); Norihiro Nabeshima, *Whitman no Kenkyû* (Tokyo, Kobe: Shinozaki Shorin, 1959); Yoshitake, *Whitman*.

7. Saburo Ota, "Walt Whitman and Japanese Literature," in Horst Frenz, ed., *Asia and the Humanities* (Bloomington: Comparative Literature Committee, Indiana University, 1959), 62–69.

Selected Bibliographies

The bibliographies that follow list the most significant translations of Whitman's work and the most important critical statements about Whitman from various cultures. We have emphasized the earliest work on Whitman as well as the most revealing recent criticism, and we have indicated those texts that contain useful bibliographies of responses to Whitman in various cultures. We have included lengthy bibliographies for China (compiled by Guiyou Huang) and Italy (compiled by Roger Asselineau), since such resources have not previously been available in English. We have added brief bibliographies for some countries not covered in the main text of *Walt Whitman and the World*, and we have not included bibliographies for English-speaking countries, since work in English has traditionally been quickly and fully incorporated into standard Whitman bibliographies.

The bibliographies are arranged by regions and language groups, following the order of the sections in *Walt Whitman and the World*: (1) Spanish and Portuguese (including Spanish-American and Brazilian); (2) Western European (German, Dutch, French, Italian); (3) Eastern European (Serbo-Croatian, Slovenian, Macedonian, Czech, Slovakian, Hungarian, Romanian, Albanian, Greek, Polish, Russian, Latvian, Ukrainian); (4) Scandinavian (Swedish, Danish, Norwegian, Finnish, Estonian, Icelandic); (5) Asian (Israeli, Indian, Kazakh, Kirghiz, Chinese, Japanese).

GENERAL TEXTS

Allen, Gay Wilson. *The New Walt Whitman Handbook*. New York: New York University Press, 1975; rev. 1986. [Chapter 5, "Walt Whitman and World Literature," 249–327, and "Selected Bibliography," 401–410.]

———, ed. *Walt Whitman Abroad*. Syracuse: Syracuse University Press, 1955.

Asselineau, Roger, and William White, eds. *Walt Whitman in Europe Today*. Detroit: Wayne State University Press, 1972.

Sill, Geoffrey, ed. *Walt Whitman of Mickle Street*. Knoxville: University of Tennessee Press, 1994. [Reprints essays from a 1988 special issue of *Mickle Street Review*, focusing on Whitman's international reputation.]

SPANISH AND SPANISH-AMERICAN

Translations

Montoliu, Cebría. *Walt Whitman: Fulles d'Herba* (*Leaves of Grass*). Barcelona: Libreria L'Avenç, 1909. [Reprinted Barcelona: Atzar, 1985.]

Vasseur, Armando. *Walt Whitman: Poemas*. Valencia: Sempere, 1912. [Reprinted Montevideo: Claudio Garcia y Cia, 1939; Buenos Aires: Schapiro, 1944, with an introduction by the translator; Valencia: Prometeo, 1968.]

Felipe, León. *Walt Whitman: Canto a mí mismo* (*Song of Myself*). Buenos Aires: Losada, 1941. [Includes verse prologue by the translator, 9–21, and biocritical epilogue by

Guillermo de Torre, 123–135; reprinted several times, including (without de Torre's epilogue) Madrid: Akal, 1990.]

Azua, Luis. *Perspectivas Democráticas* (*Democratic Vistas*). Buenos Aires: Americalee, 1944. [Introduction by Dardo Cuneo.]

Zardoya, Concha. "Walt Whitman. Cantando a la primavera." Madrid: Adonias IV, Ed. Hispanica, 1945. [Translation of "These I Singing in Spring," with an introduction.]

————. *Walt Whitman: Obras Escogidas.* Madrid: Agular, 1946. [Includes critical introduction by the translator, 21–175, and preface by John Van Horne; reprinted several times.]

Abreu Gomez, Emilio. *La ultima vez que florecieron las lilas en el patio* (*When Lilacs Last in the Dooryard Bloom'd*). Mexico: Colección Literaria de la Revista Iberoamericana, 1946.

Mendoza, Miguel R. *Walt Whitman, Cantor de la Democracia: Ensayo biográfico y breve antologia* (*Walt Whitman, Poet of Democracy: Biographical Essay and Brief Anthology*). Mexico: Secretaría de Educación Pública, 1946.

Gasman, Gregorio. *Saludo al Mundo* (*Salut au Monde!*). Chile: Libreria Negra, 1949.

Alexander, Francisco. *Walt Whitman: Hojas de Hierba* (*Leaves of Grass*). Quito, Ecuador: Casa de la Cultura Ecuatoriana, 1953. [Complete translation of 1892 *Leaves of Grass*, with major prefaces; reprinted in Mexico with introduction by Sculley Bradley; reprinted Barcelona: Novaro, 1971; Barcelona: Tesys, 1986.]

Borges, Jorge Luis. *Walt Whitman: Hojas de Hierba.* Barcelona: Lumen, 1972. [Selections from *Leaves of Grass*, Buenos Aires: Juarez, 1969; preface by the translator and critical essay by Guillermo Nolasco Juarez; reprinted by Edicomicacion, 1988.]

Mañe Garzón, Pablo. *Walt Whitman: Poesía Completa.* 4 vols. Madrid and Barcelona: Rio Nuevo, 1976–1983. [First two volumes reprinted with slight changes, Barcelona: Ediciones 29, 1992.]

Lopez Castellon, Enrique. *Walt Whitman: Canto a mí mismo.* Madrid: Busman, 1981.

————. *Walt Whitman: El Calamo, Hijos de Adan* (*Calamus* and *Children of Adam*). Madrid: Felmar, 1981.

Armiño, Mauro. *Walt Whitman: Canto de mí mismo.* Madrid: Edar, 1984. [Introduction by the translator.]

Manzano, Alberto. *Walt Whitman: Hojas de Hierba.* 2 vols. Barcelona: Teorema, 1984.

Barta, Agusti. *Walt Whitman: Canto de mi mateix.* Barcelona: Eumo, 1985. [In Catalan.]

Borges, Jorge Luis. *Walt Whitman: Hojas de Hierba.* Barcelona: Lumen, 1991. [Much richer selection than Borges's 1972 translation, with preface by Borges, 7–11.]

Wolfson, Leandro. "Walt Whitman: Cien años de vida." *Uno Mismo* (Argentina) 105 (March 1992): 4–9. [Translations of various passages from Whitman's poetry and prose.]

Criticism

Martí, José. "El Poeta Walt Whitman [1887]." In *Obras completas.* La Habana: Editorial Nacional de Cuba, 1964, 13: 129–143.

Donoso, Armando. "Walt Whitman." *Cuba Contemporánea* 7 (February 1915): 198–208.

Ferguson, John De Lancey. "Walt Whitman." In *American Literature in Spain.* New York: Columbia University Press, 1916, 170–201.

Donoso, Armando. "The Free Spirit of Walt Whitman." *Inter-America* 3 (August 1920): 340–346.

Torres-Rioseco, A. *Walt Whitman*. San José de Costa Rica: J. García Monge, 1922.

Borges, Jorge Luis. "El otro Whitman [1929]." In *Discusión*. Bueno Aires: M. Gleizer, 1932, 65–70.

Unamuno, Miguel de. "El canto adáncio." *El espejo de la muerte*. Madrid: Companía Iberoamericana de Publicaciones, 1930.

Englekirk, John E. "Notes on Whitman in Spanish America." *Hispanic Review* 6 (1938): 133–138.

Montoliu, Cebría. *Walt Whitman, el hombre y su obra*. Buenos Aires: Editorial Poseidón, 1943.

Turnia, Pepita. *Walt Whitman: cotidiano y eterno*. Santiago: Prensas de la Universidad de Chile, 1943.

Gabriel, José. *Walt Whitman, la voz democrática de América*. Montevideo: Ed. Ceibo, 1944.

Franco, Luis. *Walt Whitman*. Buenos Aires: Américalee, 1945.

Carrillo, E. Gómez. *Whitman y otras crónicas*. Washington, D.C.: Unión Panamericana, 1950.

De Moshinski, Elena Aizén. *Walt Whitman y La America Latina*. Mexico: Universidad Nacional Autonoma de Mexico, 1950.

Borges, Jorge Luis. "Nota sobre Whitman." In *Otras inquisiciones, 1937–1952*. Buenos Aires: Sur, 1952, 81–87. [Reprinted in *Other Inquisitions, 1937–1952* (Austin: University of Texas Press, 1965).]

Alegría, Fernando. *Walt Whitman en Hispanoamerica*. Mexico: Ediciones Studium, 1954. [Contains complete bibliography.]

Jaén, Didier Tisdel. *Homage to Walt Whitman: A Collection of Poems from the Spanish*. University: University of Alabama Press, 1969. [Collects and translates Spanish poems about Whitman, as well as prose statements, including a foreword by Jorge Luis Borges, xiii–xvii.]

González de la Garza, Mauricio. *Walt Whitman: Racista, Imperialista, Antimexicano*. Mexico: Colección Málaga, 1971.

Zardoya, Concha. "Walt Whitman in Spain." In Roger Asselineau and William White, eds., *Walt Whitman in Europe Today*. Detroit: Wayne State University Press, 1972, 9–12.

Bosch, Javier Yagües. "Aquí ye allí de las barbas de Whitman: un dibujo de García Lorca." *FGL* [*Boletin de las Fundacion Federico García Lorca*] 9 (June 1991): 77–117.

Martin, Eutimio. "Federico García Lorca et Walt Whitman." *Poésie 91* 40 (December 1991): 47–52.

Redondo, Ana, and Javies Azpeitia. "Versiones de Whitman." *Quimera* (Barcelona) 110 (Winter 1992): 34–39. [Compares Whitman translations by Francisco Alexánder, Jorge Luis Borges and José María Valverde, Concha Zardoya, Léon Felipe, Mauro Armiño, and A. Redondo–J. Azpeitia.]

Villar Raso, Manuel, Miguel Martínez López, and Rosa Morillas Sánchez, eds. *Walt Whitman Centennial International Symposium*. Granada: Instituto de Ciencias de la Educacion, Universidad de Granada, 1992.

Wolfson, Leandro. "Tres Veces Walt Whitman." *Indiomania* (Buenos Aires) 1 (August 1992): 18–23. [Compares Whitman translations by Armando Vasseur, Léon Felipe, Jorge Luis Borges, and Wolfson.]

Coleman, Alexander. "The Ghost of Whitman in Neruda and Borges." In Geoffrey M. Sill, ed., *Walt Whitman of Mickle Street*. Knoxville: University of Tennessee Press, 1994, 257–269.

BRAZILIAN

Translations

Ferreira, Mário D. *Saudação ao Mundo e outros poemas* (*Salut au Monde! and Other Poems*). São Paulo: Flama, 1944.

Marques, Oswaldino. *Cantos de Walt Whitman*. Rio de Janeiro: Editora José Olímpio, 1946. [Introduction by Anibal Machado.]

———. *Videntes e Sonâmbulos: Coletânea de Poemas Norte-Americanos*. Rio de Janeiro: Ministério de Educação e Cultura, 1955. [Translations of Whitman's poems, 36–79.]

Campos, Geir. *Folhas de Relva* (*Leaves of Grass*). Rio de Janeiro: Civilização Brasileira, 1964. [Selections.]

———. *Folhas das Folhas de Relva* (*Leaves from Leaves of Grass*). São Paulo: Brasiliense, 1983. [Expanded translation of all or parts of eighty poems, with introduction by Paulo Leminski; reisssued 1984, 1989, 1990.]

Criticism

Nunes Mendonça, José Antonio. *Whitman, poeta universal da América*. Academia Sergipana de Letras, 1946.

Freire, Gilberto. *O Camarada Whitman*. Rio de Janeiro: Editoria José Olympio, 1948.

Bonetti Paro, Maria Clara, *A Recepçao Literaria de Walt Whitman no Brasil: Primeiro Tempo Modernista (1917–1929)*. Master's diss., Universidade de São Paulo, 1979. [Contains annotated bibliography of Whitman references in Brazil, 1917–1929.]

Lobo, Luiza, "Walt Whitman e Sousandrade." *Letterature d'America* 3 (Autumn 1982): 101–115. [This special issue was reprinted as *Il Continente Whitman* (Rome: Bulzoni, 1986).]

Monteiro, Irineu. *Walt Whitman: Profeta da América*. São Paulo: Martin Claret, 1984.

Bonetti Paro, Maria Clara. "Mário de Andrade e Walt Whitman." In *Anais do 1 Congresso Associaçao Brasileira de Literatura Comparada*, 2: 163–171. Universidade Federal do Rio Grande do Sul, 1988.

———. "Ronald de Carvalho e Walt Whitman." *Revista de Letras* 32 (1992): 142–151.

———. "Walt Whitman in Brazil." *Walt Whitman Quarterly Review* 11 (Fall 1993): 57–66.

———. *Leituras Brasileiras da Obra de Walt Whitman*. Ph.D. diss., Universidade de São Paulo, 1995.

PORTUGUESE

Translations

Cardim, Luis. *Canção de Estrada Larga* (*Song of the Open Road*). Lisbon: Cadernos de "Seara Nova," 1947.

Baptista, José Agostino. *Cálamo* (*Calamus*). Lisbon: Assirio e Alvim, 1984.

Criticism

de Campos, Alvaro (heteronym of Fernando Pessoa). *Poesias*. Lisbon: Atica. [Volume 2 of Pessoa's *Obras Completas*, containing "Saudação a Walt Whitman," 202–212; composed in 1915.]

Hess, Ranier. "Fernando Pessoa e Walt Whitman." *Aufsätze zur Portugieschen Kulturgeschichte* 4 (1966): 181–211.

Ferreira, Luís Eugenio. *Walt Whitman: Vida e Pensamento*. Alfragida (Damaia): Galeria Panorama, 1970. [Contains translations from *Leaves of Grass*, 185–206, and a translation of "A Backward Glance O'er Travel'd Roads," 207–243.]

Lourenço, Eduardo. "Walt Whitman e Pessoa." *Quaderni Portoghesi* 1 (Autumn 1977): 155–184. [Translated into Italian by Silvano Peloso.]

Scheid, Ludwig. "A Componente Whitmaniana nas Odas de Alvaro de Campos." *Biblos* 50 (1978).

Lourenço, Eduardo. "Walt Whitman e Pessoa." *Letterature d'America* 3 (Autumn 1982): 171–176. [This special issue was reprinted as *Il Continente Whitman* (Rome: Bulzoni, 1986).]

Larsen, Neil, and Ronald W. Sousa. "From Whitman (to Marinetti) to Alvaro de Campos: A Case Study in Materialist Approaches to Literary Influence." *Ideologies and Literature: A Journal of Hispano-Luzo-Brazilian Studies* 4 (September/October 1983): 94–115.

Brown, Susan Margaret. "Whitmanian Fermentation and the 1914 Vintage Season." In *Actas de II Congresso Internacional de Estudios Pessoanos*. Porto: Centre de Estudios Pessanos, 1985, 99–109.

————. "The Poetics of Pessoa's 'Drama em Gente': The Function of Alberto Caeiro and the Role of Walt Whitman." Ph.D. diss., University of North Carolina, 1987.

Santos, Maria Irene Ramalho de Sousa. "Poetas do Atlantico: As Descobertas como metafora e Ideologia em Whitman, Crane e Pessoa." *Revista Critica de Ciencias Socials* 30 (June 1990): 113–134.

————. "A ilha incontinente: o atlantismo de Whitman e Pessoa." In *Cem Anos de Pessoa*. Lisbon: Fundação Gulbenkian, 1991.

Brown, Susan Margaret. "The Whitman/Pessoa Connection." *Walt Whitman Quarterly Review* 9 (Summer 1991): 1–14.

————. "Pessoa and Whitman: Brothers in the Universe." In Robert K. Martin, ed., *The Continuing Presence of Walt Whitman: The Life after the Life*. Iowa City: University of Iowa Press, 1992, 167–181.

GERMAN

Translations

Freiligrath, Ferdinand. "Walt Whitman: Gedichte" ("Walt Whitman: Poems"). *Augsburger Allgemeine Zeitung* 24 (1868): 369–371; 25 (1868): 385 ff. [Translations of ten poems.]

Knortz, Karl, and T. W. Rolleston. *Grashalme: Gedichte* (*Leaves of Grass: Poems*). Zürich: Verlags-Magazin, 1889. [Translations of twenty-seven poems.]

Knortz, Karl. *Walt Whitman, der Dichter der Demokratie* (*Walt Whitman, the Poet of Democracy*). Leipzig: Fleischer, 1899. [Contains translations of fifteen poems and thirteen letters.]

Federn, Karl. *Grashalme: Eine Auswahl* (*Leaves of Grass: A Selection*). Minden I.W.: Bruns, 1904. [Translation of all or parts of eighty-three poems.]

Schölermann, Wilhelm. *Grashalme*. Leipzig: Diederichs, 1904. [Translations of all or parts of fifty-one poems.]

Bertz, Eduard. "Walt Whitman: Ein Charakterbild" ("Walt Whitman: A Character-Sketch"). *Jahrbuch für sexuelle Zwischenstufen* 7 (1905): 153–287. [Contains Bertz's translations of all or parts of thirty poems.]

Lessing, O. E. *Prosaschriften (Prose Writings)*. München and Leipzig: Piper, 1905.

Schlaf, Johannes. *Grashalme*. Leipzig: Reclam, 1907. [Translations of eighty-three poems; selections reprinted 1948, 1949; whole book reprinted Stuttgart: Reclam, 1968.]

Blei, Franz. *Hymnen für die Erde (Hymns for the Earth)*. Leipzig: Insel, 1914. [Translations of all or parts of eleven poems; reprinted 1946, 1947, 1958.]

Hayek, Max. *Ich singe das Leben (I Sing Life)*. Wien: E. P. Tal, 1919. [Translations of twenty-nine poems; introductory essay by Herman Bahr.]

Schickele, René, ed. *Der Wundarzt: Briefe, Aufzeichnungen und Gedichte aus dem amerikanischen Sezessionskrieg (The Surgeon: Letters, Notes, and Poems from the American Civil War)*. Zürich: Rascher, 1919. [Prose translated by Ivan Goll; five poems translated by Gustav Landauer.]

Reisiger, Hans. *Grashalme: Neue Auswahl (Leaves of Grass: New Selection)*. Berlin: S. Fischer, 1919. [Translations of all or parts of forty-six poems.]

Hayek, Max. *Gesang von mir selbst (Song of Myself)*. Leipzig and Wien: Wiener Graphische Werkstätte, 1920. [Translation of "Song of Myself"; reprinted Wien: Steyrermühl, 1926.]

Unus, Walter, ed. *Grashalme*. Berlin: Reiss, 1920. [Thirty-eight poems translated by Johannes Schlaf, Wilhelm Schölermann, and Walter Unus; lithographs by Willi Jaeckel.]

Reisiger, Hans. *Gesang von der offenen Landstrasse (Song of the Open Road)*. Lauenberg/Elbe: A. Saal, 1921. [Translation of "Song of the Open Road."]

Landauer, Gustav. *Gesänge und Inshriften (Songs and Inscriptions)*. München: Wolff, 1921. [Translations of all or parts of twenty-eight poems.]

Reisiger, Hans. *Walt Whitmans Werk (Walt Whitman's Work)*. Berlin: S. Fischer, 1922. 2 vols. [Translations of 100 poems and selected prose; reprinted, with additions, as *Walt Whitmans Werk* (Reinbek b. Hamburg: Rowohlt, 1956), as *Grashalme* (Berlin: Aufbau, 1957), as *Grashalme* (Leipzig: Reclam, 1960; without prose), as *Walt Whitmans Werk* (München and Zürich: Droemersche Veri.-Anstalt Knaur, 1960), as *Grashalme. Eine Auswahl. Englisch und deutsch* (Leipzig: Insel, 1968), as *Grashalme* (Reinbek b. Hamburg: Rowohlt, 1968); as *Grashalme* (Zürich: Diogenes, 1985).]

———. *Gesang von mir selbst (Song of Myself)*. Berlin: Suhrkamp, 1946.

———. *Salut au Monde (Salut au Monde!)*. Berlin: Suhrkamp, 1946.

———. *Tagebuch. 1862–1864. 1876–1882 (Specimen Days)*. Berlin: Suhrkamp, 1946.

Serelmann-Küchler, Elisabeth, and Walther Küchler. *Grashalme*. Erlangen: Dipax, 1947. [Translations of 129 poems.]

Reisiger, Hans. *Demokratische Ausblicke (Democratic Vistas)*. Berlin: Suhrkamp, 1948.

Goyert, Georg. *Grashalme*. Berlin: Blanvalet, 1948. [Translations of thirty-one poems.]

Reisiger, Hans. *Auf der Brooklyn Fähre (Crossing Brooklyn Ferry)*. Berlin: Suhrkamp, 1949.

Petersen, Hans, ed. *Lyrik und Prosa*. Berlin: Volk und Welt, 1966. [One hundred and two poems translated by Erich Arendt, prose selections by Helmut Heinrich; reprinted without the prose as *Grashalme* (Leipzig: Reclam, 1970).]

Bestian, Else, and Hans Bestian. *Walt Whitman. Ein Kosmos*. Schwifting: Schwiftinger Galerie-Verlag, 1985. [Selections from various poems in English and German.]

Burghardt, Götz. *Tagebuch*. Leipzig: Reclam, 1985. [*Specimen Days*, edited by Eva Manske.]

Schaup, Susanne. *Ich rufe Erde und Meer* (*I Call Earth and Sea*). Freiburg: Herder, 1987. [Translations of twenty poems and selected prose.]

Criticism

Freiligrath, Ferdinand. "Walt Whitman." *Augsburger Allgemeine Zeitung*, Wochenausgabe 17 (April 24, 1868): 325–329.

Schlaf, Johannes. "Walt Whitman." *Freie Bühne für den Entwickelungskampf der Zeit* 3 (1892): 977–988.

Ziel, Ernst. "Walt Whitman." In *Litterarische Reliefs: Dichterportraits, Erste Reihe*. Leipzig: Wartig, 1895, 213–226.

Federn, Karl. "Walt Whitman." In *Essays zur Amerikanischen Litteratur*. Halle: Hendel, 1899, 124–140.

Bertz, Eduard. "Walt Whitman: Ein Charakterbild." *Jahrbuch für sexuelle Zwischenstufen* 7 (1905): 153–287.

Riethmüller, Richard. "Walt Whitman and the Germans." *German-American Annals* 4 (1906): 3–15, 35–49, 78–92.

Lessing, O. E. "Whitman and German Critics." *Journal of English and Germanic Philology* 9 (1910): 85–98.

Knortz, Karl. *Walt Whitman und seine Nachahmer*. Leipzig: Heichen, 1911.

Thorstenberg, Edward. "The Walt Whitman Cult in Germany." *Sewanee Review* 19 (1911): 71–86.

Bahr, Hermann. "Walt Whitman." *Die neue Rundschau* 30 (1919): 555–564.

Mann, Thomas. "Hans Reisigers Whitman-Werk. Ein Brief." *Frankfurter Zeitung* (April 16, 1922): 1.

Jacobson, Anna. "Walt Whitman in Germany Since 1914." *Germanic Review* 1 (April 1926): 132–141.

Falk, Robert P. "Walt Whitman and German Thought." *Journal of English and Germanic Philology* 40 (July 1941): 315–330.

Reisiger, Hans. *Walt Whitman*. Berlin: Suhrkamp, 1946.

Grünzweig, Walter. *Walt Whitmann: Die deutschsprachige Rezeption als interkulturelles Phänomen*. München: Wilhelm Fink, 1991. [Contains complete bibliography of Whitman translations and criticism, 259–277.]

———. "'Inundated by This Mississippi of Poetry': Walt Whitman and German Expressionism." In Geoffrey M. Sill, ed., *Walt Whitman of Mickle Street*. Knoxville: University of Tennessee Press, 1994, 244–256.

———. "'Teach Me Your Rhythm': The Poetics of German Lyrical Responses to Whitman." In Ed Folsom, ed., *Walt Whitman: The Centennial Essays*. Iowa City: University of Iowa Press, 1994, 226–239.

———. *Constructing the German Walt Whitman*. Iowa City: University of Iowa Press, 1995.

DUTCH

Translation

Wagenvoort, Maurits. *Grashalmen* (*Leaves of Grass*). Amsterdam: Wereld-Biblioteek, 1956.

FRENCH

Translations

Laforgue, Jules. *"Les Brins d'herbe*: traduit de l'étonnant poète américain Walt
   Whitman — *Dédicaces*," *La Vogue* 1 (June–July 1886): 325–328 [translations of eight
   poems]; "O Etoile de France" ("O Star of France"), *La Vogue* 1 (July 1886): 388–390;
   "Une Femme m'attend" ("A Woman Waits for Me"), *La Vogue* 2 (August 1886): 73–76.
Davray, Henry. "Walt Whitman: *Specimen Days.*" *L'Ermitage* (December 1902): 401–419;
   (January 1903): 60–72; (February 1903): 112–133; (March 1903): 201–221. [Also includes
   translations of six poems.]
Vielé-Griffin, Francis. *Thrène pour le président Lincoln.* Paris, 1908.
Bazalgette, Léon. *Walt Whitman: Feuilles d'herbe (Leaves of Grass).* Paris: Mercure de
   France, 1909. [Reprinted 1922, 1955. Bazalgette also published other collections of
   Whitman translations, including *Poèmes de Walt Whitman* (Paris, 1914), *Walt
   Whitman: Le Panseur de plaies, poèmes, lettres et fragments sur la guerre* (with
   A. M. Gossez) (Paris, 1917), and *Walt Whitman: Calamus* (Paris, 1919).]
Gide, André, Jean Schlumberger, Jules Laforgue, Louis Fabulet, Francis Vielé-Griffin, and
   Valery Larbaud. *Walt Whitman: Oeuvres choisies Poèmes and Proses.* Paris: Gallimard,
   1918. [Introduction by Valery Larbaud; reprinted 1930, 1960, and as *Walt Whitman:
   Poèmes* in 1992.]
Jamati, Paul. *Walt Whitman: Une étude, un choix de poèmes.* Paris: Seghers, 1948. [Based
   on Bazalgette's translation.]
Messiaen, Pierre. *Walt Whitman: Choix de Poèmes.* Paris: Aubier, 1951.
Asselineau, Roger. *Feuilles d'herbe.* Paris: Belles Lettres, 1956. [Selections with an
   introduction by the translator.]
Delvaille, Bernard. *Feuilles d'herbe.* Paris: Seghers, 1964. [Selections.]
Dion-Levesque, Rosaire. *Walt Whitman, ses meilleurs pages traduites de l'anglais.* Québec:
   Presses de l'Université de Laval, 1965.
Asselineau, Roger. *Chants de la terre qui tourne, poèmes et proses de Walt Whitman.* Paris:
   Nouveau Horizons, 1966.
———. *Leaves of Grass/Feuilles d'herbe.* Paris: Aubier-Flammarion, 1972. [Selections;
   bilingual edition; reprinted in larger format, 1989.]
Darras, Jacques. *Feuilles d'herbe.* Paris: Grasset, 1989. [Selections, with preface by the
   translator.]
Deleuze, Julien. *Comme des baies de genévrier: Feuilles de carnets.* Paris: Mercure de
   France, 1993. [Translation of part of *Specimen Days*, with an introduction by Philippe
   Jaworski.]
Darras, Jacques. *Feuilles d'herbe II.* Paris: Grasset, 1994. [Further selections, with an
   introduction by the translator.]

Criticism

Etienne, Louis. "Walt Whitman, poète, philosophe et 'rowdy.'" *La Revue Européene*
   (November 1, 1861): 104–117.
Bentzon, Thérèse [Madame Blanc, pseud.]. "Un poète américain, Walt Whitman: 'Muscle
   and Pluck Forever.'" *Revue de Deux Mondes* 42 (June 1, 1872): 565–582.

Blémont, Emile. "La poésie en Angleterre et aux Etats-Unis, III, Walt Whitman."
    Renaissance littéraire et artistique 7 (June 8, 1872): 54–56; 11 (July 6, 1872): 86–87; 12
    (July 13, 1872): 90–91.

Sarrazin, Gabriel. "Poètes modernes de l'Amérique, Walt Whitman." *La Nouvelle Revue* 52
    (May 1, 1888): 164–184. [Reprinted in *La Renaissance de la Poésie Anglaise 1798–1889*
    (Paris: Perrin, 1889), 235–279.]

Desjardins, Paul. "Walt Whitman." *Journal des Dèbats* (April 4, 1892).

Masson, Elsie. "Walt Whitman, ouvrier et poète." *Mercure de France* 68 (August 1907):
    385–404.

Bazalgette, Léon. *Walt Whitman: L'Homme et son oeuvre.* Paris, 1908.

Delattre, Floris. "Un poète de la démocratie." *Revue Pédagogique* 56 (May 15, 1910):
    402–420.

Lebesgue, Philéas. "Walt Whitman et la Poésie Contemporaine." In *Essai d'Expansion
    d'une Esthétique.* Le Havre, Lyon, Bordeaux: Editions de la Province, 1911, 5–26.

Arcos, René. "A propos de quelques poètes modernes." *Mercure de France* 105 (October
    1913): 697–713.

Jones, P. Mansell. "Influence of Walt Whitman on the 'vers libre.'" *Modern Language
    Review* 11 (April 1916): 186–194.

Cé, Camille. "Le poète-prophète Walt Whitman." *Grande Revue* 101 (February 1920):
    573–599.

Cestre, Charles. "Whitman poète de la nature." *La Vie des Peuples* (June 20, 1920):
    291–308.

Bazalgette, Léon. *Le Poème-Evangile de Walt Whitman.* Paris: Mercure de France, 1921.

De Tonquedec, Joseph. "Walt Whitman: Un poète de la nature aux Etats-Unis." *Etudes* 164
    (January 20, 1921): 190–207.

Jaloux, Edmond. *Figures Etrangères.* Paris: Plon-Nourrit [1925]. [Comments on Whitman,
    138–161.]

Catel, Jean. *Walt Whitman: La naissance du poète.* Paris: Editions Rieder, 1929. [Reprinted
    Saint-Clare Shores, Mich.: Scholarly Press, 1974.]

———. *Rythme et langage dans la première édition des "Leaves of Grass," 1855.* Paris:
    Editions Rieder, 1930.

De Maratray, R. *Whitmaniana, réflexions d'un adepte de la morale ouverte.* Paris, 1935.

Bidal, M. L. "Le Groupe de L'Abbaye." *Mercure de France* 283 (April 15, 1938): 333–351.

Rhodes, S. A. "The Influence of Walt Whitman on André Gide." *Romanic Review* 31 (April
    1940): 156–171.

Jones, P. Mansell. "Whitman and the Symbolists." In *The Background of Modern French
    Poetry.* Cambridge: Cambridge University Press, 1951, 69–88.

De Graaf, Daniel A. "Arthur Rimbaud et Walt Whitman." *Levende Talen* (November
    1953): 363–372.

Kanes, Martin. *La Fortune de Walt Whitman en France.* Ph.D. diss., University of Paris,
    Department of Comparative Literature, 1953.

Ramsey, Warren. *Jules Laforgue and the Ironic Inheritance.* New York: Oxford University
    Press, 1953.

Asselineau, Roger. *L'Evolution de Walt Whitman.* Paris: Didier, 1954.

Roddier, Henri. "Pierre Leroux, George Sand et Walt Whitman." *Revue de Littérature
    Comparée* 31 (January–March 1957): 5–33.

Bosquet, Alain. *Whitman*. Paris: Gallimard, 1959.

Kanes, Martin. "Whitman, Gide, and Bazalgette: An International Encounter." *Comparative Literature* 14 (Fall 1962): 341–355.

Brunel, Pierre. "A la recherche d'une influence: l'image de l'orchestre et la tentation symphonique chez Walt Whitman et Paul Claudel." *Revue des Lettres Modernes* 134–136 (1966): 49–63.

Asselineau, Roger. "On Translating Whitman into French." In Roger Asselineau and William White, eds., *Walt Whitman in Europe Today*. Detroit: Wayne State University Press, 1972, 37–40.

———. "Whitman in France in 1976." In *The Bicentennial Whitman*. Detroit: Wayne State University Press, 1976, 13–14.

Ollier, Jacqueline. "Whitman, Williams, Ginsberg: Histoire d'une filliation." *Revue Française d'Etudes Américaine* 5 (April 1978): 93–108.

Petillon, Pierre-Yves. "Le cri sur les toits du monde." In *La Grande Route: Espace et écriture en Amérique*. Paris: Seuil, 1979, 15–35.

Asselineau, Roger. *The Transcendentalist Constant in American Literature*. New York: New York University Press, 1980.

Erkkila, Betsy. *Walt Whitman among the French*. Princeton: Princeton University Press, 1980. [Contains a comprehensive chronological listing of French criticism of Whitman, 239–250, and a list of French translations of Whitman, 251–255.]

Bacigalupo, Massimo. "'Life Is an Ecstasy': A Transcendentalist Theme in Whitman, Pound and Other American Poets." *Revue du Centre de Recherche Interspace* 3 (1987): 107–120.

Fillard, Claudette. *Walt Whitman, poète des éléments*. Paris, 1987.

Pucciani, Oreste F. *The Literary Reputation of Walt Whitman in France*. New York & London: Garland, 1987. [Doctoral dissertation defended in 1943.]

Fillard, Claudette. "Quand l'herbe a des feuilles." *Etudes Anglaises* 43 (January–March 1990): 14–28.

Poésie 91, 40 (December 1991). [Special issue on Whitman, with Gilles Farcet, "Transcendentalisment vôtre," 27–34; Alain Suberchicot, "L'Homoérotisme de Walt Whitman," 36–39; and Roger Asselineau, "L'acclimatation des Feuilles de Walt Whitman," 41–46.]

Duperray, Annick. "Emancipation et parole poétique dans l'oeuvre de Walt Whitman." In *Voix et Langages aux Etats-Unis*. Aix-en-Provence: Publications de l'Université de Provence, 1992, 43–52.

Deleuze, Gilles. "Whitman." In *Critique et Clinique*. Paris: Editions de Minuit, 1993, 75–80.

Asselineau, Roger. "The Acclimatization of 'Leaves of Grass' in France." In Marina Camboni, ed., *Utopia in the Present Tense*. Rome: Il Calamo, 1994, 237–265.

———. "Quelques interprétations et lectures de *Leaves of Grass*." *Etudes Anglaises* 45 (July–September 1994): 268–274.

———. "When Whitman Was a Parisian." In Geoffrey M. Sill, ed., *Walt Whitman of Mickle Street*. Knoxville: University of Tennessee Press, 1994, 270–275.

Belgodere, Janine. "Le motif de la danse dans *Leaves of Grass*." *Etudes Anglaises* 45 (July–September 1994): 299–310.

Fillard, Claudette. "Le vannier de Camden: viellesse, poésie et les annexes de *Leaves of Grass*." *Etudes Anglaises* 45 (July–September 1994): 311–323.

Translations

Gamberale, Luigi. *Canti scelti di Walt Whitman* (*Selected Chants of Walt Whitman*). Vol. 1. Milano: Sonzogno, Biblioteca Universale, 1887. [With a preface by the translator; reprinted 1913.]

——. *Canti scelti di Walt Whitman.* Vol. 2. Milano: Sonzogno, Bibliteca Universale, 1890. [With a new preface by the translator and, in addition to the poems, a translation of the 1855 and 1872 prefaces and extracts from *Specimen Days*; reprinted 1895.]

Morandi, L., and D. Campigli, eds. "Scelta di Walt Whitman." In *Poeti stranieri.* Vol. 2. Lapi: Città di Castello, 1904, 237–241. [Five poems from "Drum-Taps" translated by F. Contaldi and E. Nencioni.]

Gamberale, Luigi. *Walt Whitman: Foglie di erba* (*Walt Whitman: Leaves of Grass*). Milano; Palermo; Napoli: Sandron, 1907. [With the additions and "Old Age Echoes" from the 1900 edition; reprinted Milano: Sandron, 1923, in two volumes under the editorship of E. P. Pavolini and later in Roma (Bernardo Lux Libraio di Sua Maestà la Regina Madre, n.d.) in three volumes.]

V. V. S. *Poesie scelte.* Milano: Signorelli, 1932.

Giachino, Enzo. *Walt Whitman: Foglie d'erba e prose.* Torino: Einaudi, 1950. [With a preface by the translator; reprinted 1965 without the prose.]

Sanesi, Roberto. *Whitman: Poesie.* Milano: Nuova Accademia, 1962.

Poli, Franco De. *Walt Whitman: Foglie d'erba.* Parma: Guanda, 1967. [With an introduction by the translator.]

Meliadò Freeth, Mariolina. *Giorni rappresentativi ed altre prose* (*Specimen Days and Other Prose*). Venezia: Neri Pozza, 1968. [With an introduction and a bibliography by the translator.]

Giachino, Enzo. *Walt Whitman: Foglie d'erba.* Milano: Mondadori, 1971. [A bilingual edition of selections from *Leaves of Grass* with a historical introduction, bibliography, preface, and extracts from critics, edited by Anna Luisa Zazo; reprinted 1972, 1981, 1985.]

——. *Foglie d'erba.* Torino: Einaudi, 1973. [Greatly expanded translation, including 1855 Preface; reprinted 1990.]

Sanesi, Roberto. *Foglie d'erba.* Verona: Giannotta, 1979. [Reprinted 1985; new edition, Verona: Edizioni del Paniere, 1991, with introduction by Sebastiano Saglimbeni.]

Tornaghi, Marina. *Calamus: Poesie d'amore per un uomo* (*Calamus: Poetry of Love for a Man*). Milano: Savelli, 1982.

Mussapi, Roberto. *Dalla culla che oscilla eternamente* (*Out of the Cradle Endlessly Rocking*). Milano: Polena, 1985.

Tedeschini-Lalli, Biancamaria, ed. *Walt Whitman: Foglie d'erba.* Milano: Rizzoli, 1988. [Bilingual edition of selections from *Leaves of Grass* translated by Ariodante Marianni, with a preface by Giorgio Manganelli and an introduction and an anthology of poems on Whitman by the editor; reprinted 1990.]

Troiano, Antonio. *O capitano, mio capitano* (*O Captain! My Captain!*). Milano: Crocetti, 1990.

Conte, Giuseppe. *Foglie d'erba.* Milano: Mondadori, 1991. [Selections, with a critical introduction.]

Troiano, Antonio. *Canti d'addio* (*Songs of Parting*). Milano: Crocetti, 1992.

Corona, Mario. Translation of the 1855 edition of *Leaves of Grass*. Milano: Granzanti [in preparation].

Criticism

Nencioni, Enrico. "Walt Whitman," *Fanfulla della Domenica* 1 (December 7, 1879): 1; "Nuovi Orizzonti Poetici," *Fanfulla della Domenica* 3 (August 21, 1881): 1–2; "Il Poeta della Democrazia," *Fanfulla della Domenica*, 5 (November 18, 1883): 1–2; "Mazzini e Whitman," *Fanfulla della Domenica* 6 (April 20, 1884): 1–2.

Carducci, Giosué. "Lettera a Nencioni" (Dec. 7, 1879); "Lettera a Nencioni" (August 25, 1881). *Lettera* 12 (Bologna: Zanichelliana).

D'Annunzio, Gabriele. "Lettere ad Enrico Nencioni, 1880–1896." *Nuova Antologia* (May 1, 1939).

Gamberale, Luigi. "Per l'ezattezza: ad Enrico Nencioni," *Il Momento* 2 (April 15, 1884): 4–6; "Walt Whitman: Indole della sua poesia," *Il Momento* 2 (May 1, 1884): 6–8; "Walt Whitman: Ideali democratici," *Il Momento* 2 (May 16, 1884): 1–3; "Walt Whitman: Il Canto dell'Esposizione," *Il Momento* 2 (June 16, 1884): 7–9.

Nencioni, Enrico. "I Poeti Americani," *Nuova Antologia* (August 16, 1885) [reprinted in *Saggi Critici di Letteratura Inglese*, with preface by Giosuè Carducci (Firenze: Le Monnier, 1897), 110–123]; review of *Antologia della opere poetiche di Walt Whitman*, E. Rhys, ed., in *Nuova Antologia* (December 16, 1888); "Il Poeta della Guerra Americana," *Nuova Antologia* (December 1, 1891) [reprinted in *Saggi Critici di Letteratura Inglese*, 204–230].

Brugi, Biagio. "Una Poesia di Walt Whitman." *Atti e Memorie della Accademia di Scienze e Arti in Padova* 9 (1894): 149–154.

Chimenti, F. "Walt Whitman." In *Note di Letteratura Americana*. Bari: Pansini, 1894, 21–36.

Jannacone, Pasquale. *La Poesia di Walt Whitman e l'Evoluzione delle Forme Ritmiche.* Torino: Roux-Frassati, 1898. [Translated by Peter Mitilineos as *Walt Whitman's Poetry and the Evolution of Rhythmic Forms*, with an introduction by Gay W. Allen. Washington, D.C.: Microcard Editions, 1973.]

Pisa, Giuliano. "Gualterio Whitman." In *Studi Letterari*. Milano: Baldini-Castoldi, 1899, 113–176.

Ragusa Moleti, Girolamo. "I Fili d'erba di Walt Whitman," *Flegréa* (October 5, 1899): 431–453; "I Canti di Walt Whitman," *Psiche* 15 (October 16, 1899): 1–3, and (November 1, 1899), 1–3; "Le 'Foglie d'erba' di Walt Whitman," *L'Ora* (September 1901): 13–14; "Le Poesia di Walt Whitman," *L'Ora* (February 1902): 9–10; "Al 'ma' di un lettore," *L'Ora* (February 1902): 16–17; "Walt Whitman," *L'Ora* (November 1902): 16–17.

Nemi, "Walt Whitman." *Nuova Antologica* series 4 (November 1, 1902) and series 5 (January 16, 1906); "Le Foglie d'erba," series 5 (December 16, 1907); "Una Biografia di Whitman" (November 1, 1908).

Gamberale, Luigi. "La Vita e le Opere di Walt Whitman." *Rivista d'Italia* 6 (February 1903): 181–207.

Rabizzani, Giovanni. "Il Mondo Poetico di Walt Whitman." *Nuova Rassegna di Letterature Moderne* 6 (1908): 113–120. [Reprinted in *Pagine di Critica Letteraria* (Pistoia: Pagnini, 1911), 111–122.]

Papini, Giovanni. "Walt Whitman." *Nuova Antologia* series 5 (June 16, 1908), 696–711. [Reprinted in *Ventiquattro Cervelli* (Firenze: Valechi, 1942), 199–239.]

Gramsci, Antonio. Unsigned article in *Ordine Nuovo* 1 (June 14, 1919). [Reprinted in *L'Ordine Nuovo* (Torino: Einaudi, 1954), 443–445.]

Pavese, Cesare. "Interpretazione di Walt Whitman poeta." *La Cultura* (July–September 1933). [Reprinted in *La Letteratura Americana e altri saggi* (Torino: Einaudi, 1953), 141–165, under the title "Poesia del far poesia."]

Alessandrini, Garibaldo. *Walt Whitman Poeta dell'Universale*. Firenze: All'Insegna del Libro, 1940.

Tenerelli, Michele. *Walt Whitman Poeta dei tempi nuovi*. Bari: Martini, 1940.

McCain, Rea. "Walt Whitman in Italy." *Italica* 20 (1943).

Alicata, Mario. "Note au Whitman." *Rinascita* 8 (May 1951): 249–254.

Bo, Carlo. "Riflessioni critiche: Whitman." *Paragone-Serie Letteratura* 22 (October 1951): 37–52.

Cambon, Glauco. "Whitman in Italia," *Aut Aut* 39 (May 1957): 244–263; "Walt Whitman e il mito di Adamo," *Aut Aut* 40 (July 1957): 315–330; "Ancora Whitman," *Aut Aut* 42 (November, 1957): 469–485.

De Maria, Federico. "Walt Whitman, poeta di ieri e di sempre." *Città di Vita* 13 (July–August 1958): 462–474.

Guidi, Augusto. "Rousseau e Pelagio nel 'Song of Myself' di Whitman." In *Occasion Americane*. Roma: Ed. Moderne, 1958.

Cambon, Glauco. "La parola come emanazione: Note marginali sullo stile di Whitman." *Studi Americani* 5 (1959): 141–160.

Meliadò, Mariolina. "La Fortuna di Walt Whitman in Italia." *Studi Americani* 7 (1961): 43–76.

Cambon, Glauco. "Presenza di Whitman nella letteratura Americana" and "Stile di Whitman: la parola come emanazione continua." In *La Lotta con Proteo*. Milano: Bompiani, 1963, 257–303.

Mondo, Lorenzo. "Fra Gozzano e Whitman: le origini di Pavese." *Sigma* 3–4 (December 1964): 3–21.

Giachino, Enzo. "Galleria dell' 800 americano, Walt Whitman." *Mondo Occidentale* 102 (March–April 1965): 52–59.

Perosa, Sergio. "Il Linguaggio di Whitman." In *Il Simbolismo nella Letteratura Nord-Americana*. Firenze: La Nuova Italia, 1965, 259–315.

Grippi, Charles S. "The Reputation of Walt Whitman in Italy." Ph.D. diss. New York University, 1971.

Meliadò-Freeth, Mariolina. "Walt Whitman in Italy." In Roger Asselineau and William White, eds., *Walt Whitman in Europe Today*. Detroit: Wayne State University Press, 1972, 20–23.

Grippi, Charles S. "Whitman in Italy." *Long Islander*, Walt Whitman supplement (June 13, 1974): 13B–14B.

Camboni, Marina. "La Molteplicità del messaggio in 'Roots and Leaves Themselves Alone.'" *Lingua e Stile* 2 (1977): 5–20.

Ludovici, Paola. "The Craftsmanship of Timelessness: A Linguistic Investigation of 'Leaves of Grass.'" *Studi Americani* 23/24 (1977–1978): 87–110.

Orestano, Francesca. *"Song of Myself," 1855–1892, la prima e l'ultima stesura a confronto*. Palermo: Vittorietti, 1979.

Rizzardi, Alfredo. "Whitman in negativo." In *Inventario di Poesia — Walt Whitman nella poesia del Novecento*. Urbino: Quattro Venti, 1980, 5–20.

D'Amico, Vittoria. "'Come up from the fields, father': lettura di un strip whitmaniana." *Siculorum Gymnasium* 33 (July–December 1980): 955–985.

Sotis, Grazia. "A Study of the Two Complete Translations of Walt Whitman's *Leaves of Grass* into Italian." Ph.D. diss., University of Connecticut, 1981.

Letterature d'America 3 (Autumn 1982). [Special issue on Whitman; all articles were reprinted in book form as *Il Continente Whitman* (Roma: Bulzoni, 1986).]

Pivano, Fernanda. "Da Whitman a Ginsberg: La Tradizione omosessuale nella letteratura americana." In *Orgoglio e Pregiudizio*. Torino, 1983.

Tedeschini-Lalli, Biancamaria. "Il Superamento dell' alterità della morte in 'Song of Myself.'" In *Letture Anglo-Americane in memoria di Rolando Anzilotti*. Pisa: Nistri-Lischi, 1986, 79–93.

Corona, Mario. "Testo e paratesto: 'Leaves of Grass' di Walt Whitman, edizione di 1855." *Nuovi Annali della Facoltà di Magisterio di Messina* 5 (1987): 421–429.

Sotis, Grazia. *Walt Whitman in Italia: La Traduzione Gamberale e la tradizione Giachino di 'Leaves of Grass.'* Napoli: Società Ed. Napoletana, 1987.

Cartosio, Bruno. "Whitman e le masse: Economia politica e idealismo democratico." *Contesti* 1 (1988): 61–82.

Camboni, Marina. *Il Corpo dell' America: 'Leaves of Grass' 1855: Introduzione all' opera di Walt Whitman*. Quaderni dell' Istituto di Lingue e Letterature Straniere, Università di Palermo, 1990.

Ricciardi, Caterina. "Walt Whitman and the Futurist Muse." In Marina Camboni, ed., *Utopia in the Present Tense: Walt Whitman and the Language of the New World*. Roma: Il Calamo, 1994, 265–284.

Benetazzo, Viviana. "Walt Whitman in Italy: Translations of *Leaves of Grass*." In Marina Camboni, ed., *Utopia in the Present Tense: Walt Whitman and the Language of the New World*. Roma: Il Calamo, 1994, 285–300. [Includes bibliography of Italian translations and criticism, 299–300.]

SERBO-CROATIAN

Translations

Ujević, Tin. *Vlati Trave* (*Leaves of Grass*). Zagreb: Zora, 1951. [Selections, including a complete translation of "Song of Myself"; preface by Gustave Krklec.]

Susko, Mario. "Pjesma o meni" ("Song of Myself"). *Forum* (Zagreb) (1967): 206–275.

Lalić, Ivan V. *Volt Vitmen: Vlati trave, Izabrane pesme* (*Walt Whitman: Leaves of Grass, Selected Poems*). Belgrade, 1985. [Complete translations of thirty-four poems, with introduction by the translator.]

Demirović, Hamdija. *Walt Whitman: Vlati trave/Respondez!* Sarajevo: Svjetlost, 1988. [Translations of sixty-one poems and various prose extracts, with introduction by the translator and selection of critical essays on Whitman, including comments by Ivo Andrić, Antun Branko Simić, Miroslav Krleža, and Miodrag Pavlović.]

Criticism

Nizeteo, Antun. "Whitman in Croatia: Tin Ujević and Walt Whitman." *Journal of Croatian Studies* 11–12 (1970–71): 105–133. [Accompanied by selection of Whitman poems translated into Croatian by Tin Ujević, 134–151.]

Bašić, Sonja. "Walt Whitman in Yugoslavia." In Roger Asselineau and William White, eds., *Walt Whitman in Europe Today.* Detroit: Wayne State University Press, 1972, 24–26.

SLOVENIAN

Translations

Žagar, Janez. "Iz *Travnih bilk*" ("From *Leaves of Grass*"). *Modra ptica* 4 (1932–33): 213–215. [Translations of five poems.]

Podbevšek, Anton. "Iz lirike Walta Whitmana" ("From Walt Whitman's Poetry"). *Modra ptica* 10 (1938–39): 359–361. [Translations of six poems.]

Levec, Peter. *Travne bilke* (*Leaves of Grass*). Ljubljana: Mladinska, 1962. [Translations of all or parts of twenty-eight poems, with introduction by the translator.]

Mozetič, Uroš. *Walt Whitman: Lirika* (*Walt Whitman: Lyrics*). Ljubljana: Mladinska Knjiga, 1989. [Translations of all or parts of twenty-nine poems, with checklist of Slovene translations of Whitman 1925–1986.]

Criticism

Cooper, Jr., Henry R. "Influence and Affinity: Walt Whitman's *Leaves of Grass* and the Early Poetry of Oton Župančič." In *Obdobje simbolizma v slovenskem jeziku, književnosti in kulturi.* Ljubljana: Univerza Edvarda Kardelja v Ljubljani, 1983, 267–276.

MACEDONIAN

Translation

Koviloska-Poposka, Ivanka. *Volt Vitman: Poezija* (*Walt Whitman: Poetry*). Skopje, 1974. [Complete translations of thirty-one poems and excerpts from "Song of Myself"; introduction by the translator; transliterated from the Cyrillic.]

CZECH

Translations

Lesehrad, Emanuel. *Walt Whitman, Vybor z básní* (*Walt Whitman: Selected Poems*). Prague: E. Weinfurter, 1900–1901. [Revised edition, with an introduction by the translator, Prague: E. sl. z Lesehradu, 1909.]

Jung, V. A. *Vyhlídky-demokracie* (*Democratic Vistas*). Prague: Jan Laichter, 1903.

Vrchlicky, Jaroslav. *Stébla trávy* (*Leaves of Grass*). Prague: B. Koci-Beaufort, 1906–1907.

Skrachová, E. K. *Vyhlídky demokracie.* Prague: Jan Laichter, 1936. [Introduction by F. X. Salda.]

Verná, B. *Stébla trávy.* Vyskov: Obzina, 1939. [Selection.]

Eisner, Pavel. *Walt Whitman: Demokracie, zeno má! Vyber ze Stebel trávy* (*Walt Whitman: Democracy, Ma Femme! and Selected Poems*). Prague: Jaroslav Podrouzek, 1945.

SLOVAKIAN

Translations

Boor, Ján. *Walt Whitman: Pozdrav Svetu (Walt Whitman: Salut au Monde!)* Bratislava:
Tatran, 1956. [Contains selections of poetry, prose, and letters.]
Boor, Ján, and Magda Seppová. *Pozdrav Svety: Vyber z diela (Leaves of Grass: Democratic
Vistas).* Bratislava: Slovenské Vydavateľstvo, Krásnej Literatúry, 1956. [Selections from
Leaves of Grass translated by Boor; *Democratic Vistas* by Seppová.]
Boor, Ján. *Tráva a trstie (Grass and Calamus).* Bratislava: Tatran, 1974.

HUNGARIAN

Translation

László, Országh, ed. *Fuszálak, Osszes Koltemények.* Budapest: Magyar Helikon, 1964.
[Selected translations by twenty-one translators.]

ROMANIAN

Translations

Poeme, Talmaciri. Bucuresti: Pro Pace, 1945. [Commentary by Vignete de Margareta
Sterian.]
Gheorghiu, Mihnea. *Walt Whitman: Opere Alese.* Bucuresti: Editura de Stat Pentru
Literatura si Arta, 1956. [Selections.]

ALBANIAN

Translation

Luarasi, Skënder. *Uollt Uitman: Fije bari: Pjese te zgjedhura (Walt Whitman: Leaves of
Grass: Selections).* Prishtine, 1971. [Translations of all or parts of thirty-one poems;
introduction by the translator.]

GREEK

Translations

Proestopoulos, Nikos. *Ekloge apo ta Phylla Chloes (Selections from Leaves of Grass).*
[Athens:] Eklekta Biblia tis Tsepis, [1936?].
———. *Phylla Chloes (Leaves of Grass).* [Athens:] "Hestia" Bookstore Publishers, [1950?].
[Complete translation of *Leaves of Grass,* with prefatory note by Angelos Sikelianos.]
Kydoniatou, Zanet S. *Opou pneuma Kyriou kai eleutheria (Where the Spirit of the Lord Is,
There Is Liberty).* Athens, 1992. [Includes several translations of Whitman's poetry by
Rita Boumi Pappa, Nikos Proestopoulos, and Yannis Sfakainnakis, 19–30, and a
lecture on Whitman by Kydoniatou.]

POLISH

Translations

Vincenz, Stanislaw. *Walt Whitman: Trzy Poematy* (*Walt Whitman: Three Poems*). Warszawa: Ignis, 1921. [Translations of "When Lilacs Last in the Dooryard Bloom'd," "Out of the Cradle Endlessly Rocking," and "Passage to India."]

Napieralski, Stefan. *Walt Whitman: 75 Poematow* (*Walt Whitman: 75 Poems*). Warszawa: J. Mortkowicz, 1934. [Preface by S. Helsztynski.]

Anonymous. "Spiacy" ("The Sleepers"). *Kamena* 3, no. 3 (1935): 51.

Milosz, Czeslaw. "Z Piesni o Sobie Samym" (From "Song of Myself"). *Odrodzenie* 12 (March 21, 1948): 3.

Lipinska, Jadwiga. *Liscie Traw (Fragmenty)* (*Leaves of Grass (fragments)*). London: Poets' and Painters', 1966.

Zulawski, Juliusz, ed. *Zbzbla Trawy* (*Leaves of Grass*). Warszawa: Panstwowy Instytut Wydawniczy, 1966. [Selections; various translators; includes selections from Whitman's prose.]

Michalski, Hieronim, ed. *Walt Whitman: Poezje Wybrane* (*Selected Poems*). Warszawa: Ludowa Spoldzielnia Wydawnicza, 1971. [Several translators.]

Szuba, Andrzej. *Kobieta Czeka Na Mnie* (*A Woman Waits for Me*). Kraków: Wydawnictwo M, 1991. [Miniature-sized book of translations of sixty-two short poems; bilingual edition.]

———. *Piesn o Sobie* (*Song of Myself*). Kraków: Wydawnictwo Literackie, 1992. [Most extensive selection of Whitman's poetry in Polish; bilingual edition.]

Criticism

Tuwim, Julian. "Manifest Powszechnej Milosci (Walt Whitman)" ("A Manifesto of General Love [Walt Whitman]"). *Pro Arte et Studio* 3, no. 8 (1917): 4–12.

Sokolicz, Antonina. "Walt Whitman." In *Warszawa 1921 Wydawnictwo Zwiazku Robotniczych Stowarzyszen Spoldzieleczych* (*Warsaw 1921 Publication of the Workers' Union and Cooperative Societies*). Warszawa: Library of Workers No. 4, 1921, 31 ff.

Dyboski, Roman. "Literatura Angielska i Anglo-Amerykanska" ("English and Anglo-American Literature"). *Przeglad Warszawski* 3 (1922): 124–132.

Helsztynski, Stanislaw. "Walt Whitman: Zyciorys i Rodowod Literacki" ("Walt Whitman: Biography and Literary Genealogy"). In *Od Szekspira do Joycea*. Warszawa: Roj, 1939, 252–277.

Zulawski, Juliusz. *Wielka podroz Walta Whitmana* (*Walt Whitman's Great Journey*). Warszawa, 1971.

RUSSIAN

Translations

Chukovsky, Kornei I. "Poet-anarkhist Walt Whitman: Perevod v stikhakh i kharakteristika" ("The Anarchist Poet Walt Whitman: A Translation in Verse and a Character Sketch"). In *Kurzhok molodykh*. St. Petersburg, 1907. [Revised and enlarged as *Poeziya*

Gryadushchei Demokratii: Uot Uitman (*Poetry of the Future Democracy: Walt Whitman*) (Moscow: I. D. Sytin, 1914), and reprinted in various versions in 1918 and 1919.]

———. *Uot Uitmen: List'ya Travy, Proza* (*Walt Whitman: Leaves of Grass, Prose*). Petersburg: "World Literature," Gos. Izd., Tip. 15-ya Gosudarstvennaya, 1922. [Expanded 5th edition of Chukovsky's translation of Whitman. Reprinted in various versions: *Uot Uitmen i Ego List'ya Travy: Poeziya Gryadushchei Demokratii* (*Walt Whitman and His Leaves of Grass: Poetry of the Future Democracy*), 1923; *Uot Uitmen: List'ya Travy*, 1931; *Uot Uitmen: Izbrannye Stikhotvoreniya* (*Walt Whitman: Selected Poems*), 1932; *Uot Uitmen: List'ya Travy, Izbrannye Stihi i Poemy*, 1935; and *Uolt Uitman: Izbrannye Stikhotvoreniya i Proza*, 1944.]

B'almont, Konstantin D. *Uol't Uitman: Pobegi Travy* (*Walt Whitman: Leaves of Grass*). Moscow: Scorpion, 1911.

———. *Iz Mirovoi Poezii* (*From the World's Poetry*). Berlin: Slovo, 1921. [Contains selected Whitman poems, 93–119.]

Uolt Uitmen: List'ya Travy. Moscow: OGIZ [Government Printing Office], 1955. [Several translators, including Chukovsky; introductions by Chukovsky and Maurice Mendelson.]

Kashkin, I. *Slushai, poyot Amerika* (*I Hear America Singing*). Moscow: Goslitizdat, 1960.

Izbrannye proizvedeniya, List'ya travy, Proza (*Selected Works, Leaves of Grass, Prose*). Moscow: Khudozhestvennaya literatura, 1970. [Introduction by Maurice Mendelson.]

Criticism

Anonymous. "Amerikansky Tolstoy" ("The American Tolstoy"). *Knizhki Nedeli* 5 (1892): 167.

B'almont, Konstantin D. "Pevets Lichnosti i Zhizni, Uol't Uitman" ("The Bard of Personality and Life, Walt Whitman"). *Vessy* 7 (July 1904): 11–32.

Chukovsky, Kornei I. "Russkaya Whitmaniana" ("Russian Whitmaniana"). *Vessy* 10 (October 1906): 43–45.

Elena, T. "Ob Uitmane, Balmonte, Narekaniyah i Dobrosovestnosti. Zametka Dokazatelnaya" ("Whitman, B'almont, Reproaches and Scrupulousness. Notes in Demonstration"). *Vessy* 12 (December 1906): 46–51.

B'almont, Konstantin D. "Polyarnost': o Tvorchestvo Uol'ta Uitmana" ("Polarity: Walt Whitman's Work"). *Sovremenny Mir* 8 (1910): 135–139.

Anonymous. "Poet Demokratii (Uot Uitman)" ("The Poet of Democracy [Walt Whitman]"). *Biulleteni Literaturi i Zhizni* 22 (July 1914): 1253–1258.

Lunacharsky, A. "Whitman i demokratia" ("Whitman and Democracy"). In Kornei Chukovsky *Poeziya gryadushchei demokratii*. Petersburg: Parus, 1918, 150–153.

Federenko, I. "Uot Uitman." *Literaturno-Naukovii Vistnik* 7 (September 1922): 53–62. [Ukrainian view.]

Parry, Albert. "Walt Whitman in Russia." *American Mercury* 33 (September 1934): 100–107.

Mirsky, D. S. "Walt Whitman: Poet of American Democracy." *Dialectics* 1 (1937): 11–29. [Tranlsated from the Russian by B. G. Guerney.]

Zverev, M. "Great American Poet: Popular in U.S.S.R." *Moscow News* (June 5, 1939), 17, 23.

Chukovsky, Kornei I. "Mayakovsky i Whitman" ("Mayakovsky and Whitman"). *Leningrad* 2 (1941): 18–19.

————. "Walt Whitman v SSSR: Bibliograficheskie zametki" ("Walt Whitman in the USSR: Bibliographical Notes"). *Internatsionalnaya literatura* 1–2 (1942): 204–206.

Mendelson, Maurice. "Walt Whitman i borba za mir i demokratiyu" ("Walt Whitman and the Struggle for Peace and Democracy"). *Znamya* 5 (1951): 170–182.

Dicharov, Z. "'Zametki o Rossii' Walt'a Whitman'a" ("Walt Whitman's 'Notes about Russia'"). *Izvestiya Akademii Nauk SSSR, Otdeleniye literatury id yazyka* 21 (1962): 245–251.

Mendelson, Maurice. *Zhizn i tvorchestvo Whitman'a* (*Life and Work of Whitman*). Moscow: Nauka, 1965. [Revised and enlarged, 1969; English-language edition, *Life and Work of Walt Whitman: A Soviet View*, translated by Andrew Bromfield (Moscow: Progress Publishers, 1976), with extensive chronological bibliography of books and articles on Whitman in Russian, 337–343, and listing of Russian translations, 343.]

Allen, Gay Wilson. "Kornei Chukovsky, Whitman's Russian Translator." In Geoffrey Sill, ed., *Walt Whitman of Mickle Street*. Knoxville: University of Tennessee Press, 1994, 276–282.

Zassoursky, Yassen. "Whitman's Reception and Influence in the Soviet Union." In Geoffrey Sill, ed., *Walt Whitman of Mickle Street*. Knoxville: University of Tennessee Press, 1994, 283–290. [Lecture originally delivered in 1986.]

LATVIAN

Translation

Skarga, Roberts. *Walt Whitman: Sahlu Steebri* (*Walt Whitman: Leaves of Grass*). Riga: Imanta, 1908.

UKRAINIAN

Translation

Listya Travy (*Leaves of Grass*). Kiev: Dnipro, 1969.

Criticism

Federenko, I. "Uot Uitman" ("Walt Whitman"). *Literaturno-Naukovii Vistnik* 7 (September 1922): 53–62.

SWEDISH

Translations

Svensson, K. A. *Strån av Gräs* (*Leaves of Grass*). Stockholm: A. B. Seelig, 1935. [Translations of sixty-seven poems, including "Song of Myself."]

Blomberg, Erik. *Modern amerikansk lyrik från Walt Whitman till våra dagar* (*Modern American Poetry from Walt Whitman to Our Days*). Stockholm: Bonniers, 1937. [Devotes thirty-seven pages to translations of all or parts of ten Whitman poems.]

Aggestam, Rolf. *Sången om Mig Själv* (*Song of Myself*). Stockholm: FIB:s Lyrikklubb, 1983. [Translation of 1855 version of "Song of Myself."]

Criticism

Butenschön, Andrea. "Walt Whitman." *Ord och Bild* 14 (1905): 351–367. [Contains translations of parts of several poems.]

Lundkvist, Artur. *Atlantvind*. Stockholm: Bonniers, 1932. [Opening essay deals at length with Whitman.]

Fridholm, Roland. "Pindaros från Paumanok." *Ord och Bild* 43 (1934): 437–443. [Translated in Gay Wilson Allen, *Walt Whitman Abroad* (Syracuse: Syracuse University Press, 1955), 127–136.]

Fleischer, Fredric. "Walt Whitman's Swedish Reception." *Walt Whitman Newsletter* 3 (1957): 19–22, 44–47, 58–62.

Åhnebrink, Lars. "Whitman and Sweden." *Walt Whitman Review* 6 (1960): 43–44.

Fleischer, Fredric. "Walt Whitman in svensksapråkig litteratur." *Nordisk tidskrift för vetenskap, konst och industri* 38 (1962): 136 ff.

———. "Walt Whitman in Sweden." In Roger Asselineau and William White, eds., *Walt Whitman in Europe Today*. Detroit: Wayne State University Press, 1972, 29–30.

Folsom, Ed. "Artur Lundkvist's Swedish Ode to Whitman." *Walt Whitman Quarterly Review* 3 (1985): 33–35.

DANISH

Translations

Jensen, Johannes V., and Otto Gelsted. *Walt Whitman: Digte*. København, Kirstiana: Nyt Nordisk Forlag, 1919.

Houmann, Børge. *Sangen om Mig Selv og Andre Digte i Udvalg*. København: Woels Forlag, 1929.

Schyberg, Frederik. *Walt Whitman: Digte*. København: Gyldendal, 1933. [Revised and reprinted 1949, 1972, 1976.]

Seeburg, P. E. *Fuldkomne Dage (Specimen Days)*. København: Steen Hasselbachs Forlag (Hasselbachs Kultur-Bibliotek, Bind 95), 1950. [Selections.]

Schmidt, Rudolf. *Demokratiske Fremblik (Democratic Vistas)*. København, 1974.

Borum, Poul, *Walt Whitman, The History of the Future: Selected Poems/ Fremtidens Historie: Digte i udvalg og oversaettelse*. København: Brøndum, 1976. [Translations of all or parts of twenty-seven poems.]

Mester, Annette, *Walt Whitman, Demokratiske Visioner (Democratic Vistas)*. København: Gyldendals Kulturbibliotek, 1991. [Foreword by Villy Sørensen.]

Criticism

Janson, Kristofer. *Amerikanske Forhold: Fem Foredrag*. København: Gyldendal, 1881. [First chapter on Whitman.]

Schmidt, Rudolf. "Walt Whitman." *Buster og Masker: Literatur-Studier*. København: F. H. Eibes Forlag, 1882, 123–192. [Translated with omissions in R. M. Bucke, Thomas Harned, Horace Traubel, eds., *In Re Walt Whitman* (Philadelphia: David McKay, 1893), 231–248.]

Hamsun, Knut. Lecture on Whitman. In *Fra det moderne Amerikas Aandsliv*. København:

Philipsens Forlag, 1889. [English-language edition, *The Cultural Life of Modern America*, translated by Barbara G. Morgridge (Cambridge: Harvard University Press, 1969), 63–85.]

Schyberg, Frederik. *Walt Whitman*. København: Gyldendal, 1933. [English-language edition translated by Evie Allison Allen (New York: Columbia University Press, 1951).]

Allen, Gay Wilson. "Walt Whitman's Reception in Scandinavia." *Papers of the Bibliographical Society of America* 40 (1946): 259–275.

Krogvig, Kjell. "Til Whitman gjennom Wergeland" ("Approach to Whitman through Wergeland"). *Samtiden* 57 (1948): 192–202.

Roos, Carl, ed. "Walt Whitman's Letters to a Danish Friend [Rudolf Schmidt]." *Orbis Litterarum* 7 (Fasc. 1–2) (1949): 31–60.

Cummings, Peter M., "Walt Whitmans 'Sang om mig selv'; et stykke af fremtidens historie." *Dansk Udaya* 57 (1977): 234–247.

NORWEGIAN

Translation

Arneberg, Per. *Walt Whitman: Sangen om Meg Selv av Leaves of Grass* (*Walt Whitman: Song of Myself from Leaves of Grass*). Oslo: Forlagt av H. Aschehoug & Co., 1947.

FINNISH

Translations

Laitinet, Viljo. *Walt Whitman: Ruohonlehtiä* (*Walt Whitman: Leaves of Grass*). Turku: Suomentajan Kustantama, 1954. [Selections, including "Song of Myself," "Song of the Open Road," and "Out of the Cradle Endlessly Rocking."]

Repo, Ville. "Crossing Brooklyn Ferry." *Parnasso* 5 (1956): 195–205.

Turtiainen, Arvo. *Ruohoa* (*Leaves of Grass*). Helsinki: Kustannusosakeyhtiö Tammi, 1965. [Selections, including "Song of Myself," "Starting from Paumanok," "Crossing Brooklyn Ferry," *Calamus*, and *Drum-Taps*.]

Criticism

Harboe, Paul. "Walt Whitman." *Euterpe* (1905): 129–131. [In Danish.]

Väinö, Valvanne. "Walt Whitman." *Sunnuntai* (1917): 3.

Nousiainen, Oskari. "Walt Whitman, Amerikan suurin runoilija" ("Walt Whitman, the Greatest American Poet"). *Jousimies* (1928): 78–80.

Viljanen, Lauri. "Walt Whitmania suomeksi." *Parnasso* 6 (1954): 278–280.

ESTONIAN

Translation

Kabur, Boris. *Rohlehed* (*Leaves of Grass*). Tallinn: Esti Riiklik Kirjastus, 1962.

ICELANDIC

Translation

Magnússon, Sigurdur A. *Song of Myself.* Reykjavik: Bjartur Press, 1994.

Criticism

Magnússon, Sigurdur A. "Whitman in Iceland." In Geoffrey Sill, ed., *Walt Whitman of Mickle Street.* Knoxville: University of Tennessee Press, 1994, 236–243.

ISRAELI

Translations

Miller, Louis. *Walt Whitman's Poems from "Leaves of Grass."* New York: Yiddish Cooperative League, 1940. [Selection of poems translated into Yiddish.]
Halkin, Simon. *Ale Esev* (*Leaves of Grass*). Tel Aviv: Sifriat Poalim, 1952. [Selection of poems translated into Hebrew, with lengthy essay on Whitman by the translator; revised edition 1984.]

Criticism

Greenberg, Uri Tsvi. *Kelape Tish'im Vetish'ah* (*Against Ninety-Nine*). Tel Aviv: Sadan, 1928.
Kahn, Sholom J. "Walt Whitman in Hebrew." *Scopus* 6 (1952): 6–7.
———. "Whitman's Sense of Evil: Criticisms." In Gay Wilson Allen, ed., *Walt Whitman Abroad.* Syracuse: Syracuse University Press, 1955, 236–253.
———. "Whitman's Wit and Wisdom." *Studies in Literature* (Jerusalem) (1982): 268–286.
Scholem, Gershom. "Reflections on the Possibility of Jewish Mysticism in Our Day." *Emot* 8 (September/October 1964).

INDIAN

Translations

Barma, Inanindra. *Durbadala* (*Leaves of Grass*). Orissa, India: Prafulla Chandra Das, 1957. [Selections in the Oriya language.]
Adiga, M. Gopalakrishna. *Hullina Dalagalu.* New Delhi: Sahitya Akademi, 1966. [Translations of 101 poems from *Leaves of Grass* into Kannada.]
Singh, Gurbakhsh. *Ghah Diyan Pattiyan.* New Delhi: Sahitya Akademi, 1968. [Selections from *Leaves of Grass* translated into Punjabi.]

Criticism

Tagore, Kshitindranath. "Walt Whitman." 1891. [In Bengali.] Translated by R. K. DasGupta in *Walt Whitman Review* 19 (1973): 3–11.
Guthrie, William N. *Walt Whitman, Camden Sage.* Cincinnati: Robert Clark, 1897, 25 ff.
Coomaraswamy, Ananda. *Buddha and the Gospel of Buddhism.* New York: Putnam's, 1916, 167 ff.

Rolland, Romain. *Prophets of the New India*. New York: Boni, 1930, 348 ff.

Mercer, Dorothy F. "*Leaves of Grass* and the Bhagavad Gita: A Comparative Study." Ph.D. diss., University of California, 1933. [Sections published include "Walt Whitman on Reincarnation," *Vedanta and the West* 9 (1946): 180–185; "Walt Whitman on Learning and Wisdom," *Vedanta and the West* 10 (1947): 57–59; "Walt Whitman on God and the Self," *Vedanta and the West* 10 (1947): 80–87; "Walt Whitman on Love," *Vedanta and the West* 10 (1947): 107–113; "Walt Whitman on Karma Yoga," *Vedanta and the West* 10 (1947): 150–153; "Whitman on Raja Yoga," *Vedanta and the West* 11 (1948): 26–31; "Whitman on Prophecy," *Vedanta and the West* 11 (1948): 118–123; "Limitations in *Leaves of Grass*," *Vedanta and the West* 12 (1949): 21–25, 82–87.]

Chari, V. K. *Whitman in the Light of Vedantic Mysticism: An Interpretation*. Lincoln: University of Nebraska Press, 1964.

Nambiar, O. K. *Walt Whitman and Yoga*. Bangalore: Jeevan Publications, 1966.

Hurwitz, Harold M. "Whitman, Tagore, and 'Passage to India.'" *Walt Whitman Review* 13 (1967): 56–60.

Nambiar, O. K. "Whitman's Twenty-Eight Bathers: A Guessing Game." In Sujit Mukherjee and D. V. K. Raghavacharyulu, eds., *Indian Essays in American Literature: Papers in Honor of Robert E. Spiller*. Bombay: Popular Prakashan, 1968, 129–137.

Das, Manoj. "The Good Gray Poet and the Last Rishi [Sri Aurobindo]." *Indian Literature* 12 (1969): 87–91.

Sharma, Mohan Lal. "Whitman, Tagore, Iqbal: Whitmanated, Under-Whitmanated, and Over-Whitmanated Singers of Self." *Walt Whitman Review* 15 (1969): 230–237.

Singh, Raman K. "Whitman: Avatar of Shri Krishna?" *Walt Whitman Review* 15 (1969): 97–102.

Ghose, Sisir. "Chari, Whitman, and the Vedantic Self: A Note." *Calamus* 4 (1970): 9–20.

Rajasekharaiah, T. R. *The Roots of Whitman's Grass*. Rutherford, N.J.: Fairleigh Dickinson University Press, 1970.

Sharma, Om Prakash. "Walt Whitman and the Doctrine of Karma." *Philosophy East and West* 20 (1970): 169–174.

Chari, V. K. "The Limits of Whitman's Symbolism." *Journal of American Studies* 5 (1971): 173–184.

———. "The Structure of Whitman's Catalogue Poems." *Walt Whitman Review* 18 (1972): 3–17.

Chinmoy, Sri. "Walt Whitman." In *America in Her Depths*. Hollis, N.Y.: Vishma Press, 1973, 21–25.

DasGupta, R. K. "Indian Response to Walt Whitman." *Revue de Litterature Comparee* 47 (1973): 58–70.

Mersch, Arnold. "Cosmic Contrast: Whitman and the Hindu Philosophy." *Walt Whitman Review* 19 (1973): 49–63.

Singh, Anritjit. "Walt Whitman in India: 1976." *The Bicentennial Walt Whitman*. Supplement to *Walt Whitman Review* (1976): 31–33.

Chari, V. K. "Whitman and the Language of the Romantics." *Etudes Anglaises* (July 1977): 314–318.

Ahliwalia, Harsharan Singh. "The Private Self and the Public Self in Whitman's 'Lilacs.'" *Walt Whitman Review* 23 (1977): 165–175.

Nambiar, O. K. *Maha Yogi Walt Whitman: New Light on Yoga*. Bangalore: Jeevan Publications, 1978.

Sachithanandan, V. *Walt Whitman and Bharati: A Comparative Study.* Madras: Macmillan Co. of India, 1978.

Sastry, C. N. "Glimpses of India in *Leaves of Grass.*" *Calamus* 16 (1978): 2–10.

Prasad, Thakur Guru. "The Orient in Whitman's 'Passage to India.'" *Calamus* 17 (1979): 4–9.

Sharma, N. K. *Walt Whitman: Vision and Art.* Delhi: Atma Ram & Sons, 1980.

Benevento, Joseph. "Whitman and the Eastern Mystic Fallacy." *Calamus* 22 (1981): 12–23.

Sastry, K. Srinivasa. *Whitman's 'Song of Myself' and Advaita: An Essay in Criticism.* Delhi: Doaba House, 1982.

Mishra, R. S. "Whitman's Sex: A Reading of 'Children of Adam.'" *Calamus* 23 (1983): 19–25.

Kumar, Sudhir. "The Gita and Walt Whitman's Mysticism." In Abhai Maurya, ed., *India and World Literature.* New Delhi: Indian Council for Cultural Relations, 1990, 524–534.

Chari, V. K. "Whitman Criticism in the Light of Indian Poetics." In Ed Folsom, ed., *Walt Whitman: The Centennial Essays.* Iowa City: University of Iowa Press, 1994, 240–250.

KAZAKH

Translation

Stikhi (Poems). Alma-Ata: Zhazushi, 1969.

KIRGHIZ

Translation

List'ya Travy (Leaves of Grass). Frunze, Kirghizstan, 1970.

CHINESE

Translations

Xi Chu. "huiteman ziyoushi xuan yi" ("Selected Translations of Whitman's Poems of Freedom"). *pingmin jiaoyu (Education of the Masses)* 20 (March 1920).

Can Hong. "yi huiteman xiaoshi wushou" ("Five Short Poems of Whitman in Translation"). *chenbao fukan (Morning Post Supplement)* (May 20, 1921).

Dong Lai. "lei" ("Tears"). *wenxue zhoubao (Literary Weekly)* 30 [1923?].

Xu Zhimo "wo ziji de ge" ("Song of Myself"). *xiaoshuo yuebao (Short Story Monthly)* 15, no. 3 (March 1924).

Wei Congwu. "huiteman shi ershou" ("Two Whitman Poems"). *mang yuan (The Wild Land)* 2 (1927).

Liu Yanling. "O Captain! My Captain!" In "linken ji qita" ("Lincoln and Others"). *dushu guwen (Reading Advisor)* 1, no. 1 (1934).

Qiu Lang. "lei" ("Tears"). *chenbao (Morning Post)* (December 5, 1934).

Wu Lifu. "kuangye zhi ge" ("Song of the Open Road"). *shijie wenxue (World Literature)* 1, no. 4 (April 1935).

Gao Han. "dalu zhi ge" ("Song of the Open Road"). *wenxue (Literature)* 8, no. 4 (January 1937).

———. "jindai de niandai" ("Years of the Modern"). *zhange* (*Battle Songs*) 1, no. 4 (December 1938).

———. "wo de fuqin de weichang" ("Come Up from the Fields Father"). *zhange* (*Battle Songs*) 1, no. 6 (February 1939).

Xu Chi. "ludi zhi ge" ("Songs of Calamus") [includes "I Hear It Was Charged Against Me," "This Moment Yearning and Thoughtful," "I Saw in Louisiana a Live-Oak Growing," "When I Peruse the Conquer'd Fame," "I Dream'd in a Dream," and "No Labor-Saving Machine"]. *wenyi zhendi* (*Literary Front*) 6, no. 1 (January 1941).

Chun Jiang. "wo zanmei yi ge ren" ("For Him I Sing"). *jiuwang ribao fukan* (*Supplement to the National Salvation Daily*) (January 18, 1941).

———. "liming de qizhi" ("Song of the Banner at Daybreak"). *wenxue yuebao* (*Literary Monthly*) 3, no. 1 (June 1941). [Special issue on American literature.]

Chen Shihuai. "zhi shibaizhe" ("To Those Who've Fail'd"). *shichuangzuo* (*Poetic Creation*) 7 (January 1942). [Special issue of translations.]

Tian Lan. "wo zuozhe er wo ningwangzhe" ("I Sit and I Look Out"). *jiefang ribao* (*Liberation Daily*) (January 13, 1942).

Wu Boxiao. "liangge laobing de zange" ("Dirge for Two Veterans"). *jiefang ribao* (*Liberation Daily*) (February 3, 1942).

———. "chuan de cheng" ("City of Ships"). *jiefang ribao* (*Liberation Daily*) (February 11, 1942).

Cao Baohua. "zou guo de daolu de huigu" ("A Backward Glance O'er Travel'd Roads"); Tian Lan, "fanpan zhi ge" ("Songs of Rebellions") [includes "Europe" and "To a Foil'd European Revolutionaire"]; Chen Shihuai, "huiteman shi sishou" ("Four Whitman Poems") [includes "I Dream'd in a Dream" and "To a Certain Cantatrice"]. *shichuanzuo* (*Poetic Creation*) 10 (April 1942). [Includes special section for the fiftieth anniversary of Whitman's death.]

Gao Han. "yishi sishou" ("Four Poems Translated") [includes "On the Beach at Night" and "For You O Democracy"]. *wenyi shenghuo* (*Literary Life*) 2, no. 1 (July 1942).

Zou Jiang. "huiteman shichao" ("Selected Poems of Whitman"). *wenhua zazhi* (*Cultural Notes*) 3, no. 3 (November 1942).

Yao Ben. "wo zuoguo yici qiyi de kanshou" ("Vigil Strange I Kept on the Field One Night"). *bizhen* (*Writing Front*) 6 (new edition, November 1942).

Jiang Xun. "yangniuzhe ji qita" ("'The Ox-Tamer' and Others"). *wenxue yibao* (*Literary Translation*) 2, no. 2 (1943).

Zhong Wei. "caoyeji xuan" (*Leaves of Grass*) [selections]. *qingnian wenyi* (*Literature and Art for Youth*) 1, no. 5 (May 1943).

Jiang Xun. "guo bulukelin dukou" ("Crossing Brooklyn Ferry"). *shi* (*Poetry*) 4, no. 1 (July 1943).

Guan Ezi, Zou Jiang. "huiteman shichao sishou" ("Four Whitman Poems"). *wenzhen xinji* (*New Collection of the Literary Front*) 2 (February 1944).

Gao Han. "dalu zhi ge" ("Song of the Open Road"). Chongqing: Dushu Press, 1944; Kexue Press, 1947.

Yang Zhouhan. "jindai meiguoshi xuanyi" ("Selected Translations of Modern American Poems") [includes "I Hear America Singing" and "When Lilacs Last in the Dooryard Bloom'd"]. *shijie wenyi jikan* (*World Literature and Art Quarterly*) 1, no. 3 (April 1946).

Yuan Shuipai. "qiutu ge sanshou" ("Three Poems of the Singer in the Prison"). *renshijian* (*The Human World*) 3 (May 1947) [Restored edition].

Tu An. *gusheng* (*Drum-Taps*). Qingtong Press, 1948. [Fifty-two poems.]

Chen Shihuai. *giulao zhong de gezhe* (*The Singer in the Prison*) [1948?]. [Thirty-one poems.]

———. *xiandai meiguo shige* (*Modern American Poetry: Famous Poems by Famous Poets*). Shanghai: Chenguang Book Company, 1949.

Gao Han. *caoyeji* (*Leaves of Grass*). Shanghai: Chenguang Book Company, 1949. [Fifty-eight poems.]

Zou Luzhi. *qichi* (*Galloping*). Shanghai: Wenhua Gongzuo Press, 1950. [Selected poems of Longfellow and Whitman.]

Chu Tunan. *caoyeji xuan* (*Selections from Leaves of Grass*). Beijing: People's Literature Press, 1955. [Reprinted, 1978.]

Huang Wu. "huiteman shi sanshou" ("Three Whitman Poems") ["A Glimpse," "To Rich Givers," and "My 71st Year"]. *wenhuibao* (*Wenhui Post*) (December 15, 1956).

Zhang Yujiu. "huiteman tan shi lunwen juou" ("Some Examples of Whitman's Writings on Poetry"). *waiguo wenxue yanjiu* (*Studies in Foreign Literature*) 1 (1978), 39–45.

———. *huiteman sanwen xuan* (*Selected Prose Works of Whitman*). Changsha: Hunan People's Press, 1986. [Thirty-nine excerpts from prose works.]

Zhao Luorui. *wo ziji de ge* (*Song of Myself*). Shanghai: Shanghai Translation Press, 1987.

Chu Tunan, Li Yeguang. *caoyeji* (*Leaves of Grass*). 2 vols. Beijing: People's Literature Press, 1987.

Tu An, Chu Tunan. *wo zai mengli mengjian* (*I Dream'd in a Dream*). Beijing: People's Literature Press, 1987. [Fifty-six poems.]

Li Shiqi (annot.). *huiteman shi xuan* (*Selected Poems of Whitman*). Taiyuan: Beiyue Literature and Art Press, 1988.

Gu Zhengkun, Guiyou Huang, et al., eds. *shijie mingshi jianshang cidian* (*A Companion to Masterpieces in World Poetry*). Beijing: Peking University Press, 1990, 623–628. [Contains translations of "When Lilacs Last in the Dooryard Bloom'd," "Song of Myself," and two essays by Li Changshan.]

Zhao Luorui. *caoyeji* (*Leaves of Grass*). Shanghai: Shanghai Translation Press, 1992. 2 vols. [Complete translation of *Leaves of Grass*; Foreign Literature Masterpieces Series.]

———. *One Hundred Lyrical Poems of Whitman*. Jinan, Shangdon: Shangdong Literature and Arts Press, 1992. [Selections from Zhao Luorui's complete translation of *Leaves of Grass*.]

Criticism

Tian Han. "pingmin shiren huiteman bainian ji" ("Poet of the Common People — Commemorating the One Hundredth Anniversary of Whitman's Birthday"). *shaonian zhongguo* (*The Young China*) 1, no. 1 (July 1919): 6–21.

Shen Yanbing. "huiteman zai faguo" ("Whitman in France"). *xiaoshuo yuebao* (*Short Story Monthly*) 12, no. 3 (1921): 8.

Liu Yanling. "meiguo de xinshi yundong" ("The New Poetic Movement in America"). *shi* (*Poetry*) 1, no. 2 (February 1922).

Sun Lianggong. "Walt Whitman." *shijie wenxuejia liezhuan* (*Biographies of Literary Writers of the World*). Zhonghua Book Company, 1926, 1930.

Jin Mingruo, trans. "Cao zhi ye — guanyu huiteman de kaocha" ("Leaves of Grass — A

Study of Whitman") [Japanese essay by You-dao-wu-lang]. *benliu* (*Racing Currents*) 1, no. 5 (October 1928).

Zeng Xubai. "Walt Whitman." *meiguo wenxue ABC* (*American Literature ABC*). Shijie Book Company, 1929.

Zheng Zhenduo. "meiguo wenxue" ("American Literature"). *wenxue dagang* (*General Outlines of Literature*); serialized in *xiaoshuo yuebao* (*Short Story Monthly*) 20, no. 12 (December 1929).

Zhu Fu. "xiandai meiguo shi gailun" ("A Survey of Modern American Poetry"). *xiaoshuo yuebao* (*Short Story Monthly*) 21, no. 5 (May 1930).

Zhang Kebiao. "Walt Whitman." In *Kaiming Literary Dictionary*. Kaiming Bookstore, 1932.

Huan Ping. "women cong huiteman xuequ shenmo?" ("What Do We Learn from Whitman?"). *shenbao* (*Shanghai Post*) (April 25, 1934).

Ruo Zhu, trans. "baifa shiren huiteman" ("The Good Grey Poet Whitman" by Upton Sinclair). *guomin wenxue* (*National Literature*) 1, no. 3 (November 1934).

Anonymous, trans. "Walt Whitman" by Edmund Gosse. *wenxue* (*Literature*) 3, no. 6 (December 1934).

Ai Qing. *shi de sanwenmei* (*The Prosaic Beauty of Poetry*). 1939. [Contains a discussion of Whitman's poetry.]

Yuan Shuipai, trans. "huiteman lun" ("On Whitman" by Milsky). *libao fukan* (*Supplement to the Power*) (March 1942, combined issue): 20–21.

Jing Wen, trans. "Walt Whitman" [Japanese essay by Gao-Chun-Gunag-Tai-Lang]; Yu Renke, trans. "buerqiaoya shi zhi xuanshou huiteman" ("Whitman — A Bourgeois Poet") [Japanese essay by Zhong-Ye-Zhong-Zhi]. *shichuangzuo* (*Poetic Creation*) 10 (April 1942). [Includes special section for the fiftieth anniversary of Whitman's death.]

Dai Menghui, trans. "huiteman zai eguo" ("Whitman in Russia"). *banyue wencui* (*Literary Digest Fortnightly*) (June 20, 1942).

Xu Chi. "meiguo shige de chuantong" ("American Poetic Tradition"). *zhong yuan* (*Central Plains*) 1, no. 1 (June 1943).

Yang Zhouhan. "lun jindai meiguo shige" ("On Modern American Poetry"). *shijie wenyi jikan* (*World Literature and Art Quarterly*) 1, no. 3 (April 1946).

Yuan Shuipai. "changqing de caoye" ("The Evergreen *Leaves of Grass*"). *remin ribao* (*People's Daily*) (February 5, 1955).

Zhou Yang. "jinian caoyeji he tangjikede" ("Commemorating *Leaves of Grass* and *Don Quixote*"). *wenyibao* (*Literature and Art Gazette*) 13 (1955).

Huang Jiade. "meiguo minzhu shiren huiteman — jinian caoyeji chuban yibai zhounian" ("American Democratic Poet Whitman: Commemorating the Centennial Publication of *Leaves of Grass*"). *wen shi zhe* (*Literature, History, and Philosophy*) (Shandong University Journal) 10 (1955): 27–31.

Yang Xianyi. "minzhu shiren huiteman" ("Democratic Poet Whitman"). *renmin wenxue* (*People's Literature*) 10 (1955): 89–93.

Zou Jiang. "jinian meiguo shiren huiteman he caoyeji chuban yibai zhounian" ("Commemorating the American Poet Whitman and the Centennial Publication of *Leaves of Grass*"). *xinan wenyi* (*Southwest Literature and Art*) 11 (1955).

Cai Qijiao. "huiteman de shenghuo he chuangzuo" ("The Life and Works of Whitman"). *jiefangjun wenyi* (*Liberation Army Literature and Art*) 10 (1955).

Huai Bing, trans. *huiteman xiangchu de rizi* (*Days with Walt Whitman* by Edward
    Carpenter). Shanghai: Wenyi Lianhe Press, 1955.

Huang Yushi, trans. *huiteman pingzhuan* (*The Critical Biography of Walt Whitman* by Abe
    Capek). Beijing: The Writers' Press, 1955.

Wang Yizhu, trans. *huiteman lun* (*Walt Whitman* by Maurice Mendelson). Beijing: The
    Writers' Press, 1955.

Huang Wu. "huiteman yu wen yiduo" ("Whitman and Wen Yiduo"). *wenhuibao* (*Wenhui
    Post*) (December 12, 1956).

Yang Yaomin. "huiteman — gesong minzhu de shiren" ("Whitman: A Poet Singing Praises
    of Democracy and Liberty"). *Collected Papers of Literary Studies*, no. 2. Beijing: People's
    Literature Press, 1957.

Zhang Yuechao. "meiguo de renmin shiren huiteman" ("Whitman — People's Poet of
    America"). *xiou jingdian zuojia yu zuopin* (*Western European Classical Writers and
    Classical Works*). Changjiang Literature and Art Press, 1957.

Hua Zhongyi. "huiteman yu gelushi" ("Whitman and Regulated Poetry"). *Fudan
    University Journal* 1, 4 (1957).

Anonymous, trans. "huiteman zai shige fangmian de geming" ("Whitman's Revolution in
    Poetry" by Abe Capek). *wenxue yanjiu* (*Literary Studies*) 2 (1958).

Li Wei, trans. *huiteman pingzhuan* (*Critical Biography of Whitman* by Maurice
    Mendelson). Beijing: People's Literature Press, 1958.

Zhou Jueliang. "ping huiteman shi wen xuanji" ("Remarks on the *The Poetry and Prose of
    Whitman*"). *xifang yuwen* (*Western Philology*) 3, no. 1 (1959).

Xu Chi. "lun caoyeji" ("On *Leaves of Grass*"). *shi yu shenghuo* (*Poetry and Life*). Beijing:
    Beijing Publishing House, 1959.

Ruan Shen. "caoyeji qianlun" ("An Introductory Study of *Leaves of Grass*"). *waiguo
    wenxue yanjiu* (*Studies in Foreign Literature*) 1 (1978): 32–37.

He Qifang. *shige xinshang* (*Appreciating Poetry*). Beijing: People's Literature Press, 1978.
    [Contains discussion of Whitman and Guo Moruo, 71–93.]

Huang Wu. "huiteman yu linken" ("Whitman and Lincoln"). *waiguo wenxue yanjiu*
    (*Studies in Foreign Literature*) 10 (1981): 100–105.

Li Yang. "Ai Qing yu oumei jindai wenxue he meishu" ("Ai Qing and Modern Euro-
    American Literature and Art"). *hongyan* (*Red Rocks*) 2 (1981): 152–159.

Qin Hong. "lu xun dui huiteman de jieshao" ("Lu Xun's Introduction of Whitman"). *lu
    xun xuekan* (*Journal of Lu Xun Studies*) 2 (1982): 101–103.

Wang Zuoliang. "du caoyeji" ("Reading *Leaves of Grass*"). *meiguo wenxue congkan*
    (*American Literature Studies*) 2 (1982).

Li Yeguang. "zhi huiteman" ("To Whitman"). *shikan* (*Journal of Poetry*) 1 (1983): 30–31.
    [A poem.]

Zhao Luorui. "huiteman 'wo ziji de ge' yihouji" ("Afterword to the Translation of
    Whitman's 'Song of Myself' "). *Peking University Journal* (Philosophy and Social
    Sciences Edition) 4 (1985): 27–32.

Pu Feng. "Guo Moruo de shi" ("Guo Moruo's Poetry"). In *Selected Works of Pu Feng*.
    Haixia Literature and Art Press, 1985. [Contains discussion of Whitman, 85 ff.]

Dong Hengxun, and Zu Hong, eds. *meiguo wenxue jianshi* (*A Short History of American
    Literature*). Beijing: People's Literature Press, 1986. [Contains a chapter on Whitman.]

Li Yeguang. *huiteman pingzhuan* (*Critical Biography of Whitman*). Shanghai: Shanghai
    Literature and Art Press, 1988.

————, ed. *huiteman yanjiu* (*Studies in Whitman*). Guilin: Li River Press, 1988.

Zhao Luorui. "yishi nan — du Han Guiliang tongzhi wen hou de yixie sikao" ("Translation, A Difficult Business: Some Reflections on Han Guiliang's article"). *Chinese Translators Journal* 4 (1991): 53–58. [Zhao's response to Han's article about her translation of "Song of Myself."]

Liu Shusen. "ping caoyeji de liuge zhongyiben: jinian huiteman shishi yibai zhounian" ("On the Six Chinese Translations of *Leaves of Grass*: Commemorating the Centennial Anniversary of Whitman's Death"). *Foreign Languages* 1 (1992): 38–44.

Criticism in English

Fang, Achilles. "From Imagism to Whitmanism in Recent Chinese Poetry: A Search for Poetics That Failed." In Horst Frenz and G. L. Anderson, eds., *Indiana University Conference on Oriental-Western Literary Relations*. Chapel Hill: University of North Carolina Press, 1955, 177–189.

Palandri, Angela Chih-ying Jung. "Whitman in Red China." *Walt Whitman Newsletter* 4 (September 1958): 94–97.

Wang, Alfred S. "Walt Whitman and Lao-Chuang." *Walt Whitman Review* 17 (1971): 109–122.

Cohen, Mark. "Whitman in China: A Revisitation." *Walt Whitman Review* 26 (March 1980): 32–35.

Huang Suyi. "English and American Literature in China." *Chinese Literature* 9 (1982): 106–119.

Kuebrich, David. "Whitman in China." *Walt Whitman Quarterly Review* 1 (September 1983): 33–35.

Li, Xilao. "Walt Whitman in China." *Walt Whitman Quarterly Review* 3 (1986): 1–8.

————. "A Backward Glance Over Traveled Roads." *West Hills Review* 6 (1986): 84–86.

Ti, Ongoey. "De Chinese Dichter Guo Moruo en Walt Whitman's 'Leaves of Grass'" ("The Chinese Poet Guo Moruo and Walt Whitman's *Leaves of Grass*"). *Maatstaf* (Amsterdam) 34 (1986): 35–36.

Li Shi Qi. "Whitman's Poetry of Internationalism." *West Hills Review* 7 (1987): 103–110.

Li, Xilao. "Whitman in China." *Mickle Street Review* 9 (1988): 67–73.

Wang Yao. "The Relation Between Modern Chinese Literature and Foreign Literature." *Chinese Literature* 8 (1988): 149–160.

JAPANESE

Translations

Naganuma, Shigetaka. *Kusa no Ha* (*Leaves of Grass*). Vol. 1. Tokyo: Nippon Dokusho Kumiai, 1946. Vol. 2. Tokyo: Mikasa Shobo, 1950. [Complete translation of *Leaves of Grass*, based on 1892 edition.]

Kimura, Sota. *Minshu-shugi Tenbo* (*Democratic Vistas*). Tokyo: Nippon Kokusho, 1947.

Shiratori, Shogo. *Whitman Shishu* (*Whitman's Poems*). Nara: Yotoku-sha, Tambashi-machi, 1947.

Yanagida, Izumi. *Waga Kuso yo Saraba* (*Good-Bye My Fancy*). Tokyo: Nippon Dokusho Kumiai, 1947.

Shiratori, Shogo. *Whitman Shishu*. Tokyo: Oizumi Shoten, 1949. [Expanded edition of 1947 translation; selection reprinted Tokyo: Shincho-sha, 1954.]

Shiga, Masaru. *Minshu-Shugi Tenbo* (*Democratic Vistas*). Tokyo: Sogen-sha, 1949.

Tomita, Saika. *Kusa no Ha*. Tokyo: Asahi Shimbunsha, 1949.

Kiguchi, Koju, and Masao Yahisa. *Whitman Shisen* (*Selected Poems of Whitman*). Tokyo: Azuma-shobo, 1949.

Asano, Akira. *Whitman Shishu*. Tokyo: Kanto-sha and Sogin-sha, 1950.

Asano, Makoto. *Whitman Shishu*. Tokyo: Sojin-sha, 1953.

Naganuma, Shigetaka. *Whitman's Letters to His Mother and Jeff.* Tokyo: Arechi Shuppan-sha, 1958.

Nabeshima, Norihiro, Masayuki Sakamoto, and Takashi Sugiki. *Kusa no Ha*. 3 vols. Tokyo: Iwanami Bookstore, 1976.

Criticism

Natsume, Soseki. "Bundan ni Okeru Byôdô Shugi no Daihyôsha Walt Whitman no Shi ni Tsuite" ("On the Poems of Walt Whitman, Representative of Equality in the Literary World"). *Tetsugaku Zasshi* 10 (October 5, 1892): 93–109.

Sugiki, Takashi. *Whitman*. Tokyo: Kenkyûsha, 1937.

Nabeshima, Norihiro. "Takeo Arishima and Walt Whitman." *Studies in Arts and Culture* (Tokyo, Ochanomizu University) 10 (December 1957): 17–68.

Matsuhara, Iwao. "Walt Whitman in Japan: From the First Introduction to the Present." *Thought Currents in English Literature* (Tokyo) 29 (January 1957); reprinted in *Leaves of Grass*, New York: Norton, 1973, 912–918.

Nabeshima, Norihiro. *Whitman no Kenkyû* (*A Study of Whitman*). Tokyo, Kobe: Shinozaki Shorin, 1959.

Ota, Saburo. "Walt Whitman and Japanese Literature." In Horst Frenz, ed., *Asia and the Humanities*. Bloomington: Comparative Literature Committee, Indiana University, 1959, 62–69.

Sadoya, Shigenobu. *Nihon ni Okeru Whitman* (*Walt Whitman in Japan: His Influence in Modern Japan*). Fukuoka, Japan: Seinan Gakuin University, 1969. [Includes abstract and bibliography in English.]

Kamei, Shunsuke. *Kindai Bungaku ni Okeru Whitman no Unmei* (*Walt Whitman in Modern Literature: A Comparative Study of Japanese and Western Appreciation*). Tokyo: Kenkyûsha, 1973.

Yoshitake, Yoshinori, ed. *Whitman Juyô no Hyakunen* (*One Hundred Years of Whitman Reception*). Tokyo: Kyôiku Shuppan Center, 1979.

Shimizu, Haruô. *Whitman no Shinzô Kenkyû* (*A Study of Whitman's Imagery*). Tokyo, Kobe: Shinozaki Shorin, 1984.

Notes on Contributors

Fernando Alegría, the Sadie Dernham Patek Professor in the Humanities, emeritus, at Stanford University, is a distinguished Chilean novelist, poet, and critic. He is the author of many books on Spanish-American literature, including *Walt Whitman en Hispanoamerica* (1955). His most recent book is *Allende: A Novel* (1993).

Gay Wilson Allen, who died in 1995, was professor emeritus at New York University and the author and editor of many books on American writers. His works on Whitman include *The Solitary Singer: A Critical Biography of Walt Whitman* (1955), *The New Walt Whitman Handbook* (1975, 1986), and *Walt Whitman Abroad* (1955). He was the general editor of *The Collected Writings of Walt Whitman*.

Carl L. Anderson, professor at Duke University, is the author of books on American and Scandinavian literature, including *Swedish Acceptance of American Literature* (1957) and *Poe in Northlight: The Scandinavian Response* (1973).

Roger Asselineau, professor emeritus at the University of Paris-Sorbonne, is the co-editor of *Etudes Anglaises* and the author of numerous books about American literature, including *L'Evolution de Walt Whitman* (1954), published in English as *The Evolution of Walt Whitman* (1960, 1962). His translation of *Leaves of Grass* (*Feuilles d'Herbe* [1956]) is the standard French version of Whitman's text.

Susan M. Brown teaches at Rhode Island College and has written several articles on the Whitman-Pessoa connection. She has taught at the University of Coimbra in Portugal and is the translator (with Edwin Honig) of *Poems of Fernando Pessoa* (1986). She is completing a translation of Pessoa's letters.

V. K. Chari, professor at Carleton University (Ottawa), is the author of *Whitman in the Light of Vedantic Mysticism* (1964) and *Sanskrit Criticism* (1990). He has taught at Banaras University in India.

Ed Folsom, professor and chair in the Department of English at the University of Iowa, has published widely in the field of American poetry. He is the editor of the *Walt Whitman Quarterly Review*, *Walt Whitman: The Measure of His Song* (1981), and *Walt Whitman: The Centennial Essays* (1994) and the author of *Walt Whitman's Native Representations* (1994).

Arthur Golden, professor emeritus at the City College of the City University of New York, currently resides in Slovenia. He is the editor of *Walt Whitman's Blue Book* (1968) and co-editor of *Leaves of Grass: A Textual Variorium of the Printed Poems* (1980).

Marija Golden, associate professor of linguistics at the University of Ljubljana in Slovenia, is the author of a book on Noam Chomsky, numerous articles, and a forthcoming book on language and linguistics.

Ezra Greenspan, professor at the University of South Carolina, has taught at Tel Aviv University and is the author of *Walt Whitman and the American Reader* (1990) and the editor of the *Cambridge Companion to Walt Whitman* (1995).

Walter Grünzweig, professor and chair of American studies at Dortmund University, is the author of *Walt Whitmann: Die deutschsprachige Rezeption als interkulturelles Phänomen* (1991) and the English version of that book, *Constructing the German Walt Whitman* (1995). He has taught at Karl-Franzens University in Graz, Austria, and at the University of Dresden.

Guiyou Huang, assistant professor of English at Kutztown University of Pennsylvania, is a translator and the author of articles on American and Chinese literature and has completed a book-length manuscript called *Cross Currents: Whitmanism, Imagism, and Modernism in China and America.*

Takashi Kodaira, professor of American literature at Yokohama City University, has published on various American writers and, with Alfred H. Marks, has translated *The Essence of Modern Haiku* by Seishi Yamaguchi (1993).

F. Lyra, professor of American studies at Warsaw University, is a prominent Polish critic who specializes in the relationship between Polish and English-language authors; his *Edgar Allan Poe* appeared in Warsaw in 1973.

Alfred H. Marks, professor emeritus at the State University of New York, College at New Paltz, is a Nathaniel Hawthorne scholar as well as the author of *Guide to Japanese Prose* (1975, 1984) and an accomplished translator of Japanese prose and poetry—most recently (with Takashi Kodaira), Yamaguchi Seishi's *The Essence of Modern Haiku: 300 Poems* (1993).

Igor Maver, assistant professor of English and American literature at the University of Ljubljana in Slovenia, has published on the translation of American texts into Slovene.

Maria Clara Bonetti Paro teaches at the Universidade Estadual Paulista (Araraquara Campus) in São Paulo, Brazil. She has published essays on Whitman's relationship with various Brazilian poets and has completed an exhaustive study of Whitman's reception in Brazil.

Niilo Peltola lives in Espoo, Finland, and is the author of *The Compound Epithet in American Poetry* (1956).

Stephen Stepanchev, professor emeritus at Queens College of the City University of New York, is a poet and critic whose books include *American Poetry Since 1945* (1965) and *Mining the Darkness* (1975).

M. Wynn Thomas is a professor at the University of Wales at Swansea and the author of numerous books on Welsh literature and of *The Lunar Light of Whitman's Poetry* (1987). He has translated Whitman's poetry into Welsh and edited *Wrenching Times: Poems from Drum-Taps* (1992).